One should hesitate to use the word 'comprehensive' about any text, but so thought-provoking, intellectually sophisticated and avowedly inter-disciplinary is Chris Greer's *Crime and Media: A Reader* that it can probably justifiably lay claim to the appellation. Dazzling in the breadth and depth of coverage, the book succeeds in bringing together key 'classics' in the field of crime and media with more obscure, idiosyncratic or simply difficult-to-get-hold of readings that are none the less essential to an understanding of the complex and nuanced relationship between crime and media. That said, the original and incisive commentaries written by the editor are worth the cover price alone. Challenging, provocative and perceptive, Greer's passion for his subject undoubtedly will enthuse students and breathe new life into sometimes stale debates. This is one of those rare books which makes anyone else's aspirations to produce a similar text in the future entirely superfluous. Quite simply, a tour de force.

Yvonne Jewkes, Professor of Criminology, University of Leicester, UK

This timely collection of classic and more recent analyses of crime and the mass media does more than simply cover a field; it is a conceptual tour de force. Greer's synthesis defines a new understanding about the relevance of new developments in cultural studies and media logic for a comprehensive critique of how the mass media packaging of crime as news and entertainment shapes practice, perceptions, and policies about crime and social control.

David L. Altheide, Regents' Professor at the School of Justice and Social Inquiry, Arizona State University, USA

The academic expression of the Sixties' imagination was to erode conventional disciplinary boundaries and to work in the new spaces where kindred interests could now meet. This was exactly the story of the meeting between, on one side, criminology, crime, deviance and social control and on the other, media studies. The result has been a flourishing of work on the many links between crime and the media. Chris Greer's selection of forty-two readings from this vast literature – from theories of simulacra to the dialectics of Dixon – strikes just the right balance between theory and research, standard and novel, normal and edgy. His selection (plus running commentary on the readings) is comprehensive enough to be a handbook for the whole field of study and coherent enough to reveal a theoretical integrity of its own. An essential guide for students and memory-aid for their teachers.

Stan Cohen, Emeritus Professor of Sociology, LSE, UK

As technology and media continue to evolve and dramatically impact all aspects of social life, it is unfortunate that crime and media research has not been more strategically integrated into criminological conversations. One reason for this neglect is that, although there is a burgeoning interdisciplinary scholarship in this area, there simply is not an easy-to-access central repository of classic and innovative works brought together with corresponding critique and analysis. Chris Greer's important new book overcomes this limitation, providing access to, and analysis of, a compilation of key works that have helped define this area of scholarship. It is a must read for students and scholars interested in crime and media issues.

Steven Chermak, Professor at the School of Criminal Justice, Michigan State University, USA

Chris Greer's Crime and Media: A Reader brings together a judicious and pedagogically useful collection of readings drawn from the fast-developing field of crime and media studies. Intelligently incorporating classic statements as well as the latest cutting-edge interventions, the collection is not only positioned at the intersection of crime and media studies, it helps to define it. An invaluable resource for students and scholars alike.

Professor Simon Cottle, Deputy Head of School, School of Journalism, Media and Cultural Studies, Cardiff University, UK

In a field where students are apt to consider the newest as the best, Greer's selection of readings proves otherwise. By mixing classic readings from the 1960s and 1970s with recent and revisionist pieces he shows that going back into a field's history is the best way to move forward. This strategy may seem counterintuitive when the problematic is an incessantly shifting mediascape, but Greer's backward glance is part of his provocative pedagogy. He clearly has a passion for his field, which instructors and students will absorb through his introduction and his 'topping' and 'tailing' of readings with commentary, context and questions. Far more than a collection of essays, this text offers a tool kit for the construction of theoretically sophisticated and methodologically rigorous approaches to crime and media research. An invaluable resource for instructors as well as students.

Carolyn Strange, Adjunct Professor Criminology and History, University of Toronto, Canada

This is a text of remarkable range and sophistication. Chris Greer understands, as few in our field do, that scholarly inquiry into 'crime and media' requires not only a sensitivity to crime's meaning and representation, but a thoroughgoing conceptualization of media dynamics in all their cultural complexity. Because of this, he offers in *Crime and Media* a collection of classic and cutting edge media scholarship that for the first time establishes a comprehensive intellectual foundation for crime and media studies. A breakthrough book, *Crime and Media* now becomes essential reading for scholars and students alike.

Jeff Ferrell, Professor of Sociology, Texas Christian University, USA and University of Kent, UK

Crime and Media: A Reader will be a vital resource for the emerging field of media criminology. Here, in one integrated volume, are found both the classics of the field as well as wonderful, cutting edge research on a wide range of topics. Because Geer has also thought seriously about the need to develop the field both theoretically and methodologically, the volume provides media criminologists with key resources to do this important work.

Meda Chesney-Lind, Professor of Women's Studies, University of Hawai'i at Manoa, Hawai'i

This is an exceptionally useful, comprehensive and stimulating collection of papers on crime and media. It skilfully blends the essential texts with less well known ones, so there is much here to interest teachers as well as students. The introductions succinctly and clearly draw out the issues concerning the ever important and increasingly salient relationship between crime and media, and the significance of each reading. The editorial commentary and the selection of materials embody a sophisticated theoretical perspective on this exciting area. The book offers a one-stop-shop for the growing number of courses studying crime and the media, and also offers a state-of-the-art synthesis of the field for scholars, practitioners or policy-makers interested in this vital topic.

Robert Reiner, Professor, School of Law, London School of Economics, UK

Crime and Media provides a welcome and exceptionally wide-ranging overview of the many issues that intersect in the rapidly changing forms of contemporary media culture. Combining the classics of media studies and the latest debates in media criminology, this book is a valuable resource for beginners and experts alike. Authoritative, bold and innovative – this is interdisciplinary criminology at its best.

Katja Franko Aas, Institute of Criminology and Sociology of Law, University of Oslo, Norway

Crime and Media: A Reader is a terrific eclectic collection of pieces. Greer has assembled a selection of influential essays prefaced with a succinct introduction. It is an exciting and diverse anthology which will provide an essential companion for students, scholars, policy makers and journalists.

Howard Tumber, Professor, Department of Journalism, City University London, UK

In the late modern world the screen reflects the street and the street the screen. This state of the art collection is the only text which fully covers the interaction and intimacy between the act of crime and its representation. Perfect for courses, a must for scholars.

Jock Young, Distinguished Professor of Criminal Justice, The Graduate Center and John Jay College, City University of New York, USA

Crime and Media

This engaging and timely collection gathers together for the first time key and classic readings in the ever-expanding area of crime and media. Comprising a carefully distilled selection of the most important contributions to the field, *Crime and Media: A Reader* tackles a wide range of issues including: understanding media; researching media; crime, newsworthiness and news; crime, entertainment and creativity; effects, influence and moral panic; and cyber-crime, surveillance and risk. Specially devised introductory and linking sections contextualize each reading and evaluate its contribution to the field, both individually and in relation to competing approaches and debates.

This book provides a single source around which criminology, media and cultural studies modules can be structured, an invaluable revision and consultation guide for students, and an extremely useful resource for scholars writing and researching across a wide range of relevant fields.

Accessible yet challenging, and packed with additional pedagogical devices, *Crime and Media: A Reader* will be an invaluable resource for students and academics studying crime, media, culture, surveillance and control.

Chris Greer is Senior Lecturer in the Department of Sociology at City University, London. His primary research interests lie at the intersections between crime, media and culture, and he has published widely in this area. Chris is also founder and co-editor of the award-winning *Crime Media Culture: An International Journal.*

Routledge Student Readers

Already in this Series:

Crime and Media

A Reader

Edited by Chris Greer

Routledge
Taylor & Francis Group

LONDON AND NEW YORK

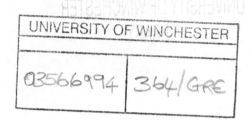
First published 2010
by Routledge
2 Park Square, Milton Park, Abingdon, Oxon, OX14 4RN

Simultaneously published in the USA and Canada
by Routledge
270 Madison Avenue, New York, NY 10016

Routledge is an imprint of the Taylor & Francis Group, an informa business

Typeset in Perpetua and Bell Gothic by Keyword Group Ltd
Printed and bound in Great Britain by TJ International Ltd, Padstow, Cornwall

British Library Cataloguing in Publication Data
A catalogue record for this book is available from the British Library

Library of Congress Cataloging in Publication Data
Greer, Chris.
Crime and media: a Reader/[edited by] Chris Greer.
p. cm.
1. Mass media and crime. I. Title.
p96.C74G74 2008
364–dc22
2008016700

ISBN10: 0-415-42238-8 (hbk)
ISBN10: 0-415-42239-6 (pbk)
ISBN10: 0-203-89478-2 (ebk)

ISBN13: 978-0-415-42238-3 (hbk)
ISBN13: 978-0-415-42239-0 (pbk)
ISBN13: 978-0-203-89478-1 (ebk)

For Mum

Contents

List of Figures

Publishers' Acknowledgements

The publishers would like to thank the following for permission to reprint their material:

Taylor & Francis Group for permission to reprint J. Habermas, 'The Public Sphere: An Encyclopedia Article', from S. Bronner and D. Kellner (eds.), *Critical Theory and Sociey: A Reader*, London: Routledge (1989).

Taylor & Francis Group for permission to reprint M. McLuhan, 'The Medium is the Message', taken from *Understanding Media*, London: Routledge (1964).

The Random House Group Ltd. for permission to reprint E. Herman and N. Chomsky, 'A Propaganda Model', an extract from *Manufacturing Consent: The Political Economy of Mass Media*, published by Vintage. Reprinted with permission of The Random House Group.

Taylor & Francis Group for permission to reprint S. Hall, 'Encoding/Decoding', from S. Hall, A. Hobson, D. Lowe and P. Willis. (eds.) *Culture, Media, Language*, London: Routledge (1981).

Taylor & Francis Group for permission to reprint M. Castells, 'An Introduction to the Information Age', from *City: analysis of urban trends, culture, theory, policy, action*, Volume 2, Issue 7, 1997, Pages 6–16. Routledge (Taylor & Francis Ltd, http://www.informaworld.com)

Semiotext(e) for permission to reprint excerpt from J. Baudrillard, *Simulcra and Simulations*, trans. P. Foss, P. Batton and P. Beitchman, New York: Semiotext(e) (1981).

Martha Millard Literary Agency for permission to reprint excerpt from W. Gibson, *Necromancer*, Ace Books (1984). Copyright © 1984 William Gibson. Used by permission of Martha Millard Literary Agency.

Richard Ericson, Patricia Baranek and Janet Chan for permission to reprint R. Ericson, P. Baranek and P. Chan, 'Research Approaches', taken from *Visualizing Deviance: A Study of News Organisation*, Milton Keynes: Open University Press (1987).

Constable & Robinson for permission to reprint S. Hall, 'The Determination of News Photographs', from S. Cohen and J. Young (eds.), T*he Manufacture of News: Social Problems, Deviance and the Mass Media*, London: Constable & Robinson (1981).

Taylor & Francis for permission to reprint Steve Neale, 'Dimensions of Genre' from *Genre and Hollywood*, London: Routledge (2000).

Transaction Publishers for permission to reprint T. Sassoon, 'Frame Analysis', an excerpt from *Crime Talk: How Citizens Construct a Social Problem*, New York: Aldine de Gruyter (1995).

Pluto Press for permission to reprint 'The Debate about Media Influence' from Jenny Kitzenger, *Framing Abuse*, London: Pluto Press (2004).

Taylor & Francis for permission to reprint David Bell, 'Researching Cybercultures' from *An Introduction to Cybercultures*, London: Routledge (2000).

Steve Chibnall for permission to reprint 'Press Ideology: The Politics of Professionalism', an excerpt from *Law and Order News: An Analysis of Crime Reporting in the British Press*, London: Tavistock (1977).

Yvonne Jewkes and Sage Publications Ltd. for permission to reprint Y. Jewkes, 'The Construction of News'. Reproduced with permission from Yvonne Jewkes, *Media and Crime*. Copyright © Yvonne Jewkes 2004, by permission of Sage Publications Ltd.

Jack Katz and Sage Publications Ltd. for permission to reprint J. Katz, 'What Makes Crime News?' Reproduced with permission from Jack Katz, *Media, Culture and Society*, 9 (1987): 47–75. Copyright © Jack Katz 1987, by permission of Sage Publications Ltd.

Macmillan Publishers Ltd. for permission to reprint S. Hall, C. Critcher, T. Jefferson, J. Clarke and B. Roberts, 'The Social Production of News', an excerpt from *Policing the Crisis: Mugging, the State and Law and Order*, London: Macmillan (1978).

Blackwell Publishing for permission to reprint P. Schlesinger, H. Tumber and G. Murdock, 'The Media Politics of Crime and Criminal Justice', from *The British Journal of Sociology*, 42, 3 (1991): 397–420.

Oxford University Press for permission to reprint E. McLaughlin, 'Recovering Blackness – Repudiating Whiteness: The Daily Mail's Construction of the Five White Suspects Accused of the Racist Murder of Stephen Lawrence', from Murji and Solomos *Racialization: Studies in Theory and Practice*, Oxford: Oxford University Press (2004).

Oxford University Press for permission to reprint Helen Benedict, 'Virgin or Vamp: How the Press Covers Sex Crimes', Oxford: Oxford University Press (1992).

Blackwell Publishing for permission to reprint T. Todorov, 'The Typology of Detective Fiction' taken from D. Lodge (ed.) *Modern Criticism And Theory: A Reader, second edition*, London and New York: Longman (1999).

Palgrave Macmillan for permission to reprint R. Reiner, 'The Dialectics of Dixon: The Changing Image of the TV Cop', from M. Stephens and S. Becker (eds.), *Police Force, Police Service: Care and Control in Britain*, London: Macmillan (1994).

Taylor & Francis Group for permission to reprint M. Valverde, 'From the Hard-Boiled Detective to the Pre-Crime Unit', an excerpt from *Law and Order: Images, Meanings, Myths*, London: Routledge (2006).

Willan Publishing for permission to reprint R. Reiner, S. Livingston and J. Allen, 'Casino Culture: Media and Crime in a Winner-Loser Society', from K. Stenson and R. Sullivan (eds.) *Crime, Risk and Justice: The Politics of Crime Control in Liberal Democracies*, Cullompton: Willan (2000).

Edinburgh University Press for permission to reprint Barry Langford 'The Gangster Film: Genre and Society' from *Film Genre: Hollywood and Beyond*, Edinburgh: Edinburgh University Press (2005).

Brian Jarvis and Sage Publications Ltd. for permission to reprint B. Jarvis, 'Monsters Inc.: Serial Killers and Consumer Culture', from *Crime, Media, Culture: An International Journal*, 3, 3 (2007): 326–344. Copyright © Brian Jarvis 2007, by permission of Sage Publications Ltd.

Jeff Ferrell: Crimes of Style, pp. 159–209, 1993, by Jeff Ferrell. Reprinted with permission of University Press of New England, Hanover, NH.

The American Psychological Association for permission to reprint A. Bandura, D. Ross and S. A. Ross, 'Imitation of film-mediated aggressive models', from *Journal of Abnormal Psychology & Social Psychology*, 66, 1 (1963): 3–11.

Taylor & Francis Group for permission to reprint D. Gauntlett, 'The Worrying Influence of 'Media Effects' Studies', from M. Barker and J. Petley (eds.), *Ill Effects: The Media/Violence Debate*, second edition, London: Routledge (2001).

Taylor & Francis Group for permission to reprint M. Barker and J. Petley, 'From Bad Media Violence Research to Good: A Guide for the Perplexed', from M. Barker and J. Petley (eds.), *Ill Effects: The Media/Violence Debate,* second edition, London: Routledge (2001).

Blackwell Publishing for permission to reprint Gerbner, G. and Gross, L., 'Living with Television: The Violence Profile', in *Journal of Communication*, 26, 1: 173–199 (1976).

Oxford University Press for permission to reprint J. Ditton, D. Chadee, S. Farrall, E. Gilchrist and J. Bannister, 'From Imitation to Intimidation: A Note on the Curious and Changing Relationship between the Media, Crime and Fear of Crime', from *The British Journal of Criminology*, 44, 4 (2004): 595–610, Oxford: Oxford University Press.

Taylor & Francis Group for permission to reprint material from Stanley Cohen, 'Folk Devils and Moral Panics: The Creation of the Mods and Rockers', London: Routledge (2002).

Blackwell Publishing Ltd. for permission to reprint Angela McRobbie and Sarah Thornton 'Rethinking "Moral Panic" for Multi-Mediated Social Worlds' and 'The Media Politics of Crime and Criminal Justice', 1991 from *The British Journal of Sociology* (1995).

Penguin Group UK and Georges Borchardt, Inc. for permission to reprint *Discipline and Punish* by Michel Foucault. English Translation copyright © 1977 by Alan Sheridan (New York: Pantheon). Originally published in French as *Surveiller et Punir*. Copyright © 1975 by Editions Gallimard. Reprinted by permission of Georges Borchardt, Inc.for Editions Gallimard.

Thomas Mathiesen and Sage Publications Ltd. for permission to reprint T. Mathiesen, 'The Viewer Society', from *Theoretical Criminology*, 1, 2 (1997): 215–34. Copyright © Thomas Mathiesen 1997, by permission of Sage Publications Ltd.

Willan Publishing for permission to reprint K. Frank Aas, 'Beyond the 'Desert of the Real': Crime Control in a Virtual(ised) Reality', in Y. Jewkes (ed.) *Crime Online*, Cullompton: Willan (2006).

Gabe Mythen, Sandra Walklate and Sage Publications Ltd. for permission to reprint G. Mythen and S. Walklate, 'Communicating the Terrorist Risk: Harnessing a Culture of Fear', from *Crime, Media, Culture: An International Journal*, 2, 2 (2006): 123–142. Copyright © Gabe Mythen and Sandra Walklate 2006, by permission of Sage Publications Ltd.

Solo Syndication for permission to reproduce the front page of *The Daily Mail* 'Murderers' 14/02/1997.

NI Syndication Ltd for permission to reproduce extract from *The Sun* 21/01/2008.

Magnus Arrevad gives non-exclusive use for image 38.2 inside *Crime and Media: A Reader* by Chris Greer, Routledge 2009, World English Language and USA rights.

Acknowledgements

As is always the case with large projects like books, there are lots people to thank. So many people, in fact, that some may inadvertently have been left off this list. For that I apologise in advance. Firstly, thanks must go to the scholars, commentators and artists whose work appears in this Reader. Engaging with and editing – hopefully in a manner that will earn approval from contributors and readers alike – 42 key and classic texts, and countless others that didn't make the final selection, was at times arduous, but always instructive. I have learned much, discovered new areas of interest, and had my eyes opened to new possibilities in media criminology. I am grateful to my colleagues and friends at City University London: Jean Chalaby, Cathie Cremin, Aeron Davis, Carrie-Anne Myers, Liza Schuster, John Solomos, Howard Tumber, Alison Wakefield, Frank Webster and Tony Woodiwiss all offered helpful criticisms and suggestions, or just a patient ear along the way. A special note of thanks goes to Eugene McLaughlin, who consistently provided all one could hope for in sound advice, good humour and 'just bloody finish it-ness'. 'It' finally was finished while on sabbatical at John Jay College of Criminal Justice, City University of New York. To Dave Brotherton, Lynn Chancer, Baz Dreisinger, Michael Flynn, Josh Freilich, Dave Green, Tony Jefferson, Andrew Karmen, Gabrielle Salfatti, Greg Snyder, Barry Spunt, Theresa Rockett, Cécile Van de Voorde, Jock Young, and the rest, thanks for making New York such an easy, stimulating and fun place to be. Jeff Ferrell and Mark Hamm, my friends and co-editors on *Crime, Media, Culture: An International Journal*, continue to amaze and inspire in equal measure. To all those who provided timely distraction, but perhaps especially to Stefi, Myrna, Orlando, Karene, Annette, Elena, Kathy, Tobes, Suzanne and the East Dulwich and Belfast crews, I am more grateful than a token mention here could ever express (and I hope you all see it that way too, though Dax probably won't). And finally, to the editorial team at Routledge: Miranda Thirkettle, Antonia Edwards and James Rabson offered helpful advice and support throughout, and Gerhard Boomgaarden remains a shining example of professionalism, conscientiousness and patience; thanks for your faith in the book.

Chris Greer, 2009

Introduction

CRIME AND MEDIA: A READER was borne out of frustration. A passion for research and teaching at the intersections of crime and media, of course. And that had lots to do with it. But it was mainly frustration. There were two sources of frustration in particular. The first was pedagogical, and related to the difficulties in finding and collating key and classic texts when teaching courses on media, crime and criminal justice. Sourcing a sufficiently wide range of appropriate readings is seldom straightforward, and all but the most well-stocked social science libraries contain a fraction of the readings included in this collection. One of the main reasons for producing this book, then, was pedagogical convenience. Now, for the first time, teachers and students can access a comprehensive selection of key and classic readings spanning the full spectrum of intersections between media and crime in a single volume. It is hoped that this book will provide a foundation upon which crime and media modules can be structured – taking in a diversity of theoretical, methodological and empirical approaches, old and new, orthodox and alternative, and along the way testing and expanding the limits of enquiry in media criminology.

The second source of frustration relates to an ongoing sense of concern about the current orthodoxy in crime and media research, and in particular about the types of research that appear increasingly to be defining the field. The other main reason for producing this book, then, is more ambitious. It is to begin a process of reorientation within media criminology towards a more fully interdisciplinary, theoretically and methodologically rigorous, qualitative engagement with the crime-media nexus. In this sense, my thinking behind the creation of *Crime and Media: A Reader* was also distinctly political. Now that the Reader has been produced and published, the pedagogical concern has been diminished, slightly, by the fact that this resource is now available for use and I can structure courses around it. The concern with the current state of media criminology, however, is still very much to the fore. In order to explain this concern further, and in so doing clarify the book's underpinning rationale, it is useful to consider the current orthodoxy within crime and media research.

The current orthodoxy in crime and media research

Quantitatively speaking, media criminology is in the ascendancy. There are more courses covering the subject, and now even full degree programmes dedicated to its exploration. There is also, it seems, more and more research being conducted on crime and media. Much of that research, however, appears to be of a less and less theoretically, methodologically and empirically rigorous nature. The current orthodoxy within crime and media research, I would suggest, has a number of negative consequences for this rapidly expanding area of scholarly interest. These consequences can be summarised in the following three points, which deal respectively with theory, methods and epistemology:

First, a consolidation of theoretical parochialism that prioritises criminological frames of reference at the expense of interdisciplinarity
    One of the most striking things about much media criminology is the imbalanced nature of the research approach taken. There is a clear tendency to prioritise the criminological, at the level of theory and method, over serious and informed consideration of the media. Indeed, despite a flourish of groundbreaking, highly interdisciplinary studies in the 1960s and 1970s, media criminology has come to be characterised by a distinct lack of attention to the theory and methods used by key thinkers on media and society. Over the last twenty years or so, as criminology has become more independent and established as a 'discipline' in its own right, so too has it become more insular and dismissive of (or perhaps just less interested in) other, non-criminological discipline bases. Jock Young (1999), in particular, has been vociferous in lamenting the detachment of criminology from its sociological roots. More recently Ferrell *et al.* have made this point with force and eloquence (2008). The tendency towards criminological parochialism has been reflected in media criminology – which, ironically enough, should by definition be interdisciplinary in nature – to the extent that serious theoretical and methodological engagement with the rapidly changing media side of the crime-media relationship has become increasingly rare. Much media criminology, therefore, is founded upon a partial theorisation of the crime-media nexus, which inevitably leads to partial analysis and partial understanding of the forces and factors that shape that nexus. This leads to, and is clearly evidenced in, a second fundamental problem with the current orthodoxy.

Second, the growing distancing between the researcher and the object of enquiry
    This second characteristic of the current orthodoxy in crime and media research is evidenced on three levels: the text, the production of the text, and the consumption of the text. At the level of the text, distancing between the researcher and the object of enquiry is made most explicit by the growing reliance on online searchable newspaper databases. Undoubtedly, these databases are extremely helpful in locating news copy. Years of coverage across scores of publications can be searched, filtered and collated by year and title, byline and headline. Indeed, a complete body of newspaper coverage for a particular case can be sourced and retrieved at the push of a button.

The advantages seem clear. The problem, however, is that online newspaper databases strip news content of its colour, style, formatting, visual imagery and surrounding context. Crime and news media research is thus increasingly based upon a 'news residue' – standardised, decontextualised words on a computer screen, light years from the brilliantly colourful and highly textured product consumed by millions every day. No wonder, then, media criminologists have had so little to say on the growing importance of the 'visual' as a defining feature of contemporary crime news (Greer, 2007). The distancing may be less apparent with respect to other forms of crime and media research – film and television studies, for example – perhaps only because a stripped down media residue is not yet available. But it is the quantitative analysis of crime news that dominates the field, and the current orthodoxy is established in these terms.

At the level of the text production, the primacy of content analysis across news, entertainment, hybrid and virtual representational forms has brought about a distancing from the social process of media production. This has amounted to nothing short of the 'death of ethnography' in media criminology. A minority of researchers is undertaking in depth qualitative analyses of media texts, which step outside the purely quantitative paradigm and seek to embrace the style, structure, form and colour of media representations. Yet virtually no one is talking to the producers of those texts in order to better understand the social processes through which media representations come into being. The study of media content can provide important insights into the role of expressive cultural forms in interpreting our social world and constructing particular versions of reality. But this research is at its richest, and surely has the greatest explanatory potential, when the *process* of production is considered as well as the *product* that results.

At the level of the consumption of the text, research on reception has tended to play a peripheral role within media criminology. Of course, within the realms of psychological positivism an entire industry has been established around media effects research, and countless studies have sought to demonstrate empirically the connection between the consumption of media violence and violence in the 'real world' (see Section Five of this Reader). The sociological analysis of media, however, tends more often to assume than actively research and evidence media influence. The main exception is research on media and fear of crime (also dealt with in Section Five). The lack of empirical engagement with media consumers is partly because the development of adequate methods for exploring the consumption, interpretation and influence of media images – of establishing their 'meaning' for media consumers – are still being developed. Nevertheless, media criminologists have been slow to capitalise on the availability of new qualitative research approaches which *can* start to make meaningful sense of the influence on consumers of media images of crime, violence and control. The current, and indeed historical, orthodoxy within media criminology is to assume and sometimes theorise media influence, but seldom to research it directly.

Third, the reification of epistemological realism within a positivistic framework of understanding

Taken together, the first two elements of media criminology's current orthodoxy – the tendency towards criminological parochialism, and the growing distancing between the researcher and the object of enquiry – create a research environment in which the breadth and depth of possible findings are severely constrained. In fact, media criminology frequently finds itself in the position where it can do little more than confirm the criminological truism that 'the media distort crime'. The nature and extent of media distortion – whether inflected through race, gender, class, or other variables – is 'objectively assessed' against a more or less explicit conception of the 'nature of reality' beyond representation. This approach is based upon a positivistic epistemological realism which insists upon, indeed relies upon, the maintenance of sharp, tangible and largely impermeable boundaries between sign and referent, represented and real. Media criminology, then, is often locked-in to a theoretical and methodological framework where the research possibilities are limited to reiterating the same findings time after time. This (re)iteration – that media distort crime – should be the starting point for a media criminology that seeks to interrogate, understand and explain, rather than just repeatedly confirm what we already know. As things stand, it is too often the outcome of the research process: the point of departure becomes the final destination.

Some may argue that this characterisation of media criminology is a little unfair; that to make these claims about the current state of research in crime in media is to subscribe to the same kind of reductionism I've just been so critical of. Quantitative research methods are essential for longitudinal analysis and, when conducted in a theoretically and methodologically rigorous manner, can shed much light on shifts and continuities in media representations of crime and criminal justice and, for example, public opinion over time. And there are of course pockets of strong, critical qualitative research, as indeed there are journals that make it their business to promote this research – *Crime, Media, Culture; An International Journal* and *Theoretical Criminology* are two such examples. But the critical, qualitative, in-depth engagement with the crime-media nexus is the clear exception rather than the rule. It is for this reason that I would advocate the development of a more fully-fledged media criminology, critical in nature and comprehensive in scope.

Media criminology

In a scathing critique of the methods that dominate within orthodox criminology, Ferrell *et al.* (2008: 165) ponder on what becomes of a field of enquiry when the researcher is so distanced from the research environment, when methods are designed for detached quantification and counting rather than engaged, in depth understanding, and the main objective is the routinised production of quick, clean datasets.

> It becomes lifeless, stale, and inhuman. Just as the broader inhumanity of modernism resulted from the reduction of human subjects to rationalized categories of work, consumption, and control, the inhumanity of orthodox criminology results in large part from methodologies designed, quite explicitly, to reduce research subjects to carefully controlled categories of counting and cross-tabulation. Just as the stale redundancy of modern work stemmed from the Taylorist exhaustion of uncertainty and possibility, the thudding boredom of orthodox criminology stems from

methodologies designed, again quite explicitly, to exclude ambiguity, surprise, and 'human error' from the process of criminological research.

The same can be said of crime and media research. More than ever it seems that the reduction of the crime-media nexus to binary oppositions and statistical tables and charts is proceeding apace. This book has been constructed in part as a response to the incursion of those pseudo-scientific research methodologies that lack a strong theoretical base and effectively quantify out of existence the complexities of the crime-media nexus – colourful, visceral, nuanced, sensational, spectacular, and unpredictable. In this sense, the philosophies and rationales underpinning this book have much in common with those that inform the wider project of cultural criminology. Indeed, given cultural criminology's concerns with aesthetic, emotion and, crucially, media and mediatisation, there are important areas of overlap. Certainly, a good many of the excerpts included in *Crime and Media: A Reader* would be equally at home in a *Reader in Cultural Criminology*. But whilst cultural criminology is, by definition and stated intention, much broader in scope and focuses on both mediatised and non-mediatised phenomena, media criminology represents a narrower, more clearly defined field of enquiry. And it is worth noting that, at the present time, cultural criminology doesn't do news media. Or at least it hasn't done so yet. Perhaps this Reader will contribute to directing the cultural criminological gaze towards that blind spot.

The tighter focus that characterises a fully-fledged media criminology is not to overlook the postmodern fluidity of mediatisation and the collapsing boundaries between the 'represented' and the 'real': a postmodern sensitisation to the hyperreal provides a strong current which runs throughout this book. Nor is it to ignore the related proposition that, today, all experience is to an extent mediatised experience – whether through direct consumption of media images, or through interpreting the social world using reference points and frameworks of understanding that are, themselves, shaped and structured through mediatised signs, symbols and codes. Within this context, media criminology could, in theory, relate to anything and everything in the late modern world. But this is perhaps a little too broad. Thus, for the purposes of this Reader, the interests of media criminology can be defined as the complex and constantly shifting intersections between crime, criminalisation and control, on the one hand, and media, mediatisation and representation on the other. It is within this broad but clearly delimited understanding of media criminology that this Reader has been structured. To further the consolidation of a media criminology, it has been produced with a number of specific aims in mind.

The aims and objectives of the Reader

The aims of this book can be outlined as follows:

1   to offer theoretically, methodologically and empirically authoritative readings on established, new and emerging debates within media criminology;
2   to promote an interdisciplinary approach to the study of crime and media by drawing from a diversity of relevant literatures, knowledge bases, and theoretical and methodological perspectives;

3   to encourage the development and application of a wide range of methodological approaches which can better capture the colour and complexity of the crime-media nexus;

4   to widen the scope and broaden the horizons of media criminology to embrace a more comprehensive appreciation of media forms and contexts and the constantly shifting boundaries between crime and media.

No single theoretical position or methodological approach can capture the complexity of what occurs at the intersections of crime and media. What is required is an interdisciplinary or multiperspectival approach that builds upon a wide diversity of theoretical, methodological and empirical perspectives. The Readings that appear in this book include the best examples of crime and media research from within mainstream academic criminology, of course. But they also foreground, in a manner that much media criminology does not, some of the most important thinkers, theorists and researchers from a diversity of fields beyond mainstream criminology, including key and classic contributions from media and cultural studies, film studies and photography. This book constitutes an acknowledgement of the acute need for a reinvigorated interdisciplinarity in crime and media research, and it is hoped that its users will approach individual readings and the wider crime-media nexus with that in mind.

The Reader's basic structure

The six Sections in this reader are intended to encourage a rethinking, redeveloping and broadening out of the traditionally narrow parameters within which the crime-media relationship has been conceptualised. It is for this reason that particular attention has been paid to theoretical and methodological approaches to understanding crime and media. These sections comprise what I consider to be key areas for consideration across any comprehensive reading of the crime-media nexus. They are: Understanding Media; Researching Media; Crime, Newsworthiness and News; Crime, Entertainment and Creativity; Effects, Influence and Moral Panic; Cybercrime, Surveillance and Risk.

These Sections have been constructed with theory, methods and applied research in mind, and variously focus on one or more of these areas. Similarly, each of the readings in this book has been included on the basis of its particular strength on one or more of these elements. Naturally, the creation of any Reader involves the inclusion of some texts to the exclusion of others. Ten different editors would no doubt have come up with ten different final listings (and possibly edited those readings differently as well). Should this book make it to a second edition the current selection will no doubt change then too. What I would maintain, however, is that the selections included here constitute key and/or classic readings – in some cases shaping or even defining a particular area of investigation, in others challenging existing knowledge and (re)establishing the terms of debate, in still others venturing into less well known theoretical, methodological and empirical territories to develop new fields of enquiry. Some of the readings are mutually supportive. Some present diametrically opposing viewpoints. Some will be familiar to many users of this book. Some less so. The aim has been to present a selection which comprehensively covers the length, breadth and depth of the crime-media nexus, and ultimately equips students with the relevant information to go out and *do research* themselves in order to develop a deeper knowledge and fuller understanding of the vast array of studies that might be conducted at the intersections of crime and media. In the final section of this Introduction, I want to offer some suggestions about how this Reader might be used.

Contexts and critical connections

The readings included in this book are not intended to be considered in isolation, though of course they can be. Rather, in putting together this Reader I have attempted to construct a narrative. This narrative aims to help students develop a cumulative appreciation and understanding of the main issues, themes and debates in media criminology, at each stage thinking critically and reflexively about the theories, methodologies and empirical approaches applied. To encourage critical reflection, and to locate readings within their wider context, each is supplemented with a variety of contextualising pieces and pedagogic devices.

Every reading in this book is topped and tailed with contextualising sections called *Introduction and Context* and *Critical Connections*. The *Introduction and Context* sections precede each reading and offer an overview of the *content* of the reading in order to establish what it is about and provide a brief summary of the main points being addressed. There is also within these sections a consideration of the theoretical, methodological and/or empirical *context* within which the excerpt can be situated, and how in that sense it fits within wider bodies of research and literature.

Following each reading, sections entitled *Critical Connections* highlight the particular strengths of readings, or challenges which have been advanced against them, in terms of the ideas, arguments or approaches being presented. In so doing they offer some sense of the reasoning behind the pieces selected for inclusion in this book. Perhaps most significantly, these sections also begin to establish *critical connections* with other readings. The aim here is to stimulate interdisciplinary, reflexive and above all critical thinking about where different readings 'sit' in relation to each other, about the different methodologies and epistemologies underpinning them, and about their respective theoretical approaches to understanding aspects of the crime-media nexus. This is a defining characteristic of this book – the desire to encourage readers, at whatever level, to *think across* theory and methods, to *work through* the relative strengths and weaknesses of different approaches in different contexts, and to *move beyond* the comfortable and safe, but arid, colourless and partial studies based around the purely quantitative classification and counting of crime and media. Of course, the critical connections I point to are not the only connections that can be made. Nor are they necessarily the definitive ones. Readers are urged to think beyond what is suggested in these pages and to seek out their own critical connections, links and pathways to further promote the interdisciplinary study of crime and media.

At the end of each individual reading, *Discussion Questions* are designed to encourage further critical reflection on the main themes and debates presented in that particular excerpt and to consolidate connections with other readings in the book. How might Manuel Castells' work on the Information Society (Reading 5) inform a reconfiguration of Jürgen Habermas' notion of the 'public sphere' (Reading 1); how could Ericson *et al.*'s ethnographic research approach (Reading 8) have influenced the development of Hall *et al.*'s *Policing the Crisis* (Reading 18) or Jack Katz's *What Makes Crime News?* (Reading 17); is it helpful or desirable to conceive of the 'war on terror' (Readings 41 and 42) as a 'moral panic' (Readings 34 and 35)?

Throughout this Reader, then, there is the underpinning aim to develop interdisciplinarity, to encourage critical reflection and cross-referencing, and to demonstrate how the use of a diversity of theoretical and methodological approaches can prepare a richer and more fertile ground for applied empirical research. In multi-mediated worlds, where signs, codes and symbols constantly loop, merge and intertwine in an endless stream of simulations and (re)presentations, crime and criminal justice *are* fundamentally mediatised phenomena. There can be no understanding of the crime-media nexus without sustained and critical engagement with the intersecting and overlapping forces that variously define, shape and inflect that nexus. Providing an interdisciplinary starting point for this journey towards a more fully-fledged media criminology and a better understanding of crime and media is the ultimate objective of this book.

References

Ferrell, J. Hayward, K. and Young, J. (2008) *Cultural Criminology: An Invitation,* London: Sage.

Greer, C. (2007) 'News Media, Victims and Crime', in P. Davies, P. Francis, C. Greer (eds) *Victims, Crime and Society,* London: Sage.

Young, J. (1999) *The Exclusive Society,* London: Sage.

SECTION ONE

Understanding media

Introduction

THE AIM IN THIS SECTION of the Reader is to push the boundaries and broaden the horizons of media criminology by beginning to think more seriously about media. The underpinning principle is straightforward. In order to adequately explore and understand the complex and myriad connections between crime and media, we must develop an adequate understanding of both 'crime' and 'media'. Perhaps understandably criminology has traditionally been more comfortable tackling the crime part of the equation. There are of course an enormous array of sometimes diametrically opposed positions on 'the problem of crime' – classical and positivist, structuralist and agentic, empiricist and rationalist, cultural and political-economic, administrative and critical, aetiological and situational, realist and idealist, modernist and postmodernist, and so on – and theoretical approaches to explaining and understanding crime and control are often underpinned by very different epistemologies. There is an equally wide diversity of approaches to understanding media and society. Yet it is much less common for criminologists to devote as much attention to theorising media as they do to theorising crime. This prioritisation of the criminological has led to an imbalance across much of the work we might describe as media criminology. And this imbalance is most clearly discernible at the level of theory and research methods. This is why the first two sections of this Reader deal specifically with theory and research methods, and place a clear emphasis on media rather than crime.

Media are fantastically diverse. Understanding media, therefore, requires a diversity of theoretical, methodological and epistemological approaches. Certainly, no single theoretical position or methodological approach can adequately capture the richness, complexity and diversity of media today. The readings included in this section have been selected in accordance with their contribution to explaining and understanding particular forms of media, or particular aspects of the relationship between media and society. Each one offers its own perspective on the structure, function, role and importance of media in everyday life.

Jürgen Habermas (1974) develops the notion of the 'public sphere' and, within this wider theoretical framework, presents a highly influential account of the importance of media for democratic administration. Marshall McLuhan (1964) explores the crucial role of media in shaping individual consciousness, culture and society, and as an active agent of historical change. Noam Chomsky and Ed Herman (1994) offer an instrumental Marxist analysis of the role of media in 'manufacturing consent' through manipulation by ruling elites – political, military and cultural – who work collectively to maintain the interests of the powerful in a class society. Stuart Hall's (1981) Encoding–Decoding model presents a theoretical and empirical approach, grounded in semiotics and Marxist theory, to understanding not just elements of media communication, but the communication process as a whole. Manuel Castells' (1997) theorisation of the Information Society develops an understanding of media in the context of recent and dramatic transformations – in particular, the rapid spread of Information and Communication Technologies (ICTs) and their role in the transition from Industrial capitalism to Information capitalism. Jean Baudrillard's (1981) *Simulacra and Simulation* is a postmodern vision of a world in which media have penetrated and saturated the everyday to such an extent that the boundaries between the 'represented' and the 'real' have dissolved away, generating a mediatised 'hyper-reality' where simulations signs and codes come to constitute everyday life. Finally, the original conception of 'cyberspace', adopted, adapted and articulated across countless contexts since, comes not from academic scholarship, but from the cyberpunk writings of novelist William Gibson (1984).

Jürgen Habermas

THE PUBLIC SPHERE:
AN ENCYCLOPEDIA ARTICLE (1974)

Introduction and context

JÜRGEN HABERMAS' key contribution to understanding media comes
from his theorising of the 'public sphere', and the role of this public sphere in
shaping the democratic administration of society. In its ideal form, the public sphere
is 'made up of private people gathered together as a public and articulating the
needs of society with the state' (Habermas, 1989: 176). Through open assembly and
rational-critical dialogue around matters of political and economic importance, the
citizenry can form a consensual 'public opinion' which, where necessary, can oppose
state power and influence state policy and practice. The 'public sphere', then, lies at
the heart of a process of participatory democracy underpinned by the values of universal access, rational debate, and disregard of rank. It is central in promoting the
liberal ideals of equality, freedom, human rights and justice. In the reading included
here, Habermas summarises the key themes and ideas from his classic *The Structural
Transformation of the Public Sphere* (1962/1989).

Habermas traces the development of the public sphere from its origins in the bourgeois coffee-houses of the eighteenth century through to the capital-driven, profit-oriented mass media of the present day. Key to the emergence of the bourgeois public
sphere was the establishment of a free political press. Newspapers and pamphlets of
the day offered important coverage of political issues and state practices, which
informed and encouraged public discussion. In this sense, the early media functioned
as instruments of rational-critical debate and the formation of public opinion. In the
latter stages of the nineteenth century, however, media became more concerned with
attracting audiences in a competitive market, and entertainment and advertising
came to replace political and social commentary as the industry's main driving force.
Media fell increasingly under the control of big business, and the public sphere was

transformed from a forum for democratic debate into a site for manipulation by corporate interests. This transformation of the media forms part of a wider 'refeudalization of the public sphere' in which the rational debating public is distanced and alienated from the processes of participatory democracy, and replaced instead by uncritical audiences more concerned with mass consumption.

As a young, second generation member of the Frankfurt School, Habermas drew much inspiration, and shared much of the pessimism, apparent in the work of his contemporaries. Early inspiration, for example, came from Max Horkheimer and Theodor Adorno's critical theorising of organised capitalism's impact on the 'culture industry'. However, Habermas is less deterministic than some of his colleagues and sees the possibility of reconstituting and re-energising a public sphere free from direct economic and state control. What is needed is a 'rational reorganisation of social and political power' between the private citizens, rival organisations and the state, along with an active citizenship that can not only articulate its political will, but also work to ensure this will is implemented by government.

The concept[*]

By "the public sphere" we mean first of all a realm of our social life in which something approaching public opinion can be formed. Access is guaranteed to all citizens. A portion of the public sphere comes into being in every conversation in which private individuals assemble to form a public body.[1] They then behave neither like business or professional people transacting private affairs, nor like members of a constitutional order subject to the legal constraints of a state bureaucracy. Citizens behave as a public body when they confer in an unrestricted fashion – that is, with the guarantee of freedom of assembly and association and the freedom to express and publish their opinions – about matters of general interest. In a large public body, this kind of communication requires specific means for transmitting information and influencing those who receive it. Today, newspapers and magazines, radio and television are the media of the public sphere. We speak of the political public sphere in contrast, for instance, to the literary one, when public discussion deals with objects connected to the activity of the state. Although state authority is, so to speak, the executor of the political public sphere, it is not a part of it.[2] To be sure, state authority is usually considered "public" authority, but it derives its task of caring for the well-being of all citizens primarily from this aspect of the public sphere. Only when the exercise of political control is effectively subordinated to the democratic demand that information be accessible to the public, does the political public sphere win an institutionalized influence over the government through the instrument of law-making bodies. The expression *public opinion* refers to the tasks of criticism and control which a public body of citizens informally – and, in periodic elections, formally as well – practices vis-à-vis the ruling structure organized in the form of a state. Regulations demanding that certain proceedings be public [*Publizitätsvorschriften*] – for example, those providing for open

*Translated by Sara Lennox and Frank Lennox.

court hearings – are also related to this function of public opinion. The public sphere as a sphere which mediates between society and state, in which the public organizes itself as the bearer of public opinion, accords with the principle of the public sphere[3] – that principle of public information which once had to be fought for against the arcane policies of monarchies and which since that time has made possible the democratic control of state activities.

It is no coincidence that these concepts of the public sphere and public opinion arose for the first time only in the eighteenth century. They acquire their specific meaning from a concrete historical situation. It was at that time that the distinction of "opinion" from "opinion publique" and "public opinion" came about. Though mere opinions (cultural assumptions, normative attitudes, collective prejudices and values) seem to persist unchanged in their natural form as a kind of sediment of history, public opinion can by definition come into existence only when a reasoning public is presupposed. Public discussions about the exercise of political power which are both critical in intent and institutionally guaranteed have not always existed – they grew out of a specific phase of bourgeois society and could enter into the order of the bourgeois constitutional state only as a result of a particular constellation of interests.

History

There is no indication that European society of the high Middle Ages possessed a public sphere as a unique realm distinct from the private sphere. Nevertheless, it was not coincidental that during that period symbols of sovereignty, for instance, the princely seal, were deemed "public." At that time there existed a public representation of power. The status of the feudal lord, at whatever level of the feudal pyramid, made it unnecessary to employ the categories "public" and "private." The holder of the position represented it publicly; he showed himself, presented himself as the embodiment of an ever-present "higher" power. The concept of this representation has been maintained up to the most recent constitutional history. Regardless of the degree to which it has loosened itself from the old base, the authority of political power today still demands a representation at the highest level by a head of state. Such elements, however, derive from a prebourgeois social structure. Representation in the sense of a bourgeois public sphere,[4] for instance, the representation of the nation or of particular mandates, has nothing to do with the medieval representative public sphere – a public sphere directly linked to the concrete existence of a ruler. As long as the prince and the estates of the realm still "are" the land, instead of merely functioning as deputies for it, they are able to "represent"; they represent their power "before" the people, instead of for the people.

The feudal authorities (Church, princes, and nobility), to which the representative public sphere was first linked, disintegrated during a long process of polarization. By the end of the eighteenth century they had broken apart into private elements on the one hand, and into public elements on the other. The position of the Church changed with the Reformation: the link to divine authority which the Church represented, that is, religion, became a private matter. So-called religious freedom came to insure what was historically the first area of private autonomy. The Church itself continued its existence as one public and legal body among others. The corresponding polarization within princely authority was visibly manifested in the separation of the public budget from the private household expenses of a ruler. The institutions of public authority, along with the bureaucracy and the military, and in part also with the legal institutions, asserted their independence from the privatized sphere of the princely court. Finally, the feudal estates were transformed as well: the nobility became the organs of public authority, parliament, and the legal institutions; while those occupied in trades and professions, insofar as they had already established urban corporations and territorial organizations, developed into a sphere of bourgeois society which would stand apart from the state as a genuine area of private autonomy.

The representative public sphere yielded to that new sphere of "public authority" which came into being with national and territorial states. Continuous state activity (permanent administration, standing army) now corresponded to the permanence of the relationships which with the stock exchange and the press had developed within the exchange of commodities and information. Public authority consolidated into a concrete opposition for those who were merely subject to it and who at first found only a negative definition of themselves within it. These were the "private individuals" who were excluded from public authority because they held no office. "Public" no longer referred to the "representative" court of a prince endowed with authority, but rather to an institution regulated according to competence, to an apparatus endowed with a monopoly on the legal exertion of authority. Private individuals subsumed in the state at whom public authority was directed now made up the public body.

Society, now a private realm occupying a position in opposition to the state, stood on the one hand as if in clear contrast to the state. On the other hand, that society had become a concern of public interest to the degree that the production of life in the wake of the developing market economy had grown beyond the bounds of private domestic authority. *The bourgeois public sphere* could be understood as the sphere of private individuals assembled into a public body, which almost immediately laid claim to the officially regulated "intellectual newspapers" for use against the public authority itself. In those newspapers, and in moralistic and critical journals, they debated that public authority on the general rules of social intercourse in their fundamentally privatized yet publicly relevant sphere of labor and commodity exchange.

The liberal model of the public sphere

The medium of this debate – public discussion – was unique and without historical pre-cedent. Hitherto the estates had negotiated agreements with their princes, settling their claims to power from case to case. This development took a different course in England, where the parliament limited royal power, than it did on the Continent, where the monarchies mediatized the estates. The Third Estate then broke with this form of power arrangement, since it could no longer establish itself as a ruling group. A division of power by means of the delineation of the rights of the nobility was no longer possible within an exchange economy – private authority over capitalist prop-erty is, after all, unpolitical. Bourgeois individuals are private individuals. As such, they do not "rule." Their claims to power vis-à-vis public authority were thus directed not against the concentration of power, which was to be "shared." Instead, their ideas infiltrated the very principle on which the existing power is based. To the principle of existing power, the bourgeois public opposed the principle of supervision – that very principle which demands that proceedings be made public [*Publizität*]. The principle of supervision is thus a means of transforming the nature of power, not merely one basis of legitimation exchanged for another.

In the first modern constitutions, the catalogues of fundamental rights were a perfect image of the liberal model of the public sphere: they guaranteed the society as a sphere of private autonomy and the restriction of public authority to a few functions. Between these two spheres, the constitutions further insured the existence of a realm of private individuals assembled into a public body who as citizens transmit the needs of bourgeois society to the state, in order, ideally, to transform political into "rational" authority within the medium of this public sphere. The general interest, which was the measure of such rationality, was then guaranteed, according to the presuppositions of a society of free commodity exchange, when the activities of private individuals in the marketplace were freed from social compulsion and from political pressure in the public sphere.

At the same time, daily political newspapers assumed an important role. In the second half of the eighteenth century, literary journalism created serious competition for the earlier news sheets, which were mere compilations of notices. Karl Bücher characterized this great development as follows: "Newspapers changed from mere institutions for the publication of news into bearers and leaders of public opinion – weapons of party politics. This transformed the newspaper business. A new element emerged between the gathering and publication of news: the editorial staff. But for the newspaper publisher it meant that he changed from a vendor of recent news to a dealer in public opinion." The publishers insured the newspapers a commercial basis, yet without commercializing them as such. The press remained an institution of the public itself, effective in the manner of a mediator and intensifier of public discussion, no longer a mere organ for the spreading of news but not yet the medium of a consumer culture.

This type of journalism can be observed above all during periods of revolution, when newspapers of the smallest political groups and organizations spring up – for instance, in Paris in 1789. Even in the Paris of 1848 every half-way eminent politician organized his club, every other his journal: 450 clubs and over 200 journals were established there between February and May alone. Until the permanent legalization of a politically functional public sphere, the appearance of a political newspaper meant joining the struggle for freedom and public opinion, and thus for the public sphere as a principle. Only with the establishment of the bourgeois constitutional state was the intellectual press relieved of the pressure of its convictions. Since then it has been able to abandon its polemical position and take advantage of the earning possibilities of a commercial undertaking. In England, France, and the United States, the transformation from a journalism of conviction to one of commerce began in the 1830s at approximately the same time. In the transition from the literary journalism of private individuals to the public services of the mass media, the public sphere was transformed by the influx of private interests, which received special prominence in the mass media.

The public sphere in the social welfare state mass democracy

Although the liberal model of the public sphere is still instructive today with respect to the normative claim that information be accessible to the public,[5] it cannot be applied to the actual conditions of an industrially advanced mass democracy organized in the form of the social welfare state. In part, the liberal model had always included ideological components, but it is also in part true that the social preconditions, to which the ideological elements could at one time at least be linked, had been fundamentally transformed. The very forms in which the public sphere manifested itself, to which supporters of the liberal model could appeal for evidence, began to change with the Chartist movement in England and the February revolution in France. Because of the diffusion of press and propaganda, the public body expanded beyond the bounds of the bourgeoisie. The public body lost not only its social exclusivity; it lost in addition the coherence created by bourgeois social institutions and a relatively high standard of education. Conflicts hitherto restricted to the private sphere now intrude into the public sphere. Group needs which can expect no satisfaction from a self-regulating market now tend toward a regulation by the state. The public sphere, which must now mediate these demands, becomes a field for the competition of interests, competitions which assume the form of violent conflict. Laws which obviously have come about under the "pressure of the street" can scarcely still be understood as arising from the consensus of private individuals engaged in public discussion. They correspond in a more or less unconcealed manner to the compromise of conflicting private interests. Social organizations which deal with the state act in the political public sphere, whether through the agency of political parties or directly in connection with the public administration. With the interweaving of the public and private realms, not only do the political authorities assume certain functions in the sphere of commodity exchange and social labor but, conversely, social powers now assume political functions. This leads to a kind of "refeudalization" of the public sphere. Large organizations strive for political compromises with the state and with one another, excluding the public sphere whenever possible. But at the same time the large organizations must assure themselves of at least plebiscitary support from the mass of the population through an apparent display of openness [demonstrative Publizität].[6]

The political public sphere of the social welfare state is characterized by a peculiar weakening of its critical functions. At one time the process of making proceedings public [Publizität] was intended to subject persons or affairs to public reason, and to make political decisions subject to appeal before the court of public opinion. But often enough today the process of making public simply serves the arcane policies of special interests; in the form of "publicity" it wins public prestige for people or affairs, thus making them worthy of acclamation in a climate of nonpublic opinion. The very words "public relations work" [Öffentlichkeitsarbeit] betray the fact that a public sphere must first be arduously constructed case by case, a public sphere which earlier grew out of the social structure. Even the central relationship of the public, the parties, and the parliament is affected by this change in function.

Yet this trend towards the weakening of the public sphere as a principle is opposed by the extension of fundamental rights in the social welfare state. The demand that information be accessible to the public is extended from organs of the state to all organizations dealing with the state. To the degree that this is realized, a public body of organized private individuals would take the place of the now-defunct public body of private individuals who relate individually to each other. Only these organized individuals could participate effectively in the process of public communication; only they could use the channels of the public sphere which exist within parties and associations and the process of making proceedings public [*Publizität*] which was established to facilitate the dealings of organizations with the state. Political compromises would have to be legitimized through this process of public communication. The idea of the public sphere, preserved in the social welfare state mass democracy, an idea which calls for a rationalization of power through the medium of public discussion among private individuals, threatens to disintegrate with the structural transformation of the public sphere itself. It could only be realized today, on an altered basis, as a rational reorganization of social and political power under the mutual control of rival organizations committed to the public sphere in their internal structure as well as in their relations with the state and each other.

Notes

1. Habermas' concept of the public sphere is not to be equated with that of "the public," i.e., of the individuals who assemble. His concept is directed instead at the institution, which to be sure only assumes concrete form through the participation of people. It cannot, however, be characterized simply as a crowd. (This and the following notes by Peter Hohendahl.)
2. The state and the public sphere do not overlap, as one might suppose from casual language use. Rather, they confront one another as opponents. Habermas designates that sphere as public which antiquity understood to be private, i.e., the sphere of nongovernmental opinion making.
3. The principle of the public sphere could still be distinguished from an institution which is demonstrable in social history. Habermas thus would mean a model of norms and modes of behavior by means of which the very functioning of public opinion can be guaranteed for the first time. These norms and modes of behavior include: a) general accessibility, b) elimination of all privileges, and c) discovery of general norms and rational legitimations.
4. The expression *represent* is used in a very specific sense in the following section, namely, to "present oneself." The important thing to understand is that the medieval public sphere, if it even deserves this designation, is tied to the *personal*. The feudal lord and estates create the public sphere by means of their very presence.
5. Here it should be understood that Habermas considers the principle behind the bourgeois public sphere, but not its historical form, as indispensable.
6. One must distinguish between Habermas' concept of "making proceedings public" [*Publizität*] and the "public sphere" [*Öffentlichkeit*]. The term *Publizität* describes the degree of public effect generated by a public act. Thus, a situation can arise in which the form of public opinion making is maintained, while the substance of the public sphere has long ago been undermined.

Critical connections

Habermas' theories have been challenged from a diversity of perspectives. Marxists, for example, have highlighted the limitations of his class analysis, and feminists have pointed to weaknesses in terms of gender (Fraser, 1992). Others have queried the existence, certainly today but also historically, of a sufficiently coherent and consensual 'public', whose opinion could be classified as the 'public opinion' (Outhwaite, 1994). And many have queried Habermas' rather idealised conception of the bourgeois public sphere, suggesting that the early print market was as much populated by booty capitalists looking for a quick profit as it was by freely engaged intellectuals in pursuit of public enlightenment (Garnham, 1990).

Despite these challanges, many of Habermas' ideas – the public sphere, political activism, rational-critical public debate – continue to resonate today. Nicholas Garnham (1990) and Craig Calhoun (1992) have considered the contemporary relevance and structure of the public sphere, and the role of media as a constituting factor. Nancy Fraser's (2007) current work on the Transnational Public Sphere considers the emergence of discursive arenas that extend beyond the boundaries of nation and state, and the significance of these for conceptualising public opinion, political citizenry, communicative power and public sphere theory. Commentators of new media and new social movements have referred to the creation of 'virtual' and 'alternative' public spheres, facilitated in part by the revolution in Information and Communication Technologies (ICTs) (Papacharissi, 2002). Habermas' concerns – whether or not they are made explicit – cut across the work of contemporary commentators on media and society such as Manuel Castells and William Gibson (Readings 5 and 7). Through the writings of these new media theorists we can gain useful insights into what an alternative public sphere might look like in the information age or the virtual society.

Discussion questions

- In a multicultural, pluralistic society, can there still be such a thing as 'public opinion'?
- Where can people go today to engage in critical-rational public debate?
- How might we conceptualise Habermas' notion of the 'public sphere' in light of media proliferation and the rapid development of Information and Communication Technologies (see especially Readings 5, 6 and 7)?

References

Calhoun, C. (ed.) (1992) *Habermas and the Public Sphere*, Cambridge: MIT Press.

Fraser, N. (2007) 'Transnationalizing the Public Sphere: On the Legitimacy and Efficacy of Public Opinion in a Post-Westphalian World', Theory, Culture & Society 2007 24: 7–30.

Fraser, N. (1992) 'Rethinking the Public Sphere: A Contribution to the Critique of Actually Existing Democracy' in C. Calhoun (ed.) *Habermas and the Public Sphere*, Cambridge, MA: MIT Press.

Garnham, N. (1990) 'The Media and the Public Sphere', in C. Calhoun (ed.) (1992) *Habermas and the Public Sphere*, Cambridge: MIT Press.

Habermas, J. (1989) *The Structural Transformation of the Public Sphere*, T. Burger and F. Lawrence (trans). Cambridge, MA: MIT Press. [German, 1962]

Outhwaite, W. (1994) *Habermas: A Critical Introduction*, Cambridge: Polity.

Papacharissi, Z. (2002) 'The Virtual Sphere: The Internet as a Public Sphere', in *New Media and Society*, 4, 1: 9–27.

Marshall McLuhan

THE MEDIUM IS THE MESSAGE (1964)

Introduction and context

MARSHALL McLUHAN'S (1964) principal aim is to understand how technology, including media technologies, shape and control 'the scale and form of human association and action' (McLuhan, 1964: 9) *Understanding Media*: *The Extensions of Man* is the highly influential book in which he developed the famous dictum, 'The Medium is the Message'. McLuhan sees media as 'any technology that creates an extension of the human body or senses': clothing is an extension of the skin, spectacles are an extension of the eye, and the wheel an extension of the foot. The 'message' refers less to the content of a medium and more to the 'change of pace or scale or pattern' (McLuhan, 1964: 8) that any new invention or idea introduces into social life. He illustrates this point with an electric light, arguing that it is 'pure information. It is a medium without a message, as it were' (1964: 23). The 'content' of electric light can be anything it happens to be shining on at the time. Yet, the 'medium' of electricity profoundly altered everyday social life by overcoming the constraints of darkness, creating new cultural spaces and facilitating new social activities. Thus, the 'medium is the message', since it is the medium that has the greatest impact on society through its very existence, largely regardless of the content. For McLuhan, media content has 'about as much importance as the stencilling on the casing of an atomic bomb' (McLuhan, 1995: 238).

To demonstrate the power of media as a key mechanism for historical change, McLuhan considers the transition from pre-modern oral culture, based on the spoken word, to the modern print culture, based on the written word, to the (post)modern electronic culture defined by electronic forms of communication and interaction. The transition from oral to print culture brought about a reorganisation of the 'human sensorium' through the 'extension', or prioritisation, of some senses over others. Whereas oral culture favoured the ear, print culture established the eye as the primary sensory organ.

This sensory shift impacted on individual consciousness, culture and society in profound ways, many of which were not always perceptible. Print culture, McLuhan argues, stimulated individualism and subjective reflection (reading is solitary), the rise of nationalism and competitive nation states (through 'seeing' one's mother tongue as a 'uniform entity', facilitating national literatures and, later, state ideology), and the industrial revolution (the printing press was the first technology of mass production, the 'prototype of all machines'). The repeatable, linear, abstract forms of printed type helped shape Western modes of thought ultimately giving rise to mass education, cities, empires, capitalism, and modernity itself.

The shift to an electronic age promised similarly dramatic changes. The invention of the telegraph, telephone, radio, television and computer, McLuhan argued, could restore the sensorial imbalance generated by the print culture through 'extending' the entire central nervous system. Furthermore, electronic media technologies allow the extension of human subjects beyond their physical bodies – from the telephone as an extension of the voice, to the computer as an extension of the brain. Thus McLuhan believed that the new media age could produce less individualistic and linear subjects who, immersed in the 'whirlpool of information' – the vivid, swirling sights, sounds and experiences of mass media – could generate a global culture that would overcome the individualism and nationalism of the previous era, establishing instead 'a new state of multitudinous tribal existences' (1995: 243).

In a culture like ours, long accustomed to splitting and dividing all things as a means of control, it is sometimes a bit of a shock to be reminded that, in operational and practical fact, the medium is the message. This is merely to say that the personal and social consequences of any medium – that is, of any extension of ourselves – result from the new scale that is introduced into our affairs by each extension of ourselves, or by any new technology. Thus, with automation, for example, the new patterns of human association tend to eliminate jobs, it is true. That is the negative result. Positively, automation creates roles for people, which is to say depth of involvement in their work and human association that our preceding mechanical technology had destroyed. Many people would be disposed to say that it was not the machine, but what one did with the machine, that was its meaning or message. In terms of the ways in which the machine altered our relations to one another and to ourselves, it mattered not in the least whether it turned out cornflakes or Cadillacs. The restructuring of human work and association was shaped by the technique of fragmentation that is the essence of machine technology. The essence of automation technology is the opposite. It is integral and decentralist in depth, just as the machine was fragmentary, centralist, and superficial in its patterning of human relationships.

The instance of the electric light may prove illuminating in this connection. The electric light is pure information. It is a medium without a message, as it were, unless it is used to spell out some verbal ad or name. This fact, characteristic of all media, means that the "content" of any medium is always another medium. The content of writing is speech, just as the written word is the content of print, and print is the content of the telegraph. If it is asked, "What is the content of speech?," it is necessary to say, "It is an actual process of thought, which is in itself nonverbal." An abstract painting represents direct manifestation of creative thought processes as they might appear in computer designs. What we are considering here, however, are the psychic and social consequences of the designs or patterns as they amplify or accelerate existing processes. For the "message" of any medium or technology is the change of scale or pace or pattern that it introduces into human affairs. The railway did not introduce movement or transportation or wheel or road into human society, but it accelerated and enlarged the scale of previous human functions, creating totally new kinds of cities and new kinds of work and leisure. This happened whether the railway functioned in a tropical or a northern environment, and is quite independent of the freight or content of the railway medium. The airplane, on the other hand, by accelerating the rate of transportation, tends to dissolve the railway form of city, politics, and association, quite independently of what the airplane is used for.

Let us return to the electric light. Whether the light is being used for brain surgery or night baseball is a matter of indifference. It could be argued that these activities are in some way the "content" of the electric light, since they could not exist without the electric light. This fact merely underlines the point that "the medium is the message" because it is the medium that shapes and controls the scale and form of human association and action. The content or uses of such media are as diverse as they are ineffectual in shaping the form of human association. Indeed, it is only too typical that the "content" of any medium blinds us to the character of the medium. It is only today that industries have become aware of the various kinds of business in which they are engaged. When IBM discovered that it was not in the business of making office equipment or business machines, but that it was in the business of processing information, then it began to navigate with clear vision. The General Electric Company makes a considerable portion of its profits from electric light bulbs and lighting systems. It has not yet discovered that, quite as much as A.T.& T., it is in the business of moving information.

The electric light escapes attention as a communication medium just because it has no "content." And this makes it an invaluable instance of how people fail to study media at all. For it is not till the electric light is used to spell out some brand name that it is noticed as a medium. Then it is not the light but the "content" (or what is really another medium) that is noticed. The message of the electric light is like the message of electric power in industry, totally radical, pervasive, and decentralized. For electric light and power are separate from their uses, yet they eliminate time and space factors in human association exactly as do radio, telegraph, telephone, and TV, creating involvement in depth.

A fairly complete handbook for studying the extensions of man could be made up from selections from Shakespeare. Some might quibble about whether or not he was referring to TV in these familiar lines from *Romeo and Juliet*:

> But soft! what light through yonder window breaks?
> It speaks, and yet says nothing.

In *Othello*, which, as much as *King Lear*, is concerned with the torment of people transformed by illusions, there are these lines that bespeak Shakespeare's intuition of the transforming powers of new media:

> Is there not charms
> By which the property of youth and maidhood

May be abus'd? Have you not read Roderigo,
Of some such thing?

In Shakespeare's *Troilus and Cressida*, which is almost completely devoted to both a psychic and social study of communication, Shakespeare states his awareness that true social and political navigation depend upon anticipating the consequences of innovation:

The providence that's in a watchful state
Knows almost every grain of Plutus' gold,
Finds bottom in the uncomprehensive deeps,
Keeps place with thought, and almost like the gods
Does thoughts unveil in their dumb cradles.

The increasing awareness of the action of media, quite independently of their "content" or programming, was indicated in the annoyed and anonymous stanza:

In modern thought, (if not in fact)
Nothing is that doesn't act,
So that is reckoned wisdom which
Describes the scratch but not the itch.

The same kind of total, configurational awareness that reveals why the medium is socially the message has occurred in the most recent and radical medical theories. In his *Stress of Life*, Hans Selye tells of the dismay of a research colleague on hearing of Selye's theory:

When he saw me thus launched on yet another enraptured description of what I had observed in animals treated with this or that impure, toxic material, he looked at me with desperately sad eyes and said in obvious despair: "But Selye, try to realize what you are doing before it is too late! You have now decided to spend your entire life studying the pharmacology of dirt!"

(Hans Selye, *The Stress of Life*)

As Selye deals with the total environmental situation in his "stress" theory of disease, so the latest approach to media study considers not only the "content" but the medium and the cultural matrix within which the particular medium operates. The older unawareness of the psychic and social effects of media can be illustrated from almost any of the conventional pronouncements.

In accepting an honorary degree from the University of Notre Dame a few years ago, General David Sarnoff made this statement: "We are too prone to make technological instruments the scapegoats for the sins of those who wield them. The products of modern science are not in themselves good or bad; it is the way they are used that determines their value." That is the voice of the current somnambulism. Suppose we were to say, "Apple pie is in itself neither good nor bad; it is the way it is used that determines its value." Or, "The smallpox virus is in itself neither good nor bad; it is the way it is used that determines its value." Again, "Firearms are in themselves neither good nor bad; it is the way they are used that determines their value." That is, if the slugs reach the right people firearms are good. If the TV tube fires the right ammunition at the right people it is good. I am not being perverse. There is simply nothing in the Sarnoff statement that will bear scrutiny, for it ignores the nature of the medium, of any and all media, in the true Narcissus style of one hypnotized by the amputation and extension of his own being in a new technical form. General Sarnoff went on to explain his attitude to the technology of print, saying that it was true that print caused much trash to circulate, but it had also disseminated the Bible and the thoughts of seers and philosophers. It has never occurred to General Sarnoff that any technology could do anything but *add* itself on to what we already are.

Such economists as Robert Theobald, W. W. Rostow, and John Kenneth Galbraith have been explaining for years how it is that "classical economics" cannot explain change or growth. And the paradox of mechanization is that although it is itself the cause of maximal growth and change, the principle of mechanization excludes the very possibility of growth or the understanding of change. For mechanization is achieved by fragmentation of any process and by putting the fragmented parts in a series. Yet, as David Hume showed in the eighteenth century, there is no principle of causality in a mere sequence. That one thing follows another accounts for nothing. Nothing follows from following, except change. So the greatest of all reversals occurred with electricity, that ended sequence by making things instant. With instant speed the causes of things began to emerge to awareness again, as they had not done with things in sequence and in concatenation accordingly. Instead of asking which came first, the chicken or the egg, it suddenly seemed that a chicken was an egg's idea for getting more eggs.

Just before an airplane breaks the sound barrier, sound waves become visible on the wings of the plane. The sudden visibility of sound just as sound ends is an apt instance of that great pattern of being that reveals new and opposite forms just as the earlier forms reach their peak performance. Mechanization was never so vividly fragmented or sequential as in the birth of the movies, the moment that translated us beyond mechanism into the world of growth and organic interrelation. The movie, by sheer speeding up the mechanical, carried us from the world of sequence and connections into the world of creative configuration and structure. The message of the movie medium is that of transition from lineal connections to configurations. It is the transition that produced the now quite correct observation: "If it works, it's obsolete." When electric speed further takes over from mechanical movie sequences, then the lines of force in structures and in media become loud and clear. We return to the inclusive form of the icon.

To a highly literate and mechanized culture the movie appeared as a world of triumphant illusions and dreams that money could buy. It was at this moment of the movie that cubism occurred, and it has been described by E. H. Gombrich (*Art and Illusion*) as "the most radical attempt to stamp out ambiguity and to enforce one reading of the picture – that of a man-made construction, a colored canvas." For cubism substitutes all facets of an object simultaneously for the "point of view" or facet perspective illusion. Instead of the specialized illusion of the third dimension on canvas, cubism sets up an interplay of planes and contradiction or dramatic conflict of patterns, lights, textures that "drives home the message" by involvement. This is held by many to be an exercise in painting, not in illusion.

In other words, cubism, by giving the inside and outside, the top, bottom, back, and front and the rest, in two dimensions, drops the illusion of perspective in favor of instant sensory awareness of the whole. Cubism, by seizing on instant total awareness, suddenly announced that the *medium is the message*. Is it not evident the moment that sequence yields to the simultaneous, one is in the world of the structure and of configuration? Is that not what has happened in physics as in painting, poetry, and in communication? Specialized segments of attention have shifted to total field, and we can now say, "The medium is the message" quite naturally. Before the electric speed and total field, it was not obvious that the medium is the message. The message, it seemed, was the "content," as people used to ask what a painting was *about*. Yet they never thought to ask what a melody was about, nor what a house or a dress was about. In such matters, people retained some sense of the whole pattern, of form and function as a unity. But in the electric age this integral idea of structure and configuration has become so prevalent that educational theory has taken up the matter. Instead of working with specialized "problems" in arithmetic, the structural approach now follows the linea of force in the field of number and has small children meditating about number theory and "sets."

Cardinal Newman said of Napoleon, "He understood the grammar of gunpowder." Napoleon had paid some attention to other media as well, especially the semaphore telegraph that gave him a great advantage over his enemies. He is on record for saying that "Three hostile newspapers are more to be feared than a thousand bayonets."

Alexis de Tocqueville was the first to master the grammar of print and typography. He was thus able to read off the message of coming change in France and America as if he were reading aloud from a text that had been handed to him. In fact, the nineteenth century in France and in America was just such an open book to de Tocqueville because he had learned the grammar of print. So he, also, knew when that grammar did not apply. He was asked why he did not write a book on England, since he knew and admired England. He replied:

> One would have to have an unusual degree of philosophical folly to believe oneself able to judge England in six months. A year always seemed to me too short a time in which to appreciate the United States properly, and it is much easier to acquire clear and precise notions about the American Union than about Great Britain. In America all laws derive in a sense from the same line of thought. The whole of society, so to speak, is founded upon a single fact; everything springs from a simple principle. One could compare America to a forest pierced by a multitude of straight roads all converging on the same point. One has only to find the center and everything is revealed at a glance. But in England the paths run criss-cross, and it is only by travelling down each one of them that one can build up a picture of the whole.

De Tocqueville, in earlier work on the French Revolution, had explained how it was the printed word that, achieving cultural saturation in the eighteenth century, had homogenized the French nation. Frenchmen were the same kind of people from north to south. The typographic principles of uniformity, continuity, and lineality had overlaid the complexities of ancient feudal and oral society. The Revolution was carried out by the new literati and lawyers.

In England, however, such was the power of the ancient oral traditions of common law, backed by the medieval institution of Parliament, that no uniformity or continuity of the new visual print culture could take complete hold. The result was that the most important event in English history has never taken place; namely, the English Revolution on the lines of the French Revolution. The American Revolution had no medieval legal institutions to discard or to root out, apart from monarchy. And many have held that the American Presidency has become very much more personal and monarchical than any European monarch ever could be.

De Tocqueville's contrast between England and America is clearly based on the fact of typography and of print culture creating uniformity and continuity. England, he says, has rejected this principle and clung to the dynamic or oral common-law tradition. Hence the discontinuity and unpredictable quality of English culture. The grammar of print cannot help to construe the message of oral and nonwritten culture and institutions. The English aristocracy was properly classified as barbarian by Matthew Arnold because its power and status had nothing to do with literacy or with the cultural forms of typography. Said the Duke of Gloucester to Edward Gibbon upon the publication of his *Decline and Fall*: "Another damned fat book, eh, Mr. Gibbon? Scribble, scribble, scribble, eh, Mr. Gibbon?" De Tocqueville was a highly literate aristocrat who was quite able to be detached from the values and assumptions of typography. That is why he alone understood the grammar of typography. And it is only on those terms, standing aside from any structure or medium, that its principles and lines of force can be discerned. For any medium has the power of imposing its own assumption on the unwary. Prediction and control consist in avoiding this sub-liminal state of Narcissus trance. But the greatest aid to this end is simply in knowing that the spell can occur immediately upon contact, as in the first bars of a melody.

A Passage to India by E. M. Forster is a dramatic study of the inability of oral and intuitive oriental culture to meet with the rational, visual European patterns of experience. "Rational," of course, has for the West long meant "uniform and continuous and sequential." In other words, we have confused reason with literacy, and rational-ism with a single technology. Thus in the electric age man seems to the conventional West to become irrational. In Forster's novel the moment of truth and dislocation from the typographic trance of the West comes in the Marabar Caves. Adela Quested's reasoning powers cannot cope with the total inclusive field of resonance that is India. After the Caves: "Life went on as usual, but had no consequences, that is to say, sounds did not echo nor thought develop. Everything seemed cut off at its root and therefore infected with illusion."

A Passage to India (the phrase is from Whitman, who saw America headed Eastward) is a parable of Western man in the electric age, and is only incidentally related to Europe or the Orient. The ultimate conflict between sight and sound, between written and oral kinds of perception and organization of existence is upon us. Since understanding stops action, as Nietzsche observed, we can moderate the fierceness of this conflict by understanding the media that extend us and raise these wars within and without us.

Detribalization by literacy and its traumatic effects on tribal man is the theme of a book by the psychiatrist J. C. Carothers, *The African Mind in Health and Disease* (World Health Organization, Geneva, 1953). Much of his material appeared in an article in *Psychiatry* magazine, November, 1959: "The Culture, Psychiatry, and the

Written Word." Again, it is electric speed that has revealed the lines of force operating from Western technology in the remotest areas of bush, savannah, and desert. One example is the Bedouin with his battery radio on board the camel. Submerging natives with floods of concepts for which nothing has prepared them is the normal action of all of our technology. But with electric media Western man himself experiences exactly the same inundation as the remote native. We are no more prepared to encounter radio and TV in our literate milieu than the native of Ghana is able to cope with the literacy that takes him out of his collective tribal world and beaches him in individual isolation. We are as numb in our new electric world as the native involved in our literate and mechanical culture.

Electric speed mingles the cultures of prehistory with the dregs of industrial marketeers, the nonliterate with the semiliterate and the postliterate. Mental breakdown of varying degrees is the very common result of uprooting and inundation with new information and endless new patterns of information. Wyndham Lewis made this a theme of his group of novels called *The Human Age*. The first of these, *The Childermass*, is concerned precisely with accelerated media change as a kind of massacre of the innocents. In our own world as we become more aware of the effects of technology on psychic formation and manifestation we are losing all confidence in our right to assign guilt. Ancient prehistoric societies regard violent crime as pathetic. The killer is regarded as we do a cancer victim. "How terrible it must be to feel like that," they say. J. M. Synge took up this idea very effectively in his *Playboy of the Western World*.

If the criminal appears as a nonconformist who is unable to meet the demand of technology that we behave in uniform and continuous patterns, literate man is quite inclined to see others who cannot conform as somewhat pathetic. Especially the child, the cripple, the woman, and the colored person appear in a world of visual and typographic technology as victims of injustice. On the other hand, in a culture that assigns roles instead of jobs to people – the dwarf, the skew, the child create their own spaces. They are not expected to fit into some uniform and repeatable niche that is not their size anyway. Consider the phrase "It's a man's world." As a quantitative observation endlessly repeated from within a homogenized culture, this phrase refers to the men in such a culture who have to be homogenized Dagwoods in order to belong at all. It is in our I.Q. testing that we have produced the greatest flood of misbegotten standards. Unaware of our typographic cultural bias, our testers assume that uniform and continuous habits are a sign of intelligence, thus eliminating the ear man and the tactile man.

C. P. Snow, reviewing a book of A. L. Rowse (*The New York Times Book Review*, December 24, 1961) on *Appeasement* and the road to Munich, describes the top level of British brains and experience in the 1930s. "Their I.Q.'s were much higher than usual among political bosses. Why were they such a disaster?" The view of Rowse, Snow approves: "They would not listen to warnings because they did not wish to hear." Being anti-Red made it impossible for them to read the message of Hitler. But their failure was as nothing compared to our present one. The American stake in literacy as a technology or uniformity applied to every level of education, government, industry, and social life is totally threatened by the electric technology. The threat of Stalin or Hitler was external. The electric technology is within the gates, and we are numb, deaf, blind, and mute about its encounter with the Gutenberg technology, on and through which the American way of life was formed. It is, however, no time to suggest strategies when the threat has not even been acknowledged to exist. I am in the position of Louis Pasteur telling doctors that their greatest enemy was quite invisible, and quite unrecognized by them. Our conventional response to all media, namely that it is how they are used that counts, is the numb stance of the technological idiot. For the "content" of a medium is like the juicy piece of meat carried by the burglar to distract the watchdog of the mind. The effect of the medium is made strong and intense just because it is given another medium as "content." The content of a movie is a novel or a play or an opera. The effect of the movie form is not related to its program content. The "content" of writing or print is speech, but the reader is almost entirely unaware either of print or of speech.

Arnold Toynbee is innocent of any understanding of media as they have shaped history, but he is full of examples that the student of media can use. At one moment he can seriously suggest that adult education, such as the Workers Educational Association in Britain, is a useful counterforce to the popular press. Toynbee considers that although all of the oriental societies have in our time accepted the industrial technology and its political consequences: "On the cultural plane, however, there is no uniform corresponding tendency." (Somervell, I. 267) This is like the voice of the literate man, floundering in a milieu of ads, who boasts, "Personally, I pay no attention to ads." The spiritual and cultural reservations that the oriental peoples may have toward our technology will avail them not at all. The effects of technology do not occur at the level of opinions or concepts, but alter sense ratios or patterns of perception steadily and without any resistance. The serious artist is the only person able to encounter technology with impunity, just because he is an expert aware of the changes in sense perception.

The operation of the money medium in seventeenth-century Japan had effects not unlike the operation of typography in the West. The penetration of the money economy, wrote G. B. Sansom (in *Japan*, Cresset Press, London, 1931), "caused a slow but irresistible revolution, culminating in the breakdown of feudal government and the resumption of intercourse with foreign countries after more than two hundred years of seclusion." Money has reorganized the sense life of peoples just because it is an *extension* of our sense lives. This change does not depend upon approval or disapproval of those living in the society.

Arnold Toynbee made one approach to the transforming power of media in his concept of "etherialization," which he holds to be the principle of progressive simplification and efficiency in any organization or technology. Typically, he is ignoring the *effect* of the challenge of these forms upon the response of our senses. He imagines that it is the response of our opinions that is relevant to the effect of media and technology in society, a "point of view" that is plainly the result of the typographic spell. For the man in a literate and homogenized society ceases to be sensitive to the diverse and discontinuous life of forms. He acquires the illusion of the third dimension and the "private point of view" as part of his Narcissus fixation, and is quite shut off from Blake's awareness or that of the Psalmist, that we become what we behold.

Today when we want to get our bearings in our own culture, and have need to stand aside from the bias and pressure exerted by any technical form of human expression, we have only to visit a society where that particular form has not been felt, or a historical period in which it was unknown. Professor Wilbur Schramm made such a tactical move in studying *Television in the Lives of Our Children*. He found areas where TV had not penetrated at all and ran some tests. Since he had made no study of the peculiar nature of the TV image, his tests were of "content" preferences, viewing time, and vocabulary counts. In a word, his approach to the problem was a literary one, albeit unconsciously so. Consequently, he had nothing to report. Had his methods been employed in AD 1500 to discover the effects of the printed book in the lives of children or adults, he could have found out nothing of the changes in human and social psychology resulting from typography. Print created individualism and nationalism in the sixteenth century. Program and "content" analysis offer no clues to the magic of these media or to their subliminal charge.

Leonard Doob, in his report *Communication in Africa*, tells of one African who took great pains to listen each evening to the BBC news, even though he could understand nothing of it. Just to be in the presence of those sounds at 7 P.M. each day was important for him. His attitude to speech was like ours to melody – the resonant intonation was meaning enough. In the seventeenth century our ancestors still shared this native's attitude to the forms of media, as is plain in the following sentiment of the Frenchman Bernard Lam expressed in *The Art of Speaking* (London, 1696):

> 'Tis an effect of the Wisdom of God, who created Man to be happy, that whatever is useful to his conversation (way of life) is agreeable to him . . . because all victual that conduces to nourishment is relishable, whereas other things that cannot be assimulated and be turned into our substance are insipid. A Discourse cannot be pleasant to the Hearer that is not easie to the Speaker; nor can it be easily pronounced unless it be heard with delight.

Here is an equilibrium theory of human diet and expression such as even now we are only striving to work out again for media after centuries of fragmentation and specialism.

Pope Pius XII was deeply concerned that there be serious study of the media today. On February 17, 1950, he said:

> It is not an exaggeration to say that the future of modern society and the stability of its inner life depend in large part on the maintenance of an equilibrium between the strength of the techniques of communication and the capacity of the individual's own reaction.

Failure in this respect has for centuries been typical and total for mankind. Subliminal and docile acceptance of media impact has made them prisons without walls for their human users. As A. J. Liebling remarked in his book *The Press*, a man is not free if he cannot see where he is going, even if he has a gun to help him get there. For each of the media is also a powerful weapon with which to clobber other media and other groups. The result is that the present age has been one of multiple civil wars that are not limited to the world of art and entertainment. In *War and Human Progress*, Professor J. U. Nef declared: "The total wars of our time have been the result of a series of intellectual mistakes . . ."

If the formative power in the media are the media themselves, that raises a host of large matters that can only be mentioned here, although they deserve volumes. Namely, that technological media are staples or natural resources, exactly as are coal and cotton and oil. Anybody will concede that society whose economy is dependent upon one or two major staples like cotton, or grain, or lumber, or fish, or cattle is going to have some obvious social patterns of organization as a result. Stress on a few major staples creates extreme instability in the economy but great endurance in the population. The pathos and humor of the American South are embedded in such an economy of limited staples. For a society configured by reliance on a few commodities accepts them as a social bond quite as much as the metropolis does the press. Cotton and oil, like radio and TV, become "fixed charges" on the entire psychic life of the community. And this pervasive fact creates the unique cultural flavor of any society. It pays through the nose and all its other senses for each staple that shapes its life.

That our human senses, of which all media are extensions, are also fixed charges on our personal energies, and that they also configure the awareness and experience of each one of us, may be perceived in another connection mentioned by the psychologist C. G. Jung:

> Every Roman was surrounded by slaves. The slave and his psychology flooded ancient Italy, and every Roman became inwardly, and of course unwittingly, a slave. Because living constantly in the atmosphere of slaves, he became infected through the unconscious with their psychology. No one can shield himself from such an influence (*Contributions to Analytical Psychology*, London, 1928).

Critical connections

McLuhan's arguments can be complex, and grasping his ideas is made more difficult by what Castells (2000: 360) refers to as 'the obscurity of his mosaic language'. That is, McLuhan tends to present his ideas, quite deliberately, in a non-linear fashion which flagrantly ignores the traditional conventions of academic writing (for which he has been attacked by some – see Miller, 1971). McLuhan has also been accused, notably by British cultural theorist Raymond Williams (1990), of 'technological determinism', in that he appears to isolate his analysis to media (as Marx was accused of isolating his analysis to the economy) at the expense of other active agents of historical change.

At the centre of McLuhan's work is the understanding that more and more aspects of culture and our own consciousness are being broken down and rendered into the form of information (see also Reading 40). With the advent of the digital era and the rapid advancement of Information and Communication Technologies (ICTs), many of the processes identified by McLuhan have accelerated enormously, and his work has taken on a renewed significance in the fields of media studies and social theory. That McLuhan's observations have, if anything, become more significant as time has progressed, has led to the Canadian Professor of English Literature being hailed the Oracle of the Electric Age, a Prophet of the Computer Age, and the High Priest of Popcult, as well as a leading analyst and critic of media culture. In 1993 he was named Patron Saint of *Wired* magazine. McLuhan's discussion of the extension through media of the human body beyond its physical limitations finds particular resonance in the writings of another proclaimed prophet, the Godfather of Cyberpunk, William Gibson (Reading 7).

Discussion questions

- What does McLuhan mean by the term 'the medium is the message'?
- How are technologies extensions of ourselves?
- What are the key sensorial and social-organisational differences between oral, print and electronic cultures?

References

Castells, M. (2000) *The Rise of the Network Society*, second edition, Oxford: Blackwell.

Kellner, D. and Gigi Durham M. (2001) *Media and Cultural Studies: Keyworks*, Oxford: Blackwell.

McLuhan, M. (1995) *Playboy interview from Essential McLuhan* Eric McLuhan and Frank Zingrone (editors), London, Routledge.

McLuhan, M. (1964) 'The Medium is the Message', excerpt from *Understanding Media; The Extensions of Man*, London: Routledge.

Miller, J. (1971) *McLuhan*, London, Fontana/Collins.

Williams, R. (1990) *Television Technology and Cultural Form* (ed. Ederyn Williams), London, Routledge.

Edward S. Herman and Noam Chomsky

A PROPAGANDA MODEL (1988)

Introduction and context

IN *MANUFACTURING CONSENT* (1988), Edward Herman and Noam Chomsky present a Marxist analysis of the influence of corporate and state power on mainstream media content. They develop what they term a propaganda model to explain how power and money effectively 'filter out the news fit to print'. Before being disseminated to a mass audience as media content, news must pass through a succession of five filters – media ownership and profit orientation, the influence of advertising, the role of experts, 'flak' as a means of disciplining the media, and anti-communism as the 'national religion'. What remains after filtering is a cleansed residue of news which marginalises oppositional views and allows government and big business to get their message across to the public in a way that reinforces the dominance of state and corporate interests.

Through meticulous research on the reporting of 'terrorism' and close consideration of the media's alleged collusion in the 'criminalisation' of non-friendly regimes, Herman and Chomsky demonstrate how economic, political, military and cultural elites effectively conspire to control the content and flow of media information. They contend that the key players in the news production process are not journalists, who in fact are seen to have little autonomous power. The real power lies with the state and large corporations. Whilst journalists may feel they are acting objectively and writing in accordance with prevailing and accepted journalistic news values, in practice they are subordinated to reproduce the interests of the ruling elite. Thus, Herman and Chomsky's radical materialist sociology casts the media as a key functionary of the 'National Security State' operating to 'manufacture consent' around elite ideas in the name of the 'national interest' and, in so doing, engendering acceptance of a social order that in fact reflects the interests of a powerful few, rather than the wider majority. The excerpt included here sets out the central characteristics of the propaganda model, and discusses the five filters that are alleged to strip the news of dissenting opinion.

The mass media serve as a system for communicating messages and symbols to the general populace. It is their function to amuse, entertain, and inform, and to inculcate individuals with the values, beliefs, and codes of behavior that will integrate them into the institutional structures of the larger society. In a world of concentrated wealth and major conflicts of class interest, to fulfil this role requires systematic propaganda.

In countries where the levers of power are in the hands of a state bureaucracy, the monopolistic control over the media, often supplemented by official censorship, makes it clear that the media serve the ends of a dominant elite. It is much more difficult to see a propaganda system at work where the media are private and formal censorship is absent. This is especially true where the media actively compete, periodically attack and expose corporate and governmental malfeasance, and aggressively portray themselves as spokesmen for free speech and the general community interest. What is not evident (and remains undiscussed in the media) is the limited nature of such critiques, as well as the huge inequality in command of resources, and its effect both on access to a private media system and on its behavior and performance.

A propaganda model focuses on this inequality of wealth and power and its multilevel effects on mass-media interests and choices. It traces the routes by which money and power are able to filter out the news fit to print, marginalize dissent, and allow the government and dominant private interests to get their messages across to the public. The essential ingredients of our propaganda model, or set of news "filters," fall under the following headings: (1) the size, concentrated ownership, owner wealth, and profit orientation of the dominant mass-media firms; (2) advertising as the primary income source of the mass media; (3) the reliance of the media on information provided by government, business, and "experts" funded and approved by these primary sources and agents of power; (4) "flak" as a means of disciplining the media; and (5) "anticommunism" as a national religion and control mechanism. These elements interact with and reinforce one another. The raw material of news must pass through successive filters, leaving only the cleansed residue fit to print. They fix the premises of discourse and interpretation, and the definition of what is newsworthy in the first place, and they explain the basis and operations of what amount to propaganda campaigns.

The elite domination of the media and marginalization of dissidents that results from the operation of these filters occurs so naturally that media news people, frequently operating with complete integrity and goodwill, are able to convince themselves that they choose and interpret the news "objectively" and on the basis of professional news values. Within the limits of the filter constraints they often are objective; the constraints are so powerful, and are built into the system in such a fundamental way, that alternative bases of news choices are hardly imaginable. It requires a macro, alongside a micro- (story-by-story), view of media operations, to see the pattern of manipulation and systematic bias.

Let us turn now to a more detailed examination of the main constituents of the propaganda model.

Size, ownership, and profit orientation of the mass media: the first filter

It has long been noted that the media are tiered, with the top tier – as measured by prestige, resources, and outreach – comprising somewhere between ten and twenty-four systems. It is this top tier, along with the government and wire services, that defines the news agenda and supplies much of the national and international news to the lower tiers of the media, and thus for the general public. [...]

Many of the large media companies are fully integrated into the market, and for the others, too, the pressures of stockholders, directors, and bankers to focus on the bottom line are powerful. These pressures have intensified in recent years as media stocks have become market favorites, and actual or prospective owners of newspapers and television properties have found it possible to capitalize increased audience size and advertising revenues into multiplied values of the media franchises – and great wealth. This has encouraged the entry of speculators and increased the pressure and temptation to focus more intensively on profitability. Family owners have been increasingly divided between those wanting to take advantage of the new opportunities and those desiring a continuation of family control, and their splits have often precipitated crises leading finally to the sale of the family interest.

This trend toward greater integration of the media into the market system has been accelerated by the loosening of rules limiting media concentration, cross-ownership, and control by non-media companies. There has also been an abandonment of restrictions – previously quite feeble anyway – on radio-TV commercials, entertainment-mayhem programming, and "fairness doctrine" threats, opening the door to the unrestrained commercial use of the airwaves.

The greater profitability of the media in a deregulated environment has also led to an increase in takeovers and takeover threats, with even giants like CBS and Time, Inc., directly attacked or threatened. This has forced the managements of the media giants to incur greater debt and to focus ever more aggressively and unequivocally on profitability, in order to placate owners and reduce the attractiveness of their properties to outsiders. They have lost some of their limited autonomy to bankers, institutional investors, and large individual investors whom they have had to solicit as potential "white knights." [...]

The large media companies all do business with commercial and investment bankers, obtaining lines of credit and loans, and receiving advice and service in selling stock and bond issues and in dealing with acquisition opportunities and takeover threats. Banks and other institutional investors are also large owners of media stock. These holdings, individually and collectively, do not convey control, but these large investors can make themselves heard, and their actions can affect the welfare of the companies and their managers. If the managers fail to pursue actions that favor shareholder returns, institutional investors will be inclined to sell the stock (depressing its price), or to listen sympathetically to outsiders contemplating takeovers. These investors are a force helping press media companies toward strictly market (profitability) objectives.

So is the diversification and geographic spread of the great media companies. Many of them have diversified out of particular media fields into others that seemed like growth areas. Many older newspaper-based media companies, fearful of the power of television and its effects on advertising revenue, moved as rapidly as they could into broadcasting and cable TV. [...]

The large media companies have also diversified beyond the media field, and non-media companies have established a strong presence in the mass media. [...]

Another structural relationship of importance is the media companies' dependence on and ties with government. The radio-TV companies and networks all require government licenses and franchises and are thus potentially subject to government control or harassment. [...]

The great media also depend on the government for more general policy support. All business firms are interested in business taxes, interest rates, labor policies, and enforcement and nonenforcement of the antitrust laws. [...]

In sum, the dominant media firms are quite large businesses; they are controlled by very wealthy people or by managers who are subject to sharp constraints by owners and other market – profit-oriented – forces; and they are closely interlocked, and have important common interests, with other major corporations, banks, and government. This is the first powerful filter that will affect news choices.

The advertising license to do business: the second filter

Before advertising became prominent, the price of a newspaper had to cover the costs of doing business. With the growth of advertising, papers that attracted ads could afford a copy price well below production costs. This put papers lacking in advertising at a serious disadvantage: their prices would tend to be higher, curtailing sales, and they would have less surplus to invest in improving the salability of the paper (features, attractive format, promotion, etc.). For this reason, an advertising-based system will tend to drive out of existence or into marginality the media companies and types that depend on revenue from sales alone. [...]

In fact, advertising has played a potent role in increasing concentration even among rivals that focus with equal energy on seeking advertising revenue. A market share and advertising edge on the part of one paper or television station will give it additional revenue to compete more effectively – promote more aggressively, buy more salable features and programs – and the disadvantaged rival must add expenses it cannot afford to try to stem the cumulative process of dwindling market (and revenue) share. The crunch is often fatal, and it helps explain the death of many large-circulation papers and magazines and the attrition in the number of newspapers.

From the time of the introduction of press advertising, therefore, working-class and radical papers have been at a serious disadvantage. Their readers have tended to be of modest means, a factor that has always affected advertiser interest. One advertising executive stated in 1856 that some journals are poor vehicles because "their readers are not purchasers, and any money thrown upon them is so much thrown away." [...]

In short, the mass media are interested in attracting audiences with buying power, not audiences per se; it is affluent audiences that spark advertiser interest today, as in the nineteenth century. The idea that the drive for large audiences makes the mass media "democratic" thus suffers from the initial weakness that its political analogue is a voting system weighted by income! [...]

Working-class and radical media also suffer from the political discrimination of advertisers. Political discrimination is structured into advertising allocations by the stress on people with money to buy. But many firms will always refuse to patronize ideological enemies and those whom they perceive as damaging their interests, and cases of overt discrimination add to the force of the voting system weighted by income. [...]

In addition to discrimination against unfriendly media institutions, advertisers also choose selectively among programs on the basis of their own principles. With rare exceptions these are culturally and politically conservative. Large corporate advertisers on television will rarely sponsor programs that engage in serious criticisms of corporate activities, such as the problem of environmental degradation, the workings of the military-industrial complex, or corporate support of and benefits from Third World tyrannies. [...]

Television networks learn over time that such programs will not sell and would have to be carried at a financial sacrifice, and that, in addition, they may offend powerful advertisers. With the rise in the price of advertising spots, the forgone revenue increases; and with increasing market pressure for financial performance and the diminishing constraints from regulation, an advertising-based media system will gradually increase advertising time and marginalize or eliminate altogether programming that has significant public-affairs content.

Advertisers will want, more generally, to avoid programs with serious complexities and disturbing controversies that interfere with the "buying mood." They seek programs that will lightly entertain and thus fit in with the spirit of the primary purpose of program purchases – the dissemination of a selling message. [...] There are exceptional cases of companies willing to sponsor serious programs, sometimes a result of recent embarrassments that call for a public-relations offset. But even in these cases the companies will usually not want to sponsor close examination of sensitive and divisive issues – they prefer programs on Greek antiquities, the ballet, and items of cultural and national history and nostalgia. [...]

Television stations and networks are also concerned to maintain audience "flow" levels, i.e., to keep people watching from program to program, in order to sustain advertising ratings and revenue. Airing program interludes of documentary-cultural matter that cause station switching is costly, and over time a "free" (i.e., ad-based) commercial system will tend to excise it. Such documentary-cultural-critical materials will be driven out of secondary media vehicles as well, as these companies strive to qualify for advertiser interest, although there will always be some cultural-political programming trying to come into being or surviving on the periphery of the mainstream media.

Sourcing mass-media news: the third filter

The mass media are drawn into a symbiotic relationship with powerful sources of information by economic necessity and reciprocity of interest. The media need a steady, reliable flow of the raw material of news. They have daily news demands and imperative news schedules that they must meet. They cannot afford to have reporters and cameras at all places where important stories may break. Economics dictates that they concentrate their resources where significant news often occurs, where important rumors and leaks abound, and where regular press conferences are held. The White House, the Pentagon, and the State Department, in Washington, D.C., are central nodes of such news activity. On a local basis, city hall and the police department are the subject of regular news "beats" for reporters. Business corporations and trade groups are also regular and credible purveyors of stories deemed newsworthy. These bureaucracies turn out a large volume of material that meets the demands of news organizations for reliable, scheduled flows. [...]

Another reason for the heavy weight given to official sources is that the mass media claim to be "objective" dispensers of the news. Partly to maintain the image of objectivity, but also to protect themselves from criticisms of bias and the threat of libel suits, they need material that can be portrayed as presumptively accurate. This is also partly a matter of cost: taking information from sources that may be presumed credible reduces investigative expense, whereas material from sources that are not prima facie credible, or that will elicit criticism and threats, requires careful checking and costly research.

The magnitude of the public-information operations of large government and corporate bureaucracies that constitute the primary news sources is vast and ensures special access to the media. [...]

To consolidate their preeminent position as sources, government and business-news promoters go to great pains to make things easy for news organizations. They provide the media organizations with facilities in which to gather; they give journalists advance copies of speeches and forthcoming reports; they schedule press conferences at hours well-geared to news deadlines; they write press releases in usable language; and they carefully organize their press conferences and "photo opportunity" sessions. It is the job of news officers "to meet the journalist's scheduled needs with material that their beat agency has generated at its own pace."

In effect, the large bureaucracies of the powerful *subsidize* the mass media, and gain special access by their contribution to reducing the media's costs of acquiring the raw materials of, and producing, news. The large entities that provide this subsidy become "routine" news sources and have privileged access to the gates. Non-routine sources must struggle for access, and may be ignored by the arbitrary decision of the gatekeepers. [...]

Because of their services, continuous contact on the beat, and mutual dependency, the powerful can use personal relationships, threats, and rewards to further influence and coerce the media. The media may feel obligated to carry extremely dubious stories and mute criticism in order not to offend their sources and disturb a close relationship. It is very difficult to call authorities on whom one depends for daily news liars, even if they tell whoppers. Critical sources may be avoided not only because of their lesser availability and higher cost of establishing credibility, but also because the primary sources may be offended and may even threaten the media using them. [...]

Perhaps more important, powerful sources regularly take advantage of media routines and dependency to "manage" the media, to manipulate them into following a special agenda and framework. Part of this management process consists of inundating the media with stories, which serve sometimes to foist a particular line and frame on the media and at other times to help chase unwanted stories off the front page or out of the media altogether. This strategy can be traced back at least as far as the Committee on Public Information, established to coordinate propaganda during World War I, which "discovered in 1917–18 that one of the best means of controlling news was flooding news channels with 'facts,' or what amounted to official information."

The relation between power and sourcing extends beyond official and corporate provision of day-to-day news to shaping the supply of "experts." The dominance of official sources is weakened by the existence of highly respectable unofficial sources that give dissident views with great authority. This problem is alleviated by "co-opting the experts" – i.e., putting them on the payroll as consultants, funding their research, and organizing think tanks that will hire them directly and help disseminate their messages. In this way bias may be structured, and the supply of experts may be skewed in the direction desired by the government and "the market." […]

The mass media themselves also provide "experts" who regularly echo the official view. […] By giving these purveyors of the preferred view a great deal of exposure, the media confer status and make them the obvious candidates for opinion and analysis.

Another class of experts whose prominence is largely a function of serviceability to power is former radicals who have come to "see the light." The motives that cause these individuals to switch gods, from Stalin (or Mao) to Reagan and free enterprise, is varied, but for the establishment media the reason for the change is simply that the ex-radicals have finally seen the error of their ways. In a country whose citizenry values acknowledgement of sin and repentance, the turncoats are an important class of repentant sinners. […] The steady flow of ex-radicals from marginality to media attention shows that we are witnessing a durable method of providing experts who will say what the establishment wants said.

Flak and the enforcers: the fourth filter

"Flak" refers to negative responses to a media statement or program. It may take the form of letters, telegrams, phone calls, petitions, lawsuits, speeches and bills before Congress, and other modes of complaint, threat, and punitive action. It may be organized centrally or locally, or it may consist of the entirely independent actions of individuals.

If flak is produced on a large scale, or by individuals or groups with substantial resources, it can be both uncomfortable and costly to the media. Positions have to be defended within the organization and without, sometimes before legislatures and possibly even in courts. Advertisers may withdraw patronage. Television advertising is mainly of consumer goods that are readily subject to organized boycott. During the McCarthy years, many advertisers and radio and television stations were effectively coerced into quiescence and blacklisting of employees by the threats of determined Red hunters to boycott products. Advertisers are still concerned to avoid offending constituencies that might produce flak, and their demand for suitable programming is a continuing feature of the media environment. If certain kinds of fact, position, or program are thought likely to elicit flak, this prospect can be a deterrent.

The ability to produce flak, and especially flak that is costly and threatening, is related to power. Serious flak has increased in close parallel with business's growing resentment of media criticism and the corporate offensive of the 1970s and 1980s. Flak from the powerful can be either direct or indirect. The direct would include letters or phone calls from the White House or the FCC to the television networks asking for documents used in putting together a program, or from irate officials of ad agencies or corporate sponsors to media officials asking for reply time or threatening retaliation. The powerful can also work on the media indirectly by complaining to their own constituencies (stockholders, employees) about the media, by generating institutional advertising that does the same, and by funding right-wing monitoring or think-tank operations designed to attack the media. They may also fund political campaigns and help put into power conservative politicians who will more directly serve the interests of private power in curbing any deviationism in the media. [...]

Although the flak machines steadily attack the mass media, the media treat them well. They receive respectful attention, and their propagandistic role and links to a larger corporate program are rarely mentioned or analyzed. [...] This reflects the power of the sponsors, including the well-entrenched position of the right wing in the mass media themselves.

The producers of flak add to one another's strength and reinforce the command of political authority in its news-management activities. The government is a major producer of flak, regularly assailing, threatening, and "correcting" the media, trying to contain any deviations from the established line. News management itself is designed to produce flak. [...]

Anticommunism as a control mechanism: the fifth filter

A final filter is the ideology of anticommunism. Communism as the ultimate evil has always been the specter haunting property owners, as it threatens the very root of their class position and superior status. The Soviet, Chinese, and Cuban revolutions were traumas to Western elites, and the ongoing conflicts and the well-publicized abuses of Communist states have contributed to elevating opposition to communism to a first principle of Western ideology and politics. This ideology helps mobilize the populace against an enemy, and because the concept is fuzzy it can be used against anybody advocating policies that threaten property interests or support accommoda-tion with Communist states and radicalism. It therefore helps fragment the left and labor movements and serves as a political-control mechanism. If the triumph of communism is the worst imaginable result, the support of fascism abroad is justified as a lesser evil. Opposition to social democrats who are too soft on Communists and "play into their hands" is rationalized in similar terms.

Liberals at home, often accused of being pro-Communist or insufficiently anti-Communist, are kept continuously on the defensive in a cultural milieu in which anticommunism is the dominant religion. If they allow communism, or something that can be labeled communism, to triumph in the provinces while they are in office, the political costs are heavy. Most of them have fully internalized the religion anyway, but they are all under great pressure to demonstrate their anti-Communist credentials. This causes them to behave very much like reactionaries. [...]

It should be noted that when anti-Communist fervor is aroused, the demand for serious evidence in support of claims of "communist" abuses is suspended, and charlatans can thrive as evidential sources. Defectors, informers, and assorted other opportunists move to center stage as "experts," and they remain there even after exposure as highly unreliable, if not downright liars. [...]

The anti-Communist control mechanism reaches through the system to exercise a profound influence on the mass media. In normal times as well as in periods of Red scares, issues tend to be framed in terms of a dichotomized world of Communist and anti-Communist powers, with gains and losses allocated to contesting sides, and rooting for "our side" considered an entirely legitimate news practice. [...]

Dichotomization and propaganda campaigns

The five filters narrow the range of news that passes through the gates, and even more sharply limit what can become "big news," subject to sustained news campaigns. By definition, news from primary establishment sources meets one major filter requirement and is readily accommodated by the mass media. Messages from and about dissidents and weak, unorganized individuals and groups, domestic and foreign, are at an initial disadvantage in sourcing costs and credibility, and they often do not comport with the ideology or interests of the gatekeepers and other powerful parties that influence the filtering process.

Thus, for example, the torture of political prisoners and the attack on trade unions in Turkey will be pressed on the media only by human-rights activists and groups that have little political leverage. The U.S. government supported the Turkish martial-law government from its inception in 1980, and the U.S. business community has been warm toward regimes that profess fervent anticommunism, encourage foreign investment, repress unions, and loyally support U.S. foreign policy (a set of virtues that are frequently closely linked). Media that chose to feature Turkish violence against their own citizenry would have had to go to extra expense to find and check out information sources; they would elicit flak from government, business, and organized right-wing flak machines, and they might be looked upon with disfavor by the corporate community (including advertisers) for indulging in such a quixotic interest and crusade. They would tend to stand alone in focusing on victims that from the standpoint of dominant American interests were *unworthy*.

In marked contrast, protest over political prisoners and the violation of the rights of trade unions in Poland was seen by the Reagan administration and business elites in 1981 as a noble cause, and, not coincidentally, as an opportunity to score political points. Many media leaders and syndicated columnists felt the same way. Thus information and strong opinions on human-rights violations in Poland could be obtained from official sources in Washington, and reliance on Polish dissidents would not elicit flak from the U.S. government or the flak machines. These victims would be generally acknowledged by the managers of the filters to be *worthy*. The mass media never explain *why* Andrei Sakharov is worthy and José Luis Massera, in Uruguay, is unworthy – the attention and general dichotomization occur "naturally" as a result of the working of the filters, but the result is the same as if a commissar had instructed the media: "Concentrate on the victims of enemy powers and forget about the victims of friends."

Reports of the abuses of worthy victims not only pass through the filters; they may also become the basis of sustained propaganda campaigns. If the government or corporate community and the media feel that a story is useful as well as dramatic, they focus on it intensively and use it to enlighten the public. This was true, for example, of the shooting down by the Soviets of the Korean airliner KAL 007 in early September 1983, which permitted an extended campaign of denigration of an official enemy and greatly advanced Reagan administration arms plans. As Bernard Gwertzman noted complacently in the *New York Times* of August 31, 1984, U.S. officials "assert that worldwide criticism of the Soviet handling of the crisis has strengthened the United States in its relations with Moscow." In sharp contrast, the shooting down by Israel of a Libyan civilian airliner in February 1973 led to no outcry in the West, no denunciations for "cold-blooded murder," and no boycott. This difference in treatment was explained by the *New York Times* precisely on the grounds of utility: "No useful purpose is served by an acrimonious debate over the assignment of blame for the downing of a Libyan airliner in the Sinai peninsula last week." There was a very "useful purpose" served by focusing on the Soviet act, and a massive propaganda campaign ensued. [...]

Conversely, propaganda campaigns will *not* be mobilized where victimization, even though massive, sustained, and dramatic, fails to meet the test of utility to elite interests. Thus, while the focus on Cambodia in the Pol Pot era (and thereafter) was exceedingly serviceable, as Cambodia had fallen to the Communists and useful lessons could be drawn by attention to their victims, the numerous victims of the U.S. bombing *before* the Communist takeover were scrupulously ignored by the U.S. elite press. After Pol Pot's ouster by the Vietnamese, the United States quietly shifted support to this "worse than Hitler" villain, with little notice in the press, which adjusted once again to the national political agenda. Attention to the Indonesian massacres of 1965–66, or the victims of the Indonesian invasion of East Timor from 1975 onward, would also be distinctly unhelpful as bases of media campaigns, because Indonesia is a U.S. ally and client that maintains an open door to Western investment, and because, in the case of East Timor, the United States bears major responsibility for the slaughter. The same is true of the victims of state terror in Chile and Guatemala, U.S. clients whose basic institutional structures, including the state terror system, were put in place and maintained by, or with crucial assistance from, U.S. power, and who remain U.S. client states. Propaganda campaigns on behalf of these victims would conflict with government-business-military interests and, in our model, would not be able to pass through the filtering system. [...]

Using a propaganda model, we would not only anticipate definitions of worth based on utility, and dichotomous attention based on the same criterion, we would also expect the news stories about worthy and unworthy victims (or enemy and friendly states) to differ in *quality*. That is, we would expect official sources of the United States and its client regimes to be used heavily – and uncritically – in connection with one's own abuses and those of friendly governments, while refugees and other dissident sources will be used in dealing with enemies. We would anticipate the uncritical acceptance of certain premises in dealing with self and friends – such as that one's own state and leaders seek peace and democracy, oppose terrorism, and tell the truth – premises which will not be applied in treating enemy states. We would expect different criteria of evaluation to be employed, so that what is villainy in enemy states will be presented as an incidental background fact in the case of oneself and friends. What is on the agenda in treating one case will be off the agenda in discussing the other. We would also expect great investigatory zeal in the search for enemy villainy and the responsibility of high officials for abuses in enemy states, but diminished enterprise in examining such matters in connection with one's own and friendly states.

The quality of coverage should also be displayed more directly and crudely in placement, headlining, word usage, and other modes of mobilizing interest and outrage. In the opinion columns, we would anticipate sharp restraints on the range of opinion allowed expression. Our hypothesis is that worthy victims will be featured prominently and dramatically, that they will be humanized, and that their victimization will receive the detail and context in story construction that will generate reader interest and sympathetic emotion. In contrast, unworthy victims will merit only slight detail, minimal humanization, and little context that will excite and enrage.

Meanwhile, because of the power of establishment sources, the flak machines, and anti-Communist ideology, we would anticipate outcries that the worthy victims are being sorely neglected, that the unworthy are treated with excessive and uncritical generosity, that the media's liberal, adversarial (if not subversive) hostility to government explains our difficulties in mustering support for the latest national venture in counterrevolutionary intervention.

In sum, a propaganda approach to media coverage suggests a systematic and highly political dichotomization in news coverage based on serviceability to important domestic power interests. This should be observable in dichotomized choices of story and in the volume and quality of coverage. Such dichotomization in the mass media is massive and systematic: not only are choices for publicity and suppression comprehensible in terms of system advantage, but the modes of handling favored and inconvenient materials (placement, tone, context, fullness of treatment) differ in ways that serve political ends.

Critical connections

Herman and Chomsky's propaganda model, which exemplifies an instrumental Marxist approach to understanding media has been challenged on theoretical and methodological grounds, and even dismissed as a conspiratorial exercise in (anti-state) propaganda itself. Critics such as Hallin (1986) and Schlesinger (1989) find their analysis too deterministic. They question the very existence of an 'elite consensus' – amounting to a unified 'dominant ideology' – that can be reproduced in mainstream media discourses, as well as the extent to which the US national media are closed to alternative viewpoints. Elsewhere in this Reader, Hall *et al.* (Reading 18) draw from structural Marxism and seek to develop a less deterministic interpretation of the news media as a contested terrain upon which elite ideas must continually compete for ideological supremacy, legitimacy and definitional control. In the final instance, however, and despite significant methodological and theoretical differences, their insistence on the state's capacity to achieve discursive closure around matters of national importance shares much in common with the findings of Chomsky and Herman's analysis. Though their study appears to have attracted praise and criticism in equal measure, not least because of its radical, uncompromising and condemnatory stance on the national security state, Herman and Chomsky offer a powerful counter to liberal pluralist conceptions of a free press in a democratic society (see Greer, 2003; McNair, 1998).

Discussion questions

- Outline and evaluate the central tenets of the propaganda model of media production.
- What are the implications of the spread of the Internet for Herman and Chomsky's proposition that elite groups can achieve discursive closure around issues of national security?
- Is the state winning the propagandistic 'war on terror' (see especially Readings 18, 19 and 40)?

References

Greer, C. (2003) Sex Crime and the Media: Sex Offending and the Press in a Divided Society, Cullompton: Willan.
Hallin, D. (1986) The Uncensored War, Oxford: Oxford University Press.
McNair, B. (1998) The Sociology of Journalism, London: Arnold.
Schlesinger, P. (1989) 'From Production to Propaganda', in Media, Culture and Society, 11, 3: 286–306.

Stuart Hall

ENCODING–DECODING (1980)

Introduction and context

PRIOR TO STUART HALL'S MODEL OF ENCODING–DECODING (1980, though first published in 1973 as 'Encoding and Decoding in the Television Discourse'), accounts of the encoding and decoding of media texts tended to be structured in accordance with a 'transmission model' of communication, whereby a sender transmits a message to a receiver who is viewed as interpreting the message largely as intended by its producer. Though people may of course relate to media texts in different ways, meaning still tended to be conceived of as something that exists only within fixed packages of media content. Hall's significant intervention was to insist that the active construction (rather than passive reception) of meaning is a socially structured process, and that in order to fully comprehend its complexities, the communication process as a whole needed to be considered, with each stage – or 'moment' – of that process being given due attention. Hall thus rejected the linearity and textual determinism of previous models, since these could not account for differential interpretations between receivers of the same message, nor for why heterogeneous audiences may variously derive pleasure or discomfort from very diverse sources of media content. In essence, Hall argues that media texts are 'polysemic' – they can have multiple meanings in different social and cultural contexts – and that there is no necessary connection between the encoded meaning intended by the producer and the decoded meaning ultimately arrived at by the receiver.

In a clear nod to pioneering semiotician Ferdinand de Saussure's turn of the twentieth-century notion of the 'speech circuit', and drawing from Marx's discussion of commodity production, Hall produces a model that he calls the 'circuit of communication'. This circuit captures the various stages of the communication process, from message production to audience perception and, continuing the Marxist analogy, consists of a series of distinctive 'moments' – production, circulation, distribution/

consumption, reproduction. How media texts are decoded depends not only, or even primarily, on the content of the message itself. It is also shaped by the social positioning of the receiver and the various codes, skills and experiences they have access to and draw from as a result. Adapting Frank Parkin's (1972) 'meaning systems', Hall proposes three hypothetical interpretive positions for readers of media texts – dominant-hegemonic, negotiated and oppositional. The identification of three interpretive positions acknowledges that there is often a 'preferred reading' in media texts, but insists that media audiences can adopt alternative stances and develop alternative readings.

Traditionally, mass-communications research has conceptualized the process of communication in terms of a circulation circuit or loop. This model has been criticized for its linearity – sender/message/receiver – for its concentration on the level of message exchange and for the absence of a structured conception of the different moments as a complex structure of relations. But it is also possible (and useful) to think of this process in terms of a structure produced and sustained through the articulation of linked but distinctive moments – production, circulation, distribution/consumption, reproduction. This would be to think of the process as a 'complex structure in dominance', sustained through the articulation of connected practices, each of which, however, retains its distinctiveness and has its own specific modality, its own forms and conditions of existence. This second approach, homologous to that which forms the skeleton of commodity production offered in Marx's *Grundrisse* and in *Capital*, has the added advantage of bringing out more sharply how a continuous circuit – production-distribution-production – can be sustained through a 'passage of forms'. It also highlights the specificity of the forms in which the product of the process 'appears' in each moment, and thus what distinguishes discursive 'production' from other types of production in our society and in modern media systems.

The 'object' of these practices is meanings and messages in the form of sign-vehicles of a specific kind organized like any form of communication or language, through the operation of codes within the systematic chain of a discourse. The apparatuses, relations and practices of production thus issue, at a certain moment (the moment of 'production/circulation'), in the form of symbolic vehicles constituted within the rules of 'language'. It is in this discursive form that the circulation of the 'product' takes place. The process thus requires, at the production end, its material instruments – its 'means' – as well as its own sets of social (production) relations – the organization and combination of practices within media apparatuses. But it is in the *discursive* form that the circulation of the product takes place, as well as its distribution to different audiences. Once accomplished, the discourse must then be translated – transformed, again – into social practices if the circuit is to be both completed and effective. If no 'meaning' is taken, there can be no 'consumption'. If the meaning is not articulated in practice, it has no effect. The value of this approach is that while each of the moments, in articulation, is necessary to the circuit as a whole, no one moment can fully guarantee the next moment with which it is articulated. Since each has its specific modality and conditions of existence, each can constitute its own break or interruption of the 'passage of forms' on whose continuity the flow of effective production (that is, 'reproduction') depends.

Thus while in no way wanting to limit research to 'following only those leads which emerge from content analysis', we must recognize that the discursive form of the message has a privileged position in the communicative exchange (from the viewpoint of circulation), and that the moments of 'encoding' and 'decoding', though only 'relatively autonomous' in relation to the communicative process as a whole, are *determinate* moments. A 'raw' historical event cannot, *in that form*, be transmitted by, say, a television newscast. Events can only be signified within the aural-visual forms of the televisual discourse. In the moment when a historical event passes under the sign of discourse, it is subject to all the complex formal 'rules' by which language signifies. To put it paradoxically, the event must become a 'story' before it can become a *communicative event*. In that moment the formal sub-rules of discourse are 'in dominance', without, of course, subordinating out of existence the historical event so signified, the social relations in which the rules are set to work or the social and political consequences of the event having been signified in this way. The 'message form' is the necessary 'form of appearance' of the event in its passage from source to receiver. Thus the transposition into and out of the 'message form' (or the mode of symbolic exchange) is not a random 'moment', which we can take up or ignore at our convenience. The 'message form' is a determinate moment; though, at another level, it comprises the surface movements of the communications system only and requires, at another stage, to be integrated into the social relations of the communication process as a whole, of which it forms only a part.

From this general perspective, we may crudely characterize the television communicative process as follows. The institutional structures of broadcasting, with their practices and networks of production, their organized relations and technical infrastructures, are required to produce a programme. Using the analogy of *Capital*, this is the 'labour process' in the discursive mode. Production, here, constructs the message. In one sense, then, the circuit begins here. Of course, the production process is not without its 'discursive' aspect: it, too, is framed throughout by meanings and ideas: knowledge-in-use concerning the routines of production, historically defined technical skills, professional ideologies, institutional knowledge, definitions and assumptions, assumptions about the audience and so on frame the constitution of the programme through this production structure. Further, though the production structures of television originate the television discourse, they do not constitute a closed system. They draw topics, treatments, agendas, events, personnel, images of the audience, 'definitions of the situation' from other sources and other discursive formations within the wider socio-cultural and political structure of which they are a differentiated part. Philip Elliott has expressed this point succinctly, within a more traditional framework, in his discussion of the way in which the audience is both the 'source' and the 'receiver' of the television message. Thus – to borrow Marx's terms – circulation and reception are, indeed, 'moments' of the production process in television and are reincorporated, via a number of skewed and structured 'feedbacks', into the production process itself. The consumption or reception of the television message is thus also itself a 'moment' of the production process in its larger sense, though the latter is 'predominant' because it is the 'point of departure for the realization' of the message. Production and reception of the television message are not, therefore, identical, but they are related: they are differentiated moments within the totality formed by the social relations of the communicative process as a whole.

At a certain point, however, the broadcasting structures must yield encoded messages in the form of a meaningful discourse. The institution-societal relations of production must pass under the discursive rules of language for its product to be 'realized'.

This initiates a further differentiated moment, in which the formal rules of discourse and language are in dominance. Before this message can have an 'effect' (however defined), satisfy a 'need' or be put to a 'use', it must first be appropriated as a meaningful discourse and be meaningfully decoded. It is this set of decoded meanings which 'have an effect', influence, entertain, instruct or persuade, with very complex perceptual, cognitive, emotional, ideological or behavioural consequences. In a 'determinate' moment the structure employs a code and yields a 'message': at another determinate moment the 'message', via its decodings, issues into the structure of social practices. We are now fully aware that this re-entry into the practices of audience reception and 'use' cannot be understood in simple behavioural terms. The typical processes identified in positivistic research on isolated elements – effects, uses, 'gratifications' – are themselves framed by structures of understanding, as well as being produced by social and economic relations, which shape their 'realization' at the reception end of the chain and which permit the meanings signified in the discourse to be transposed into practice or consciousness (to acquire social use value or political effectivity).

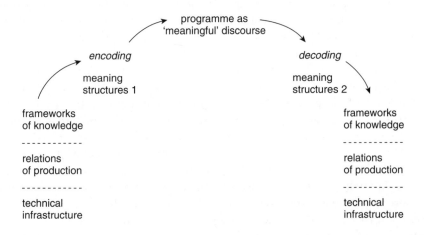

Clearly, what we have labelled in the diagram 'meaning structures 1' and 'meaning structures 2' may not be the same. They do not constitute an 'immediate identity'. The codes of encoding and decoding may not be perfectly symmetrical. The degrees of symmetry – that is, the degrees of 'understanding' and 'misunderstanding' in the communicative exchange – depend on the degrees of symmetry/asymmetry (relations of equivalence) established between the positions of the 'personifications', encoder-producer and decoder-receiver. But this in turn depends on the degrees of identity/non-identity between the codes which perfectly or imperfectly transmit, interrupt or systematically distort what has been transmitted. The lack of fit between the codes has a great deal to do with the structural differences of relation and position between broadcasters and audiences, but it also has something to do with the asymmetry between the codes of 'source' and 'receiver' at the moment of transformation into and out of the discursive form. What are called 'distortions' or 'misunderstandings' arise precisely from the *lack of equivalence* between the two sides in the communicative exchange. Once again, this defines the 'relative autonomy', but 'determinateness', of the entry and exit of the message in its discursive moments.

The application of this rudimentary paradigm has already begun to transform our understanding of the older term, television 'content'. We are just beginning to see how it might also transform our understanding of audience reception, 'reading' and response as well. Beginnings and endings have been announced in communications research before, so we must be cautious. But there seems some ground for thinking that a new and exciting phase in so-called audience research, of a quite new kind, may be opening up. At either end of the communicative chain the use of the semiotic paradigm promises to dispel the lingering behaviourism which has dogged mass-media research for so long, especially in its approach to content. Though we know the television programme is not a behavioural input, like a tap on the knee cap, it seems to have been almost impossible for traditional researchers to conceptualize the communicative process without lapsing into one or other variant of low-flying behaviourism. We know, as Gerbner has remarked, that representations of violence on the TV screen 'are not violence but messages about violence': but we have continued to research the question of violence, for example, as if we were unable to comprehend this epistemological distinction.

The televisual sign is a complex one. It is itself constituted by the combination of two types of discourse, visual and aural. Moreover, it is an iconic sign, in Peirce's terminology, because 'it possesses some of the properties of the thing represented'. This is a point which has led to a great deal of confusion and has provided the site of intense controversy in the study of visual language. Since the visual discourse trans-lates a three-dimensional world into two-dimensional planes, it cannot, of course, *be* the referent or concept it signifies. The dog in the film can bark but it cannot bite! Reality exists outside language, but it is constantly mediated by and through language: and what we can know and say has to be produced in and through discourse. Discursive 'knowledge' is the product not of the transparent representation of the 'real' in language but of the articulation of language on real relations and conditions. Thus there is no intelligible discourse without the operation of a code. Iconic signs are therefore coded signs too – even if the codes here work differently from those of other signs. There is no degree zero in language. Naturalism and 'realism' – the appar-ent fidelity of the representation to the thing or concept represented – is the result, the effect, of a certain specific articulation of language on the 'real'. It is the result of a discursive practice.

Certain codes may, of course, be so widely distributed in a specific language community or culture, and be learned at so early an age, that they appear not to be constructed – the effect of an articulation between sign and referent – but to be 'naturally' given. Simple visual signs appear to have achieved a 'near-universality' in this sense: though evidence remains that even apparently 'natural' visual codes are culture-specific. However, this does not mean that no codes have intervened; rather, that the codes have been profoundly *naturalized*. The operation of naturalized codes reveals not the transparency and 'naturalness' of language but the depth, the habitua-tion and the near-universality of the codes in use. They produce apparently 'natural' recognitions. This has the (ideological) effect of concealing the practices of coding which are present. But we must not be fooled by appearances. Actually, what naturalized codes demonstrate is the degree of habituation produced when there is a fundamental alignment and reciprocity – an achieved equivalence – between the encoding and decoding sides of an exchange of meanings. The functioning of the codes on the decoding side will frequently assume the status of naturalized perceptions. This leads us to think that the visual sign for 'cow' actually *is* (rather than *represents*) the animal, cow. But if we think of the visual representation of a cow in a manual on animal husbandry – and, even more, of the linguistic sign 'cow' – we can see that both, in different degrees, are *arbitrary* with respect to the concept of the animal they represent. The articulation of an arbitrary sign – whether visual or verbal – with the concept of a referent is the product not of nature but of convention, and the conventionalism of discourses requires the intervention, the support, of codes. Thus Eco has argued that iconic signs 'look like objects in the real world because they reproduce the conditions (that is, the codes) of perception in the viewer'. These 'conditions of perception' are, however, the result of a highly coded, even if virtually unconscious, set of operations – decodings. This is as true of the photographic or televisual image as it is of any other sign. Iconic signs are, however, particularly vulnerable to being 'read' as natural because visual codes of perception are very widely distributed and because this type of sign is less arbitrary than a linguistic sign: the linguistic sign, 'cow', possesses *none* of the properties of the thing represented, whereas the visual sign appears to possess *some* of those properties.

This may help us to clarify a confusion in current linguistic theory and to define precisely how some key terms are being used in this article. Linguistic theory frequently employs the distinction 'denotation' and 'connotation'. The term 'denotation' is widely equated with the literal meaning of a sign: because this literal meaning is almost universally recognized, especially when visual discourse is being employed, 'denotation' has often been confused with a literal transcription of 'reality' in language – and thus with a 'natural sign', one produced without the intervention of a code. 'Connotation', on the other hand, is employed simply to refer to less fixed and therefore more conventionalized and changeable, associative meanings, which clearly vary from instance to instance and therefore must depend on the intervention of codes.

We do *not* use the distinction – denotation/connotation – in this way. From our point of view, the distinction is an *analytic* one only. It is useful, in analysis, to be able to apply a rough rule of thumb which distinguishes those aspects of a sign which appear to be taken, in any language community at any point in time, as its 'literal' meaning (denotation) from the more associative meanings for the sign which it is possible to generate (connotation). But analytic distinctions must not be confused with distinc-tions in the real world. There will be very few instances in which signs organized in a discourse signify *only* their 'literal' (that is, near-universally consensualized) meaning. In actual discourse most signs will combine both the denotative and the connotative *aspects* (as redefined above). It may, then, be asked why we retain the distinction at all. It is largely a matter of analytic value. It is because signs appear to acquire their full ideological value – appear to be open to articulation with wider ideological discourses and meanings – at the level of their 'associative' meanings (that is, at the connotative level) – for here 'meanings' are *not* apparently fixed in natural perception (that is, they are not fully naturalized), and their fluidity of meaning and association can be more fully exploited and transformed. So it is at the connotative *level* of the sign that situational ideologies alter and transform signification. At this level we can see more clearly the active intervention of ideologies in and on discourse: here, the sign is open to new accentuations and, in Vološinov's terms, enters fully into the struggle over meanings – the class struggle in language. This does not mean that the denotative or 'literal' meaning is outside ideology. Indeed, we could say that its ideological value is strongly *fixed* – because it has become so fully universal and 'natural'. The terms 'denotation' and 'connotation', then, are merely useful analytic tools for distinguishing, in particular contexts, between not the presence/absence of ideology in language but the different levels at which ideologies and discourses intersect.

The level of connotation of the visual sign, of its contextual reference and positioning in different discursive fields of meaning and association, is the point where *already coded* signs intersect with the deep semantic codes of a culture and take on additional, more active ideological dimensions. We might take an example from advertising discourse. Here, too, there is no 'purely denotative', and certainly no 'natural', representation. Every visual sign in advertising connotes a quality, situation, value or inference, which is present as an implication or implied meaning, depending on the connotational positioning. In Barthes's example, the sweater always signifies a 'warm garment' (denotation) and thus the activity/value of 'keeping warm'. But it is also possible, at its more connotative levels, to signify 'the coming of winter' or 'a cold day'. And, in the specialized sub-codes of fashion, sweater may also connote a fashionable style of *haute couture* or, alternatively, an informal style of dress. But set against the right visual background and positioned by the romantic sub-code, it may connote 'long autumn walk in the woods'. Codes of this order clearly contract relations for the sign with the wider universe of ideologies in a society. These codes are the means by which power and ideology are made to signify in particular discourses. They refer signs to the 'maps of meaning' into which any culture is classified; and those 'maps of social reality' have the whole range of social meanings, practices, and usages, power and interest 'written in' to them. The connotative levels of signifiers, Barthes remarked, 'have a close communication with culture, knowledge, history, and it is through them, so to speak, that the environmental world invades the linguistic and semantic system. They are, if you like, the fragments of ideology'.

The so-called denotative *level* of the televisual sign is fixed by certain, very complex (but limited or 'closed') codes. But its connotative level, though also bounded, is more open, subject to more active *transformations*, which exploit its polysemic values. Any such already constituted sign is potentially transformable into more than one connotative configuration. Polysemy must not, however, be confused with pluralism. Connotative codes are *not* equal among themselves. Any society/ culture tends, with varying degrees of closure, to impose its classifications of the social and cultural and political world. These constitute a *dominant cultural order*, though it is neither univocal nor uncontested. This question of the 'structure of discourses in dominance' is a crucial point. The different areas of social life appear to be mapped out into discursive domains, hierarchically organized into *dominant or preferred meanings*. New, problematic or troubling events, which breach our expectancies and run counter to our 'common-sense constructs', to our 'taken-for-granted' knowledge of social structures, must be assigned to their discursive domains before they can be said to 'make sense'. The most common way of 'mapping' them is to assign the new to some domain or other of the existing 'maps of problematic social reality'. We say *dominant*, not 'determined', because it is always possible to order, classify, assign and decode an event within more than one 'mapping'. But we say 'dominant' because there exists a pattern of 'preferred readings'; and these both have the institutional/political/ideological order imprinted in them and have themselves become institutionalized. The domains of 'preferred meanings' have the whole social order embedded in them as a set of meanings, practices and beliefs: the everyday knowledge of social structures, of 'how things work for all practical purposes in this culture', the rank order of power and interest and the structure of legitimations, limits and sanctions. Thus to clarify a 'misunderstanding' at the connotative level, we must refer, *through* the codes, to the orders of social life, of economic and political power and of ideology. Further, since these mappings are 'structured in dominance' but not closed, the communicative process consists not in the unproblematic assignment of every visual item to its given position within a set of pre-arranged codes, but of *performative rules* – rules of competence and use, of logics-in-use – which seek actively to *enforce* or *prefer* one semantic domain over another and rule items into and out of their appropriate meaning-sets. Formal semiology has too often neglected this practice of *interpretative work*, though this constitutes, in fact, the real relations of broadcast practices in television.

In speaking of *dominant meanings*, then, we are not talking about a one-sided process which governs how all events will be signified. It consists of the 'work' required to enforce, win plausibility for and command as legitimate a *decoding* of the event within the limit of dominant definitions in which it has been connotatively signified. Terni has remarked:

> By the word *reading* we mean not only the capacity to identify and decode a certain number of signs, but also the subjective capacity to put them into a creative relation between themselves and with other signs: a capacity which is, by itself, the condition for a complete awareness of one's total environment.

Our quarrel here is with the notion of 'subjective capacity', as if the referent of a televisional discourse were an objective fact but the interpretative level were an individualized and private matter. Quite the opposite seems to be the case. The televisual practice takes 'objective' (that is, systemic) responsibility precisely for the relations which disparate signs contract with one another in any discursive instance, and thus continually rearranges, delimits and prescribes into what 'awareness of one's total environment' these items are arranged.

This brings us to the question of misunderstandings. Television producers who find their message 'failing to get across' are frequently concerned to straighten out the kinks in the communication chain, thus facilitating the 'effectiveness' of their communication. Much research which claims the objectivity of 'policy-oriented analysis' reproduces this administrative goal by attempting to discover how much of a message the audience recalls and to improve the extent of understanding. No doubt misunderstandings of a literal kind do exist. The viewer does not know the terms employed, cannot follow the complex logic of argument or exposition, is unfamiliar with the language, finds the concepts too alien or difficult or is foxed by the expository narrative. But more often broadcasters are concerned that the audience has failed to take the meaning as they – the broadcasters – intended. What they really mean to say is that viewers are not operating within the 'dominant' or 'preferred' code. Their ideal is 'perfectly transparent communication'. Instead, what they have to confront is 'systematically distorted communication'.

In recent years discrepancies of this kind have usually been explained by reference to 'selective perception'. This is the door via which a residual pluralism evades the compulsions of a highly structured, asymmetrical and non-equivalent process. Of course, there will always be private, individual, variant readings. But 'selective perception' is almost never as selective, random or privatized as the concept suggests. The patterns exhibit, across individual variants, significant clusterings. Any new approach to audience studies will therefore have to begin with a critique of 'selective perception' theory.

It was argued earlier that since there is no necessary correspondence between encoding and decoding, the former can attempt to 'prefer' but cannot prescribe or guarantee the latter, which has its own conditions of existence. Unless they are wildly aberrant, encoding will have the effect of constructing some of the limits and parameters within which decodings will operate. If there were no limits, audiences could simply read whatever they liked into any message. No doubt some total misunderstandings of this kind do exist. But the vast range must contain *some* degree of reciprocity between encoding and decoding moments, otherwise we could not speak of an effective communicative exchange at all. Nevertheless, this 'correspondence' is not given but constructed. It is not 'natural' but the product of an articulation between two distinct moments. And the former cannot determine or guarantee, in a simple sense, which decoding codes will be employed. Otherwise communication would be a perfectly equivalent circuit, and every message would be an instance of 'perfectly transparent communication'. We must think, then, of the variant articulations in which encoding/decoding can be combined. To elaborate on this, we offer a hypothetical analysis of some possible decoding positions, in order to reinforce the point of 'no necessary correspondence'.

We identify *three* hypothetical positions from which decodings of a televisual discourse may be constructed. These need to be empirically tested and refined. But the argument that decodings do not follow inevitably from encodings, that they are not identical, reinforces the argument of 'no necessary correspondence'. It also helps to deconstruct the common-sense meaning of 'misunderstanding' in terms of a theory of 'systematically distorted communication'.

The first hypothetical position is that of the *dominant-hegemonic position* When the viewer takes the connoted meaning from, say, a television newscast or current affairs programme full and straight, and decodes the message in terms of the reference code in which it has been encoded, we might say that the viewer is *operating inside the dominant code*. This is the ideal-typical case of 'perfectly transparent communication' – or as close as we are likely to come to it 'for all practical purposes'. Within this we can distinguish the positions produced by the *professional code*. This is the position (produced by what we perhaps ought to identify as the operation of a 'metacode') which the professional broadcasters assume when encoding a message which has *already* been signified in a hegemonic manner. The professional code is 'relatively independent' of the dominant code, in that it applies criteria and transformational operations of its own, especially those of a technico-practical nature. The professional code, however, operates *within* the 'hegemony' of the dominant code. Indeed, it serves to reproduce the dominant definitions precisely by bracketing their hegemonic quality and operating instead with displaced professional codings which foreground such apparently neutral-technical questions as visual quality, news and presentational values, televisual quality, 'professionalism' and so on. The hegemonic interpretations of, say, the politics of Northern Ireland, or the Chilean *coup* or the Industrial Relations Bill are principally generated by political and military elites: the particular choice of presentational occasions and formats, the selection of personnel, the choice of images, the staging of debates are selected and combined through the operation of the professional code. How the broadcasting professionals are able *both* to operate with 'relatively autonomous' codes of their own *and* to act in such a way as to reproduce (not without contradiction) the hegemonic signification of events is a complex matter which cannot be further spelled out here. It must suffice to say that the professionals are linked with the defining elites not only by the institutional position of broadcasting itself as an 'ideological apparatus', but also by the structure of *access* (that is, the systematic 'over-accessing' of selective elite personnel and their 'definition of the situation' in television). It may even be said that the professional codes serve to reproduce hegemonic definitions specifically by *not overtly* biasing their operations in a dominant direction: ideological reproduction therefore takes place here inadvertently, unconsciously, 'behind men's backs'. Of course, conflicts, contradictions and even misunderstandings regularly arise between the dominant and the professional significations and their signifying agencies.

The second position we would identify is that of the *negotiated code* or position. Majority audiences probably understand quite adequately what has been dominantly defined and professionally signified. The dominant definitions, however, are hegemonic precisely because they represent definitions of situations and events which are 'in dominance' (*global*). Dominant definitions connect events, implicitly or explicitly, to grand totalizations, to the great syntagmatic views-of-the-world: they take 'large views' of issues: they relate events to the 'national interest' or to the level of geopolitics, even if they make these connections in truncated, inverted or mystified ways. The definition of a hegemonic viewpoint is (a) that it defines within its terms the mental horizon, the universe, of possible meanings, of a whole sector of relations in a society or culture; and (b) that it carries with it the stamp of legitimacy – it appears coterminous with what is 'natural', 'inevitable', 'taken for granted' about the social order. Decoding within the *negotiated version* contains a mixture of adaptive and oppositional elements: it acknowledges the legitimacy of the hegemonic definitions to make the grand significations (abstract), while, at a more restricted, situational (situated) level, it makes its own ground rules – it operates with exceptions to the rule. It accords the privileged position to the dominant definitions of events while reserving the right to make a more negotiated application to 'local conditions', to its own more *corporate* positions. This negotiated version of the dominant ideology is thus shot through with contradictions, though these are only on certain occasions brought to full visibility. Negotiated codes operate through what we might call particular or situated logics: and these logics are sustained by their differential and unequal relation to the discourses and logics of power. The simplest example of a negotiated code is that which governs the response of a worker to the notion of an Industrial Relations Bill limiting the right to strike or to arguments for a wages freeze. At the level of the 'national interest' economic debate the decoder may adopt the hegemonic definition, agreeing that 'we must all pay ourselves less in order to combat inflation'. This, however, may have little or no relation to his/her willingness to go on strike for better pay and conditions or to oppose the Industrial Relations Bill at the level of shop-floor or union organization. We suspect that the great majority of so-called 'misunderstandings' arise from the contradictions and disjunctures between hegemonic-dominant encodings and negotiated-corporate decodings. It is just these mismatches in the levels which most provoke defining elites and professionals to identify a 'failure in communications'.

Finally, it is possible for a viewer perfectly to understand both the literal and the connotative inflection given by a discourse but to decode the message in a *globally* contrary way. He/she detotalizes the message in the preferred code in order to retotalize the message within some alternative framework of reference. This is the case of the viewer who listens to a debate on the need to limit wages but 'reads' every mention of the 'national interest' as 'class interest'. He/she is operating with what we must call an *oppositional code*. One of the most significant political moments (they also coincide with crisis points within the broadcasting organizations themselves, for obvious reasons) is the point when events which are normally signified and decoded in a negotiated way begin to be given an oppositional reading. Here the 'politics of signification' – the struggle in discourse – is joined.

Critical connections

Hall's model of Encoding and Decoding has been criticised for its implicit assumption – made explicit in the theory of 'primary definition' advanced in *Policing the Crisis* (see Reading 18) – that media texts are encoded in accordance with the dominant hegemonic discourse. For this reason, some have suggested that the model may work better for news media. But even when isolated to news programmes, the model risks over-predicting the hegemony of the dominant code. Others have queried how we can establish with any certainty what the 'preferred reading' of a text actually is, and what negotiated and oppositional readings might look like in that context (Moores, 1993). Nonetheless, Hall's model of Encoding and Decoding has been hugely influential within cultural and media studies, and remains central to contemporary audience research. It formed the theoretical basis, for example, for David Morley's (1980) *Nationwide* study, which examined how people's differing responses to the popular British current affairs programme might be understood as a function of their socio-economic positioning and political interests, alongside other demographic characteristics. In this Reader, the influence of Encoding–Decoding is also apparent in Jenny Kitzinger's discussion of focus group work and audience research (Reading 13). It is, of course, also clear in Hall's (1973) 'The Determination of News Photographs', which applies some of the central concerns with the circuit of communication to the interpretation of images presented in news media (Reading 10).

Discussion questions

- Explain Hall's criticisms of previous research on media consumption and, therefore, his rationale for theorising and researching the complete 'circuit of communication'.
- Select a newspaper crime story and, considering both the words and pictures (see also Reading 10), try to identify what the 'hegemonic', 'negotiated' and

'oppositional' readings might be. Does your interpretation match that of your fellow students?
- Now try applying Hall's theoretical model of Encoding-Decoding to magazine advertisements.

References

de Saussure, F. (1972) Course in *General Linguistics*, Open Court Publishing Company. LaSalle, Illinois. (Translated by: Roy Harris.)

Moores, S. (1993): *Interpreting Audiences: The Ethnography of Media Consumption.* London: Sage.

Morley, D. (1980): *The 'Nationwide' Audience: Structure and Decoding.* London: BFI.

Parkin, F. (1972): *Class Inequality and Political Order.* London: Granada.

Manuel Castells

AN INTRODUCTION TO THE INFORMATION AGE (1997)

Introduction and context

THEORISING THE SHIFT towards the Information Age receives its most sophisticated and highly developed articulation in the work of Manuel Castells, who has been writing on the issue for several decades. Fundamentally, Castells is interested in understanding the shift from one mode of capitalist production and development to another. The shift in question is from 'industrial capitalism' to 'informational capitalism'. The latter is a very different form of capitalism driven by the rapid expansion of Information and Communications Technologies (ICTs) which, in turn, has created new and unprecedented capacities for information processing and the global exchange of symbols. The result has been the emergence of a society organised around 'information flows' – what Castells terms the 'Network Society' (2000). It is a society in which cultural, technical and financial information circulates globally in real time, simultaneously interacting with, driving and drawing from other key changes – the transformation of labour and employment, the mediatisation of politics, the shift to a global economy, the influence of social and cultural movements – on a planetary scale, and with enormous consequences. The Network Society is reshaping political, cultural and economic relations. In so doing, it is reshaping our ways of life.

In *An Introduction to the Information Age*, Castells offers an overview of the defining characteristics of the Information Age and the main lines of his argument. The reading is excerpted from a Castells speech first reproduced in the urban studies journal *City*. In this distillation of key themes and ideas, Castells identifies nine features or processes which help to delineate the structure and dynamics of the Network Society. Several of these – the globalised economy, the mediatisation of politics, the rise in social polarisation and social exclusion, the simultaneous oligopolisation of media and fragmentation of consumer audiences – are of direct relevance to criminologists because they impact profoundly on definitions, understandings, experiences of media, crime and social control locally, nationally and globally. Indeed, elsewhere Castells has taken some time to discuss the impact of the Information Age on global organised crime (Castells, 1998 in McLaughlin et al., 2003). Castells' work on the Information Age is included in this Reader, therefore, because of its commentary of the key changes which are shaping the Information Age and the potentially enormous impact of these changes for crime and media, and media criminology.

In the last decade I was struck, as many have been, by a series of major historical events that have transformed our world/our lives. Just to mention the most important: the diffusion and deepening of the information technology revolution, including genetic engineering; the collapse of the Soviet Union, with the consequent demise of the international Communist movement, and the end of the Cold War that had marked everything for the last half a century; the restructuring of capitalism; the process of globalization; emergence of the Pacific as the most dynamic area of the global economy; the paradoxical combination of a surge in nationalism and the crisis of the sovereign nation-state; the crisis of democratic politics, shaken by periodic scandals and a crisis of legitimacy; the rise of feminism and the crisis of patriarchalism; the widespread diffusion of ecological consciousness; the rise of communalism as sources of resistance to globalization, taking in many contexts the form of religious fundamentalism; last, but not least, the development of a global criminal economy that is having significant impacts in international economy, national politics, and local everyday life.

I grew increasingly dissatisfied with the interpretations and theories, certainly including my own, that the social sciences were using to make sense of this new world. But I did not give up the rationalist project of understanding all this, in a coherent manner, that could be somewhat empirically grounded and as much as possible theoretically oriented. Thus, for the last 12 years I undertook the task of researching and understanding this wide array of social trends, working in and on the United States, Western Europe, Russia, Asian Pacific, and Latin America. Along the way, I found plenty of company, as researchers from all horizons are converging in this collective endeavour.

My personal contribution to this understanding is the book in three volumes that I have now completed, *The Information Age*, with the first volume already published, and the two others scheduled for publication in 1997. The first volume analyses the new social structure, the network society. The second volume studies social movements and political processes, in the framework of and in interaction with the network society. The third volume attempts an interpretation of macro-social processes, as a result of the interaction between the power of networks and the power of identity, focusing on themes such as the collapse of the Soviet Union, the emergence of the Pacific, or the ongoing process of global social exclusion and polarization. It also proposes a general theoretical synthesis.

I will take this opportunity to share with you the main lines of my argument, hoping that this will help a debate that I see emerging from all directions in the whole world. I see coming a new wave of intellectual innovation in which, by the way, British researchers are at the forefront.

Trying to summarize a considerable amount of material within one hour I will follow a schematic format. I will focus on identifying the main features of what I consider to be the emerging, dominant social structure, the network society, that I find characteristic of informational capitalism, as constituted throughout the world. I will not indulge in futurology: everything I say is based on what I have perceived, rightly or wrongly, already at work in our societies. I will organize my lecture, in one disclaimer, nine hypotheses, and one conclusion.

Disclaimer

I shall focus on the structure/dynamics of the network society, not on its historical genesis, that is how and why it came about, although in my book I propose a few hints about it. For the record: in my view, it resulted from the historical convergence of three *independent* processes, from whose interaction emerged the Network Society:

- The Information Technology Revolution, constituted as a paradigm in the 1970s.
- The restructuring of capitalism and of statism in the 1980s, aimed at superseding their contradictions, with sharply different outcomes.
- The cultural social movements of the 1960s, and their 1970s aftermath (particularly feminism and ecologism).

The Information Technology Revolution DID NOT create the Network Society. But without information technology, the Network Society would not exist.

Rather than providing an abstract categorization in what this Network Society is, let me summarize its main features and processes, before attempting a synthesis of its embedded logic in the diversity of its cultural/institutional variations. There is no implied hierarchy in the sequence of presentation of these features. They all interact in, guess what, a network.

1. An informational economy

It is an economy in which sources of productivity and competitiveness for firms, regions, countries depend, more than ever, on knowledge, information, and the technology of their processing, including the technology of management, and the management of technology. This is not the same as a service economy. There is informational agriculture, informational manufacturing, and different types of infor-mational services, while a large number of service activities, e.g. in the developing world, are not informational at all.

The informational economy opens up an extraordinary potential for solving our problems, but, because of its dynamism and creativity, it is potentially more exclusionary than the industrial economy if social controls do not check the forces of unfettered market logic. [...]

2. A global economy

This is not the same as a world economy. That has existed, in the West, at least since the sixteenth century. The global economy is a new reality: it is an economy whose core, strategically dominant activities have the potential of working as a unit in real time on a planetary scale. This is so for financial and currency markets, advanced business services, technological innovation, high technology manufacturing, media communication.

Most economic activity in the world and most employment are not only national but regional or local. But, except for subsistence economies, the fate of these activities, and of their jobs, depend ultimately on the dynamics of the global economy, to which they are connected through networks and markers. Indeed, if labour tends to be local, capital is by and large globalized – not a small detail in a capitalist economy. This globalization has developed as a fully fledged system only in the last two decades, on the basis of information/communication technologies that were previously not available.

The global economy reaches out to the whole planet, but it is not planetary, it does not include the whole planet. In fact, it excludes probably a majority of the population. It is characterized by an extremely uneven geography. It scans the whole world, and links up valuable inputs, markets, and individuals, while switching off unskilled labour and poor markets. For a significant part of people around the world, there is a shift, from the point of view of dominant systemic interests, from exploitation to structural irrelevance. [...]

This is different from the traditional First World/Third World opposition, because the Third World has become increasingly diversified, internally, and the First World has generated social exclusion, albeit in lesser proportion, within its own boundaries. Thus, I propose the notion of the emergence of a Fourth World of exclusion, made up not only of most of Africa, and rural Asia, and of Latin American shanties, but also of the South Bronx, La Courneuve, Kamagasaki, or Tower Hamlets of this world. A fourth world that, as I document extensively in volume three, is predominantly populated by women and children.

3. The network enterprise

At the heart of the connectivity of the global economy and of the flexibility of informational capitalism, there is a new form of organization, characteristic of economic activity, but gradually extending its logic to other domains and organizations: the **network enterprise**. This is not the same as a network of enterprises. It is a network made either from firms or segments of firms, or from internal segmentation of firms. Multinational corporations, with their internal decentralization, and their links with a web of subsidiaries and suppliers throughout the world, are but one of the forms of this network enterprise. But others include strategic alliances between corporations, networks of small and medium businesses (such as in Northern Italy or Hong Kong), and link-ups between corporations and networks of small businesses through subcontracting and outsourcing.

So, the network enterprise is the specific set of linkages between different firms or segments, organized ad hoc for a specific project, and dissolving/reforming after the task is completed, e.g. IBM, Siemens, Toshiba. This ephemeral unit, The Project, around which a network of partners is built, is the actual operating unit of our economy, the one that generates profits or losses, the one that receives rewards or goes bust, and the one that hires and lays off, via its member organizations. [...]

4. The transformation of work and employment: the flexi-workers

Work is at the heart of all historical transformations. And there is no exception to this. But the coming of the Information Age is full of myths about the fate of work and employment.

With the exception, and an important one, of Western Europe, there is no major surge of unemployment in the world after two decades of diffusion in information technology. Indeed, there is much higher unemployment in technologically laggard countries, regions, and sectors.

All evidence and analysis points to the variable impact of technology on jobs depending on a much broader set of factors, mainly firms' strategies and governments' policies. Indeed, the two most technologically advanced economies, the US and Japan, both display a low rate of unemployment. In the US in the last four years there is a net balance of 10 million new jobs, and their educational content for these new jobs is significantly higher than that of the pre-existing social structure: many more information-intensive jobs than hamburger flippers' jobs have been created. Even manufacturing jobs are at an all time high on a global perspective: between 1970 and 1989, manufacturing jobs in the world increased by 72 per cent, even if OECD countries, particularly the US and the UK, have indeed de-industrialized.

There is certainly a major unemployment problem in the European Union, as a result of a combination of rigidities in the institutional environment, strategies of global redeployment by firms and, more importantly, the restrictive macro-economic policies induced by an insane obsession with fitting in the Maastricht criteria that nobody, and particularly not Germany, will be able to qualify for, in an incredible example of collective alienation in paying respect to gods of economic orthodoxy that have taken existence independently from us.

There is indeed a serious unemployment problem in the inner cities of America, England, or France, among the uneducated and switched off populations, or in low technology countries around the world, particularly in the rural areas.

For the majority of people in America, for instance, unemployment is not a problem. And yet, there is a tremendous anxiety and discontent about work. There is a real base for this concern:

(a) There is the transformation of power relationships between capital and labour in favour of capital, through the process of socio-economic restructuring that took place in the 1980s, both in a conservative environment (Reagan, Thatcher) and, to a lesser but real extent, in a less conservative environment (Spain, France). In this sense, new technologies allowed business to either automate or [undertake] offshore production or outsource supplies or to subcontract to smaller firms or to obtain concessions from labour or all the above.

(b) The development of the network enterprise translates into downsizing, sub-contracting, and networking of labour, inducing flexibility of both business and labour, and individualization of contractual arrangements between management and labour. So, instead of layoffs what we often have are layoffs followed by subcontracting of services on an ad hoc, consulting basis, for the time and task to be performed, without job tenure and without social benefits provided by the firm. [...]

This is indeed the general trend, exemplified by the rapid growth in all countries of self-employment, temporary work, and part-time, particularly for women. In England, between 40 and 45 per cent of the labour force seems to be already in these categories, as opposed to full-time, regularly salaried employment, and is growing. Some studies in Germany project that in 2015, about 50 per cent of the labour force would be out of stable employment. And in the most dynamic region in the world, Silicon Valley, a recent study we have just completed shows that, in the midst of a job creation explosion, in the last ten years, between 50 per cent at least and 90 per cent of new jobs, most of them highly paid, are of this kind of non-standard labour arrangement.

The most significant change in work in the Information Age is the reversal of the socialization/salarization of labour that characterized the industrial age. The 'organization man' is out, the 'flexible woman' is in. The individualization of work, and therefore of labour's bargaining power, is the major feature characterizing employment in the network society. [...]

5. Social polarization and social exclusion

The processes of globalization, business networking, and individualization of labour weaken social organizations and institutions that represented/protected workers in the Information Age, particularly labour unions and the welfare state. Accordingly, workers are increasingly left to themselves in their differential relationship to management and to the market place.

Skills and education, in a constant redefinition of these skills, became critical in valorizing or devaluing people in their work. But even valuable workers may fall down for reasons of health, age, gender discrimination, or lack of capacity to adapt to a given task or position.

As a result of these trends, most societies in the world, and certainly OECD countries, with the US and the UK at the top of the scale, present powerful trends towards increasing inequality, social polarization, and social exclusion. There is increasing accumulation of wealth at the top, and of poverty at the bottom.

In the US inequality has regressed to the pre-1920s period. In the limit, social exclusion creates pockets of dereliction with various entry points, but hardly any exits. It may be long-term unemployment, illness, functional illiteracy, illegal status, poverty, family disruption, psychological crisis, homelessness, drugs, crime, incarceration, etc. Once in this underworld, processes of exclusion reinforce each other, requiring a heroic effort to pull out from what I call the black holes of informational capitalism, that often have a territorial expression. The proportion of people in these black holes is staggering, and rapidly growing. In the US, it may reach above 10 per cent of the population, if you consider that simply the number of adults under the control of the justice system in 1966 was 5.4 million, that is almost 3 per cent of the population, while the proportion of people below the poverty line is 15 per cent.

The Information Age does not have to be the age of stepped-up inequality polarization and social exclusion. But for the moment it is.

6. The culture of real virtuality

Shifting to the cultural realm, we see the emergence of a similar pattern of networking, flexibility, and ephemeral symbolic communication, in a culture organized around electronic media, including in this communication system the computer-mediated communication networks. Cultural expressions of all kinds are increasingly enclosed in or shaped by this world of electronic media. But the new media system is not characterized by the one-way, undifferentiated message through a limited number of channels that constituted the world of mass media. And it is not a global village.

Media are extraordinarily diverse, and send targeted messages to specific segments of audiences and to specific moods of the audiences. They are increasingly inclusive, bridging from one to another, from network TV to cable or satellite TV, radio, VCR, musical video, walkman type of devices, connected throughout the globe, and yet diversified by cultures, constituting a hypertext with extraordinary inclusive capacity. Furthermore, slowly but surely, this new media system is moving towards interactivity, particularly if we include CMC [computer mediated communication] networks, and their access to text, images, and sounds, that will eventually link up with the current media system.

Instead of a global village we are moving towards mass production of customized cottages. While there is oligopolistic concentration of multimedia groups around the world, there is at the same time, market segmentation, and increasing interaction by and among the individuals that break up the uniformity of a mass audience. These processes induce the formation of what I call *the culture of real virtuality*. It is so, and not virtual reality, because when our symbolic environment is, by and large, structured in this inclusive, flexible, diversified hypertext, in which we navigate every day, the virtuality of this text is in fact our reality, the symbols from which we live and communicate. [...]

7. Politics

This enclosure of communication in the space of flexible media does not only concern culture. It has a fundamental effect on **politics**. In all countries, the media have become the essential space of politics. Not all politics takes place through the media, and imagemaking still needs to relate to real issues and real conflicts. But without significant presence in the space of media, actors and ideas are reduced to political marginality. This presence does not concern only, or even primarily, the moments of political campaigns, but the day-to-day messages that people receive by and from the media.

I propose the following analysis:

- To an overwhelming extent people receive their information, on the basis of which they form their political opinion, and structure their behaviour, through the media, particularly television and radio.
- Media politics needs to simplify the message/proposals.
- The simplest message is an image. The simplest image is a person.
- Political competition revolves around personalization of politics.
- The most effective political weapons are negative messages. The most effective negative message is character assassination of opponents' personalities. The politics of scandal, in the US, in Europe, in Japan, in Latin America etc. is the predominant form of political struggle. [...]
- Political marketing is the essential means to win political competition in democratic politics. In the Information Age it involves media advertising, telephone banks,

targeted mailing, image making, image unmaking, image control, presence in the media staging of public appearances etc. This makes it an excessively expensive business, way beyond that of traditional party politics, so that mechanisms of political financing are obsolete, and parties use access to power as a way to generate resources to stay in power or to prepare to return to it. This is the fundamental source of political corruption, to which intermediaries add a little personal twist. This is also at the source of systemic corruption, that feeds scandal politics. The use of scandal as a weapon leads to increased expense and activity in intelligence, damage control, and access to the media. Once a market is created intermediaries appear to retrieve, obtain, or fabricate information, offering it to the highest bidder. Politics becomes a horse race, and a soap opera motivated by greedy backstage manoeuvres, betrayals and, often, sex and violence, becoming hardly distinguishable from TV scripts.

- Those who survive in this world become politically successful, for a while. But what certainly does not survive, after a few rounds of these tricks, is political legitimacy, not to speak of citizens' hope.

8. Timeless time

As with all historical transformations, the emergence of a new social structure is necessarily linked to the redefinition of the material foundations of life, **time and space**. Time and space are related in society as in nature. Their meaning, and manifestations in social practice, evolve throughout histories and across cultures, as Giddens, Thrift, Harvey, Adams, Lash, and Urry, among others, have shown.

I propose the hypothesis that the network society, as the dominant social structure emerging in the Information Age, is organized around new forms of time and space: timeless time, the space of flows. These are the dominant forms, and not the forms in which most people live, but through their domination, they affect everybody. Let me explain, starting with time, then with some greater detail on space given the specific interests of many in this conference.

In contrast to the rhythm of biological time of most of human existence, and to the clock time characterizing the industrial age, a new form of time characterizes the dominant logic of the network society: **timeless time**. It is defined by the use of new information/communication technologies in a relentless effort to annihilate time, to compress years in seconds, seconds in split seconds. Furthermore the most fundamental aim is **to eliminate sequencing of time**, including past, present, and future in the same hypertext, thus eliminating the 'succession of things' that, according to Leibniz, characterizes time, so that without things and their sequential ordering there is no longer time in society. We live, as in the recurrent circuits of the computer networks in the encyclopedia of historical experience, all our tenses at the same time, being able to reorder them in a composite created by our fantasy or our interests.

David Harvey has shown the relentless tendency of capitalism to eliminate barriers of time. But I think in the network society, that is indeed a capitalist society but something else at the same time, all dominant processes tend to be constructed around timeless time. I find such a tendency in the whole realm of human activity. I find it certainly in the split second financial transactions of global financial markets but I also find it, for instance, in instant wars, built around the notion of a surgical strike that devastates the enemy in a few hours, or minutes, to avoid politically unpopular, costly wars. Or in the blurring of the life cycle by new reproductive techniques, allowing people a wide range of options in the age and conditions of parenting, even storing their embryos to eventually produce babies later either by themselves, or through surrogate mothers, even after their procreators are dead. I find it in the twisting of working life by the variable chronology of labour trajectories and time schedules in increasingly diverse labour markets. And I find it in the vigorous effort to use medical technology, including genetic engineering and computer-based medical care to exile death from life, to bring a substantial proportion of the population to a high level of life expectancy, and to diffuse the belief that, after all, we are eternal, at least for some time.

As with space, timeless time characterizes dominant functions and social groups, while most people in the world are still submitted to biological time and to clock time. Thus, while instant wars characterize the technological powers, atrocious, lingering wars go on and on for years, around the planet, in a slow-motion destruction process, quasi-ignored by the world until they are discovered by some television programme.

I propose the notion that a fundamental struggle in our society is around the redefinition of time, between its annihilation or desequencing by networks, on one hand, and, on the other hand, the consciousness of glacial time, the slow-motion, inter-generational evolution of our species in our cosmological environment, a concept suggested by Lash and Urry, and a battle undertaken, in my view, by the environmental movement. [...]

9. The space of flows

Many years ago (or at least it seems to me as many) I proposed the concept of Space of Flows to make sense of a body of empirical observation: dominant functions were increasingly operating on the basis of exchanges between electronic circuits linking up information systems in distant locations. Financial markets, global media, advanced business services, technology, information. In addition, electronically based, fast transportation systems reinforced this pattern of distant interaction by following up with movements of people and goods. Furthermore, new location patterns for most activities follow a simultaneous logic of territorial concentration/decentralization, reinstating the unity of their operation by electronic links, e.g. the analysis proposed in the 1980s on location patterns of high tech manufacturing; or the networked articulation of advanced services throughout the world, under the system labelled as 'global city'.

Why keep the term of space under these conditions? Reasons: (1) These electronic circuits do not operate in the territorial vacuum. They link up territorially based complexes of production, management, and information, even though the meaning and functions of these complexes depend on their connection in these networks of flows. (2) These technological linkages are material, e.g. depend on specific telecommunication/transportation facilities, and on the existence and quality of information systems, in a highly uneven geography. (3) The meaning of space evolves – as the meaning of time. Thus, instead of indulging in futurological state-ments such as the vanishing of space, and the end of cities, we should be able to reconceptualize new forms of spatial arrangements under the new technological paradigm. [...]

To proceed with this conceptualization I build on a long intellectual tradition, from Leibniz to Harold Innis, connecting space and time, around the notion of space as a coexistence of time. Thus, my definition: space is the material support of time-sharing social practices.

What happens when the time-sharing of practices (be it synchronous or asynchro-nous) does not imply contiguity? 'Things' still exist together, they share time, but the material arrangements that allow this coexistence are inter-territorial or transterritorial: **the space of flows is the material organization of time-sharing social prac-tices that work through flows**. What concretely this material organization is depends on the goals and characteristics of the networks of flows, for instance I can tell you what it is in the case of high technology manufacturing or in the case of global networks of drug traffic. However, I did propose in my analysis some elements that appear to characterize the space of flows in all kinds of networks: electronic circuits connecting information systems; territorial nodes and hubs; locales of support and social cohesion for dominant social actors in the network (e.g. the system of VIP spaces throughout the world).

Dominant functions tend to articulate themselves around the space of flows. But this is not the only space. **The space of places continues to be the predomi-nant space of experience**, of everyday life, and of social and political control. Places root culture and transmit history. (A place is a locale whose form, function, and meaning, from the point of view of the social actor, are contained within the boundaries of physical contiguity.)

In the network society, a fundamental form of social domination is **the prevalence of the logic of the space of flows over the space of places**. The space of flows structures and shapes the space of places, as when the differential fortunes of capital accumulation in global financial markets reward or punish specific regions, or when telecom systems link up CBDs to outlying suburbs in new office development, bypassing/marginalizing poor urban neighbourhoods. The domi-nation of the space of flows over the space of places induces intra-**metropolitan dualism** as a most important form of social/territorial exclusion, that has become as significant as regional uneven development. The simultaneous growth and decline of economies and societies within the same metropolitan area is a most fun-damental trend of territorial organization, and a key challenge to urban management nowadays. [...]

But there is still something else in the new spatial dynamics. Beyond the opposition between the space of flows and the space of places. As information communication networks diffuse in society, and as technology is appropriated by a variety of social actors, segments of the space of flows are penetrated by forces of resistance to domi-nation, and by expressions of personal experience. Examples:

(a) Social movements, Zapatistas and the Internet (but from the Lacandona forest). But also American Militia.

(b) Local governments, key agents of citizen representation in our society, linking up through electronic networks, particularly in Europe (see research by Stephen Graham).

(c) Expressions of experience in the space of flows.

Thus, we do witness an increasing penetration, and subversion, of the space of flows, originally set up for the functions of power, by the power of experience, inducing a set of contradictory power relationships. Yes, it is still an elitist means of communication, but it is changing rapidly. The problem is to integrate these observations in some theory, but for this we still lack research, in spite of some insightful elaborations, such as the one by Sherry Turkle at MIT.

The new frontier of spatial research is in examining the interaction between the space of flows, the space of places, function, meaning, domination, and challenge to domination, in increasingly complex and contradictory patterns. Homesteading in this frontier is already taking place, as shown in the pioneering research by Graham and Marvin, or in the reflections of Bill Mitchell, but we are clearly at the beginning of a new field of study that should help us to understand **and to change** the currently prevailing logic in the space of flows.

Conclusion: the Network Society

So, what is the Network Society? It is a society that is structured in its dominant functions and processes around networks. In its current manifestation it is a capitalist society. Indeed, we live more than ever in a capitalist world, and thus an analysis in terms of capitalism is necessary and complementary to the theory of the network society. But this particular form of capitalism is very different from industrial capitalism, as I have tried to show.

The Network Society is not produced by information technology. But without the Information Technology Revolution it could not be such a comprehensive, persuasive social form, able to link up, or de-link, the entire realm of human activity.

So, is that all? Just a morphological transformation? Well, historically, transformation of social forms has always been fundamental, both as expressions and sources of major social processes, e.g. standardized mass production in the large factory as characteristic of the so-called Fordism, as a major form of capitalist social organization; or the rational bureaucracy as the foundation of modern society, in the Weberian conception.

But this morphological transformation is even more significant because the network architecture is particularly dynamic, open-ended, flexible, potentially able to expand endlessly, without rupture, bypassing/disconnecting undesirable components following instructions of the networks' dominant nodes. Indeed, the February 1997 Davos meeting titled the general programme of its annual meeting 'Building the Network Society'.

This networking logic is at the roots of major effects in our societies. Using it:

- capital flows can bypass controls
- workers are individualized, outsourced, subcontracted
- communication becomes at the same time global and customized
- valuable people and territories are switched on, devalued ones are switched off.

The dynamics of networks push society towards an endless escape from its own constraints and controls, towards an endless supersession and reconstruction of its values and institutions, towards a meta-social, constant rearrangement of human institutions and organizations.

Networks transform power relationships. Power in the traditional sense still exists: capitalists over workers, men over women, state apparatuses still torture bodies and silence minds around the world.

Yet, there is some order of power: the power of flows in the networks prevails over the flows of power. Capitalists are dependent upon uncontrollable financial flows; many workers are at the same time investors (often unwillingly through their pension funds) in this whirlwind of capital; networkers are inter-related in the logic of the network enterprise, so that their jobs and income depend on their positioning rather than on their work. States are bypassed by global flows of wealth, information, and crime. Thus, to survive, they band together in multilateral ventures, such as the European Union. It follows the creation of a web of political institutions: national, supranational, international, regional, and local, that becomes the new operating unit of the information age: the network state. [...]

In this complexity, the communication between networks and social actors depends increasingly on shared CULTURAL CODES. If we accept certain values, certain categories that frame the meaning of experience, then the networks will process them efficiently, and will return to each one of us the outcome of their processing, according to the rules of domination and distribution inscripted in the network.

Thus, the challenges to social domination in the Network Society revolve around the redefinition of cultural codes, proposing alternative meaning and changing the rules of the game. This is why the affirmation of IDENTITY is so essential, because it fixes meaning autonomously vis-à-vis the abstract, instrumental logic of networks. I am, thus I exist. In my empirical investigation I have found identity-based social movements aimed at changing the cultural foundations of society to be the essential sources of social change in the Information Age, albeit often in forms and with goals that we do not usually associate with positive social change. Some movements, that appear to be the most fruitful and positive, are proactive, such as feminism and environmentalism. Some are reactive, as in the communal resistances to globalization built around religion, nation, territory, or ethnicity. But in all cases they affirm the preeminence of experience over instrumentality, of meaning over function, and, I would dare to say, of use value of life over exchange value in the networks. [...]

The implicit logic of the Network Society appears to end history, by enclosing it into the circularity of recurrent patterns of flows. Yet, as with any other social form, in fact it opens up a new realm of contradiction and conflict, as people around the world refuse to become shadows of global flows and project their dreams, and sometimes their nightmares, into the light of new history making. [...]

Critical connections

Though Castells' work has reflected Marxist thinking to varying degrees, his influences are diverse – Marshall McLuhan (see Reading 2), Harold Innis (McLuhan's colleague and mentor) and Daniel Bell among them. There are also explicit links to postmodern theorising, for which Castells has been roundly criticised by some (see Garnham, 1998). His postmodern tendencies are clearly manifest, for example, in his discussions of 'timeless time', the end of class struggle, and the 'culture of real virtuality'. He notes (Castells, 2000:403):

> Culture is made up of communications processes. And all forms of com-munication, as Roland Barthes and Jean Baudrillard taught us many years ago, are based on the production and consumption of signs.

Diversification, interconnectedness and global inclusiveness of media forms create a hypertext that increasingly structures and constitutes the symbolic environment that we navigate through and interact within every day. For Castells, this media hypertext is not a virtual reality. It is more than that. The hypermediatised symbolic environment is so inclusive, flexible and pervasive that it comes to constitute the very conditions of our daily existence: 'the virtuality of this text is actually our reality, the symbols from which we live and communicate'. This idea, as the preceding quote suggests, owes a considerable theoretical debt to Jean Baudrillard (see Reading 6).

Discussion questions

- What does Castells mean by the term 'The Information Age'?
- Identify and discuss the main structures and processes that constitute the shift to the Network Society.
- Compare and contrast Castells' notion of 'real virtualty' with Baudrillard's (Reading 6) notion of 'hyperreality'.

References

Castells, M. (2000) *The Rise of the Network Society*, second edition, Oxford: Blackwell.
Castells, M. (1998) 'The Global Criminal Economy', in E. McLaughlin, J. Muncie and G. Hughes (eds) *Criminological Perspectives: Key Readings*, London: Sage.
Garnham, N. (1998) 'Information Society Theory as Ideology', in *Loisir et Société*, 21, 1: 97–120.

Jean Baudrillard

SIMULACRA AND SIMULATIONS (1981)

Introduction and context

BAUDRILLARD'S WORK on culture is rooted in the deconstuctionist analysis of advertising and consumption. In modern society, Baudrillard contends, it was possible to distinguish between the represented and the real, between the 'sign' and the actual 'thing' in reality it referred to – the referent. In the postmodern world, signs and referents no longer have any clear or logical connection as sign systems become recodified and detached from the modernist logic that previously connected them. The shift from the modern to the postmodern world is a shift from societies structured around production to societies structured around simulation. A simulation is more than just a copy, and is distinct from feigning or dissimulation. As Baudrillard notes, 'feigning or dissimulation leaves the reality principle intact: the difference is always clear, it is only masked; whereas simulation threatens the difference between "true" and "false", between "real" and "imaginary"'.

Thus in the postmodern world the modernist notion of an original and a copy disintegrates: the original is displaced and then replaced by the copy, in the end becoming obsolete as the copy comes to represent and ultimately constitute the 'real'. Consider, for example, as Durham and Kellner (2006) have, the efforts of media consumers all over the world to emulate the impossible perfection exhibited by the artificial, digitally enhanced, highly simulated images of models on the front pages of glossy magazines. The simulation of the model comes to represent the real for thousands of people who invest considerable time, energy and money – undertaking cosmetic surgery or rigorous dietary regimes, spending hour upon hour in the gym – to recreate and 'make real' that which never really existed in the first place. Thus the image becomes the reality – a mediatised 'hyperreality' – in which simulations, signs and codes come to structure and constitute everyday life. This, for Baudrillard, is the 'simulacrum' – a copy without an original, a representation 'more real than real'.

Disneyland provides the paradigmatic illustration of Baudrillard's simulacrum. This world-famous holiday destination and theme park constitutes an idealised imaginary – a Utopian America and a perfect world. It has its own ideals, role models, structures of living and codes of practice. It is also, for Baudrillard, a replica of a fantasy which serves to distract attention from the Disney-like qualities of the rest of the United States. Disneyland, Baudrillard argues, exists to make us believe that the rest of America is real, when in fact the rest of America is no longer real, but a simulation. It is an artificial universe, an 'immense script', resembling Hollywood movies and television advertisements. Disneyland, he declares, is the 'real' country: the rest of America *is* Disneyland.

If we were able to take as the finest allegory of simulation the Borges tale where the cartographers of the Empire draw up a map so detailed that it ends up exactly covering the territory (but where, with the decline of the Empire this map becomes frayed and finally ruined, a few shreds still discernible in the deserts – the metaphysical beauty of this ruined abstraction, bearing witness to an imperial pride and rotting like a carcass, returning to the substance of the soil, rather as an aging double ends up being confused with the real thing), this fable would then have come full circle for us, and now has nothing but the discrete charm of second-order simulacra.[1]

Abstraction today is no longer that of the map, the double, the mirror or the concept. Simulation is no longer that of a territory, a referential being or a substance. It is the generation by models of a real without origin or reality: a hyperreal. The territory no longer precedes the map, nor survives it. Henceforth, it is the map that precedes the territory – *precession of simulacra* – it is the map that engenders the territory and if we were to revive the fable today, it would be the territory whose shreds are slowly rotting across the map. It is the real, and not the map, whose vestiges subsist here and there, in the deserts which are no longer those of the Empire, but our own. *The desert of the real itself.*

In fact, even inverted, the fable is useless. Perhaps only the allegory of the Empire remains. For it is with the same imperialism that present-day simulators try to make the real, all the real, coincide with their simulation models. But it is no longer a question of either maps or territory. Something has disappeared: the sovereign difference between them that was the abstraction's charm. For it is the difference which forms the poetry of the map and the charm of the territory, the magic of the concept and the charm of the real. The representational imaginary, which both culminates in and is engulfed by the cartographer's made project of an ideal coextensivity between the map and the territory, disappears with simulation, whose operation is nuclear and genetic, and no longer specular and discursive. With it goes all of metaphysics. No more mirror of being and appearances, of the real and its concept; no more imaginary coextensivity: rather, genetic miniaturization is the dimension of simulation. The real is produced from miniaturized units, from matrices, memory banks and command models – and with these it can be reproduced an indefinite number of times. It no longer has to be rational, since it is no longer measured against some ideal or negative instance. It is nothing more than operational. In fact, since it is no longer enveloped by an imaginary, it is no longer real at all. It is a hyperreal: the product of an irradiating synthesis of combinatory models in a hyperspace without atmosphere.

In this passage to a space whose curvature is no longer that of the real, nor of truth, the age of simulation thus begins with a liquidation of all referentials – worse: by their artificial resurrection in systems of signs, which are a more ductile material than meaning, in that they lend themselves to all systems of equivalence, all binary oppositions and all combinatory algebra. It is no longer a question of imitation, nor of reduplication, nor even of parody. It is rather a question of substituting signs of the real for the real itself; that is, an operation to deter every real process by its operational double, a metastable, programmatic, perfect descriptive machine which provides all the signs of the real and short-circuits all its vicissitudes. Never again will the real have to be produced: this is the vital function of the model in a system of death, or rather of anticipated resurrection which no longer leaves any chance even in the event of death. A hyperreal henceforth sheltered from the imaginary, and from any distinction between the real and the imaginary, leaving room only for the orbital recurrence of models and the simulated generation of difference.

The divine irreference of images

To dissimulate is to feign not to have what one has. To simulate is to feign to have what one hasn't. One implies a presence, the other an absence. But the matter is more complicated, since to simulate is not simply to feign: "Someone who feigns an illness can simply go to bed and pretend he is ill. Someone who simulates an illness produces in himself some of the symptoms" (Littre). Thus, feigning or dissimulating leaves the reality principle intact: the difference is always clear, it is only masked; whereas simulation threatens the difference between "true" and "false", between "real" and "imaginary". Since the simulator produces "true" symptoms, is he or she ill or not? The simulator cannot be treated objectively either as ill, or as not ill. Psychology and medicine stop at this point, before a thereafter undiscoverable truth of the illness. For if any symptom can be "produced," and can no longer be accepted as a fact of nature, then every illness may be considered as simulatable and simulated, and medicine loses its meaning since it only knows how to treat "true" illnesses by their objective causes. Psychosomatics evolves in a dubious way on the edge of the illness principle. As for psychoanalysis, it transfers the symptom from the organic to the unconscious order: once again, the latter is held to be real, more real than the former; but why should simulation stop at the portals of the unconscious? Why couldn't the "work" of the unconscious be "produced" in the same way as any other symptom in classical medicine? Dreams already are.

The alienist, of course, claims that "for each form of the mental alienation there is a particular order in the succession of symptoms, of which the simulator is unaware and in the absence of which the alienist is unlikely to be deceived." This (which dates from 1865) in order to save at all cost the truth principle, and to escape the specter raised by simulation: namely that truth, reference and objective cause have ceased to exist. What can medicine do with something which floats on either side of illness, on either side of health, or with the reduplication of illness in a discourse that is no longer true or false? What can psychoanalysis do with the reduplication of the discourse of the unconscious in a discourse of simulation that can never be unmasked, since it isn't false either?[2]

What can the army do with simulators? Traditionally, following a direct principle of identification, it unmasks and punishes them. Today, it can reform an excellent simulator as though he were equivalent to a "real" homosexual, heart-case or lunatic. Even military psychology retreats from the Cartesian clarities and hesitates to draw the distinction between true and false, between the "produced" symptom and the authentic symptom. "If he acts crazy so well, then he must be mad." Nor is it mistaken: in the sense that all lunatics are simulators, and this lack of distinction is the worst form of subversion. Against it, classical reason armed itself with all its categories. But it is this today which again outflanks them, submerging the truth principle.

Outside of medicine and the army, favored terrains of simulation, the affair goes back to religion and the simulacrum of divinity: "I forbade any simulacrum in the temples because the divinity that breathes life into nature cannot be represented." Indeed it can. But what becomes of the divinity when it reveals itself in icons, when it is multiplied in simulacra? Does it remain the supreme authority, simply incarnated in images as a visible theology? Or is it volatilized into simulacra which alone deploy their pomp and power of fascination – the visible machinery of icons being substituted for the pure and intelligible Idea of God? This is precisely what was feared by the iconoclasts, whose millennial quarrel is still with us today.[3] Their rage to destroy images rose precisely because they sensed this omnipotence of simulacra, this facility they have of erasing God from the consciousnesses of people, and the overwhelming, destructive truth which they suggest: that ultimately there has never been any God; that only simulacra exist; indeed that God himself has only ever been his own simulacrum. Had they been able to believe that images only occulted or masked the Platonic idea of God, there would have been no reason to destroy them. One can live with the idea of a distorted truth. But their metaphysical despair came from the idea that the images concealed nothing at all, and that in fact they were not images, such as the original model would have made them, but actually perfect simulacra forever radiant with their own fascination. But this death of the divine referential has to be exorcised at all cost.

It can be seen that the iconoclasts, who are often accused of despising and denying images, were in fact the ones who accorded them their actual worth, unlike the iconolaters, who saw in them only reflections and were content to venerate God at one remove. But the converse can also be said, namely that the iconolaters possessed the most modern and adventurous minds, since, underneath the idea of the apparition of God in the mirror of images, they already enacted his death and his disappearance in the epiphany of his representations (which they perhaps knew no longer represented anything, and that they were purely a game, but that this was precisely the greatest game – knowing also that it is dangerous to unmask images, since they dissimulate the fact that there is nothing behind them).

This was the approach of the Jesuits, who based their politics on the virtual disappearance of God and on the worldly and spectacular manipulation of consciences – the evanescence of God in the epiphany of power – the end of transcendence, which no longer serves as alibi for a strategy completely free of influences and signs. Behind the baroque of images hides the grey eminence of politics.

Thus perhaps at stake has always been the murderous capacity of the images: murderers of the real; murderers of their own model as the Byzantine icon could murder the divine identity. To this murderous capacity is opposed the dialectical capacity of representations as a visible and intelligible mediation of the real. All of

Western faith and good faith was engaged in this wager on representation: that a sign could refer to the depth of meaning, that a sign could *exchange* for meaning and that something could guarantee this exchange – God, of course. But what if God himself can be simulated, that is to say, reduced to the signs which attest his existence? Then the whole system becomes weightless; it is no longer anything but a gigantic simulacrum: not unreal, but a simulacrum, never again exchanging for what is real, but exchanging in itself, in an uninterrupted circuit without reference or circumference.

So it is with simulation, insofar as it is opposed to representation. Representation starts from the principle that the sign and the real are equivalent (even if this equivalence is Utopian, it is a fundamental axiom). Conversely, simulation starts from the Utopia of this principle of equivalence, *from the radical negation of the sign as value*, from the sign as reversion and death sentence of every reference. Whereas representation tries to absorb simulation by interpreting it as false representation, simulation envelops the whole edifice of representation as itself a simulacrum.

These would be the successive phases of the image:

1   It is the reflection of a basic reality.
2   It masks and perverts a basic reality.
3   It masks the *absence* of a basic reality.
4   It bears no relation to any reality whatever: it is its own pure simulacrum.

In the first case, the image is a *good* appearance: the representation is of the order of sacrament. In the second, it is an *evil* appearance: of the order of malefice. In the third, it *plays at being* an appearance: it is of the order of sorcery. In the fourth, it is no longer in the order of appearance at all, but of simulation.

The transition from signs which dissimulate something to signs which dissimulate that there is nothing, marks the decisive turning point. The first implies a theology of truth and secrecy (to which the notion of ideology still belongs). The second inaugurates an age of simulacra and simulation, in which there is no longer any God to recognize his own, nor any last judgement to separate truth from false, the real from its artificial resurrection, since everything is already dead and risen in advance.

When the real is no longer what it used to be, nostalgia assumes its full meaning. There is a proliferation of myths of origin and signs of reality; of second-hand truth, objectivity and authenticity. There is an escalation of the true, of the lived experience; a resurrection of the figurative where the object and substance have disappeared. And there is a panic-stricken production of the real and the referential, above and parallel to the panic of material production. This is how simulation appears in the phase that concerns us: a strategy of the real, neo-real and hyperreal, whose universal double is a strategy of deterrence.

Hyperreal and imaginary

Disneyland is a perfect model of all the entangled orders of simulation. To begin with it is a play of illusions and phantasms: pirates, the frontier, future world, etc. This imaginary world is supposed to be what makes the operation successful. But, what draws the crowds is undoubtedly much more the social microcosm, the miniaturized and *religious* revelling in real America, in its delights and drawbacks. You park outside, queue up inside, and are totally abandoned at the exit. In this imaginary world the only phantasmagoria is in the inherent warmth and affection of the crowd, and in that sufficiently excessive number of gadgets used there to specifically maintain the multitudinous effect. The contrast with the absolute solitude of the parking lot – a veritable concentration camp – is total. Or rather: inside, a whole range of gadgets magnetize the crowd into direct flows; outside, solitude is directed onto a single gadget: the automobile. By an extraordinary coincidence (one that undoubtedly belongs to the peculiar enchantment of this universe), this deep-frozen infantile world happens to have been conceived and realized by a man who is himself now cryogenized; Walt Disney, who awaits his resurrection at minus 180 degrees centigrade.

The objective profile of the United States, then, may be traced throughout Disneyland, even down to the morphology of individuals and the crowd. All its values are exalted here, in miniature and comic-strip form. Embalmed and pacified. Whence the possibility of an ideological analysis of Disneyland (L. Marin does it well in *Utopies, jeux d'espaces*): digest of the American way of life, panegyric to American values, idealized transposition of a contradictory reality. To be sure. But this conceals something else, and that "ideological" blanket exactly serves to cover over a *third-order simulation*: Disneyland is there to conceal the fact that it is the "real" country, all of "real" America, which *is* Disneyland (just as prisons are there to conceal the fact that it is the social in its entirety, in its banal omnipresence, which is carceral). Disneyland is presented as imaginary in order to make us believe that the rest is real, when in fact all of Los Angeles and the America surrounding it are no longer real, but of the order of the hyperreal and of simulation. It is no longer a question of a false representation of reality (ideology), but of concealing the fact that the real is no longer real, and thus of saving the reality principle.

The Disneyland imaginary is neither true nor false: it is a deterrence machine set up in order to rejuvenate in reverse the fiction of the real. Whence the debility, the infantile degeneration of this imaginary. It is meant to be an infantile world, in order to make us believe that the adults are elsewhere, in the "real" world, and to conceal the fact that real childishness is everywhere, particularly among those adults who go there to act the child in order to foster illusions of their real childishness.

Moreover, Disneyland is not the only one. Enchanted Village, Magic Mountain, Marine World: Los Angeles is encircled by these "imaginary stations" which feed reality, reality-energy, to a town whose mystery is precisely that it is nothing more than a network of endless, unreal circulation: a town of fabulous proportions, but without space or dimensions. As much as electrical and nuclear power stations, as much as film studios, this town, which is nothing more than an immense script and a perpetual motion picture, needs this old imaginary made up of childhood signals and faked phantasms for its sympathetic nervous system.

Political incantation

Watergate. Same scenario as Disneyland (an imaginary effect concealing that reality no more exists outside than inside the bounds of the artificial perimeter): though here it is a scandal-effect concealing that there is no difference between the facts and their denunciation (identical methods are employed by the CIA and the *Washington Post* journalists). Same operation, though this time tending towards scandal as a means to regenerate a moral and political principle, towards the imaginary as a means to regenerate a reality principle in distress.

The denunciation of scandal always pays homage to the law. And Watergate above all succeeded in imposing the idea that Watergate *was* a scandal — in this sense it was an extraordinary operation of intoxication: the reinjection of a large dose of political morality on a global scale. It could be said along with Bourdieu that: "The specific character of every relation of force is to dissimulate itself as such, and to acquire all its force only because it is so dissimulated"; understood as follows: capital, which is immoral and unscrupulous, can only function behind a moral superstructure, and whoever regenerates this public morality (by indignation, denunciation, etc.) spontaneously furthers the order of capital, as did the *Washington Post* journalists.

But this is still only the formula of ideology, and when Bourdieu enunciates it, he takes "relation of force" to mean the *truth* of capitalist domination, and he *denounces* this relation of force as itself a *scandal*: he therefore occupies the same deterministic and moralistic position as the *Washington Post* journalists. He does the same job of purging and reviving moral order, an order of truth wherein the genuine symbolic violence of the social order is engendered, well beyond all relations of force, which are only elements of its indifferent and shifting configuration in the moral and political consciousnesses of people.

All that capital asks of us is to receive it as rational or to combat it in the name of rationality, to receive it as moral or to combat it in the name of morality. For they are *identical*, meaning *they can be read another way*: before, the task was to dissimulate scandal; today, the task is to conceal the fact that there is none.

Watergate is not a scandal: this is what must be said at all cost, for this is what everyone is concerned to conceal, this dissimulation masking a strengthening of morality, a moral panic as we approach the primal (mise-en-)scene of capital: its instantaneous cruelty; its incomprehensible ferocity; its fundamental immorality — these are what are scandalous, unaccountable for in that system of moral and economic equivalence which remains the axiom of leftist thought, from Enlightenment theory to communism. Capital doesn't give a damn about the idea of the contract which is imputed to it: it is a monstrous unprincipled undertaking, nothing more. Rather, it is "enlightened" thought which seeks to control capital by imposing rules on it. And all that recrimination which replaced revolutionary thought today comes down to reproaching capital for not following the rules of the game. "Power is unjust; its justice is a class justice; capital exploits us; etc." — as if capital were linked by a contract to the society it rules. It is the left which holds out the mirror of equivalence, hoping that capital will fall for this phantasmagoria of the social contract and fulfill its obligation towards the whole of society (at the same time, no need for revolution: it is enough that capital accept the rational formula of exchange).

Capital in fact has never been linked by a contract to the society it dominates. It is a sorcery of the social relation, it is a *challenge to society* and should be responded to as such. It is not a scandal to be denounced according to moral and economic rationality, but a challenge to take up according to symbolic law.

Moebius: spiralling negativity

Hence Watergate was only a trap set by the system to catch its adversaries – a simulation of scandal to regenerative ends. This is embodied by the character called "Deep Throat," who was said to be a Republican grey eminence manipulating the leftist journalists in order to get rid of Nixon – and why not? All hypotheses are possible, although this one is superfluous: the work of the Right is done very well, and spontaneously, by the Left on its own. Besides, it would be naive to see an embittered good conscience at work here. For the Right itself also spontaneously does the work of the Left. All the hypotheses of manipulation are reversible in an endless whirligig. For manipulation is a floating causality where positivity and negativity engender and overlap with one another; where there is no longer any active or passive. It is by putting an *arbitrary* stop to this revolving causality that a principle of political reality can be saved. It is by the *simulation* of a conventional, restricted perspective field, where the premises and consequences of any act or event are calculable, that a political credibility can be maintained (including, of course, "objective" analysis, struggle, etc.). But if the entire cycle of any act or event is envisaged in a system where linear continuity and dialectical polarity no longer exist, in a field *unhinged by simulation*, then all determination evaporates, every act terminates at the end of the cycle having benefited everyone and been scattered in all directions.

Is any given bombing in Italy the work of leftist extremists; or of extreme right-wing provocation; or staged by centrists to bring every terrorist extreme into disrepute and to shore up its own failing power; or again, is it a police-inspired scenario in order to appeal to calls for public security? All this is equally true, and the search for proof – indeed the objectivity of the fact – does not check this vertigo of interpretation. We are in a logic of simulation which has nothing to do with a logic of facts and an order of reasons. Simulation is characterized by a *precession of the model*, of all models around the merest fact – the models come first, and their orbital (like the bomb) circulation constitutes the genuine magnetic field of events. Facts no longer have any trajectory of their own, they arise at the intersection of models; a single fact may even be engendered by all the models at once. This anticipation, this precession, this short-circuit, this confusion of the fact with its model (no more divergence of meaning, no more dialectical polarity, no more negative electricity or implosion of poles) is what each time allows for all the possible interpretations, even the most contradictory – all are true, in the sense that their truth is exchangeable, in the image of the models from which they proceed, in a generalized cycle.

The communists attack the socialist party as though they wanted to shatter the union of the Left. They sanction the idea that their reticence stems from a more radical political exigency. In fact, it is because they don't want power. But do they not want it at this conjuncture because it is unfavorable for the Left in general, or because it is unfavorable for them within the union of the Left – or do they not want it by definition? When Berlinguer declares, "We mustn't be frightened of seeing the communists seize power in Italy," this means simultaneously:

1   That there is nothing to fear, since the communists, if they come to power, will change nothing in its fundamental capitalist mechanism.

2   That there isn't any risk of their ever coming to power (for the reason that they don't want to); and even if they do take it up, they will only ever wield it by proxy.

3   That in fact power, genuine power, no longer exists, and hence there is no risk of anybody seizing it or taking it over.

4   But more: I, Berlinguer, am not frightened of seeing the communists seize power in Italy – which might appear evident, but not so evident, since:

5   It can also mean the contrary (no need for psychoanalysis here): *I am frightened* of seeing the communists seize power (and with good reason, even for a communist).

All the above is simultaneously true. This is the secret of a discourse that is no longer only ambiguous, as political discourses can be, but that conveys the impossibility of a determinate position of power, the impossibility of a determinate position of discourse. And this logic belongs to neither party. It traverses all discourses without their wanting it.

Who will unravel this imbroglio? The Gordian knot can at least be cut. As for the Moebius strip, if it is split in two, it results in an additional spiral without there being any possibility of resolving its surfaces (here the reversible continuity of hypotheses). Hades of simulation, which is no longer one of torture, but of the subtle, maleficent, elusive twisting of meaning[4] – where even those condemned at Burgos are still a gift from Franco to Western democracy, which finds in them the occasion to regenerate its own flagging humanism, and whose indignant protestation consolidates in return Franco's regime by uniting the Spanish masses against foreign intervention. Where is the truth in all that, when such collusions admirably knit together without their authors even knowing it?

The conjunction of the system and its extreme alternative like two ends of a curved mirror, the "vicious" curvature of a political space henceforth magnetized, circularized, reversibilized from right to left, a torsion that is like the evil demon of commutation, the whole system, the infinity of capital folded back over its own surface: transfinite? And isn't it the same with desire and libidinal space? The conjunction of desire and value, of desire and capital. The conjunction of desire and the law; the ultimate joy and metamorphosis of the law (which is why it is so well received at the moment): only capital takes pleasure, Lyotard said, before coming to think that *we* take pleasure in capital. Overwhelming versatility of desire in Deleuze: an enigmatic reversal which brings this desire that is "revolutionary by itself, and as if involuntarily, in wanting what it wants," to want its own repression and to invest paranoid and fascist systems? A malign torsion which reduces this revolution of desire to the same fundamental ambiguity as the other, historical revolution.

All the referentials intermingle their discourses in a circular, Moebian compulsion. Not so long ago sex and work were savagely opposed terms: today both are dissolved into the same type of demand. Formerly the discourse on history took its force from opposing itself to the one on nature, the discourse on desire to the one on power: today they exchange their signifiers and their scenarios.

It would take too long to run through the whole range of operational negativity, of all those scenarios of deterrence which, like Watergate, try to revive a moribund principle by simulated scandal, phantasm, murder – a sort of hormonal treatment by negativity and crisis. It is always a question of proving the real by the imaginary; proving truth by scandal; proving the law by transgression; proving work by the strike; proving the system by crisis and capital by revolution; and for that matter proving ethnology by the dispossession of its object (the Tasaday). Without counting: proving theater by anti-theater; proving art by anti-art; proving pedagogy by anti-pedagogy; proving psychiatry by anti-psychiatry, etc., etc.

Everything is metamorphosed into its inverse in order to be perpetuated in its purged form. Every form of power, every situation speaks of itself by denial, in order to attempt to escape, by simulation of death, its real agony. Power can stage its own murder to rediscover a glimmer of existence and legitimacy. Thus with the American presidents: the Kennedys are murdered because they still have a political dimension. Others – Johnson, Nixon, Ford – only had a right to puppet attempts, to simulated murders. But they nevertheless needed that aura of an artificial menace to conceal that they were nothing other than mannequins of power. In olden days the king (also the god) had to die – that was his strength. Today he does his miserable utmost to pretend to die, so as to preserve the *blessing* of power. But even this is gone.

To seek new blood in its own death, to renew the cycle by the mirror of crisis, negativity and anti-power: this is the only alibi of every power, of every institution attempting to break the vicious circle of its irresponsibility and its fundamental nonexistence, of its déjà-vu and its déjà-mort.

Strategy of the real

Of the same order as the impossibility of rediscovering an absolute level of the real, is the impossibility of staging an illusion. Illusion is no longer possible, because the real is no longer possible. It is the whole *political* problem of the parody, of hyper-simulation or offensive simulation, which is posed here.

For example: it would be interesting to see whether the repressive apparatus would not react more violently to a simulated hold up than to a real one? For a real hold up only upsets the order of things, the right of property, whereas a simulated hold up interferes with the very principle of reality. Transgression and violence are less serious, for they only contest the *distribution* of the real. Simulation is infinitely more dangerous since it always suggests, over and above its object, that *law and order themselves might really be nothing more than a simulation*.

But the difficulty is in proportion to the peril. How to feign a violation and put it to the test? Go and simulate a theft in a large department store: how do you convince the security guards that it is a simulated theft? There is no "objective" difference: the same gestures and the same signs exist as for a real theft; in fact the signs incline neither to one side nor the other. As far as the established order is concerned, they are always of the order of the real.

Go and organize a fake hold up. Be sure to check that your weapons are harmless, and take the most trustworthy hostage, so that no life is in danger (otherwise you risk committing an offence). Demand ransom, and arrange it so that the operation creates the greatest commotion possible. In brief, stay close to the "truth", so as to test the reaction of the apparatus to a perfect simulation. But you won't succeed: the web of artificial signs will be inextricably mixed up with real elements (a police officer will really shoot on sight; a bank customer will faint and die of a heart attack; they will really turn the phoney ransom over to you). In brief, you will unwittingly find yourself immediately in the real, one of whose functions is precisely to devour every attempt at simulation, to reduce everything to some reality: that's exactly how the established order is, well before institutions and justice come into play.

In this impossibility of isolating the process of simulation must be seen the whole thrust of an order that can only see and understand in terms of some reality, because it can function nowhere else. The simulation of an offence, if it is patent, will either be punished more lightly (because it has no "consequences") or be punished as an offence to public office (for example, if one triggered off a police operation "for nothing") – but *never as simulation*, since it is precisely as such that no equivalence with the real is possible, and hence no repression either. The challenge of simulation is irreceivable by power. How can you punish the simulation of virtue? Yet as such it is as serious as the simulation of crime. Parody makes obedience and transgression equivalent, and that is the most serious crime, since it *cancels out the difference upon which the law is based*. The established order can do nothing against it, for the law is a second-order simulacrum whereas simulation is a third-order simulacrum, beyond true and false, beyond equivalences, beyond the rational distinction upon which function all power; and the entire social stratum. Hence, *failing the real*, it is here that we must aim at order.

This is why order always opts for the real. In a state of uncertainty, it always prefers this assumption (thus in the army they would rather take the simulator as a true madman). But this becomes more and more difficult, for it is practically impossible to isolate the process of simulation; through the force of inertia of the real which surrounds us, the inverse is also true (and this very reversibility forms part of the apparatus of simulation and of power's impotency): namely, *it is now impossible to isolate the process of the real*, or to prove the real.

Thus all hold ups, hijacks and the like are now as it were simulation hold ups, in the sense that they are inscribed in advance in the decoding and orchestration rituals of the media, anticipated in their mode of presentation and possible consequences. In brief, where they function as a set of signs dedicated exclusively to their recurrence as signs, and no longer to their "real" goal at all. But this does not make them inoffensive. On the contrary, it is as hyperreal events, no longer having any particular contents or aims, but indefinitely refracted by each other (for that matter like so-called historical events: strikes, demonstrations, crises, etc.[5]), that they are precisely unverifiable by an order which can only exert itself on the real and the rational, on ends and means: a referential order which can only dominate referentials, a determinate power which can only dominate a determined world, but which can do nothing about that indefinite recurrence of simulation, about that weightless nebula no longer obeying the law of gravitation of the real – power itself eventually breaking apart in this space and becoming a simulation of power (disconnected from its aims and objectives, and dedicated to *power effects* and mass simulation).

The only weapon of power, its only strategy against this defection, is to reinject realness and referentiality everywhere, in order to convince us of the reality of the social, of the gravity of the economy and the finalities of production. For that purpose it prefers the discourse of crisis, but also – why not? – the discourse of desire. "Take your desires for reality!" can be understood as the ultimate slogan of power, for in a nonreferential world even the confusion of the reality principle with the desire principle is less dangerous than contagious hyperreality. One remains among principles, and there power is always right.

Hyperreality and simulation are deterrents of every principle and of every objective; they turn against power this deterrence which is so well utilized for a long time itself. For, finally, it was capital which was the first to feed throughout its history on the destruction of every referential, of every human goal, which shattered every ideal distinction between true and false, good and evil, in order to establish a radical law of equivalence and exchange, the iron law of its power. It was the first to practice deterrence, abstraction, disconnection, deterritorialization, etc.; and if it was capital which fostered reality, the reality principle, it was also the first to liquidate it in the extermination of every use value, of every real equivalence, of production and wealth, in the very sensation we have of the unreality of the stakes and the omnipotence of manipulation. Now, it is this very logic which is today hardened even more *against* it. And when it wants to fight this catastrophic spiral by secreting one last glimmer of reality, on which to found one last glimmer of power, it only multiplies the *signs* and accelerates the play of simulation.

As long as it was historically threatened by the real, power risked deterrence and simulation, disintegrating every contradiction by means of the production of equivalent signs. When it is threatened today by simulation (the threat of vanishing in the play of signs), power risks the real, risks crisis, it gambles on remanufacturing artificial, social, economic, political stakes. This is a question of life or death for it. But it is too late.

Whence the characteristic hysteria of our time: the hysteria of production and reproduction of the real. The other production, that of goods and commodities, that of *la belle epoque* of political economy, no longer makes any sense of its own, and has not for some time. What society seeks through production, and overproduction, is the restoration of the real which escapes it. That is why *contemporary "material" production is itself hyperreal*. It retains all the features, the whole discourse of traditional production, but it is nothing more than its scaled-down refraction (thus the hyperrealists fasten in a striking resemblance a real from which has fled all meaning and charm, all the profundity and energy of representation). Thus the hyperrealism of simulation is expressed everywhere by the real's striking resemblance to itself.

Power, too, for some time now produces nothing but signs of its resemblance. And at the same time, another figure of power comes into play: that of a collective demand for *signs* of power – a holy union which forms around the disappearance of power. Everybody belongs to it more or less in fear of the collapse of the political. And in the end the game of power comes down to nothing more than the critical obsession with power: an obsession with its death; an obsession with its survival which becomes greater the more it disappears. When it has totally disappeared, logically we will be under the total spell of power – a haunting memory already foreshadowed everywhere, manifesting at one and the same time the satisfaction of having got rid of it (nobody wants it any more, everybody unloads it on others) and grieving its loss. Melancholy for societies without power: this has already given rise to fascism, that overdose of a powerful referential in a society which cannot terminate its mourning.

But we are still in the same boat: none of our societies know how to manage their mourning for the real, for power, for the *social itself*, which is implicated in this same breakdown. And it is by an artificial revitalization of all this that we try to escape it. *Undoubtedly this will even end up in socialism*. By an unforeseen twist of events and an irony which no longer belongs to history, it is through the death of the social that socialism will emerge – as it is through the death of God that religions emerge. A twisted coming, a perverse event, an unintelligible reversion to the logic of reason. As is the fact that power is no longer present except to conceal that there is none. A simulation which can go on indefinitely, since – unlike "true" power which is, or was, a structure, a strategy, a relation of force, a stake – this is nothing but the object of a social *demand*, and hence subject to the law of supply and demand, rather than to violence and death. Completely expunged from the *political* dimension, it is dependent, like any other commodity, on production and mass consumption. Its spark has disappeared; only the fiction of a political universe is saved.

Likewise with work. The spark of production, the violence of its stake no longer exists. Everybody still produces, and more and more, but work has subtly become something else: a need (as Marx ideally envisaged it, but not at all in the same sense), the object of a social "demand," like leisure, to which it is equivalent in the general run of life's options. A demand exactly proportional to the loss of stake in the work process.[6] The same change in fortune as for power: the *scenario* of work is there to conceal the fact that the work-real, the production-real, has disappeared. And for that matter so has the strike-real too, which is no longer a stoppage of work, but its alternative pole in the ritual scansion of the social calendar. It is as if everyone has "occupied" their work place or work post, after declaring the strike, and resumed production, as is the custom in a "self-managed" job, in exactly the same terms as before, by declaring themselves (and virtually being) in a state of permanent strike.

This isn't a science-fiction dream: everywhere it is a question of a doubling of the work process. And of a double or locum for the strike process – strikes which are incorporated like obsolescence in objects, like crises in production. Then there are no longer any strikes or work, but both simultaneously, that is to say something else entirely: a wizardry of work, a trompe l'oeil, a scenodrama (not to say melodrama) of production, collective dramaturgy upon the empty stage of the social.

It is no longer a question of the *ideology* of work – of the traditional ethic that obscures the "real" labour process and the "objective" process of exploitation – but of the scenario of work. Likewise, it is no longer a question of the ideology of power, but of the *scenario* of power. Ideology only corresponds to a betrayal of reality by signs; simulation corresponds to a short-circuit of reality and to its reduplication by signs. It is always the aim of ideological analysis to restore the objective process; it is always a false problem to want to restore the truth beneath the simulacrum.

This is ultimately why power is so in accord with ideological discourses and discourses on ideology, for these are all discourses of *truth* – always good, even and especially if they are revolutionary, to counter the mortal blows of simulation.

Notes

1. Counterfeit and reproduction imply always an anguish, a disquieting foreignness: the uneasiness before the photograph, considered like a witch's trick – and more

generally before any technical apparatus, which is always an apparatus of reproduction, is related by Benjamin to the uneasiness before the mirror-image. There is already sorcery at work in the mirror. But how much more so when this image can be detached from the mirror and be transported, stocked, reproduced at will (cf. *The Student of Prague*, where the devil detaches the image of the student from the mirror and harasses him to death by the intermediary of this image). All reproduction implies therefore a kind of black magic, from the fact of being seduced by one's own image in the water, like Narcissus, to being haunted by the double and, who knows, to the mortal turning back of this vast technical apparatus secreted today by man as his own image (the narcissistic mirage of technique, McLuhan) and that returns to him, cancelled and distorted – endless reproduction of himself and his power to the limits of the world. Reproduction is diabolical in its very essence; it makes something fundamental vacillate. This has hardly changed for us: simulation (that we describe here as the operation of the code) is still and always the place of a gigantic enterprise of manipulation, of control and of death, just like the imitative object (primitive statuette, image of photo) always had as objective an operation of black image.

2. There is furthermore in Monod's book a flagrant contradiction, which reflects the ambiguity of all current science. His discourse concerns the code, that is the third-order simulacra, but it does so still according to "scientific" schemes of the second-order – objectiveness, "scientific" ethic of knowledge, science's principle of truth and transcendence. All things incompatible with the indeterminable models of the third-order.

3. "It's the feeble 'definition' of TV which condemns its spectator to rearranging the few points retained into a kind of *abstract work*. He participates suddenly in the creation of a reality that was only just presented to him in dots: the television watcher is in the position of an individual who is asked to project his own fantasies on inkblots that are not supposed to represent anything." TV as perpetual Rorshach test. And furthermore: "The TV image requires each instant that we 'close' the spaces in the mesh by a convulsive sensuous participation that is profoundly kinetic and tactile."

4. "The Medium is the Message" is the very slogan of the political economy of the sign, when it enters into the third-order simulation – the distinction between the medium and the message characterizes instead signification of the second-order.

5. The entire current "psychological" situation is characterized by this short-circuit.

Doesn't emancipation of children and teenagers, once the initial phase of revolt is passed and once there has been established the *principle* of the *right* to emancipation, seem like the *real* emancipation of parents? And the young (students, high-schoolers, adolescents) seem to sense it in their always more insistent demand (though still as paradoxical) for the presence and advice of parents or of teachers. Alone at last, free and responsible, it seemed to them suddenly that other people possibly have absconded with their true liberty. Therefore, there is no question of "leaving them be." They're going to hassle them, not with any emotional or material spontaneous demand, but with an exigency that has been premeditated and corrected by an implicit oedipal knowledge. Hyperdependence (much greater than before) distored by irony and refusal, *parody of libidinous original mechanisms*. Demand without content, without referent, unjustified, but for all that all the more severe – naked demand with no possible answer. The contents of knowledge (teaching) or of affective relations, the pedagogical or familial referent having been eliminated in the act of emancipation, there remains only a demand linked to the empty form of the institution – perverse demand, and for that reason all the more obstinate. "Transferable" desire (that is to say non-referential, un-referential), desire that has been fed by lack, by the place left vacant, "liberated," desire captured in its own vertiginous image, desire of desire, as pure form, hyperreal. Deprived of symbolic substance, it doubles back upon itself, draws its energy from its own reflection and its disappointment with itself. This is literally today the "demand," and it is obvious that unlike the "classical" objective or transferable relations this one here is insoluble and interminable.

Simulated Oedipus.

François Richard: "Students asked to be seduced either bodily or verbally. But also they are aware of this and they play the game, ironically. 'Give us your knowledge, your presence, you have the word, speak, you are there for that.' Contestation certainly, but not only: the more authority is contested, vilified, the greater the need for authority as such. They play at Oedipus also, to deny it all the more vehemently. The 'teach', he's Daddy, they say; it's fun, you play at incest, malaise, the untouchable, at being a tease – in order to de-sexualize finally." Like one under analysis who asks for Oedipus back again, who tells the "oedipal" stories, who has the "analytical" dreams to satisfy the supposed request of the analyst, or to resist him? In the same way the student goes through his oedipal number, his seduction number, gets chummy, close, approaches, dominates – but this isn't desire, it's simulation. Oedipal psychodrama of simulation (neither less real nor less dramatic for all that). Very different from the real libidinal stakes of knowledge and power or even of a real mourning for the absence of same (as could have happened after 1968 in the universities). Now we've reached the phase of desperate reproduction, and where the stakes are nil, the simulacrum is maximal – exacerbated and parodied simulation at one and the same time – as interminable as psychoanalysis and for the same reasons.

The interminable psychoanalysis.

There is a whole chapter to add to the history of transference and countertransference: that of their liquidation by simulation, of the impossible psychoanalysis because it is itself, from now on, that produces and reproduces the unconscious as its institutional substance. Psychoanalysis dies also of the exchange of the *signs* of the unconscious. Just as revolution dies of the exchange of the critical signs of political economy. This short-circuit was well known to Freud in the form of the gift of the analytic dream, or with the "uninformed" patients, in the form of the gift of their analytic knowledge. But this was still interpreted as resistance, as detour, and did not put fundamentally into question either the process of analysis or the principle of transference. It is another thing entirely when the unconscious itself, the discourse of the unconscious becomes unfindable – according to the same scenario of simulative anticipation that we have seen at work on all levels with the machines of the third order. The analysis then can no longer end, it becomes logically and historically interminable, since it stabilizes on a puppet-substance of reproduction, an unconscious programmed on demand – an impossible-to-breakthrough point around which the whole analysis is rearranged. The messages of the unconscious have been short-circuited by the psychoanalysis "medium." This is libidinal hyperrealism. To the famous categories of the real, the symbolic and the imaginary, it is going to be necessary to add the hyperreal, which captures and obstructs the functioning of the three orders.

6.   Athenian democracy, much more advanced than our own, had reached the point where the vote was considered as payment for a service, after all other repressive solutions had been tried and found wanting in order to insure a quorum.

Critical connections

Baudrillard's influence on social theory has been enormous, and his work still consti-tutes a key pillar in the postmodern theorisation of media, identity and social reality. He has also come under considerable criticism, however, for creating a nihilistic 'epis-temological void', and producing work that favours intellectual transgression over the insightful theorising of contemporary social transformation (King, 1998). While some may challenge the view that intellectual transgression is necessarily a bad thing, it can also be suggested that Baudrillard overstates the completeness of the historical break with modernity, viewing the society of simulation as transcending the society of production rather than remaining closely interconnected with it. His dissolution of reality, and along with it the disintegration of identity and meaning, conjures a world in which the unstable, the flexible and the fluid are given too much precedence, and the tangible, the sensory and the emotional become too illusory. Nevertheless, many have been seduced, in part if not completely, by the notions of simulation and the hyperreal. Manuel Castells (Reading 5), drew heavily from Baudrillard in his concep-tualisation of real virtuality. In Reading 40, Katja Franko Aas similarly applies his concepts to an exploration of changing forms of social control and governance in the virtual world.

In addition to his influence within academy, Baudrillard's combative social theory has also infiltrated popular culture. Clearly illustrating the fluidity of the boundaries between academic and popular discourses, as well as the represented and the real, his work provided one major source of inspiration for the hugely successful trilogy of *Matrix* films (*The Matrix* (1999), *The Matrix: Reloaded* (2003) *and The Matrix: Revolutions* (2003)). In this dystopian view of the future, the reality per-ceived by humans is actually a computer simulation generated by sentient machines which are farming humans and using them as energy sources. The films' writers and directors, Larry and Andy Wachowski, cited Baudrillard's *Simulacra and Simulations* as a powerful influence. Not only did they borrow many of his key ideas, they also adopted his term 'the desert of the real' to describe the devastated war torn Chicago landscape Neo encounters when he awakens from the virtual simulation which, until now, had been his 'reality'. However, since it is possible to step outside the Matrix and experience 'real life', whilst in Baudrillard's postmodern media-driven society there is *only* 'hyperreality', the French philosopher reputedly claimed that the films repre-sented a *mis*understanding of his work.

Discussion questions

● Discuss Baudrillard's notion of 'hyperreality' and try to think of some contempo-rary examples that illustrate the blurring of the boundaries between the repre-sented and the real.

- For Baudrillard, Disneyworld is the perfect simulacrum: consider the look, design and purpose of Disneyworld and discuss this proposition.
- Throughout the 1980s, Baudrillard was hailed as the new Marshall McLuhan (Reading 2). Compare and contrast Baudrillard's and McLuhan's contributions to our understanding of media and society.

References

Durham G. and Kellner, D. (2001) *Media and Cultural Studies: Keyworks,* Oxford: Blackwell.

King, A (1998) 'A Critique of Baudrillard's Hyperreality: Towards a Sociology of Postmodernism, in *Philosophy and Social Criticism,* 24, 6: 47–66.

William Gibson

NEUROMANCER (1984)

Introduction and context

SOMETIMES REFERRED to as the Godfather or 'noir prophet' of Cyberpunk, William Gibson is not an academic scholar in the traditional sense. His visionary writing on the techno worlds of the near future, however, in addition to winning a string of literary awards'[1] has for many earned the status of social and cultural theory (see Burrows, 1997; Brown, Reading 39). Gibson's work is underpinned by the idea that technology and the human are no longer dichotomous. People develop intimate relationships with machines, thinking about them in psychological and often emotional terms, partly because they are both an extension of the self and part of the external world (Turkle 2005). As Burrows (1997: 239) notes: 'The boundaries between subjects, their bodies and the outside world are, like everything else, being radically reconfigured ... The division between technology and nature is dissolving as the analytic categories we draw upon to give structure to our world – the biological, the technological, the natural, the artificial, *and* the human – begin to blur.' Prosthetic limbs and medical implants merge machine and organism to produce hybrids, or 'cyborgs', that make the stuff of science fiction a contemporary reality (Haraway, 1991). The rapid development of nanotechnologies and Artificial Intelligence (AI) further promise the physical transformation of the human body, and may be ushering in an era of a 'postbiological humanity'.

---

[1] Gibson's first novel *Neuromancer* (1984) won the Nebula Award, Hugo Award and Philip K. Dick Award for Science Fiction writing.

Beyond the body's physical transformation lies its virtual transcendence . . . and Cyberspace. It was in his debut novel *Neuromancer* that Gibson (1984: 51) first developed the concept of 'Cyberspace':

> Cyberspace. A consensual hallucination experienced daily by billions of legitimate operators, in every nation . . . A graphic representation of data abstracted from the banks of every computer in the human system. Unthinkable complexity. Lines of light ranged in the nonspace of the mind, clusters and constellations of data. Like city lights, receding.

Central to the Gibsonian vision of cyberspace is the possibility of interactive, fully sensorial representation in a virtual world – a new, virtual reality. For Gibson, cyberspace is constituted by a global network of computer information called 'the matrix' (see also Readings 6 and 41). Operators can 'jack-in' to the matrix via 'trodes' (headsets) attached to 'cyberspace decks' (computer terminals). Once inside, it is possible to 'fly' to and explore any part of the three-dimensional datasystem, laid out as a brilliantly coloured cityscape of information blocks. In 'the matrix', it is also possible to interact with other sentient forms, whether previously downloaded personality constructs of humans, or independent and autonomous Artificial Intelligences (AIs).

Case sat in the loft with the dermatrodes strapped across his forehead, watching motes dance in the diluted sunlight that filtered through the grid overhead. A countdown was in progress in one corner of the monitor screen.

Cowboys didn't get into simstim, he thought, because it was basically a meat toy. He knew that the trodes he used and the little plastic tiara dangling from a simstim deck were basically the same, and that the cyberspace matrix was actually a drastic simplification of the human sensorium, at least in terms of presentation, but simstim itself struck him as a gratuitous multiplication of flesh input. The commercial stuff was edited, of course, so that if Tally Isham got a headache in the course of a segment, you didn't feel it.

The screen bleeped a two-second warning.

The new switch was patched into his Sendai with a thin ribbon of fiberoptics.

And one and two and –

Cyberspace slid into existence from the cardinal points. Smooth, he thought, but not smooth enough. Have to work on it . . .

Then he keyed the new switch.

The abrupt jolt into other flesh. Matrix gone, a wave of sound and color . . . She was moving through a crowded street, past stalls vending discount software, prices feltpenned on sheets of plastic, fragments of music from countless speakers. Smells of urine, free monomers, perfume, patties of frying krill. For a few frightened seconds he fought helplessly to control her body. Then he willed himself into passivity, became the passenger behind her eyes.

The glasses didn't seem to cut down the sunlight at all. He wondered if the built-in amps compensated automatically. Blue alphanumerics winked the time, low in her left peripheral field. Showing off, he thought.

Her body language was disorienting, her style foreign. She seemed continually on the verge of colliding with someone, but people melted out of her way, stepped sideways, made room.

'How you doing, Case?' He heard the words and felt her form them. She slid a hand into her jacket, a fingertip circling a nipple under warm silk. The sensation made him catch his breath. She laughed. But the link was one-way. He had no way to reply.

Two blocks later, she was threading the outskirts of Memory Lane. Case kept trying to jerk her eyes toward landmarks he would have used to find his way. He began to find the passivity of the situation irritating.

The transition to cyberspace, when he hit the switch, was instantaneous. He punched himself down a wall of primitive ice belonging to the New York Public Library, automatically counting potential windows. Keying back into her sensorium, into the sinuous flow of muscle, senses sharp and bright.

He found himself wondering about the mind he shared these sensations with. What did he know about her? That she was another professional; that she said her being, like his, was the thing she did to make a living. He knew the way she'd moved against him, earlier, when she woke, their mutual grunt of unity when he'd entered her, and that she liked her coffee black, afterward . . .

Her destination was one of the dubious software rental complexes that lined Memory Lane. There was a stillness, a hush. Booths lined a central hall. The clientele were young, few of them out of their teens. They all seemed to have carbon sockets planted behind the left ear, but she didn't focus on them. The counters that fronted the booths displayed hundreds of slivers of microsoft, angular fragments of colored silicon mounted under oblong transparent bubbles on squares of white cardboard. Molly went to the seventh booth along the south wall. Behind the counter a boy with a shaven head stared vacantly into space, a dozen spikes of microsoft protruding from the socket behind his ear.

'Larry, you in, man?' She positioned herself in front of him. The boy's eyes focused. He sat up in his chair and pried a bright magenta splinter from his socket with a dirty thumbnail.

'Hey, Larry.'

'Molly.' He nodded.

'I have some work for some of your friends, Larry.'

Larry took a flat plastic case from the pocket of his red sportshirt and flicked it open, slotting the microsoft beside a dozen others. His hand hovered, selected a glossy black chip that was slightly longer than the rest, and inserted it smoothly into his head. His eyes narrowed.

'Molly's got a rider,' he said, 'and Larry doesn't like that.'

'Hey,' she said, 'I didn't know you were so . . . sensitive. I'm impressed. Costs a lot, to get that sensitive.'

'I know you, lady?' The blank look returned. 'You looking to buy some softs?'

'I'm looking for the Moderns.'

'You got a rider, Molly. This says.' He tapped the black splinter. 'Somebody else using your eyes.'

'My partner.'

'Tell your partner to go.'

'Got something for the Panther Moderns, Larry.'

'What are you talking about, lady?'

'Case, you take off,' she said, and he hit the switch, instantly back in the matrix. Ghost impressions of the software complex hung for a few seconds in the buzzing calm of cyberspace.

'Panther Moderns,' he said to the Hosaka, removing the trodes. 'Five minute precis.'

'Ready,' the computer said.

It wasn't a name he knew. Something new, something that had come in since he'd been in Chiba. Fads swept the youth of the Sprawl at the speed of light; entire subcultures could rise overnight, thrive for a dozen weeks, and then vanish utterly. 'Go,' he said. The Hosaka had accessed its array of libraries, journals, and news services.

The precis began with a long hold on a color still that Case at first assumed was a collage of some kind, a boy's face snipped from another image and glued to a photograph of a paint-scrawled wall. Dark eyes, epicanthic folds obviously the result of surgery, an angry dusting of acne across pale narrow cheeks. The Hosaka released the freeze; the boy moved, flowing with the sinister grace of a mime pretending to be a jungle predator. His body was nearly invisible, an abstract pattern approximating the scribbled brickwork sliding smoothly across his tight onepiece. Mimetic polycarbon.

Cut to Dr Virginia Rambali, Sociology, NYU, her name, faculty, and school pulsing across the screen in pink alphanumerics.

'Given their penchant for these random acts of surreal violence,' someone said, 'it may be difficult for our viewers to understand why you continue to insist that this phenomenon isn't a form of terrorism.'

Dr Rambali smiled. 'There is always a point at which the terrorist ceases to manipulate the media gestalt. A point at which the violence may well escalate, but beyond which the terrorist has become symptomatic of the media gestalt itself. Terrorism as we ordinarily understand it is inately media-related. The Panther Moderns differ from other terrorists precisely in their degree of self-consciousness, in their awareness of the extent to which media divorce the act of terrorism from the original sociopolitical intent . . .'

'Skip it,' Case said.

Case met his first Modern two days after he'd screened the Hosaka's precis. The Moderns, he'd decided, were a contemporary version of the Big Scientists of his own late teens. There was a kind of ghostly teenage DNA at work in the Sprawl, something that carried the coded precepts of various short-lived subcults and replicated them at odd intervals. The Panther Moderns were a softhead variant on the Scientists. If the technology had been available, the Big Scientists would all have had sockets stuffed with microsofts. It was the style that mattered and the style was the same. The Moderns were mercenaries, practical jokers, nihilistic technofetishists.

The one who showed up at the loft door with a box of diskettes from the Finn was a soft-voiced boy called Angelo. His face was a simple graft grown on collagen and shark-cartilage polysaccharides, smooth and hideous. It was one of the nastiest pieces of elective surgery Case had ever seen. When Angelo smiled, revealing the razor-sharp canines of some large animal, Case was actually relieved. Toothbud transplants. He'd seen that before.

'You can't let the little pricks generation-gap you,' Molly said. Case nodded, absorbed in the patterns of the Sense/Net ice.

This was it. This was what he was, who he was, his being. He forgot to eat. Molly left cartons of rice and foam trays of sushi on the corner of the long table. Sometimes he resented having to leave the deck to use the chemical toilet they'd set up in a corner of the loft. Ice patterns formed and reformed on the screen as he probed for gaps, skirted the most obvious traps, and mapped the route he'd take through Sense/Net's ice. It was good ice. Wonderful ice. Its patterns burned there while he lay with his arm under Molly's shoulders, watching the red dawn through the steel grid of the skylight. Its rainbow pixel maze was the first thing he saw when he woke. He'd go straight to the deck, not bothering to dress, and jack in. He was cutting it. He was working. He lost track of days.

And sometimes, falling asleep, particularly when Molly was off on one of her reconnaissance trips with her rented cadre of Moderns, images of Chiba came flooding back. Faces and Ninsei neon. Once he woke from a confused dream of Linda Lee, unable to recall who she was or what she'd ever meant to him. When he did remember, he jacked in and worked for nine straight hours.

The cutting of Sense/Net's ice took a total of nine days.

'I said a week,' Armitage said, unable to conceal his satisfaction when Case showed him his plan for the run. 'You took your own good time.'

'Balls,' Case said, smiling at the screen. 'That's good work, Armitage.'

'Yes,' Armitage admitted, 'but don't let it go to your head. Compared to what you'll eventually be up against, this is an arcade toy.'

'Love you, Cat Mother,' whispered the Panther Modern's link man. His voice was modulated static in Case's headset. 'Atlanta, Brood. Looks go. Go, got it?' Molly's voice was slightly clearer.

'To hear is to obey.' The Moderns were using some kind of chickenwire dish in New Jersey to bounce the link man's scrambled signal off a Sons of Christ the King satellite in geosynchronous orbit above Manhattan. They chose to regard the entire operation as an elaborate private joke, and their choice of comsats seemed to have been deliberate. Molly's signals were being beamed up from a one-meter umbrella dish epoxy-ed to the roof of a black glass bank tower nearly as tall as the Sense/Net building.

Atlanta. The recognition code was simple. Atlanta to Boston to Chicago to Denver, five minutes for each city. If anyone managed to intercept Molly's signal, unscramble it, synth her voice, the code would tip the Moderns. If she remained in the building for more than twenty minutes, it was highly unlikely she'd be coming out at all.

Case gulped the last of his coffee, settled the trodes in place, and scratched his chest beneath his black t-shirt. He had only a vague idea of what the Panther Moderns planned as a diversion for the Sense/Net security people. His job was to make sure the intrusion program he'd written would link with the Sense/Net systems when Molly needed it to. He watched the countdown in the corner of the screen. Two. One.

He jacked in and triggered his program. 'Mainline,' breathed the link man, his voice the only sound as Case plunged through the glowing strata of Sense/Net ice. Good. Check Molly. He hit the simstim and flipped into her sensorium.

The scrambler blurred the visual input slightly. She stood before a wall of gold-flecked mirror in the building's vast white lobby, chewing gum, apparently fascinated by her own reflection. Aside from the huge pair of sunglasses concealing her mirrored insets, she managed to look remarkably like she belonged there, another tourist girl hoping for a glimpse of Tally Isham. She wore a pink plastic raincoat, a white mesh top, loose white pants cut in a style that had been fashionable in Tokyo the previous year. She grinned vacantly and popped her gum. Case felt like laughing. He could feel the micropore tape across her ribcage, feel the flat little units under it: the radio, the simstim unit, and the scrambler. The throat mike, glued to her neck, looked as much as possible like an analgesic dermadisk. Her hands in the pockets of the pink coat, were flexing systematically through a series of tension-release exercises. It took him a few seconds to realize that the peculiar sensation at the tips of her fingers was caused by the blades as they were partially extruded, then retracted.

He flipped back. His program had reached the fifth gate. He watched as his icebreaker strobed and shifted in front of him, only faintly aware of his hands playing across the deck, making minor adjustments. Translucent planes of color shuffled like a trick deck. Take a card, he thought, any card.

The gate blurred past. He laughed. The Sense/Net ice had accepted his entry as a routine transfer from the consortium's Los Angeles complex. He was inside. Behind him, viral subprograms peeled off, meshing with the gate's code fabric, ready to deflect the real Los Angeles data when it arrived.

He flipped again. Molly was strolling past the enormous circular reception desk at the rear of the lobby.

12:01:20 as the readout flared in her optic nerve.

At midnight, synched with the chip behind Molly's eye, the link man in Jersey had given his command. 'Mainline.' Nine Moderns, scattered along two hundred miles of the Sprawl, had simultaneously dialed MAX EMERG from pay phones. Each Modern delivered a short set speech, hung up, and drifted out into the night, peeling off surgical gloves. Nine different police departments and public security agencies were absorbing the information that an obscure subsect of militant Christian fundamentalists had just taken credit for having introduced clinical levels of an outlawed psychoactive agent known as Blue Nine into the ventilation system of the Sense/Net Pyramid. Blue Nine, known in California as Grievous Angel, had been shown to produce acute paranoia and homicidal psychosis in eighty-five percent of experimental subjects.

Case hit the switch as his program surged through the gates of the subsystem that controlled security for the Sense/Net research library. He found himself stepping into an elevator.

'Excuse me, but are you an employee?' The guard raised his eyebrows. Molly popped her gum. 'No,' she said, driving the first two knuckles of her right hand into the man's solar plexus. As he doubled over, clawing for the beeper on his belt, she slammed his head sideways, against the wall of the elevator.

Chewing a little more rapidly now, she touched CLOSE DOOR and STOP on the illuminated panel. She took a blackbox from her coat pocket and inserted a lead in the keyhole of the lock that secured the panel's circuitry.

The Panther Moderns allowed four minutes for their first move to take effect, then injected a second carefully prepared dose of misinformation. This time, they shot it directly into the Sense/Net building's internal video system.

At 12:04:03, every screen in the building strobed for eighteen seconds in a frequency that produced seizures in a susceptible segment of Sense/Net employees. Then something only vaguely like a human face filled the screens, its features stretched across asymmetrical expanses of bone like some obscene Mercator projection. Blue lips parted wetly as the twisted, elongated jaw moved. Something, perhaps a hand, a thing like a reddish clump of gnarled roots, fumbled toward the camera, blurred, and vanished. Subliminally rapid images of contamination: graphics of the building's water supply system, gloved hands manipulating laboratory glassware, something tumbling down into darkness, a pale splash . . . The audio track, its pitch adjusted to run at just less than twice the standard playback speed, was part of a month-old newscast detailing potential military uses of a substance known as HsG, a bio-chemical governing the human skeletal growth factor. Overdoses of HsG threw certain bone cells into overdrive, accelerating growth by factors as high as one thousand percent.

At 12:05:00, the mirror-sheathed nexus of the Sense/Net consortium held just over three thousand employees. At five minutes after midnight, as the Moderns' message ended in a flare of white screen, the Sense/Net Pyramid screamed.

Half a dozen NYPD Tactical hovercraft, responding to the possibility of Blue Nine in the building's ventilation system, were converging on the Sense/Net Pyramid. They were running full riot lights. A BAMA Rapid Deployment helicopter was lifting off from its pad on Riker's.

Case triggered his second program. A carefully engineered virus attacked the code fabric screening primary custodial commands for the sub-basement that housed the Sense/Net research materials. 'Boston,' Molly's voice came across the link, 'I'm downstairs.' Case switched and saw the blank wall of the elevator. She was unzipping the white pants. A bulky packet, exactly the shade of her pale ankle, was secured there with micropore. She knelt and peeled the tape away. Streaks of burgundy flickered across the mimetic polycarbon as she unfolded the Modern suit. She removed the pink raincoat, threw it down beside the white pants, and began to pull the suit on over the white mesh top.

12:06:26.

Case's virus had bored a window through the library's command ice. He punched himself through and found an infinite blue space ranged with color-coded spheres strung on a tight grid of pale blue neon. In the nonspace of the matrix, the interior of a given data construct possessed unlimited subjective dimension; a child's toy calculator, accessed through Case's Sendai, would have presented limitless gulfs of nothingness hung with a few basic commands. Case began to key the sequence the Finn had purchased from a mid-echelon sarariman with severe drug problems. He began to glide through the spheres as if he were on invisible tracks.

Here. This one.

Punching his way into the sphere, chill blue neon vault above him starless and smooth as frosted glass, he triggered a sub-program that effected certain alterations in the core custodial commands.

Out now. Reversing smoothly, the virus reknitting the fabric of the window.

Done.

Critical connections

Whilst the technological fulfilment of the full Gibsonian vision of cyberspace is still some way away, we are already surrounded by examples in which the human body can be transcended and allowed to interact, with sensorial stimulation, with other operators in a virtual space. Indeed the preconditions for a cyberspace have arguably already been established through the proliferation of digital equipment as a means of everyday communication and interaction. Mobile phones, email devices Internet chat rooms and online social networking sites like Facebook, MySpace and Bebo are transforming consciousness, culture, social organisation and interaction (see also McLuhan, Reading 2). Inspired by the Cyberpunk movement, and in particular by Neil Stephenson's novel *Snow Crash* (1992), the Internet-based *Second Life* offers a powerful illustration. In this 3D virtual world, imagined and created entirely by its residents, people appoint and adopt virtual personas which can interact and participate in individual and group activities through motional 'avatars' (a term borrowed directly from Stephenson). Spending on average 20–40 hours a week in-world (Alter, 2007), residents can establish and break-up virtual relationships, start virtual business with virtual business meetings and transactions, and make real millions buying and selling virtual real estate and other services. *Second Life* is characterised by 'disembodied subjectivities' capable in some sense of transcending the 'the meat' of the human body. The latest development is Nintendo's promise of the first mind controlled game in 2009. Using an electro-encephalographic headset remarkably similar to the 'trodes' Case uses to jack into the matrix, players will be able to 'spin, push, pull, and lift objects on a computer monitor, simply by thinking' (Ayers, 2008). This level of control is already a reality for some quadriplegic patients. For as long as the material body needs to be sustained for human existence to be possible, it will continue to impede a complete separation of virtual and physical worlds (Gies, 2009). Nevertheless, new and rapidly emerging computer technologies are beginning to facilitate some crude form of Gibsonian 'net-consciousness', and to open up new opportunities for self-identity, mobility and interaction.

Thus in the sense that Gibson's vision of cyberspace provides a framework for understanding many of the shifts and changes that characterise the postmodern condition, it can for many be read seriously as social and cultural theory (Burrows, 1997). Indeed, Douglas Kellner (1995) has argued that Gibson's contribution to postmodern theory ultimately transcends that of Jean Baudrillard (see Reading 6). 'When Baudrillard dropped the theoretical ball', Kellner argues, 'losing his initiative, Gibson and cyberpunk picked it up, beginning their explorations of the new theoretical world Baudrillard had been exploring' (Kellner, 1995: 327, cited in Burrows, 1997). It might thus be suggested that William Gibson's *Neuromancer* transcends the novel. It represents the conceptualisation of a new mode of communication and social existence, the shift towards virtual communities and virtual reality, and the possibility of an alternative public sphere: in Habermasian terms, historically constituted by those engaging in public discussion in eighteenth-century salons and coffee houses (Reading 1); in Gibsonian terms, reconstituted by a global discursive community that transcends body and space, reconfigures notions of self and social, and redefines the concepts of citizenship and participatory democracy.

References

Alter, A. (2007) Is This Man Cheating on His Wife?, *New York Times* (http://online.wsj.com/public/article/SB118670164592393622.html, accessed 17th June 2008).

Ayers, C. (2008) 'Thought Control: It's the Computer World's Latest Game Plan', *The Times*, July 18th,

Burrows, R. (1997) 'Cyberpunk as Social Theory: William Gibson and the Sociological Imagination', in S. Westwood and J. Williams (eds) *Imagining Cities: Scripts, Signs, Memory,* London: Routledge.

Gies, L. (2009) How material are cyberbodies? Broadband Internet and embodied subjectivity, in *Crime, Media, Culture: An International Journal,* 4, 3: 311–330.

Haraway, D. (1991) *Simians, Cyborgs and Women: The Reinvention of Nature,* New York: Routledge.

Stephenson, N. (1992) *Snow Crash,* New York: Bantam Books.

Turkle, S. (2005) *The Second Self: Computers and the Human Spirit,* Twentieth Anniversary Edition, Massachusetts: MIT Press.

Discussion questions

- Think about and discuss current technologies that enable sensorial interaction in virtual space.
- To what extent do online experiences like *Second Life* encapsulate Gibson's vision of cyberspace?
- How might Gibson's articulation of cyberspace inform a reconceptualisation of Habermas' 'public sphere' (Reading 1) for the twenty-first century?

SECTION TWO

Researching media

Introduction

IN ORDER TO 'DO' RESEARCH on crime and media it is necessary to develop a repertoire of tools to facilitate the research process. The aim in this section is to set out some of the diverse methodological approaches which have informed, or might usefully inform, the work of media criminologists. Some of the readings in this section cover fairly well research approach trodden ground in crime and media research. Content analysis, for example, is by far the most commonly employed research approach within the crime and media literature. Yet content analysis embraces a wide range of methods – quantitative and qualitative, lexical-verbal (focusing on words) and visual. Most studies have tended to favour quantitative, lexical-verbal analysis over anything else, and this trend appears to be increasing.

Ericson, Baranek and Chan's reading on Content Analysis, therefore, evaluates the relative strengths and weaknesses of quantitative and qualitative approaches to researching news content, and insists that a qualitative approach is required if we are to appreciate the complexity of the cultural form – in this case crime news – under investigation. Most of the other readings in this section outline and discuss approaches which today are seldom if ever used by the majority of researchers working at the crime-media nexus. Currently, for example, there is virtually no sociological research being conducted in newsrooms. Nor are media criminologists engaging with audiences (either in terms of media effects or discursive practices), whether they are consumers of crime news or film, the Internet, graphic video games, or television violence. Research on the consumption of crime and violence tends to be located within the realm of psychological positivism (some of the main exemplars of this approach are included in Section Five).

It is with this deficit of methodological diversity in mind that the readings in this section on Researching Media have been selected. There are two readings by Richard

Ericson, Janet Chan and Patricia Baranek (1987, 1991) of simply because their discussion of researching the newsroom and conducting content analysis, across two books within their now classic trilogy – *Visualising Deviance, Negotiating Control*, and *Representing Order* – has yet to be surpassed. Stuart Hall's (1973) seminal piece on reading news photographs builds on a solid foundation of semiotic, cultural and social theory and presents a model for understanding how news photographs can become ideologically loaded, and how they might be deconstructed and read in that context. Steve Neale (2000) is included here for his explication of the concept of film genre and the idea of verisimilitude, which could be employed by media criminologists to great effect. Theodore Sasson's (1995) work on crime talk presents a social constructionist's understanding not of the objective nature of 'the crime problem' – inasmuch as that can ever be known – but of the discursive frames that citizens variously accept and apply, negotiate or oppose or rebut (see also Hall's Encoding–Decoding in Reading 4). Jenny Kitzinger (2004) presents a critical overview of the long and often conflictful history of audience research, before mapping out her own approach to researching media influence which combines consideration of the power of media and audiences in order to develop a more holistic analysis of media influence. Finally, David Bell (2000) discusses some key concerns when researching the Internet, both as a resource for conducting research, and as a varied and fascinating research site in its own right.

Richard Ericson, Patricia Baranek and Janet Chan

RESEARCH APPROACHES (1987)

Introduction and context

ERICSON *ET AL.*'S (1987) central contention is that the analysis of deviance and control news offers key insights into the process of understanding how cultural workers – journalists and news sources – reproduce order in the knowledge society. With respect to researching the news, what is most striking about their approach is their strong support for ethnographic method. Indeed, they insist that engagement within the newsroom is the only way researchers can develop a sufficiently deep and nuanced appreciation of the internal and external factors that shape the news production process (see also Greer, 2003, 2007). Their commitment to immersing themselves in the field of study epitomises a long and distinguished tradition of 'appreciative' research which is strikingly rare in media criminology. One of the pioneers of appreciative or ethnographic methods, Robert Park, Director of the Department of Sociology in the University of Chicago, urged his graduate students to 'Go and sit in the lounges of the luxury hotels and on the doorsteps of the flophouses; sit on the Gold Coast settees and on the slum shakedowns; sit in Orchestra Hall and in the Star and Garter Burlesque. In short, gentlemen, go get the seats of your pants dirty in real research' (Park, 1927 cited in Bulmer 1984).

Borrowing from pioneering anthropologist Clifford Geertz, Ericson *et al.* argue that understanding news as knowledge requires an 'ethnography of modern thought'. In this sense, they seek to look inside not only the news product itself, but also the social processes through which that product comes to be formed, inflected and framed in terms of particular cultural norms, political ideologies and professional values. Thus Ericson *et al.'s* approach is one which seeks to marry or reengage the processes whereby both text and text creation become the focus of empirical enquiry. They insist that 'some aspects of newsmakers' orientations can be gleaned from content, but the inferences will be weak without knowledge of the actual methods of news-makers'. News content analysis can generate rich data and discussion about what *has* been selected, produced and ultimately reported as news. Only newsroom analyses allow the researcher to understand and explore what *has not*. Furthermore, ethno-graphic techniques such as observation and interviewing are essential to discovering the different organisation, structure and working cultures between agencies within the same medium – for example, competing newspapers – and between agencies spe-cialising in different media – such as television and radio.

Research questions and methodological requirements

Research questions

Our discussion of how news is organized, of how news-as-knowledge is focused on aspects of deviance and control, and of how the media institution is central to the knowledge society has raised basic issues, concepts, and questions. However, theoriz-ing about these matters can only be advanced through sustained empirical inquiry that is interpretive and critical in approach (Bernstein, 1978; Giddens, 1984).

   Our central concerns are how news of deviance and control is produced; how the organization of production articulates with the product; and how the news product plays back into the organizations that report and are reported on. How do sources and journalists as newsmakers in the knowledge society reproduce culture? What is their relation to the texts they produce ('intentionality')? How do the parts of a news text relate to each other ('coherence')? How does a news text relate to other culturally associated texts ('intertextuality')? How do news products relate to other realities ('reference')? (cf Geertz, 1983: 32). [...]

Deviance and control

Studying the production and products of deviance and control news is a fruitful vehicle for understanding how cultural workers reproduce order in the knowledge society. Researching deviance and control news in the broadest sense helps us to understand news workers, assumptions about organizational order, social order, and processes of social change. It reveals how reporters work in concert with others whose job it is to police organizational life, symbolically constructing the moral boundaries of stability as well as the reform politics of change. It makes evident how the organizational cultures of reporters and sources intersect to accomplish particular interests in the name of objectivity, neutrality, and balance. In the process the relation between organizational cultures and dominant cultures is addressed. There is nothing like operating conceptions of good and bad to reveal the beliefs, values, and understandings which underlie representations of reality.

News process stages

Research must respect the entire news process. The central research question in this respect is the extent to which one can speak of a somewhat discrete process from occurrence, to news event, to news product, to the reception of news by the news organizations and source organizations concerned. Is it a discrete communication process, or are there several different processes along the way, with each one requiring explanation in its own terms because it is associated with a unique set of organizational activities?

This question is a matter for empirical inquiry. Existing wisdom suggests, 'It is relatively rare for original source, mass communicator, and audience member to be united and co-operating in the same activity with a common perception of it at the same time or in a connected sequence' (McQuail and Windahl, 1981: 8). Any text written within an organization is a 'situated production,' 'the concrete medium and outcome' of its work activities (Giddens, 1979: 40–4). The author of the text draws upon the tacit knowledge of his experience to construct the text, especially what sort of account is required to achieve accountability with the 'audience' (organizational superior, client, regulating agency, etc.) to whom it is directed, The author must be studied in this connection, for he as the subject becomes bound up in the text as object (ibid, 1979: 43). This is not a matter of considering the author's personal characteristics and competence alone, but of considering how the individual author's knowledge and practices in producing texts are a property of the organizational relations in which he finds himself.

Furthermore, once a text is produced, whatever meaning it had to the author, or others immediately involved in the account, can 'escape' them as the text is interpreted and used within other contexts of organizational relations. As the text becomes objective knowledge, it is interpreted and used by others in a manner which is external to, and independent of, its creators (Popper, 1972). Its transformation as objective knowledge, impacting on other persons and organizations, may have been unintended or unanticipated by the author. Additionally the use of the objective knowledge in the new organizational context may ultimately affect the original author, forcing him to give it new interpretations and to incorporate it for use in further accounts, and so on.

In sum, it seems likely that the social and cultural organization of the reporting process varies at each stage. A particular constellation of social and cultural organization will affect what source activities are considered legitimate news events in the first place; another constellation affects what reporters attend to, choose, produce, and publish; and, yet another constellation relates to what published news items sources and reporters choose from and make further use of within their respective organizations.

Inside news organizations

Examination of how news texts are situated products of organizational relations, and yet escape authors at successive stages, necessarily entails detailed scrutiny of practices inside news organizations. To what extent do internal social and cultural aspects influence reporters and the directions their news organization takes? To what extent are the news texts produced by journalists, or by their colleagues in the same news organization, used to construct interpretations and meanings about their organization? To what extent are the texts of other news organizations used by journalists to construct meanings and interpretations about their own work and news organization? Other questions flow from these considerations. To what extent and how is competition in the production of news a matter of what is happening among members of a particular news organization? To what extent and how is competition a matter internal to the practice of journalism? As a consequence, to what extent and how does the news constitute knowledge that is essentially internal to the news-media institution?

Inside source organizations

The same questions need to be asked of members of source organizations who are involved in the situated production of occurrences which become news events, and whose texts also escape them in the news-reporting process. In particular, what social and cultural processes in their organizations lead them to transform occurrences into news events? What are their strategies and tactics to draw reporter attention to their events and to ensure prominent and favourable publication? What is the influence of news texts in constructing interpretations and meanings within their own organization? How are news texts interpreted and used as a vehicle for further contact and influence with news organizations (e.g., provision of additional information, letters to the editor, efforts at remedy for unreasonable coverage)?

Nature of knowledge

Process and product must both be understood to appreciate the nature of news as knowledge. On the level of process, inquiry must be made into the minutiae of everyday transactions. '[B]y examining routine procedures, it is possible to develop an account of the material and sources used regularly in media production. Such an account is necessary to any sociological analysis of the type of knowledge and culture the media convey' (Elliott, 1979: 159). These transactions bear the imprint of the organizational structures and systems within which news as knowledge is reproduced; indeed, it is these organizational elements which permit newsmakers to define reality in their particular symbolic form.

In Geertz's (1983: chap. 7) terms, the nature of news as knowledge requires 'an ethnography of modern thought.' Thinking must be regarded as a social process as well as an individual one, in which people actively manipulate cultural forms to sustain their activities. An ethnography of thought requires a description of the contexts in which the thought, or knowledge in use, makes sense (ibid: 152; see also Holy and Stuchlik, 1983: chap. 3). The study of news production seems particularly suited to the task because news workers span most spheres of organized life and most aspects of the common sense. News workers' practices and the knowledge associated with them display the very elements which Geertz (1983: 153) recommends should be attended to in an ethnography of thought: 'the representation of authority, the marking of boundaries, the rhetoric of persuasion, the expression of commitment, and the registering of dissent.' More generally, the work of news sources and journalists seems particularly suited to address central theoretical questions about the production of knowledge. These questions focus on 'translation, how meaning gets moved, or does not, reasonably intact from one sort of discourse to the next; about intersubjectivity, how particular individuals come to conceive, or do not, reasonably similar things; about how frames change ... how thought provinces are demarcated ... how thought norms are maintained, thought models acquired, thought labor divided. The ethnography of thinking, like any other sort of ethnography ... is an attempt not to exalt diversity but to take it seriously as itself an object of analytic description and interpretive reflection' (ibid: 154). [...]

The overall news product can also be used to descriptively display the system which is structured by news workers. For example, in relation to news of deviance and control, many of the aspects of interest to us can be described statistically through systematic content analysis. What topics of deviance are published or broadcast? What topics of social control are published or broadcast? Who is involved as sources? In what news formats are they represented? Do these vary by different news media? Do these vary by different news organizations within a medium? Having shown the patterns in this respect, the analyst can explain them in terms of the processes of production he has captured via observation, interviewing, and scrutiny of other organizational texts (documents, memos, manuals, etc.).

News-media variation

The question of whether all news media are relatively similar in their practices of knowledge production and in the knowledge conveyed is one which is central in the research literature. Many persons have called for research comparing media. For example, Fishman cautions that his study of newspapers is limited: 'It remains an open question just how general my findings are with respect to news produced through other forms of mass media (notably television and radio) and news produced outside American society' (1980: 19). On the specific topic of crime news, Garofalo (1981) stresses the need for media comparisons.

Those who have compared media vary in the extent to which they see differences. This variance of course depends on what they have looked for. Those who have studied ethnographically the production process have generally argued that there is little difference across media. This is the impression given, for example, by Tuchman (1978) in her studies of newspapers and television, and the finding of Schlesinger (1978) in his studies of BBC radio and television. Hirsch (1977) goes to the extent of criticizing those who emphasize differences in print and broadcast news, asserting that there are a number of organizational similarities across media. However, some of those who have engaged in systematic analysis of news content have shown media differences. [...] In the area of crime news, Sheley and Ashkins (1981) and Graber (1980) have shown divergence in television and newspaper coverage.

News-organization variation

An attendant series of research questions concern how news organizations within a medium, or across media, vary. Again research is divergent in this area, and there has been too little research to enunciate general trends. Are any two organizations within a medium more similar in process and product than any two organizations in different media? Or, are two organizations in different media that have a similar orientation and audiences (for example, a quality newspaper and a quality radio station) likely to be more similar to each other than two organizations in the same medium that have a different orientation and audiences (for example, a quality newspaper and a popular newspaper)?

Again, the degree of convergence or divergence is likely to be related to the questions asked. [...] We now turn to a more specific consideration of the methodological requirements to address the many research questions we have raised in this section.

Methodological requirements

[...] A combination of social-science research techniques, including observation, interviewing, scrutiny of organizational documents, and systematic analysis of organizational products, is a requirement for a full view of the news-media institution.

There has been a traditional division between those in the humanities, who study individual texts, and those in the social sciences, who study processes of text creation. 'The study of inscriptions is severed from the study of inscribing, the study of fixed meaning is severed from the study of the social processes that fix it. The result is a double narrowness. Not only is the extension of text analysis to nonwritten materials blocked, but so is the application of sociological analysis to written ones' (Geertz, 1983: 32). As argued previously, knowledge can be broadened by appreciating that textual production and texts themselves are part of continuing social processes, in which texts feed back into the production of further texts, and so on. A full range of methodologies are required to capture this process/product relation, including those associated with the techniques of ethnography and those associated with the techniques of content analysis.

Ethnographic approaches which employ observation, interviewing, and document-analysis techniques are essential for our purposes. Whether it is across the world or around the corner, the social scientist is better equipped to convey understanding of his subject matter if he has been immersed in the world of which it is a part. As Runciman (1983: 296–7) asks, 'How can the armchair sociologist presume to pronounce on the experience of people to whom he has never spoken, in whose institutions and practices he has never played a part, and whose manners and mores are far removed from his own?' While ethnographic approaches are no guarantee that understanding will be forthcoming, and while other methods can add to their richness, they are a necessary part of any organizational or institutional analysis.

Nevertheless, some of the more influential cultural analyses of the news media have been presumptuous enough not to include ethnographies of the social relations of production (e.g., Hall *et al.*, 1978; for a critique in this regard, see Sumner, 1981). Some researchers were excluded from ethnographic research by the news organizations they sought to scrutinize, and were therefore left to undertake content analyses exclusively (e.g., GUMG, 1976, 1980, 1982). They at least appreciate the point that ethnographic approaches are a particularly important part of research on the news, and of cultural studies more generally (GUMG, 1980: 407–10).

Ethnographic methods are especially suited to recording 'the cultural' at the level of human activity, allowing 'a sensitivity to meanings and values as well as an ability to represent and interpret symbolic articulations, practices, and forms of cultural production' (Willis, 1981: 3). Indeed, ethnographic methods are essential if we accept that the core concerns of cultural studies compared to behavioural studies are understanding rather than explanation; the interpretion of significance rather than underlying causal forces; diagnosis rather than prediction; and descent into the empirical world rather than ascent to abstract empiricism and high theory (Carey, 1979: 418–19). [...]

Immersion in the organizational culture of one's subjects is also an aid to understanding data of different kinds. Unless the researcher has a fairly extensive grasp of the background knowledge which his subjects have to give meaning to their particular utterances, pieces of organizational 'paper,' and so on, he will be unable to understand his bits of data and how they represent notions held by his subjects (cf Holy and Stucklik, 1983: 56–60). Moreover, once the researcher has acquired such knowledge he can make better sense of data, such as formal interview materials, which are obtained in conditions somewhat removed from the actual setting.

The development of various kinds of data allows them to be put alongside one another for comparison, so that better sense can be made of them than would have been possible with one isolated type of data (cf Weick, 1983: 16). It is of course necessary to keep different types of data distinct, to exercise caution with regard to the 'seeing is believing' (observed data) and 'believing is seeing' (what subjects' present, usually verbally) problems that plague ethnographies (Van Maanen, 1979; Holy and Stuchlik, 1983: chap. 2). However, the fact of having been in the world under study to obtain detailed background knowledge, and the derivation of different types of data through different methods to be compared and contrasted with one another, is the best guarantee of veracity and accuracy known to us.

Researchers 'in organizational communication … have spent very little time observing and describing the communicative activities of organizational members' (Trujillo, 1983: 73). The ethnographic approaches are the only means of acquiring knowledge in this regard. Moreover, they are especially suited to the study of interorganizational processes since these are usually dependent upon a small number of trusting, reciprocal relations between people strategically placed in their respective organizations. In the case of journalists, the nature of their information source networks and elements of negotiation and reciprocity with sources cannot be gleaned from analysis of news content. For example, court clerks are key informants on the court beat but they are rarely if ever cited in news stories (Drechsel, 1983: 50).

Ethnography is also *the* means for acquiring knowledge about what it is like to be a member of the organization under study. 'The ethnographer becomes part of the situation being studied in order to feel what it is like for the people in that situation' (Sandy, 1979: 527). This is what Runciman terms 'tertiary understanding,' and it is this type of understanding which is particularly needed in the study of cultural production and products (Runciman, 1983: 183–4).

The ethnographer is also well situated to suspend belief in what his subjects take as common place and common sense, and to analyse these common elements as functions of the ideological paradigms his subjects bring to bear on the objects of their world. He can examine at first hand the relation between the observing ideologies of his subjects and the observed appearances of their objects, a necessary step towards appreciation of the ideological effects under study.

While news-media content can be analysed to reveal the conventions of published or broadcast communications, these are not the conventions employed by newsmakers in producing content. Some aspects of newsmakers' orientations can be gleaned from content, but the inferences will be weak without knowledge of the actual methods and activities of newsmakers. Content analysis reveals nothing about critical decisions to report on something: about assignment editors who decide not to give coverage; about sources who decide not to send a release to a news organization, or not to respond to requests for interviews, or to give only selected information; about reporters who decide not to contact particular sources, to abandon a story, to work at making a non-newsworthy event into a newsworthy one, to change an angle; about desk editors who alter a story, incorporate wire material into it, make it into a minor item; about legal advisers who recommend alterations or no publication; and so on. Bias is built into these everyday decisions and ethnographic methods are best suited to ascertaining the nature and direction of this bias.

Exclusive reliance on content analysis yields a picture of news work as being much more structured and rational than it actually is. Moreover, the rationality presented through aggregate data is certainly not that which informs news workers as they work on a given story. Content analysis is ultimately directed at the communicators' consciousness and intentions, but inferences from content are unsuitable for understanding consciousness and intentions. Quantitative content analysis consists of the counting of appearances, and correlating these, often without any theory about the significance of what is being counted (Sumner, 1979). One way of developing a theory of significance, and therefore of making content studies more than just speculation about repetition, is to examine at first hand the relations among journalists and sources at different levels in various source organizations and news organizations, and working with different media.

Related to the practices of newsmaking, both qualitative and systematic quantitative content analyses are of significance, indeed necessary for an adequate analysis of the news-media institution. Aggregate data on content do show systematically what is published and broadcast and what is not. For example, these data might show that most violent crime reported is 'street crime,' rather than domestic violence, the violence on workers resulting from unsafe working conditions, or the violence on citizens caused by environmental pollution. The reasons for this can then be pursued ethnographically in terms of the social relations of cultural production, for example, is it related to what material journalists are fed routinely from the police and other regular sources? Is it related to the values and ideology of journalists and their regular or more influential sources, regarding what is the greatest source of actual risk or public fear?

In terms of our central focus on how the news media report on and contribute to organizational life through accounts of deviance and control, systematic content analysis can be most revealing. By systematically indicating who are the authorized knowers, what organizations they represent, and what are their preferred problems of deviance and their preferred control remedies, a great deal can be made evident about the nature of news ideology and the media institution. As Hirsch (1977: 35–6) observes, content studies 'afford a rare opportunity for researchers to link occupational, organizational and institutional nexes and cross-pressures.' Drechsel (1983: 142) has stated as a future research priority the need for quantitative analysis of deviance and control news content that focuses upon who the sources are and what type of information is attributed to them. [...]

Content analysis offers a way of knowing that adds to our knowledge of the process/product relation. It is a necessary component of research on this relation although it is very limited in what it can reveal about the social relations of production. At best, analysis of what does not get presented can suggest aspects of the scheme of conceptualization with which information is presented; and, the uses of authorized knowers and organizations in relation to topics within their command suggests the news media's main frames, and where the ethnographer might search to learn the conventions by which they are framed.

References

Bernstein, R. (1978) *The Restructuring of Social and Political Theory.* Philadelphia: University of Pennsylvania Press.

Carey, J. (1979) 'Mass Communication Research and Cultural Studies: An American View', in J. Curran *et al.*, eds., *Mass Communication and Society*, pp. 409–25. Beverly Hills: Sage.

Drechael, R. (1983) *News Media in the Trial Courts.* New York: Longman.

Elliott, P. (1979) 'Media Organizations and Occupations: An Overview,' in J. Curran. ed., *Mass Communication and Society*, pp. 142–73. Berverly Hills: Sage.

Fishman, M. (1980) *Manufacturing the News.* Austin: University of Texas Press.

Garofalo, J. (1981) 'Crime and the Mass Media: A Selective Review of Research,' *Journal of Research in Crime and Delinquency*, 18: 319–50.

Geertz, C. (1983) *Local Knowledge.* New York: Basic Books.

Giddens, A. (1979) *Central Problems in Social Theory: Action, Structure, and Contradiction in Social Analysis.* London: Macmillan.

Giddens, A. (1984) *The Constitution of Society.* Cambridge: Policy.

Glasgow University Media Group. (1976) *Bad News.* London: Routledge.

Glasgow University Media Group (1980) *More Bad News.* London: Routledge.

Glasgow University Media Group (1982) *Really Bad News*, London: Writers and Readers.

Graber, D. (1980) *Crime News and the Public.* New York: Praeger.

Hall, S., C. Critcher, T. Jefferson, J. Clarke, and B. Roberts. (1978) *Policing the Crisis.* London: Macmillan.

Hirsch, P. (1977) 'Occupational, Organizational and Institutional Models in Mass Media Research: Toward an Integrated Framework,' in P. Hirsch *et al.*, eds., *Strategies for Communication Research*, pp. 13–42. Beverly Hills: Sage.

Holy, L., and M. Stuchlik (1983) *Actions, Norms and Representations: Foundations of Anthropological Inquiry.* Cambridge: Cambridge University Press.

McQuail, D. and S. Windahl (1981) *Communication Models: For the Study of Mass Communications.* London: Longman.

Popper, K. (1972) *Objective Knowledge.* Oxford: The Clarendon Press.

Runciman, W. (1983) *A Treatise on Social Theory: Volume One. The Methodology of Social Theory.* Cambridge: Cambridge University Press.

Sandy, P. (1979) ' The Ethnographic Paradigm(s).' *Administrative Science Quarterly*, 24: 527–38.

Schlesinger, P. (1978) *Putting 'Reality' Together: B.B.C News.* London: Constable.

Sheley, J., and C. Ashkins. (1981) 'Crime, Crime News and Crime Views,' *Public Opinion Quarterly* 45: 492–506.

Sumner, C. (1979) *Reading Ideologies.* London: Academic Press.

Sumner, C. (1981). 'Race, Crime and Hegemony,' *Contemporary Crises*, 5: 277–91.

Trujillo, N. (1983) "Performing' Mintzberg's Roles: The Nature of Managerial Communication,' in L. Putnam and M. Pacanowsky, eds. *Communication and Organizations: An Interpretive Approach*, pp. 73–97. Beverly Hills: Sage.

Tuchman, G. (1978) *Making News.* New York: Free Press.

Van Maanen, J. (1979) 'The Fact of Fiction in Organizational Ethnography,' *Administrative Science Quarterly*, 24: 539–50.

Weick, K. (1983) 'Organizational Communication: Toward a Research Agenda,' in L. Putnam and M. Pacanowsky, eds, *Communication and Organizations*, pp. 13–29. Beverly Hills: Sage.

Willis, P. (1981) *Learning to Labor: How Working Class Kids Get Working Class Jobs,* New York: Columbia University Press.

Critical connections

Ericson *et al.* observe that 'there has been too little research to enunciate trends'. This observation still pertains today, perhaps more than ever given the massive changes which have occurred within and beyond newsrooms over the past 15 or 20 years, and the dearth of ethnographic research seeking to explain and understand them. There have been fundamental transformations within the news media environment at both national and global levels since Ericson *et al.* conducted their research in the mid-1980s. Though there remain important differences between the US and the UK press markets, Anglo-American news production – and news production across many European countries – has been characterized by increasing market competition, the intensified commodification of news, transformations in journalistic practice, the professionalisation of news sources, the diversification and fragmentation of news audiences and, perhaps above all, the massively increased technological capacity for the sourcing, production and dissemination of 'news' (McNair, 2006). These changes carry important implications for how crime is reported across the twenty-first century global news mediasphere (Greer, 2009). Though the journalistic and organizational practices they explore may now appear somewhat outdated, Ericson *et al.*'s discussion of researching the newsroom prefaces what remains one of the most penetrating and theoretically sophisticated studies of crime reporting, or indeed reporting in general, and sets the bar at a height few media criminologists have reached since.

Discussion questions

- What precisely do Ericson *et al.* mean when they call for an 'ethnography of modern thought', and how do they advocate achieving it within the context of press reporting?
- Why is it so important for news media criminologists to conduct research inside newsrooms?
- How has news production changed in recent decades, and what is driving these changes (see also Readings 5, 7 and 16)?

References

Bulmer, M. (1984) *The Chicago School of Sociology: Institutionalization, Diversity and the Rise of Sociological Research,* Chicago: University of Chicago Press.

Greer, C. (2003) *Sex Crime and the Media*: Sex Offending and the Press in a Divided Society, Cullompton: Willan.

Greer, C. (2007) 'News Media, Victims and Crime', in P. Davies, P. Francis, C. Greer (eds) *Victims, Crime and Society*, London: Sage.

Greer, C. (2009) 'Crime and Media: Understanding the Connections' in C. Hale, K. Hayward, A. Wahadin and E. Wincup (eds) *Criminology*, second edition, Oxford: Oxford University Press.

McNair, B. (2006) *Cultural Chaos: News, Journalism and Power in a Globalised World*, London: Routledge.

Richard Ericson, Patricia Baranek and Janet Chan

READING THE NEWS (1991)

Introduction and context

ERICSON *ET AL.*'S (1991) discussion of content analysis is driven by the commitment to understand the relationship of news texts, as an expressive cultural form, to social order, and to indicate the complex and variable nature of this relationship. Their particular approach to cultural analysis, which in places echoes Stuart Hall's *Encoding-Decoding* (see Reading 4), seeks to establish how meanings become embedded in news texts: to 'make sense of the ways in which the news, mediated by journalists and sources, makes sense of our lives'. They are insistent that focusing on news content alone is not an adequate means of comprehending the news process. Indeed, they contest that 'one can no more deduce fully what journalists and sources do from a reading of news content than one can deduce fully what law-enforcement officials do from a reading of statutes, law reports, and police occurrence reports'. Nevertheless, the systematic analysis of news content is a crucial part of the analytical process, and a requirement of understanding the construction of crime and deviance as a news product. Their attention to the pros and cons of both quantitative and qualitative content analysis, and the full engagement with the original printed product, is of particular significance given current trends in crime and news media research.

Research questions

[. . .] There are several questions regarding how the representation and use of sources vary by medium and markets. Some of these questions also address variation in format across media and markets. Do news organizations operating in different media and markets vary in the number of sources they use, the types of sources they use, and the types of knowledge provided by their sources? Do news organizations vary in their use of different contexts for presenting sources? Do news organizations vary in the extent to which sources back up their statements with reference to evidence, and in the types of evidence referred to in this regard? How do news organizations operating in different media and markets vary in their use of visuals and sound in representing sources?

It is important to establish the proportion of total news content that involves crime, law, and justice stories, and how this varies by medium and market. A related question is how concordant stories of crime, law, and justice are across news outlets. Do most news outlets cover the same events and issues in crime, law, and justice in similar ways? Alternatively, are there some differences, for example, in terms of medium, with substantial overlap in broadcast news and a much greater variety in newspapers?

There are several key questions about the specifics of news topics of crime and deviance and how these vary by media and markets. Do news organizations operating in different media and markets vary in the areas and types of crime and deviance they focus on? Do they vary in their targeting of particular institutional contexts and fields in which crime and deviance occur? Do they vary in the types of knowledge about crime and deviance they emphasize? Do they vary in the types of explanations of crime and deviance they offer? Do they vary in their use of headlines, teasers, and leads, regarding the type of knowledge about crime and deviance these devices convey?

There are also several key questions about the specifics of news topics of legal control and justice, and how these vary by media and markets. Do news organizations operating in different media and markets vary in the extent to which they focus on legal control actions that have taken place, are projected, or are recommended? Do they give varying emphasis to particular legal control or justice models, styles, and mechanisms? Do news organizations vary in the institutional contexts and fields they present as being mobilized in legal control actions? Do they vary in their focus on institutional contexts and fields of persons involved in legal control actions? Do they vary in their selection of institutional contexts and fields as targets for legal control actions? Finally, do news organizations vary in the explanations or reasons for legal control actions offered?

Research designed to answer these questions involves an approach to cultural analysis explicated in our earlier research (Ericson, Baranek, and Chan 1987, 1989). Journalists and their sources re-create the texts of the social world, in effect producing texts about social texts. Our task is to understand the relationship of news texts, as an expressive cultural form, to social order, and to indicate the complex and variable nature of this relationship. In news content, journalists have already fixed meaning from the flow of events, and it is this fixation we seek to clarify and analyse. The questions raised above are essentially questions of intra- and intertextuality readable from news content. What is the relation of a text's parts to each other? What is the relation of the text to other texts? What is the relation of the text to those who participated in constructing it? What is the relation of the text to realities conceived of as lying outside of it? What empirical patterns are evident in these intra- and intertextual relations and what do these indicate about the meaning of news discourse?

In addressing these questions, our goal is to pick apart what is usually taken for granted. Through the very mechanisms by which news serves to represent order, it appears as common sense. Through 'simple truth . . . artlessly apprehended,' and through 'things that anybody properly put together cannot help but think' (Geertz 1983: 10), news as common sense tells the consumer how to deal with the world. Our task is to make sense of the ways in which the news, mediated by journalists and sources, makes sense of our lives. This includes making evident not only the parameters of common sense, but also what it overlooks. This is the task of the critic, not the poet (Kermode 1966: 3).

Some critics might contend that reading the news for the commonsensical properties by which it represents order requires studying the people who consume it. We will deal with this consideration in more detail later in the chapter. An understanding of news content is necessary before we can pose meaningful questions regarding the effects of content on consumers. As Gitlin, (1980: 14) has argued, 'Since the media aim at least to influence, condition and reproduce the activity of audiences by reaching into the symbolic organization of thought, the student of mass media must pay attention to the symbolic content of media messages before the question of effects can even be sensibly posed.'

Critics might also contend that the questions we have posed cannot be addressed adequately through a reading of news content, but instead must be grounded in an understanding of the process by which the news is produced. Many researchers (e.g., Hall *et al.* 1978) have tried to deduce social relations from a reading of the cultural form of news. Our view is that one can no more deduce fully what journalists and sources do from a reading of news content than one can deduce fully what law-enforcement officials do from a reading of statutes, law reports, and police occurrence reports (Ericson 1981, 1982), or what scientists do from a reading of journal articles, textbooks, and reviews (Mulkay 1979: 69, 91). News, like law and science, is a socially constructed product that is highly self-referential in nature. That is, news content is used by journalists and sources to construct meanings and expectations about their organizations. This means that the analyst of news content must examine the meanings used by news producers in the construction of their product. We have, in fact, undertaken such an examination through a series of fine-grained ethnographies of journalists and news sources at work (Ericson, Baranek, and Chan 1987, 1989). Our present analysis draws upon our previous work, especially in helping us to explain the aggregate patterns in news content that we identify. In our previous work, we dealt more with the phenomenological, subjective, and interactional processes by which the signs of news are constructed, while, in the present work, we move to the objectified signs of language, ritual, and classification available in news texts. This movement from contexts of production to patterns in texts provides us with a more complete view of sign or symbol use in action, and a more developed ethnography of modern thought.

Research requirements

[. . .] Traditionally there has been a distinction between quantitative content analysis, which seeks to show patterns or regularities in content through repetition, and qualitative content analysis, which emphasizes the fluidity of text and context in the interpretive understanding of culture. Each of these approaches has strengths and limitations.

Our purpose in this section is to show how the methodological issues and problems associated with quantitative and qualitative content analysis are entwined with theoretical
concerns, including considerations of epistemology and ontology. This discussion highlights the relative value of quantitative and qualitative approaches, and thereby indicates
the value we assigned to each in designing our research.

Quantitative content analysis

Quantitative content analysis is a valuable means of revealing patterns in news content, and making evident previously unarticulated assumptions about how the news is
structured and presented. It assumes repetition is the most valuable indicator of significance. Therefore the emphasis is on what can be reasonably classified so that it can
be counted. Even narrative data are placed into predefined categories and thereby
transformed into numerical data. Within this format, emphasis is on verification and
reliability of data as classified. Data that prove recalcitrant because they are lacking in
verification or reliability are discarded, rather than focused upon to discover alternative or new understandings.

Traditionally the patterns of regularities revealed in quantitative content analysis
have been compared to other measures of reality. Since the main purpose of quantitative content analysis has been to comment on what is not presented, wrongly
presented, and/or underrepresented, there is a need for data indicating the norm in
relation to which the news content is compared. The basic questions in this regard
concern the extent to which, and the ways in which, news mirrors reality. Does the
cultural product reflect the social reality? For example, do the types of crimes, criminals, and disposition of cases covered in news stories reflect the patterns revealed in
official statistics, or what the public thinks (e.g., Davis 1973; Roshier 1973; Jones
1976; Sherizen 1978; Ditton and Duffy 1982; Doob 1984)?

In setting out to show that news content in a particular area is distorted or biased
in particular ways, quantitative content analysis is ideologically and politically charged.
'Content analysis, like the mass media generally, is the product of social conflict'
(McCormack 1982:145). A lot of research in this area has been sponsored by interest
groups wanting to show how the news is slanted against their interests. News organizations also sponsor such research, especially when they themselves are subject to
research indicating their content is slanted or distorted. One notorious example is
the large research expenditures of the Independent Broadcasting Association and the
British Broadcasting Corporation to counter the Glasgow University Media Group's
analyses of industrial news on television (Towler 1984).

Quantitative content analysis has many limitations, several of which are made
evident in our subsequent discussion of qualitative content analysis. A basic limitation
is that content analysis can deal only with what has been disseminated. Only observational methodologies based in newsrooms and source organizations can tell us what is
considered for inclusion but is not published, and why.

Quantitative content analysis is further restricted in that it is limited to what can
be quantified. What counts analytically is what can be counted. This limitation leads to
a concentration on aspects that are simple, measurable, and subject to standardization.
Important dimensions are likely to be overlooked. Instead of searching for the anomaly

and focusing upon its significance, the researcher looks no farther than what his or her predefined categories have told him or her to see. Magnification of the novel discovery gives way to standardization of the obvious category. In consequence, quantitative content analysis often results in a rather barren counting of repetition without adequate attention to its significance. In studies where there is no effort to theorize the significance of what is being counted, quantitative content analysis ends up as no more than 'repetition speculation . . . since its practitioners are merely speculating about the significance of repetition . . . Clearly, with no theory of significance, the method is *arbitrary* and *unsystematic*, and could not be anything else. Content analysis is based on empiricist thinking which provides that the truth is self-evident and visible – a provision which conceals the operation of its own highly political concept of ideology' (Sumner 1979: 69, 71). This is not to say that quantitative-content analysts are precluded from theorizing about the significance of what they count, as more sophisticated research has shown (for a review, see McCormack 1982). Rather, it indicates that most research in this tradition is obsessed with methodological concerns (validity, reliability, statistical significance) and ideological concerns (showing the news is distorted and slanted against particular political interests) to the relative exclusion of theoretical concerns (especially about the significance of what is being counted).

The narrow focus on standardizing categories and counting them also leads to simplification. The quantitative-content analyst is forced to reconstruct the commonsense categories in the news, instead of deconstructing these categories and analysing them in the particular. The analyst thereby reproduces the formats and language of journalists and of official news sources. This analytical task is easy, but not very enlightening. 'A thinker who classifies the phenomenon to be examined according to known and visible institutions saves himself the trouble of justifying the classification' (Douglas 1986: 94).

The most significant aspects of news content are not simple or easy to standardize. Indeed, the whole effort to standardize categories is thrown into doubt by the well-known fact that different people assign different meaning and significance to the same text. 'We know nothing of things beyond their significance to us' (Ames 1960: 4), as judged from where we 'sit' in space and time. Even the news – which is prepared to be simplistic and commonsensical so that it can be comprehended by someone with a primary-school education – is open to a wide range of interpretations and uses by different readers in various settings (Snow 1983; Robinson and Levy 1986; Fiske 1987; Ericson, Baranek, and Chan 1989; Ericson 1991).

The fact that even the simplest texts are open to multiple interpretation poses serious difficulties for quantitative content analysis. Surveys of news content, in keeping with positivistically oriented social surveys in general, are based on the assumption that everyone (respondents, readers, coders) has the same understanding of what he or she sees and hears. The research coders are trained to seek and to see things in common. If there are frequent 'misunderstandings' or 'misinterpretations,' then items are discarded, or simplified until a consensus is arrived at. In other words, a consensus is forged among coders through their training and accumulative experience. Obviously this is not the way people normally read the news.

The reality of reading the news is that people in various settings at different times give it significance according to their circumstances and their selves. The news fosters pluralism, varying opinion, and different uses, in different settings. This approach is the antithesis of that taken by researchers in most quantitative content analyses, which involve a methodological construction of consensus through prolonged discussion that culminates in forcing everyone either to 'see it this way' or to not see it at all. The failure of quantitative-content analysts to accept the reality of how texts are a matter of consumers' contexts means that their analyses are not only reified but fictive. Acceptance of the reality that news texts have differential meaning according to consumers' contexts is necessary for a full appreciation of what the news has to offer. As Molotch and Lester (1975: 240–1) state, 'Our general theoretical schema . . . assumes that there can be no such thing as intercoder reliability, because each individual receives a unique observational world . . . Our coders are competent social members, each of whom has a world as valid as any other. The intervention of such coders' worlds into the coding process is a fact which must be acknowledged, not obscured through assertions of objective intercoder reliability.'

These points about the socially constructed and interpreted nature of texts have implications for the effort by quantitative-content analysts to compare news texts with other textually mediated versions of reality such as official statistics or public opinion surveys. These studies do not compare news signs and symbols in relation to some more basic and fundamental reality, but rather in relation to other signs and symbols that are themselves socially constructed. While it might be argued that some of these constructs are closer to the thing being observed than others (Wieck 1983), this is a complex matter. It is certainly problematic to assume that news accounts are at a more distant level of sign-reproduction than, say, official documents about an event. For example, a police reporter often has a more direct and detailed account of a crime from investigating officers than is available in police documents (Ericson, Baranek, and Chan 1989: chap. 3). News accounts may also be at a less distant level of sign-reproduction than public opinion surveys, in which the opinion of citizens is often based on what they have seen or heard on the news, and then textually mediated by the organizational practice of social science. Ultimately what is being compared in these 'Does the news mirror reality?' studies is the news genre as an institutional discourse and some other genre (e.g., legal, official) as an institutional discourse. The social constructs and appearances produced within the genre capacities and purposes of news discourse are compared with the social constructs and appearances produced within the genre capacities and purposes of another institutional discourse (e.g., police statistics). Ultimately a judgment is made about discrepancies in these appearances – for example, that the news is sensational because it dwells on violent crime – that does not reflect the distribution of types of crime as shown in police statistics. However, this judgment is vacuous because it is based on the association of appearances that have been generated in other contexts for other purposes.

Again, there is a need to appreciate the practices that lead to the appearances in terms of the genre capacities of each form of institutional discourse. This shifts the focus from a simple and standardized objectification of texts to an interpretive understanding of how people perceive and use texts. 'The relationship between observer and observed achieves a kind of primacy. It becomes the only thing that *can* be observed . . . The true nature of things may be said to be not in things themselves, but in the relationship we construct and then perceive, *between* them' (Hartley 1982: 13; Hawkes 1977: 17). This relationship is at the core of qualitative content analysis.

Qualitative content analysis

Qualitative content analysts view written and electronically mediated texts as human action, and human action as a text. What is inscribed in written documents and electronic media is action, as is the process by which inscription takes place. As they participate in the construction of documented realities, actors are self-conscious that their actions are being inscribed as part of the overall performance of their roles. Thus they pay careful attention to the scripts, constructing interpretations that will spotlight a competent performance (Gusfield 1981; Geertz 1983; Wagner-Pacifici 1986; Ericson, Baranek, and Chan 1989). In this light, the role of the content analyst is 'to construct a "reading" of the text. The text itself is a sequence of symbols – speech, writing, gesture – that contain interpretations. Our task, like that of the literary critic, is to interpret the interpretations' (Carey 1979: 421).

> The great virtue of the extension of the notion of a text beyond things written on paper or carved into stone is that it trains attention on pre-cisely this phenomenon: on how the inscription of action is brought about, what its vehicles are and how they work, and on what the fixation of meaning from the flow of events . . . implies for sociological interpreta-tions. To see social institutions, social customs, social changes as in some sense 'readable' is to alter our whole sense of what social interpretation is and shift it toward modes of thought rather more familiar to the transla-tor, the exegete, or the iconographer than to the test-giver, the factor analyst, or the pollster. (Geertz 1983:31)

Qualitative analysis, aimed at understanding how human expression articulates social order, begins by picking apart the order that is presented to us as common sense. In the process, the analyst picks out what is relevant for analysis and pieces it together to create tendencies, sequences, patterns, and orders. The process of decon-struction, interpretation, and reconstruction breaks down many of the assumptions dear to quantitative analysts, such as the separation of theory and data, maintaining an objective language cleansed of subjective reference and claims to moral neutrality (Geertz 1983: 34). While the qualitative analyst tries to understand *with* the produc-ers and users of texts he or she studies, he or she must engage in 'constructive inter-pretation' as he or she produces his or her own texts (Dworkin 1986: 62–5; Goodrich 1986). Interpretation, understanding, and application are all part of the same process in which the analyst makes judgments and ultimately presents claims that compete with those of the people involved in the practices he or she is analysing. This construc-tive interpretation is inevitable because the analyst is already dealing with the pre-interpreted knowledge of those he or she is studying, and is not interested in simply reproducing their constructions. Inevitable also in this process is a melding of theory and data, subjective reference, and moral evaluation. The human action of reading and producing texts, in social-scientific analysis as in everyday life, selects and privileges meanings and thereby constitutes preferred texts. It is a social and political activity.

Recognition of the interpretive, subjective, and evaluative dimensions of textual analysis does not diminish the requirement of systematic evidence that is reliable and valid. As ethnographers of texts, qualitative-content analysts are primarily concerned with discovery and verification through quasi-experimental reasoning. They search for suggestive contrasts that 'may either test or extend a theory which has application over as much as possible of the range of events, processes or states of affairs which have been chosen for study' (Runciman 1983:168; see also Glaser and Strauss 1967; Altheide 1987a). There is what Geertz (1983:69) has termed an 'intellectual perpetual motion' from the concrete context of particular formats, meanings, styles, and images to general theoretical claims. Movement from the concrete to the general requires the detection and construction of regularities and patterns. This construction is usually accomplished through narrative description and commentary, although numerical data are also valuable. Whether numerical or narrative, the data are 'built up' into patterns over the course of the research through a process of reflexive and circular comparison, validation, and discovery. Many of these features are summarized by Hall (1975: 15).

> [Qualitative-content analysts] point, in detail, to the text on which an interpretation of latent meaning is based; they indicate more briefly the fuller supporting or contextual evidence which lies to hand; they take into account material which modifies or disproves the hypotheses which are emerging; and they *should* (they do not always) indicate in detail why one rather than another reading of the material seems to the analyst the most plausible way of understanding it . . . [They use] recurrence as one critical dimension of significance though these recurring patterns may not be expressed in quantifiable terms . . . These recurring patterns are taken as pointers to latent meanings from which inferences as to the sources can be drawn . . . [The qualitative-content] analyst has another string to his bow; namely, strategies for noting and taking into account emphasis. Position, placing, treatment, tone, stylistic intensification, striking imagery, etc., are all ways of registering emphasis. The really significant item may not be the one which continually recurs, but the one which stands out as an exception from the general pattern – but which is *also* given, in its exceptional content, the greatest weight.

Qualitative-content analysts focus on each of the questions of intra- and intertextuality raised earlier. Regarding how the components of the same text are related to each other, analysts focus on, for example, how news sources are juxtaposed and cited to 'drop' particular inferences and innuendo. Especially in stories aimed at policing organizational life (Ericson, Baranek, and Chan 1987, 1989), some sources are given a dominant place in the lead and throughout the item, allowing them to frame both the preferred definition of the problem and the control solution. Other sources, 'forced' into this frame, are variously used to underpin it or are themselves marginalized, excluded, or shown to be part of the problem.

Qualitative content analysis is also capable of pin-pointing the subtle ways in which news operatives combine different items and stories to create new meanings and new themes. The newspaper layout juxtaposes stories on the same page or on facing pages to suggest more than is available in each item taken individually (for examples, see Hartley 1982; Voumvakis and Ericson 1984). The same effect is achieved in the broadcast line-up by 'wrapping' several items into a segment to create a theme (for examples, see Fishman 1978; Ericson, Baranek, and Chan 1987). Moreover, within the same newspaper publication or radio or television broadcast, there are different types of items – news stories, features, editorials, letters to the editor, opinion columns, and advertising – that nevertheless are on the same topic or themes and reinforce each other in the aggregate.

The same intertextual relation of different types of items occurs over time in the presentation of continuing stories. Some stories continue for months and even years, and questions of balance, range of opinion, and which sources are setting the agenda become difficult to address because coverage intensifies and then lapses, and some sources and their version of events are in favour but then go out of favour. Researchers have shown that when analysing continuing stories and news themes, some patterns and systematic relationships can be captured only through qualitative research techniques. Quantitative content analysis, which promises to be systematic and to reveal patterns, would in fact miss systematic and patterned aspects if its random or stratified sampling techniques were used to study continuing stories and themes. This point is underscored, for example, in Altheide's (1985, 1987b) analysis of television coverage of the taking of American hostages in Iran; Chibnall's (1977) research on the 'violent society' theme in England; and various studies of particular moral panics, such as Hall and associates' (1978) analysis of the 'mugging' panic in England, and Ng's (1982) research on a sexual-assault-against-children panic in Toronto.

Qualitative content analysis is also valuable for comparing the content of different news outlets as they cover a continuing story or theme. Differences among news outlets in layouts or line-ups, priorities, and sources used are often difficult to capture quantitatively, and again may be lost if standard sampling strategies for quantitative analysis are employed.

Qualitative-content analysts are also sensitive to the relation of texts to those who participate in construing and using them. Texts always escape their authors as they become used by different people in different contexts. Sources find their material taken over by journalists and put into different contexts; they are always taken out of context, literally. Journalists always find their material taken over by consumers, including sources and other journalists; they, too, are always taken out of context, literally. This means that an analyst of the text must remain sensitive to the various contexts in which it is used: once the text escapes its author, what matters is what it says to those who are using it rather than what the author meant to say or what influence he or she hoped it would bear. How does the regular source use it (Ericson, Baranek, and Chan 1989)? How does the journalist use it to produce more news (Tuchman 1978; Altheide 1985; Ericson, Baranek, and Chan 1987)? As Altheide (1987a: 74) directs, 'The aim . . . is to place documents in context just as members do, in order to theoretically relate products to their organizational production.'

Sensitivity to the organizational contexts of textual reproduction also bears awareness about how the text is related to other constructions of reality. For example, it instructs about how news is intertextually related to official documents. To what extent does the news reproduce the performative and presentational character of official discourse (Altheide and Johnson 1980; Fishman 1980)? How do people represent themselves and their organizations in the news, compared to the representations they made in official forms and publications internal to their organization (Ericson, Baranek, and Chan 1989)? Addressing such questions is part of the general task of the ethnographer to make evident how people represent themselves: 'searching out and analysing the symbolic forms – words, images, institutions, behaviours – in terms of which, in each place, people actually represented themselves to themselves and to one another' (Geertz 1983:58).

The dimensions of openness and sensitivity in qualitative content analysis foster discovery, but not always solid evidence and analytical rigour. All readings, including those of media analysts, are subjective and speculative, particular and relative. All readers have to take the part for the whole, and the question becomes what they will fill in the blanks with. In this respect, qualitative content analysis is in the realm of literary and textual criticism, with attendant debates about the proper procedures for reading texts and which readings seem preferable. These debates centre upon 'preferred readings' and whose preferences win out, i.e., which readers are able to convince others that their readings are preferable and that these others should join them. In academic circles, as in other circles, such debates are partially settled by dimensions of knowledge/power, including cogent arguments about such things as evidence, objectivity, systematization of data, and generalizability of findings. This is illustrated, for example, in the reaction to the work of Hall and associates (1978) by media analysts representing different theoretical persuasions (e.g., Sumner 1981; Waddington 1986; Schlesinger 1988).

The fluidity of interpretation and ritual of debate are not exclusive to qualitative analyses, *vide* the money and psychic energy expended on efforts to discredit the work of the Glasgow University Media Group (1976,1980, 1982; Towler 1984). Moreover, qualitatively oriented researchers with an ethnographic sensibility would predict such debates over the analysis of texts. These debates are not only healthy, but inevitable, given the fact that analysts must always engage in constructive interpretations that claim a superiority to interpretations of subjects or other textual analysts. Qualitative-content researchers do not exalt the reality of interpretive pluralism – particularism, subjectivism, idealism, relativism – but they do take pluralism seriously as a matter worthy of interpretive description and analysis. And, of course, to be honest, such interpretive description and analysis should be applied as much to their own work as to the work of other producers and readers of texts they may see fit to study.

References

Altheide, D. (1985) *Media Power*. Beverly Hills: Sage

Altheide, D. (1987a) 'Ethnographic Content Analysis', *Qualitative Sociology* 10: 65–77.

Altheide, D. (1987b) 'Format and Symbols in TV Coverage of Terrorism in the United States and Great Britian', *International Studies Quarterly* 31: 161–76.

Altheide, D. and J. Johnson. (1980) *Bureaucratic Propaganda. Boston:* Allyn and Bacon.

Ames, A. (1960) *The Morning Notes of Adelbert Ames*. Hadley Centril, ed. New Brunswick, NJ: Rutgers University Press.

Carey, J. (1979) 'Mass Communication Research and Cultural Studies: An American View,' in J. Curran *et al.*, eds., *Mass Communication and Society*, pp. 409–25, Beverly Hills: Sage.

Chibnall, S. (1977) *Law-and-Order News*. London: Tavistock.

Davis, F. (1973) 'Crime News in Colorado Newspapers,' in S. Cohen and J. Young, eds, *The Manufacture of News*, pp. 127–35. London: Constable.

Ditton, J., and J. Duffy. (1982) *Bias in Newspaper Crime Reports: Selected and Distorted Reporting of Crime News in 6 Scottish Newspapers during March, 1981*. Background Paper Number 3, Department of Sociology, University of Glasgow.

Doob, A. (1984) 'The Many Realities of Crime,' in A. Doob and E. Greenspan, eds, *Perspectives in Criminal Law*, pp. 61–80. Toronto: Canada Law Book.

Douglas, M. (1986) *How Institutions Think*. Syracuse: Syracuse University Press.

Dworkin, R. (1986) *Law's Empire*. Cambridge, Mass.: Harvard University Press.

Ericson, R. (1981) *Making Crime: A Study of Detective Work*. Toronto: Butterworths.

Ericson, R. (1982) *Reproducing Order: A Study of Police Patrol Work*. Toronto: University of Toronto Press.

Ericson, R. (1991) 'Mass Media, Crime, Law and Justice: An Institutional Approach,' *British Journal of Criminology* forthcoming.

Ericson, R., P. Baranek, and J. Chan (1987) *Visualizing Deviance: A Study of News Organization*. Toronto: University of Toronto Press; Milton Keynes: Open University Press.

Ericson, R., P. Baranek, and J. Chan (1989) *Negotiating Control: A study of News Sources*. Toronto: University of Toronto Press; Milton Keynes: Open University Press.

Fishman, M. (1978) 'Crime Waves as Ideology,' *Social Problems* 25: 531–43.

Fishman, M. (1980) *Manufacturing the News*, Austin: University of Texas Press.

Fiske, J. (1987) *Television Culture*. London: Methuen.

Geertz, C. (1983) *Local Knowledge*. New York: Basic Books.

Gitlin, T. (1980) *The Whole World Is Watching*. Berkeley: University of California Press.

Glaser, B., and A. Strauss. (1967) *The Discovery of Grounded Theory: Strategies for Qualitative Research*. Chicago: Aldine.

Glasgow University Media Group. (1976) *Bad News*. London: Routledge.

Glasgow University Media Group. (1980) *More Bad News*. London: Routledge.

Glasgow University Media Group. (1982) *Really Bad News*. London: Writers and Readers.

Goodrich, P. (1986) *Reading the Law*. Oxford: Blackwell.

Gusfield, J. (1981) *The Culture of Public Problems*. Chicago: University of Chicago Press.

Hall, S. (1975) 'Introduction,' in A. Smith, E. Immirzi, and T. Blackwell, eds, *Paper Voices: The Popular Press and Social Change, 1935–1965*, pp. 11–24. London: Chatto and Windus.

Hall, S., C. Critcher, T. Jefferson, J. Clarke, and B. Roberts. (1978) *Policing the Crisis*. London Macmillan.

Hartley, J. (1982) *Understanding News*. London: Methuen.

Hawkes, T. (1977) *Structuralism and Semiotics*. London: Methuen.

Jones, E. (1976) 'The Press as Metropolitan Monitor,' *Public Opinion Quarterly* 40: 239–44.

Kermode, F. (1966) *The Sense of an Ending: Studies in the Theory of Fiction*. Bloomington: Indiana University Press.

McCormack, T. (1982) 'Content Analysis: The Social History of a Method,' in T. McCormack, ed., *Studies in Communications*, 2, pp. 143–78. Greenwich, Conn.: JAI Press.

Molotch, H., and M. Lester. (1975) 'Accidental News: The Great Oil Spill,' *American Journal of Sociology* 81: 235–60.

Mulkay, M. (1979) *Science and the Sociology of Knowledge*. London: Allen and Unwin.

Ng, Y. (1982) 'Ideology, Media and Moral Panics: An Analysis of the Jacques Murder,' MA thesis, Centre of Criminology, University of Toronto.

Robinson, J., and M. Levy. (1986) *The Main Source: Learning from Television News*. Beverly Hills: Sage.

Roshier, B. (1973) 'The Selection of Crime News by the Press,' in S. Cohen and J. Young, eds, *The Manufacture of News*, pp. 28–39. London: Constable.

Runciman, W. G. (1983) *A Treatise on Social Theory*. Vol. 1: The *Methodology of Social Theory*. Cambridge: Cambridge University Press.

Schlesinger, P. (1988) 'Rethinking the Sociology of Journalism: Source Strategies and the Limits of Media Centrism,' Paper to the Economic and Social Research Council Workshop on Classic Issues of Mass Communication Research, Madingley Hall, Cambridge.

Sherizen, S. (1978) 'Social Creation of Crime News: All the News Fitted to Print,' in C. Winick, ed., *Deviance and Mass Media*, pp. 205–24. Beverly Hills: Sage.

Snow, R. (1983) *Creating Media Culture*. Beverly Hills: Sage.

Sumner, C. (1979) *Reading Ideologies*. London: Academic Press.

Sumner, C. (1981) 'Race, Crime and Hegemony,' *Contemporary Crises* 5: 277–91.

Towler, R. (1984) 'Television and Its Audiences,' Mass Communication and Modern Culture Seminar Series, Social and Political Studies Committee, Cambridge, England.

Tuchman, G. (1978) *Making News*. New York: Free Press.

Voumvakis, S., and R. Ericson. (1984) *News Accounts of Attacks on Women: A Comparison of Three Toronto Newspapers*. Toronto: Centre of Criminology, University of Toronto.

Waddington, P. (1986) 'Mugging as a Moral Panic: A Question of Proportion,' *British Journal of Sociology* 37: 245–59.

Wagner-Pacifici, R. (1986) *The Moro Morality Play: Terrorism as Social Drama*. Chicago: University of Chicago Press.

Weick, K. (1983) 'Organizational Communication: Toward a Research Agenda,' in L. Putnam and M. Pacanowsky, eds, *Communication and Organizations*, pp. 13–29. Beverly Hills: Sage.

Critical connections

Crime and news media content analysis has traditionally favoured quantitative over qualitative research methods (Greer, 2009; Reiner, 2007; Jewkes, 2004). Quantitative analyses can be very effective at identifying changing trends and patterns in media content over time. But the fundamental problem with the purely quantitative analysis of content is that it cannot grasp the complexities of media colour, context and meaning. It results, ultimately, in a methodological distancing from that which is actually being studied. The quantitative approach is most completely encapsulated in analyses of content gleaned from online searchable newspaper databases, which enable researchers to access and analyse, for example, newspaper crime coverage from the comfort and convenience of their desktop. Such technological developments present undeniable advantages. Years of coverage across scores of publications can be searched, filtered and collated by year and title, byline and headline. But there is a cost, and this cost is significant.

Online searchable databases also strip news media content of much of its form, style and colour. Though the development of full-form media databases may not be far away, the current series of packages reduces news content to words reproduced on a computer screen in standardised font. Decontextualised. Arid. Colourless. And, crucially, without images. Of course, not all crime news stories contain images; though all high profile ones do. The point is that at a time when the visual is becoming increasingly important in crime news production, it remains methodologically and theoretically marginalised in crime and media research.

Thus, the emerging orthodoxy of computer-assisted, online quantitative content analysis produces results based on what is at best a partial reproduction of a much more colourful, complex and interesting cultural form. Using a partial empirical platform inevitably leads to a partial analysis. Consider the difference between Figures 9.1 and 9.2. Both present the same newspaper story – the putative descent into a lawless Britain where murderous youths run wild – but the extent to which these cultural forms offer a platform for in-depth research differs enormously. Ericson *et al.* insist that due attention must be paid to the quantitative element and indeed that this is a requirement, for example, in longitudinal analysis. However, they make a convincing case – in line with the methodological position advocated in this book – that it is only through qualitative engagement with the complete news product, in its original format, that the richness of the source material, its ideological underpinnings, context nuance, colour and style, can be revealed, explained and understood.

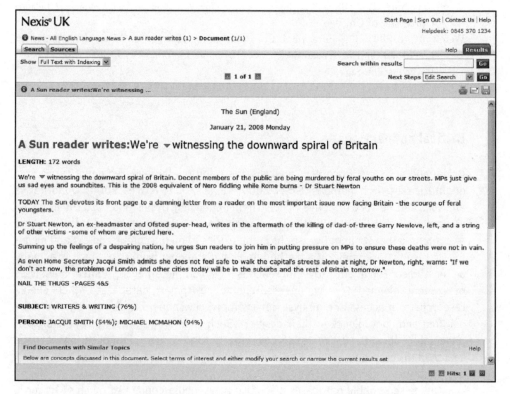

Figure 9.1 The 'news residue' produced by computerised newspaper databases.

Figure 9.2 *The Sun*: 'The downward spiral of Britain', 21 January 2008.

Discussion questions

● What are the main advantages and disadvantages of quantitative and qualitative approaches to researching news content?
● Why might sustained academic attention to the visual remain such a rarity within media criminology?
● Conduct your own content analysis of newspaper crime coverage, incorporating both quantitative and qualitative methods to explore the constituent words and images (see also Readings 8 and 10).

References

Greer, C. (2009) 'Crime and Media: Understanding the Connections' in C. Hale, K. Hayward, A. Wahadin and E. Wincup (eds) *Criminology*, second edition, Oxford: Oxford University Press.

Jewkes, Y. (2004) *Media and Crime: An Introduction*, London: Sage.

Reiner, R. (2007) 'Media Made Criminality: The representation of crime in the mass media', in M. Maguire, R. Morgan and R. Reiner (eds) *The Oxford Handbook of Criminology* (4th edn). Oxford: Oxford University Press.

Stuart Hall

THE DETERMINATIONS OF
NEWS PHOTOGRAPHS (1973)

Introduction and context

STUART HALL BEGINS HIS ANALYSIS of news photographs with
the line 'In the modern newspaper, the text is still an essential element, the photograph an optional one' (Hall, 1973: 226). Some 35 years later it might be suggested
that this position has changed. Perhaps the most significant development in news
production over the last ten years has been the growing prominence of the visual as
a defining feature of contemporary news journalism. The rapid development of
Information and Communication Technologies (ICTs) has permitted the instantaneous packaging and transmission of visual images as news commodities. Stories may
be run or dropped on the strength of the images available to accompany them. Yet
despite the increasing significance of visual images in the news, and all around us,
there is a dearth of methodologically sound media criminology focusing on the visual.
To be sure, analysing images is neither simple nor straightforward. The investigation
of visual culture, dating back decades, has generated a distinct and varied set of
theoretical and methodological approaches grounded not in criminology, but in other
disciplines such as media, cultural and film studies.

Building on classic semiotic theory of Roland Barthes and others, Hall maps out
the relations between signifier and signified, denotation and connotation, cultural
codes and modes of interpretation, and explores these within the context of the news
photograph. Of particular significance are the formal and ideological levels on which
news images operate to produce first and second order meanings. Hall explores how
a photo can, via meanings generated at the level of connotation, serve as an index
of an ideological theme, effectively becoming an ideological sign which reinforces
a particular view of the world – in Gramscian terms, the dominant ideology. Thus the

news-photo of anti-war protesters kicking a police officer works on a number of connotative and ideological levels, interacting with the text and headlines, and circulating around and reinforcing dominant discourses of law and order, public safety, and national security.

The level of signification in photographs

In the modern newspaper, the text is still an essential element, the photograph an optional one. Yet photographs, when they appear, add new dimensions of meaning to a text. As Roland Barthes has observed, 'pictures . . . are more imperative than writing, they impose meaning at one stroke, without analysing or diluting it'.[1]

The codes of connotation

First, we must turn to the *codes* which make signification possible. It is principally codes of connotation which concern us here. Connotative codes are the configurations of meaning which permit a sign to signify, in addition to its denotative reference, *other, additional implied meanings*. These configurations of meaning are forms of social knowledge, derived from the social practices, the knowledge of institutions, the beliefs and the legitimations which exist in a diffused form within a society, and which order that society's apprehension of the world in terms of dominant meaning-patterns. Codes of denotation are precise, literal, unambiguous: the photo-image of a sweater *is* (denotes) an object to be worn, recognizable as a sweater and not as a coat, a hat or a walking stick. Codes of connotation are more open-ended. In the connnotative domain of everyday speech *sweater* may also connote 'keeping warm', a 'warm garment' – and thus by further elaboration 'the coming of winter', a 'cold day', and so on. But in the domain of the specialized discourse (sub-code) of fashion, *sweater* may connote 'a fashionable style of *haute couture*', a certain 'informal style' of dress, and so on. Set against the right background, and positioned in the domain of romantic discourse, *sweater* may connote 'long autumn walk in the woods'.[2]

At the expressive level, the photo signifies within the lexicon of expressive features distributed throughout the culture of which the reader is a member. This lexicon is not restricted to photography, or indeed to the domain of visual representation. The same 'cues' which allow us to decode the expressive features of the photographed subject are also employed by almost everyone when they 'read' everyday subjects and occasions in an expressive way. Expressive codes depend on our competence to resolve a set of gestural, non-linguistic features (signifiers) into a specific expressive configuration (signified) – an accomplishment which is cultural, not technical. It is part of the 'social stock of knowledge at hand' in any culture that a set of bodily or physical features serves as indices of recognizable expressions. Members of a culture are competent to use this 'knowledge' whether face-to-face with the living subject or a visual transcription of it. The main difference is that in social situations we have available to us a richer set of signifying cues from which to distinguish an expressive pattern: in addition to body position, facial expression, gesture, we have movement, situation, interaction and speech. The photograph therefore represents a *truncated version* of this cultural code. [. . .]

The signification of news

It is necessary to distinguish *two aspects* to the signification of news. The first is the *news value* of the photographic sign. The second is the *ideological level* of the photographic sign. 'News value' consists of the elaboration of the story (photo + text) in terms of the professional ideology of news – the common-sense understandings as to what constitutes the news in the newspaper discourse. The ideological level consists of the elaboration of the story in terms of its connoted themes and interpretations. *Formal* news values belong to the world and discourse of the newspaper, to newsmen as a professional group, to the institutional apparatuses of news-making. *Ideological* news values belong to the realm of moral-political discourse in the society as such. Ideological themes will be inflected in different ways according to the particular construction which each newspaper selects. This *inflection* will, in turn, be governed by the newspaper's policy, political orientation, its presentational values, its tradition and self-image. But behind the particular inflections of a particular news 'angle' lie, not only the 'formal' values as to 'what passes as news in our society', but the ideological themes of the society itself. Thus the death of the Duke of Windsor meets the requirement of 'formal news values' because it is unexpected, dramatic, a recent event, concerning a person of high status. But, at the ideological level, this event connotes a powerful, resonant 'set' of themes: 'Prince Charming', the 'King with the people at heart', the monarch who 'gave up the throne for the woman I love', the celebrity life of the Windsors in retirement, the late reconciliation with the Queen, the death and national burial – 'the King who came Home'.

Different newspapers will inflect the news-story differently, by picking up one or more of these ideological themes. Nevertheless, in general, *any* of these particular 'news angles' intersects directly with the great ideological theme: *the Monarchy itself*. This is a point which that great chronicler of the British ideology, Bagehot, would have relished:

> The best reason why Monarchy is a strong government is that it is an intelligible government. The mass of mankind understand it, and they hardly in the world understand any other. It is often said that men are ruled by their imaginations; but it would be truer to say they are governed by the weakness of their imaginations . . . We have no slaves to keep down by special terrors and independent legislation. But we have whole classes unable to comprehend the idea of a constitution – unable to feel the least attachment to impersonal laws . . . A republic has only difficult ideas in government; a Constitutional Monarchy has an easy idea too; it has a comprehensible element for the vacant many, as well as complex laws and notions for the inquiring few.[3]

The structure of 'news values' appears as a neutral, operational level in news production. It 'naturally' connects stories and events with persons: it attaches qualities, status, positions in the social world to anonymous events: it searches out the 'drama', the 'human interest', behind impersonal historical forces. Yet, these operational values are not, in the end, neutral values. As Althusser has argued, it is precisely by operating with 'the category of the *subject*', and by producing in the reader 'familiar recognitions', that a discourse becomes ideological.[4]

THE KICK-PHOTO

Figure 10.1 The kick-photo.

It appears, then, that the news-photo must lend itself to exploitation at the level of what we have called 'formal news values' first, before – secondly – it can signify an ideological theme. Thus the photo of a demonstrator kicking a policeman has news value because it witnesses to a recent event, which is dramatic, unusual, controversial. It is then possible, by linking this so-to-speak 'completed message' with an interpretation, to produce 'second-order meanings' with powerful ideological content: thus AND THEY TALK ABOUT PROVOCATION! *(The Sketch)*, WHAT THE BOBBIES FACED *(Express)*, VICTORY FOR POLICE *(Telegraph)*, THE DAY THE POLICE WERE WONDERFUL *(Mirror)*. Halloran, Elliott and Murdock[5] note how this 'kick-photo' (taken by a free-lance photographer for Keystone Agency) selectively reinforced both a previous interpretation – that the demonstration against the Vietnam War would be a 'violent' one – and a specific 'news angle' – 'the editorial decision to make the police the centre of the story'.[5] In news-value terms, the police are signified as the 'centre' for the story – that is its *formal* news exploitation, grounded by the 'Kick-Photo'. In ideological terms, the police are signified as the *heroes* of the story – an interpretation connotatively amplified by the photo.

In practice, there is probably little or no distinction between these two aspects of news production. The editor not only looks at and selects the photo in terms of impact, dramatic meaning, unusualness, controversy, the resonance of the event signified, etc. (formal news values): he considers at the same time how these values will be treated or 'angled' – that is, interpretatively coded.

It is this double articulation – formal news values/ideological treatment – which binds the inner discourse of the newspaper to the ideological universe of the society. It is via this double articulation that the institutional world of the newspaper, whose manifest function is the profitable exchange of news values, is harnessed to the latent function of reproducing 'in dominance' the major ideological themes of society. The formal requirements of 'the news' thus appear as 'the operator' for the reproduction of ideology in the newspaper. Via 'news angles', the newspaper articulates the core

themes of bourgeois society in terms of *intelligible representations*. It *translates* the legitimations of the social order into faces, expressions, subjects, settings and legends. As
Bagehot observed, 'A royal family sweetens politics by the seasonable addition of nice
and pretty events. It introduces irrelevant facts into the business of government, but
they are facts which speak to "men's bosoms" and employ their thoughts.'

Newspapers trade in news stories. But though the need to harness a multitude of
different stories and images to the profitable exchange of news values is 'determining
in the last instance', this economic motive never appears on its own. The ideological
function of the photographic sign is always hidden within its exchange value. The
news/ideological meaning is the *form* in which these sign-vehicles are exchanged.
Though the economic dialectic, here as elsewhere, determines the production and
appropriation of 'symbolic' values, it is 'never active in its pure state'. The exchange
value of the photographic sign is, necessarily, over-determined.

News values

By news values we mean the operational practices which allow editors, working
over a set of prints, to select, rank, classify and elaborate the photo in terms of his
'stock of knowledge' as to what constitutes 'news'. 'News values' are one of the most
opaque structures of meaning in modern society. All 'true journalists' are supposed to
possess it: few can or are willing to identify and define it. Journalists speak of 'the
news' as if events select themselves. Further, they speak as if which is the 'most
significant' news story, and which 'news angles' are most salient are divinely inspired.
Yet of the millions of events which occur every day in the world, only a tiny proportion ever become visible as 'potential news stories': and of this proportion, only a
small fraction are actually produced as the day's news in the news media. We appear
to be dealing, then, with a 'deep structure' whose function as a selective device is un-
transparent even to those who professionally most know how to operate it.

A story, report or photo which has the potential of being used to signify the news,
seems, in the world of the daily newspaper, to have to meet at least *three* basic criteria.
The story must be linked or linkable with an event, a happening, an occurrence: the
event must have happened recently, if possible yesterday, preferably today, a few hours
ago: the event or person 'in the news' must rank as 'newsworthy'. That is to say, news
stories are concerned with *action*, with '*temporal recency*' and '*newsworthiness*'. [. . .]

News values *do* have something to do with 'what is not (yet) widely known': with
the scarce, rare, unpredictable event. In French the news – *les nouvelles* – means
literally 'the new things'. This suggests that news values operate against the structured
ignorance of the audience. They take for granted the restricted access of people to power,
and mediate this scarcity. News stories often pivot around the unexpected, the problematic. But an event is only unexpected because it 'breaches our expectations about
the world'. In fact, most news stories report minor, unexpected developments in the
expected continuity of social life and of institutions. They *add to* what we already
know or could predict about the world. But, whether the news dramatizes what we
really do not know, or merely adds an unexpected twist to what is already known, the
central fact is that news values operate as a foreground structure with a hidden 'deep
structure'. News values continually play against the set of on-going beliefs and constructions about the world which most of its readers share. That is, news values require

consensus knowledge about the world. The preoccupation with change/continuity in the news can function at either a serious or a trivial level: the breaking of the truce by the IRA or the latest model on the bonnet of the latest model at the Motor Show. Either the wholly a-typical (the IRA) or the over-typical (the Motor Show) constitute 'news' because, at the level of 'deep structure', it is the precariousness or the stability of the social order which most systematically produces visible news stories.[6]

Without this background consensus knowledge – our 'routine knowledge of social structures' – neither newsmen nor readers could recognize or understand the foreground of news stories. Newspapers are full of the actions, situations and attributes of 'elite persons'. The prestigious are part of the necessary spectacle of news production – they people and stabilize its environment. But the very notion of 'elite persons' has the 'routine knowledge of social structures' inscribed within it. Prime Ministers are 'elite persons' because of the political and institutional power which they wield. Television personalities are 'newsworthy' because celebrities serve as role-models and trend-setters for society as a whole. 'Elite persons' make the news because power, status and celebrity are monopolies in the institutional life of our society. In C. Wright Mills' phrase, 'elite persons' have colonized 'the means of history making' in our society.[7] It is this distribution of status, power and prestige throughout the institutional life of class societies which makes the remarks, attributes, actions and possessions of 'elite persons' – their very being-as-they-are – naturally newsworthy. The same could be said of 'elite nations'. If we knew nothing about Britain's historical connections throughout the world, or the preferred map of power relations, it would be difficult to account for the highly skewed structure to the profile of foreign news in British newspapers. In setting out, each day, to signify the world in terms of its most problematic events, then, newspapers must always *infer what is already known*, as a present or absent structure. 'What is already known' is not a set of neutral facts. It is a set of common-sense constructions and ideological interpretations *about* the world, which holds the society together at the level of everyday beliefs.

Regularly, newspapers make news values salient by *personifying* events. Of course people are interesting, can be vividly and concretely depicted in images, they possess qualities and so on. Personalization, however, is something else: it is the isolation of the person from his relevant social and institutional context, or the constitution of a personal subject as exclusively the motor force of history, which is under consideration here. Photos play a crucial role in this form of personification, for people – human subjects – are *par excellence* the content of news and feature photographs. 'There is no ideology except for the concrete subjects, and the destination for ideology is only made possible by the subject: meaning, *by the category of the subject* and its functioning.'[8] A newspaper can account for an event, or deepen its account, by attaching an individual to it, or by bringing personal attributes, isolated from their social context, to bear on their account as an explanation. Individuals provide a universal 'grammar of motives' in this respect – a grammar which has as its suppressed subject the universal qualities of 'human nature', and which manipulates subjects in terms of their 'possessive individualism'.[9]

The most salient, operational 'news value' in the domain of political news is certainly that of *violence*. Events not intrinsically violent can be augmented in value by the attribution of violence to them. Most news editors would give preference to a photo signifying violence in a political context. They would defend their choice on the grounds that violence represents conflict, grips the reader's interest, is packed with action, serious in its consequences. These are formal news values. But at the level of 'deep structure', political violence is 'unusual' – though it regularly happens – because it signifies the world of politics *as it ought not to be*. It shows conflict in the system at its most extreme point. And this 'breaches expectations' precisely because in our society conflict is supposed to be regulated, and politics is exactly 'the continuation of social conflict without resort to violence': a society, that is, where the legitimacy of the social order rests on the absolute inviolability of 'the rule of law'.

Formal news criteria, though operated by professionals as a set of 'rules of thumb', are no less rooted in the ideological sphere because these transactions take place out of awareness. Events enter the domain of ideology as soon as they become visible to the news-making process. Unless we clarify what it is members of a society 'normally and naturally' take as predictable and 'right' about their society, we cannot know why the semantization of the 'unpredictable' in terms of violence, etc., can, in and of itself, serve as a criterion of 'the news'.

The ideological level

This brings us directly to the second aspect of news construction – the elaboration of a news photo or story in terms of an interpretation. Here, the photo, which already meets and has been exposed within the formal criteria of news, is linked with an interpretation which exploits its connotative value. We suggest that, rhetorically, the ideological amplification of a news photo functions in the same manner as Barthes has given to the exposition of 'modern myths'.[10] By ideological elaboration we mean the insertion of the photo into a set of thematic interpretations which permits the sign (photo), via its connoted meanings, to serve as the index of an ideological theme. Ideological news values provide a second level of signification of a ideological type to an image which already (at the denotative level) signifies. By linking the completed sign with a set of themes or concepts, the photo becomes an ideological sign. [. . .]

We may take two examples here. (i) The photo of the Nixons, arm in arm, walking in the White House garden. The President is smiling, giving an 'it's O.K.', 'spot on' gesture. Here the ideological message requires little or no further elaboration. The President's in a happy mood: a figure of world prominence relaxes just like other men: Nixon's on top of the world. There is no accompanying text, only a caption: and the caption, apart from identifying the actors and occasion (their daughter Tricia's wedding), redundantly mirrors the ideological theme: 'Everything in the garden's lovely'. This is very different from (ii) the 'kick-photo', where the denoted message – 'a man in a crowded scene is kicking a policeman' – is ideologically 'read' – 'extremists threaten law-and-order by violent acts', or 'anti-war demonstrators are violent people who threaten the state and assault policemen unfairly'. This second-order message is fully amplified in the captions and headlines. But note also that it is slightly inflected to suit the position, presentational tradition, history and self-image of each individual newspaper. It is the linking of the photo with the themes of *violence, extremists and law-and-order, confrontation* which produces the ideological message. But this takes somewhat different forms in each paper: *The Times* inflects it *formally* – POLICE WIN BATTLE OF GROSVENOR SQUARE; the *Express* inflects it *sensationally*, accenting the 'marginal' character of the demonstrators – FRINGE FANATICS FOILED AT BIG DEMONSTRATION; the

Mirror inflects it *deferentially* — THE DAY THE POLICE WERE WONDERFUL. Here the text is crucial in 'closing' the ideological theme and message.

It is difficult to pin down precisely how and where the themes which convert a photo into an ideological sign arise. Barthes argues that 'The concept is a constituting element of myth: if I want to decipher myths, I must somehow be able to name concepts.' But he acknowledged that 'there is no fixity in mythical concepts: they can come into being, alter, disintegrate, disappear completely'. This is because the dominant ideology, of which these themes or concepts are fragments, is an extremely plastic, diffuse and apparently a historical structure. Ideology, as Gramsci argued, seems to consist of a set of 'residues' or preconstituted elements, which can be arranged and rearranged, *bricoleur*-fashion, in a thousand different variations.[11] The dominant ideology of a society thus frequently appears redundant: we know it already, we have seen it before, a thousand different signs and messages seem to signify the same ideological meaning. It is the very mental environment in which we live and experience the world — the 'necessarily imaginary distortion' through which we continually represent to ourselves 'the [imaginary] relationship of individuals to the relations of production and the relations that derive from them'.[12] The ideological concepts embodied in photos and texts in a newspaper, then, do not produce new knowledge about the world. They produce *recognitions* of the world as we have already learned to appropriate it: 'dreary trivialities or a ritual, a functionless creed'.

Barthes suggests[13] that we can only begin to grasp these ideological concepts reflexively, by the use of ugly neologisms: e.g. 'French-ness', 'Italian-ness'. Or by the naming of very general essences: e.g. militarism, violence, 'the rule of law', the-state-of-being-on-top-of-the-world. Such concepts appear to be 'clearly organized in associative fields'. Thus 'Italian-ness' belongs to a certain axis of nationalities beside 'French-ness', 'German-ness' or 'Spanish-ness'. In any particular instance, then, the item — photo or text — perfectly indexes the thematic of the ideology it elaborates. But its general sphere of reference remains diffuse. It is there and yet it is not there. It appears, indeed, as if the general structure of a dominant ideology is almost impossible to grasp, reflexively and analytically, *as a whole*. The dominant ideology always appears, precisely, diffused in and through the particular. Ideology is therefore both the specific interpretation which any photo or text *specifies*, and the general ambience within which ideological discourse itself is carried on. It is this quality which led Althusser to argue that, while ideologies have histories, ideology as such has none.

Ideological themes exhibit another quality which makes them difficult to isolate. They appear in their forms to link or join *two* quite different levels. On the one hand they classify out the world in terms of immediate political and moral values: they give events a specific ideological reference in the here-and-now. Thus they ground the theme *in* an event: they lend it faces, names, actions, attributes, qualities. They provide ideological themes with actors and settings — they operate above all in the realm of the *subject*. The photo of the demonstrators and the policeman is thus *grounded* by its particularity, by its relation to a specific event, by its temporal relevance and immediacy to a particular historical conjuncture. In that photo the general background ideological value of the 'rule of law', the generalized ethos of attitudes against 'conflict by violent means' were *cashed* at a moment in the political history of this society when the 'politics of the street' was at its highest point, and where the whole force of public discourse and disapproval was mobilized against the rising tide of extra-parliamentary opposition movements. Yet, in that very moment, the ideological theme is distanced and universalized: it becomes *mythic*. Behind or within the concrete particularity of the event or subject we seem to glimpse the fleeting forms of a more archetypal, even archaeological-historical, knowledge which universalizes its forms. The mythic form seems, so to speak, to hover within the more immediate political message. The smiling face of Nixon is of that very time and moment – an American President at a particular moment of his political career, riding the storms of controversy and opposition of a particular historical moment with confidence. But, behind this, is the universal face of the home-spun family man of all times, arm in arm with his lady-wife, taking a turn in the garden at his daughter's wedding. In the handling of the 'kick-photo', *The Times* picks out and specifies the immediate political ideological theme – POLICE WIN BATTLE OF GROSVENOR SQUARE. But, within that message, the *Mirror* glimpses, and elaborates, a more mythic, universal theme – one which may underpin a hundred different photographs: the myth of 'our wonderful British police'.

We seem here to be dealing with a double movement within ideological discourse: the movement towards propaganda, and the movement towards myth. On the one hand, ideological discourse shifts the event towards the domain of a preferred political/moral explanation. It gives an event an 'ideological reading' or interpretation. Barthes puts this point by saying that the ideological sign connects a mythical schema to history, seeing how it corresponds to the interests of a definite society. At this level, the rhetoric of connotation saturates the world of events with ideological meanings. At the same time, it disguises or *displaces* this connection. It asks us to imagine that the particular inflection which has been imposed on history *has always been there*: is its universal, 'natural' meaning. Myths, Barthes argues, dehistoricize the world so as to disguise the motivated nature of the ideological sign. They do not 'unveil historical realities': they inflect history, 'transforming it into nature'. At the ideological level, news photos are continually passing themselves off as something different. They interpret historical events ideologically. But in the very act of grounding themselves in fact, in history, they become 'universal' signs, part of the great storehouse of archetypal messages, nature not history, myth not 'reality'. It is this conjuncture of the immediate, the political, the historical and the mythic which lends an extraordinary complexity to the deciphering of the visual sign.

News photos have a specific way of passing themselves off as aspects of 'nature'. They repress their ideological dimensions by offering themselves as literal visual-transcriptions of the 'real world'. News photos witness to the *actuality* of the event they represent. Photos of an event carry within them a meta-message: 'this event really happened and this photo is the proof of it'. Photos of people – even the 'passport' type and size – also support this function of *grounding and witnessing*: 'this is the man we are talking about, he really exists'. Photos, then, appear, as records, in a literal sense, of 'the facts' and speak for themselves. This is what Barthes calls[14] the 'having-been-there' of all photographs. News photos operate under a hidden sign marked, 'this really happened, see for yourself'. Of course, the choice of *this* moment of an event as against that, of *this* person rather than that, of *this* angle rather than any other, indeed, the selection of this photographed incident to represent a whole complex chain of events and meaning, is a highly ideological procedure. But, by appearing literally to reproduce the event as it *really* happened, news photos suppress their selective/interpretive/ideological function. They seek a warrant in that ever pre-given, neutral structure, which is beyond question, beyond interpretation: the 'real world'. At this level, news photos not only support the credibility of the newspaper as an accurate medium. They also guarantee and underwrite its *objectivity* (that is, they neutralize its ideological func-tion). This 'ideology of objectivity' itself derives from one of the most profound myths in the liberal ideology: the absolute distinction between fact and value, the distinction which appears as a common-sense 'rule' in newspaper practice as 'the distinction between facts and interpretation': the empiricist illusion, the utopia of naturalism.

The ideological message of the news photo is thus frequently displaced by being *actualized*. At first this seems paradoxical. Everything tends to locate the photo in historical time. But historical time, which takes account of development, of struc-tures, interests and antagonisms, is a different modality from 'actuality time', which, in the newspaper discourse, is foreshortened time. The characteristic *tense* of the news photo is the *historic instantaneous*. All history is converted into 'today', cashable and explicable in terms of the immediate. In the same moment, all history is mythified – it undergoes an instantaneous mythification. The image loses its motivation. It appears, 'naturally', to have selected itself.

But few news photos are quite so unmotivated. The story of the Provisional IRA leader, Dutch Doherty, under the headline ULSTER WANTS DOHERTY EXTRADITED, speculates within the story-text on moves against IRA men in the Republic, pressures on the Lynch Government not to shelter wanted men, and so on: but it carries only a small, head-and-shoulders 'passport-photo' of the man in question, with the simple caption *Anthony 'Dutch' Doherty*. Yet the 'passport photo', with its connotation of 'wanted men', prisoners and the hunted, is not without ideological significance. This photo may not be able, on its own, to produce an ideological theme. But it can *enhance, locate* or *specify* the ideological theme, once it has been produced, by a sort of recipro-cal *mirror-effect*. Once we know who the story is about, how he figures in the news – once, that is, the text has added the themes to the image – the photo comes into its own again, refracting the ideological theme at another level. Now we can 'read' the meaning of its closely-cropped, densely compacted composition: the surly, saturnine face: the hard line of the mouth, eyes, dark beard: the tilted angle so that the figure appears hunched, purposefully bent: the black suit: the bitter expression. These formal, compositional and expressive meanings reinforce and amplify the ideological message. The ambiguities of the photo are here not resolved by a caption. But once the ideological theme has been signalled, the photo takes on a signifying power of its own – it adds or situates the ideological theme, and grounds it at another level. This, it says, is the face of one of the 'bombers and gunmen': this is what today's headline, of another 'senseless' explosion in downtown Belfast, is all about. This its subject, its author. It is *also* a universal mythic sign – the face of all the 'hard men' in history, the portrait of Everyman as a 'dangerous wanted criminal'.

References

1.   Roland Barthes, 'Myth today', *Mythologies* (London, Cape, 1972).
2.   The example is from Barthes, *Elements of semiology* (London, Cape, 1967).
3.   Walter Bagehot, 'The English constitution'. *Walter Bagehot*, ed. N. St John Stevas (London, Eyre & Spottiswoode, 1959).
4.   L. Althusser, 'Ideology and the State', *Lenin and philosophy and other essays* (London, New Left Books, 1971).

5.   J. Halloran, P. Elliott & G. Murdock, *Demonstrations and communication* (Harmondsworth, Penguin, 1970).
6.   Cf. Jock Young, 'Mass media, drugs & deviancy', in McIntosh and Rock, op. cit.
7.   C. Wright Mills, *The power elite* (Oxford, Univ. Press, 1956).
8.   L. Althusser, 'Ideology and the State', op. cit.
9.   Cf. J. O'Neil, *Sociology as a skin trade* (London, Heinemann, 1972). The phrase is from C.B. MacPherson, *The political theory of possessive individualism* (OUP, 1962).
10.   R. Barthes, 'Myth today', *Mythologies*, op. cit.
11.   Gramsci, *Selections from the Prison Notebooks*. Ed. G. Nowell-Smith (London, Lawrence & Wishart, 1971). Cf. also *Beliefs in society*, Nigel Harris (London, Watts, 1968).
12.   L. Althusser, op. cit.
13.   R. Barthes, 'Rhetoric of the image', *Working papers in Cultural Studies* no. 1 (Birmingham, Centre for Cultural Studies).
14.   R. Barthes, ibid.

Critical connections

At around the same time that Stuart Hall was working on the news photograph, Susan Sontag was arguing for the special place of the photograph as a cultural and emotional form. For Sontag (1977:161):

> ... the true modern primitivism is not to regard the image as a real thing: photographic images are hardly that real. Instead reality has come more and more to seem like what we are shown by cameras. It is common now for people to insist about their experience of a violent event in which they were caught up – a plane crash, a shoot-out, a terrorist bombing – that 'it seemed like a movie'. This is said, other descriptions seeming insufficient, in order to explain how real it was. While many people in non-industrialised countries still feel apprehensive when being photographed, divining it to be some sort of trespass, an act of disrespect, a sublimated looting of the personality or the culture, people in industrialised countries seek to have their photographs taken – feel that they are images, and are made real by photographs.

Sontag's comments on the power of the photograph and the profound influence that media have on our conceptions of the 'real' make clear theoretical connections with the work of Stuart Hall, Jean Baudrillard (Reading 6) and Manuel Castells (Reading 5), among others. Writing about the September 11 2001 attacks on the Twin Towers in New York, Castells (2004:139) argues,

> Ultimately ... action is geared toward human minds, toward transforming consciousness. The media, local and global, are the means of communication through which the public mind is formed. Therefore, *action has to be media-oriented*, it has to be spectacular, provide good footage, so the whole world can see it: like a Hollywood movie because this is what has trained the human mind in our times.

At a time when the image has arguably become as indispensable to print news as the text (one wonders which between an all-text or all-pictures newspaper would sell more copy!), it is vital for researchers of crime and media to 'take the image seriously'. Stuart Hall's (1973) *Determinations of News Photographs* offers a useful starting point in this endeavour. Susan Sontag's commentary on images of torture in Abu Ghraib prison (Reading 42) offers an alternative approach to understanding the symbolic and formal power of the visual.

Discussion questions

- What do the terms 'denotation' and 'connotation' mean, and how can they be elevated to the level of ideology?
- Why is the visual such a key determinant of newsworthiness and a defining characteristic of news production?
- Take a front page crime story from any newspaper and, using Hall's methodological approach, conduct your own semiotic analysis (see also Readings 4 and 9).

References

Castells, M. (2004) *The Power of Identity* (2nd edn). Oxford: Blackwell.
Sontag, S. (1977) *On Photography*, New York: Picador.

Steve Neale

DIMENSIONS OF GENRE (2000)

Introduction and context

GIVEN THAT SO MUCH concern about the pernicious influence of media targets violence in film, it is important to develop a grasp of some of the conceptual and methodological tools underpinning sociological film analysis. Film studies, of course, is a well-established discipline in its own right, and there is insufficient space in this Reader to discuss even a selection of its domain assumptions and key methodological approaches. One area of particular interest, however, is genre analysis. Excerpted from his book *Genre and Hollywood* (2000), Steve Neale sets out the key elements in defining and subsequently analysing different genres of movie, including the crime film. One crucial requirement of genre analysis is that researchers become versed in the tropes and conventions they subsequently set out to explore. Media criminologists should be well equipped to analyse the crime and justice aspects of Cop or Gangster movies, and to locate these within a wider moral-political, socio-economic or cultural context in order to explain, for example, changes in representation over time. Few, however, may be as comfortable locating the crime and justice elements of those same movies within the conventions of film production. Steve Neale's contribution to this Reader is intended to equip researchers with some of the conceptual and methodological tools to probe deeper, combining criminological expertise with a deeper understanding of the workings and narrative construction of crime film.

The argument that genre is ubiquitous, a phenomenon common to all instances of discourse, clearly must modify the perception, and to some extent also the location, of Hollywood's genres. No longer the sole or even the principal site of genre in the cinema, Hollywood instead becomes just one particular site, its genres specific instances – not necessarily paradigms – of a much more general phenomenon. Genre in Hollywood also expands. It now encompasses 'the feature film', 'the newsreel', 'the cartoon', 'the B film', 'the A film' and 'the serial' as well as – and often at the same time as – 'the western', 'the musical', 'the gangster film' and the others. In addition, the argument that genre is multi-dimensional means that attention now needs to be paid as much to the factors that impinge on audience expectations, the construction of generic corpuses, and the processes of labelling and naming as to those that impinge on the films themselves. This chapter will pursue some of these points, and in doing so will introduce a number of further concepts, terms and topics of debate. The first of these is verisimilitude.

Verisimilitude

To reiterate an earlier point. Genres do not consist solely of films. They consist also of specific systems of expectation and hypothesis which spectators bring with them to the cinema and which interact with films themselves during the course of the viewing process. These systems provide spectators with means of recognition and understanding. They help render individual films, and the elements within them, intelligible and, therefore, explicable. They offer a way of working out the significance of what is happening on the screen: a way of working out why particular actions are taking place, why the characters are dressed the way they are, why they look, speak and behave the way they do, and so on. Thus if a character in a film suddenly bursts into song, spectators (or at least spectators accustomed to Hollywood films) are likely to hypothesize that the film is a musical, a particular kind of film in which otherwise unmotivated singing is likely to occur. This hypothesis offers grounds for further anticipation: if a film is a musical, more singing is likely, and the plot is liable to follow some directions rather than others.

Inasmuch as this is the case, these systems of expectation and hypothesis involve a knowledge of, indeed they partly embody, various regimes of verisimilitude – various systems and forms of plausibility, motivation and belief. 'Verisimilitude' means 'probable', 'plausible' or 'likely'. In addition, it entails notions of propriety, of what is appropriate and *therefore* probable (or probable and therefore appropriate) (Brewster 1987; Genette 1969; Todorov 1977: 42–52, 80–8, 1981: 118–19. See also Aumont *et al.* 1992: 117–21). Regimes of verisimilitude vary from genre to genre. Bursting into song is appropriate, therefore probable – therefore believable – in a musical, but not in a war film or a thriller. Killing one's lover is possible in a gangster film, a thriller, or even a romantic drama, but unlikely in romantic comedy. And so on. As such, these regimes entail rules, norms and laws. Singing in a musical is not just probable, it is obligatory; it is not just likely to occur, it is bound to.

As Todorov (1981) has pointed out, there are two basic types of verisimilitude: generic verisimilitude, on the one hand, and social or cultural verisimilitude on the other. Neither equates in any direct sense with 'reality' or 'truth':

> If we study the discussions bequeathed us by the past, we realize that a work is said to have verisimilitude in relation to two chief kinds of norms. The first is what we call *rules of the genre*: for a work to be said to have verisimilitude, it must conform to these rules. In certain periods, a

comedy is judged 'probable' only if, in the last act, the characters are discovered to be near relations. A sentimental novel will be probable if its outcome consists in the marriage of hero and heroine, if virtue is rewarded and vice punished. Verisimilitude, taken in this sense, designates the work's relation to literary discourse: more exactly, to certain of the latter's subdivisions, which form a genre.

But there exists another verisimilitude, which has been taken even more frequently for a relation with reality. Aristotle, however, has already perceived that the verisimilar is not a relation between discourse and its referent (the relation of truth), but between discourse and what readers believe is true. The relation is here established between the work and a scattered discourse that in part belongs to each of the individuals of a society but of which none may claim ownership; in other words to *public opinion*. The latter is of course not 'reality' but merely a further discourse, independent of the work.

(Todorov 1981: 118–19)

Drawing on Todorov's work, Jonathan Culler has gone on to propose five types of verisimilitude, five levels of *vraisemblance*,

five ways in which a text may be brought into contact with and defined in relation to another text which helps make it intelligible. First there is the socially given text, that which is taken as the 'real world'. Second, but in some cases difficult to distinguish from the first, is a general cultural text: shared knowledge which would be recognized by participants as part of culture and hence subject to correction or modification but which none the less serves as a kind of 'nature'. Third there are the texts or conventions of a genre . . . Fourth, comes what might be called the natural attitude to the artificial, where the text explicitly cites and exposes *vraisemblance* of the third kind so as to reinforce its own authority. And finally, there is the complex *vraisemblance* of specific intertextualities, where one work takes another as its basis or point of departure and must be assimilated in relation to it.

(Culler 1975: 140)

Culler cites the detective story to illustrate the workings of generic *vraisemblance*, highlighting in addition the extent to which generic conventions are as much a property of expectations as they are of works themselves:

The detective story is a particularly good example of the force of genre conventions: the assumption that characters are psychologically intelligible, that the crime has a solution which will eventually be revealed, that the relevant evidence will be given but that the solution will be of some complexity, are all essential to the enjoyment of such books. In fact, these conventions are especially interesting because of the large place they grant to the irrelevant. It is only at the level of the solution that coherence is required: everything deviant and suspicious must be explained by the resolution which produces the key to the 'real' pattern, but all other details can at this point be set aside as of no consequence. The conventions make possible the adventure of discovering and producing a form, of finding the pattern amid a mass of details, and they do so by stipulating what kind of pattern one is reading towards.

(Culler 1975: 148)

Todorov (1977) also uses the detective story, and what he calls 'the murder mystery', to illustrate the concept of verisimilitude. One of the major points he makes is that the *generic* verisimilitude of the murder mystery entails a flaunting or trangression of *cultural* (or 'ordinary') verisimilitude, the second of Culler's categories of *vraisemblance*:

We find the same 'regularity' in any whodunit; a crime has been committed, the criminal must be found. Given several isolated clues, a whole is reconstructed. But the law of reconstruction is never the law of verisimilitude; on the contrary, precisely the obvious suspects turn out to be innocent, and the innocent are 'suspect'. The guilty man in a murder mystery is the man who does not seem guilty. In his summing up, the detective will invoke a logic which links the hitherto scattered clues; but such logic derives from a scientific notion of possibility, not from one of verisimilitude. The revelation must obey these two imperatives: possibility and absence of verisimilitude.

(Todorov 1977: 85)

Hence, if 'every discourse enters into a relation of verisimilitude with its own laws, the murder mystery takes verisimilitude for its very theme; verisimilitude is not only its law but also its object' (ibid.: 85).

The detective story and the murder mystery may well be special cases, instances in which the relationship, and in particular the gap, between generic and socio-cultural regimes of verisimilitude are brought to the fore in a systematic way. But as Culler points out, the *vraisemblance* of any artistic genre is always 'artificial' (1975: 140). This particular relationship and this particular gap are therefore always at stake, always in play. They are always at stake, for instance, in the musical, at those moments and points at which characters burst into otherwise unmotivated song. And they are always at stake, as Frank Krutnik and I have argued, in the comic events and moments that dominate most forms of comedy (Neale and Krutnik 1990: 83–94). Such events and such moments are founded on transgressions and gaps of this kind, whether they involve deviations from the norms of sense and logic, or departures from dominant cultural models of action, speech and behaviour.

It is arguably the case that most Hollywood genres, as traditionally defined, involve transgressions of socio-cultural verisimilitude – for the sake of particular kinds of aesthetic pleasure (as derived, for instance, from the song or from the gag), and in the name not of 'art', but entertainment. Nevertheless, there is in any individual genre always a balance between generic and socio-cultural verisimilitude, and some genres appeal more to the latter than to the former. Gangster films, war films and police procedural thrillers in particular often mark that appeal by drawing on and quoting 'authentic' (or authenticating) discourses, artefacts, and texts: maps, newspaper headlines, memoirs, archival documents, and so on. Other genres – sword-and-sorcery adventure films, space operas and supernatural horror films, for instance – appeal much less to this kind of authenticity. The discourses, artefacts and texts that they cite – like the Book of Revelation in *The Omen* (1974) or the lore of the Jedi in the *Star Wars* films – tend either to be blatantly fictional or else treated as such within our culture. Midway between these extremes lie such instances of science fiction as *Tarantula* (1955) and *Them* (1954), films which draw on the authentic, factual and verisimilitudinous status of science (and contemporary atomic technology) in order to motivate otherwise non-verisimilitudinous actions and events.

Of particular relevance here is Todorov's work on 'the fantastic' (1975), a category founded on the existence of different regimes of verisimilitude. For Todorov the fantastic is defined in relation to two neighbouring categories, 'the marvellous' and 'the uncanny'. In the former, events are explained and understood as supernatural, in the latter in terms of the laws of the natural world. The fantastic involves a 'hesitation' between the two, often on the part of a fictional protagonist, but crucially always on the part of the reader:

> In a world which is indeed our world, the one we know, a world without devils, sylphides, or vampires, there occurs an event which cannot be explained by the laws of this same familiar world. The person who experiences the event must opt for two possible solutions: either he is the victim of an illusion of the senses, of a product of the imagination – and the laws of the world remain what they are; or else the event has indeed taken place, it is an integral part of reality – but then this reality is controlled by laws unknown to us. Either the devil is an illusion, an imaginary being; or else he really exists, precisely like other living beings – with this reservation, that we encounter him infrequently.
>
> The fantastic occupies the duration of this uncertainty. Once we choose one answer or the other, we leave the fantastic for a neighboring genre, the uncanny or the marvelous. The fantastic is that hesitation experienced by a person who knows only the laws of nature, confronting an apparently supernatural event.
>
> (Todorov 1975: 25)

It should be pointed out that although many works involve the hesitation to which Todorov refers, very few sustain it throughout. Todorov himself cites *The Saragossa Manuscript* and *The Turn of the Screw*. Aside from adaptations of these works, cinematic examples are few and far between. Examples include *Vampyr* (1928) (Nash 1976), *Martin* (1978) (Grant 1994: 114–15) and *The Birds* (1963).

Negotiating the balance between different regimes of verisimilitude plays a key role in the relations established between spectators, genres and individual films. In markedly non-verisimilitudinous genres these relations can be particularly complex – and particularly fragile (Neale 1980: 36–47, 1990b). The predominance of ideologies of realism in our culture tends to mean that, unless marked as high art, many avowedly non-realist genres are viewed as frivolously escapist, as 'mere fantasy', and thus as suitable only for children, or for 'mindless', 'irresponsible' adults. This, of course, is to refuse to acknowledge the generic status of realism itself (Todorov 1981: 18–20), and the element of fantasy inherent in all forms of artistic representation (Cowie 1984; Freud [1908] 1985a). However, such refusals have consequences. One is that adults who find themselves viewing examples of these genres have often to disown their enjoyment by maintaining that such genres – and such pleasures – are not really for them, but for children, teenagers, others less 'responsible' (less 'adult') than they are themselves (Bergala 1978). Another is that films which are modelled on these genres often take account of disavowals of this kind by overtly addressing the topics of adulthood and responsibility, childhood and the infantile, and credulity, fantasy and belief.

There are numerous manifestations and examples of this. Noel Carroll (1981) has identified two plot structures characteristic of horror films and of horror/sci-fi hybrids. The first he calls 'the Discovery Plot'. It has four main stages, 'onset', 'discovery', 'confirmation' and 'confrontation', and it is worth noting that as Carroll describes them, 'discovery' involves not just the testing – and failure – of responsibility and the capacity for belief of those in (adult) authority, but an identification of the one with the other, while 'confirmation' involves their eventual realignment. Thus the structure as a whole involves not only a 'play between knowing and not knowing', but an articulation of that play across themes and positions of responsibility, power and belief. It is also worth noting, particularly in the light of Carroll's concluding remarks, that 'teen horror' variants like *A Nightmare on Elm Street* (1984) nearly always insist on the adult status of those in authority, on the 'non-adult' status of those who really know and who are most under threat, on the culpability, irresponsibility and ignorance of the former, and on the extent to which the latter have to assume power themselves in order to survive:

> Perhaps the most serviceable narrative armature in the horror film genre is what I call the Discovery Plot. It is used in *Dracula, The Exorcist, Jaws I and II, It Came from Outer Space, Curse of the Demon, Close Encounters of the Third Kind, It Came from Beneath the Sea* and myriad other films. It has four essential movements. The first is onset: the monster's presence is established, e.g., by an attack, as in *Jaws*. Next, the monster's existence is discovered by an individual or group, but for one reason or another its existence or continued existence, or the nature of the threat it actually poses, is not acknowledged by the powers that be. 'There are no such things as vampires,' the police chief might say at this point. Discovery, therefore, flows into the next plot movement which is confirmation. The discoverers or believers must convince some other group of the existence and proportions of the mortal danger at hand. Often this section of the plot is the most elaborate, and suspenseful. As the UN refuses to accept the reality of the onslaught of killer bees or invaders from Mars, precious time is lost, during which the creature or creatures often gain power and advantage . . .
>
> After the hesitations of confirmation, the Discovery Plot culminates in confrontation. Mankind meets its monster, most often winning, but on occasion, like the remake of *Invasion of the Body Snatchers,* losing. What is particularly of interest in this plot structure is the tension caused by the delay between discovery and confirmation. Thematically, it involves the audience not only in the drama of proof but also in the play between knowing and not knowing, between acknowledgement and nonacknowledgement, that has

the growing awareness of sexuality in the adolescent as its archetype. This conflict can become very pronounced when the gainsayers in question — generals, police chiefs, scientists, heads of institutions, etc. — are obviously parental authority figures.

(Carroll 1981: 23)

The second plot is the Overreacher Plot. Where the Discovery Plot involves endowing childlike or adolescent credulity, rather than adult scepticism, with the virtues of true responsibility, the Overreacher Plot makes a virtue of childlike powerlessness and superstition, and vilifies adult, scientific knowledge:

> Another important plot structure is that of the Overreacher. *Frankenstein, Jeckyll and Hyde* [sic], and *Man with the X-Ray Eyes* [sic] are all examples of this approach. Whereas the Discovery Plot often stresses the shortsightedness of science, the Overreacher Plot criticizes science's will to knowledge. The Overreacher Plot has four basic movements. The first comprises the preparation for the experiment, generally including a philosophical, popular-mechanics explanation or debate about the experimenter's motivation. The overreacher himself (usually Dr. Soandso) can become quite megalomaniacal here, a quality commented upon, for instance, by the dizzyingly vertical laboratory sets in *Frankenstein* and *Bride of Frankenstein*. Next comes the experiment itself, whose partial success allows for some more megalomania. But the experiment goes awry, leading to the destruction of innocent victims and/or to damage or threat to the experimenter or his loved ones. At this point, some overreachers renounce their blasphemy; the ones who don't are mad scientists. Finally, there is a confrontation with the monster, generally in the penultimate scene of the film.

(Carroll 1981: 23)

Films using neither of these plots are nevertheless marked by the same set of concerns. *Curse of the Cat People* (1943), for example, sets up an opposition between the imaginative sensitivity of a young girl and the prosaic matter-of-factness of her father. The girl believes she has an 'invisible companion' in the form of the ghost of her father's first wife. Her father refuses to believe her and threatens her with punishment. But his disbelief places her in danger when she subsequently runs away. It is thus seen not only as repressive and cruel, but also as irresponsible, a mark of failure in his role as adult and father. Only when he tells his daughter that he believes her, only when he acknowledges her invisible companion, is he seen to be a truly responsible adult. Only then does he become a proper father — a *visible* companion for his child. In this way the film works to justify itself in terms of adult issues and concerns as well as in terms of childish or childlike ones.

A further set of remarks might be made at this point about non-verisimilitudinous genres and audience expectations. Viewers of horror or science fiction may expect the unlikely. But precisely for this reason they will often also be unable to anticipate the norms, rules and laws that govern the fictional world in any one particular instance. And this means that the films themselves will have to explain them.

Of course, all fiction films involve exposition, the provision of information about the nature and state of the fictional world. But many films are able to rely on the norms, rules and laws – the systems of 'everyday knowledge' – embodied in regimes of socio-cultural verisimilitude in accounting at a fundamental level for the actions, events and behaviour they represent: most films do not have to explain the laws of gravity, or that humans are mortal, or that they are incapable of mutating into the life forms they ingest. However, in horror films and science fiction such laws may well not apply. Other laws, other norms, may have taken their place. Not only that, but these laws and norms may well be specific to one particular film, to one particular fictional universe. Thus they have to be explained; and thus the expositional burden carried by films of this kind is increased. Aside from their role in scenarios of scepticism, power, authority, belief and credulity, this is another reason why such films are so full of scientists, sages, doctors, seers and other experts in arcane norms and laws.

So far, verisimilitude, expectation and knowledge have only been considered in relation to genres as traditionally defined and conceived. However, in addition to the likes of the detective film, the horror film and science fiction, they are also relevant to the feature film, the documentary, the serial and the newsreel. For instance, if we know that the film we are watching is a feature film, we expect it to last a minimum – and also a maximum – amount of time. And certainly in the case of a Hollywood feature, we expect that time to be filled by a narrative. Thus if we were to go to a local commercial cinema and were to find ourselves watching *Empire* (1964), a film which is eight hours long, and which lacks narrative, characters and movement, we might well be nonplussed. For on these grounds alone, *Empire* would not qualify as a 'real' or 'proper' feature film. And even though it is essentially a filmed 'record' of the Empire State Building in New York, we would probably not consider it a proper documentary either – it is too long; its length appears to exceed the degree of interest or information its image track can provide; it lacks the conventional guidance usually provided by editing and a commentary; and so on.

Maybe, for all these reasons, we would not even consider *Empire* to be a real, a proper, a verisimilitudinous film at all. But this would depend upon the repertoire of genres with which we are familiar, and the institutional context within which we encountered the film. If instead of the local commercial cinema we were to encounter *Empire* at the Museum of Modern Art in New York or at the Filmmakers' Co-op in London, our expectations, and the generic systems around which they were organized, might well be very different. For in these contexts generic categories like 'the feature film' and 'the documentary' are not institutionalized as either dominant, or even particularly relevant. Here, the genres and regimes of verisimilitude associated with avant-garde art are more appropriate. The key term here is 'institutionalized'. These genres and regimes are made known to audiences in a number of ways: through statements, manifestos, programme notes, lectures, introductions, discussions and the like. Though different in many ways from the means by which Hollywood's genres are made known, they nevertheless perform a similar institutional function: they help provide a generic framework within which to comprehend films. It is important to bear this in mind when considering the institutional practices of Hollywood itself.

Institutional aspects of genre and Hollywood

As John Ellis has pointed out, central to the practices of Hollywood is the construction of a 'narrative image' for each individual film: 'An idea of the film is widely circulated and promoted, an idea which can be called the "narrative image" of the film, the cinema's anticipatory reply to the question, "What is the film like?"' (1981: 30). As he goes on to note, the institutionalized public discourse of the press, television and radio often plays an important part in the construction of such images. So, too, do the 'unofficial', 'word of mouth' discourses of everyday life. But a key role is also played by the discourse of the industry itself, especially in the earliest phases of a film's public circulation, and in particular by those sectors of the industry concerned with publicity and marketing: distribution, exhibition, studio marketing departments, and so on.

Genre is, of course, an important ingredient in any film's narrative image. The indication and circulation of what the industry considers to be the generic framework – or frameworks – most appropriate to the viewing of a film is therefore one of the most important functions performed by advertising copy, and by posters, stills and trailers. In addition, reviews nearly always contain terms indicative of a film's generic status, while posters and trailers often offer verbal generic description – 'The Greatest War Picture Ever Made', 'The Comedy of the Decade', 'The Drama of the Year', and so on – as anchorage for the generically pertinent iconography they almost always also contain. Advertising campaigns, posters, stills and marquee displays in cinemas help comprise what Lukow and Ricci (1984) have called cinema's 'inter-textual relay'. They mention credit sequences and titles as well, and certainly it is hard from a generic point of view to think of the credit sequence of *The Wild Bunch* (1969) as the opening sequence in a musical, or of films with titles like *Night of the Living Dead* (1968) and *Fright Night* (1985) as anything other than horror films.

Cinemas, cinema programming and cinema specialization could also be considered components in the relay, especially if broader conceptions of genre, conceptions that include the short, the newsreel and the feature film, are taken into account. During Hollywood's studio era most cinemas in the United States showed mixed programmes of films: not just musicals or horror films, but also detective films, comedies and dramas; not just feature films, but also newsreels and shorts of various kinds. According to Douglas Gomery (1992: 137–54) and Barbara Stones (1993: 82–3, 119–23) there were cinemas, and even small circuits, which specialized in westerns and action films, and one or two cinemas, particularly in New York, which specialized in cartoons and newsreels. They and their names would thus have functioned as generic cues in their own right. But alongside cinemas and circuits which showed 'ethnic' films, 'art' films, and later – increasingly – pornography, they were, and are, the exception. The precise structure of the programmes shown in most cinemas during the studio era is unclear, and probably varied considerably. However, it *is* clear that if you had just sat through two feature films, a newsreel, short or trailer was likely to follow. Hence you would probably have had to adjust your generic expectations.

In addition to the provision of generic images for individual films, the industry's inter-textual relay also provides images of and for genres themselves. This is the case whatever the genre, feature film or short, musical or thriller. The former are genres which are, or were, exclusive to the cinema (they can now be found in television too).

The latter also exist in the theatre and/or in popular fiction. Some can be found in television and radio. And some predate the cinema itself. The inter-textual relays that accompany the theatre, the publishing industry and other sectors of media thus also play a part in the circulation of such images. It is therefore worth drawing attention both to the general circulation of personnel from one institutional relay to another (an increasing phenomenon in an era of synergy and conglomeration), and to specific individuals like Warren William Baumgarter, Dean Cornwell, John Held Junior and William Rose, who not only designed film posters but also designed illustrations and covers for comic books, paperbacks and pulp magazines (and who were thus responsible in a literal sense for the images associated with a number of popular genres).

Labels and names

In additition to images, Hollywood's inter-textual relay also circulates a number of generic labels, terms and names. The importance of labels and names has been touched on already. Their existence is one of the hallmarks of a genre, one of the signs of its institutional and social existence. This point has been stressed by Ryan (1981). During the course of her argument she refers to the work of Ben-Amos (1976) on folklore genres, and draws on the distinction he makes between 'ethnic' and 'analytical' categories, concepts and terms. Ben-Amos 'opposes the "ethnic genres" yielded by native taxonomy to the "analytical categories" made up by the specialist for their description and classification', she writes. In addition, 'he warns against the danger of "changing folk taxonomies, which are culture-bound and vary according to the speaker's cognitive system, into culture-free, analytical, unified and objective models of folk literature"' (1981: 113). Ryan herself reinforces this point. However, she goes on to propose a compromise, a way in which analytical categories and terms can still be of use:

> even if the generic system of every culture should be studied in its own right, there is no need to give up the possibility of describing its genres by means of cross-culturally applicable concepts. The gap between ethnic and analytical approaches to the problem of genre can be bridged by viewing analytical categories as building blocks for the characterization of genres, rather than as abstract generic concepts in themselves.
>
> (Ryan 1981: 113)

A similar compromise is adopted by Altman (1987) during the course of one of the few comparable discussions to be conducted in relation to the topic of genre in the cinema.

Altman is writing about culturally familiar – or 'native' – genres. His central concern is with the establishment of a generic corpus for subsequent analysis. In this context, he argues that the categories and terms provided by Hollywood and by the reviewers of its films have only a limited role to play. They may indicate the possible presence of a genre, but beyond that they are of little further use:

> The fact that a genre has previously been posited, defined, and delimited by Hollywood is taken only as *prime facie* evidence that generic levels of meaning are operative within or across a group of texts roughly designated

by the Hollywood term and its usage. The industrial/journalistic term thus founds a hypothesis about the presence of meaningful activity, but does not necessarily contribute a definition or delimitation of the genre in question.

(Altman 1987: 13)

Thus the location of industrial and journalistic terms is for Altman just the first step in a multi-stage process – and the only one in which such terms have a role to play. Having established an initial corpus, the task of 'the genre critic' is to subject the corpus to analysis, and to find a means by which to define and describe the structures, functions and systems specific to most of the films within it. Thus far, institutional terms and analytical categories more or less dovetail with one another. However, the next stage that Altman proposes involves the redefinition and reconstruction of the corpus itself:

Texts which correspond to a particular understanding of the genre, that is which provide ample material for a given method of analysis, will be retained within the generic corpus. Those which are not illuminated by the method developed . . . will simply be excluded from the final corpus.

(Altman 1987: 14)

At this point, institutional and analytic categories begin to diverge. 'The genre critic' replaces the former with the latter and includes or excludes films on that basis. He or she, though, is at this point in danger of producing a version of the gap identified by Ryan and Ben-Amos and of separating genre and genre analysis from the conditions and the features that define genres themselves. To that extent he or she risks undermining the two final tasks that Altman proposes: the construction of a history of the genre itself, and an analysis of the ways in which it is 'moulded by, functions within, and in turn informs the society of which it is a part' (ibid.: 14–15). For genres, as Todorov (1990) has pointed out, are public and institutional – not personal or critical – in nature.[1] It is 'always possible', he writes,

to discover a property common to two texts, and thus to put them together in a class. Is there any virtue in calling such a combination a 'genre'? I believe we will have a useful and operative notion that remains in keeping with the prevailing usage of the word if we agree to call genres only the classes of texts that have been historically perceived as such. Evidence of such perception is found first and foremost in discourse dealing with genres (metadiscursive discourse) and, sporadically and indirectly, in literary texts themselves.

(Todorov 1990: 17)

It is precisely because they 'exist as an institution' that genres can 'function as "horizons of expectation" for readers and as "models of writing" for authors' (ibid.: 17, note 9). (The term 'horizons of expectation' derives from Jauss 1982.)

It should be noted that Todorov's argument here is, as he himself points out, at odds with arguments he had previously made in favour of the notion of 'theoretical genres' – types or categories of work deducible as logical variants on the properties or conventions of particular forms of representation (Todorov 1975: 13–15; Ducrot and Todorov 1979: 149–52). Aside from Todorov's own work on the marvellous, the uncanny and the fantastic (all of which are defined as variants on a set of motivational conventions), the notion of theoretical genres has rarely been explored. In her Ph.D. thesis on a category of films she calls 'the apocalyptic', Sylvia Lynne Foil (1991) argues in favour of a 'conceptual approach' to genre, though in the end her own approach is closer to Altman's than it is to Todorov's. While further work in this area may be possible, it is probably best to distinguish theoretical genres from genres proper by renaming the former 'theoretical categories'.

In the passage cited above, Todorov is writing about literature, and High Literature at that. The 'metadiscursive discourse' to which he refers may therefore include the writings of critics and theorists, and the discourse produced by academies, universities, and other institutions of a similar kind. But as far as Hollywood is concerned, it is principally located in the industry's inter-textual relay. Testimony to the existence of genres – and evidence as to the boundaries of any particular generic corpus – is to be found primarily there. Moreover, it is only on the basis of this testimony that the history of any one genre and an analysis of its social functions and social significance can begin to be produced. For a genre's history is as much the history of a term as it is of the films to which the term has been applied; is as much a history of the consequently shifting boundaries of a corpus of texts as it is of the texts themselves.[2] The institutionalization of any generic term is a key aspect of the social existence – and hence the potential social significance – of any genre, the provenance or use of a term in Hollywood's inter-textual relay precisely an index of Hollywood's social presence and cultural power. In addition, sometimes the conjunction of a generic term, a corpus of films and the inter-textual relay can be of wider social and historical significance, a point exemplified by the early history of the western.

The early western

According both to Eric Partridge's *Dictionary of Slang and Unconventional English* (1961: 1345) and to the researches of Jean-Louis Leutrat (1987), the first use of the term 'western' as a generic noun (rather than as an adjective) occurred in or around 1910. Leutrat draws attention to the fact that this terminological event coincided with a number of important developments in the American film industry, among them the shooting of increasing numbers of 'western' films in and around California, and the increasing specialization of a number of companies, in particular Selig, Essanay, Bison and Flying A, in the production of such films. He also notes that it was not until the 1920s that the term itself was fully established:

> It was in that same year, 1910, that we encounter one of the first uses of the word 'Western' as a noun. The study of genres has as its point of departure testimony as to the existence of genres. A genre is what it is collectively believed to be at any given point in time. Up until the mid-1920s, the word 'Western' mostly enabled one to be more precise about a traditional generic term. It remained an adjective. In his 1915 book, *Buck Purvin and the Movies*, Charles E. Van Loan includes a director named

Jimmy Montague who 'had a reputation for making sensational cinemato-graphic dramas'. These *dramas* are films which concern themselves indiscriminately with the civil war, with the circus, with Indians, with animals, etc. They are set just as effectively at sea as in the American West, the Great North, or the deserts of Africa and Asia. And in order to designate these groups of films, categories inherited from the theatre and the novel of the preceding century are used: melodrama, drama, comedy, romance . . . 'Western' can further characterize any of these terms: it allows the specification of an atmosphere, a setting. In 1904, the Kleine Optical Company's catalogue proposed five generic categories – the Western was not among them. An article on nickelodeons published in the *Saturday Evening Post* in 1907 reprinted the publicity material produced by a film production company: each film title is followed by a brief phrase in parenthesis indicating its genre – the word 'western' does not appear at all. In 1910, an article in the *Moving Picture World* notes that 'There seems to exist among the exhibitors we questioned a powerful and increasing demand for [. . .] Indian and Western subjects [. . .].' In another article published in the same journal a year later, there is a report on films (Western and Indian films) being shot around Los Angeles: it is noted that most of Selig's, Kalem's and Biograph's films are 'westerns'.

(Leutrat 1987: 127–8; my translation)

One of the implications of Leutrat's research is that a film like *The Great Train Robbery* (1903), often retrospectively hailed as an early example of the western, is unlikely, in fact, to have been perceived as a western at the time the film was made.[3] Charles Musser makes a similar point, arguing that the contemporary success of *The Great Train Robbery* was due to its location within generic paradigms provided by melodrama, 'the chase film', 'the railway genre' and 'the crime film' rather than the western:

Kenneth McGowan attributed this success . . . to the fact that the film was 'the first important Western', William Everson and George Fenin find it important because it is 'the blueprint for all Westerns'. These, however, are retrospective readings. One reason for *The Great Train Robbery's*, popularity was its ability to incorporate so many trends, genres and strategies fundamental to the institution of cinema at that time. The film includes elements of both re-enactment of contemporary events (the train hold-up was modeled after recently reported crimes) and refers to a well-known stage melodrama by its title. Perhaps most importantly, *The Great Train Robbery* was part of a violent crime genre which had been imported from England a few months earlier. Porter [the film's director] was consciously working (and cinema patrons viewing) within a framework established by Sheffield Photo's *Daring Daylight Burglary*, British Gaumont/Walter Haggar's *Desperate Poaching Affair* [sic] and R. W. Paul's *Trailed by Bloodhounds* . . . [Thus] When initially released, *The Great Train Robbery* was not primarily perceived in the context of the Western. Its success did encourage the production of other Westerns but other films of crime – Lubin's *Bold Bank Robbery*, Paley and Steiner's *Burned at the Stake*, and

Porter's own *Capture of the Yegg Bank Robbers* . . . It was only when the
Western genre emerged in the nickelodeon era that *The Great Train Robbery*
was interpreted from this new perspective.

(Musser 1984: 56–7)[4]

The importance of 'the nickelodeon era' is also stressed in Robert Anderson's
account of the early western (1979). Anderson is particularly concerned with the
role played by the western in shifting the balance of power between American and
non-American film companies in the domestic market in the US in the latter half of the
1900s. Like Leutrat, he stresses the role of companies like Selig and the American Film
Manufacturing Company and the importance of shooting on location in the West. (An
advertisement for the latter's Flying A westerns in the *Moving Picture World* (8 April
1911: 779) draws attention to the fact that they were 'made IN the West – OF the West –BY
our Western Company'. Emphases in original.) And like Leutrat, he sees 1910 as 'a
pivotal year' (1979: 25). The key period overall is the period between 1907 and 1911.
It is then that the western emerges as a 'uniquely American product':

> The explosive increase in production and popularity of perhaps the
> most definitively American type of narrative film, the Western, from
> 1907–1911 was accomplished through the successful manipulation of
> the American marketplace by domestic film companies who by self-
> consciously promoting a uniquely American product (in marked contrast
> to the stage dramas of European art photoplays), corralled the nickels and
> enthusiasm of motion picture patrons nationwide. By late 1909, in an
> article entitled 'An American School of Picture Drama', *Moving Picture
> World* referred to the Western as the 'foundation' of American dramatic
> narrative and recognized those pictures with Wild West or Indian themes
> as being 'the most popular subjects'.

(Anderson 1979: 22)

The emergence of 'An American School of Moving Picture Drama', and of a
generic term for its product, is, then, coincident with the emergence of American
film companies – and the American film industry in general – as the dominant force
in the domestic market in America itself. It is coincident too, as Leutrat and as Abel
(1998) point out, both with a resurgence of American nationalism and American
imperialism and, in the wake of the official closure of the frontier in 1890, with the
emergence of what Leutrat calls the 'synthetic' western (and a synthetic West) across
an array of cultural practices in America, from rodeos and Wild West Shows to novels
and pulp magazines, from comic books and paintings to the work of ethnographers,
photographers, folklore societies and academic historians.[5] The appearance of the
western as a body of films, and the appearance of 'the western' as a term at this time,
is therefore of crucial and multiple national significance.[6]

The same kind of significance cannot, of course, be claimed for all generic terms.
Nevertheless, the emergence and use of such terms is always of *some* significance, if
only within the industry itself. Of significance too, as is implied by Musser's argument,
is the distinction between terms used retrospectively by critics and theorists, and the
terms in use within the industry's relay when a particular film – or when a particular

group of films – is made. Two terms of particular interest here are '*film noir*', a critical term first used in the mid-to-late 1940s in France to describe a number of then contemporary Hollywood films, and 'melodrama', a term used both by Hollywood's relay and by a number of recent critics and theorists, though with rather different emphases and meanings.

Notes

1. Of course, viewers, spectators and fans often devise their own 'unofficial' or improvised terms. Richard Maltby cites the example of a reader of *Picturegoer* magazine who expressed a preference for 'Love and Romance' films, but distinguished between 'Boy-meets-girl' romances and 'triangle stories' (1995: 108). As always, terms like these perform a generic function for the person – or the people – concerned. The same is true of the terms devised by critics and theorists. That does not mean, though, that they are always indicative of production trends or of genres as such.

2. Rick Altman unwittingly confirms this point when he notes that 'the first musicals built around entertainers and their music were not identified as "musicals"', that 'the use of "musical" as a free-standing term designating a specific genre did not achieve general acceptance until the 1930–1 season', and that 'Not until 1933, with the definitive merger of music-making and romantic comedy, did the term "musical" abandon its adjectival, descriptive function and become a noun' (1996a: 277). He himself argues that early musical films already constituted 'the type of category we call film genre', but that they had yet to become 'genre films'. However, it could be argued that early musical films were far too disparate in kind to constitute a genre, and that this is precisely reflected in the lack of a noun to describe them. See Barrios (1995), in particular the chapter headed 'Is It a Musical?' (309–22).

3. This does not mean, of course, that representations of 'the West' or of 'the frontier' did not exist, or that these representations were unfamiliar to audiences in the early 1900s. Far from it. What it does mean is that they had yet to cohere into anything resembling a single genre. For a survey of the earliest films representing western scenes, views and activities, see Jones (1980). For a survey of representations of the West and the frontier prior to the advent of the western itself, see Buscombe (1988b: 18–22). For other short surveys, see the essays in Truettner (1991), in Aquila (1996: 21–105, 243–68), and in Milner, O'Connor and Sandweiss (1994: 671–833).

4. The references here are to MacGowan (1965: 114) and Fenin and Everson (1962: 49).

5. Leutrat's thesis is thus consonant with the work of Richard W. Etulain and Lee Clark Mitchell on the western novel. Etulain argues that 'the Western was born in the first twenty-five years of the present century' (1973: 76), and Mitchell that most of the fundamental codes of the western, especially those to do with landscape and gender, were either established or synthesized in recognizably modern generic form by Owen Wister in *The Virginian* in 1902 and by Zane Grey in *Riders of the Purple Sage* in 1912. He writes: 'Not until Owen Wister's *The Virginian* . . . does the Western reach its acknowledged embodiment, the first in a line of narratives that stretch throughout this century' (1996: 9). However, the extent to which these codes hegemonized all western films or only some, and hence the extent to which the synthetic western was – and is – a heterogeneous rather than a homogeneous phenomenon, remains a matter of research and debate.

6. The popularity of the western in Europe at this time, as noted by Vasey among others (1997: 274 n. 2), merely augments this significance: the western clearly helped establish a distinctively American presence in the European market and on European screens as well as American ones.

References

Abel, R. (1998) '"Our Country"/Whose Country? The "Americanisation" Project in Early Westerns', in Buscombe and Pearson 1998, 77–95.

Altman, R. (ed) (1987) *The American Film Musical,* Bloomington: Indiana University Press.

Altman, R. (ed) (1996a) 'Cinema and Genre', in Nowell-Smith 1996, 294–85.

Andersen, R. (1979) 'The Role of the Western Film Genre in Industry Competition, 1907–1911', *Journal of the University Film Association* 31, 2: 19–27.

Aquila, R. (ed.) (1996) *Wanted Dead or Alive: The American West in Popular Culture,* Urbana: University of Illinios Press.

Aumont, J., Bergala, A., Marie, M. and Vernet, M. (1992) *Aesthetics of Film,* trans. R. Neupert, Austin: University of Texas Press.

Barrios, R. (1995) *A Song in the Dark: The Birth of the Musical Film,* New York: Oxford University Press.

Ben-Amos, D. (1976) 'Analytical Categories and Ethnic Genres', in D. Ben-Amos (ed.), *Folklore Genres,* Austin: University of Texas Press 215–42.

Bergala, A. (1978) '*Dora et la Lanterne Magique*', *Cahiers du Cinèma* 287: 52–3.

Brewster, B. (1987) 'Film', in D. Cohn-Sherbok and M. Irwin (eds), *Exploring Reality,* London: Allen and Unwin, 145–67.

Buscome, E. (1988b) 'The Western: A Short History', in Buscombe 1998a, 15–54.

Carroll, N. (1981) 'Nightmare and the Horror Film: The Symbolic Biology of Fantastic Beings' *Film Quarterly* 34, 3: 16–25.

Cowie, E. (1984) 'Fantasia', *m/f* 9: 71–105.

Culler, J. (1975) *Structuralist Poetics. Structuralism, Linguistics and the Study of Literature,* London: Routledge.

Ducrot, O. and Todorov, T. (1979) *Encyclopedic Dictionary of the Sciences of Language,* trans. C. Porter. Baltimore: Johns Hopkins University Press.

Ellis, J. (1981) *Visible Fictions: Cinema: Television: Video,* London: Routledge

Etulain, R. W. (1973) 'The Historical Development of the Western', *Journal of Popular Culture* 7, 3: 75–84.

Fenin, G. and Everson, W. K. (1962) *The Western: From Silents to Cinemera,* New York: Orion Press.

Foil, S. L. (1991) *An Examination of the Conceptual Approach to Film Genre with a Specific Application to the Definition of the Apocalyptic,* Northwestern University Ph.D. thesis, 1989, Ann Arbor: UMI Dissertation Information Service.

Frend, S. ([1908] 1985a) 'Creative Writers and Day-Dreaming', trans. J. Strachey, in *Art and Literature,* The Pelican Freud Library, Vol. 14, Harmondsworth: Penguin, 129–41.

Genette, G. (1969) 'Vraisemblance et Motivation', in *Figures II,* Paris: Seuil, 71–99.

Gomenry, D. (1992) *Shared Pleasures: A History of Movie Presentation in the United States,* London: British Film Institute.

Grant, M. (1994) 'James Whale's *Frankenstein*: The Horror Film and the Symbolic Biology of the Cinematic Monster', in S. Bann (ed.), *Frankenstein: Creation and Monstrosity*, London: Reaktion Books, 113–35.

Jones, D. E. (1980) 'The Earliest Western Films', *Journal of Popular film and Television* 8, 2: 42–6.

Leutrat, J.-L. (1987) Le Western: Archèologie d'un Genre, Lyon: Presses Universitaires de Lyon.

Lukow, G. and Ricci, S. (1984) 'The "Audience" Goes "Public": Inter-Textuality, Genre and the Responsibilities of Film Literacy', *On Film* 12: 29–36.

MacGowan, K. (1965) *Behind the Screen*, New York: Deiacorte.

Maltby, R. (1995) *Hollywood Cinema: An Introduction*, Oxford: Blackwell.

Milner, C. A. II, O' Connor, C. A. and Sandweiss, M. A. (eds) (1994) *The Oxford History of the American West*, New York: Oxford University Press.

Mitchell, L. C. (1996) *Westerns: Making the Man in Fiction and Film*, Chicago: Chicago University Press.

Musser, C. (1984) 'The Travel Genre in 1903–1904: Moving Toward Fictional Narratives', *Iris* 2, 1: 47–59.

Nash, M. (1976) '*Vampyr* and the Fantastic', *Screen* 17, 3: 29–67.

Neale, S. (1980) *Genre*, London: British Film Institute.

Neale, S. and Krutnik, F. (1990) *Popular Film and Television Comedy*, London: Routledge.

Partridge, E. (1961) *Dictionary of Slang and Unconventional English*, 2 vols, London: Routledge and Kegan Paul.

Ryan, M.-L. (1981) 'Introduction: On the Why, What and How of Generic Taxonomy', *Poetics* 10: 127–47.

Stones, B. (1993) *America Goes to the Movies: 100 Years of Motion Picture Exhibition*, Hollywood: National Association of Theatre Owners.

Todorov, T. (1975) *The Fantastic: A Structural Approach to a Literary Genre*, trans. R. Howard, Ithaca: Cornell University Press.

Todorov, T. (1977) *The Poetics of Prose,* trans. R. Howard, Ithaca: Cornell University Press.

Todorov, T. (1981) *Introduction to Poetics,* trans. R. Howard, Brighton: Harvester Press.

Todorov, T. (1990) *Genres in Discourse*, trans. C. Porter, Cambridge: Cambridge University Press.

Truettner, W. H. (ed.) (1991) *The West as America: Reinterpreting Images of the Frontier, 1820–1920,* Washington, DC: Smithsonian Institution Press.

Vasey, R. (1997) *The World According to Hollywood*, 1918–1939, Exeter: University of Exeter Press.

Critical connections

Hall (Readings 4 and 10) defines cultural codes as a common stock of social knowledge, assumed to be shared by members of a particular culture, which help to orient how people make sense of the world around them. Film genres work in a similar way. They have their own cues, codes and patterns of recognition and understanding that spectators bring with them to the viewing process. Musicals, westerns, detective, gangster and war films all embody their own regimes of verisimilitude – the conventions of the genre which indicate what is probable, plausible, appropriate, even obligatory, within that particular film genre. Whereas westerns and gangster films are likely to contain gunplay and violent conflict, musicals will feature singing. Of course, there can be, and is, considerable interplay and overlap between genres, and directors have made an artform of cutting across and playing with particular genre (and wider social and cultural) conventions. Quentin Tarantino's films (for example, *Pulp Fiction* (1994) or *Kill Bill – Volumes I and II* (1993, 1994)) creating highly stylised post-modern pastiches that blend the conventions of 1950s detective films and Japanese Kung Fu movies. In *Blue Velvet* (1986) David Lynch mixed the genres of film noir and horror to considerable effect, playing with sound, camera placement and pacing to create a kind of horror noir.

The usefulness of genre analysis as a method for reading narrative texts is illustrated elsewhere in this book. These texts are not confined to the medium of film. Indeed, as Neale notes, the seminal statement in genre analysis came from within literary criticism. Tzvetan Todorov's *Typology of Detective Fiction* (Reading 22) uses the detective story to illustrate the concepts of genre, sub-genre and verisimilitude. Barry Langford (Reading 26) and Brian Jarvis (Reading 27) use genre to examine gangster and serial killer movies respectively. It is useful for media criminologists to understand film genres and regimes of verisimilitude because, just like the analyses of crime news discussed above, a more comprehensive grasp of expressive cultural forms, whether news, film or literature, comes from exploring not only the media text is isolation, but also the methods, rules and social processes that contributed to shaping its construction and intelligibility to its audiences.

Discussion questions

- How can concepts like 'genre' and 'verisimilitude' help media criminologists 'read' crime film?
- Try to identify the principal characteristics of different genres of crime film – for example, gangster, detective, film noir, or Western (see also Readings 22 and 26).
- In what ways have recent crime films played on the postmodern 'knowingness' of media-savvy movie consumers?

Theodore Sasson

FRAME ANALYSIS (1995)

Introduction and context

ONE OF THE KEY WAYS of understanding how people think about crime and justice is by investigating how they talk about it. This excerpt from Theodore Sasson's (1995) *Crime Talk: How Citizens Construct a Social Problem* describes one method of establishing what crime means to people through considering how they articulate and express their views about it in open conversation. Influenced by symbolic interactionism, labelling, and the defining work of Spector and Kitsuse in the 1970s, Sasson's study is located within the constructionist paradigm for social problems research. Unlike objectivist scholars (and the vast majority of social scientists are in some sense objectivist),[1] constructionists are largely unconcerned with examining the objective nature of social problems (i.e. their sources, dimensions and possible remedies). Rather, they are interested primarily in how issues like crime come to be viewed as a social problem in the first place, and how they are shaped in media discourses and the public imagination. Constructionists thus argue that a given social condition – whether it be mugging, infanticide, nuclear pollution, child sex abuse, or global warming – only becomes a social problem when groups and individuals engage in 'claims-making' about it, both 'defining some putative condition as a problem, and asserting the need for eradicating, ameliorating, or otherwise changing that condition' (Kitsuse and Spector, 1973: 415).

Of central significance to this kind of analysis are the different 'frames' people may draw from or deploy in order to 'make sense' of the problem of crime.

[1] Notions of objectivism do play a pivotal role in constructionist debates, and have led to fundamental rifts within the constructionist project (Woolgar and Pawluch, 1985; Spector and Kistuse, 1977).

Is it a question, for example, of the state being soft on crime, or more a matter of people offending because of structurally limited opportunities? How people talk about crime offers clear and important insights into their understanding of the nature, causes and consequences of criminal offending, and their impressions of the most (and least) suitable remedies to the 'crime problem'. To locate crime talk within a suitable analytical framework, Sasson draws from media discourse and the speeches and publications of various partisan stakeholders – for example, politicians and activists – in order to identify publicly competing crime 'frames'. These frames are: faulty system, blocked opportunities, social breakdown, media violence and racist system. Focus group discussions are then used to track the relative prevalence and success of the different 'frames' within participants' crime talk. Qualitative focus groups are chosen over quantitative survey methods since, as Sasson puts it, 'human consciousness is bound up with social context and language, both rife with shades of symbolic meaning . . . Surveys, in spite of the best efforts of skilled researchers, cannot adequately deal with this complexity'. This prioritisation of qualitative over quantitative methods to explore how people actively assemble meaning from personal experience, accepted wisdom, media representations and other sources, closely echoes the research philosophy of Jenny Kitzinger (Reading 13), who offers an historical overview of audience research from its origins to the present day.

Frame analysis

The research strategy adopted for this study builds on the work of Gamson (1988, 1992), Gamson and Modigliani (1989, 1987), Neuman *et al.* (1992) and Beckett (1994a). Known as "frame analysis," the strategy is best regarded as a methodology for conducting research in the constructionist paradigm. It rests on three basic premises.

1   People should be regarded as active assemblers of meaning. In constructing accounts of public issues, they draw upon the resources at their disposal including popular wisdom, their personal experiences, and bits of media discourse. To assemble this raw material into coherent and meaningful accounts, they select from the range of interpretive frameworks available in the culture for making meaning on the issue at hand (cf. Miller and Holstein, 1993). [. . .]

    Frames on public problems typically feature a diagnostic component that identifies a condition as intolerable and attributes blame or causality, and a prognostic component that prescribes one or more courses of ameliorative action (cf. Snow and Benford, 1988; Gusfield, 1981). Frames can be evoked through catch-phrases, historical exemplars, public figures and other types of condensing symbols (Gamson, 1988). Finally, frames tend to have more or less standard rebuttals.

2   The creation of meaning through the work of framing occurs in various forums, including academic journals, the mass media, and everyday conversation (cf. Ibarra and Kitsuse, 1993). These ought best be treated as discrete cultural systems each with its own norms and vocabularies and each deserving of study in its own right. [. . .]

3   Political conflicts on particular issues are fought out as symbolic contests
      between contesting frames. Politicians, grass roots activists, journalists and
      other claimsmakers vie with one another to get their preferred frames before
      the public and to rebut those of their rivals. They measure their own success in
      this venture by the degree of visibility they win for their preferred frames
      (Gamson *et al.*, 1992). [. . .]

The contesting frames

In order to establish a catalogue of culturally available frames on street crime, I examined the speeches and publications of partisans on various "sides" of the issue.
There are two advantages to this strategy: First, frame sponsors tend to express their
views in an ideologically coherent manner, thus presenting relatively "pure" or unadulterated frames. Second, by first consulting sponsors rather than mass media products,
I could create a catalogue that comes close to including all culturally available frames
rather than only those that enjoy prominence in the mass media.

My review of the activist and partisan discourse yielded a working catalogue of
frames. I then tested the "fit" of this catalogue on the sample of media discourse assembled
for the study. My aim at this stage was to make sure that the frame catalogue offered
the right balance between precision (it should represent all of the important views and
ideas in the crime debate) and economy (it should summarize and simplify the debate).
The final, revised catalogue included five basic frames that I labeled *Faulty System, Blocked
Opportunities, Social Breakdown, Media Violence* and *Racist System*.

Faulty System

The "law and order" perspective described in the introduction is best captured in the
frame *Faulty System*. This frame regards crime as a consequence of impunity: People
do crimes because they know they can get away with them. The police are handcuffed
by liberal judges. The prisons, bursting at their seams, have revolving doors for
serious offenders. [. . .] The only way to enhance public safety is to increase the swift-
ness, certainty and severity of punishment. [. . .] Adequate funding for police, courts
and prisons must be made available. In our failure to act, warns political scientist
James Q. Wilson, "We thereby trifle with the wicked, make sport of the innocent, and
encourage the calculating" (P.A.F., 1993:15).

Faulty System is sponsored by Republican politicians, conservative policy analysts,
and most criminal justice professionals. It can be symbolically condensed with the
mug-shot of the convicted rapist Willie Horton, or by the image of inmates passing
through a revolving door on a prison gate (both symbols courtesy of commercials
aired on behalf of George Bush in the 1988 presidential campaign).

Blocked Opportunities

The frame *Blocked Opportunities* depicts crime as a consequence of inequality and
discrimination, especially as they manifest themselves in unemployment, poverty,
and inadequate educational opportunities. People commit crimes when they discover
that the legitimate means for attaining material success are blocked. In the words of

President Lyndon B. Johnson, "Unemployment, ignorance, disease, filth, poor housing, congestion, discrimination – all of these things contribute to the great crime wave that is sweeping through our nation" (Beckett, 1994a). [. . .] Since the 1960s the deindustrialization of American cities and attendant disappearance of good paying blue-collar jobs has steadily worsened prospects for the urban poor. Growing desperation promotes violence as well as property crime; in the words of criminologist David Bruck, "If you're going to create a sink-or-swim society, you have to expect people to thrash before they go down" (P.A.F., 1993:22). To reduce crime, government must ameliorate the social conditions that cause it. [. . .] *Blocked Opportunities* is sponsored by liberal and Left policy analysts and by some liberal Democrat politicians. It can be symbolically condensed through references to the dead-end jobs reserved for inner-city youth, such as "flipping burgers at McDonald's."

Social Breakdown

The frame *Social Breakdown* depicts crime as a consequence of family and community disintegration. Witness the skyrocketing rates of divorce and out-of-wedlock births. Witness the indifference of urbanites to the crime that plagues their communities. Family breakdown in the context of urban indifference has loosened the moral and social bonds that in better times discouraged crime. As President Clinton explained in his 1994 State of the Union message, "In America's toughest neighborhoods, meanest streets, and poorest rural areas, we have seen a stunning breakdown of community, family and work – the heart and soul of civilized society. This has created a vast vacuum into which violence, drugs and gangs have moved." The remedy for the problem can be found in collective efforts to reconstitute family and community through moral exhortation, neighborhood associations, crime watches and community policing. [. . .] The frame can be symbolically condensed through laments over the decline of "family values" and by the figure of Kitty Genovese, the New York woman who was stabbed to death while her neighbors looked passively on.

Social Breakdown is typically expressed in a neutral, ostensibly non-ideological fashion, but the frame also has conservative and liberal versions. The conservative versions attribute family and community breakdown to "permissiveness," the protest movements of the 1960s and 70s (e.g., civil rights, feminism) and government-sponsored antipoverty initiatives (e.g., "welfare"). [. . .] The liberal versions, in contrast, attribute family and community breakdown to unemployment, racial discrimination, deindustrialization and capital flight.

Media Violence

The frame *Media Violence* depicts crime as a consequence of violence on television, in the movies and in popular music. Violence in the mass media undermines respect for life. By the time the average child reaches age 18, notes Dr. Thomas Elmendorf in testimony before the House Subcommittee on Communication, "he will have witnessed . . . some 18,000 murders and countless highly detailed incidents of robbery, arson, bombings, shooting, beatings, forgery, smuggling and torture." As a result, "Television has become a school of violence and a college for crime" (1976:764). To reduce violence in the society we must first reduce it in the mass media.

Media Violence can be symbolically condensed through reference to violent television programs (e.g., *Miami Vice*) or musicians whose lyrics are said to promote violence (e.g., "Guns N' Roses," "2 Live Crew"). The frame is sponsored by citizen lobby organizations (e.g., the Massachusetts-based group Action for Children's Television), and, periodically, by members of Congress and the Department of Justice.

Racist System

The fifth frame, *Racist System*, derives its essence from a depiction of the criminal justice system rather than an attribution of responsibility for crime. The frame depicts the courts and police as racist agents of oppression. In the words of Johnson Administration Undersecretary of State Nicholas deB. Katzenbach, "We have in these United States lived under a dual system of justice, one for the white, one for the black" (1968:616). Police resources are dedicated to the protection of low crime white neighborhoods rather than high crime minority ghettos. Black offenders are more likely to be arrested, convicted and sentenced to prison than whites who commit comparable offenses. And the death penalty is administered in a racist fashion. In some versions of this frame, the putative purpose of the criminal justice system is to suppress a potentially rebellious underclass.

Racist System is sponsored by civil rights and civil liberties activists and by Left intellectuals. It can be condensed by reference to Rodney King or other well-known targets of racially motivated police violence.

Rebuttals

Each of these five frames has a number of standard rebuttals. *Faulty System*, for example, is frequently negated with the claim that imprisonment "hardens" offenders; *Blocked Opportunities* with the claim that most poor people are straight as an arrow; *Social Breakdown* with the claim that rhetoric about the "nuclear family" is in fact thinly veiled hostility for feminism; and so on. [. . .] Table 1 illustrates the frames' key components.

There is one more matter to clarify concerning my catalogue of frames. In contemporary discourse, crime is often attributed to drugs and guns. I made an early decision that drugs and guns are part of the crime problem – things that demand explanation and not explanations in themselves. If in the account that follows "drugs" and "guns" are conspicuously absent as "causes" of crime, it is for this reason. [. . .]

Popular discourse

The shortcomings of survey research for gathering data on public opinion are widely recognized: Surveys tend to produce findings that reflect the concepts and categories of their authors rather than their subjects (Reinharz, 1984); they treat opinions as stable when in fact opinions vary with context (Potter and Wetherell, 1987; Bennett, 1980); and they foster an image of people as isolated individuals rather than members of particular cultures and subcultures (Blumer, 1948). At the root of the problem is that survey research rests on a faulty depiction of the research subject. It assumes that each

Table 1 Crime Frames

	Diagnosis	Prognosis	Condensing Symbols
Faulty System	Crime stems from criminal justice leniency and inefficiency	The criminal justice system needs to "get tough"	Willie Horton "Handcuffed police" "Revolving door justice"
Blocked Opportunities	Crime stems from poverty and inequality	The government must address the "root causes" of crime by creating jobs and reducing poverty	"Flipping Burgers" at McDonald's
Social Breakdown	Crime stems from family and community breakdown	Citizens should band together to recreate traditional communities	"Take back the streets" Kitty Genovese "Family values"
Media Violence	Crime stems from violence in the mass media	The government should regulate violent imagery in the media	"Life imitates art" 2 Live Crew Guns n' Roses
Racist System	The criminal justice system operates in a racist fashion	African Americans should band together to demand justice	Rodney King Crown Heights Charles Stuart

person carries about in her head a fixed and relatively simple structure of attitudes. But in the real world, human consciousness is bound up with social context and language, both rife with shades of symbolic meaning. What people think and say depends in part on who is asking, who is listening, how the question is posed, and a host of related details. Surveys, in spite of the best efforts of skilled researchers, cannot adequately deal with this complexity.

Michael Billig's (1987, 1991) depiction of the research subject is perhaps the alternative most compatible with the constructionist approach to public opinion. He contends that thinking is nothing more than a dialogue or an argument occurring in a single self. Hence public conversation and private thinking can be treated analytically as part and parcel of the same process. The best way to analyze both is to regard people as orators and to examine the rhetorical components of their arguments. Prominent among the latter are "common-places" – the contrary themes, maxims, folk wisdom, values, and so forth, that together comprise a culture's common sense. But how can we sample the work of everyday orators?

Peer group discussions

Peer group discussions (Gamson, 1992) are ideally suited to producing discourse for the kind of analysis Billig proposes. Like the conventional focus group (Morgan, 1988), of which they are a variation, they permit the researcher to listen in as subjects use their own categories and vocabularies to cooperatively create meaning. But unlike conventional focus groups, the participants in the peer group are acquainted with one another *outside* of the research setting. This difference offers two advantages: First, peer group participants typically interact with greater intensity and less reserve than their focus group counterparts. This, in turn, permits the facilitator to minimize his or her involvement in the discussion and results in richer transcripts. Second, because the peer groups have a social existence independent of the sociologist's contrivance, their discourse can be regarded with greater confidence as reflective of the particular subcultures from which they are drawn.

Recruitment

I decided to constitute peer groups from a sample of neighborhood crime watch groups because the latter are venues in which urbanites regularly meet to talk about crime. Working from a list provided by the crime watch division of the Boston Police Department, I contacted group organizers by mail and telephone and asked them to host a discussion with four to six members of their group. To achieve a racial balance in group type I recruited both from communities of color and neighborhoods that are mostly white. In all, I contacted about 60 organizers and arranged 20 successful interviews (I also conducted several pilot sessions to rehearse the format). My effort to achieve racial balance proved successful: Of the twenty interview groups, eight were white, nine black, and three mixed.

The groups were from the working and middle class residential areas of seven Boston neighborhoods. [. . .]

These neighborhoods have in common their close proximity to what Wilson (1987) describes as "underclass" zones. The frontier dividing the shady streets and well-kept houses of the former from the vacant lots and boarded up buildings of the latter is sometimes as narrow as a single street. This is especially true for several of the black groups. But even in these cases the distinction between the two areas is real enough.

Boston neighborhoods endure a great deal of crime, a fact that becomes especially apparent when we compare the rates of street crime offenses within the city with those statewide. The city comprises less than 10% of Massachusetts's population, but approximately one third of all homicides statewide, one fourth of all rapes, and nearly one half of all robberies, occur within the city (U.S. Department of Justice, 1992). Notably, however, while most city neighborhoods suffer crime rates that are higher than those statewide, the aggregate figures reported here mask the disproportionate concentration of street crime in Boston's minority neighborhoods. In 1990, for example, 81% of all homicides, 54% of all rapes and 46% of all robberies occurred in Roxbury, Dorchester and Mattapan, the three neighborhoods from which all of the black groups participating in this study were drawn (Boston Police Department, 1992).

The discussions

The discussions were structured around six questions aimed at generating discourse on the dimensions of the crime problem, its sources, and its most promising remedies. They were run by a facilitator whose race matched that of the group members. Matching the race of the facilitator and group members was important because doing so minimized the influence that norms of politeness – or against the airing of "dirty laundry" – might otherwise have had on the discussions. The first pilot discussion was conducted in the Fall of 1991; the final discussion was in the Winter of 1993.

The interview schedule was designed with two goals in mind: First, I wanted to ensure that the conversationalists would have ample opportunity to come up with their own shared frames on crime. Second, I wanted to be sure to get their reactions to the frames that are the subject of this study. Accordingly, the schedule began with two general questions aimed at sparking open conversation on the dimensions and sources of the crime problem. These questions were followed by a series of three statements, one representing each of the first three frames described above. The conversationalists were asked to state whether they agreed or disagreed with each of the statements, and to explain their viewpoints.

The frame *Racist System* was not prompted with a statement; instead, reaction to it was elicited separately through a question about a highly publicized murder investigation that occasioned public discourse on police violations of civil rights. I decided to trigger *Racist System* using this *indirect* approach because of the highly charged nature of its claims. [. . .]

In contrast to the other frames, *Media Violence* was not prompted in any fashion whatsoever. Where it emerged in the discussions it did so spontaneously. In fact, it was only after examining the discussion transcripts that I decided to code for the presence of the frame.

The facilitators did not participate in the discussions in any way, beyond asking the interview questions. Upon arrival at each session, they explained to the participants that they would be audiotaping the discussion and taking notes in order to keep track of who was speaking. After asking each question, they broke off eye contact by attending to the task of note-taking. The conversationalists were thus, in effect, left to negotiate their own response to each question.

Typicality of the sample

Who participated in the discussions? To what population can we generalize from this sample? In all, 110 Boston residents participated in the peer group discussions. The profile that follows is based on information provided by the participants in a brief questionnaire filled out at the conclusion of each session. The sample population is more racially balanced than the larger population of Boston (50% of the participants are white, 47% African American) but underrepresents Hispanic and Asian Americans (less than 3% of the sample). It is also more female (71%) and a bit better educated than the larger population (40% finished college). With respect to age, it is right on target for people 60 and older (21%), but overrepresents people in the 40–59 bracket at the expense of younger residents (42 and 26% of the sample, respectively).

The most intuitively significant characteristic of the sample is that it is comprised of participants in crime watch groups. But for three reasons, this turns out to be less important than at first it might seem. First, the participants in this study are not anticrime zealots. For most, crime watch membership involves no more than attending meetings in a neighbor's living room a few times each year. Second, while the participants are certainly fearful of crime, survey research (Stinchcombe *et al.*, 1980; Cullen, Clark, Cullen, and Mathers, 1985) has failed to identify any relationship between this variable and attitudes about crime's causes and remedies. Third, research has also failed to sustain the common sense notion that people who participate in crime watch are either unusually fearful or unusually punitive. After reviewing the best studies in this area, Lewis and Salem (1986:129) conclude that "there is no systematic evidence that an individual's attitude toward crime is associated with participation in collective responses."

Thus, with respect to the issue of generalizability, the fact that the participants attend crime watch meetings is likely a red herring. But there is no getting around the limitations associated with my choice of a qualitative research strategy. In general, qualitative techniques afford greater accuracy with respect to a given sample population ("internal validity"), but they do so at the cost of precision when generalizing to some larger population ("external validity"). This tradeoff is somewhat less troubling when studying consciousness about crime than when attempting to predict the outcome of a closely contested election (cf. Roberts, 1992). Nevertheless, the relatively small and nonrandom nature of the study sample means that we ought not use it as a basis for making claims about Americans as a whole.

Who, then, do the study participants represent? A reasonable supposition is that they are typical of their neighbors and the kinds of people who live in neighborhoods of the same type. For whites, this means urban neighborhoods that are racially integrated (if primarily white) and that adjoin high crime "underclass" areas. For blacks, this means the nicer streets and blocks in segregated minority communities. [. . .]

There is one final point to be made concerning the study sample and design. The peer group technique is itself a device for minimizing the kind of sample bias that bedevils qualitative researchers who use more conventional interviewing techniques. Because the discussion created by the group is a collective product, it tends to reflect the common sense of the subculture from which its participants are drawn. Indeed, as Gamson points out (1992:192), meaningful interaction within a group is only possible to the extent that its members share taken-for-granted assumptions about the world – *intersubjectivity*, in Schutz's (1967) term. Group interaction dynamics thus tend to discourage the expression of marginal ideas, encouraging instead ideas that are in broad currency within a particular subculture. This tends to be the case regardless of the precise composition of the group. While the presence of a few "outliers" (individuals with idiosyncratic views) can badly skew the results of conventional interview research, their presence within a peer group tends not to pose so much of a problem.

References

Beckett, Katherine. 1994a. *Crime and Drugs in Contemporary American Politics.* Unpublished Doctoral Dissertation. University of California at Los Angeles.

Bennett, W. Lance. (1990) *Public Opinioin in American Politics*. New York: Harcourt, Brace, Javanovich.

Billig, Michael. (1987) *Arguing and Thinking*. Cambridge, UK: Cambridge University Press.

Billig, Michael. (1991) *Ideology and Opinions*. Newbury Park, CA: Sage.

Blumer, Herbert. (1948) "Public Opinion and Public Opinion Polling." *American Sociological Review* 13:542–54.

Boston Police Department (B.P.D.). (1992) Office of Strategic Planning and Policy Development, Boston, M.A.

Cullen, Francis T., and Gregory A. Clark, John B. Cullen an Richard A. Mathers, 1985. "Attribution, Salience and Attitudes Toward Criminal Sanctioning." *Criminal Justice and Behavior* 12(3):305–31.

Elmendrof, Thomas. (1976) "Violence on TV." *Vital Speeches of the Day* 42(24):764–67.

Gamson, William A. (1992) *Talking Politics*. New York: Cambridge University Press.

———. (1988) "A Construction Approach to Mass Media and Public Opinion." *Symbolic Interaction* 11(2):161–74.

Gamson, William A. and Andre Modigaliani. (1989) "Media Discourse and Public Opinion on Nuclear Power," *American Journal of Sociology* 95:1–37.

Gamson, William A., David Croteau, William Hoynes, and Theodore Sasson. (1992) "Media Images and the Social Construction of Reality," *Annual Review of Sociology* 18:373–93.

Gusfield, Joseph R. (1981) *The Culture of Public Problems*. Chicago: University of Chicago Press.

Ibarra, Peter and John Kitsuse. (1993) "Vernacular Constituents of Moral Discourse: An Interactionist Proposal for the Study of Social Problems," Pp. 21–54 in Gale Miller and James A. Holstein, eds., *Constructionist Controversies*. Hawthorne, N.Y.: Aldine de Gruyter.

Katzenbach, Nicholas.deB. (1968) "Violence," *Vital Speeches of the Day* 34(20):615–17.

Lewsis, Dan A. and Greta Salem. 1986. *Fear of Crime*. New Brunswick, NJ: Transaction Books.

Miller, Gale and James A. Holstein. (1993) "Social Constructionism as Social Problems Work," Pp. 131–152 in Gale Miller and James A. Holstein, eds., *Constructionist Controversies*. Hawthorne, NY: Aldine de Gruyter.

Morgan, David L. (1988) *Focus Groups as Qualitative Research*. Newbury Park, CA: Sage.

Neuman, Russell W., Marion R. Just, and Ann N. Crigler. (1992) *Common Knowledge: News and the Constructions of Political Meaning*. Chicago: University of Chicago Press.

Potter, Jonathan and Margaret Wetherell. (1987) *Discourse and Social Psychology*. Newbury Park, CA: Sage.

Public Agenda Foundation (PAF). (1993) *Criminal Violence: What Direction Now for the War on Crime?* New York: McGraw-Hill.

Reinharz, Shulamit. (1984) *On Becoming a Social Scientist*. New Brunswick, NJ: Transaction Publishers.

Roberts, Julian V. (1992) "Public Opinion, Crime, and Criminal Justice," Pp. 99–180 in Michael Tonry, ed., *Crime and Justice: A Review of Research*. Chicago: University of Chicago Press.

Schutz, Alfred. (1967) *The Phenomenology of the Social World*. Evanston, IL: North-western University Press.

Snow, David A. and Robert Benford. (1988) "Ideology, Frame Resonance, and Participant Mobilization." *International Social Movement Research* 1:197–217.

Stinchcombe, A. L. and R. Adams, C. A. Heimer, K. L. Schepple, T. W. Smith, and D. G. Taylor.
    (1980) *Crime and Punishment: Changing Attitudes in America.* San Francisco: Josey-Bass.
U.S. Department of Justice, *Uniform Crime Report*, 1992.
Wilson, William J. 1987. The Truly Disadvantaged, Chicago: University of Chicago Press.

Critical connections

For social constructionists, the very existence of social problems is contingent upon the continued existence of interested individuals or groups – the 'claims-makers' – that identify a condition as problematic and attempt to do something about it. What is crucial here is that a given objective condition need not even exist in order to be constituted or defined as socially problematic. A good example is the witch-hunts of Renaissance Europe and colonial New England (Erikson, 1966). Only the most fanciful would today maintain that the women executed for witchcraft were actually cohorts of the devil. In this Reader, Hall *et al.*'s (1978) study *Policing the Crisis,* and the theory of primary definition developed therein (Reading 18), is an examination of the political activities which engendered a moral panic around mugging in 1970s England. Hall *et al.* argue that the social reaction to the newly defined, though scarcely new, problem was 'all out of proportion with the actual level of threat' it posed (1978: 29). Waddington (1986), and others, have challenged this assertion, arguing that the increase in public and political concern did in fact coincide with an actual increase in the levels of street crime. But from a social constructionist perspective, whether or not there was a mugging epidemic is not the important issue (Goode and Ben-Yehuda, 1994). What matters is the fact that public concern was mobilised to such an extent that – real or imagined – the problem was *made real* in the minds of the general public; it was constituted by the definitional process. Social problems are thus constituted by the interpretative processes through which social conditions come to be seen as problematic and in need of correction. In short, they are the product of 'collective definition' (Blumer, 1971).

Discussion questions

- What are the central tenets of the constructionist approach to social problems research?
- How would you go about conducting a 'frame' analysis around the problems of 'gang violence', 'drugs offences' or 'sexual assault'?
- What frames can you identify in your own thinking on the problem of crime, and to what extent do they match or conflict with those identified by Theodore Sasson?

References

Blumer, H. (1971) 'Social Problems as a Collective Behaviour', in *Social Problems,*
    18:298–306. Berkeley, CA: University of California Press.
Erikson, K. (1966) Wayward Puritans: A Study in the Sociology of Deviance, London:
    Macmillan.

Goode, E. and Ben-Yehuda, N. (1994) *Moral Panics: The Social Construction of Deviance.* Oxford: Blackwell.

Kitsuse, J. and Spector, M. (1973) 'Toward a Sociology of Social Problems: Social Conditions, Value Judgements and Social Problems', in *Social Problems,* 20: 407–419.

Sasson, T. (1995) *Crime Talk: How Citizens Construct a Social Problem,* New York: Aldine de Gruyter.

Spector, M. and Kitsuse, J. (1977) *Constructing Social Problems,* Hawthorne, NY: Aldine de Gruyter.

Waddington (1986) 'Mugging as a Moral Panic: A Question of Proportion', in *British Journal of Sociology,* 37, 2: 245–59.

Woolgar, S. and Pawluch, D. (1985) 'Ontological Gerrymandering: The Anatomy of Social Problems Explanations', in *Social Problems,* 32, 3: 214–227.

Jenny Kitzinger

THE DEBATE ABOUT
MEDIA INFLUENCE (2004)

Introduction and context

THE FIELD OF AUDIENCE RESEARCH is one of the most contested in the social sciences. Given the epistemological and methodological rifts and divisions that have characterised audience research, it is perhaps not surprising that media criminologists have tended to steer clear. In an excerpt from her book *Framing Abuse: Media Influence and Public Understanding of Sexual Violence Against Children* (2004), Jenny Kitzinger outlines and evaluates the key approaches to audience research. The dominant approaches can be divided into those that foreground the power of the media and those that prioritise the power and activity of audiences. The former category includes, for example, the hypodermic syringe model of the Frankfurt School, George Gerbner's cultivation analysis (see Reading 32), and agenda setting and framing. The active audience approaches notably include Stuart Hall's Encoding–Decoding circuit of communication (see Reading 4), and the later work of David Morley, as well as the more recent developments in active audience research (Reading 31). Despite media crimonologists' reluctance to engage with audiences, it is undeniable that understanding media consumption remains absolutely fundamental to understanding the crime-media relationship. In order to pick a way through what is characterised as an almost circular argument between media and active audience researchers, Kitzinger outlines her own approach to audience research, which seeks to accommodate both the influence of media texts on audiences and the power of audiences to actively engage with media texts.

A review of some key approaches to audience research

The history of debate about audiences can be characterised as a series of pendulum swings. In some periods theorists have emphasised the media's impact, at other times they have argued that media influence is quite weak and is highly mediated by other social factors. The following section reviews theories about the power of the mass media divided under the two headings: approaches that focus on the power of the media, and approaches that focus on the power and activity of audiences.[1]

Approaches focusing on the power of the media

The Frankfurt School and hypodermic model: The origins of contemporary media studies are often identified as being located in 1930s Germany with the work of scholars such as Adorno, Marcuse and Horkheimer. These writers propose a very powerful model of media effects known as the hypodermic model because it suggests that media messages are directly injected into the hearts and minds of the masses. The Frankfurt School coined the term 'mass culture', a concept originally suggested by the Nazi propaganda machine but then applied to the American capitalist media. Their theories were developed in response to Germany's descent into fascism and the apparent failure of the revolutionary social change predicted by Marx. They were also informed by their observations (having fled Germany for the USA) of the manipulative popular culture of the USA. Popular culture which, they argue, infiltrates our every way of being:

> The way in which a girl accepts and keeps the obligatory date, the inflection on the telephone or in the most intimate situation, the choice of words in conversation, and the whole inner life . . . bear witness to [people's] attempt to make [themselves] a proficient apparatus, similar (even in emotions) to the model served up by the cultural industry (Adorno and Horkheimer 1983:383).[2]

The behavioural effects tradition: The behavioural effects tradition refers to a much more empirically grounded approach to studying audiences, adopted by psychologists using laboratory-based, experimental research techniques. This often relies on methods such as testing people before and after viewing a particular film to measure changes in attitude or behaviour. Alternatively these researchers compare a control group (not exposed to the stimulus) to a group of subjects who were exposed. This work tests whether people (particularly children) are stimulated into aggressive excitement that might be acted out in violence, or whether they are influenced by role models and may imitate what they see in the media. A famous example of such work is Bandura's experiments during the 1950s. He tested children's aggression towards Bobo dolls following viewing of a violent film. (For a discussion see Livingstone 1990/98:14–15.)[3]

Cultivation theory: A very different approach to researching media effects, called 'cultivation theory', was developed by George Gerbner at the University of Pennsylvania during the 1960s. Gerbner hypothesised that media impacts were likely to be much more long-term, subtle and cumulative than laboratory-based research methods implied. The power of the media, he argues, lies in its pervasiveness and its ability to cultivate a general view of reality over time. This poses a problem for traditional experimental effects research because if 'the messages are so stable, the medium is so ubiquitous, and the accumulated total exposure is what counts, then almost everyone should be affected. It is clear, then, that the cards are stacked against finding evidence of effects' (Gerbner *et al.* cited in Livingstone 1996:311). In order to explore this Gerbner adopted a large-scale quantitative research method based on analysing patterns in mass media content and using surveys to assess people's beliefs. He then looked for any statistical correlation between their beliefs about the world and the amount of television they watched. For example, a character on TV is much more likely to be involved in violence than a real person would be. Gerbner's analysis shows that statistical analysis of audiences, divided into 'heavy' and 'light' viewers, suggests that heavy viewers are more likely to overestimate the frequency of violence in the real world.

Agenda-setting: A whole new paradigm developed in the 1970s with agenda-setting theory (McCombs and Shaw 1972). The question pursued here is not what people believe about an issue but how they rank its importance. Agenda-setting theorists argue that although we might not be able to measure the media impact on what people think, it is possible to identify their impact on what people think about. 'In one sense the media only record the past and reflect a version of the present but, in doing so, they can affect the future, hence the significance of the "agenda" analogy' (McQuail 1977/83:84). Using quantitative techniques measuring the extent of media attention to diverse social issues (such as welfare, famine and drug abuse) investigators are able to show that this correlates with the degree of salience of these issues for the public. They are also able to show that public concern and policy attention rises and falls in response to shifts in media coverage (rather than changes in the actual size of the problem in the real world). In addition some scholars designed experimental research. Iyengar and Kinder, for example, produced doctored videotapes of news broadcasts by inserting extra coverage of some particular issues. They then compared research participants who viewed these tapes with a control group. They found that respondents who viewed the videotapes containing the extra news coverage rated those issues as more important than those who had not (Iyengar and Kinder 1987). Developing out of agenda-setting theory, media scholars also introduced the notion of 'priming'. This refers to the effect of a prior context on the interpretation and retrieval of information. Priming can, for example, influence the criteria by which people assess their political leaders depending on whether or not they address the concerns that people have been 'primed' to consider of key importance.

Framing: The notion of framing developed alongside agenda-setting theory as another key way of examining media power. Framing focuses on the nature of the coverage rather than the sheer amount of media attention given to an issue. Although framing has been used mainly to analyse media texts it is increasingly being used to study audiences too. This concept, as my book title implies, is a key strand in my own work and will therefore be introduced here in a little more depth than the approaches I have outlined so far.

Terms such as 'frames', 'frameworks' and 'frame analysis' are used in a variety of overlapping ways in various disciplines (sociology, linguistics, psychology and fine arts) (Fisher 1997). One key contributor to the concept of framing is Erving Goffman.

In his book *Frame Analysis* (1974) he argues that a framework is something that 'allow[s] its user to locate, perceive, identify and label a seemingly infinite number of concrete occurrences defined in its terms' (Goffman 1974:21). Other authors have defined frames as 'cognitive windows' through which stories are 'seen' (Pan and Kosicki 1993:59) or 'maps' helping us to navigate through a forest of multiple realities (Gamson 1992:117). It is not simply a question of bias or what is said or left unsaid; frames are about how an account organises reality. In editorial terms this includes the 'angle' that journalists adopt in their approach to a story.

Ideas about how stories are framed feature in many classic studies of news coverage. Chibnall, in his analysis of crime reporting, identifies 'ideological frameworks' as 'structures through which the subjective reality of things is fashioned and meaning is imposed on the social world' (Chibnall 1977:13). Gitlin, in his study of reporting of the New Left, defines frames as 'tacit theories about what exists, what happens, and what matters' which inform the ways in which we negotiate, manage and comprehend reality (Gitlin 1980:6). A similar definition features in early work by the Glasgow University Media Group. The group explored 'inferential frameworks' in economic and industrial reporting and argued that the relation between wages and prices was presented as the key factor in explaining inflation. Wage negotiations were seen as threatening and the normal workings of the economic system 'are never treated as if they themselves generate serious problems. Rather the causes of economic problems are sought largely in the activities of trade unionists' (Glasgow University Media Group 1980:112).

This area of research continues to thrive in more recent studies. These include research projects that range from examining the framing of hate speech (Miller and Andsager 1997) and 'political correctness' (Dickerson 2001) to the framing of the US peace movement (Marullo *et al.* 1996) or Clinton's attempts at health care reforms (Pan and Kosicki 2001).

Most of this work (including early studies by the Glasgow group and that by Chibnall and by Gitlin) focuses on analysing media texts and/or examining the claims-making activity of various stake holders. Far less research has actually addressed people's responses. The studies that have attempted to do this usually adopt survey methods and/or a quasi-experimental approach (Shah *et al.* 2001; Nelson and Willey 2001; Rhee 1997). In one classic study Iyengar explored the potential consequences of the whole style of news reporting. He was interested in how news reporting that is 'episodic' (depicting concrete events) might impact on people and compared this to reporting that is 'thematic' (presenting collective or general evidence). He showed some groups episodic reporting, and others thematic reporting and then examined how each group responded. He concludes that episodic framing (the most common form of news framing) reinforces prevailing conventional wisdom and diverts attention from societal responsibility (Iyengar 1991:137).

In spite of such important work there is a lack of in-depth understanding of how media frames might operate upon or in interaction with audiences in a broader cultural context. As Hertog and McLeod conclude:

> A great deal more effort in determining how social framing of controversies affects public understandings of those controversies is needed. This research needs to move out of the laboratory and into the realm of popular culture (Hertog and McLeod 2001:160).

In fact, this task has been (and is being) addressed by an overlapping strand of work which, although not necessarily rooted in the framing tradition, offers complementary insights into this whole area. This research breaks from the survey and experimental tradition. Instead it involves in-depth qualitative analysis of how people discuss key social issues (in interviews, focus group discussions or natural settings). This research (including more recent work by the Glasgow Media Group), examines the integration of, and interaction between, media representations and everyday ways of knowing about issues ranging from AIDS to nuclear power, from gun control to racism, from economics to human genetics. I call this scattered but substantial body of work: 'New Media Influence Research'. As this emerging strand of research actually bridges the traditional division between research that prioritises the power of the text, and work that focuses on the power of the audience, I will not discuss it in any greater depth here. As it is central to my own approach, however, I will return to a discussion of such work in my conclusion.

The approaches outlined above, all, in their different ways, focus on how the nature of the media message can influence people. Throughout the same time periods, however, alternative approaches were being developed which primarily focus instead on the activities of audiences. These are outlined below.

Approaches focusing on the power and activity of audiences

Two-step model of media influence: The two-step model of media influence was developed by American researchers in the 1940s and 1950s in direct opposition to the pessimistic generalisations of the Frankfurt School and its hypodermic thesis. Much of this research was based on a much narrower focus than the broad critique of popular culture which formed the basis of the hypodermic model. The two-step model developed out of empirical research into the impact of political campaigns on people's voting intentions. This suggested that the media had a much weaker and more indirect influence than had previously been thought. It highlighted the role of social networks in mediating responses to media messages. Merton's work on mass persuasion (1946) focuses on the importance of reference groups in influencing the messages that people accepted from political campaigns. Similar findings were emphasised in work by Lazarsfeld, Berelson and Gaudet, who tracked a panel of people over six months during the 1940 US presidential campaign battle between Roosevelt and Willkie. This study revealed that most people already knew how they were going to vote before the presidential campaign began, and their intentions did not alter, although they were sometimes influenced by people whose political views they trusted (Lazarsfeld et al. 1944). Katz and Lazarsfeld's research on personal influence (1955) reiterates this point, posing a two-step model of media effects whereby media messages are mediated by opinion leaders who influence how ideas are taken up by members of their communities.[4]

Uses and gratifications: Uses and gratifications theory was another approach developed in opposition to those who highlighted the power of the media to shape public understandings of the world. This approach turns traditional ways of thinking about media effects on their head. It replaces the question 'what do the media do to people?' with the question 'what do people do with media?' Uses and gratifications scholars explore how people actively use and process media materials in accordance with their own needs, emphasising the ways in which individuals make a conscious selection between the various items of media content, choosing what they will watch and for what purposes. The degree and kind of media effect will therefore depend on the need of the audience member concerned and is more likely to reinforce rather than change beliefs. The uses and gratifications (U and G) approach thrived during the 1970s and 1980s. However, the earliest example of U and G theory is evident in Herzog's pioneering work with radio listeners in the 1940s USA. She examined women's consumption of radio serials (the earliest form of soap opera). Her research is based on interviews with 100 women from a variety of age and income groups and provides a fascinating portrait of women's lives at that time. She demonstrates how listeners could use and interpret the same radio serial quite differently according to their own needs and identifies the types of gratification obtained from these programmes. These gratifications included: an outlet for pent-up anxieties in giving the listener a 'chance to cry', a wishful escape from isolation and drudgery and using the radio serials to help them understand the world and provide 'recipes for adjustment' (Herzog 1941:69).[5]

Reception analysis and audience decodings: Both the two-step model and Uses and gratifications theory highlight people's choices and social interactions as important factors in how they relate to media messages. However, the most radical and influential break in theorising about media influence came in the 1970s with a new model of understanding text-audience relations that focused on how people interpret, read or 'decode' texts. This involved a reconfiguration of the whole model of communication from one which implied transmission of a fixed object (the message) from producer to receiver to one which emphasised the social and symbolic processes involved in encoding and decoding a text. The emphasis on audience decodings led to an increasing interest in 'reception research' and 'active audience' studies which explore how people responded to the same media output in different (sub)cultures, the skills people bring to their cultural consumption and how they wrest pleasure or positive images from unexpected sources. This is the body of work which (particularly within Europe) defines the contemporary audience research agenda. It is, therefore, worth addressing this theme in some detail and outlining how it has evolved.

The foundations for studying audience reception processes are usually located in the Birmingham Centre for Contemporary Cultural Studies (BCCCS) in the UK, led by Stuart Hall and, later, David Morley. It should be acknowledged, however, that parallel and overlapping insights were developing (or were already established) across continental Europe. Reception theory drew on the 1920s tradition of empirical studies of literature (Rosengren 1996:23) and the German branch of literary theory that focuses on the role of the reader in the reading process; a tradition developed at the University of Konstanz (Hagen and Wasko 2000:7). The emphasis on the audience (rather than the text) also built on the insights of Roland Barthes, the French philosopher and linguist, who, in 1968, famously announced the 'death of the author'. Texts, he argued, should no longer be seen as messages dispatched by their inventors, but as sites of multiple writings. Since their socially active meanings were constructed 'not in [their] origin but in [their] destination', it was time to announce 'the demise of the producer and the birth of the reader' (Barthes 1977:148).

Whatever the correct history of how reception analysis was 'discovered' across different disciplines, it is clear that the BCCCS became an innovative centre of activity developing this analysis. Stuart Hall's paper 'Encoding and decoding in the television discourse' (1973) undoubtedly served as a key intervention in the debate within media studies. This paper stresses the need to take the communicative process as a whole, with the moment of programme making at one end and the moment of audience perception at the other. Hall argues that texts are 'polysemic', being open to more than one reading, and that there is no necessary correspondence between the message encoded by the film or programme maker and that decoded by audiences.

Hall clearly sees texts as carrying a 'preferred meaning' but proposes three hypothetical positions from which decodings might be constructed in practice: the dominant, the negotiated and the oppositional (terms derived from Parkin 1971). The dominant-hegemonic position is where:

> [the audience] takes the connoted meaning from, say, a television newscast or current affairs programme full and straight, and decodes the message in terms of the reference code in which it has been encoded, we might say that the viewer is operating inside the dominant code (Hall 1973:101).

The negotiated position involves accepting the legitimacy of the dominant framework in the abstract, but negotiating the application of this framework to local conditions. For example, a worker may accept a news broadcast's hegemonic definition of the economic necessity of freezing wages in the national interest in order to avoid inflation, but still be willing to oppose such measures at the level of the shop-floor. The oppositional position, by contrast, challenges the broader hegemonic framing of the problem, questioning whether wage freezes do indeed serve the national interest or only the interest of the dominant class.

Hall's distinction between encoding and decoding highlights the possibility that meaning does not lie in the text alone. Researchers cannot accurately predict how people will relate to and interpret a particular cultural product simply by analysing headlines and photographs, camera angles, lighting, sound track and scripts. Paying attention to the process of decoding also opens questions of audience diversity and allows that 'other discourses are always in play besides those of the particular text in focus – discourses . . . brought into play through "the subject's" placing in other practices – cultural, educational, institutional' (Morley 1980:163).

In other words, people are not blank slates who approach a film without any pre-existing identity, experience or resources. They come to the cinema (or TV set) with sets of prior opinions, views and ideas of themselves. In order to understand the role of the media it is therefore, Hall argues, imperative to discover how different groups respond to and interpret any particular programme, to explore the resources they bring to bear on their interpretation and the discourse to which they have access.

It was this understanding which laid the groundwork for a flowering of qualitative work with audiences during the 1980s and 1990s; quite different from the text based, survey or experimental work which had preceded it. One of the first and most influential of these studies was Morley's research into responses to the popular current affairs programme *Nationwide*. David Morley and Charlotte Brundson had already conducted a textual analysis of the programme. Morley (1980) then decided to study ordinary viewers' interpretations. His aim was to produce a typology of different responses and examine how these related to people's varying socio-economic position. To this end, he showed video recordings of an episode of *Nationwide* to 29 groups of people including managers, students, apprentices and trade unionists. The video showings were followed by group discussions.

Morley's work confirms Hall's theory that there are at least three possible readings of a text: the dominant reading (accepting the preferred reading of the text), a negotiated reading and an oppositional reading. His findings show that people differed in their critique of the style of the programme and their critique of the content/ framework and that this was related to class. For example, managers objected to the style of *Nationwide* but accepted the content, whereas trade unionists did the opposite. Morley also found that many people across a range of groups were well aware of the preferred meanings embedded in the programme and that 'awareness of the construction by no means entails the rejection of what is constructed' (Morley 1980:140). He also found that class alone was inadequate to explain the diversity of audience responses. There were differences between working-class people active within the trade union movement and those who were not. There were also additional cross-cutting differences to do with age, gender and ethnicity.

Domestic consumption processes: During the 1980s and 1990s researchers also engaged with the processes of consumption itself (Moores 1993). Moving on from his study of the *Nationwide* audience Morley became increasingly interested in the context of media consumption. He was concerned about the unnatural settings in which his study of *Nationwide* audiences had been conducted. His research participants might never have chosen to watch *Nationwide* in the first place, and were unlikely to have engaged in such in-depth discussion and analysis of the programme in the normal course of events. He also hypothesised that the reading a shop steward makes in company with other shop stewards may be very different from the interpretation he might make at home, the most usual viewing situation. His next study therefore focused on how people actually watched television at home and he subsequently went on to scrutinise the impact of the media as technological hardware (e.g. the effect of having a television in the home alongside other technologies such as the computer or telephone) (Morley and Silverstone 1990).

Examining how people consume cultural products has now become a thriving area of media research. Researchers examine the television set itself as a cultural object which carries symbolic meaning. For example, one's choice of media hardware can indicate status, disposable income and taste or the lack of it (Morley 1995). They also explore how cultural consumption may be integrated into people's day-to-day lives and serve particular purposes in the social organisation of the home (Hobson 1980; Modleski 1984; Winship 1987). Throughout the 1980s (in the context of second wave feminism and challenges to traditional patriarchal ways of organising family life) there was intense interest in how men and women negotiated gender relations. This research shows how men take possession of the remote control or mock women's preferred choice of programmes as trivial (Morley 1986). It also highlights the gendered division of labour in relation to different technologies, for example, men may profess to find setting the controls on the washing machine 'too complicated' but claim supremacy over the video machine (Gray 1987). Other researchers have explored the creative way in which women engage in cultural consumption in the context of traditional family life in ways which assert their own needs. 'Addiction' to soap operas, for example, may allow women to establish times when they are not available and attentive to the needs of others (Brunsdon 1981; Hobson 1982; Seiter *et al*. 1989).

Some scholars argue that this is the cutting edge of media studies, the way forward for theorising about media audience. According to proponents such as Ang, this approach enables us to conceive of 'the ideological operations of television in a much more radical way than has hitherto been done'. It allows us to see that 'If television is an "ideological apparatus" . . . this is not so much because its texts transmit "messages" as because it is a cultural form through which those constraints [on structuring social relationships, identities and desires] are negotiated and those possibilities take shape' (Ang 1989:109).

The broader field of active audience studies: Research into how people engage with media technologies was paralleled by a continued fascination with audience reception processes. In particular, researchers were interested in how people might read cultural products differently depending on their own pre-existing cultural resources and competencies.

Some researchers wanted to test out the cultural colonialism thesis. (Cultural colonialism refers to the idea that the export of American cultural products will also export American cultural values.) Comparative research often seemed to challenge a simple notion of cultural colonialism because it highlighted how the same media output could be read quite differently in diverse cultures. Katz and Liebes, for example, studied how different audiences in Israel responded to *Dallas* (an internationally successful US-made soap about a Texan oil family that was seen to celebrate conspicuous consumption). Their findings contradict the cultural colonialism thesis. They found that Russian Jews, newly arrived in Israel, read *Dallas* as capitalism criticising itself, while a Moroccan Jew learned from the series that Jewishness was the right way to be, because it was clear that non-Jews lived messy and immoral lives (Katz and Liebes 1985). This supports the argument presented by the Italian theorist Eco, for example, that audiences may engage in 'semiological guerrilla warfare' (Eco 1974) and that advertising could serve as a revolutionary message in depressed areas. This is because 'For a Milanese bank clerk a TV ad for a refrigerator represents a stimulus to buy, but for a peasant in Calabria the same image means the confirmation of a world of prosperity that doesn't belong to him' (Eco 1986:141).[6]

Other researchers were fuelled by a commitment to exploring social diversity and inequalities (e.g. by age and ethnicity). This spawned a great deal of work with minority or oppressed groups. It showed that it was possible for people to take mainstream offerings and use them to reflect constructively on their own lives. Bobo's work with black women viewers of the film *The Color Purple* was a classic study informing this strand of work.[7] She aimed to 'examine the ways in which a specific audience creates meanings from a mainstream text and uses the reconstructed meaning to empower themselves and their social group' (Bobo 2003:307). A similar approach is evident in Gillespie's richly ethnographic study of TV use by British Asians. She found that *Neighbours*, an Australian soap featuring an all-white cast, attracted young British Asians who perceived it as offering 'a complex metaphor for their own social world' (Gillespie 1995:207). *Neighbours* explores the tensions that exist between families and their neighbours in a way which resonated with those young people's experiences of their communities (1995:164). Such findings parallel research with lesbians and gay men that highlights the way in which even the most mainstream heterosexual media text can be used creatively to construct positive gay identities (Whitiker 1985; Dyer 1986; Jay and Glasgow 1992; Doty 1993; Griffen 1993). Similarly, research with children shows how they use mainstream media in ways which help them to make sense of their own structural position (Hodge and Tripp 1986). Studies of *Prisoner Cell Block H*, for example, the Australian soap set in a woman's prison, found that the programme provided school students with language and cultural categories with which to think through their experiences. Teachers were given nicknames from the cast of prison guards and the children used the programme as a way of understanding and articulating their powerlessness (Curthoys and Docker 1989; Palmer 1986).

Many scholars at this time were interested in questioning the privileged status of 'highbrow' (i.e. white, male, middle class) cultural tastes. Many feminist scholars, for example, also wanted to challenge the status accorded to watching 'serious' ('masculine') television genre and attempted to reclaim disparaged pleasures and skills (Ang 1985). Extensive work was conducted on soap fans.[8] Dorothy Hobson, for example (based at the BCCCS), went to women's homes to watch a phenomenally popular soap opera called *Crossroads* with them and to discuss their enjoyment of the programme. She found that women enjoyed hypothesising about the future actions of characters and would engage in sophisticated games with soap opera characters, including them in their 'gossip' even though fully cognisant of their fictional status. Hobson emphasises how women were actively involved in bringing meaning to the programme by drawing on experiences in their own lives. Attending to audience pleasure and acknowledging their active engagement with the text challenges traditional analysis of media content. Hobson concludes:

> To look at a programme like *Crossroads* and criticise it on the basis of a conventional literary/media analysis is obstinately to refuse to understand the relationship which it has with its audience [. . .] To try to say what *Crossroads* means to its audience is impossible for there is no single *Crossroads*, there are as many different *Crossroads* as there are viewers (Hobson 1982:135–6).

Such statements are less an evolution from Hall's notion of audience decodings than a challenge. Hobson's formulation breaks with the notion that there is a preferred reading built into the text at all (see Barker and Brooks 1998). At its boldest, active audience research can sometimes suggest that questions of media influence are irrelevant or, at best, impossible to research. The production of meaning is so dependent on what people bring to their engagement with the media that attempts to generalise about the impact of media coverage, or to predict how texts might influence people, are misguided, or at least doomed to failure.

The current impasse: media influence versus active audiences

Given the diverse approaches outlined above it is perhaps not surprising that media studies in general, and audience research in particular, is a very volatile and unsettled field (see, for example, the 1983 issue of *Journal of Communication*, entitled *Ferment in the Field*; see also Corner *et al.* 1997:2). Theorising about media influence has been condemned as a messy pot-pourri with inconsistent or inconclusive conclusions (Livingstone 1999:14). The terms 'media' and 'audience' themselves incorporate such diverse conceptualisations that some of this work is barely recognisable as addressing the same object of study at all. Some studies concentrate on the impact of one type of media (e.g. television); some examine a particular genre (e.g. soap) or an individual text (e.g. a cartoon or film). Others are concerned with an altogether broader canvas (e.g. the impact of popular culture or general news reporting). Studies in this field often investigate different types of media (from radio to digital television) and consider diverse time frames (from the immediate aftermath of viewing to the long-range absorption of ideas). They are looking for very different types of effect (ranging from imitation of violent acts to the framing of general ideas about 'the ways of the world'). Sometimes they are asking entirely different questions altogether (e.g. what people do with television rather than what it does to them).

Some of the divisions about study design and methodology follow geographical and cultural borders. For example, research which emphasises the power of the media is stronger in the USA while that which emphasises the activity of the audiences is better established within western Europe. The former has traditionally been based on quantitative and experimental work rooted in the disciplines of social and political science or mainstream experimental psychology. The latter favours in-depth qualitative research and draws more on the disciplines of arts and humanities (including cultural studies, literary theory and social anthropology).

The gap between those who theorise about media influence and those who prioritise active audience research has become a seemingly unbridgeable gulf. Sometimes each side simply ignores the other, a stance made easier by the ways in which the fault-lines in this debate coincide with national, disciplinary and methodological boundaries. At other times communication across the divide takes the form of sniping (Morley 1998). Those who study active audiences accuse those who focus on media influence of a crude approach to textual interpretation, insensitivity to people's diversity and a failure to attend to nuances of gender, ethnic and sexual identity. They attack research addressing the potential effects of media coverage for casting people as 'cultural dupes', objectifying them, being elitist and pessimistic and promoting condescending attitudes to 'vulnerable' audiences (especially children and young people) (Barker and Petley 1997/2001). Theorists concerned with media influence, for their part, often challenge their opponents for romanticising audience resistance and failing to attend to systematic asymmetries in the distribution of power and resources. (For critiques see Barry 1993; Corner 1991; Eldridge *et al.* 1997; Gitlin 1991; Jakubowicz *et al.* 1994; Kitzinger 1993; McGuigan 1992; McLaughlin 1993; Morris 1988; Seaman 1992; Philo and Miller 1997.)

Each side accuses the other of failure to address the real sites of power, for example focusing on the macro at the expense of the micro, or vice versa (Corner 1991; Gray 1999). Active audience theorists are criticised for their tendency to concentrate on fictional genres and questions of pleasure, hence sometimes being seen to sideline the 'serious' public issues of the day (Barry 1993:489; Jakubowicz *et al.* 1994:23). Media influence theorists are accused of underestimating the importance of non-news genre and failing to understand complex issues around identity and the role of fantasy. Each side in the conflict accuses the other of misreading the literature, misrepresenting history and failing to understand the social and political context within which particular polemics were published (Curran 1990, 1996; Morley 1996). Each side also accuses the other of using methodologies rooted in oppressive histories or alleges that the other is pursuing an agenda which serves the powers-that-be. On the one hand, for example, it is clear that research that highlights media influence can serve institutional interests in justifying censorship and state control or allowing the media to be used as a scapegoat for social problems more properly linked to issues such as poverty and injustice. On the other hand, it is equally clear that a focus on audience creativity can be used by multi-national media conglomerates to defend monopolies or oppose efforts to maintain 'quality'. The celebration of difference can also become the mantra of global capitalism, a goldmine, rather than a threat (McLaughlin 1993:61; McGuigan 1992:164,183; Klein 2000:115).

Some of the accusations flung across the barricades between the two sides are true for some of the theories (or for some individual theorists) at least some of the time. The fierce polemics about the history and future of audience research have served an important role in clarifying potential dangers and highlighting differences. However, the debate becomes unproductive when the argument is reduced to simplistic binaries. There is a danger of producing highly selective accounts that oppose simple 'pro-media effects' against 'active audience' division (labels, that as the above outlines show, can cover a multitude of diverse work). Emphasising competing brands of thought also tends to play up the differences rather than areas of convergence. Thus, for example, in spite of the apparently unbridgeable gulf between theorists often cited in relation to the different positions outlined above, they can each agree on some core issues. In particular commentators on both sides now often seem to concur that the constraints of how texts are produced, and how people read them, are important, and that the power of audience activity should not be exaggerated. Compare, for example, the statements below that come from John Corner who has contributed a great deal to work on media influence, David Morley (of *Nationwide* fame) and Umberto Eco, a theorist more usually associated with celebrating semiological guerrilla warfare.

> 'so much effort has been centred on audiences' interpretative activity that even the preliminary theorisation of influence has become *awkward*' (Corner 1991:267–9, emphasis in original).
>   '. . . the rights of the interpreters have been overstressed [as if] interpretation has no context and there is a failure to examine the limitations or constraints of readings' (Eco 1990:7).
>   'The power of viewers to reinterpret meanings is hardly equivalent to the discursive power of centralised media institutions to construct the texts which the viewer then interprets; to imagine otherwise is simply foolish' (Morley 1996:291).

Polemics can also have the unfortunate effect of ignoring work that is more nuanced or that has tried to address the problems highlighted in the attacks and counterattacks. Research into the active audience, for example, is sometimes summarised by reference to the more extreme statements of its more radical proponents, while studies into the influence of the media are often reviewed simply in terms of 'the effects tradition'. The effects tradition is defined predominantly by behavioural experiments and the Frankfurt School, sometimes including cultivation theory. When proponents of an active audience review research on media effects/influence they rarely give any attention to work on agenda-setting or framing, and have not taken into account the range of work that I categorise as 'New Media Influence Research'.

My research approach

My desire to bring together a range of my own research projects into this single volume was born out of frustration with this debate. We seem to be going round in circles. Old battles are endlessly revisited while new developments are ignored. There are plenty of detailed criticisms of old effects paradigms or attacks on active audience theory and plenty of calls for research which combines attention to both textual and audience power. It is much rarer to find reviews that actually address such research as it exists. I think it is time to move on. I hope the research presented in this volume will help us to do precisely this (and, as I have already pointed out, there is plenty of other research that can also be brought into play in this debate). [. . .]

My interviews with incest survivors in the 1980s, although not informed by media studies scholarship, were conducted in the context of the Women's Liberation Movement. This movement insisted that women should be viewed as survivors rather than victims and challenged traditional methodological approaches. In particular, feminist theorists objected to traditional ways of objectifying research subjects. My concern, during the course of this research, was thus in how women (re)constructed their identities and took back control from their abusers. My questions focused on the process of survival and resistance, rather than the acts of victimisation. In addition, I approached women as experts on their own lives and I tried to engage with them as 'participants' in, rather than objects of, my research. (For example, I sent interviewees transcripts of their interviews for comment and discussion.)

The two main focus group studies presented in this volume also address people as active participants in the construction of meaning. These groups were conducted after I had been initiated into the debates about active audience theory. One of the studies (involving 30 focus groups) explored people's reactions to a particular social awareness campaign. The other (involving 49 focus groups) had a broader remit, exploring the role of the mass media in general.[9] Both focus group studies were explicitly designed to attend to potential influence and also to explore how people actively engage with media texts. I wanted to explore how people use the media as a resource in their day-to-day lives and to address the multiple alternative sources people might bring to bear on their readings of a text. These concerns informed my sampling strategies, the way in which the groups were composed, the choice of location in which discussion sessions were held, the games used in the focus groups and the ways in which I facilitated them. My interest in the audience's active engagement in these issues, rather than mere 'receivers' of messages, also informs my analytical approach and the way in which I have presented my data.

- My sampling strategies: Following in the footsteps of researchers such as Morley (1980), I selected the sample in order to include people with a wide range of experiences. The aim here was to maximise potential diversity, especially in relation to the specific issue under discussion. Some groups were chosen because they might be expected to have particular knowledge of, or perspectives on, sexual abuse (e.g. social workers and incest survivors support groups). Others were chosen because, as a group, they were not necessarily expected to have any special interest in this issue (e.g. a group of people attending the same community centre or youth club). Efforts were also made to meet with groups in diverse settings (social, occupational and educational) and include participants with a range of demographic characteristics. Thus some groups were specifically targeted to ensure the sample included old people as well as young, English people as well as Scottish and black people as well as white. Community centres, clubs, youth groups and schools were also approached in different areas ranging from middle-class suburbia to areas of 'inner-city deprivation' and including some rural as well as urban locations.

- The composition of the focus groups: The groups were based on pre-existing groups of people who already knew each other through living, working or socialising together. These are, after all, the 'interpretive communities' in which people might normally discuss (or evade) the sorts of issues raised in the research session (Morgan 1988; Barbour and Kitzinger 1999). I also kept the groups small, an average of five or six participants per group, in order to allow for in-depth discussion during the sessions (which usually lasted between one and three hours).

- The design of exercises used in the focus groups: Various exercises and games were used to engage people in the debates. These included games that encouraged people to actively construct and deconstruct campaign or media messages, positioning them as expert commentators upon, not just victims of the text. [. . .] For fuller discussion of this exercise, see Kitzinger 1990.

- The way the group discussions were facilitated: Focus groups have one major advantage over interviews; they are forums within which research participants can (indeed should) address each other much more than they address the researcher. This can allow closer access to everyday forms of talk. Rather than adopting a very controlling 'group leader' role, I therefore adopted a more low-key facilitating position. For example, instead of asking questions of each person in turn, group participants were encouraged to talk to one another; ask questions, exchange anecdotes, and comment on each others' experiences and points of view. I allowed 'natural' conversation to develop and evolve in the group, and was tolerant of apparent 'digressions' in an effort to gain access to the context within which people discussed this issue with one another. (For full discussion of the focus group method see Kitzinger 1994.)

- Transcription, coding and qualitative analysis: Focus groups are only really focus groups, rather than simply group interviews, when interaction between participants is explicitly used to generate data as part of the analytical process. Analysis of transcripts should include, for example, attention to the difference between argumentative and complementary interactions (Kitzinger 1994), and attend to the differences between common and shared knowledge. Detailed focus group analysis also pays attention to issues such as how people talk and what counts as sensitive or unusual information (Kitzinger and Farquhar 1999).

In order to allow for such analysis a full transcription is invaluable. The focus groups and interviews were fully transcribed to facilitate close examination of how talk developed in interaction over the progress of the discussion. The transcripts were also coded for themes (e.g. all references to a particular scandal) but also for types of speech or interaction (e.g. jokes, laughter, declared changes of mind). For similar reasons I often present examples of the conversational exchanges between people, rather than just statements from individuals taken out of context. I also tried to attend to different notions about the nature of talk, including thinking about talk as performance, as self-narration and as action (see Gillespie 1995:205; McKinley 1997).

- Systematic examination of patterns and deviation: Most of the focus group data is indexed on computer. This allows for rigorous comparison of themes, across thousands of pages of transcript. Such quantification is sometimes seen to be out of keeping with qualitative approaches and respect for the nuances of how people talk. However, in my experience, used in the right way, such computer-assisted analysis can complement such approaches. While always keeping the context in mind, computer coding allows for a very systematic way of locating recurring themes in a very large dataset. This gave me a basis from which to present meaningful quantification alongside in-depth qualitative analysis. (This includes detailed attention to the nuances of talk.)

Throughout the book I have thus been able to indicate where ideas were common across a variety of groups, or where they were only expressed by a few people. Even if unable to precisely enumerate the number of individuals who express a certain point of view, it is important to give an idea of the distribution of ideas across groups. As Lewis argues:

> It matters whether the discourse whose presence we identify during a focus group interview is widespread within the culture (or subculture). It is important for us to know, roughly, the number of people who construct one reading of a TV programme rather than another [. . .] We may not be able to enumerate it, but in describing its presence we assume that it is, in some form, quantifiable. We assume that it counts (Lewis 1997:87).

In addition, computer indexing transcripts allows one to locate and attend to deviant examples and to systematically examine all examples of types of speech and interaction (e.g. jokes, unease, declared changes of mind).

I hope the approach outlined above will provide some useful suggestions for future research and that I have provided sufficient detail to help readers to evaluate and reflect on my findings. My research demonstrates that it is possible to identify how certain aspects of media coverage can influence us, sometimes even in spite of our own 'better judgement'. It is also possible to track how specific media coverage can tap into pre-existing cultural images, experiences and expectations in ways that provoke powerful responses. The mass media are rarely our sole source of information and we actively interpret and consume the media for our own purposes and pleasures. The paradox is, as this book will show, that in spite and sometimes even because of such audience engagement, the media can have a very powerful role in defining, maintaining, and even transforming the way we see the world.

Notes

1. All histories are a form of story-telling told from a standpoint in the present and summaries inevitably end up glossing over subtleties in the original texts (Gray 1999). My review is a partial history in the sense that, like any other history, it can be neither comprehensive nor entirely impartial. In my first draft of this chapter my efforts to 'be true' to the original studies and not simply reproduce secondary accounts led me into a maze of complexity and contradictions. In the end I decided to adopt a conventional way of categorising and summarising the key approaches, because it is precisely these conventional categories that help to underpin contemporary debate in much of Europe and North America. Such accounts therefore have a 'truth' regardless of what happened at the time. I would, however, urge readers who want to develop a thorough understanding of each approach to read the primary materials for themselves.

2. Alternative trajectories can be tracked through looking at the history of film studies. For example, the Payne Fund studies (1929–32) sought to assess the effects on audiences of exposure to the themes and messages of motion pictures. According to some writers it is these studies which 'gave birth to the scientific study of mass communication' (Lowry and DeFleur 1955, cited in Mosco and Kaye 2000:37). This review also does not discuss the dominant research paradigm emerging out of film theory in Britain during the 1970s and 1980s, although this contributed to the dialogue in developing approaches to television audience research. For a discussion of this dialogue see Eldridge *et al.* 1997:127–9.

3. The hypodermic model and the experimental behavioural approach are now both often seen as out-dated. Although such strong notions of media effect continue to thrive within mainstream psychology and to influence policy decisions, some of this work has been severely criticised on methodological grounds. (See Gauntlett 1995, 1998; Barker and Petley 1997/2001.)

4. The two-step model of media influence was pioneered in actual practice much earlier. It was used in 1918 by Parkes who directed British propaganda in the USA. Parkes started his campaigns by first singling out influential and eminent people of every profession as targets in order to encourage American involvement in the First World War (Kubey 1996:197).

5. The 'recipe for adjustment' category is a particularly interesting one and it is fascinating to revisit Herzog's data from a modern perspective. A remark by one of Herzog's interviewees that the radio stories give her 'an idea of how a wife should be to a husband' and warns her of the danger of being a busy-body is interpreted by Herzog as the woman 'using' the media for her own ends. It could equally be used to illustrate the ideological power of media representations (Herzog 1941:90).

6. Within a single country, different cultural interpretations may also produce quite distinct readings of a single film or programme. A study of women's reactions to representations of violence against women reports that a group of British Asian women 'learned' from *The Accused* (a film about a gang rape and the subsequent trial) that drinking and flirting was dangerous. 'They seemed to view the film almost anthropologically as a report upon the wider society', comment Schlesinger *et al.*, '... their

reading of the film validated their differences, showing how their culture could operate to protect them from danger' (Schlesinger *et al.* 1992:64). This is in spite of the
fact that the film was framed by the western feminist ideals about women's rights and
designed to challenge the idea that women who drank and flirted were 'asking for it'.

7.   Alice Walker's book was not a straightforward mainstream text. It was at the forefront of addressing sexual violence against girls and was extremely important for
incest survivors when it first came out (see Chapter 3). However, the film
(produced by the white male director, Steven Spielberg) was the focus of a major
controversy about the image of black people in the media, 'the likes of which had
not been seen since the films *The Birth of a Nation* (1915) and *Gone with the Wind*
(1939)' (Bobo 2003:307).

8.   In Latin America the telenovellas are phenomenally popular with both men and
women. Leading theorist Martin-Barbero theorises that their appeal in Latin
America is due to the fact that melodrama 'speaks to many people who search for
their identity in the primordial sociability of family relations and in the social
solidarity of the neighbourhood, region, and friend networks' (Martin-Barbero
2000:152). This work highlights the telenovela as providing a language for popular
forms of hope (Tufte 2000; Martin-Barbero 1999).

9.   This study was designed on the premise that people do not view individual media
messages in isolation, but as part of a patchwork of messages over time. I was also
interested in how people might draw on different genre (news, soaps, documenta-
ries, discussion shows) in constructing views on a topic or negotiating with different media messages. The research was also essentially retrospective. Where other
researchers have used in-depth observation to explore the immediate interaction
between audiences and their television sets, I wanted to tap into people's memories
and their uses and understandings of media messages long after the naturally occurring media-watching event, and in a broader social context. Rather than assuming
that 'consumption' and the relationship between text and audience is confined to
the moment of viewing/reading (and the conversations which take place in the
family sitting room or on the bus the next day) my research examined what people
were left with long after the images had faded from the TV screen.

References

Adorno, T. and Horkheimer, M. (1983) The Culture Industry: Enlightenment as Mass
Deception. In: Curran, J. *et al.* eds. *Mass Communications and Society*. London: Arnold.
pp. 349–384.

Ang, I. (1985) *Watching 'Dallas': Soap Opera and the Melodramatic Imagination*. London:
Methuen.

Ang, I. (1989) Wanted: Audiences. On the politics of Empirical Audience Studies. In:
Seiter, E. *et al.* eds. *Remote Control: Television, Audiences and Cultural power*. London:
Routledge, pp. 96–115.

Ayish, M. (2003) Beyond Western-oriented Communication Theories. A Normative
Arab–Islamic Perspective. *Javnost* x(2), pp. 79–92.

Barker, M. and Brooks, K. and Petley, J. eds. 2001. *Ill Effects: the Media/Violence*. 2nd edn.
London: Routledge.

Barbour, R. and Kitzinger, J. eds. (1999) *Developing Focus Group Research*. London: Sage.

Barry, A. (1993) Television, Truth and Democracy. *Media, culture and Society* 15(3),
pp. 487–496.

Barthes, R. (1966/1977) The Death of the Author. In: Barthes, R. ed. *Image, Music, Text*. London: Fontana.

Bobo, J. (2003) The color Purple: Black Women as Cultural Readers. In: Brooker, W. and Jermyn, D. eds. *The Audience Studies Reader*. London: Routledge, pp. 305–314.

Brunsdon, C. (1981) 'Crossroads': Notes on Soap Opera. *Screen* 22(4), pp. 32–37.

Chibnall, S. (1977) *Law-and-Order News: an Analysis of crime Reporting in the British Press*. London: Tavistock Press.

Corner, J. (1991) Meaning, Genre and Context: the Problematics of 'Public Knowledge' in the New Audience Studies. In: Curran, J. and Gurevitch, M. eds. *Mass Media and Society*. London: Edward Arnold.

Corner, J. *et al*. (1997) Introduction. In: Corner, J. *et al*. eds. *International Media Research: A Critical Survey*. London: Routledge.

Curran, J. (1990) The New Revisionism in Mass Communication Research: A Reappraisal. *European Journal of Communication* 5, pp. 135–164.

Curran, J. (1996) Media Dialogue: a Reply. In: Curran, J. *et al*. eds. *Cultural Studies and Communications*. London: Edward Arnold, pp. 294-299.

Curthoys, A. and Docker, J. (1989) In 'Praise of Prisoner'. In: Tulloch, J. and Turner, G. eds. *Australian Television: Programmes, Pleasures and Politics*. Sydney: Allen and Unwin.

Dickerson, D. (2001) Framing 'Political Correctness': The New York Times' Tale of Two Professors. In: Reese, S. *et al*. eds. *Framing Public Life*. Mahwah, New Jersey: Lawrence Erlbaum Associates. pp. 163–174.

Doty, A. (1993) *Making Things Perfectly Queer: Interpreting Mass Culture*, Minnesota: University of Minnesota Press.

Dyer, R. (1986) *Heavenly Bodies*. London: Macmillan.

Eco, U. (1974) Semiological Guerrilla Warfare, In: Eco, U. ed. *Faith in Fakes: Travels in Hyper-reality*. London: Picador.

Eco, U. (1986) *Faith in Fakes: Travels in Hyper-Reality*. London: Picador.

Eco, U. (1990) *The Limits of Interpretation*. Indianapolis: Indiana University Press.

Eldridge, J. *et al*. (1997) *The Mass Media and Power in Modern Britain*. Oxford: Oxford University Press.

Fisher, K. (1997) Locating Frames in the Discursive Universe. *Sociological Research Online* 2(3).

Gamson, W. (1992) *Talking Politics*. Cambridge: Cambridge University Press.

Gauntlett, D. (1995) *Moving Experiences: Understanding Television's Influences and Effects*. London: John Libbey.

Gauntlett, D. (1998) Ten Things Wrong with the 'Effects' Model. In: Dickinson, R. *et al*. eds. *Approaches to Audiences: A Reader*. London: Arnold.

Gillespie, M. (1995) *Television, Ethnicity and Cultural Change*. London: Routledge.

Gitlin, T. (1980) *The Whole World is Watching: Mass Media in the Making and Unmaking of the New Left*. Berkeley, USA: University of California.

Gitlin, T. (1991) The Politics of Communication and the Communication of Politics. In: Curran, J. and Gurevitch, M. eds. *Mass Media and Society*. London: Edward Arnold.

Glasgow University Media Group (1980) *More Bad News*, London: Routledge and Kegan Paul.

Goffman, E. (1974) *Frame Analysis: An Essay on the Organization of Experience*. New York: Harper and Row.

Gray, A. (1987) Behind Closed Doors: Video Recorders in the Home. In: Baehr, H. and Dyer, G. eds. *Boxed In: Women and Television*. London: Pandora.

Gray, A. (1999) Audience and Reception Research in Retrospect: the Trouble with Audiences. In: Alsuutari, P. ed. *Rethinking the Media Audience*. London: Sage, pp. 22–37.

Griffen, G. ed. (1993) *Outwrite: Lesbianism and Popular Culture*. London: Pluto Press.

Hagen, I. and Wasko, J. eds. (2000) *Consuming Audiences? Production and Reception in Media Research*. Cress Hill, N.J.: Hampton Press.

Hall, S. (1981/1973) Encoding and Decoding in the Television Discourse. In: Hall, S. *et al*. eds. *Culture, Media, Language: Working Papers in Cultural Studies 1972–79*. London: Hutchinson.

Hertog, J. and McLeod, D. (2001) A Multiperspectival Approach to Framing Analysis: A Field Guide. In Reese, S. *et al*. eds. *Framing Public Life*. Mahwah, New Jersey: Lawrence Erlbaum Associates.

Herzog, H. (1941) On Borrowed Experience: an Analysis of Listening to Daytime Sketches. *Studies in Philosophy and Social Science* 9(1), pp. 65–95.

Hobson, D. (1981, 1980) Housewives and the Mass Media. In: Hall, S. *et al*. eds. *Culture, Media, Language: Working Papers in Cultural Studies 1972–79*. London: Hutchinson.

Hobson, D. (1982) *'Crossroads': The Drama of Soap Opera*. London: Methuen.

Hodge, R. and Tripp, D. (1986) *Children and Television*. Cambridge: Polity Press.

Iyengar, S. (1991) *Is Anyone Responsible? How Television Frames Political Issues*. Chicago: University of Chicago Press.

Iyengar, S. and Kinder, D. (1987) *News that Matters; Television and American Opinion*. Chicago: University of Chicago Press.

Jakubowicz, A. *et al*. (1994) *Racism, Ethnicity and the Media*. St Leonards, Australia: Allen and Unwin.

Jay, C. and Glasgow, J. eds. (1992) *Lesbian Texts and Contexts:* Radical Revisions. London: Onlywomen.

Katz, E. Lazarsfeld, P. (1955) *Personal Influence: the Part Played by People in the Flow of Mass Communication*. New York: Free Press.

Katz, E. Lazarsfeld, P. and Liebes, T. (1988, 1985) Mutual Aid in Decoding Dallas: Preliminary Notes for a Cross-culture Study. In: Drummond, P. and Paterson, R. eds. *Television and its Audience: International Research Perspectives*. London: B.F.I.

Kitzinger, J. (1990) Who Are You kidding?: Children, Power and the Struggle Against Sexual Abuse. In: James A. and Prout, A. eds. *Constructing and Reconstructing Childhood*. London: Falmer Press, pp. 157–183.

Kitzinger, J. (1993) Understanding AIDS–Media Messages and What People know about AIDS. In: Eldridge, J. ed. *Getting the Message*. London: Routledge.

Kitzinger, J. (1994) Challenging Sexual Violence Against Girls: A Public Awareness Approach. *Child Abuse Review* 3(4), pp. 246–248.

Kitzinger, J. and Farquhar, C. (1999) The Analytical Potential of 'Sensitive Moments'. In: Barbour, R. and Kitzinger, J. eds. *Developing Focus Group Research: Politics, Theory and Practice*. London: Sage.

Klein, N. (2000) *No Logo*. London: HarperCollins/Flamingo.

Kubey, R. (1996) On Not Finding Media Effects: Conceptual Problems in the Notion of an 'Active Audience'. In: Hay, J. eds. *The Audience and its Landscapes*. Boulder: Westview Press, pp. 187–205.

Lazarsfeld, P.F. *et al*. (1944) *The People's Choice. How the Voter Makes Up his Mind in a Presidential Campaign*. New York: Duell, Sloan and Pearce.

Lewis, J. (1997) What Counts in Cultural Studies. *Media, Culture and Society 19*, pp. 83–97.

Livingstone, S. (1990) Interpreting a Television Narrative: How Different Viewers See a Story. *Journal of Communication* 40, pp.72–85.

Livingstone, S. (1996) On the Continuing Problem of Media Effects Research. In: Curran, J. and Gurevitch, M. eds. *Mass Media and Society*. 2nd edn. London: Edward Arnold.

Livingstone, S. (1998) *Making Sense of Television: The Psychology of Audience Interpretation*. 2nd edn. London: Routledge.

Livingstone, S. (1999) Mediated knowledge: Recognition of the Familiar, Discovery of the New. In: Gripsrud, J. ed. *Television and Common Knowledge*. London: Routledge, pp. 91–107.

Martin-Barbero, J. (2000) Cultural Mediations of Television Consumption. In: Hagen, I. and Wasko, J. eds. *Consuming Audiences? Production and Reception in Media Research*. Cresshill N.J.: Hampton Press, pp. 145–161.

Marullo, S. *et al*. (1996) Frame Changes and Social Movement Contraction: U.S Peace Movement Framing after the Cold War. *Sociological Inquiry* 66, pp. 1–28.

McCombs, M. and Shaw, D. (1972) The Agenda-Setting Functions of the Mass Media. *Public Opinion Quarterly* 36, pp. 176–187.

McGuigan, J. (1992) *Cultural Populism*. London: Routledge.

McKinley, E. G. (1997) *Beverly Hills, 90210: Television, Gender and Identity*. Philadelphia: University of Pennsylvania Press.

McLaughlin, L. (1993) Feminism, the Public Sphere, Media and Democracy. *Media Culture and Society* 15, pp. 599–620.

McQuail, D. (1977/83) The Influence and Effects of Mass Media. In: Curran, J. *et al*. eds. *Mass Communication and Society*. London: Arnold.

Merton, R. (1946) *Mass Persuasion*: The Social Psychology of a War Bond Drive. New York: Harper Brothers.

Miller, D. and Andsager, J. (1997) Protecting 1st Amendment? Newspaper Coverage of Hate Speech. *Newspaper Research Journal* 18(3-4), pp.2–15.

Modleski, T. (1984) *Loving With a Vengeance – Mass-produced Fantasies for Women*. London: Methuen.

Moores, S. (1993) *Interpreting Audiences: The Ethnography of Media Consumption*. London: Sage.

Morgan, D. (1988) *Focus Groups as Qualitative Research*. London: Sage.

Morley, D. (1980) *The 'Nationwide' Audience: Structure and Decoding*. London: B.F.I.

Morley, D. (1986) *Family Television: Cultural Power and Domestic Leisure*. London: Comedia.

Morley, D. (1995) Theories of Consumption in Media Studies. In: Miller, D. ed. *Acknowledging Consumption: A Review of New Studies*. London: Routledge.

Morley, D. (1998) So-Called Cultural Studies: Dead Ends and Reinvented Wheels. *Cultural Studies* 12(4), pp. 476–497.

Morley, D. and Silverstone, R. (1990) *Domestic Communications: Technologies and Meanings*. London: Sage.

Morris, M. (1988) Banality in Cultural Studies. *Black* 14, pp. 15–25.

Mosco, V. and Kaye, L. (2000) Questioning the Concept of the Audience. In: Hagen, I. and Wasko, J. eds. (1991) *Consuming Audiences? Production and Reception in Media Research*. Cresshill N.J.: Hampton Press, pp. 31–46.

Palmer, P. (1986) *The Lively Audience: A Study of Children around the TV Set*. Sydney: Allen and Unwin.

Pan, Z. and Kosicki, G. (1993) Framing Analysis: An Approach to News Discourse. *Political Communication* 10(1), pp. 55–75.

Pan, Z. and Kosicki, G. (2001) Framing as a Strategic Action in Public Deliberation. In: Reese, S et al. eds. *Framing Public Life*. Mahwah, New Jersey: Lawrence Erlbaum Associates, pp. 35–65.

Parkin, F. (1971) *Class Inequality and Political Order*. London: McGibbon and Kee.

Philo, G. and Miller, D. (1997) *Cultural Compliance: Dead Ends of Media / Cultural Studies and Social Science*. Glasgow: Glasgow Media Group.

Rhee, J. (1997) Strategy and Issue Frames in Election Campaign Coverage: A Social Cognitive Account of Framing Effects. *Journal of Communication* 47(3), pp. 26–48.

Rosengren, K. (1996) Combinations, Comparisons and Confrontations: Towards a Comprehensive Theory of Audience Research. In: Hay, J. et al. eds. *The Audience and its Landscapes*. Boulder: Westview Press, pp. 23–51.

Schlesinger, P., Dobash, R.E., Dobash, R. and Weaver, C.K. (1992) *Women Viewing Violence*. London: British Film Institute.

Seaman, W. (1992) Active Audience Theory: Pointless Populism. *Media, Culture and Society* 14, pp. 301–311.

Seiter, E. et al. eds. (1989) *Remote Control: Television and Cultural Power*. London: Routledge.

Shah, D. et al. (2001). The Effects of Value-Framing on Political Judgement and Reasoning. In: Reese, S. et al. eds. *Framing Public Life*. Mahwah, New Jersey: Lawrence Erlbaum Associates, pp. 227–243.

Tufte, T. (2000) The Popular Forms of Hope: About the Force of Fiction Among TV Audiences in Brazil. In: Hagen, I. and Wasko, J. eds *Consuming Audiences? Production and Reception in Media Research*. Cresshill N.J.: Hampton Press, pp. 275–295.

Whitiker, C. (1985) Hollywood Transformed: Interviews with Lesbian Viewers. In: Staven, P. ed. *Jump Cut: Hollywood, Politics and Counter Cinema*. New York: Praeger Scientific.

Winship, J. (1987) *Inside Women's Magazines*. London: Pandora.

Critical connections

Kitzinger remains one of the key figures in UK audience research. For more than 20 years her work has explored how relationships of power, especially as inflected through gender, ethnicity and sexuality, influence the reception and interpretation of media messages. Kitzinger previously was a member of the Glasgow Media Group (GMG), based in Glasgow University, Scotland. One of the GMG's greatest strengths was its institutionalisation of media research. Though members came and went, the specialist focus of a critical mass of GMG researchers on media and communications facilitated the development of a clear theoretical identity, methodological approach and research agenda over a period of decades. The institutionalisation of qualitative sociological research within criminology has yet to be established. Instead, a great deal of media criminology appears to be conducted in a piecemeal or haphazard fashion, with little sustained attention from groups of dedicated researchers. Audience research, in particular, tends to be avoided. This dearth of audience studies in media criminology can be partly understood by the difficulty of conducting this type of research well, and by the time it takes to do so in a professional academic environment geared toward quick and quantifiable publication outputs. Whatever the reasons, media criminologists seldom research media influence through engaging directly with audiences, more often reiterating 'assumptions' – often empirically untested – about the influence images of crime and control have on those that consume them.

Discussion questions

- What are the main points of conflict and tension within current debates on audience research?
- What are the relative advantages and disadvantages of focus group work when exploring how people actively assemble meaning about social issues?
- To what extent is Kitzinger's research approach informed by Hall's Encoding–Decoding model (Reading 4), and in what ways does Kitzinger develop or enhance it?

Reference

Kitzinger, J. (2004) 'The Debate About Media Influence', in *Framing Abuse: Media Influence and Public Understanding of Sexual Violence Against Children*, London: Polity.

David Bell

RESEARCHING CYBERCULTURES (2000)

Introduction and context

THE FINAL READING IN THIS SECTION explores ground that is less well trodden by sociological researchers. In an era of Google books and escalating cases of online plagiarism among the student populace, and relentless popular and academic debate about the relative freedoms and dangers of the virtual environment (see Readings 7, 39 and 40), the Internet has become central both as an information resource for doing research, and as a place of research interest in its own right. Yet the methods for doing online research are still in their relatively formative stages. It is largely a case, as Nina Wakeford (2000: 31) puts it, of 'plundering existing research for emerging methodological ideas which have been developed in the course of diverse research projects, and weighing up whether they can be used or adapted for our own study'.

David Bell's contribution on 'Researching Cybercultures' is as much about defining what research on cybercultures might look like and identifying the broad approaches that might be taken when conducting that research, as it is about providing specific methodological tools. Doing research *in* cyberspace and conducting research *on* cyberspace present interesting challenges for researchers because they are characterised by the same debates that shape and constrain other forms of research, whilst simultaneously raising issues and dilemmas peculiar to the online world. For example, conducting an online content analysis of web pages can tell us much about web texts. But, to paraphrase Ericson *et al.* from Reading 9, one can no more deduce fully what web designers do from a reading of web content than one can deduce fully what journalists do from a reading of newspaper content. Since both the content of web materials and the context of production, distribution and consumption are of interest, Bell spends some time discussing methods of researching both – focusing on textual analysis of web content and ethnographic studies of cyberspace, or cyber-ethnographies.

Hot links and cool sites

> The ontology of the World Wide Web is more than simply a question of space, sites, or pages; it is fundamentally concerned with links and motion.
>
> (Shields 2000: 145)

Computers have become valuable (if contested) tools in information-gathering, especially now they are networked and configured to be 'user-friendly'. We have been provided with the means to access huge amounts of information of all different kinds, and with help in finding what we want – up to a point. A frequent complaint voiced by student users (among others) is that searching the web for useful stuff is a time-consuming and sometimes overwhelming task. Moreover, the helpmates we have been given, such as search engines, aren't (yet) smart enough to really be of help. As my colleague Tracey Potts (1999: 82) says, the trouble with the search engine is that it 'discriminates only at the level of the signifier and does not distinguish between contextual use of words'. David Deacon and his colleagues (1999: 332) call search engines 'the catalogue of the Internet', adding that they have 'none of the librarian's informed discretion, or the sensitivity to users' needs found in a good library cata-logue'. While intelligent search agents are promised in the futurology of artificial intelligence research, current search engines are anything but smart. Let me give you an example: some time ago, while researching a paper on lesbian and gay life in rural areas, I went looking on-line for a book called *Below the Belt: sexuality, religion and the American South* (Wilson 2000). I located the book on an Internet bookseller's site, and was offered the opportunity to 'click' for related sites. Thinking this would yield valuable extra research materials, I duly clicked, and was linked to a site selling authentic leather belts! Now, while these were very nice, and very reasonably priced, the ridiculousness of the link, connecting only at the level of the word 'belt', makes Potts' point very clearly.

Of course, this is a lazy commercial link, and not all links are like that. Looking at links is, in fact, one interesting way of thinking about websites, information and knowl-edge. Deborah Heath and her colleagues discuss the use of links to think about 'inter-active knowledge production', arguing that hyperlinks are simultaneously 'vehicles for travel within and between Internet domains and online documents, and *part of the con-tent* of such areas' (Heath *et al.* 1999: 456; my emphasis). Links are, therefore, much more than a technical, infrastructural device – they carry important information in their code. In their research on websites about medical genetics, Heath *et al.* show how links work as content and context, for example in joining 'official' medical database sites to support groups for people with particular genetic conditions. The networks mapped by hyperlinks gave them important 'clues' for understanding the intersections and the blockages between users of different kinds of sites, as well as revealing the kinds of 'tricks' that skilled users could utilize in order to 'decode' links.

Links are, in fact, a central component of the experience of the Web; we have got used to using them, clicking on them out of curiosity, moving around in cyberspace through these digital wormholes. Steven Johnson reminisces about the early experience of using hyperlinks:

> The eureka moment for most of us came when we first clicked on a link, and found ourselves jettisoned across the planet. The freedom and imme- diacy of that moment — shuttling from site to site across the info-sphere, following trails of thought wherever they led us — was genuinely unlike anything before it.
>
> (Johnson 1997: 110)

Hypertext reconfigures the architecture of knowledge, and the practices of writing and reading; as Rob Shields (2000: 151) writes, 'links cannot be treated as merely thresholds or passages to other pages. The link is both part of the text and an index caught on the threshold of departure, signaling to another page or text' — links are 'arrows frozen in flight, but still imbued with an overall sense of being in flight, between here and there' (152).

In an effort to get a sense of this structure, some researchers have mapped hyper- links between sites, tracing the dense and often serendipitous trails that those frozen arrows lead us through. Forms of software have now been devised to show us these tracings, such as Footprints and cookies, which can track a user through sites. As Dodge and Kitchin argue, such programs yield useful data on movement in cyberspace, as well as potentially reframing the activity of browsing or surfing the net:

> Web browsing is currently a solitary activity with users unaware of others who may also be looking at the same page, and unaware of the many pre- vious users. This kind of knowledge, however, can be used to improve navigation, with current users benefiting from the efforts of those who have explored the space before. The integration of this information would transform solitary surfing into a more collaborative, social activity like walking around a busy city centre.
>
> (Dodge and Kitchin 2001: 120)

While many people will still want to walk the road less travelled, others will surely welcome seeing traces of other travellers, and maybe decide to follow in their footsteps. Think of your own experiences: you visit a site, and spot an intriguing link. One quick click and you're there, then you spot another link . . . Like travelling without a map, or doing the situationist *derive* (meandering the city streets as the mood takes you), clicking through links can take you into strange territories (Sadler 1998). It can bring dead-ends as well as treasure troves — fine if you're out for an amble, but less satisfactory if, like Howcroft's (1999) respondents, you need a quick answer to some burning question. Luckily, for those of us who don't want to surrender to the mysteries of cyberspace, it's also possible to retrace your steps, and get to home (page) again, thanks to the 'Back' button. As Wise (2000) reminds us, hypertext was developed to reflect the nonlinearity of human thought processes — and the complexity of maps that trace links clearly illustrates this. These maps are, there-fore, fascinating documents, since they reveal the *higgledy-piggledy* business of thinking.

Moreover, as the study by Heath *et al*. of 'genetic knowledge production' shows, the links that we need to attend to extend beyond the hyperlinks between web pages and other online sites. As their work suggests, 'methodological strategies for mapping these emergent technosocial processes must be attentive to the nodes and interven-tions that link online and offline sites' (Heath *et al*. 1999: 451). Tracing these links is equally important if we are to understand how knowledge is produced, in acknowledge-ment that online resources are patched into offline worlds and lives in complex ways. For Heath and her co-researchers, this demands 'an itinerant methodological approach that traces connections between on- and off-line milieux' (452). We shall explore the implications of this in more detail later in this chapter. But before that, I want to think through one of the other prominent ways of examining the contents of cyberspace that I have already alluded to: the 'reading' of things like web pages as 'texts'.

Textual approaches to cybercultures

One interesting attempt to outline strategies for analysing the web is that by Mitra and Cohen (1999), which focuses on textual analysis. While it is important to remem-ber that the web is more than text, their essay is useful in picking through the key features of 'web textuality' and suggesting ways to think about them. Their proposal for a kind of 'critical text work' considers semiotic analyses of content (layout, style, etc.), a consideration of intertextuality (the relationships between texts) and the role of different reading positions in making the text (web page) meaningful. Borrowing from literary criticism and discourse analysis, Mitra and Cohen proceed to highlight six key features of web texts: intertextuality, nonlinearity, a blurring of the reader/writer distinction, 'multimedieness', 'globalness' and ephemerality. The intertextual-ity of web pages – the extent to which any text makes reference to other texts – is especially manifest through hyperlinks, and these determine most of the remaining characteristics, too. Pages are nonlinear since hyperlinks make nonsense of begin-nings and ends – there is no origin-point (first page) and no final destination (last page). The text is, therefore, open, potentially infinite, and rhizomatic. The blurring of the reader/writer distinction arises since (i) anyone with the (increasingly avail-able) technical knowledge can make their own site (Cheung 2000); and (ii) each reader 'constructs' the text through their use of links, customizing the connections between pages in a way the page's producer has little or no control over. The convergence of text, sound and image on the web gives pages their 'multimedieness', redefining the ways we interact with information in cyberspace, and giving websites a polysemous character in terms of content (Wise 2000). The potential for links to criss-cross the globe in disjunctive ways also brings polysemy, by opening the text up to different potential meanings. For example, both Mitra's (CR) work on 'India on the Internet' and Zickmund's (CR) on neo-nazi sites illustrates the heterogeneity of postings, responses and links between sites scattered geographically (and ideologically). Finally, web pages can appear and vanish without warning, rendering the web unstable – and thereby also destabilizing any 'text' we construct in it. As we can see, the 'hypertextuality' of web texts is their key characteristic, from which all the others emanate. As Mitra and Cohen show, these characteristics all have implications for the ways in which we conduct research on web texts.

The first problem is: where to begin? As there is no beginning in the interlinked, nonlinear web, we either have to hope for the best and dive in, or devise some frame-work for deciding where a suitable starting-point might be. Web mapping tools and hit counters, Mitra and Cohen suggest, might indicate to us the popularity of some websites – and this might be a good place to start. But, as they say, to get over-bothered by the question of beginnings is to miss the point of the web – and in any case, given the ephemerality of pages and sites, the starting-point may vanish before you're done. Related to the question of where to start is the question of where (and when) to stop. There are always more links to follow – even if we hit a dead-end, we can back-track and choose a new route. But how many links do we need to follow in order to get a sense of an 'area' of the web? If we look at ten sites on a topic, does it matter that there might be a hundred more we haven't seen? Lastly, what are the implications of web texts' ephemerality? What if the site we've been focusing on suddenly one day disappears, replaced by the familiar '404' error message? Where the remains of past sites are archived, it might be possible to do some archaeological work (Wilbur CR) – but in many cases, sites simply disappear without a trace.

In answer to all these questions, Mitra and Cohen take a pragmatic approach, which is to emphasize the *provisional*, *located* and *contingent* nature of any findings: awareness of these issues means that research on the web is always a snapshot, from a particular time, of a limited number of sites, stitched together uniquely. Just as an anthropologist has to realize that her or his fieldwork is embedded in the locale and the period of their visit, so researchers exploring web texts must be mindful of the modesty of their knowledge-claims. As we shall see in the next section, similar issues and questions arise for those researchers attempting ethnographic work on or in cyberspace.

Ethnographies in/of cybercultures

> While any ethnography is methodologically risky, cyberspace ethno-graphy is vulnerable to unique disruptions.
>
> (Hakken 1999: 37)

Perhaps more than any other research strategy, ethnography has come to occupy a central yet controversial position in studies of cybercultures. There are serious methodological questions raised by the attempt to transplant ethnographic research into cyberspace that we need to explore here. These must also be set in the broader context of debate about ethnography as a research practice more broadly, notably in disciplines such as anthropology and sociology – and of the percolation of ethnog-raphy into popular domains such as docusoaps and other 'reality' programmes on television. This leads Ken Plummer (1999) to conclude that we now inhabit an 'ethnographic society', all of us 'people watching' (or at least docusoap watching). Debates about the status and practices of ethnography can't all be squeezed into this chapter comprehensively; instead, we shall address those that come up as and when we meet them in the specific context of ethnography in cyberculture (and see also Hine 2000).

The very existence of the Internet and its easy accessibility make it a very attractive 'site' for fieldwork. As Steve Jones (1999b: 11) says, there has been something of an academic land-rush into cyberspace, matching those colonists who want to claim it as a community-space or an economic resource. Our senses of discovery and wonder, Jones writes, are 'titillated by the sheer scale and penetration of the Internet', as we marvel at the opportunities it offers us, from the comfort of our offices, to explore strange new worlds:

> the sheer availability of chat sessions, MUD/MOO sessions, e-mail, and the like provide us with a seductive data set, and it takes little effort to be of the belief that such data represent . . . well, *something*, some semblance of reality, perhaps, or some 'slice of life' on-line.
>
> (Jones 1999b: 12; emphasis in original)

Furthermore, in these days of tight finances in higher education, the Internet is a cheap-and-easy way to reach these worlds (a point reiterated a number of times by Paccagnella 1997). This can mean, of course, that researchers have less invested in their field sites, and can merely swoop in and out, grabbing data for their projects, or spend time 'lurking' – observing interaction without getting involved. Jones worries about the ethical implications of what he names an '"easy come, easy go" opportunity for sociological work' (18), and I share those worries. We shall return to the ethics of online fieldwork in a moment. First, let me introduce one of the most hotly-debated aspects of online fieldwork (and something that has long troubled ethnography more broadly) – the question of verifiability. This becomes particularly controversial when it comes to the relationship between online and offline worlds: is it possible to do ethnography wholly in cyberspace?

Proponents of what is variously called virtual ethnography, cyberethnography and cyberspace ethnography argue that cyberspace is a distinct and discrete world, and should therefore be treated as such. Luciano Paccagnella (1997: 5), for example, writes that in 'ethnographic research on virtual communities the on-line world has its own dignity'. T. L. Taylor (1999: 443) makes the same argument in her work on virtual bodies and identities – that if we take seriously the phenomenology of on-line life, then we need not be too hung up on 'verifying' our findings IRL: 'the idea that verifiability can be achieved offline is often embedded in a larger epistemological claim I am less willing to accept'. This issue links us back to older methodological worries about 'truth', authenticity, validity, as already noted – arguments that have rumbled on for a very long time (Plummer 1999). In the end, Taylor argues that we should resist sliding back to a position that unproblematically replicates an offline/online boundary. Instead, she urges scholars to become as fully immersed in virtual worlds as the participants we are researching:

> being willing to fully inhabit the spaces we are researching, and adapting ourselves to the new methodological challenges they present, is likely the

best (and possibly the only) way we will begin to make sense of life in these fluid landscapes.

(Taylor 1999: 448)

This stance contrasts with that taken by Sherry Turkle (1995) in *Life on the Screen*, and by Danny Miller and Don Slater (2000) in *The Internet: an ethnographic approach*. Turkle only reported findings where she had met respondents face-to-face as well as on-line – or, in her terms, 'in person as well as in persona' (Turkle 1995: 324) – acknowledging that this may make her work seem conservative. Miller and Slater confess to a similar outlook on ethnography:

> An ethnographic approach is . . . one that is based on a long-term and multifaceted engagement with a social setting. In this regard we are both relatively conservative in our defence of traditional canons of ethnographic enquiry. This seems particularly important at the present time, when the term 'ethnography' has become somewhat fashionable in many disciplines. In some fields, such as cultural studies, it has come to signify simply a move away from purely textual analysis. In other cases, the idea of an Internet ethnography has come to mean almost entirely the study of online 'community' and relationships – the ethnography of cyberspace . . . We assume that *ethnography means a long-term involvement amongst people, through a variety of methods, such that any one aspect of their lives can be properly contextualized in others. . . . An ethnography is much more than fieldwork.*
>
> (Miller and Slater 2000: 21–2; my emphasis)

David Hakken (1999: 45) echoes Miller and Slater too, chastizing those wayward academics guilty of 'donning the mantle of an anthropology of the contemporary but wearing it loosely', adding that 'misappropriation of ethnography is one reason why intellectuals find it hard to construct a convincing account of culture in cyberspace'. Like Miller and Slater, Hakken advocates multi-sited ethnography, with online and offline elements (see also Heath *et al.* 1999). Lyman and Wakeford (1999: 363) ask the pertinent question here: 'How much do we need to know about nonvirtual manifestations ("the real") to interpret the data that we collect online ("the virtual")?' We need, however, to broaden this question out, and think about (for example) the usefulness of seeing 'real' sites where people interact with the 'virtual' – as in Miller and Slater's time spent huddled round computers in Trinidad, or Wakeford's (1999) own work on cybercafés.

One way of reading this debate is as a predictable academic 'turf war' over the method of ethnography – as we see in Miller and Slater's dig at cultural studies, or Hakken's loose-fit anthropology. It's beyond the scope of my discussion here to join in with that spat. Instead, let's take the view that we're comfortable with different ways of doing ethnography, and focus instead on what seems to me to be the key issue here. To reiterate: *can we do ethnography solely online?* Christine Hine (2000) picks through this debate, siding with the more generous interpretation of ethnography, but (like Taylor) recommending active participation rather than passive observation. As she writes, this also means recognizing the distinctiveness of online life (and online research): 'how can you live in an online setting? Do you have to be logged on 24 hours a day, or can you visit the setting at periodic intervals?' (Hine 2000: 21). The researcher's depth of involvement should match participants' — indeed, in some respects, this distinction should disappear. Probably the most productive statement that Hine makes is to distinguish between different research contexts: 'the settings where we might observe Internet culture are different from the ones in which we would observe the Internet in use. One setting is virtual and the other a physical place' (40). While this maintains a distinction between real and virtual worlds that some scholars would want to contest (Taylor 1999), I feel that Hine's suggestion provides a useful practical solution to this particular problem. Moreover, to require face-to-face 'verification' of online ethnography may be unreflective of the context one is researching:

> Many inhabitants of cyberspace . . . have never met face-to-face and have no intention of doing so. To instigate face-to-face meetings in this situation would place the ethnographer in an asymmetric position, using more varied and different means of communication to understand informants than are used by informants themselves.
>
> (Hine 2000: 48)

This point reminds us of one key ethical issue in cyberspace ethnography — again echoing similar debates about power in the research process more broadly. Virtual ethnography restages some of these on-going debates, but also brings with it new ethical questions. It is important to sketch some of these here.

Ethics in cybercultures research

> Every ethnography needs a warrant (what right do I have to tell this story?) and a credo (what are the damages I could do and how are they to be avoided?).
>
> (Plummer 1999: 645)

Qualitative methods like ethnography have a long history of wrestling with ethical questions of all sorts. There are serious issues to confront about the role and power that a researcher has, as someone who enters a social setting to conduct research in it — and this methodological baggage is carried into cyberspace, too. Let's start by considering the positioning of the researcher in cyberspace. As Hine (2000) says, the arrival on our desktops of computers through which to access cyberspace has made online research virtually irresistible. At the practical level, computers let scholars overcome time, money and other constraints that often prevent us from conducting the kind of in-depth ethnographies associated with anthropology. Here, through the wires, we have instant access to countless potential field sites and informants — and we don't even have to leave our offices! Moreover, we can be almost completely invisible, simply silently watching what's going on — something that's impossible in real life, unless we engage in the ethically problematic practice of so-called covert research (entering the field site in disguise, masquerading as a participant and not disclosing our real reasons for being there). The observer who only observes – who 'stays on the verandah' (Hine 2000) – has become an untenable role to occupy in 'real world' ethnography. When we enter cyberculture, however, the opportunities to stay on the *virtual verandah* can be seductive. There's even a ready-made role for us – that of the 'lurker'. Lurkers are people who watch things like chat rooms or MUDs without actively participating – a kind of virtual voyeurism. Before you set off to lurk, however, it's important to note that this is a discussion of ethics, and that lurking as a research technique is widely condemned by virtual ethnographers. At the very least, as Heath *et al.* (1999) suggest, lurking is not acceptable since it puts the researcher in a powerful and distant position – the academic is someone who gazes on others, appropriating their actions for the purposes of research. Lurking is a one-way process, and one of the strengths of ethnography is its emphasis on *dialogue* with respondents – recasting research as collaboration rather than appropriation. More-over, the practice of lurking and then using material collected in research brings out questions of privacy in cyberspace: are chat rooms, discussion lists and so on 'public' or 'private'? There are different standpoints on this, and concepts of public and private vary across and between different kinds of online site (Mann and Stewart 2000). Given issues of database anxiety in this information age (Poster 1995), it seems sensible (and responsible) that researchers do not add to feelings of panic about unauthorised uses of information mined in cyberspace. Mann and Stewart (2000) survey arguments about ethics, confidentiality and lurking, and provide a broad ethical framework for online research, which highlights consent, confidentiality and the observance of netiquette, as well as offering practical advice on how to address these.

Set against research from the virtual verandah, then, is participation rather than observation. However, we should not simply see participation as the cure-all to ethical questions. For a start, we need to remember a distinction between overt and covert research – while many researchers have been disgruntled by the way that declaring their research aims means that no-one'll talk to them online (Ward 2000), there are immense ethical problems associated with covert participation. Again, this requires a mode of masquerade that amounts to deception, perhaps doubly so if we are attempting to pass as something we are not: if we are an 'outsider' rather than an 'insider' to the setting we're researching. That the act of masquerade is made easier in cyberspace does not mean that it is less ethically troublesome; neither does hiding behind the fact that everyone else could be lying about who they are. To rewire one of cyberspace's famous aphorisms, the fact that in *cyberspace no-one knows you're an ethnographer* does not answer the question of whether participants have a *right* to know that you are. Even if, as Daniel Tsang (CR: 432) says, it 'pays to have a sense of "healthy paranoia" on-line', researchers shouldn't be aggravating that.

In addition, we have to remember that participation in any social setting trans-forms it – even if we do declare our intentions, our presence impacts on the behav-iour of those around us. In some cases of overtly collaborative research, part of the agenda is to effect change – to intervene in the lives of respondents to enhance their well-being (Heath *et al.* 1999). Even when this is not the case, researchers have to recognize the effects that they have just by being there. While there are substantial practical gains in online research, such as comparative ease of access, there are also new limitations: the kind of sporadic involvement with a virtual field setting means we might miss some of the unintended impacts that our presence has. In common with offline participant observation, an awareness of these issues is paramount (Kendall 1999).

There are other serious ethical questions raised in cyberspace ethnography, but I do not have time to work through them all here. Ultimately, while David Hakken (1999: 210) argues that 'it may be more difficult for everyone to act ethically in cyberspace', it is important that scholars consider the ethical implications for different research strategies. Like the choice of methods, the exact shape of any ethical framework is context-specific; what's important is that it must be in tune with the field site, and must be accountable. Finally, we should remember what Howcroft (1999) wrote about information overload, and Poster's (1995) comments on database anxiety. Firing off endless intrusive questions contributes to both these problems, and can be considered a form of spamming (Selwyn and Robson 1998). The machine on your desktop might seem like a trouble-free gateway into limitless social phenomena, but all research online relies on the generosity of those we are researching (or, to put it more collaboratively, those we are *researching with*).

A manifesto for cyberethnographers?

To round off our discussion of the pleasures and pitfalls of ethnography in cyberspace, I want to return to Hine's (2000) important work. *Virtual Ethnography* presents, I think, one of the best discussions and illustrations of the principles and practices of this kind of fieldwork. Hine picks her way through many of the methodological questions that arise, based on the experience of researching online activities around the trial of British nanny Louise Woodward in the US in 1997. From the benefit of that experience she formulates a set of principles for virtual ethnography that I'd like to look at here. There are ten points (see Hine 2000: 64–5):

1   Virtual ethnography interrogates taken-for-granted assumptions about the Internet.
2   We need to see the Internet as both culture and cultural artefact.
3   The Internet transforms the notion of the field site, making the research mobile rather than spatially located.
4   Contesting the idea of the field site also means concentrating on flow and connectivity.
5   Virtual ethnography focuses attention on boundaries as well as connections – especially between the 'virtual' and the 'real'.
6   Virtual ethnography is 'interstitial' temporally – it is not inhabited 24 hours a day, so immersion can only be intermittent.
7   Virtual ethnography can only ever be partial, and can never reflect the totality of the Internet.
8   The ethnographer is also a participant in using the media of cyberspace, and so reflexivity about online experiences should be foregrounded.
9   The ethnographer and informants are both present and absent to each other; virtual ethnography is 'ethnography *in*, *of* and *through* the virtual', so face-to-face interaction is unnecessary.

10   Virtual ethnography also means 'not quite' ethnography in purists' terms; it is adaptive, and 'adequate for the practical purpose of exploring the relations of mediated interaction'.

Hine concludes with pragmatics rather than principles, in response to the last point made – the one principle is that there are no once-and-for-all principles in an *adaptive* methodology:

> There are no set of rules to follow in order to conduct the perfect ethnography, and defining the fundamental components of the ethnographic approach is unhelpful. The focus of ethnography on dwelling within a culture demands adaptation and the possibility of overturning prior assumptions.
>
> (Hine 2000: 65–6)

In addition, and reinforcing points 4 (emphasis on connections) and 7 (about the partial nature of any virtual ethnography), Hine draws up a list of different sites 'in which the Internet is enacted and interpreted', to stress the need for mobile or multi-sited ethnography – or at least, the need to recognize the dense and complex sites that comprise the Internet. While she acknowledges that this list is incomplete, it's worth looking at here:

- Web pages
- Accounts of making web pages
- Instructions on how to make web pages
- Programs to help in making web pages
- Reviews of web pages
- Media reports on Internet events
- Magazines and newspaper supplements devoted to the Internet
- Fictionalized accounts of Internet-like technologies
- Computer equipment retailers
- Software developers
- Stock markets
- Newsgroups
- MUDs
- IRC
- Video conferences
- Accounts of the purpose of newsgroups
- Internet service providers' advertising and introductory materials
- Internet gateways and search engines
- Homes and workplaces where the Internet is used, and the practices we find there
- Training courses
- Conversations between friends, families and work colleagues
- Academic Internet studies like this one

(Hine 2000: 62–3)

In the case of her ethnography, Hine chose to focus on the Woodward case, and to incorporate from this list the dimensions relevant to exploring how the Internet shaped the discourses around the British nanny's trial. Depending on the specific focus of any research project, different aspects will become more or less significant. One dimension that Hine doesn't figure very prominently is the infrastructure of cyberspace – like Latour's (1992) missing masses, ethnography has tended to miss nonhuman elements. However, Susan Leigh Star (1999: 379) argues that we should 'attend ethnographically to the plugs, settings, sizes, and other profoundly mundane aspects of cyberspace', since in programs and protocols are embedded issues of power, culture and the potential for change.

That last component is, in fact, a key aspect of many discussions of online research: that it should embody a political commitment to change (Escobar CR). By showing how things are, issues of power, inequality and injustice are made visible, so that they can be addressed. Heath *et al.* (1999) refer to such acts as 'modest interventions', reflecting their contingency and partiality. Their modesty does not, however, diminish their importance. As Hakken concludes:

> The ultimate intent of an ethnographically led cyberspace studies . . . is to ground the process of imagining cyberspace on both a rich empirical understanding of what is actually taking place and to articulate ethically formulated intellectual rules of thumb to guide further imaginings. I believe it also to be a responsibility of cyberspace ethnography to explore diligently what the empirical study suggests regarding how best to imagine the future – *to help create cyberspace, not just be created by it* . . . Because its imaginings can affect the future, cyberspace ethnography has a distinct moral charge. We study what is not because it will tell us what will be in any simple way, but *because in understanding what is (and what has been) we can learn ways of imagining that discourage practices that should be hindered, as ways that help us set goals we can attain*.
>
> (Hakken 1999: 228; my emphasis)

References

Cheung, C. (2000) 'A home on the web: presentations of self on personal homepages', in D. Gauntlett (ed.) *Web.Studies: rewiring media studies for the digital age*, London: Arnold.

Deacon, D., Pickering, M., Golding , P. and Murdock, G. (1999) *Researching Communications: a practical guide to methods in media and cultural analysis*, London: Arnold.

Dodge, M. and Kitchin, R. (2001) *Mapping Cyberspace*, London: Routledge.

Hakken, D. (1999) *Cyborgs@Cyberspace? An ethnographer looks to the future*, London: Routledge.

Heath, D., Koch, E., Ley, B. and Montoya, M. (1999) 'Nodes and queries: linking locations in networked fields on inquiry', *Americon Behavioral Scientist*, 43: 450–63.

Hine, C. (2000) *Virtual Ethnography*, London: Sage.

Howcroft, D. (1999) 'The hyperbolic age of information: an empirical study of internet usage', *Information, Communication and Society*, 2: 277–99.

Johnson, S.(1997) *Interface Culture: how new technology transforms the way we create and communicate*, New York: HarperCollins.

Jones, S. (1999b) 'Studying the Net: intricacies and issues', in S. Jones (ed.) *Doing Internet Research: critical issues and methods for examining the Net*, London: Sage.

Kendall, L. (1999) 'Recontextualizing "cyberspace": methodological considerations for on-line research', in S. Jones (ed.) *Doing Internet Research: critical issues and methods for examining the net*, London: Sage.

Latour, B. (1992) 'Where are the missing masses? A sociology of a few mundane artefacts', in W. Bijker and J. Law (eds) *Shaping Technology/Building Society*, Cambridge MA: MIT Press.

Lyman, P. and Wakeford, N. (1999) 'Introduction: going into the (virtual) field', *American Behavioral Scientist*, 43: 359–76.

Mann, C. and Stewart, F. (2000) *Internet Communication and Qualitative Research: a handbook for researching online*, London: Sage.

Miller, D. and Slater, D. (2000) *The Internet: an ethnographic approach*, Oxford: Berg.

Mitra, A. and Cohen, E. (1999) 'Analyzing the Web: directions and challenges', in S. Jones (ed.) *Doing Internet Research: critical issues and methods for examining the net*, London: Sage.

Paccagnella, L. (1997) 'Getting the seats of your pants dirty: strategies for ethnographic research on virtual communities', *Journal of Computer-Mediated Communication*, 3, available at http://www.ascusc.org/jcmc/vol3/issue1/paccagnella.html (accessed January 2001).

Plummer, K. (1999) 'The "ethnographic society" at century's end: clarifying the role of public ethnography', *Journal of Contemporary Ethnography*, 28: 641–9.

Poster, M. (1995) *The Second Media Age*, Cambridge: Polity Press.

Potts, T. (1999) 'Thrift-shop blues', *Things*, 11: 81–4.

Sadler, D. (1998) *The Situationist City*, Cambridge MA: MIT Press.

Selwyn, N. and Robson, K. (1998) 'Using e-mail as a research tool', *Social Research Update* 21, available at http://www.soc.surrey.ac.uk/sru/SRU21.html (accessed January 2001).

Shields, R. (2000) 'Hypertext links: the ethic of the index and itd space-time effects', in A. Herman and T. Swiss (eds) *The World Wide Web and Contemporary Cultural Theory*, London: Routledge.

Star, S. L. (1999) 'An ethnography of infrastructure', *American Behaviorial Scientist*, 43: 377–91.

Taylor T. L. (1999) 'Life in virtual worlds: plural existence, multimodalities, and other online research challenges', *American Behavioral Scientist*, 43: 436–49.

Turkle, S. (1995) *Life on the Screen: identity in the age of the Internet*, London: Phoenix.

Wakeford, N. (1999) 'Gender and the landscapes of computing in an Internet café', in M. Crang, P. Crang and J. May (eds) *Virtual Geographies: bodies, space and relations*, London: Routledge.

Wakeford, N. (2000) New Media, New Methodologies: Studying the Web', in D. Gauntlett (ed.) *web.studies: Rewiring Media Studies for the Digital Age,* London: Arnold.

Ward, K. (2000) 'A cyber-ethnographic analysis of the impact of the internet on community, feminism and gendered relations', unpublished PhD thesis, Staffordshire University.

Wilson, A. (2000) *Below the Belt: sexuality, religion and the American South*, London: Cassell.

Wise, R. (2000) *Multimedia: a critical introduction*, London: Routledge.

Critical connections

Many of the thinkers and theorists featured in this Reader can contribute much to explorations of the cyber. Habermas' 'public sphere' (Reading 1), McLuhan's 'extension of the human sensorium' (Reading 2), Castells' 'real virtuality' (Reading 5), Baudrillard's 'hyperreality' (Reading 6), and Gibson's cyberpunk imaginings of 'jacking in' to 'the matrix' (Reading 7) all provide potential theoretical platforms from which to launch empirical journeys into cyberspace. Indeed, the theoretical and, based on Bell's discussion here, methodological routes into the cyber seem almost as plentiful and diverse as the opportunities and dangers that might be encountered while there. It is curious, then, as Katja Franko Aas (Reading 40) has observed, that 'While research on cyberspace has been experiencing a steady growth, there is still a clear boundary between the field of cybercrime and what might be termed 'terrestrial criminology', with the latter receiving the vast majority of criminological attention' (see Reading 40). Aas' analysis of online and offline social governance, and Sheila Brown's exploration of virtual aspects of crime, media and law, represent two clear exceptions to this trend (Reading 40 and 39 respectively). Invoking a number of those pioneering theorists noted above, both take as their starting point the crucial issue of the blurring of the boundaries between the virtual and the real. The self, of course, can in myriad ways be extended and transcended beyond the physical body into virtuality. But the two cannot yet be separated entirely, and this carries important implications for how crimes and criminality are defined, perpetrated, experienced, policed and responded to in the virtual world.

Discussion questions

- What ethical dilemmas are raised by conducting online research on cybercultures (see also Reading 39)?
- How might Ericson et al.'s call for an 'ethnography of modern thought' (Reading 8) be extended to the virtual world?
- In what ways can the Internet be viewed as both culture and cultural artefact?

SECTION THREE

Crime, newsworthiness and news

Introduction

CRIME HAS ALWAYS BEEN, and will probably always be, a prominent feature of news media content. This is because crime news serves particular social, cultural, political, moral and economic purposes, the reading of which may vary considerably depending on the theoretical approach adopted. For Durkheimian functionalists, for example, crime reporting can help to reinforce moral boundaries and promote social cohesion among the law-abiding by publicly labelling and denunciating particular forms of criminal transgression. For Marxists, it contributes to strengthening the legitimacy of 'law and order' and the authoritarian state, helping to manufacture mass political consent around the interests of a powerful minority. For Feminists, crime news can contribute to the wider subjugation of women in a patriarchal society by reifying the predatory dominance of males and the victim status of women, and reinforcing gender stereotypes that maintain unequal power relations. Of course, there may also be considerable variation within and degrees of overlap between these broad theoretical approaches: instrumental and structural Marxists, for example, though both problematise the authoritarian state, disagree fundamentally regarding the coercive or ideological nature of law, the relations of the state to more or less unified ruling elites, and the forces and constraints that shape the news production process (see Readings 3 and 18 for different Marxist interpretations of crime news). There may also be considerable differences between, say, radical and liberal feminist readings of crime news, since the former generally maintain a much broader spectrum of behaviours that might be classified as male violence (see Reading 21 for a radical feminist interpretation of crime reporting). What all these approaches share in common, however, is their acknowledgement that news media representations of crime and criminal justice are a crucial, yet highly selective and unrepresentative, source of information about crime, control and social order.

Indeed, what is perhaps most striking about news representations of crime is their unrepresentative nature. Crime news presents a picture of criminal offending and victimisation which is the direct inverse of that portrayed by official criminal statistics. The vast majority of crime reporting relates to serious cases of interpersonal violence, most often between strangers, and only a tiny proportion covers the everyday property crimes that make up around three-quarters of offences recorded by the police (though official crime statistics are by no means an accurate indicator of actual crime levels either). Estimates of the precise proportion of crime news that relates to violent interpersonal attacks, property crimes, or other offences, will vary across studies depending on the particular definitions adopted and the methodological approaches employed (see Section Two on Researching Media). This section introduces readers to a range of theoretical, methodological and empirical approaches to researching and understanding crime news. The readings explore crime reporting in terms of news content and the complex and varied processes that determine how that content is produced and consumed. The influence of crime consumption is considered in Section Five.

In the first book-length sociological analysis of crime reporting in Britain, Steve Chibnall (1977) maps out the professional imperatives or 'news values' that shape the reporting of crime, and locates these within a wider ideology of the press and professional journalistic practice. Jewkes (2004) draws extensively on contemporary examples of crime and crime reporting to update Chibnall's professional imperatives and develop a list of news values suited to crime reporting in the twenty-first century. Unlike Chibnall and Jewkes, Katz (1987) locates the attractiveness of crime news in its capacity for enabling readers to engage in 'daily moral workouts', serving symbolically to help them work through the existential challenges faced in everyday life. Hall *et al.'s* (1978) model of 'primary definition' understands crime reporting in terms of the routine requirements of the news production process and the unequal power relations that exist between journalists and the institutional sources they rely on daily for information. Schlesinger, Tumber and Murdoch (1991) are critical of what they see as the overly deterministic nature of 'primary definition' and offer an alternative approach that seeks to overcome the media-centricity of previous research by considering the news production process from the perspective of sources as well as journalists. McLaughlin (2005) develops an in-depth case study analysis of the complex structural, cultural and moral processes that shaped how one British national newspaper reported the high profile murder of a black London teenager, and the police investigation and court proceedings that followed. Finally, Benedict's (1992) investigation of how the US news media covered the gang rape of a Portuguese woman interweaves feminist analysis with sociology, media studies and professional journalistic experience, and exemplifies the all too rare ethnographic approach to researching crime news reporting.

Steve Chibnall

PRESS IDEOLOGY: THE POLITICS OF PROFESSIONALISM (1977)

Introduction and context

IN KEEPING WITH the intellectual traditions that defined much British critical media research at that time, Steve Chibnall's *Law and Order News* is situated within a Marxist framework for understanding media, power and ideology.[1] Chibnall draws from a wide range of sources, however, and weaves a rich theoretical tapestry merging political economy, semiotics and media studies to explore the codes or rules that shape journalistic practice and, ultimately, underpin the reporting of crime. Through a combination of content analysis and ethnographic method (see Section Two of this Reader on Researching Media), he identifies eight *professional news impera-tives of journalism* – or 'news values' – that guide journalists' selection and construc-tion of newsworthy stories. These news values are seldom written down (outside academic research, at least) and journalists generally experience considerable diffi-culty articulating them when asked. Nevertheless, a sense of news values is inter-nalised to some extent by all journalists, and acts implicitly to provide a professional stock of knowledge that enables informed assessments about what is newsworthy and what is not. The eight news values Chibnall identifies are: immediacy, dramatisation, personalisation, simplification, titillation, conventionalism, structured access, and novelty.

---

[1] Critical media and cultural studies in 1970s Britain were heavily influenced by Marxist thinking, but there were important differences between the approaches taken by different insti-tutional centres. Whereas the Birmingham Centre for Contemporary Cultural Studies, then under Stuart Hall, espoused a Marxist cultural studies that drew heavily from Althusser and Gramsci, work emanating from Leicester was more informed by a political economy of the media. Whilst the Birmingham Centre developed a primarily theoretical model of how consumers actively make meaning from ideologically loaded media content, the Glasgow Media Group sought to establish a framework within which the influence of media bias could be evidenced empirically.

These overarching professional journalistic imperatives can be refined, inflected and augmented by other news criteria to gain greater insight into the reporting of particular 'types' of newsworthy event. Accordingly, Chibnall (1977: 77) identifies 'at least five sets of informal rules of relevancy in the reporting of violence [which] . . . guide journalists' treatment of violence by asserting the importance of': visible and spectacular acts, sexual and political connotations, graphic presentation, individual pathology, and deterrence and repression. Understanding these professional imperatives helps to make sociological sense of crime news content. For example, it helps explain why public violence between strangers tends to be newsworthy, whilst domestic violence between intimates does not. It also helps explain why news tends to focus on particular criminal events, rather than the more complex and intractable social-structural conditions that might provide a causal context. What it cannot illuminate is what these imperatives – and the wider practice of newsmaking – mean to working journalists. This level of insight can only be achieved through ethnographic engagement with the news-making process. It is the combination of theoretical sophistication and ethnographic method that distinguishes Chibnall's *Law and Order News* as one of the most significant studies of crime journalism conducted to date.

We can now identify the master concepts of the framework – the British way of life, the national interest, the democratic process, the rule of law, anarchy, law and order, subversion, militants and moderates, minority and majority, the public, private property, free enterprise, state interference and monopoly, and perhaps a handful of others such as

Positive, Legitimating Values	*Negative, Illegitimate Values*
Legality	Illegality
Moderation	Extremism
Compromise	Dogmatism
Co-operation	Confrontation
Order	Chaos
Peacefulness	Violence
Tolerance	Intolerance
Constructiveness	Destructiveness
Openness	Secrecy
Honesty	Corruption
Realism	Ideology
Rationality	Irrationality
Impartiality	Bias
Responsibility	Irresponsibility
Fairness	Unfairness
Firmness	Weakness
Industriousness	Idleness
Freedom of choice	Monopoly/uniformity
Equality	Inequality

family life. The dominant values of the ideology are set out in the table below. [1] They provide criteria for evaluating existing and emergent forms of behaviour.

Those actors who want their actions and beliefs signified as legitimate by the news media must contrive to associate themselves with the positive legitimating values. The politician seeking a 'good press' must appear 'firm but fair', his approach must seem honest and open, his policies moderate and flexible, never allowing dogmatism to distort his perception of economic and political realities, and finally in his public and private behaviour he must be seen to uphold the values of family life – love, respect, loyalty, faithfulness, consideration, etc. Similarly, the legitimacy of emergent forms of behaviour is assessed according to criteria derived from positive values. Their aims can be identified as constructive or destructive, open or secret, rational or irrational, responsible or irresponsible and so on; while the means employed in pursuit of those aims can be identified as legal or illegal, moderate or extreme, violent or peaceful, fair or unfair, etc. This process of evaluation can only be accomplished, of course, by means of shared background assumptions concerning the meaning of 'fairness', 'violence', 'moderation', and so on in typical contexts. These background assumptions constitute the most unconscious part of any ideological system. They are part of a stock of common sense knowledge (Schutz and Luckmann 1974) and as such they really only become accessible when realized in concrete evaluations. [2]

The professional news imperatives of journalism

By and large, journalists share the same stock of common sense knowledge as their readers. They are not responsible for its creation, although they do contribute towards its stability and survival. It is not part of the *professional* component of press ideology. The operation of the framework of concepts and values is ordered and controlled by at least eight professional imperatives which act as implicit guides to the construction of news stories:

1. Immediacy
2. Dramatization
3. Personalization
4. Simplification
5. Titillation
6. Conventionalism
7. Structured access
8. Novelty

1. Immediacy

News is about what is new, what has just happened. This means that it is centrally concerned with the present rather than the past, change rather than inertia, and events rather than long-term processes. This means large and important segments of reality are not communicated because they cannot be successfully cast in the conventional news form. The process of selection is constrained both by the medium of news and the timetable of newspaper production. Newspapers predominantly report 'developments' occurring between the two most recent printing deadlines, supplying only enough 'background' information to make the foreground event intelligible at a mundane level. [. . .]

News, then, is a form of communication which encourages what Barthes (1972:151) has described as the 'miraculous evaporation of history' from events. When cast as news stories events tend to be denuded of the historical context and history of development which gives them meaning for their participants. As Marx (1846) pointed out, without history reality becomes vulnerable to the interpretations of a dominant ideology: '. . . we must pay attention to this history, since ideology boils down to either an erroneous conception of this history, *or to a complete abstraction from it.*' [. . .] Reality becomes as immediate and convenient as instant coffee. The processes of its production and the social conditions within which they take place are rendered irrelevant to the purposes of consumption. Things happen, get described by newsmen and are ingested by passive consumers with their coffee and cornflakes. They are understandable, not as historical developments, but as manifestations of the peculiar present, the strange times in which we live. If we feel that this level of 'explanation' supplies an insufficient depth of understanding we are invited to buy the packaged interpretations of newspaper ideology displayed in the leader columns and littering the shelves of the news stores.

2. Dramatization

The event-orientation of news is reinforced by an emphasis on the dramatic. News is commercial knowledge designed in a situation of competition with profit in mind. Its purveyors are concerned with grabbing the attention of prospective audiences by making an 'impact'. This stress on impact contributes towards the predisposition to communicate concrete happenings and to neglect underlying patterns of motivation and belief. Actions lend themselves far more easily to sensational treatment than do thoughts. This is a consideration essential to the understanding of the manner in which, for instance, political dissent is reported. It leads to a concentration on the form rather than the content of opposition. As John Whale (1971:48) put it: 'Journalists are better at reporting the fact than the matter of protest. The antics of the unilateral nuclear disarmers were always better copy than their arguments.'

But the 'antics' of protesters are not only good copy, they form the basis for the evaluation of the general worth of the protest. The presence or absence of violence during a demonstration becomes perhaps the most significant factor in judging and signifying the legitimacy of the cause it represents, as dramatization directs attention away from the meaning of the event for its participants. The search for impact sensitizes the reporter to any violent form of expression which is then taken up and isolated from underlying political convictions. Meaningful action is transformed into spectacle for passive consumers of news. [. . .]

Thus the imperative of dramatization has the effect of trivializing dissent and focusing public attention on the symptoms rather than the causes of 'social problems'. [. . .]

3. Personalization

News is not simply about instantly packaging drama, it is about personalities. The cult of the star is perhaps the most pervasive product of the cultural fetishism of modern society. Modernization brings with it a proliferation of celebrities (Alberoni 1972; Taylor *et al.* 1975). [. . .]

The celebrity is increasingly a focus of attention not because of what he does but because of what he is or what he represents. He is an image, an embodiment of popular fantasy, a projection of the ideal and an object of commercial interest and exploitation. [. . .] The more that news enters the market place of entertainment the more it is obliged to recognize and promote the cult of the star. The consequence of this is not merely that front pages are occupied by the famous arriving at Heathrow, but that issues increasingly become defined and presented in terms of personalities, catering for the public desire for identification fostered by the entertainment media. Politics becomes a gladiatorial spectacle in which the conflict of policies is reduced to the clash of personalities. [. . .] Events are to be understood not by reference to certain structural arrangements and social processes but either (a) as the work of individuals or (b) through their effects on individuals. [3]

The first mode of understanding is obviously consonant with those components in the press's ideological framework which interpret collective deviant activity as a consequence of the work of corrupters, the tiny minority of wreckers who play on the weaknesses of the normally moderate and reasonable majority. The professional imperative of personalization encourages their identification and isolation as objects for the projection of negative popular fantasies. A whole social demonology is established and the genre of exposé journalism is enriched by stories of the form 'We name the men behind the . . . industrial chaos/drugs and pornography racket/student unrest/land speculation', etc. [. . .] The effect is to direct attention away from structural causes and deviant motivations, and this is also true of the second mode of understanding events and processes – through their impact on individuals. This appears to be based first on the tacit assumption that 'ordinary people' can only grasp the meaning of abstractions when they are presented in vivid personalized terms which allow for identification. Thus inflation becomes intelligible by examining its effect on the housekeeping of a Greater London housewife, while violence can be understood through an interview with a mugger's victim. Now, I am not suggesting that this type of approach is irrelevant to an understanding of the phenomena of inflation and violence, but rather that it conveys only one dimension of the phenomena. Moreover, it tends to merely reinforce the 'everyday, common sense' impressions which the reader already has of the phenomena. This is because the professional socialization of popular journalism encourages the reporter to adopt the perspective of his readers, recording those aspects of news events which are directly relevant to their practical activities. [. . .] The victims or structural conflicts and collective motivations are of 'human interest' in a way in which the conflicts and motivations are not.

4. Simplification

A fourth tendency inherent in journalists' conceptions of news is the oversimplification of reality, the elimination of the shades of grey that lie between black and white, the glossing over of the subtle complexities of motivation and situation which make human action intelligible at a level beyond the mundane one of 'common-sense', 'cliché', 'folk wisdom', and taken-for-granted assumption. This simplifying tendency is intimately bound up with practical standards of professional competence. The popular news story must be quickly assimilable and easily comprehended by readers of widely differing intellectual abilities. Arthur Christiansen, one of the most successful editors of the *Daily Express*, defined a bad news story as: '. . . a story that cannot be absorbed on the first time of reading. It is a story that leaves questions unanswered. It is a story that has to be read two or three times to be comprehended.'

For the popular journalist, then, good reporting involves 'pruning down' the reality of a situation, trimming its rough edges and moulding its shape to fit the pre-existing forms of news. Reality must accommodate news, just as news must trade off reality. Whenever possible, social situations must be reduced to the binary opposi-tions which provide the materials and dynamics of spectacle and drama – good vs bad/pros vs antis/unions vs Government/moderates vs extremists. Loose ends must be tied up and the story must remain uncluttered by 'unnecessary' impediments to immediate comprehension. [. . .]

Simplification, then, is an accommodation to perceived audience needs which tends to dichotomize complex reality, facilitating the presentation of events in a dramatic and personalized form.

5. Titillation

Jock Young writes of newspaper journalists:

> They have discovered that people read avidly news which titillates their sensibilities and confirms their prejudices . . . They hold their readers' attention by presenting material and sexual desiderata in an alluring, although forbidden, form . . . They fascinate, titivate, and then reassure by finally condemning.
>
> (Young 1974:239)

This may not apply so much to the *Financial Times* as it does to the *Sun*, but it is a generaliza-tion of considerable importance in understanding the genre of popular journalism. [4]

The advertising executives of monopoly capitalism have long realized that, carefully handled, sexual titillation can sell anything from cars to carpets. It also sells newspapers. [. . .] If the press lives by disclosure, it thrives on scandal. The popular press has turned salacious gossip into an art, providing its readers with vicarious enjoyment without the need for involvement, the age-old recipe of the voyeur. But while the press develops and caters for the voyeuristic predilections of its readers it studiously distances itself from the activities portrayed. It maintains a self-righteous moral rectitude which denies the desirability of illicit pleasure. The *News of the World*, of course, supplies the classic example of this combination of titillation and condemnation. Its present owner, Rupert Murdoch, has said of the paper: 'The "News of the World" used to be like a morality play. It used to write about people who were in trouble for doing wrong, or for being adul-terous with their neighbour's wife, or whatever, and they always came to a sticky end' (*Guardian* 28.8.74). Ignoring the implication that the paper is no longer like that, this is a very clear statement of the *News of the World*'s commercial formula – the simultaneous portrayal and condemnation of the more exotic and lurid forms of deviance. This applies primarily to expressions of sexuality but it also operates with regard to other forms of illicit hedonism such as drug taking or occultism. Such deviations become a spectacle which may be glimpsed without involvement or contamination. The reader can sit over his cornflakes in mild moral indignation while today's SHOCK HORROR PROBE into yesterday's SEX/DRUGS/WITCHCRAFT ORGY unfolds its unseemly content.

Titillation becomes a suitably commercial context in which to set the activities of personalities – pop stars, footballers, actors, criminals, and even, occasionally, politicians. [. . .]

It might equally be argued that the commercial imperative of titillation trivializes reality and diverts attention from politics and social problems, substituting superficial salacity for genuine understanding and thus clearing the ground for the interpretations of newspaper ideology.

6. Conventionalism

The interpretations of newspaper ideology provide the basic materials for the operation of conventionalism – the situating of emergent phenomena in existent structures of meaning. [. . .]

The need for interpretative reporting is now widely recognized and justified by a belief in the need to reduce the ambiguity of news by organizing the immediate chaos of isolated news events into a more coherent framework of knowledge, i.e., in a world of complex and fast-moving events, the public require expert interpretative aid if they are to successfully understand the meaning and significance of the news. To some extent, background information must be provided and the historical nature of news remedied by supplying the reader with an interpretative context. But if this context is to be immediately intelligible it must be familiar. Thus, there is a tendency for new events to be cast as well-known scenarios. We are offered a normalization of the potentially problematic, a collection of familiar images. [. . .]

This was succinctly expressed by a crime reporter who suggested that news stories were really 'simple clichés set to music – you select the right cliché and you write it up to suit the particular circumstances'.

Thus we receive our news extensively predigested, coded, and packaged in conventional parcels. As Burgelin (1971:323) has observed: 'Mass communications are plainly not just so much raw material of which the consumer . . . can make absolutely anything he likes; they are products which have already been extensively pre-structured . . . by the conditions under which they were manufactured.' In part, this pre-structuring takes the form of standardized formats and conventionalized selection procedures but it is also reflected in recurrent explanations, legitimations and evaluations of social phenomena.

These structures of meaning have become incorporated into journalism's stock of knowledge and as conventional wisdoms they constitute both a source on which the journalist may draw in arriving at understandings of phenomena, and a conservative constraint on the construction of stories in that they provide 'ready-made' interpretations of new phenomena. [. . .]

The journalist's conventional interpretations, then, both inform and reflect a somewhat fragmented, but more-or-less hegemonic, ideology. [. . .] By employing these interpretations the journalist can be sure that he is on tested ground, that he will not give offence and that his reporting is likely to be seen as 'responsible' by editors as well as reputable and influential individuals outside the news organization.[5] Moreover, conventional interpretations are convenient. They allow the journalist working under deadline pressures to produce copy rapidly with a minimum of thought and preparation. But, whether the reporter internalizes or distances himself from these interpretations, the imperative of conventionalism (like the other professional imperatives) is so closely bound up with the phenomenon of 'news' that it will exert a significant influence on his perceptual apparatus and subsequent construction of stories. They will tend to act as 'inferential structures' (Lang and Lang 1965) filtering acceptable reality and moulding events to fit pre-conceptions. Interpretative conventions, in short, contribute towards overall frames of reference within which phenomena are defined and signified. The study by Halloran and his colleagues of the 1968 London anti-Vietnam war demonstration provides a striking example of the operation of inferential structures:

> During the month or so prior to 27 October . . . the newspapers defined the event as likely to be a violent confrontation of the forces of law and order (as represented by the Police) and the forces of anarchy (as represented by the radical groups participating), with the result that when these predictions were contradicted by the peaceful behaviour of the vast majority of the marchers, the discrepancy was resolved by concentrating attention upon those aspects of the event which were violent.
>
> (Halloran et al. 1970:90)

The reality of the event was subordinated to considerations of the 'event as news'.

7. Structured access

The imperative of structured access is a residue of the objectivity paradigm in journalism which requires that news stories be firmly grounded in the authoritative pronouncements of experts in the fields covered by the stories. It survives largely because it helps to situate the media within the State's framework of power, defining their relationship to the plurality of institutional elites in the wider society. In the press the structure of access ensures that newspaper accounts and representations are 'structured in dominance'; that there is a systematic tendency to take up definitions of situations and events articulated by those in legitimate institutional positions, and to exclude definitions developed by those who lack formal qualifications to comment (Hall 1972, 1973). [. . .]

The structure of access mediates between the reality and the public signification of events, and causes the media to systematically 'over-assess' (a) accredited spokesmen of the State and powerful organizations and (b) certificated experts who are looked to to provide 'impartial' comment and evaluation. This structure of access has its ultimate and implicit base in what Howard Becker has termed society's 'hierarchy of credibility'.

> In any system of ranked groups, participants take it as given that members of the highest group have the right to define the way things really are . . . those at the top have access to a more incomplete picture of what is going on than anybody else. Members of lower groups will have incomplete information and their view of reality will be partial and distorted in consequence.
>
> (Becker 1967)

Thus, it is argued, members of society tend to place greater reliance on the state-ments of those in powerful positions of authority, those who are in possession of all the 'facts'. Journalists do tend to be less credulous than most when it comes to believ-ing the accounts supplied by the 'official sources' they cultivate, but it does not pre-vent them reproducing those accounts in preference to those of less powerful sources. They will often take informal accounts to official sources for confirmation or denial. One Fleet Street crime correspondent told me that whenever possible he uses his police contacts to test the veracity of information derived from other sources: 'you don't know what to believe because they [the non-police sources] are all on the fringes of criminal activity'. But despite the rhetoric of truth-seeking with which he may surround his activity, the journalist is primarily interested in the acquisition of official accounts (irrespective of their veracity) because his editors expect him to obtain them, and to obtain them quickly. Thus the production demands of the news organi-zation largely dictate the reporter's priorities and relevance structures and encourage the fairly uncritical reliance on official sources reported by this *Guardian* journalist: 'I think we accept Scotland Yard statements too easily, for the sake of convenience. They must feed us information that they want to put out which we accept because it's convenient.' [. . .]

8. *Novelty*

Each of the professional news imperatives discussed so far intermesh to support and articulate newspaper ideology. But there is at least one imperative which introduces an element of randomness into newspaper accounts, even though it too may facilitate the use of the ideological interpretations and stereotypes. That imperative is the one which demands that stories be 'kept alive' by the search for fresh 'news angles':

> When you're working for a pop paper where there is always this desperate search for a thing called an angle, it isn't enough that something has happened, there must be an angle, there must be something different, we must have something that somebody else hasn't got, and because we've got something that somebody else hasn't got it must be right up the top. The plain facts are distorted round to suit this particular angle.
>
> (Crime Correspondent)

The imperative of novelty encourages speculation, often speculation supported by only slender evidence. In some cases when deadlines become oppressively close, almost any story may suffice, almost any fresh twist of interpretation may become acceptable. At times like this reporters occasionally file copy which is distinguished by little more than the doubtful reliability of its sources. [. . .]

It should now be clear that the professional news imperatives of journalism provide the necessary support for newspaper ideology. They add to the plausibility of ideological accounts and representations through the provision of working definitions of news and practical rules for the accomplishment of reportorial work. But this social organization of reporting can only supply *foundations* for the plausibility of newspaper accounts to those whose practical purposes are bound up with the assembling of those accounts i.e., newspapermen themselves. The consumer of news will have different practical purposes and will utilize different criteria in judging the plausibility of the interpretations he meets in his newspaper. These consumer criteria of plausibility are not really the subject of this study but it is perhaps worth speculating that they are also likely to make reference to the utility of interpretations for various practical accomplishments. Paramount among these accomplishments is probably common-sense understanding. That is, as recent commentators have suggested (Mepham 1973; Morley 1974), the power of newspaper interpretations lies in their ability to make events intelligible at a mundane, 'commonsense' level, to provide a guide for practical activity and to alleviate the need for further investigation and consideration. The self-confident and assertive style in which the interpretations are communicated complements their general claim to represent the opinions of all right-minded people and encourages their ready acceptance as self-evident and 'obvious'. They may be absorbed as part of a routine and habitualized way of making sense of the world which typically operates below the threshold of consciousness. This commonsense mode of understanding trades off myths and stereotypes which provide simple, comfortable, ready-made pictures and explanations of things. It does this because it is grounded in everyday practical concerns which allow no time to probe beneath the surface of things. The interpretations of popular newspapers tend to fit admirably into the commonsense world of everyday life because they make few intellectual demands on the reader. They promote a peculiarly restricted mode of understanding by signifying the definitional characteristics of a phenomenon and its causation by reference to highly selective aspects of the phenomenon. This process 'works', it is suggested, because the aspects selected are ones to which most readers can easily relate. [. . .] I do not wish to imply that readers are necessarily credulous in their approach to news. On the contrary, suspicion of newspaper accounts is deeply ingrained in our culture – it is part of 'what everybody knows' that one has to take what the papers say 'with a pinch salt. But I would suggest that it is easier for most readers to reject the open, substantive (factual) content of newspaper accounts than the more latent and implicit interpretive schema in which that content is embedded. These schema are easily absorbed into the common stock of knowledge in a largely subliminal fashion. [. . .]

Notes

1.   This should not be considered an exhaustive list.
2.   These concrete evaluations will be further analyzed in due course.
3.   As Galtung and Ruge (1965) point out, this approach fits very well with modern techniques of newsgathering and presentation: 'It is easier to take a photo of a person than of a structure . . . and, whereas one interview yields a necessary and sufficient basis for a one person-centred news story, a structure-centred news story will require many interviews, observation techniques, data gathering etc.'
4.   However, the 'quality' press should not be thought immune from the temptation to titllate. The reader is invited to examine, for example, the *Daily Telegraph*'s 'full and frank' coverage of the case of 'the topper and the copper' in 1974 (the rape of a show girl by a policeman).

5.   Specialist correspondents usually employ conventionalized interpretations in their private as well as their public constructions of reality. The discontinuity between private thoughts and public words is characteristic of the generalist rather than the specialist – the strong element of natural selection in specialist recruitment sees to this (Sigalman 1973).

References

Alberoni, F. (1972) The Powerless 'Elite': Theory and Sociological Research on the Phenomenon of the Stars. In D. McQuail (ed.), *Sociology of Mass Communications*. Harmondsworth: Penguin.

Backer, H. (1967) Whose Side Are We On?. *Social Problems* 14: 239–47.

Burgelin, O. (1971) Structural Analysis of Mass Communication. In D. McQuail (ed.), *Sociology of Mass Communications*. Harmondsworth: Penguin.

Galtung, J. and Ruge M. (1965) The Structure of Foreign News. *Journal of International Peace Research* 1(1): 64–90.

Hall, S. (1972) External Influences on Broadcasting, Stencilled *Occasional Paper No. 4*. Centre for Contemporary Cultural Studies. University of Birmingham.

Hall, S. (1973) The Structured Communication of Events. Stencilled *Occasional Paper No. 5*. Centre for Contemporary Cultural Studies, University of Birmingham.

Halloran J, Elliot, P., and Murdock, G. (1970) *Demonstrations and Communication: A Case Study*. Harmondsworth: Penguin.

Lang, K. and Lang, L (1965) The Inferential Structure of Political Communications. *Public Opinion Quarterly* 19.

Marx, K. and Engels, F. (1846) *The German Ideology*. London: Lawrence & Wishart 1965.

Mepham, J. (1973) The Theory of Ideology in Capital. *Radical Philosophy* 6.

Morley, D. (1974) Industrial Conflict and the Mass Media. Stencilled *Occasional Paper No. 8*. Centre for Contemporary Cultural Studies, University of Birmingham.

Roshier, R. (1971) Crime and the Press. *New Society* 16.9.71:502–6.

Schutz, A. and Luckmann, T. (1974) *The Structures of the Life World*. London: Heinemann.

Sigalman, J. (1973) Reporting the News: An Organizational Analysis. *American Journal of Sociology* 79:132–51.

Taylor, I., Walton, P., and Young, J. (eds), (1975) *Critical Criminology*. London: Routledge and Kegan Paul.

Whale, J. (1971) *Journalism and Government*. London: Macmillan.

Young, J. (1974) Mass Media, Drugs, and Deviance. In P. Rock and M. McIntosh (eds.), *Deviance and Social Control*. London: Tavistock.

Critical connections

It is only through Chibnall's ethnographic approach that it becomes possible to research the subtleties and contradictions embedded in the practice of crime journalism (see also Reading 8). In the final chapter of the book he offers the example of a Sunday reporter who expresses a profound commitment to his own 'integrity and sense of professional responsibility' in 'not writing stories I don't believe in', only to declare moments later that he is 'in much the same position as the man who goes to work for Ford in Dagenham — I do my work, how it's sold by the company is someone else's business' (Chibnall, 1977: 221). The strong ethnographic element of *Law and Order News* is often overlooked in textbook summaries of the study, which tend instead merely to list the news values Chibnall identifies. The ethnography comes through clearly in the excerpt included here, in which Chibnall maps out the key determinants of newsworthiness, not only through close analysis of the crime news that is produced, but also by engaging with those who produce it. Chibnall's *Law and Order News* (1977) remains one of the classic, and indeed one of the very few, in-depth ethnographies of British crime journalism.

Discussion questions

- Can Chibnall's news values be ranked in order of importance?
- Think of a high profile criminal event that received sustained front-page media coverage and discuss its 'newsworthiness' in terms of Chibnall's news values.
- What does Chibnall's ethnographic approach to researching crime reporting contribute to our understanding that content analysis alone could not (see Readings 8, 9 and 10)?

Yvonne Jewkes

THE CONSTRUCTION OF CRIME NEWS (2004)

Introduction and context

SINCE THE PUBLICATION of *Law and Order News,* very little work has been done to chart changes in the professional imperatives or news values that determine the newsworthiness of crime. In part, this is because many of those key criteria identified by Chibnall still apply today. There are certain core or fundamental news values – for example, dramatisation, personalisation, immediacy – which appear to transcend place and time and survive even the most dramatic shifts in the socio-political and cultural environment, and the nature of the information market place. However, as Bronwyn Naylor (2001) has pointed out, news values are also to an extent culturally specific in that they reflect the historical and social moment in which they are situated. Yvonne Jewkes' (2004) work constitutes one of the few recent attempts to develop an updated list of news values more suited to crime reporting in the twenty-first century. The excerpt included here lists all of Jewkes' news values, but includes discussion only of those that mark a significant departure from or develop-ment of Chibnall's original listing. Six from a list of twelve news values are discussed in detail: risk, sex, proximity, violence, spectacle and graphic imagery, and children.

The first people to attempt to systematically identify and categorize the news values that commonly determine and structure reported events were Galtung and Ruge (1965/1973). Their concern was with news reporting generally, rather than crime news per se, but their view that incidents and events were more likely to be reported if they were, for example, unexpected, close to home, of a significant threshold in terms of dramatic impact, and negative in essence, clearly made them relevant to crime reporting. Following their classic analysis, another influential study was published in 1977 by Steve Chibnall. Despite it being nearly 30 years old, and being concerned with journalistic priorities in the post-War period from 1945 to 1975, *Law and Order News* arguably remains the most influential study of news values relating to crime reporting and has led to numerous applications of the concept of news values in a myriad of different contexts (including Hall et al., 1978; Hartley, 1982; Hetherington, 1985; Ericson et al., 1987, 1989, 1991; Cavender and Mulcahy, 1998; Surette, 1998; Manning, 2001; Greer, 2003).

However, Britain is a very different place now than it was half a century ago. The prison population has soared from just over 40,000 in 1977 to 73,850 in April 2003 (expected to rise to in excess of 99,300 by June 2009), and contemporary news reports contain references to crimes – road rage, joyriding, car-jacking, ecstasy dealing, identity theft – not heard of 30 years ago. Conversely, non-violent crimes such as property offences which, in the post-War period constituted nearly a quarter of stories in *The Times* (Reiner, 2001; Reiner et al., 2001) are now so common-place that they are rarely mentioned in the national media. The media landscape has itself changed almost beyond recognition. In 1977 there were just three television channels, a fraction of the newspaper and magazine titles, and although e-mail had just been developed it was the preserve of a handful of academics sitting in computer labs on either side of the Atlantic. The structures of ownership and control have altered and news, like all other media output, is significantly more market-driven and dictated by ever-looming deadlines than it was previously. Politics is not as polarized as it was in the 1970s when the ideological battlefield was fiercely contested between capitalists and socialists. At the same time, contemporary audiences are arguably more knowledgeable, more sophisticated and more sceptical than at any time previously, and are certainly sufficiently media-savvy to know when they are on the receiving end of political 'spin' (Manning, 2001). What is more, some critics argue that the pressure on media professionals to produce the ordinary as extraordinary shades into the postmodern, and that what was historically described as news gathering has, in the new millennium, begun to take on the same '"constructed-for-television" quality that postmodernists refer to as "simulation"' (Osborne, 2002: 131). The time seems right, then, for a reassessment of the criteria that structure the news that we read, hear, watch and download at the beginning of the 21st century. [. . .]

Of course, some of the criteria identified by Galtung and Ruge in 1965 and Chibnall in 1977 still broadly hold true. [. . .] It is also important to remember that different values may determine the selection and presentation of events by different news media (and, for that matter, by different or competing organizations), and that the broadcast media tend to follow the news agenda of the press in deciding which stories are newsworthy. Not surprisingly, the news values of the *Sun* are likely to be somewhat different from those of the *Independent* and different again from those of the BBC. Even among news organizations which appear to be very similar, such as the British tabloid press, there may be differences in news reporting which are largely accounted for by the house style of the title in question. For example, some stress the 'human interest' angle of a crime story (with first-hand accounts from victims and witnesses, an emphasis on tragedy, sentimentality and so on) and may be primarily designed to appeal to a female readership, while others sensationalize crime news, emphasizing sex and sleaze, but simultaneously adopting a scandalized and prurient tone. [. . .]

News values for a new millennium

Six of the 12 news structures and news values that shape crime news listed below are discussed in the rest of this chapter:

- Threshold
- Predictability
- Simplification
- Individualism
- Risk
- Sex
- Celebrity or high-status persons
- Proximity
- Violence
- Spectacle and graphic imagery
- Children
- Conservative ideology and political diversion [. . .]

Risk

Given that the notion of modern life being characterized by *risk* has become such a widespread and taken-for-granted assumption, it is surprising to find that the media devote little attention to crime avoidance, crime prevention or personal safety. The exception to this is if a message about prevention can be incorporated into an ongoing narrative about a serious offender 'at large', in which case the story will be imbued with a sense of urgency and drama (Greer, 2003). The vast majority of serious offences, including murder, rape and sexual assault, are committed by people known to the victim. There are also clearly discernible patterns of victimization in certain socio-economic groups and geographical locations. Yet the media persist in present-ing a picture of serious crime as random, meaningless, unpredictable and ready to strike anyone at any time (Chermak, 1994: 125). Such discourse as exists in the media (particularly the popular press) regarding prevention and personal safety invariably relates to offences committed by strangers, thus implicitly promoting stereotypes of dangerous criminals prepared to strike indiscriminately (Soothill and Walby, 1991; Greer, 2003).

The idea that we are all potential victims is a relatively new phenomenon. After the Second World War, news stories encouraged compassion for offenders by provid-ing details designed to elicit sympathy for their circumstances, thus endorsing the rehabilitative ideal that dominated penal policy at that time (Reiner, 2001). In today's more risk-obsessed and retributive times, crime stories have become increasingly victim-centred. Perceived vulnerability is emphasized over actual victimization so that fear of crime might be more accurately conceived as a fear for personal safety (Bazelon, 1978). Sometimes, the media exploit public concerns by exaggerating potential risks in order to play into people's wider fears and anxieties. Following the September 11th terrorist attacks in America, the British media fuelled a vision of apocalyptic meltdown with a series of stories ranging from terrorist plots to target the UK, to warnings about falling meteorites heading for earth. Yet it must be remembered that audiences are not passive or undiscriminating. Many crime scares and moral panics simply never get off the ground, and while it might be argued that the media fail to provide the public with the resources to independently construct alternative definitions and frameworks (Potter and Kappeler, 1998), people's sense of personal risk will usually correspond to their past personal experiences and a realistic assessment of the likelihood of future victimization above and beyond anything they see or hear in the media.

Sex

One of the most salient news values – especially in the tabloid press, but also to a significant degree in the broadsheets and other media – is that of sex. Studies of the press by Ditton and Duffy (1983) in Strathclyde, by Smith (1984) in Birmingham, and by Greer (2003) in Northern Ireland, reveal that newspapers over-report crimes of a sexual nature, thus distorting the overall picture of crime that the public receives, and instilling exaggerated fears among women regarding their likelihood of being victims of such crimes (see also Cameron and Frazer, 1987; Soothill and Walby, 1991; Carter, 1998; Naylor, 2001). Ditton and Duffy found that when reporting assaults against women, the press frequently relate sex and violence, so that the two become virtually indistinguishable. Furthermore, the over-reporting of such crimes was so significant that in Strathclyde in March 1981, crimes involving sex and violence accounted for only 2.4 per cent of recorded incidents, yet occupied 45.8 per cent of newspaper coverage (Ditton and Duffy, 1983). So interlinked are the themes of sex and violence, and so powerfully do they combine to illustrate the value of 'risk', that the prime example of newsworthiness is arguably the figure of the compulsive male lone hunter, driven by a sexual desire which finds its outlet in the murder of 'innocent' victims (Cameron and Frazer, 1987). As such, sexually motivated murders by someone unknown to the victim invariably receive substantial, often sensational, attention. On the other hand, sexual crimes against women where violence is not an overriding component of the story (bluntly, sex crimes that are non-fatal) and sexual assaults by someone known or related to the victim are generally regarded as routine and 'pedestrian' and may contain only limited analysis (Carter, 1998; Naylor, 2001). Moreover, the sexually motivated murder of prostitutes – who do not conform to media constructions of 'innocent' victims – also invariably receive considerably less coverage than those of other women.

Bronwyn Naylor (2001) argues that the frequency with which articles appear about apparently random stranger violence against 'ordinary' women and girls not only indicates that such stories fulfil key news values, but also that they permit highly sexualized, even pornographic representations of women. At the same time, these narratives tend to be highly individualized so that offences involving females – whether as victims or perpetrators – are rarely reported by the popular media without reference, often sustained and explicit, to their sexualities and sexual histories. Victims are frequently eroticized: for example, the conviction of Stuart Campbell in December 2002 for the sexually-motivated murder of his 15-year-old niece, Danielle Jones, was accompanied by media reports of their 'inappropriate', that is, abusive, sexual relationship, and photographs of a pair of blood-stained, white lace-topped stockings belonging to the girl found at Campbell's home. Meanwhile, female offenders are often portrayed as sexual predators – even if their crimes have no sexual element. This narrative is so widely used that it leads Naylor to question the purpose of such stories and how readers consume them:

> These stories draw on narratives about particular kinds of masculinity and about violent pornography, reiterating a discourse about masculine violence as a 'natural force', both random and inevitable. They normalize this violence, drawing on and repeating the narrative that all men are potentially violent and that all women are potentially and 'naturally' victims of male violence (2001: 186).

She goes on to suggest that not only does the media's obsession with 'stranger-danger' give a (statistically false) impression that the public sphere is unsafe and the private sphere is safe, but also that it influences government decisions about the prioritization of resources, resulting in the allocation of funding towards very visible preventative measures (such as street lighting and CCTV cameras) and away from refuges, 'or indeed from any broader structural analysis of violence' (Naylor, 2001: 186). [. . .]

Proximity

Proximity has both spatial and cultural dynamics. Spatial proximity refers to the geographical 'nearness' of an event, while cultural proximity refers to the 'relevance' of an event to an audience. These factors often intertwine so that it is those news stories which are perceived to reflect the recipient's existing framework of values, beliefs and interests and occur within geographical proximity to them that are most likely to be reported. Proximity obviously varies between local and national news. For example, a relatively 'ordinary' crime like mugging or arson may be reported in local media but might not make the national news agenda unless it conforms to other news values, for example, it was especially violent or spectacular or involved a celebrity. The converse of this trend is that events that occur in regions which are remote from the centralized bases of news organization or in countries that are not explicitly linked (in alliance or in opposition) to the UK or US rarely make the news. For example, the extended global coverage of two hijacked passenger jets ploughing into the twin towers of the New York World Trade Center on 11 September 2001, like earlier footage taken in Dallas in October 1965 of the assassination of President John F. Kennedy, illustrates the degree to which America is regarded a world super-power. Their news is our news in a truly global sense, and both these crimes cast a long shadow in the collective memory of people with no connection, however tenuous, with the events of those days. But as others have pointed out, for those not of the 'First World', there have been other 'September 11ths' which have received little, if any, media coverage in the West (Brown, 2002; Hogg, 2002; Jefferson, 2002).

Cultural proximity also changes according to the political climate and cultural mood of the times. There was little media coverage of the Iran–Iraq war in the 1980s, but more recently Iraq has rarely been out of the news. In short, there may be a domestication of foreign news whereby events in other areas of the world will receive media attention if they are perceived to impinge on the home culture of the reporter and his or her audience. If there is no discernible relevance to the target audience, a story has to be commensurately bigger and more dramatic in order to be regarded as newsworthy. Novelist Michael Frayn comments facetiously:

> The crash survey showed that people were not interested in reading about road crashes unless there were at least 10 dead. A road crash with 10 dead, the majority felt, was slightly less interesting than a rail crash with one dead . . . Even a rail crash on the Continent made the grade provided there were at least 5 dead. If it was in the United States the minimum number of dead rose to 20; in South America 100; in Africa 200; in China 500. But people really preferred an air crash . . . backed up with a story about a middle-aged housewife who had been booked to fly aboard the plane but who had changed her mind at the last moment. (Frayn, 1965: 60)

Cultural proximity also pertains to perpetrators and victims of crime within the UK. When an individual goes missing (whether or not foul play is immediately suspected) the likelihood of the national media lending their weight behind a campaign to find the missing person depends on several inter-related factors. If the individual in question is young, female, white, middle-class and conventionally attractive, the media are more likely to cover the case than if the missing person is, say, a working-class boy or an older woman. Even in cases where abduction and/or murder is immediately suspected, the likelihood of media interest will vary in accordance with the background of the victim. If the victim is male, working class, of African Caribbean or Asian descent, a persistent runaway, has been in care, has drug problems, or is a prostitute (or any combination of these factors), reporters perceive that their audience is less likely to relate to, or empathize with, the victim, and the case gets commensurately lower publicity. The compliance of the victim's family in giving repeated press conferences and making themselves a central part of the story is also a crucial factor in determining its newsworthiness, as is their willingness to part with photographs and home video footage of their missing child. [. . .]

A short time after the disappearance of 14-year-old Milly Dowler from Surrey in March 2002, the body of a teenage girl was recovered from a disused quarry near Tilbury Docks. Before the body had even been identified, sections of the tabloid press were carrying headlines announcing that Milly had been found. But it turned out to be the corpse of another 14-year-old girl, Hannah Williams, who had disappeared a year earlier. Yet it was the hunt for Milly that continued to dominate the news for the weeks and months to follow. Almost as soon as she was found, Hannah was forgotten. Quite simply, unlike Milly who was portrayed as the 'ideal' middle-class teenager, Hannah's background made it difficult to build a campaign around her. She was working class and had run away before. Furthermore, her mother – a single parent on a low income – 'wasn't really press-conference material' according to a police spokeswoman (Bright, 2002: 23).

Violence

The news value which is arguably most common to all media is that of 'violence'. Violence fulfils the media's desire to present dramatic events in the most graphic possible fashion, and even the most regulated media institutions are constantly pushing back the boundaries of acceptable reportage when it comes to depicting acts of violence. In *Policing the Crisis: Mugging, the State and Law and Order*, Hall et al. comment:

> Any crime can be lifted into news visibility if violence becomes associated with it, since violence is perhaps the supreme example of . . . 'negative consequences'. Violence represents a basic violation of the person; the greatest personal crime is 'murder', bettered only by the murder of a law-enforcement agent, a policeman. Violence is also the ultimate crime against property and against the State. It thus represents a fundamental rupture in the social order. The use of violence marks the distinction between those who are *of* society and those who are *outside* it . . . The State, and the State only has the monopoly of legitimate violence, and this 'violence' is used to safeguard society against 'illegitimate' uses. Violence thus constitutes a critical threshold in society; all acts, especially criminal ones, which transgress that boundary are, by definition, worthy of news attention. It is often complained that 'the news' is too full of violence; an item can escalate to the top of the news agenda simply because it contains a 'Big Bang'. Those who so complain do not understand what 'the news' is about. It is impossible to define 'news values' in ways which would not rank 'violence' at or near the summit of news attention. (Hall et al., 1978: 68)

Despite its 'big bang' potential, in the years since Hall and his colleagues made this assertion, violence has become so ubiquitous that – although still considered newsworthy – it is frequently reported in a routine, mundane manner with little follow-up or analysis. Unless a story involving violence conforms to several other news values or provides a suitable threshold to keep alive an existing set of stories, even the most serious acts of violence may be used as 'fillers' and consigned to the inside pages of a newspaper (Naylor, 2001). Yet whether treated sensationally or unsensationally, violence – including violent death – remains a staple of media reporting. According to research, the British press devote an average of 65 per cent of their crime reporting to stories involving interpersonal violence, although police statistics indicate that only around 6 per cent of recorded crime involves interpersonal violence (Williams and Dickinson, 1993).

Postmodernists might argue that one of the reasons for the expansion in depictions of violence to gain audience attention in crime news is that real life has become increasingly saturated with images of violence, humiliation and cruelty. For cultural criminologists like Presdee (2000), crime and violence have become objectified and commodified, and thus desired, to the extent where they are widely distributed through all forms of media to be pleasurably consumed. Presdee offers numerous examples of the commodification of violence, humiliation and cruelty which, he claims, are evidence of the consumer's need for privately enjoyed, carnivalesque transgression. From 'sports' that, having all but disappeared, are now enjoying a dramatic upturn in popularity (albeit underground), such as bareknuckle fighting, badger-baiting and dog-fighting, to 'Reality TV' and gangsta rap, the evidence of our lust for pain and humiliation is all around us:

> The mass of society bare their souls to the media who, in turn, transform them into the commodity of entertainment. Confidentialities are turned against the subject, transforming them into the object of hurt and humiliation as their social being is commodified ready for consumption. (Presdee, 2000: 75)

Little wonder then, that news has followed a similarly dramatic and vicarious path. With an increasing imperative to bring drama and immediacy to news production, the caveat 'You may find some of the pictures that follow distressing' seems to preface an increasing number of television news reports. This leads us to consider the spectacle of violence as portrayed through graphic imagery.

Spectacle and graphic imagery

Television news is generally given greater credence by the public than newspapers, partly because it is perceived to be less partisan than the press, but also because it offers higher quality pictures which are frequently held to demonstrate the 'truth' of a story or to verify the particular angle from which the news team has chosen to cover it. As described above, violence is a primary component of news selection. But there are many different types of violence and it tends to be acts of violence that have a strong visual impact and can be graphically presented that are most likely to receive extensive media coverage. In his study of the professional codes governing popular news reporting, Chibnall (1977) suggests that the violence most likely to receive media attention is that which involves sudden injury to 'innocent others', especially in public places. Emotive language such as 'brutal thugs', 'rampaging hooligans' and 'anarchy' frequently accompany the reporting of crimes and disorder and serve to whip up public hysteria about the 'enemy' within. But such definitions serve to impose severe limitations on public discourses and debates about crime, so that it is 'spectacular' crimes (joyriding, rioting, arson, clashes between police and citizens and so on) that get most attention. They make good copy and are visually arresting on television. But those crimes which occur in private spheres, or which are not subject to public scrutiny, become even more marginalized, even more invisible. Hence, crimes like domestic violence, child abuse, elder abuse, accidents at work, pollution of the environment, much white collar crime, corporate corruption, state violence and governments' denial or abuse of human rights, all receive comparatively little media attention, despite their arguably greater cost to individuals and society. Similarly, long-term developments, which may be more important than immediate, dramatic incidents in terms of their effects, may not be covered because they cannot be accompanied by dramatic visual imagery.

The 'spectacle' of news reporting has [. . .] blurred the lines between 'real' and 'fake' and made it increasingly difficult to distinguish between 'fact' and 'fiction', especially in television programming. This is the age of 'fake TV'; a 'relentless and grotesque' drive towards infotainment (Osborne, 2002: 131). Channel 4 caused controversy in 2001 when it broadcast *Brass Eye*, a spoof current affairs programme in which celebrities were duped into condemning paedophilia in the most ludicrous terms, and the same station was prosecuted for passing off actors as 'real' participants in a documentary about male prostitution. Furthermore, not only do programmes like *Big Brother* blur the line between entertainment and reality and call into question the extent to which people behave 'normally' while being watched on television, but televised court trials in the US have made celebrities out of lawyers and judges, and led to accusations that they, too, are not immune to playing up for the cameras. In addition, 'real' footage of the kind captured on CCTV or on video cameras by witnesses and bystanders as a criminal event unfolds, is increasingly used in news broadcasts to visually highlight the event's immediacy and 'authenticity'. Such images have graphically and poignantly contributed to the spectacle of crime and violence in the postmodern era. Many of the most shocking events that occurred in the last few years of the 20th century entered the collective consciousness with such horrifying impact precisely because news reports were accompanied by images of the victim at the time of, immediately prior to, or soon after, a serious violent incident. The video footage of black motorist Rodney King being beaten up by four white LA police officers, and the live broadcast of O.J. Simpson being chased for miles down the freeway by police following the brutal murder of his wife, are examples from the US of graphic imagery being used to heighten the drama of already newsworthy stories. In this country, the last moments of the lives of Diana, Princess of Wales leaving the Ritz Hotel in Paris, James Bulger being led out of a Bootle shopping centre, Jill Dando shopping in Hammersmith, and Damilola Taylor skipping down a Peckham street, are all forcefully etched on the British psyche. Combining the mundane ordinariness of everyday life with the grim inevitability of what is about to unfold, CCTV footage – played out by the media on a seemingly endless loop – appeals to the voyeuristic elements in all of us, while at the same time reinforcing our sense of horror, revulsion and powerlessness. [. . .] In 2001 the Oklahoma bomber, Timothy McVeigh, exploited these conflicting emotions by urging Americans to watch him die at the hands of the State. Victims, relatives and witnesses were allocated tickets for a CCTV showing of his execution (McCahill, 2003); an event which many predict will soon lead to executions routinely being broadcast on US television networks.

Children

Writing in 1978, Stuart Hall and his colleagues argued that any crime can be lifted into news visibility if violence becomes associated with it, but three decades later it might be said that any crime can be lifted into news visibility if children are associated with it. In fact, Philip Jenkins (1992) argues precisely this, suggesting that *any* offence, particularly those that deviate from the *moral* consensus, are made eminently more newsworthy if children are involved. This is true whether the children at the centre of the story are victims or offenders, although Jenkins concentrates on child victims who, he says, not only guarantee the newsworthiness of a story, but can ensure the media's commitment to what might be called 'morality campaigns'. This amounts to what Jenkins describes as the 'politics of substitution'. In the 1970s, those who wished to denounce and stigmatize homosexuality, the sale of pornography or religious deviation (for example, satanism) found little support in the prevailing moral climate. But the inclusion of children in stories about these activities makes it impossible to condone them within any conventional moral or legal framework. Thus we have witnessed over the last 30 years a process of escalation whereby morality campaigns are now directed 'not against homosexuality but at paedophilia, not pornography but child pornography, not satanism but ritual child abuse' (Jenkins, 1992: 11). The focus on children means that deviant behaviour automatically crosses a higher threshold of victimization than would have been possible if adults alone had been involved (1992: 11). Nevertheless, despite Jenkins's assertion that the involvement of children guarantees news coverage of a story, this is not necessarily the case. Sexual abuse within the family remains so low down on the media's agenda as to render it virtually invisible, and as we shall see in later chapters, the mass media persist in preserving the image of the ideal family and underplaying or ignoring the fact that sexual violence exists – indeed, is endemic – in *all* communities, and that sexual abuse of children is more likely to occur within the family than at the hands of an 'evil stranger'.

Children who commit crimes have [. . .] become especially newsworthy since the murder of two-year-old James Bulger by two 10-year-olds in 1993, which was the first case for at least a generation in which the media constructed pre-teenage children as 'demons' rather than as 'innocents' (Muncie, 1999: 3). The case also proved a watershed in terms of criminal justice and crime prevention. The 10-year-olds were tried in adult court and the case was the impetus for a massive expansion of CCTV equipment in public spaces throughout the country (Norris and Armstrong, 1999; McCahill, 2003). But at a more fundamental level, it presented a dilemma for the mass media. Childhood is a *social construction*; in other words, it is subject to a continuous process of (re)invention and (re)definition and, even in the modern period, has gone through numerous incarnations from 18th-century romantic portrayals of childhood as a time of innocence, to more recent conceptions of childhood as a potential site of psychological and psychiatric problems (Muncie, 1999). But with the exception of a brief period in the early 19th century when children were viewed as inherently corrupt and in need of overt control and moral guidance (which coincided with a period when child labour was the norm among the working classes, before legislation took children out of factories, mills and mines and relocated them in schools and reformatories), the notion of children being 'evil' has not been prominent. By and large, childhood has been seen as fundamentally separate from adulthood, and children regarded as requiring nurture and protection, whether by philanthropic reformers, educators, parents, welfare agencies, the medical profession or the law. But with the murder of James Bulger by two older children, the notion of childhood innocence gave way to themes of childhood horror and evil. Public outrage was fuelled, in part, by sensational and vindictive press reporting which variously described the 10-year-olds as 'brutes', 'monsters', 'animals' and 'the spawn of Satan' (1999). As far as the British media were concerned, these children were not 'innocents'. Yet neither were they uniquely deviant. While the Bulger case provided 'the strongest possible evidence to an already worried public that there was something new and terrifying about juvenile crime' (Newburn, 1996: 70), it was merely the apex of a wave of hysteria that, in the early 1990s, incorporated young joyriders, truants, drug users, burglars, gang members and, memorably, 'Ratboy';

a child of 14 with a string of offences to his name who had absconded from local authority care and was reportedly living in a sewer (1996:70). [. . .] The young are frequently used as a kind of measuring stick or social barometer with which to test the health of society more generally. Children and adolescents represent the future, and if they engage in deviant behaviour it is often viewed as symptomatic of a society that is declining ever further into a moral morass. For the media, then, deviant youth is used as a shorthand ascription for a range of gloomy and fatalistic predictions about spiralling levels of crime and amoral behaviour in society at large. [. . .]

News values and crime news production: some concluding thoughts

[. . .] The time and space available for news is not infinite and journalism is, of necessity, a selective account of reality (McNair, 1993, 1998). No story can be told without judgements being made about the viability of sending costly resources to film, photograph and report it, or without implicit suppositions being made about the beliefs and values of the people who will be reading, viewing or listening to it. [. . .]

The news media do not cover systemically all forms and expressions of crime and victimization, and that they pander to the most voyeuristic desires of the audience by exaggerating and dramatizing relatively unusual crimes, while ignoring or downplaying the crimes that are most likely to happen to the 'average' person. At the same time, they sympathize with some victims while blaming others. Nevertheless, the tabloidization of news (on television and radio as well as in print) is arguably a cultural expression of democratic development, giving voice to new forms of political engagement with issues such as environmentalism, health and sexuality (McNair, 1998; Manning, 2001). And while the interests and priorities of the contemporary audience may be regarded as populist and trivial, the fact is that more people consume news today than have at any time previously. Furthermore, there is a valuable investigative tradition in journalism which continues to play an important role, not least in the spheres of crime control, crime prevention and uncovering police corruption and miscarriages of justice.

References

Bazelon, D. (1978) 'The hidden politics of American criminology', in J. Conrad (ed.) *The Evolution of Criminal Justice*, Newbury Park, CA: Sage.

Bright, M. (2002) 'The vanishing', *Observer Magazine*, 15 December.

Brown, D. (2002) '"Losing my religion": reflections on critical criminology in Australia', in K. Carrington and R. Hogg (eds) *Critical Criminology: Issues, Dabates, Challenges*, Cullompton: Willan.

Cameron, D. and Frazer, E. (1987) *The Lust to Kill: A Feminist Investigation of Sexual Murder*, Cambridge: Polity Press.

Carter, C. (1998) 'When the "extraordinary" becomes "orinary": everyday news of sexual violence', in C. Carter, G. Branston and S. Allen (1998) *News, Gender and Power*, London: Routledge.

Cavender, G. and Mulcahy, A. (1998) 'Trial by fire: media constructions of corporate deviance', *Justice Quarterly*, 15(4): 697–719.

Chibnall, S. (1977) *Law and Order News*, London: Tavistock.

Ditton, J. and Duffy, J. (1983) 'Bias in the newspaper reporting of crime news', *British Journal of Criminology*, 23(2).

Ericson, R., Baranek, P. and Chan, J. (1987) *Visualising Deviance: A Study of News Organizations*, Buckingham: Open University Press.

Ericson, R., baranek, P. and Chan, J. (1989) *Negotiating Control: A study of News Sources*, Buckingham: Open University Press.

Ericson, R., Baranek, P. and Chan, J. (1991) *Representing Order: Crime, Law and Justice in the News Media*, Buckingham: Open University Press.

Frayn, M. (1965) *The Tin Men*, London: Colins.

Galtung, J. and Ruge, M. (1973) 'Stucturing and selecting the news', in S. Cohen and J. Young (eds) *The Manufacture of News: Deviance, Social Problems and the Mass Media*, London: Constable.

Greer, C. (2003) *Sex Crime and the Media: Sex Offending and the Press in a Divided Society*, Cullompton: Willan.

Hall, S., Critcher, C., Jefferson, T., Clarke, J. and Roberts, B. (eds) (1978) *Policing the Crisis: Mugging, the State and Law and Order*, London: Macmillan.

Hartley, J. (1982) *Understanding News*, London: Routledge.

Hetherington, A. (1985) *News, Newspapers and Television*, London: Macmillan.

Hogg, R. (2002) 'Criminology beyond the nation state: global conflicts, human rights and the "new world order"', in K. Carrington and R. Hogg (eds) *Critical Criminology: Issues Debates, Challenges*, Cullompton: Willan.

Jefferson, T. (2002) 'For a psychosocial criminology', in K. Carrington and R. Hogg (eds) *Critical Criminology: Issues, Dabates, Challenges*, Cullompton: Willan.

Jenkins, P. (1992) *Intimate Enemies: Moral Panics in Contemporary Great Britain*, New York: Aldine de Gruyter.

McCahill, M (2003) 'Media representations of surveillance', in P. Mason (ed.) *Criminal Visions: Media Representations of Crime and Justice*, Cullompton: Willan.

McNair, B. (1993) *News and Journalism in the UK*, London: Routledge

McNair, B. (1998) *The Sociology of Journalism*, London: Arnold.

Manning, P. (2001) *News and News Sources: A Critical Introduction*, London: Sage.

Muncie, J. (1999) *Youth and Crime: A Critical Introduction*, London: Sage.

Naylor, B. (2001) 'Reporting violence in the British print media: gendered stories', in *Howard Journal*, 40(2): 180–194.

Newburn, T. (1996) 'Back to the future? Youth crime, youth justice and the rediscovery of "authoritarian populism"', in J. Pilcher and S. Wagg (eds) *Thatcher's Children*, London: Falmer.

Norris, C. and Armstrong, G. (1999) *The Maximum Surveillance Society: The Rise of CCTV*, Oxford: Berg.

Osborne, R. (2002) *Megawords*, London: Sage.

Potter, G. W. and Kappeler, V. E. (1998) *Constructing Crime: Perspectives on Making News and Social Problems*, Prospect Heights, IL: Waveland Press.

Presdee, M. (2000) *Cultural Criminology and the Carnival of Crime*, London: Routledge.

Reiner, R. (2001) 'The rise of virtual vigilantism: crime reporting since World War II', *Criminal Justice Matters*, 43, Spring.

Reiner, R., Livingstone, S. and Allen, J. (2001) 'Casino culture: media and crime in a winner-losser society', in K. Stenson and R.R. Sullivan (eds) *Crime, Risk and Justice: the Politics of Crime Control in Liberal Democracies*, Cullompton: Willan.

Smith, S. J. (1984) 'Crime in the news', *British Journal of Criminology*, 24(3).

Soothill, K. and Walby, S. (1991) *Sex Crime in the News*, London: Routledge.

Surette, R. (1998) *Media, Crime and Criminal Justice*, Belmont, CA: West/Wadsworth

Williams, P. and Dickinson, J. (1993) 'Fear of crime: read all about it?, *British Journal Criminology*, 33(1).

Critical connections

One issue discussed briefly by Jewkes, but absent from the vast majority of studies on crime newsworthiness, is the growing primacy of the visual. Facilitated by techno- logical developments and consolidated by the shift to a more explicitly visual culture, the 'image' has come increasingly to constitute a defining influence on perceived newsworthiness. As I have argued elsewhere, crime stories are today 'increasingly selected and "produced" as *media events* on the basis of their visual (how they can be portrayed in images) as well as their lexical-verbal (how they can be portrayed in words) potential' (Greer, 2007: 29). The availability of an image may determine whether or not a story is run. The availability of the right image can help elevate a crime victim or offender to iconic status.

Of course, television stations are primarily concerned with producing an 'appealing visual product' (Chermak, 1995: 110). But press representations too have become intensely visual phenomena, incorporating: photographs of victims, offenders, or loved ones; diagrams mapping out a route taken, a geographical area, a weapon, or a crime scene; graphic illustrations of offending rates, prison populations, and police numbers; satirical cartoons lampooning bungling criminal justice professionals; the list goes on. Images depict immediately, dramatically, and often in full colour, what it may take several paragraphs to say in words. If the visual has always played an important part in the manufacture of crime news (Hall, 1973, Reading 10), today its importance is greater than ever.

Discussion questions

- What are the key changes in 'news values' and 'newsworthiness' that Jewkes identifies, and can you think of any further examples to illustrate them?
- Why might it be that so few media criminologists have actively researched the visual?
- Examine the crime reporting in one local or national newspaper and consider the visual representation of offenders, victims and criminal justice practitioners (see also Readings 4, 9 and 10.)

References

Chermak, S. (1995) 'Crime in the news media: a refined understanding of how crimes become news', in G. Barak (ed.) *Media, Process, and the Social Construction of Crime*, New York: Garland.

Greer, C. (2007) 'News Media, Victims and Crime', in P. Davies, P. Francis, C. Greer (eds.) *Victims, Crime and Society*, London: Sage.

Jack Katz

WHAT MAKES CRIME 'NEWS'? (1987)

Introduction and context

JACK KATZ'S (1987) EXPLANATION of crime newsworthiness differs significantly from those advanced by both Steve Chibnall (Reading 15) and Yvonne Jewkes (Reading 16). Chibnall (1977), for example, uses ethnographic methods to deconstruct crime news and identify its component parts, locating crime reporting within the wider context of press ideology and the political economy of news production. The main focus here is on the background factors – institutional, ideological, economic – that shape the selection and production of crime as news, before it is disseminated to a mass audience. Katz, in contrast, considers newsworthiness from the perspective of the consumer, and is more interested in understanding the symbolic relevance and psycho-social utility of crime news. The principal focus here, then, is on the foreground factors – existential, moral, emotional – that make crime news 'required reading' for people on a daily basis. In contrast with the institutional journalist-centred, Marxist approach that characterises Chibnall's (1977) *Law and Order News* (Reading 15) and to a lesser extent Hall *et al.*'s (1978) *Policing the Crisis* (Reading 18), Katz adopts a phenomenological, consumer-centred approach, informed by a critical appreciation of Durkheimian sociology.

Whilst 'novelty' had been identified as a key determinant of crime newsworthiness in a number of studies, with Hall *et al.* (Reading 20) elevating it to the status of 'cardinal news value', Katz offers a different interpretation. He suggests that, in fact, the most newsworthy crimes seldom appear to be particularly unexpected or novel. Political scandals and stories of high-level corruption confirm for many what they knew all along, yet such stories invariably attract considerable media attention. Banks are routine targets for robberies, yet they continue to generate substantial media interest when they hit. If the key to understanding crime newsworthiness is not its unexpectedness, Katz argues, a more fruitful approach may be to consider crime's 'symbolic value in articulating the normatively expected'. From this perspective, crime is not newsworthy because it appeals to readers' base or morbid interests. Rather, crime is newsworthy because its reporting presents readers with the opportunity to engage in a daily ritual moral workout, allowing them to question and confirm (or otherwise) their own moral fortitude. In essence, crime news 'speaks dramatically to issues that are of direct relevance to readers' existential challenges, whether or not readers are preoccupied with the possible personal misfortune of becoming victims to crime'.

Ambiguities of 'the unexpected' in crime news

[. . .] As almost all sociologists of the news have noted, there is an urgency with which a story must be published lest it lose its character as 'news'. (Tuchman, 1978: 51, on 'hard' versus 'soft' news; Hughes, 1940: 67, on 'big' versus 'little' news; and Roshco, 1975: 10–12, on the 'recency', 'immediacy' and 'currency' of the news.) But if in the reporting of crime it is taken for granted that something newsworthy should have happened in the immediate past, the necessary something is in fact only rarely the crime itself. Of the 200 crimes reported in the [. . .] sample of New York area newspapers, about 100 were common crimes and seventy white-collar crimes. Only 6 percent of the initial reports of white-collar crimes clearly described the crimes as occurring within six months of the date of publication, in part because the criminality indicated was typically a pattern of fraud or corruption that did not appear to begin or end on any particular date. But even for common crimes, such as robberies, thefts from post offices or at airports, and contraband sales, only 30 percent were described as occurring within six months of the first article on the given offence.

A similar indication appeared in our examination of about 1,400 crime articles appearing in the *Los Angeles Times* in 1981, 1982 and 1983. Incidents and cases were coded separately: crimes were coded as cases if they had been processed to the point of arrest or beyond (indictment, trial, sentence, post-prison release, etc.). Of these news articles on crime, only 45 percent reported criminal incidents, or crimes that had not been officially processed to the point of arrest. If the newsworthiness of crime could be explained by expectations violated by crimes themselves – the *victim's* experience of the unexpected in the form of surprise, or the shock waves set off in public consciousness when the crime was committed, we should find an overwhelming predominance of recent criminal incidents in crime news.

While the news emphasizes yesterday's events, the crimes covered in daily newspapers did not necessarily happen yesterday nor even in the recent past. Some feature of the story signals a currency that makes the crime newsworthy, but the current element is less often and less clearly the incidence of the crime than a feature of the criminal case, a subsequent event affecting the victim, or a vicissitude of the alleged criminal's life. If a violation of 'the unexpected' somehow must qualify crime to be newsworthy, the necessary element of surprise is a matter neither of the victim's experience nor of the reader's empathic shock that something so awful might also happen to him.

More directly, we should question whether surprise is a common, much less essential, feature in the experience of reading crime news. Here I would ask the reader to review his or her own experience for evidence that the most avid readers of stories on particular crimes may be those who are least surprised. During Watergate, it was not necessarily Republican readers who were the most religious followers; many left-wing Americans rejoiced in the daily unfolding of what they regarded as more proof for what they had long believed.

Especially newsworthy crimes do not appear to be especially unexpected, either to victims or to readers. According to highly publicized opinion polls, Americans believe that a substantial proportion of unindicted congressmen are corrupt. Yet a new official charge of corruption against a congressman will always generate news coverage. Banks are robbed more than many other types of commercial establishment, yet they remain distinctively newsworthy sites of crime.

In short, if crime news inevitably carries a sense of the unexpected, just what that sense is, is not obvious. Perhaps, following Durkheim, we should turn the explanation around and consider whether crime is newsworthy for its symbolic value in articulating the normatively expected.

The historical limitations of the Durkheimian view

Durkheim (1958: 67; 1964: 108) argued that in violating social order, deviants may actually promote collective consensus – normative cohesion, the moral integration of society, a widespread sense of order in society – by providing occasions for mass reactions against deviance. Crime news may be the best contemporary example of what Durkheim had in mind. The reading of crime news is a collective, ritual experience. Read daily by a large portion of the population, crime news generates emotional experiences in individual readers, experiences which each reader can assume are shared by many others. Although each may read in isolation, phenomenologically the experience may be a collective, emotional 'effervescence' of moral indignation. But the application of the Durkheimian perspective to crime news requires a tortured reasoning.

There is a fundamental, historical difference between the social meanings of contemporary crime news and those of the public ceremonies of labelling deviants that Durkheim had in mind and that Kai Erikson (1966) documented in his celebrated book on seventeenth-century Puritans. Contemporary news stories on crime focus on stages in the criminal justice process before punishment. In our data set of crime news stories published in New York area newspapers between 1974 and 1979, the perspective of official authority, as represented by a description of an action or comment by a law enforcement agent, was present in less than half of the articles. About 65 percent of the articles appeared before disposition, when the outcome of official investigation and allegation was still unclear. Less than 12 percent of the cases first appeared in the news at or after the stage of sentencing. On the surface, the contemporary reading of crime news disconcerts rather than reassures.

The previously noted study of the *Los Angeles Times* provides additional support. About 45 percent of the articles for 1981, 1982 and 1983 (*n* = 1,384) were on incidents or criminal events as distinguished from crime cases or crimes reported as officially processed to the point of arrest or beyond. There are thus a variety of indicators that crime news raises perhaps as many questions about collective integrity as it resolves; its structure seems as likely to increase doubts about social order, by publicizing crimes that are still open criminal cases, as to strengthen a sense of collective order by celebrating a triumph of collective will over deviants and disorder.[1]

In a long historical perspective, the modern newspaper appears as a distinctive social structure for collectively observing deviance, a structure dramatically different from that existing before the nineteenth century. Shortly before a mass Sunday newspaper was created in England in the 1830s, crime news was circulated on broadsheets. One of the last and most successful broadsheets was widely disseminated in the 1820s; the 'Last Dying Speech and Confession' of the murderer of Maria Marten sold more than 1,100,000 copies (Williams, 1978: 43). Before the nineteenth century, in western and in primitive societies, among Erikson's Puritans and among the primitives Durkheim examined in his book on religion (1965), deviance was made a mass public symbol most emphatically, through exemplary forms of punishment and subsequent gossip, after doubt about criminal responsibility was resolved. Broadsheets were written to detail the behaviour of the condemned on the scaffold: 'The best sellers were the literature of the gallows. These were the last dying confessions of murderers and an account of their execution' (Hughes, 1940: 140). The wayward Puritan was put on trial, then in stocks on public display and made the subject of sermonizing, primarily after punishment was decided upon and delivered by officials symbolizing the collective identity of the society. Witchcraft trials in the American colonies and throughout medieval Europe were means of dramatizing the execution of collective will, not processes in which a problematic outcome was subject to adversary skill (see Currie, 1968).

In western societies, mass media for disseminating news about crime at first threatened confidence in collective order, then with the rise of print media came to serve the official interest in order, and then with the advent of the daily newspaper once again took on an unsettling role. Chibnall (1980:180) notes that in Great Britain in the middle ages, before the advent of printed media for conveying crime news, ballads often disserved a social control function by dramatizing the heroic defiance of outlaws. Then, in the late seventeenth century, when pamphlets and broadsheets emerged to give a written form to crime news, they emphasized 'dying speeches' in which official authority, often through the quoted (or invented) words of the condemned, displayed the terrible costs of crime and praised the path of virtue. But the twentieth-century newspaper offers a much less moralistic format for news about crime. In many respects it more clearly celebrates than excoriates criminals.[2]

As Foucault (1979) has analysed historical change in the social meaning of deviance, in pre-Enlightenment society adjudication was private (as symbolized by 'star chamber' proceedings) and punishment was public (as exemplified by elaborate torture and execution ceremonies); in post-Enlightenment society, trials became the public drama of criminal justice, while punishment retreated to the privacy of prisons, emerging into publicity only rarely and then in shame. Before the nineteenth century, public viewing of deviance may have had a morally integrative effect on the community; but to make the same analysis of today's crime news is to ignore its distinctive contemporary social organization. Metropolitan daily news stories on victimization and arrest are routine and are only in the exceptional case followed up by stories on conviction and punishment.

A social class sub-pattern is notable in this context. The higher the educational and economic level of a newspaper's readers, the more it appears to employ a form that provokes rather than resolves its readers' moral anxieties. Comparing New York's *Times* and *Daily News*, studies have found the latter to be more sensational in that it contains a higher proportion of crime news (Deutschmann, 1959). But comparing the crime stories published in the two papers, there is little difference in reported fact. Both papers draw on essentially the same police sources and records. The difference lies in the language used to describe the crime.

The *Daily News* moralizes while the *Times* uses what are conventionally regarded as emotionally neutral, technical terms, in particular the formally non-prejudicial, officially constrained language of courts and lawyers (Meyer, 1975). Thus the *Daily News* reports the illegal harvesting of undersized clams as clams that were 'copped', while the *Times* refers to a 'theft'. The *Times*, under a headline of moderate size, describes an arrangement by which GTE-Sylvania officials paid money to public transit officials in order to ensure acceptance of bulbs not meeting specifications, as a bribery; while the *News* runs a large front-page title: 'Subway Bulb Gyp'. The difference, which becomes even more pronounced if one compares contemporary daily US newspapers with those published sixty years ago, is that newspapers with readers of a higher social class level leave moral execration to readers, at least as a matter of form; while newspapers with relatively lower-class readers lead the chorus of invective. Thus it appears that the more modern the newspaper, or the more formally educated the readership, the more that crime news is styled to provoke rather than resolve doubt.[3]

Daily crime news reading as a ritual moral exercise

Although the frequency of news stories on homicides, violent robberies and rapes might seem evidence of a 'lowbrow' insensitivity in the modern public, an opposite interpretation is more revealing and more consistent with the overall patterns in crime news. The interest is less morbid than inspirational. If portrayals of violent crime show in the extreme the lack of sensibility with which members of our society may treat each other, readers' appetites for such stories suggest that they are not so coarse as to take for granted destructive personal insensitivity. The fact that assaults on property are far less newsworthy than assaults on the person indicates that readers' fundamental concerns are more humanistic than material. Or rather, by picking up the paper to read about yet another brutal crime, readers can attempt to sustain their conviction that their own moral sensibility has not yet been brutalized into a jaded indifference. The predominance of stories on violent crime in contemporary newspapers can be understood as serving readers' interests in re-creating daily their moral sensibilities through shock and impulses of outrage.

Instead of the empirically ambiguous idea that crime becomes interesting to the extent that it is 'unexpected', and in place of a simple invocation of Durkheim's ideas, I would argue that crime news is taken as interesting in a process through which adults in contemporary society work out individual perspectives on moral questions of a quite general yet eminently personal relevance.

Each of the categories of crime news relates to a type of non-criminal, moral question that adults confront daily, First, crime stories with implications about personal competence and sensibility are taken as interesting because readers sense that they must deal with analogous questions in everyday life. In routine interactions with others, we must make assumptions about their essential qualities, assumptions about the age competencies of the young or old, about qualities related to gender, or about qualities like intelligence (which today are less politically controversial but no more visible than the competencies supposedly associated with age and sex). If children can hold up banks, should we take as serious the statement by our 7-year-old that he would like to kill his younger brother? If there is a 'Grandma Mafia', should we be concerned that the elderly woman behind us in the supermarket line may have a lethal intent as she rams her cart into our rear?

We must also make assumptions constantly about our own essential competencies and sensibilities. The question of audacity is faced not only by criminals. How daring, how ingenious, can I be? Would it be admirably daring; just reasonably cautious; or really, recklessly foolish to submit a paper for publication in its current draft? Crime news is of widespread interest because it speaks dramatically to issues that are of direct relevance to readers' existential challenges, whether or not readers are preoccupied with the possible personal misfortune of becoming victims to crime.

Similarly, the second group of crime news stories, those that depict threats to sacred centres of society, are deemed interesting because readers understand that they themselves must work, day after day, to define moral perspectives on questions about elusive collective entities. The interest in such stories comes not just from the practical necessity of evaluating the physical safety of different places, but from inescapable encounters with enigmas of collective identity. In contemporary bourgeois life, questions of physical safety are of minor relevance compared to questions about collective moral character – mundane, recurrent questions such as: What's a 'nice' (morally clean) place to take the family to dinner?

The question raised by this type of crime news – is society holding together? – is the global form of questions asked more narrowly by readers in their daily routines. In everyday, concrete work settings, do you sense the collective identity of the university in which you are employed? If so, your behaviour will have a significance otherwise lacking: you will shape your behaviour somehow to fit into or against the character of the whole. Sociologists have long argued that social facts are real, that there is a reality to collective identity that transcends individual experience. The debate about the reality of collective identity is bothersome not only to sociological theorists, but to laymen as well as sociologists in their everyday, practical action.

The forms of the issue, as it appears in the lives of each member of society, are extremely diverse. Some worry about the level of 'strength' or 'health' of 'the economy' (or 'the military', or their 'family'). In this anxiety, 'the economy' is addressed as a whole, a thing that presumably exists objectively, not only as a convenient metaphoric shorthand for summarizing some arbitrary aggregation of individual economic events. But the objective measure of 'its' identity is always in dispute. 'The economy' is recurrently experienced as a precarious collective entity whose integrity may be threatened by hidden forces, an entity which goes up and down in response to pressures that no one has been able to locate precisely. Many news readers shape their everyday emotional mood as well as their consumption and investment decisions upon a sense of optimism or pessimism about the fate of 'the economy'.

As members of society continuously confront issues of personal and collective competence, they develop an appetite for crime news. Worrying about miscalculating their own and others' personal abilities, people find interesting the questioning of personal moral competence that is often intensely dramatized in crime stories. Repeatedly assessing whether, how, and how effectively certain people, organizations and places represent collective identity, members of society consume tales about the vulnerable integrity of personages, institutions, and sites.

As to the third category of crime news, stories reflecting preexisting tensions among groups, people in persistent political conflict often hunger for moral charges to use against the character of their opponents. They find satisfying morsels in crime news.

Finally, what process of daily stimulation might be behind the widespread taste for news of white-collar crime? I would suggest that the newsworthiness of white-collar crime is constructed in a dialectical relationship to the moral routines of everyday life. The crimes of people in high white-collar occupations are especially newsworthy, not because they are shocking or surprising – not because such people are presumed to be more conforming, decent; respectable or trustworthy than blue-collar workers or the unemployed; but because *they have to be treated as if they are.*

It is certainly inadequate to attribute the newsworthiness of white-collar crime to shocked expressions of honour. News readers maintain appetites for stories of white-collar crime, day after day – another congressman caught taking bribes!; another multinational corporation caught corrupting foreign governments! – while common crimes committed by poor, young, minority males continue in their redundant, typically non-newsworthy procession, because every day, in infinite ways, news readers only feel forced to enact trust in and deference towards the former. However cynical a person's view of the morality of business, political, and civic institutional leaders, he or she lives surrounded by symbols of their superior status: their towering offices, their advertised qualities on subway or bus placards or on TV commercials, their names on hospitals. Readers of a news story about white-collar crime recall that they have made many payments to that firm; that they were moved around by that airplane or bus company; that they have had their neighbourhood or recreational environment defined by those politicians or lay leaders; that each day at work they must defer to a person in that type of superior status. The newsworthiness of white-collar crime owes much to the routine moral character of the division of labour. (On the 'moral division of labour', see Hughes, 1971.)

I have argued that crime news takes its interest from routinely encountered dilemmas, not from concerns focused on crime. The reading of crime news is not a process of idle moral reflection on past life; it is an eminently practical, future-oriented activity. In reading crime news, people recognize and use the moral tale within the story to orient themselves towards existential dilemmas they cannot help but confront. What level of competence should I impute to that 10-year-old? Is the economy strengthening or weakening? Should the political arguments of the PLO be heard with respect? Am I wise to defer to the boss in earnest, or should I balance apparent fealty with self-respecting cynicism?

The content of crime news provides no solutions, not even advice on how the reader should resolve the dilemmas he will confront. Instead, crime news provides material for a literal working out of the moral perspectives that must be applied to dilemmas of everyday life. Crime is in today's newspaper, not because it contradicts the beliefs readers had yesterday, but because readers seek opportunities to shape-up moral attitudes they will have to use today.

The idea that crime news serves readers' interests in performing a daily moral workout explains not only the content but several features of the structure of crime news. Crime news features details on the identities of victim and offender, and on time and place. As such, it encourages readers to see the event as potentially within his or her own experience. Its form serves to mobilize the reader's response by providing a shock or inviting outrage; it is a type of 'hot news' (Hughes, 1940: 234), specifically provoking an emotional experience, inducing a response of the 'whole organism' (Park, 1940: 670). The focus of crime news on the early criminal justice stages, stages before formal adjudication and punishment, when questions of guilt have been raised but not resolved, also provokes readers' emotions by challenging them to react against the face of uncertainty.

As several studies have documented (Graber, 1980: 49; Sherizen, 1978), crime news focuses on criminals much more than on victims. In our New York area data set from the mid-1970s, a comment by the victim or a representative of the victim was reported in only twenty-one of 527 articles, compared to 162 comments from the defence side and 185 comments by the prosecutor. A focus on victims would have substantial practical relevance for readers, were they concerned with learning how to avoid the costs of crime. Some neighbourhood 'throwaway' papers respond directly to these concerns. Unlike the major metropolitan dailies, the neighbourhood newspapers often present crime news under the by-line of a local policeman who begins the story from the victim's perspective (e.g. 'When driving back to her house at 11 p.m. on September 5, a resident of the 600 block of Lucerne noticed an unfamiliar car in her driveway. As she exited her car . . .') and concludes with annotated advice on what the victim might have done to avoid vulnerability. The same readers, picking up the metropolitan daily and inspecting its crime news, are no less pragmatic in their perspectives on crime news, but their practical concerns appear to be different — larger and more pervasively relevant.

The emphasis of the city papers on the criminal rather than the victim is understandable if we understand the reader's concerns as less with avoiding victimization than in working out moral positions on which his own behaviour will be based. If the victim's behaviour is often as important as the criminal's for understanding the causality of victimization, a focus on the criminal's behaviour stimulates moral sensitivities with which the reader may wish to identify. Each day in myriad ways the metropolitan news reader must work out his position on dimensions of moral callousness, personal audacity and faith in collective enterprises, and these are the very matters which the news depicts criminals as testing.

This perspective on interest in crime news makes understandable the apparent contradiction of substantive redundancy and constantly sustained reader interest. Laid side by side, stories about violent crime published over a sequence of days may appear quite similar. But they are experienced as new, as 'new-s', because the questions they tap re-emerge daily in readers' social lives.

The experience of reading crime news induces the reader into a perspective useful for taking a stand on existential moral dilemmas. The dilemmas of imputing personal competence and sustaining one's own moral sensibility, of honouring sacred centres of collective being, of morally crediting and discrediting political opponents, and of deferring to the moral superiority of elites, cannot be resolved by deduction from rational discourse. In these moral areas, a measure of faith – of understanding a position or making a commitment that underlies the reasons that can be given for one's beliefs – is an essential part of everyday social life. Crime news accordingly moves the reader through emotions rather than discursive logic, triggering anger and fear rather than argumentation.

Like vitamins useful in the body only for a day, like physical exercise whose value comes from its recurrent practice, crime news is experienced as interesting by readers because of its place in a daily moral routine. The very location of crime stories in the newspaper indicates that editors and readers understand this. Although minor local crime stories have a regular place in 'Metro' sections, crime stories may be scattered in unpredictable places throughout the general news sections; they are not as neatly confined to a substantial, specialized section as are sports and financial news. The structural location of crime news re-creates the unpredictable character of the phenomenon, and transfers to the reader a measure of responsibility to organize its place in his life.

Modern newspapers appear to emphasize this role. The more modern or sophisticated the newspaper, the less it moralizes in style; the more it imposes responsibility for moral reaction on the reader as a matter of form. Another modern feature of crime news, its focus on the early stages of the criminal justice system, places the responsibility for 'conviction', in both its narrow, criminal justice sense and in its broader, existential sense of commitment through faith, on the reader.

This responsibility is not necessarily one desired by readers, yet it appears to be one they acknowledge they cannot ignore or escape. Although people often fear crime and criticize the news as too negative and disturbing, they apparently find it even more unsettling not to read. To understand what makes crime 'news', one must explain the voluntary affliction of disturbing emotional experience on the self, on a mass level, day after day, throughout modern society. The reading of crime news appears to serve a purpose similar to the morning shower, routine physical exercise, and shaving (cf. Douglas, 1966): the ritual, non-rational value of experience that is, to a degree, shocking, uncomfortable, and self-destructive, and that is voluntarily taken up by adults in acknowledgment of their personal burden for sustaining faith in an ordered social world.

Notes

This paper stems from a programme of research at Yale Law School which was guided by Stanton Wheeler and supported by LEAA Grant 78 NIAX 0017. Points of view or opinions stated are those of the author and do not necessarily represent the official position or policies of US Department of Justice. Additional support came from the Academic Senate of UCLA. Elizabeth Sammis provided extensive bibliographic research assistance and, with William Shipley, she coded the Los Angeles newspapers. I wish to thank David G. Trager for his gracious assistance in providing the New York data.

1. See also Garofalo (1981): 'the press gives very little attention to the postdispositional processes of the criminal justice system', citing three studies. But cf. Roshier (1973: 33),

on British papers: 'all the newspapers gave an exaggerated impression of the chances of getting caught and, when caught, of getting a serious punishment'.

2. Crimes in the entertainment media, however, may follow the Durkheimian pattern. On TV, but not in the news, the audience learns that 'evil is always punished in the end'. See Schattenberg (1981).

3. Cf. Schudson (1978: 119): 'Perhaps . . . the *Times* established itself as the "higher journalism" because it adapted to the life experience of persons whose position in the social structure gave them the most control over their own lives.'

References

Chermak, S. (1995) *Victims in the News: Crime and the American News Media,* Boulder, CO: Westview Press.

Chibnall, S. (1980) 'Chronicles of the Gallows: The Social History of Crime Reporting', pp. 179–217 in H. Christian (ed.), *The Sociology of Journalism and the Press* (Sociological Review Monograph 29). Stoke-on-Trent: J.H, Brookes.

Currie, E. (1968) 'Crimes Without Criminals; Witchcraft and its Control in Renaissance Europe', *Law & Society Review,* 3: 7–32.

Deutschmann, P.J. (1959) *News Page Content of Twelve Metropolitan Dailies.* Cincinnati: Scripps-Howard Research Center.

Douglas, M. (1966) *Purity and Danger.* London: Routledge & Kegan Paul.

Durkheim, E. (1958) *The Rules of Sociological Method.* Glencoe, Illinois: Free Press.

Durkheim, E. (1964) *The Division of Labor in Society.* New York: Free Press.

Durkheim, E. (1965) *The Elementary Forms of the Religious Life.* New York: Free Press.

Erikson, K.T. (1966) *Wayward Puritans.* New York: Wiley.

Foucault, M. (1979) *Discipline and Punishment.* New York: Vintage Books.

Garofalo, J. (1981) 'Crime and the Mass Media: A Selective Review of Research', *Journal of Research in Crime and Delinquency,* 18: 319–49.

Graber, D. (1980) *Crime News and the Public.* New York: Praeger.

Hughes, E.C. (1971) 'The Study of Occupations', pp. 283–97 in E.G. Hughes, *The Sociological Eye,* Vol. 1. Chicago: Aldine-Atherton.

Hughes, H.M. (1940) *News and the Human Merest Story.* Chicago: University of Chicago Press.

Meyer, J. (1975) 'Newspaper Reporting of Crime and Justice', *Journalism Quarterly,* 52: 731–4.

Park, R.E. (1940) 'Introduction' to H.M. Hughes, *News and the Human Interest Story.* Chicago: University of Chicago Press.

Roshco, B. (1975) *Newsmaking.* Chicago: University of Chicago Press.

Roshier, B. (1973) 'The Selection of Crime News by the Press', pp. 28–39 in S. Cohen and J. Young (eds), *The Manufacture of News.* Beverly Hills: Sage.

Schattenberg, G. (1981) 'Social Control Functions of Mass Media Depictions of Crime', *Sociological Inquiry,* 51: 71–7.

Schudson, M. (1978) *Discovering the News.* New York: Basic.

Sherizen, S. (1978) 'Social Creation of Crime News', pp. 203–24 in C. Winick (ed.), *Deviance and Mass Media.* Beverly Hills: Sage.

Tuchman, G. (1978) *Making News.* New York: Free Press.

Williams, R. (1978) 'The Press and Popular Culture; An Historical Perspective', pp. 41–50 in G. Boyce, J. Curran and P. Wingate (eds), *Newspaper History.* London: Constable.

Critical connections

The news media landscape has changed enormously since Katz's research was conducted in the mid-1980s, and the reporting of crime and justice has changed with it. Katz's observation that 'crime news focuses on criminals much more than on victims' is simply no longer true, as Reiner *et al.* (2001, Reading 25) make clear in their post-War analysis of crime in news and popular culture (Reading 25; see also Chermak, 1995). The increasing focus on and active idealisation of (certain types of) crime victim is perhaps *the* most significant change in crime reporting in the past 20 years. Rather than undermining Katz's central thesis, however, this shift in media attention raises interesting questions about the changing nature of the moral dilemmas people are faced with in the twenty-first century. By reading across the three excerpts of crime newsworthiness included here readers of this book should begin to develop a more comprehensive, critical sense of the complex processes that shape the production of crime news as a deeply ideological, yet highly marketable news product, that carries a particular symbolic relevance in everyday life.

Discussion questions

- How does Jack Katz's phenomenological approach to understanding the newsworthiness of crime differ from Steve Chibnall's Marxist analysis?
- How might the 'ritual moral workout' offered by crime news be affected by the shift from offender-centred to victim-centred news stories and what, in Katz's terms, does this say about the 'existential moral dilemmas' people face today?
- Why might we feel better about ourselves through reading tales of other people's criminal offending and victimisation?

Stuart Hall, Chas Critcher, Tony Jefferson, John Clarke and Brian Roberts

THE SOCIAL PRODUCTION OF NEWS (1978)

Introduction and context

*P*OLICING THE CRISIS is a highly influential Marxist analysis of state power, the politicisation of law and order, the racialisation of crime, and the criminalisation of youth. The backdrop is a context of deepening economic recession and rising social and cultural tension across Britain's inner cities in the 1970s. Drawing from Louis Althusser's theory of the state and Antonio Gramsci's theory of hegemonic control (state control through consent rather than coercion), the authors identify this particular period in British history with a 'crisis in hegemony'. They argue that the state, in short, was losing its grip on society, and something needed to be done to get it back. One clear manifestation of this crisis in hegemony was a 'moral panic' (see Readings 34 and 35) around street robberies, or, as the media termed them, 'muggings'. Hall *et al.* (1978) are interested in understanding how the relatively autonomous institutions of the state – the police, the judiciary and the media (Althusser's (1977) ideological state apparatus) – contributed to the panic independently, whilst simultaneously functioning collectively to reproduce the ideas of the ruling elite, and reinforce the dominant ideology. It is Hall *et al.*'s analysis of the social production of news, and in particular the theory of 'primary definition', central to this ideological process, that provides the focus for the reading included here.

Building on Leslie Wilkins' (1964) symbolic interactionism and Howard Becker's (1967) 'hierarchy of credibility', and introducing Gramsci's notion of hegemonic struggle, Hall *et al.* constructed a contextual analysis of the social and political processes through which news is manufactured in accordance with the dominant ideology, and the cultural processes through which that ideology comes to be objectified and normalised throughout wider society. They argue that the ideas of the powerful are perpetually constructed and reconstructed in the media as a result of the virtual monopoly of certain 'privileged' elite sources, those members of society who collectively represent and command institutional power; the expert knowers. By investing in the relationship with those who are 'recognised socially to be in a position to know' (Ericson *et al.*, 1989: 4), the media appeal to the elite knowledge of control agencies (police, courts and penal system) and various other professionals (politicians, academics, care workers, hospital administrators) which establish 'an initial definition or *primary interpretation* of the topic in question'. Once the parameters are set they are extremely difficult to alter, and all coverage of future debate takes place within a forum of 'controlled discourse', governed by the primary definers.

The media do not simply and transparently report events which are 'naturally' newsworthy in *themselves*. 'News' is the end-product of a complex process which begins with a systematic sorting and selecting of events and topics according to a socially constructed set of categories. As MacDougall puts it:

> At any given moment billions of simultaneous events occur throughout the world. . . . All of these occurences are potentially news. They do not become so until some purveyor of news gives an account of them. The news, in other words, is the account of the event, not something intrinsic in the event itself.[1]

One aspect of the structure of selection can be seen in the routine organisation of newspapers with respect to regular types or areas of news. Since newspapers are committed to the regular production of news, these organisational factors will, in turn, affect what is selected. For example, newspapers become predirected to certain types of event and topic in terms of the organisation of their own work-force (e.g. specialist correspondents and departments, the fostering of institutional contacts, etc.) and the structure of the papers themselves (e.g. home news, foreign, political, sport, etc.).[2]

Given that the organisation and staffing of a paper regularly direct it to certain categories of items, there is still the problem of selecting, from the many contending items within any one category, those that are felt will be of interest to the reader. This is where the *professional ideology* of what constitutes 'good news' – the newsman's sense of *news values* – begins to structure the process. At the most general level this involves an orientation to items which are 'out of the ordinary', which in some way breach our 'normal' expectations about social life, the sudden earthquake or the moon-landing, for example. We might call this the *primary* or *cardinal news value*. Yet, clearly 'extraordinariness' does not exhaust the list, as a glance at any newspaper will reveal: events which concern elite persons or nations; events which are dramatic; events which can be personalised so as to point up the essentially human characteristics of humour, sadness, sentimentality, etc.; events which have negative consequences, and events which are part of, or can be made to appear part of, an existing newsworthy theme, are all possible news stories.[3] Disasters, dramas, the everyday antics – funny and tragic – of ordinary folk, the lives of the rich and the powerful, and such perennial themes as football (in winter) and cricket (in summer), all find a regular place within the pages of a newspaper. Two things follow from this: the first is that journalists will tend to *play up* the extraordinary, dramatic, tragic, etc. elements in a story in order to enhance its newsworthiness: the second is that events which score high on a number of these news values will have greater news potential than ones that do not. And events which score high on *all* dimensions, such as the Kennedy assassinations (i.e. which are *unexpected* and *dramatic*, with *negative* consequences, as well as *human trage-dies* involving *elite persons* who were heads of an extremely *powerful nation*, which possesses the status of a *recurrent theme* in the British press), will become *so* newsworthy that programmes will be interrupted – as in the radio or television news-flash – so that these items can be communicated immediately.

When we come later to consider the case of mugging, we will want to say something about how these news values tend to operate together, as a structure. For our present purposes, however, it is sufficient to say that news values provide the criteria in the routine practices of journalism which enable journalists, editors and newsmen to decide routinely and regularly which stories are 'newsworthy' and which are not, which stories are major 'lead' stories and which are relatively insignificant, which stories to run and which to drop.[4] Although they are nowhere written down, formally transmitted or codified, news values seem to be widely shared as between the different news media (though we shall have more to say later on the way these are differently *inflected* by particular newspapers), and form a core element in the professional socialisation, practice and ideology of newsmen.

These two aspects of the social production of news – the bureaucratic organisation of the media which produces the news in specific types or categories and the structure of news values which orders the selection and ranking of particular stories within these categories – are only part of the process. The third aspect – the moment of the *construction* of the news story itself – is equally important, if less obvious. This involves the presentation of the item to its *assumed* audience, in terms which, as far as the presenters of the item can judge, will make it comprehensible to that audience. If the world is not to be represented as a jumble of random and chaotic events, then they must be identified (i.e. named, defined, related to other events known to the audience), and assigned to a social context (i.e. placed within a frame of meanings familiar to the audience). This process – identification and contextualisation – is one of the most important through which events are 'made to mean' by the media. An event only 'makes sense' if it can be located within a range of known social and cultural identifications. If newsmen did not have available – in however routine a way – such cultural 'maps' of the social world, they could not 'make sense' for their audiences of the unusual, unexpected and unpredicted events which form the basic content of what is 'newsworthy'. Things are newsworthy because they represent the changefulness, the unpredictability and the conflictful nature of the world. But such events cannot be allowed to remain in the limbo of the 'random' – they must be brought within the horizon of the 'meaningful'. This bringing of events within the realm of meanings means, in essence, referring unusual and unexpected events to the 'maps of meaning' which already form the basis of our cultural knowledge, into which the social world is *already* 'mapped'. The social identification, classification and contextualisation of news events in terms of these background frames of reference is the fundamental process by which the media make the world they report on intelligible to readers and viewers. This process of 'making an event intelligible' is a social process – constituted by a number of specific journalistic practices, which embody (often only implicitly) crucial assumptions about what society is and how it works.

One such background assumption is the *consensual* nature of society: the process of *signification* – giving social meanings to events – *both assumes and helps to construct society as a 'consensus'*. We exist as members of one society *because* – it is assumed – we share a common stock of cultural knowledge with our fellow men: we have access to the same 'maps of meanings'. Not only are we all able to manipulate these 'maps of meaning' to understand events, but we have fundamental interests, values and concerns in common, which these maps embody or reflect. We all want to, or do, maintain basically the same perspective *on* events. In this view, what unites us, as a society and a culture – its consensual side – far outweighs what divides and distinguishes us as groups or classes from other groups. Now, at one level, the existence of a cultural consensus is an obvious truth; it is the basis of all social communication.[5] If we were not members of the same language community we literally could not communicate with one another. On a broader level, if we did not inhabit, to some degree, the same classifications of social reality, we could not 'make sense of the world together'. In recent years, however, this basic cultural fact about society has been raised to an extreme ideological level. Because we occupy the same society and belong to roughly the same 'culture', it is assumed that there is, basically, only *one* perspective on events: that provided by what is sometimes called *the* culture, or (by some social scientists) *the* 'central value system'. This view denies any major structural discrepancies between different groups, or between the very different maps of meaning in a society. This 'consensual' viewpoint has important political consequences, when used as the taken-for-granted basis of communication. It carries the assumption that we also all have roughly the same *interests* in the society, and that we all roughly have an equal share of power in the society. This is the essence of the idea of the political consensus. 'Consensual' views of society represent society as if there are no major cultural or economic breaks, no major conflicts of interests between classes and groups. Whatever disagreements exist, it is said, there are legitimate and institutionalised means for expressing and reconciling them. The 'free market' in opinions and in the media is supposed to guarantee the reconciliation of cultural discontinuities between one group and another. The political institutions – parliament, the two-party system, political representation, etc. – are supposed to guarantee equal access for all groups to the decision-making process. The growth of a 'consumer' economy is supposed to have created the economic conditions for everyone to have a stake in the making and distribution of wealth. The rule of law protects us all equally. This consensus view of society is particularly strong in modern, democratic, organised capitalist societies; and the media are among the institutions whose practices are most widely and consistently predicated upon the assumption of a 'national consensus'. So that, when events are 'mapped' by the media into frameworks of meaning and interpretation, it is assumed that we all equally possess and know how to use these frameworks, that they are drawn from fundamentally the same structures of understanding for all social groups and audiences. Of course, in the formation of opinion, as in politics and economic life, it is conceded that there will be differences of outlook, disagreement, argument and opposition; but these are understood as taking place within a broader basic framework of agreement – 'the consensus' – to which everyone subscribes, and within which every dispute, disagreement or conflict of interest can be reconciled by discussion, without recourse to confrontation or violence. The strength of this appeal to consensus was vividly encapsulated in Edward Heath's prime ministerial broadcast, following the settlement of the miners' strike in 1972 (suggesting that open appeals to consensus are particularly prevalent when conflict is most visible):

> In the kind of country we live in there cannot be any 'we' or 'they'. There is only 'us'; all of us. If the Government is 'defeated', then the country is defeated, because the Government is just a group of people elected to do what the majority of 'us' want to see done. That is what our way of life is all about. It really does not matter whether it is a picketline, a demonstration or the House of Commons. We are all used to peaceful argument. But when violence or the threat of violence is used, it challenges what most of us consider to be the right way of doing things. I do not believe you elect any government to allow that to happen and I can promise you that it will not be tolerated wherever it occurs.[6]

Events, as news, then, are regularly interpreted within frameworks which derive, in part, from this notion of *the consensus* as a basic feature of everyday life. They are elaborated through a variety of 'explanations', images and discourses which articulate what the audience is assumed to think and know about the society. The importance of this process, in *reinforcing* consensual notions, has been recently stressed by Murdock:

> This habitual presentation of news within frameworks which are already familiar has two important consequences. Firstly, it recharges and extends the definitions and images in question and keeps them circulating as part of the common stock of taken-for-granted knowledge. . . . Secondly, it 'conveys an impression of eternal recurrence, of society as a social order which is made up of movement, but not innovation'.[7] Here again, by stressing the continuity and stability of the social structure, and by asserting the existence of a commonly shared set of assumptions, the definitions of the situation coincide with and reinforce essential consensual notions.[8]

What, then, is the underlying significance of the framing and interpretive function of news presentation? We suggest that it lies in the fact that the media are often presenting information about events which occur outside the direct experience of the majority of the society. The media thus represent the primary, and often the only, source of information about many important events and topics. Further, because news is recurrently concerned with events which are 'new' or 'unexpected', the media are involved in the task of making comprehensible what we would term 'problematic reality'. Problematic events breach our commonly held expectations and are therefore threatening to a society based around the expectation of consensus, order and routine. Thus the media's mapping of problematic events within the conventional understandings of the society is crucial in two ways, The media define for the majority of the population *what* significant events are taking place, but, also, they offer powerful interpretations are of *how* to understand these events. Implicit in those interpretations are orientations towards the events and the people or groups involved in them.

Primary and secondary definers

In this section we want to begin to account for the 'fit' between dominant ideas and professional media ideologies and practices. This cannot be simply attributed – as it sometimes is in simple conspiracy theories – to the fact that the media are in large part capitalist-owned (though that structure of ownership is widespread), since this would be to ignore the day-to-day 'relative autonomy' of the journalist and news producers from direct economic control. Instead we want to draw attention to the more routine *structures* of news production to see how the media come in fact, in the 'last instance', to *reproduce the definitions of the powerful*, without being, in a simple sense, in their pay. Here we must insist on a crucial distinction between *primary* and *secondary definers* of social events.

The media do not themselves autonomously create news items; rather they are 'cued in' to specific new topics by regular and reliable institutional sources. As Paul Rock notes:

> In the main journalists position themselves so that they have access to institutions which generate a useful volume of reportable activity at regular intervals. Some of these institutions do, of course, make themselves visible by means of dramatization, or through press releases and press agents. Others are known to regularly produce consequential events. The courts, sports grounds and parliament mechanically manufacture news which is . . . assimilated by the press.[9]

One reason for this has to do with the internal pressures of news production – as Murdock notes:

> The incessant pressures of time and the consequent problems of resource allocation and work scheduling in news organisations can be reduced or alleviated by covering 'pre-scheduled events'; that is, events that have been announced in advance by their convenors. However, one of the consequences of adopting this solution to scheduling problems is to increase the newsmen's dependance on news sources willing and able to preschedule their activities.[10]

The second has to do with the fact that media reporting is underwritten by notions of 'impartiality', 'balance' and 'objectivity'. This is formally enforced in television (a near-monopoly situation, where the state is directly involved in a regulatory sense) but there are also similar professional ideological 'rules' in journalism.[11] One product of these rules is the carefully structured distinction between 'fact' and 'opinion'. [. . .]

The important point is that these professional rules give rise to the practice of ensuring that media statements are, wherever possible, grounded in 'objective' and 'authoritative' statements from 'accredited' sources. This means constantly turning to accredited representatives of major social institutions – M.P.s for political topics, employers and trade-union leaders for industrial matters, and so on. Such institutional representatives are 'accredited' because of their institutional power and position, but also because of their 'representative' status: either they represent 'the people' (M.P.s, Ministers, etc.) or organised interest groups (which is how the T.U.C.

and the C.B.I. are now regarded). One final 'accredited source' is 'the expert': his calling – the 'disinterested' pursuit of knowledge – not his position or his representativeness, confers on his statements 'objectivity' and 'authority'. Ironically, the very rules which aim to preserve the impartiality of the media, and which grew out of desires for greater professional neutrality, also serve powerfully to orientate the media in the 'definitions of social reality' which their 'accredited sources' – the institutional spokesmen – provide.

These two aspects of news production – the practical pressures of constantly working against the clock and the professional demands of impartiality and objectivity – combine to produce a systematically structured *over-accessing* to the media of those in powerful and privileged institutional positions. The media thus tend, faithfully and impartially, to reproduce symbolically the existing structure of power in society's institutional order. This is what Becker has called the 'hierarchy of credibility' – the likelihood that those in powerful or high-status positions in society who offer opinions about controversial topics will have their definitions accepted, because such spokesmen are understood to have access to more accurate or more specialised information on particular topics than the majority of the population.[12] The result of this structured preference given in the media to the opinions of the powerful is that these 'spokesmen' become what we call the *primary definers* of topics.

What is the significance of this? It could rightly be argued that through the requirement of 'balance' – one of the professional rules we have not yet dealt with – alternative definitions do get a hearing: each 'side' *is* allowed to present its case. In point of fact, . . . the setting up of a topic in terms of a debate within which there are oppositions and conflicts is also one way of *dramatising* an event so as to enhance its newsworthiness. The important point about the structured relationship between the media and the primary institutional definers is that it permits the institutional definers to establish the initial definition or *primary interpretation* of the topic in question. This interpretation then 'commands the field' in all subsequent treatment and sets the terms of reference within which all further coverage or debate takes place. Arguments *against* a primary interpretation are forced to insert themselves into *its* definition of 'what is at issue' – they must begin from this framework of interpretation as their starting-point. This initial interpretative framework – what Lang and Lang have called an 'inferential structure'[13] – is extremely difficult to alter fundamentally, once established. For example, once race relations in Britain have been defined as a 'problem of numbers' (i.e. how many blacks there are in the country), then even liberal spokesmen, in proving that the figures for black immigrants have been exaggerated, are nevertheless obliged to subscribe, implicitly, to the view that the debate is 'essentially' *about numbers*. Similarly, Halloran and his co-workers have clearly demonstrated how the 'inferential structure' of violence –once it became established in the lead-up period – dominated the coverage of the second Anti-Vietnam Rally and the events of Grosvenor Square, despite all the first-hand evidence directly contradicting this interpretation.[14] Effectively, then, the primary definition *sets the limit* for all subsequent discussion by *framing what the problem is*. This initial framework then provides the criteria by which all subsequent contributions are labelled as 'relevant' to the debate, or are 'irrelevant' – beside the point. Contributions which stray from this framework are exposed to the charge that they are 'not addressing the problem'.[15]

The media, then, do not simply 'create' the news; nor do they simply transmit the ideology of the 'ruling class' in a conspiratorial fashion. Indeed, we have suggested that, in a critical sense, the media are frequently not the 'primary definers' of news events at all; but their structured relationship to power has the effect of making them play a crucial but secondary role in *reproducing* the definitions of those who have privileged access, as of right, to the media as 'accredited sources'. From this point of view, in the moment of news production, the media stand in a position of structured subordination to the primary definers.

It is this structured relationship – between the media and its 'powerful' sources – which begins to open up the neglected question of the *ideological role* of the media. It is this which begins to give substance and specificity to Marx's basic proposition that 'the ruling ideas of any age are the ideas of its ruling class'. Marx's contention is that this dominance of 'ruling ideas' operates primarily because, in addition to its ownership and control of the means of material production, this class also owns and controls the means of 'mental production'. In producing their definition of social reality, and the place of 'ordinary people' within it, they construct a particular image of society which represents particular class interests as the interests of all members of society. Because of their control over material and mental resources, and their domination of the major institutions of society, this class's definitions of the social world provide the basic rationale for those institutions which protect and reproduce their 'way of life'. This control of mental resources ensures that theirs are the most powerful and 'universal' of the available definitions of the social world. Their universality ensures that they are shared to some degree by the subordinate classes of the society. Those who govern, govern also through ideas; thus they govern with the consent of the subordinate classes, and not principally through their overt coercion. Parkin makes a similar point: 'the social and political definitions of those in dominant positions tend to become objectified in the major institutional orders, so providing the moral framework for the entire social system.'[16]

In the major social, political and legal institutions of society, coercion and constraint are never wholly absent. This is as true for the media as elsewhere. For example, reporters and reporting *are* subject to economic and legal constraints, as well as to more overt forms of censorship (e.g. over the coverage of events in Northern Ireland). But the transmission of 'dominant ideas' depends *more* on non-coercive mechanisms for their reproduction. Hierarchical structures of command and review, informal socialisation into institutional roles, the sedimenting of dominant ideas into the 'professional ideology' – all help to ensure, within the media, their continued reproduction in the dominant form. What we have been pointing to in this section is *precisely how one particular professional practice ensures that the media, effectively but 'objectively', play a key role in reproducing the dominant field of the ruling ideologies.*

Media in action: reproduction and transformation

So far we have considered the processes through which the 'reproduction of the dominant ideologies' is secured in the media. As should be clear, this reproduction, in our view, is the product of a set of *structural imperatives*, not of an open conspiracy with those in powerful positions. However, the whole cycle of 'ideological reproduction' is not completed until we have shown the process of *transformation* which the media themselves must perform on the 'raw materials' (facts *and* interpretations) which the powerful provide, in order to process these 'potential' stories into their finished commodity news form. If the former section stressed a relatively passive orientation to powerful 'authoritative' definitions, in this section we are concerned to examine those aspects of news creation in which the media play a more autonomous and active role.

The first point at which the media actively come into their own is with respect to *selectivity*. Not every statement by a relevant primary definer in respect of a particular topic is likely to be reproduced in the media; nor is every part of each statement. By exercising selectivity the media begin to impose their own criteria on the structured 'raw materials' – and thus actively appropriate and transform them. We emphasised earlier how the criteria of selection – a mixture of professional, technical and commercial constraints – served to orientate the media in general to the 'definitions of the powerful'. Here, on the other hand, we wish to stress that such criteria – common to all newspapers – are, nevertheless, *differently* appropriated, evaluated and made operational by each newspaper. To put it simply, each paper's professional sense of the newsworthy, its organisation and technical framework (in terms of numbers of journalists working in particular news areas, amount of column space routinely given over to certain kinds of news items, and so on), and sense of audience or regular readers, is different. Such differences, taken together, are what produce the very different 'social personalities' of papers. The *News of the World*'s dominant orientation towards the 'scandalous' and the sexual, and the *Daily Mirror*'s concern with the 'human-interest' aspect of stories, are but two obvious examples of such internal differences in 'social personalities'. It is here – as each paper's own 'social personality' comes into play – that the transformatory work proper begins.[17]

An even more significant aspect of 'media work' is the activity of transforming an event into a finished news item. This has to do with the way an item is *coded* by the media into a particular language form. Just as each paper, as we have just argued, has a particular organisational framework, sense of news and leaderdership, so each will also develop a regular and characteristic *mode of address*. This means that the same topic, sources and inferential structures will appear differently even in papers with a similar outlook, since the different rhetorics of address will have an important effect in inflecting the original item. Of special importance in determining the particular mode of address adopted will be the particular part of the readership spectrum the paper sees itself as customarily addressing: its target audience. The language employed will thus be the *newspaper's own version of the language of the public to whom it is principally addressed*: its version of the rhetoric, imagery and underlying common stock of knowledge which it assumes its audience shares and which thus forms the basis of the reciprocity of producer/reader. For this reason we want to call this form of address – different for each news outlet – the *public idiom* of the media.

Although we have stressed here the *different* languages of different papers, this emphasis should not be taken too far. It is not the vast pluralistic range of voices which the media are sometimes held to represent, but a range *within certain distinct ideological limits*. While each paper may see itself as addressing a different section of the newspaper-reading public (or different types of newspapers will be in competition for different sectors of the public), the 'consensus of values' which is so deeply embedded in all the forms of public language is *more limited* than the variety of the forms of public 'language in use' would suggest. Their publics, however distinct, are assumed to fall within that very broad spectrum of 'reasonable men', and readers are addressed broadly in those terms.

The coding of items and topics into variations of the public language provides a significant element of variation in the process of transforming the news into its finished form; but, as with 'objectivity' and 'impartiality' before, this variation is not necessarily structurally at odds with the process we have called 'ideological reproduction' – for translating a news item into a variant of the public language serves, also, to *translate into a public idiom the statements and viewpoints of the primary definers*. This translation of official viewpoints into a public idiom not only makes the former more 'available' to the uninitiated; it invests them with popular force and resonance, naturalising them within the horizon of understandings of the various publics. The following example will serve as an illustration. The *Daily Mirror* of 14 June 1973 reported the presentation by the Chief Inspector of the Constabulary of his *Annual Report*, in which he claimed that 'the increase in violent crimes in England and Wales had aroused justifiable public concern'. What the *Mirror* does in this case is to *translate* the Chief Inspector's concern with rising violent crime amongst the young into a more dramatic, more connotative and more popular form – a news headline which runs, simply, 'AGGRO BRITAIN: "Mindless Violence" of the Bully Boys Worries Top Policeman'. This headline invests the sober *Report* with dramatic news value. It transposes the *Report*'s staid officialese into more newsworthy rhetoric. But it also inserts the statement *into* the stock of popular imagery, established over long usage, including that usage created by the paper's own previous coverage of the activities of 'aggro' football hooligans and skinhead 'gangs'. This transformation into a public idiom thus gives the item an *external public reference and validity* in images and connotations already sedimented in the stock of knowledge which the paper and its public share. The importance of this external public reference point is that it serves to *objectify* a public issue. That is, the publicising of an issue in the media can give it more 'objective' status as a *real* (valid) issue of public concern than would have been the case had it remained as merely a report made by experts and specialists. Concentrated media attention confers the status of high public concern on issues which are highlighted; these generally become understood by everyone as the 'pressing issues of the day'. This is part of the media's *agenda-setting* function. Setting agendas also has a reality-confirming effect.

The significance of using a public idiom with which to 'set the agenda' is that it inserts the language of everyday communication *back into the consensus*. While it is true that 'everyday' language is already saturated with dominant inferences and interpretations, the continual process of translating formal official definitions into the terms of ordinary conversation reinforces, at the same time as it disguises, the links between the two discourses. That is, the media 'take' the language of the public and, on each occasion, return it to them *inflected with dominant and consensual connotations*.

This more 'creative' media role is not obviously fully autonomous. Such translations depend on the story's potential-for-translation (its newsworthiness) and on its anchorage in familiar and long-standing topics of concern – hooliganism, crowd violence, 'aggro' gang behaviour. This process is neither totally free and unconstrained, nor is it a simple, direct reproduction. It is a transformation; and such transformations require active 'work' on the part of the media. Their over-all effect is nevertheless to help close the circle by which the definitions of the powerful become part of the taken-for-granted reality of the public by translating the unfamiliar into the familiar world. All this is entailed in the over-simple formula that journalists, after all, know best how to 'get things across to the public'.

Notes

1. MacDougall, *Interpretative Reporting* (New York: Macmillan, 1968) p. 12.
2. For a fuller account of the impact of these 'bureaucratic' factors in news production, see P. Rock, 'News as Eternal Recurrence', in *The Manufacture of News: Social Problems, Deviance and the Mass Media*, ed. S. Cohen and J. Young (London: Constable, 1973).
3. See J. Galtung and M. Ruge, 'Structuring and Selecting News' in *The Manufacture of News*, ed. Cohen and Young.
4. See ibid; K. Nordenstreng, 'Policy for News Transmission', in *Sociology of Mass Communications*, ed. D. McQuail (Harmondsworth: Penguin, 1972); W. Breed, 'Social Control in the Newsroom? A Functional Analysis', *Social Forces*, vol. 33, May 1955; and S. M. Hall, 'Introduction' in *Paper Voices*, ed. Smith *et al*.
5. L. Wirth, 'Consensus and Mass Communication', *American Sociological Review*, vol. 13, 1948.
6. *The Times*, 28 February 1973; quoted in G. Murdock, 'Political Deviance: the Press Presentation of a Militant Mass Demonstration', in *The Manufacture of News*, ed. Cohen and Young, p. 157.
7. Rock, 'News as Eternal Recurrence'.
8. G. Murdock, 'Mass Communication and the Construction of Meaning', in *Rethinking Social Psychology*, ed. N. Armistead (Harmondsworth: Penguin, 1974) pp. 208-9; but see also S. M. Hall, 'A World at One with Itself', *New Society*, 18 June 1970; and J. Young, 'Mass Media, Deviance and Drugs', in *Deviance and Social Control*, ed. Rock and McIntosh.
9. Rock, 'News as Eternal Recurrence', p. 77.
10. Murdock, 'Mass Communication', p. 210.
11. For a historical account of the evolution of those rules, see J. W. Carey, 'The Communications Revolution and the Professional Communicator', *Sociological Review Monograph*, vol. 13, 1969.
12. H. Becker, 'Whose Side are We on?', in *The Relevance of Sociology*, ed. J. D. Douglas (New York: Appleton-Century-Crofts, 1972).
13. K. Lang and G. Lang, 'The Inferential Structure of Political Communications', *Public Opinion Quarterly*, vol. 19, Summer 1955.
14. J. D. Halloran, P. Elliott and G. Murdock, *Demonstrations and Communication: a Case Study* (Harmondsworth: Penguin, 1970).
15. See S. M. Hall, 'The "Structured Communication" of Events', paper for the Obstacles to Communication Symposium, UNESCO/Division of Philosophy (available from centre for Contemporary Cultural Studies, University of Birmingham); Clarke *et al*., 'The Selection of Evidence and the Avoidance of Racialism'.
16. F. Parkin, *Class Inequality and Political Order* (London: MacGibbon & Kee, 1971) p. 83.
17. On the *Mirror*'s transformations, see Smith *et al*., *Paper voices*.

Critical connections

Policing the Crisis is an ambitious and wide-reaching sociological analysis that draws from an eclectic mix of influences, connecting 'new deviancy theory, news media studies and research on urban race relations with political economy, state theory and notions of ideological consent' (McLaughlin, 2008:146). For some critical criminologists, it represents the high point of Marxist theorising about crime, law and order and the state. It was also perhaps the first sociological analysis of the racialisation of law and order. Yet the book has attracted its fair share of critics (Crime, Media, Culture Special Section, 4,1). With specific regard to 'primary definition', it is undoubtedly significant that the theory was developed without speaking directly to any sources or journalists. Some of the major criticisms of 'primary definition' are outlined by Schlesinger, Tumber and Murdock[1] (Reading 19). Nonetheless, whilst their approach has been challenged, one of Hall *et al.*'s (1978) most lasting and significant contributions to media criminology is their attempt to take seriously and to seriously theorise the news media.

Discussion questions

● Discuss the assertion that 'in the moment of news production, the media stand in a position of structured subordination to the primary definers' (Hall *et al.* 1978: 59)?
● Who, if anyone, are the primary definers of crime news today?
● Consider Steve Chibnall's (Reading 15) *Law and Order News* alongside Stuart Hall *et al.*'s (Reading 18) *Policing the Crisis* – what points of theoretical and methodological similarity and difference can you identify

References

Althusser, L. (1977) "Lenin and Philosophy" and Other Essays. London: New Left Books.
Becker, H. (1967) 'Whose Side Are We On', in *The Relevance of Sociology,* Douglas, J. D., (ed.), (1970) New York, Appleton-Century Crofts.
Crime, Media, Culture: An International Journal (2008) 4,1: Special section on 'Policing the Crisis Thirty Years On'.
Ericson, R., Baranek, P. and Chan, J. (1989) *Negotiating Control: A Study of News Sources,* Milton Keynes: Open University Press.
McLaughlin, E. (2008) Hitting the panic button: policing/'mugging'/media/crisis', in *Crime, Media, Culture: An International Journal,* 4, 1: 145–154.
Wilkins, L. (1964) 'Information and the Definition of Deviance', in S. Cohen and J. Young. (eds.) (1973), *The Manufacture of News: Social Problems, Deviance and Mass Media.* Constable, London.

[1] Stuart Hall was Director of the Birmingham Centre for Contemporary Cultural Studies throughout the 1970s. For much of the same period, Graham Murdock was a leading member of the Leicester Centre for Mass Communication Research. The different approaches adopted in Readings 18 and 19 bear some of the hallmarks of the theoretical and methodological differences that distinguished the Centres.

Philip Schlesinger, Howard Tumber and Graham Murdock

THE MEDIA POLITICS OF CRIME AND CRIMINAL JUSTICE (1991)

Introduction and context

PHILIP SCHLESINGER, Howard Tumber and Graham Murdock take up a position which is critical of dominant ideology readings of news production – including both hegemonic (Reading 17) and propaganda (Reading 3) variants. Their contention is that the media-centric approach traditionally adopted in such studies takes inadequate account of the news production process from the perspective of sources. The privileging of journalist accounts obfuscates the organisational realities of source-media management strategies, inter-source competition and journalist-source power relations. Whilst not eschewing the clear insights that arise through Marxist readings, their approach draws from a diverse range of theoretical and empirical influences – for example, Habermas' public sphere (1962, and Reading 1) and Bourdieu's (1986) notion of 'cultural capital', as well as Ericson *et al.*'s (1987) classic newsroom ethnography (Reading 8). The resulting context allows for an analysis of news production which is less ideologically and structurally deterministic and more wide-reaching in its understanding of journalist-source relations and definitional power.

Adopting a research approach that combines in-depth content analysis *and* interviews with both journalists and sources, Schlesinger and Tumber uncover a more nuanced and contested process of news production than more overtly Marxist analyses tend to suggest. 'Primary definition', they assert, 'which ought to be an empirically ascertainable outcome, is taken instead to be an a priori effect of the privileged access of the powerful'. Through an analysis of different sources' media strategies, they find that definitional advantage may be structurally determined to an extent, but it can seldom if ever be guaranteed. Access to the media is not simply granted 'as of right', but must be won through a variety of often carefully managed media methods and practices. Furthermore, off-the-record disclosures, internal leaks and other unplanned knowledge transactions all diminish the extent to which powerful institutions can achieve discursive closure around newsworthy matters. Nor are journalists always in a position of 'structured subordination' to the sources upon which they rely for a steady stream of reportable information. Schlesinger *et al.* insist that flows of information between journalists and sources are more complex than the original articulation of primary definition suggests, and that more attention needs to be paid to 'the communication process as a whole'.

Introduction

The relationship between crime and the media has long been a matter of recurrent controversy. Social scientific research on this topic dates from the early part of this century, and one notable theme has been the press coverage of crime.

Such work grew out of a broader concern with the role of the mass media in liberal democracies, prompted by the rapid growth of a popular daily press. Many commentators perceived there to be a growing tension between the press's idealised political role and the proprietor's audience-building strategies. [. . .]

Much recent media research has been based upon a 'dominant ideology thesis'.[1] Using either a neo-Gramscian theory of hegemony[2] or a 'propaganda model',[3] it has been argued that the power of politically and economically dominant groups in the society defines the parameters of debate, ensures the privileged reproduction of their discourse, and by extension, largely determines the contours of the dominant ideology – of what is socially thinkable.

Whether culturalist or political-economic in emphasis, such work has paid inadequate attention to the communication process as a whole. Specifically, it has neglected the conflictual processes that lie behind the moment of definition both inside central social institutions and within the media themselves. Furthermore, such work has been characterized by a tendency to treat media as homogeneous, as *the* media. This largely ignores the distinctiveness of particular media (say, the press or television) and the ways in which such media are internally differentiated (e.g., the 'popular' vs the 'quality' press).

In recent years, sociological arguments about communication have developed against the backdrop of wider theoretical disputes between Marxists and pluralists. At the heart of the matter is whether the workings and output of the media are seen (more or less sophisticatedly) as subject to the control of the ruling class in capitalist societies or alternatively, whether they are seen as enjoying substantial autonomy vis-à-vis contending forces and interests.[4] The resultant tendency has been to pose either 'Marxist' or 'pluralist' questions for research.

Such inflexibility has its shortcomings, for it is necessary to consider questions of both structure and agency. For instance, whilst recognising structured inequalities of access to the media, one should not ignore the competitive strategies for media attention employed by news sources.

Virtually all research to date on this question has been media centric: that is, it has failed to focus on the relations between news sources and news media from the standpoint of the *sources* themselves. Thus, in Stuart Hall's well-known formulation, official sources' access to the media is presented as essentially guaranteed by their structural positions within the political and economic system and as therefore affording them a 'primary defining' role.[5] One effect of this standpoint is that the sociological question of how sources might organise *media strategies* and compete with one another is entirely neglected. 'Primary definition', which ought to be an empirically ascertainable outcome, is taken instead to be an a priori effect of the privileged access of the powerful. For its part, the empirical sociology of journalism, whilst more sensitive to the existence of source competition (which unquestionably takes place on unequal terms), has still remained largely trapped within methodological frameworks that preclude the direct investigation of source strategies.[6] [. . .]

Discourse about crime and criminal justice is produced in a social space in which the contending social actors range from government departments through to pressure groups. They pursue their communicative goals in what Jürgen Habermas calls the 'public sphere', namely a realm in which 'something approaching public opinion can be formed' and where, ideally, access 'is guaranteed to all citizens'.[7]

But the normative ideal hardly matches contemporary conditions. As Habermas himself notes, organised groups rather than individual citizens prevail in what is essentially 'a field for the competition of interests'.[8] Indeed, others have observed that the contemporary public sphere is under threat from the concentration of media ownership and control, the weakening of public service goals in broadcasting and the internationalizing tendencies of media production and distribution.[9] Moreover, in Britain, recent legislation and overt political intervention have tended to reinforce both state secrecy and a climate of journalistic caution.

For present purposes, this highly pressured public sphere of capitalist democracies may usefully be seen as divided into numerous discursive fields that are subject to symbolic struggle. Such ideological conflict involves an incessant mobilisation of resources by social actors in pursuit of their strategies and tactics, during the course of which they manipulate what Pierre Bourdieu[10] terms their 'cultural capital' in an effort to impose an orthodoxy of interpretation upon public attitudes and judgments about matters in dispute.

Discursive competition in the public sphere requires social actors to seek contexts for their messages that may enable them to shape the public agenda. As there is a scarcity of public spaces relative to the number of views competing for recognition, what Hilgartner and Bosk[11] call the 'carrying capacity of public institutions' – amongst which the media are of major importance – acts as an important constraint upon access.

Richard Ericson and his colleagues [12] have amply demonstrated in a cognate study of Canadian media and the criminal justice process that the state and its agencies must be at the centre of any analysis of competition for media attention. However, at the same time, as they also show, it is essential to recognize that other organized forces may also have the capacity to intervene with varying effect in the public domain.

The crime and criminal justice fields

[. . .] So far as news sources are concerned, apart from considering the organization and media strategies of state institutions, our study has focused upon pressure groups such as those dealing with prison and penal reform, civil liberties, and police accountability. Thus, the aim has been to investigate what John Kingdon[13] terms the 'policy community', namely those with specialized interests in the areas of crime and criminal justice.

The role played by resources is fundamental. First, there is the extent to which any given source is institutionalized. The most advantageous locations within the field are occupied by the apparatuses of the state such as the Home Office and the Metropolitan Police. These are locuses of permanent activity for which the routine dissemination of official information is important. In competition for space in the media, but relatively disadvantaged by comparison, are long-standing pressure groups such as the National Council for Civil Liberties (NCCL, which in May 1990 renamed itself Liberty) and the Howard League for Penal Reform. At the other end of the continuum are the least institutionalized actors, consisting of *ad hoc* issue-oriented groups or bodies such as police monitoring groups, whose base of public support is narrow and weak.

Second, the investment in media and public relations by a given actor is extremely important. As the development of media strategies has become increasingly common, the impact of symbolic media-oriented action has more and more become a crucial criterion of effectiveness. However, this can pose problems, even for the best resourced: for instance, where the Home Office and the police have invested in media monitoring and public relations, this has come up against internal budgetary limitations and has required explicit thinking about goals that might justify substantial expansion. Criteria of success in publicity are not as clear-cut as a rational-utilitarian set of assumptions might predict. Ensuring the attention desired is not just a matter of filling space and time but of achieving an impact, which is very difficult to assess.

Social actors' information management activities (and specifically their media strategies) are not solely intended to influence the policy agenda, that is those 'items which decision makers have formally accepted for serious consideration'.[14] Other reasons and motives may be discerned. For example, organizational imperatives such as the need to increase resources, to aid recruitment, and particularly in the case of professional associations and trade unions, to boost membership morale. For voluntary and pressure groups media coverage can also enhance feelings of solidarity, dissipate isolationist tendencies and give a fillip to staff confidence. [. . .]

For the police, it has been the crisis of confidence both inside the force and amongst the general public that has led them to redevelop their press and public relations operations. In fact, the 1980s were not a very good time for the police in Britain. Their handling of the inner-city riots of the early years of the decade came in for heavy criticism in some quarters. Violent confrontations during the course of industrial relations disputes were also at the forefront of political debate. The most important such instances were the coal miners' strike in 1984–85 and the print workers' disputes with newspaper proprietor Eddie Shah at his Warrington plant in 1983, and the subsequent much more serious confrontations with News International's Rupert Murdoch at his new Wapping plant in 1987. The shooting of innocent citizens in the course of police operations also caused great public concern, as did allegations of corruption and accusations of beatings to obtain confessions. All of these contributed to a widespread shaking of public confidence and a diminution of support. [. . .]

In a recent move aimed at boosting support, the current Commissioner of the Metropolitan Police, Sir Peter Imbert, hired one of the best-known design consultancies and corporate image specialists, Wolff Olins, to make an audit of internal and external attitudes towards 'the Met'. The designers' belief is that a change in image will produce more favourable public opinion with the eventual outcome of a changed impression of police effectiveness (whether genuine or not). [. . .]

Such image-building has characterized many of the social actors involved in the crime and criminal justice field. It is a version of the mobilization model used by political leaderships to gain support for their objectives which has spread to those on the outer rim of the policy-making circle. [. . .]

Returning to the question of the policy agenda, we found that while some groups were targeting the wider public in order to arouse attention, many concentrated their efforts on influencing the political elites or liberal elements in the establishment in order to achieve their objectives. The Prison Reform Trust is an example of a group that attempts to do both. They accept, however, that because most of their contact with the media is with the quality press and with television current affairs and documentary teams, this inevitably means that their audience is relatively restricted. This is not seen as a problem, however, since like many pressure groups, their prime objective is to influence people in the Home Office and in Parliament, and to inform policy and opinion makers amongst the readers of the quality press. Getting the message across to the wider public is achieved either through occasionally being mentioned in the tabloids or through popular television fiction.

At first glance, the actions of this group, and others that behave similarly, suggests that policy initiatives or changes are purely a top-down phenomenon. However, our research has shown that the situation is much more complex. Oppositional and alternative entry into the policy agenda process does take place, and raises questions about a conception of 'primary definition' that tends to assume a largely closed circle of definers. The influential analysis of Hall *et al*. failed to examine the multifold processes whereby the definitions of the powerful were themselves at times partially shaped by negotiations with those outside official circles. For example, even though we found that many of the radical groups were treated as marginal, some of their ideas were adopted by the more reformist groups, who in turn treated with state agencies. The question of where 'primary definitions' originate and the ultimate 'authorship' of policy discourse may therefore be less obvious than would appear from studying media content alone. [. . .]

Some features of media content

Media representations are a key moment in the process whereby public discourses concerning crime and justice are made available for general consumption. They are the end result of the strategies and practices deployed by sources and media personnel . . . and one of the means whereby audiences make sense of this domain. Consequently, we have aimed to provide an account of patterns of coverage in the two major mass media, the national press and television. We were particularly interested in charting the similarities and divergencies in coverage *within* and *between* these two media. Did tabloid, mid-market and quality newspapers differ significantly in their patterns of attention and exclusion and in the ways in which they presented material? Did broadcast television 'hold the middle ground'?

Our content analysis has built upon (but also goes beyond) previous British studies of crime and criminal justice, as for the first time we have sampled both national newspapers and national broadcasting. The study reported here included all national newspapers (both dailies and Sundays) and television programmes on all four terrestrial channels broadcast between 5.45p.m. and close-down.[15] A full account of the findings is beyond the scope of the present article, in which we limit ourselves to presenting some basic results relating to differences within and between the national press and the television channels.

The study of news content, as pointed out above, can be traced back to the very beginnings of social scientific interest in the media coverage of crime and justice. Some investigators set about deepening and systematizing the casual and anecdotal observations of general commentators by undertaking detailed studies of how particular cases were being handled in the press.[16] Others employed systematic sampling and column inch counts to describe the general pattern of newspaper coverage,[17] and some years later, began to use official crime statistics as a point of comparison with the situation on the ground.[18]

This approach became standard after World War Two. From James Davis' pioneering study of Colorado papers onwards,[19] a succession of American studies covering a wide variety of newspaper markets has shown that interpersonal crimes, particularly those involving violence, are consistently over-reported in relation to the official statistics, whereas routine property crimes are under-reported. Ditton and Duffy's analysis of Scottish newspapers – the closest British equivalent to the US work, most of which deals with regional markets – reaches the same basic conclusion.[20]

Surprisingly, given its centrality as a source of public knowledge, there are virtually no British studies of national press coverage of crime. A rare exception is Roshier's study of the *Daily Mirror*, *Daily Express*, and *Daily Telegraph*, which found the expected over-reporting of crimes against the person (particularly murder) but also made two other important points.[21] First, up to one third of the stories analysed concerned a variety of trivial offences. This suggests that instead of talking about 'crime news' as though it were a unitary category, it is necessary to distinguish between two types of story. On the one hand, there are 'sensational' stories which are given extended treatment, often on the front page and with accompanying pictures. On the other hand, there are the short, terse, 'mundane' items which are tucked away on the inside pages.[22] Roshier's second suggestive finding is the over-reporting of fraud, indicating that although white collar crimes receive less attention than interpersonal violence, they are by no means neglected.

A similar pattern emerged from Doris Graber's study of local and network television news in Chicago in the late 1970s in which official corruption accounted for between 20 and 24 per cent of all crimes mentioned.[23] Her argument that this was a product of the sensitizing effects of the Watergate scandal is certainly part of the explanation, but it may also be that covering the 'crimes of the powerful' taps into and articulates a strong streak of populism in the audience. There was a parallel instance during the sample period of our own study when the Guinness share scandal and other instances of 'insider dealing' attracted a great deal of coverage.

Turning now to our own results, as Tables 1 and 2 show, between 18 and 29 per cent of all crime-related items recorded for the national daily press and

Table 1 Percentage of crime-related items in national daily newspapers mentioning various types of offence

Type of Offence	Type of Newspaper		
	Quality	Mid-market	Tabloid
Non-sexual violence against the person	24.7%	38.8%	45.9%
Sexual offences	7.2%	9.3%	11.3%
Non-violent offences against the person	3.7%	5.1%	4.4%
Drug offences	3.1%	5.4%	6.4%
Offences against animals	0.4%	0.2%	0.3%
Property offences	25.7%	23.2%	18.8%
Corporate offences	5.6%	2.9%	2.1%
Public order offences	5.3%	5.9%	4.1%
Offences against the justice system	1.9%	2.4%	2.3%
Offences against the state	5.0%	4.6%	2.8%
Number of items	835	410	388

Notes: (1) More than one type of offence could be recorded for each item.
(2) Only items dealing with the UK are represented in these figures.

national television news mentioned offences against property, and more detailed analysis revealed that most of these were related to City scandals rather than to more routine property offences such as burglary and theft.

Recent American studies of prime-time fiction and entertainment programming also show a strong bias towards the misdeeds of the powerful with the majority of offenders being white males aged between 20 and 50 in white collar jobs. Conversely, blacks, young people and members of the working class are under-represented.[24] We need to be cautious in applying this argument directly to British television however, since it takes no account of the mediating effects of genre.[25]

Also noteworthy is the distribution of attention to different kinds of discourse in the print media. This is somewhat crudely indicated by variations in the space allocated to the views of different groups and individuals. As Table 3 shows, there are important differences between the top and bottom ends of the newspaper market, particularly amongst daily titles. Whilst the quality dailies are focused upon Parliament and government, and offer space to the views of experts, elites and pressure groups, tabloid newspapers give far greater play to the opinions and perspectives offered by the victims of crime and their relatives and by those suspected or convicted of crimes. They are more oriented, that is, to 'common sense' thinking and discourse, and less to professionalized debate and the evaluation of policy. These variations throw light upon the complexity of the process of 'secondary definition' through the media, as they suggest that the distribution and hierarchy of discourses between different types of daily newspaper may vary significantly in relation to different readerships.

Table 2 Percentage of crime-related television news items mentioning various types of offence

Type of Offence	News Items on		National News Bulletins on		
	National Bulletins	Local Bulletins	ITV	BBC1	Channel 4
Non-sexual violence against the person	40.0%	63.2%	43.5%	42.3%	18.2%
Sexual offences	5.5%	8.8%	8.7%	–	9.1%
Non-violent offences against the person	8.3%	8.8%	10.1%	5.8%	9.1%
Drug offences	4.8%	1.8%	5.8%	3.8%	4.5%
Offences against animals	0.7%	5.3%	–	1.9%	–
Property offences	23.4%	12.3%	20.3%	26.9%	27.3%
Corporate offences	2.1%	1.8%	2.9%	1.9%	–
Public order offences	18.6%	5.3%	14.5%	23.1%	18.2%
Offences against the justice system	7.6%	7.0%	10.1%	7.7%	–
Offences against the state	6.2%	–	4.3%	9.6%	4.5%
Number of items	145	57	69	52	22

Notes: (1) More than one type of offence could be recorded for each item.
(2) Only items dealing with the UK are represented in these figures.
(3) This table refers solely to news bulletins and excludes daily current affairs programmes. Consequently, BBC2, which does not carry a nightly bulletin, has not been included in the channel columns. However, two news flashes on BBC are included in the item total for all national bulletins.

The second major set of differences concerns variations in the general pattern of attention to crime within the national press. As Table 1 shows, the overall distribution confirms the commonsense distinctions made between quality, mid-market and tabloid newspapers. Whereas almost half (46 per cent) of crime-related items in the daily tabloids mention violent crimes against the person, the corresponding figure for the quality dailies is only 25 per cent, with mid-market papers falling almost exactly in between. A similar, though far less dramatic pattern emerges in the coverage of sexual offences and offences involving drugs.

As Table 4 shows, these differences are also evident in variations in the prominence given to stories featuring different kinds of crime. Although their smaller page size results in mid-market and tabloid dailies carrying far fewer crime-related items on their front pages than the quality titles, those that do appear are twice as likely to feature violent crimes against the person (45 per cent as against 22 per cent). Tabloids and mid-market papers are also far more likely to feature sexual offences on the front page than are quality papers. In other words, the world of front-page crime in the 'popular' press (both tabloid and mid-market) is primarily oriented towards

Table 3 Percentage of crime-related items in national daily newspapers containing the views or comments of selected groups

	Type of Newspaper		
Group	Quality	Mid-market	Tabloid
Members of the Government and Conservative MPs	15.7%	8.0%	5.7%
MPs from Opposition parties	11.9%	8.0%	3.6%
Local government officials and local politicians	3.8%	3.4%	1.0%
Judges, lawyers and court officials	19.9%	17.6%	18.8%
Police and law enforcement sources	12.2%	15.1%	16.2%
Probation and prison workers	1.3%	1.0%	1.8%
Experts/elites/members of lobby and pressure group	21.7%	17.3%	11.3%
Victims, suspects' relatives and criminals	13.4%	22.9%	24.2%
Vox pops, members of general public	3.0%	4.4%	7.0%
Number of items	835	410	388

Notes: (1) More than one type of offence could be recorded for each item.
(2) Only items dealing with the UK are represented in these figures.

Table 4 Percentage of crime-related items on the front pages of national daily newspapers mentioning various types of offence

	Type of Newspaper		
Type of Offence	Quality	Mid-market	Tabloid
Non-sexual violence	22.0%	45.0%	45.5%
Sexual offences	2.8%	20.0%	22.7%
Non-violent offences against the person	5.5%	10.0%	22.7%
Drug offences	—	5.0%	4.5%
Property offences	35.8%	40.0%	27.3%
Corporate offences	6.4%	—	—
Public order offences	6.4%	5.0%	—
Offences against the justice system	0.9%	—	13.6%
Offences against the state	8.3%	10.0%	—
Number of items	109	20	22

Notes: (1) More than one type of offence could be recorded for each item.
(2) Only items dealing with the UK are represented in these figures.

personalized crime affecting identifiable individuals, with a strong emphasis on interpersonal violence.

Turning now to some of the findings for television news (shown in Table 2), several points are worth noting. First, the overall pattern of attention to different kinds of violent crimes against the person, drug offences, and property offences in national television news approximates to the pattern established for the mid-market dailies, lending weight to the argument that in certain key areas television news seeks the 'middle ground'. However, as Table 2 also shows, this pattern is by no means consistent across all categories of offence. Compared to all types of national daily paper, television news pays rather more attention to offences relating to public order, to the justice system and to the state.

Second, compared to the national bulletins, local news gives markedly more attention to violent crimes against the person, which perhaps suggests a heavy reliance on the police and courts (and the local press) as sources of news items. Third, there are some important differences between channels, with violent crimes against the person attracting many more mentions on the two 'popular' channels, BBC1 and ITV, than on the more 'upmarket' Channel 4. Indeed, the pattern for ITV more closely approximates to the pattern displayed by the tabloid dailies – particularly in the areas of interpersonal violence, sexual crimes, and drug offences.

These different patterns of emphasis in coverage have important implications for our understanding of audience perceptions, since they suggest that differences in newspaper readership and television viewing may regulate access to significant variations in discourses about crime. [. . .]

Notes

1.   N. Abercrombie, S. Hill, and B. S. Turner, *The Dominant Ideology Thesis*, London, George Allen and Unwin, 1980, and *ibid., Sovereign Individuals of Capitalism*, London, Allen and Unwin, 1986.

2.   S. Hall, C. Critcher, T. Jefferson, J. Clarke and B. Roberts, *Policing the Crisis: Mugging, the State and Law and Order*, London, Macmillan, 1978.

3.   E. H. Herman and N. Chomsky, *Manufacturing Consent: The Political Economy of the Mass Media*, New York, Pantheon Books, 1988.

4.   J. Curran, M. Gurevitch and J. Woollacott, 'The study of the media: theoretical approaches' in M. Gurevitch, T. Bennett, J. Curran and J. Woollacott (eds), *Culture, Society and the Media*, London and New York, Methuen, 1982, pp. 11–29.

5.   Cf. Hall *el al.*, 1978, *op. cit.* and S. Hall, 'Media power and class power', in J. Curran, J. Ecclestone, G. Oakley and A. Richardson (eds), *Bending Reality: The State of the Media*, London, Pluto Press, 1986, pp. 5–14.

6.   For fuller criticisms of both Hall's and Herman and Chomsky's positions (amongst others), cf. P. Schlesinger, 'From production to propaganda?', *Media, Culture and Society*, vol. 11, no. 3, July 1989, pp. 283–306, and *ibid.*, 'Rethinking the sociology of journalism: source strategies and the limits of media-centrism', in M. Ferguson (ed.), *Public Communication: The New Imperatives*, London, Sage, 1989, pp. 61–83.

7.   J. Habermas, 'The public sphere', in A. Mattelart and S. Siegelaub (eds), *Communication and Class Struggle*, vol. 1, New York, International General, 1979, p. 198.

8.   *Ibid.*, p. 200.

9. Cf. P. Elliott, 'Intellectuals, the "information society" and the disappearance of the public sphere', *Media, Culture and Society,* vol. 4, no.3, July 1982, pp. 243–53; N. Garnham, 'The media and the public sphere', in P. Golding, G. Murdock and P. Schlesinger (eds), *Communicating Politics: Mass Communications and the Political Process,* Leicester University Press, 1986, pp. 37–53; and P. Scannell, 'Public service broadcasting and modern public life', *Media, Culture and Society,* vol. 11, no. 2, April 1989, pp. 135–66.

10. Cf. P. Bourdieu, *Distinction: A Social Critique of the Judgement of Taste,* London and New York, Routledge and Kegan Paul, 1986. The concept of 'strategy' has become increasingly important in contemporary sociological analysis across a wide range of social actors. G. Crow, 'The use of the concept of "strategy" in recent sociological literature', *Sociology,* vol. 23, no. 1, pp. 1–24 points out rightly that the use of strategic analysis has become somewhat over-extended, and that many of the problems of how it relates to institutional analysis remain unresolved. Nevertheless, in the present study we believe that there is demonstrable utility in applying strategic analysis to the inter-relations between media and news sources in the crime and criminal justice fields.

11. S. Hilgartner and C. L. Bosk, 'The rise and fall of social problems: a public arenas model', *American Journal of Sociology,* vol. 94, 1988, pp. 53–78.

12. R. V. Ericson, P. M. Baranek and J. L. Chan, *Negotiating Control: A Study of News Sources,* Toronto, Buffalo, London, University of Toronto Press, 1989.

13. J. Kingdon, *Agendas, Alternatives and Public Policies,* Boston, Toronto, Little, Brown and Co., 1984.

14. R. W. Cobb, J-K. Ross and M. H. Ross, 'Agenda-building as a comparative political process', *American Political Science Review,* vol. 70, no. 1, 1976, p. 126.

15. The sample covered two full weeks of seven days each spread over a total period lasting from 11 January to 21 March 1987, made up of one continuous seven day period and a further seven days sampled at intervals. Constructing the sample in this way allowed for a systematic overview of coverage in the two major national media over a sufficiently long time period to compensate for any special circumstances during the initial week. It worked well for forms of output with a daily cycle, such as news, but had the disadvantage of yielding comparatively few examples of relevant current affairs, documentary and fictional programmes.

   The sample included all programmes or newspaper items which mentioned or featured any aspect of crime, policing, the legal system and the treatment of offenders. All relevant dimensions of all items were coded. For example, a report of a court case could be coded under courts and policing (if police evidence was featured) as well as under crime. In order to ensure that the analysis was as comprehensive as possible, up to four separate crimes could be recorded for each news item featuring crime.

16. J. L. Holmes, 'Crime and the press', *Journal of Criminal Law,* vol. 20, 1929, pp. 246–93.

17. F. Fenton, *The Influence of Newspaper Presentations upon the Growth of Crime and Other Anti-Social Activity,* The University of Chicago Press, 1911.

18. F. Harris, *Presentation of Crime in Newspapers,* Hanover, New Hampshire, The Sociological Press, 1932.

19. F. J. Davis, 'Crime news in Colorado newspapers', *American Journal of Sociology,* vol. 57, 1951, pp. 325–30.

20. J. Ditton and J. Duffy, 'Bias in newspaper reporting of crime news', *British Journal of Criminology,* vol. 23, 1983, pp. 159–65.

21.   B. Roshier, 'The selection of crime news by the press', in S. Cohen and J. Young (eds), *The Manufacture of News: Deviance, Social Problems and the Mass Media,* London, Constable, 1973, pp. 28–39.
22.   P. Dahlgren, 'Crime news: the fascination of the mundane', *European Journal of Communication,* vol. 3, no. 2, 1988, pp. 189–206.
23.   D. Graber, *Crime News and the Public,* New York, Praeger, 1980.
24.   L. S. Lichter and S. R. Lichter, *Prime Time Crime: Criminals and Law Enforcers in TV Entertainment,* Washington DC, The Media Institute, 1983.
25.   Crime is shown in a greater variety of contexts on this side of the Atlantic because the system supports a wider range of programme formats – from the street-level inner city policing of *The Bill,* through the complexly contextualised offences in *EastEnders,* to the boardroom struggles of *Howard's Way.* Different formats organize discourse and imagery diversely though their patterns of exclusion and emphasis and their construction of varying points of view of the actions presented. In soap operas such as *Brookside* or *EastEnders,* routine crimes emerge out of well-established situations and milieux and are committed by characters the audience knows well. In contrast, the action in *The Bill* (which shares many of the basic features of a soap opera) is viewed through the eyes of the police. We see only the incident or its aftermath. It is something to be dealt with. The motivations involved often remain obscure. These variations suggest a possible link between differences in patterns of media consumption and differences in public perceptions and attitudes.

Critical connections

Especially today, when the tabloid print media seem increasingly inclined to flex their adversarial muscles, calling government and the state agencies of control to account and routinely taking the scalps of senior state officials, the notion that definitional closure can be secured around all but the most straightforward and uncontroversial of issues seems untenable. Crime, certainly, is not one of these issues. Indeed, much has changed since Schlesinger *et al.*'s research which calls into question the continued usefulness of modernist conceptions of news production grounded in radical or liberal pluralist understandings of power relations and information flows. With globalisation and the emergence of the 24-7 news media environment, some suggest we are now faced with conditions best described as 'cultural chaos' (McNair, 2006) A global news mediasphere is characterised by the intensified commodification of news and counter-culture, increasing market competition, a hyper-adversarial news media, and the rapid rise of 'mediated access' to public participation broadcasting (for example, Talk Radio and live television debates). Ideological hegemony is replaced by ideological dissolution, and journalistic consensus around elite ideas – whether manufactured in the radical sense or organic in the liberal pluralist sense – is replaced by journalistic *dissensus.* The emergence of a highly diversified, widely accessible and ultimately chaotic media environment has changed the terrain upon which struggles over media power and influence are played out. These changes, in turn, are transforming the ways in which news is sourced, selected, produced, disseminated, consumed and interpreted.

Discussion questions

- What are Schlesinger and Tumber's main criticisms of Hall *et al.*'s thesis of 'primary definition'?
- Why is it so important to consider news production from the perspective of both journalists and sources (see also Reading 8)?
- What challenges face traditional or modernist understandings of news production in the 24-7 global news mediasphere (see also Readings 5 and 6)?

References

Bourdieu, P. (1986) *Distinction: A Social Critique of the Judgement of Taste*, London: Routledge.

Ericson, R. Baranek, P. and Chan, J. (1989) *Negotiating Control: A Study of News Sources*, Milton Keynes: Open University Press.

McNair, B. (2006) *Cultural Chaos: Journalism, News and Power in a Globalised World*, London: Routledge.

Eugene McLaughlin

RECOVERING BLACKNESS/
REPUDIATING WHITENESS (2005)

Introduction and context

EUGENE McLAUGHLIN EXPLORES the racialisation of crime in the British print media. McLaughlin demonstrates how the *Daily Mail*'s reporting of the 1993 racist murder in South London of black teenager Stephen Lawrence articulated a 'psychopathical version of whiteness that made the racist murder comprehensible to the ethnoracial imaginary of Middle England'. Adopting a qualitative case study approach, he systematically examines the *Daily Mail*'s coverage of the case from the murder through to the final outcome of the second trial and aftermath. The *Mail* – known for its traditionally reactionary stance on race issues in Britain – constructed the Lawrence family in a manner which obscured their 'race' to the point of writing it 'out of the script'. This deracialisation allowed Stephen and his parents to be idealised *within* a shared system of Middle England values, but in a manner that did not immediately interrupt the ethnoracial master-narrative espoused by the *Daily Mail*, and disseminated throughout its Middle England readership. The deracialisation of the Lawrence family and their subsequent portrayal as innocent, proud and respectable, was paralleled by the racialisation of the five suspects as racist, violent 'white trash'. At the same time, the *Mail*'s construction of violent racism as a localised problem confined to an underclass of thugs distanced the readership from the uncomfortable 'reality' of normalised racism, thus absolving Middle England of any responsibility in the murder of Stephen Lawrence.

Richard Dyer (1997) has noted that official and cultural constructions of race within white societies are often underpinned by a more or less implicit assumption that only non-white people are 'raced'. White people, by contrast, are not 'raced', and tend only to think of themselves in racial terms when they feel threatened by racial difference. He continues, 'In Western representation whites are overwhelmingly and disproportionately predominant ... Yet precisely because of this and their placing as norm they seem not to be represented to themselves *as* whites but as people who are variously gendered, classed, sexualised and abled. At the level of racial representation, in other words, whites are not of a certain race, they're just the human race' (Dyer, 1997: 2–3). With this in mind, McLaughlin's analysis of the *Daily Mail*'s deracialisation of Stephen Lawrence and parallel racialisation of the white males accused of killing him marks a highly original contribution to the study of race in media discourses. The reporting of the Stephen Lawrence case, McLaughlin argues, changed how the mainstream British press 'do' race. It set a precedent and established that ethnic minority (murder) victims can secure media attention, public sympathy and legitimate victim status. The resulting Macpherson Enquiry (Macpherson, 1999), which branded the London Metropolitan Police 'institutionally racist', reconfigured British race relations on a much broader canvas.

Stuart Hall (1982: 35) has famously argued that the media is not only a powerful source of ideas about race, 'they are also one place where these ideas are articulated, worked on, transformed and elaborated'. The media is not unbiased or neutral: it provides the connecting words, ideas, and images out of which we fashion 'our very identities, our sense of selfhood; our notion of what it means to be male or female; our sense of class, of ethnicity and race, of nationality, of sexuality, of "us" and "them." Media images help shape our view of the world and our deepest values. Media stories provide the symbols, myths and resources through which we constitute a common culture and through the appropriation of which we insert ourselves into this culture' (Kellner 1995: 25). To be sure, it is virtually impossible to prove the effects of media coverage on what the public thinks and does about race. However, there is evidence that print and broadcast news media discourses are a constitutive part of everyday family and communal conversational interactions.

Consequently, an understandable place to start to address the tricky question of how and whether racialization works is to probe how the media's 'boundless appetite for racial image and narrative is crucial to its capacity to signify' (Torres 1998: 4). Numerous research studies have demonstrated how the racialized images and representational tropes circulating in the news media can transform complex human identities and social issues into one-dimensional, colour-coded stereotypes and caricatures (see Martindale 1986; Dates and Barlow 1990; Gray 1995; Wilson and Gutierrez 1995; Gabriel 1998; Hunt 1999; Entman and Rojecki 2001; Jacobs 2000; Law 2002). However, to date researchers have paid scant attention to exploring the few moments when mainstream journalism and prime time television news decide to address whiteness explicitly (see Neal 1999; van Loon 1999).

I have elected to situate my discussion of how the racialization of whiteness works with the *Daily Mail*'s role in the campaign to bring the murderers of Stephen Lawrence to justice. The *Daily Mail* is one of the United Kingdom's most successful and politically conservative mass circulation newspapers. When it chooses to do so, this mid-market tabloid can embrace more than two million readers, via headline stories, editorials, opinion essays, and human interest features, in a heated conversation on the changing nature of race relations in the United Kingdom. Put bluntly, what we might describe as its working within whiteness 'race work' does more than tell its readers *what* to think about race; it also uses well-established reportorial cues and structures to tell its readers *how* they might want to think about race. Although several broadsheet newspapers and independent television companies had investigated the Stephen Lawrence murder, it was the *Daily Mail*'s high-profile campaign that set the agenda for the terms of the public debate about who and what was responsible for the killing. Never before had a racist murder been so graphically and repeatedly described and condemned by a right-wing newspaper in the United Kingdom. Equally importantly, this newspaper campaign offered 'Middle England' the possibility of thinking differently about both the racial injustices of everyday life and the reasons why a young man could be murdered on a suburban street because of the colour of his skin. In the Stephen Lawrence case, I will attempt to demonstrate how the *Daily Mail* produced what is best described as a psychopathological version of whiteness that made the racist murder comprehensible to the ethnoracial imaginary of Middle England. [. . .]

Before proceeding, I need briefly to remind readers of the basic details of this notorious stab-and-run murder that continues to define debates on British race relations. On the night of Thursday, 22 April 1993, Stephen Lawrence, an eighteen-year-old black student, was stabbed to death by a group of young white men in the southeast London semi-suburb of Eltham. Stephen and his friend Duwayne Brooks had been waiting for a bus to take them home. He did not know his killers and his killers did not know him. According to Duwayne the only words uttered on that fateful night were 'what, what, nigger?' In the years to follow, the remarkable campaign organized by his parents Doreen and Neville Lawrence to bring the murderers of their son to justice transformed yet another unsolved racist murder with limited newsworthiness into a national conversation on race and justice. In a news media frenzy, on 24 February 1999, the report of Sir William Macpherson's public inquiry into the murder declared that professional incompetence, institutional racism, and a failure of leadership within the Metropolitan Police had allowed the murderers to escape justice. Against a backdrop of blanket news media coverage, Prime Minister Tony Blair and the then Home Secretary, Jack Straw, declared that the Macpherson report would serve as a watershed to British society's attitudes to racism. Despite the media frenzy, there has been a relative lack of critical commentary on the news media's coverage of this extraordinary moment in the post-war history of UK race relations (see Cathcart 1999; Alibhai-Brown 2000; Cottle 2000; Law 2002). This is particularly the case concerning what I would argue is the racialized framing of those held responsible for the murder of Stephen Lawrence. These five young white men are in effect a taboo topic for scholars, their racist words and violent actions to be condemned rather than analysed.

Working within whiteness: the *Daily Mail*'s ethnoracial imaginary of Middle England

[. . .]Crime is an emblematic issue for the *Daily Mail*, fostering fear and anger among readers. It provides graphic coverage that enables its readers to discuss the causes and solutions to the United Kingdom's crime problem within a racialized 'something-must-be-done' framework. [. . .] At the same time, an innumerable number of crime problems receive little, if any, coverage in the newspaper. Most controversially, it stands accused of systematically under-reporting racist violence. The *Daily Mail*'s coverage of racist violence is premised upon the notion that tolerance and fair play are defining features of British society. Overt racism is not a part of Middle England and racist incidents are exceptional events perpetuated by fringe neo-fascist and white supremacist groups or almost the inevitable result of inner city racial tensions. It is therefore a 'switch off' issue for Middle England. However, in addition to strategic omission and/or distancing, the *Daily Mail* is also capable of 'reality check' stories that seek to turn public discussion of 'only whites can be violent racists' on its head. The newspaper periodically declares that an unspoken aspect of racist violence in contemporary Britain is one of anti-white street crime perpetrated by predatory young black men. It also condemns what it defines as the politically correct criminal justice and media establishment for suppressing or attempting to explain away the extent and seriousness of black-on-white criminal violence. The dramatic visual imprinting of 'black crime' stories on the public imagination, has led critics of the newspaper to accuse it of racially coding the United Kingdom's crime problem. [. . .]

Recovering blackness: the assimilation of Stephen Lawrence

The *Daily Mail*'s initial reporting of the murder of Stephen Lawrence was true to form. On 8 May 1993, a 'news in brief' story noted that three white teenagers were being questioned by the police about the killing of Stephen Lawrence. There was 'no front page on the horror of it all. No shouting headlines or a demand for an end to racial injustice. No mention of the fact that it could even be a racially motivated attack. Just one short news story' (Ahmed 1999). However, two days later the newspaper spotlighted the murder as 'a family tragedy' to which many of its readers could relate. As it turned out, the *Mail* was in the process of not just putting faces to names but testing whether Stephen Lawrence and his family might be worthy of the support of Middle England. According to the news story and the associated editorial, Stephen Lawrence was a devout Christian and a hard-working sixth-former who wanted to train as an architect. His parents, Doreen and Neville Lawrence, were decent, moderate people who had encouraged his ambitions and were proud of his achievements. The Lawrences assured the newspaper that they had [. . .] brought their son up to respect the law and not to see colour as an issue. Indeed, they went so far as to declare that neither they nor their children had experienced racial harassment, let alone violence.

The paper was therefore able to draw a categorical distinction between the Middle England values of the Lawrence family home and those of the anti-racist and 'rent-a-mob' groups who had taken to the streets in the aftermath of the killing and were talking of reprisal attacks. The editorial line was clear:

> Racism is abominable. Those of the neo-nazi persuasion who preach and provoke it should be condemned. But is there not also something contemptible about professional protestors who capitalise on grief to fuel confrontation? Such street agitators of the right and left need each other. Most of us in Britain – whatever our colour – need them like the plague.

A follow-on exclusive interview with Doreen and Neville Lawrence which the newspaper ran on 12 May provided more intimate details of the strain placed on this ordinary family by the murder of their eldest son. [. . .] The grieving parents once more distanced themselves from the extremists who were trying to hijack the murder of their son for political ends. As the first arrests were made and court appearances took place, the *Daily Mail*'s representation of Stephen Lawrence as the innocent victim of a racist attack was consolidated:

> Stephen, an A-Level student who hoped to become an architect, was killed on April 22 at a bus stop in Eltham, South-East London. He was waiting with a friend for a bus to return to his home in nearby Plumstead when he was stabbed by a gang of between 4 and 6 white youths who had apparently made racist remarks. (*Daily Mail*, 22 December 1993)

The newspaper had little to say about the collapse of the public prosecution case against the suspects and the subsequent decision of the Lawrence family to launch a private prosecution in April 1996. However, the emotional scenes accompanying the collapse of the private prosecution in April 1996 and the reconvening of the inquest of February 1997 allowed the paper to remind readers of what had happened and who was involved. Although the photographic and discursive image of Stephen Lawrence's innocence and the quiet dignity of his parents was by now firmly established in the public imagination, because of legal restrictions very little information was available about the young white men accused of his murder. However, all this would change as a result of the *Daily Mail*'s frame-breaking decision to invest its moral authority, political clout, and considerable investigative resources in a high-profile crusade to bring the murderers of Stephen Lawrence to justice.

Repudiating whiteness: the psychopathologization of the five suspects

In a blaze of publicity, on 13 February 1997 the five suspects reluctantly presented themselves at the reconvened inquest to be cross-examined about their alleged involvement in the murder of Stephen Lawrence. The decision by the suspects to exercise the legal right to refuse to answer any question that might incriminate them frustrated and infuriated all involved in the inquest process. It also most likely contributed to the inquest verdict that Stephen Lawrence had been killed 'in a completely unprovoked racist attack by five white youths'. The following day, the *Daily Mail* recorded a journalistic first in the United Kingdom, attracting approval and condemnation in equal measure for printing a front page banner headline – 'Murderers: The Mail accuses these men of killing. If we are wrong let them sue us.' The most significant factors in the *Daily Mail*'s decision to print the names and the photographs of the prime suspects seem to have been that the extensive Metropolitan Police investigation and various unsuccessful court hearings confirmed that Stephen Lawrence was the victim of an unprovoked racially motivated attack: he did not have a criminal record, was not associated with drug dealing or a member of a street gang. He had been stabbed repeatedly and left to die because of the colour of his skin. The newspaper's preliminary investigations into the murder also confirmed that Stephen's parents were 'ordinary', 'decent', and 'dignified' people who had refused to allow race extremists to make political capital out of their son's death. The newspaper was also

Figure 20.1 *The Daily Mail*: 'Murderers', 14 February, 1997.

concerned that the suspects' manipulation of the legal process and the atmosphere of fear and intimidation surrounding the unresolved murder were threatening to lock Middle England into a racial crisis comparable to anything that had been seen in the United States in the aftermath of the Rodney King case.

In a complicated double movement, the *Daily Mail*'s subsequent 'Justice for Stephen Lawrence' campaign repeatedly acclaimed the Lawrences as a grief-stricken family that had been left with the knowledge that a grave injustice had been allowed to prevail. In the process, Doreen and Neville Lawrence were transformed into a couple of extraordinary moral authority and respectability and their son Stephen idealized as an icon for Middle England. He was the gifted black schoolboy whose dream of becoming an architect had been brutally ended on a south London street in April 1993. These images would stand in pointed contrast to the *Daily Mail*'s depiction of Neil Acourt, Jamie Acourt, Gary Dobson, Luke Knight, and David Norris, as the five white 'racist savages', the 'pack of bigots', the 'gang of evil killers', the 'moronic thugs' 'overflowing with hatred' who were 'walking free and smirking at the thrill of getting away with it'. In conjunction with its own investigations, the newspaper used the evidence that had emerged in earlier court hearings as the basis for its relentless hounding of the prime suspects. As a result, they would be transformed into a portrait of white psychopathological savagery that threatened all that Middle England stood for.

Acting it out I: video footage of natural born racists

The newspaper's overall construction of the suspects was based on police video evidence showing the five men expressing extremely violent racist views. In December 1994, as part of the Metropolitan Police investigation, a camera and a microphone had been hidden in a rented flat occupied by one of the suspects. The blurred footage with its 'yob culture' background 'of loud music, blaring TV shows and foul and racist language' provided *Daily Mail* readers with an insight into the private lives and thoughts of the suspects. It reveals 'a group of violent depraved men almost insane with hatred of people they called "Pakis and coons"' and 'a soundtrack of sickening racist obscenities'. The *Daily Mail*, along with the other newspapers and broadcasters, would subsequently make extensive use of this 'reality TV' footage as it illustrated 'the gang's love of knives and violence', predilection for 'racist thuggery', and 'psychopathic hatred of blacks'. And there is no doubt that the raging, racialized anger, and paranoia articulated in this video makes for disturbing viewing and listening. Throughout, the suspects brandish knives and practise stabbing moves and shout racist abuse at black entertainers and athletes as they are watching television. A couple of the suspects attempt to outdo each other in their stream of consciousness fantasies about the extreme violence they want to enact on 'fucking niggers' and 'Pakis' who they hold responsible for their predicament and all the ills of contemporary multiculturalized Britain.

What exactly is being acted out in this edited videotape, as well as why, has generated heated discussion. The suspects always claimed that they knew that the flat had been bugged and that they had used extreme language deliberately and acted provocatively both to undermine this supposedly covert police operation and express their anger about being unfairly hounded for a crime they did not commit. It therefore proved nothing. Indeed, on the video, they go to strenuous lengths to deny any involvement in the murder and distance themselves from the neo-fascist groups operating in the locality. However, for the *Daily Mail* the video footage provided incontrovertible evidence that the suspects were foul mouthed, uneducated, hardcore racists who gloried in the doing of extreme violence. These were the sort of 'natural born racists' who could have murdered Stephen Lawrence for no reason other than because of the colour of his skin. In the following months, the repetition of the contents of the video footage across the newspaper and the rest of the news media magnified the identikit racist views and transparent guilt of the five suspects.

The murder scene: the racist badlands of South London

Equally significantly, the *Daily Mail* produced expansive investigative reports on the disconcerting racial dynamics of the 'sprawling' working class Brook council estate in Eltham, that tightened its representational grip on the 'natural born racists'. These 'heart of darkness' and 'badlands', 'be grateful you do not live here', reports from the murder scene tapped into and voiced local gossip and rumour about the murder of Stephen Lawrence. They implanted the notion that the murder was not a random act of mindless violence but the outcome of a geographically isolated white working class culture of racism. This was a murder waiting to happen. Other newspapers and television programmes had already run investigative features on the semi-suburban locality identifying it as 'a smouldering cauldron of race hatred' and the 'race hate capital of Britain'. Now the *Daily Mail* confirmed that the five suspects and the 'white place' they lived in were mutually constitutive:

> If you ask decent law abiding residents questions about the Stephen Lawrence murder you will 'taste the fear' in this locality. This is because the Brook council estate is also home to a group of aggressive young men who delight in calling themselves the Firm. Violent and racist, they rule the area 'like cockerels'. In one of the very few uncared for houses lives Neil and Jamie Acourt, the uneducated, 'jobless brothers' who modelled themselves on the Kray Twins. This group exulted in their title. For several years the Firm had 'strutted the streets, drinking heavily and spending freely' in the pubs, clubs and bars of south London. (*Daily Mail*, 14 February 1997)

The gang had known each other since childhood. In their early years they were regarded by classmates as 'wimps, useless at football and academically poor'. However:

> they transformed themselves, by a kind of group osmosis, into fearsome young thugs who both used and allegedly dealt in soft and hard drugs. They were tutored in this by some members of their families, at least one of whom has been involved in major crime.
>
> Only Norris and Knight have ever held jobs since leaving school, and then only briefly. Yet they always have large amounts of money which they enjoy flashing around. On the estate where most vehicles are second hand, they are seen driving expensive cars.
>
> They enjoy buying fashionable clothes. For night clubs four-buttoned tight suits and narrow ties, like the anti-heroes from the film *Reservoir Dogs*. For days spent wandering the parks, drinking and smoking cannabis, they wear Polo shirts and Hugo Boss jeans. (*Daily Mail*, 15 February 1997)

The disreputable value system that permeated this white working class estate was the reason why the police investigation had run into a 'wall of silence' even though many law-abiding residents were disgusted by what had happened.

The Acourts' personal terror campaign against black residents was the reason why the Brook estate was predominantly white. Although the *Daily Mail* could not find evidence that they were members of local neo-fascist groups, it was in no doubt that the primary focus and pleasure in the five's otherwise pointless unemployed lives involved seeking out young blacks and Asians and deploying their 'vicious brand of designer racism'. For the 'innocent and unfortunate Stephen Lawrence, whose family had until that day four years ago never experienced serious racism in Britain, the Firm's sick pleasure exploded into murder outside the doors of Eltham Parish Church'.

The reports also found evidence of their love of violence. One resident informs the newspaper that the suspects enjoyed flashing the knives they routinely carried. 'I always had a feeling they were all acting out some kind of movie in their heads. Because they were so fast in their movements. And because they were either drunk or drugged up most days, they were scary kids.' Neil Acourt is identified locally as the 'completely fearless' and 'on the very edge of extreme violence' leader of this tightly bonded gang.

> Neil with his close cropped hair and permanent half smile, was widely feared by other gang members because of his mood changes. He was the most ferocious racist in the group and was said to be involved in several vendettas against other youths, mostly black, on the rival Ferrier estate.

On 16 March 1998, the newspaper revisited Eltham, the by now, 'grimy', 'desolate' southeast London suburb 'which earned unwanted notoriety when the studious black teenager Stephen Lawrence was killed by a gang of white thugs'. Sitting outside multicultural London this is an area 'blighted by racism, sometimes crude and violent, sometimes casual and unthinking, but always lurking there like a malignant cancer'. Away from the High Street with its chain stores and McDonald's many of the shops have closed down and are smeared with graffiti and the area has experienced some of the worst racist violence in the country. Blacks and Asians avoid the area after dark. The reporter encounters John, '6ft tall, built like a tank with shorn hair, rippling muscles and several tattoos' who aggressively denies there is racism in the area and a nervous elderly Asian shopkeeper 'wearing an immaculate grey suit who does not want to get dragged into a discussion about racism'. The cause of this racism was identified:

> There are lots of single mothers around here, and many of the kids have problems. When they finish school, they find there are no jobs, so many of them turn to crime or racism. Lots of them hang around and get their kicks trying to intimidate you.

Investigating the locality further the reporter also identified the rougher estates:

> My first stop, the Ferrier Estate, surrounded by a 5ft high wall, reminded me of a prison. Nonetheless, I made my way inside. Its long corridors were deathly quiet and the air was oppressive. Two hard faced youths approached me and gave me such a cold, sustained stare that I turned on my heels and left. It was a terrifying hint of menace that even I, as a white person, would be foolish to ignore. And it gave me a chilling glimpse of

the daily nightmare of life faced by so many decent families in these bad-lands of south London just because their faces don't match the required colour. Clearly, even now, five years after a pointless stabbing shocked the nation, little has changed in Eltham.

Readers were left in little doubt that the intrinsic violently racist culture of the semi-suburban racist working class estate that had bred the five suspects was a place at odds with not just nearby multicultural London but Middle England.

Acting it out II: the public inquiry

At the end of June 1998, one of the most eagerly anticipated news media events of the year took place at the public inquiry into the murder of Stephen Lawrence. The appearance and performance of the uneducated, unemployed, lower class white suspects who had expressed such extreme racist sentiments delivered the most dramatic episode of the inquiry. They also created the definitive visual images that have been reproduced and commented upon on countless occasions. An atmosphere had been created that bore a remarkable resemblance to a racially charged show trial. Fighting broke out among protestors and police as the five suspects made their way into the inquiry. At one stage, during the first day of cross-examination of the suspects, police officers used tear gas when members of the Nation of Islam demanded to be admitted to the already packed inquiry. The exit of the five from the public inquiry sparked public disorder in the surrounding streets.

Rather than breaking under concentrated questioning the suspects toughed it out, refusing to account for their whereabouts on the night of the murder and denying that they had murdered Stephen Lawrence. They also repudiated the assertion that the racist words and violent actions detailed on the police videotape evidenced their pathological hatred of black people. Neil Acourt, for example, admitted using the word 'nigger' but denied this attested to his racism; 'Black people call each other niggers, so why does it matter if white people say that?': He declared that the language he had used in the video was the result of the stress and harassment he had suffered after being accused of the murder. He had been stupid to react as he did. He also drew a distinction between words and actions. He was just going through the motions: 'It is not as if I'm going to do it, is it? I've been through a lot and when you have been through a lot you say things you don't mean.' In addition, 'when you watch the video you can see laughing and joking going on . . . it's a joke . . . everybody makes jokes about everyone else . . . when you're young at that stage and you are angry and you are laughing and joking, you say things, you don't mean them'. The other suspects put their performance down to immaturity and being very angry about being accused of a murder they did not commit.

Intense news coverage was given to what was defined as an outrageous perform-ance of white working class defiance and arrogance. The *Daily Mail* (30 June 1998) reported on how the suspects, in their sharp suits, crisply ironed shirts, greased hair, and sunglasses, had 'strutted into the emotion-charged inquiry' past a chanting mob to resist all attempts to implicate themselves in the murder of Stephen Lawrence. Gary Dobson, 'a crew cut young white man gazed back at the learned QC with impu-dence in his eyes. He had nothing to fear unless he lied in court, and most of the time he wasn't able to lie because he "couldn't remember". . . . His use of the word "cannot" instead of can't was fascinating. It was the one piece of standard English in a sea of cockney. Who could have taught him that one wondered?'

The newspaper also provided details of the suspects' family members who had the audacity to show up to support their murderous offspring. Again its description reinforced a powerful image of 'white trash' culture. 'Teresa "Tracy" Norris . . . wore a blue blazer and check shirt. A blue velvet band held back her bottle-blonde hair . . . Luke Knight's mother was also there, another bottle blonde in brown leggings, suede jacket and gold bangle earrings.' The *Daily Mail* also made much of the 'flash lifestyle' of Clifford Norris, the well-known south London criminal who was supposed to have protected the suspects. On the chaotic scenes that erupted as the suspects made their final departure from the inquiry, the *Daily Mail* commented:

> Their faces were contorted with hatred as they lashed out at anybody within reach. These were the five men named by the *Daily Mail* as the murderers of Stephen Lawrence as they came face to face with a riot yesterday. Greeted by a baying mob and a hail of bottles, bricks, stones and punches outside the public inquiry into the black teenager's death, the sullen contempt they had shown earlier vanished and was replaced by anger. Undaunted by two days of questions and accusations before a hostile audience, they shouted racist abuse at the crowd and revelled in the conflict as they made their getaway. They even fought with the policemen there to ensure their safety.

[. . .]

Conclusion

The main purpose of this chapter was to re-emphasize the need to conduct case study research on the role played by the news media in racializing public debate. The vanguard role played by the *Daily Mail*, the self-declared guardian of Middle England, heightened the public profile of the racist murder of Stephen Lawrence and armed the Lawrence family with the moral authority and political clout to persuade the incoming New Labour government that it was politically safe to establish a judicial inquiry. The newspaper's decision to embrace the Lawrence family can be seen as part of a highly complex and volatile reworking of the coverage of race relations in the UK news media. 'Black Britons' are no longer homogeneously the 'alien other' or quintessentially 'different' because of their 'non-whiteness'. Rather the *Daily Mail*, in accepting the integratedness of Doreen and Neville Lawrence, is involved in redefining the conventional ethnoracial imaginary of Middle England. In memorializing Stephen Lawrence the newspaper broke out of its knee jerk framing of young black men as 'muggers' and 'yardies'. This particular young black man moved from being just another violent crime statistic to being one of the most powerful images of end-of-the-century Middle England. Hence, the newspaper was making its own conservative readjustment to the multiculturalism and cosmopolitanism that was transforming post-colonial British society.

References

Ahmed, K. (1999) 'Lawrence Inquiry: How Murder Became a Media Event'. *Guardian*, 25 February.

Alibhai-Brown, Y. (2000) *Who do We Think We Are? Imagining the New Britain*. London: Penguin.

Cathcart, B. (1999) *The Case of Stephen Lawrence*. London: Viking Press.

Cottle, S. (ed.) (2000) *Ethnic Minorities and the Media: Changing Cultural Boundaries*. Buckingham: Open University Press.

Dates, J. L. and Barlow, W. (1990) *Split Image: African Americans in the Mass Media*. Washington, DC: Howard University Press.

Entman, R. M. and Rojecki, A. (2001) *The Black Image in the White Mind: Media and Race in America*. Chicago: University of Chicago Press.

Gabriel, J. (1998) *Whitewash: Racialised Politics and the Media*. London: Routledge.

Gray, H. (1995) *Watching Race: Television and the Struggle for 'Blackness'*. Minneapolis: University of Minnesota Press.

Hall, S. (1982) 'The Whites of their Eyes: Racist Ideologies and the Media', in G. Bridges and R. Brunt (eds), *Silver Linings: Some Strategies for the Eighties*. London: Lawrence and Wishart.

Hunt, D. M. (1999) *OJ Simpson Facts and Fictions: News Rituals in the Construction of Reality*. Cambridge: Cambridge University Press.

Jacobs, R. N. (2000) *Race, Media and the Crisis of Civil Society*. Cambridge: Cambridge University Press.

Law, I. (2002) *Race in the News*. Basingstoke: Palgrave Macmillan.

Kellner, D. (1995) 'Cultural studies, multiculturalism and media culture', in G. Dines and J. M. Hamez (eds.), *Gender, Race and Class in Media*. Thousand Oaks, CA: Sage

Martindale, C. (1986) *The White Press and Black America*. New York: Greenwood Press.

Neal, S. (1999) 'Populist Configurations of "Race" and "Gender": The Case of Hugh Grant, Liz Hurley and Divine Brown', in A. Brah et al. (eds), *Thinking Identities: Ethnicity, Racism and Culture*. Basingstoke: Macmillan.

Torres, S. (ed.) (1998) *Living Color: Race and Television in the United States*. Durham, NC: Duke University Press.

van Loon, J. (1999) 'Whiter Shades of Pale: Media Hybridies of Rodney King', in A. Brah, M. Hickman, and M. Mac an Ghaill (eds), *Thinking Identities: Ethnicity, Racism and Culture*. Basingstoke: Macmillan.

Wilson, C. C. and Gutierrez, F. (1995) *Race, Multiculturalism and the Media*. Thousand Oaks, CA: Sage.

Critical connections

McLaughlin makes some bold assertions about the impact of the Stephen Lawrence case coverage, and questions might be raised over the suggestion that the reporting of a single case in one newspaper has such a profound impact on how the news media report race in Britain. Whereas McLaughlin and Benedict (Reading 21) are more concerned to conduct in depth analyses of single cases, the research focus, for example, of Reiner *et al.*'s (2000, Reading 25) work, is to identify broader changes in reporting trends and patterns over time. This is one of the tensions inherent in the case study vs. longitudinal approaches to news media research – there is an inevitable trade-off between the depth of analysis that can be achieved in longitudinal studies and the extent to which the findings from case study approaches can be generalised. Reinforcing the argument for building research teams dedicated to the ongoing exploration of phenomena at the intersections of crime and media – in this case murder news – the cumulative knowledge acquired through the systematic development of qualitative case study analyses could answer many questions. The Glasgow Media Group, led by Gregg Philo at Glasgow University (and at one point providing a research home for Jenny Kitzinger – Reading 13), exemplified the development of this critical research mass and produced study after study and book after book espousing their own particular form of critical media analysis (see Eldridge, 1995, Philo, 1995). Such institutional organisation and commitment has yet to be paralleled in media criminology, perhaps partly due to the current orthodoxy in pseudo-scientific, quantitative crime-media research discussed in Section Two of this Reader.

Discussion questions

● Describe and discuss the processes of 'racialisation' and 'deracialisation' identified by McLaughlin in the *Daily Mail's* coverage of the murder of Stephen Lawrence?

● How might we define the contemporary 'ideal victim' in a multi-mediated, multicultural society (see also Readings 16)?

● Can the British or American news media be meaningfully accused of 'institutional racism'?

References

Dyer, R. (1997) *White,* London: Routledge.
Eldridge, J. (ed.) (1995) News Content, Language and Visuals: Glasgow University Media Reader (Communication and Society), London: Routledge.
Philo, G. (ed.) (1995) Industry, Economy, War and Politics: Glasgow University Media Reader: 2 (Communication and Society), London: Routledge.

Helen Benedict

'SHE SHOULD BE PUNISHED': THE 1983–1984 NEW BEDFORD 'BIG DAN'S' GANG RAPE (1992)

Introduction and context

HELEN BENEDICT'S IN-DEPTH analysis of the reporting of five high profile sex crime cases in the US views news production through a radical feminist lens. The excerpt included here is taken from Benedict's analysis of media coverage of the 'Big Dan's' Gang Rape case in Massachusetts 1983–84. The canon of feminist media criminology is extensive, and varies enormously in scope and depth (Cameron and Fraser, 1987; Soothill and Walby, 1991; Kitzinger and Skidmore, 1995; Meyers 1997; Chancer, 2003). *Virgin or Vamp* is included here because of the comprehensive nature of the approach and the depth of the subsequent analysis. Benedict was herself a working journalist and rape counsellor before turning to academia, and so brings to the study a well-developed understanding both of the news production process and the impact of rape. This professional insight is combined with a rigorous content analysis of the case coverage, interviews with many of the journalists and editors who produced the actual news reports, and an academic feminist reading of power, gender, race and class. One of *Virgin or Vamp*'s greatest strengths, then, is the extent to which Benedict gets *inside* the news production process to explore the structural, cultural, professional and ideological arrangements that shaped the press construction of a vicious gang rape. The particular case is significant, in Benedict's view, because it exemplifies gender stereotyping and class prejudice both by press and public, it demonstrates the racial tensions and moral sensitivities within a racially mixed immigrant community, and it raises questions of fairness in the reporting of an offence, trial and verdict in which two opposing viewpoints were vociferously expressed.

One Sunday night in March 1983, in the small city of New Bedford, Massachusetts, a young woman ran, screaming, out of Big Dan's Tavern. Wearing only a sock and a jacket, she flagged down a passing pickup truck for help. Sobbing and shaking, she told the driver that she had been gang-raped.

The story was quickly labeled the "Big Dan's pool table rape" by the local press and became a national fixation within days. The case was disturbing not only because the woman had been attacked by at least six men in a public place, but because she had told police that a roomful of men had cheered during the rape instead of helping her. [. . .]

The case was taken up by feminists and a huge candlelight march was held in New Bedford protesting violence against women a week after the rape, Gloria Steinem sent a letter to be read to the crowd, local feminists spoke, and grandmothers, men, and children turned out to lend their support. The press covered the march at length and the country was reminded that [. . .] this was the 1980s and women were enlightened and angry about rape. Meanwhile, another vocal group was waiting in the wings with a very different point of view: the local Portuguese.

New Bedford is known as a home for first and second generation immigrants from Portugal. Their presence is so prominent (about 60 percent of the population) that the telephone book is thick with Portuguese names, and many of the local stores display signs in Portuguese only. It is not surprising, then, that most of the people involved in the case were Portuguese themselves: the six accused men were all first generation immigrants, the victim was of Portuguese descent, the district attorney, the police chief, and half the jury were Portuguese-Americans, and the leader of the local feminist protest had a Portuguese surname. Nevertheless, the New Bedford Portuguese saw the coverage of the case as a slight to their community and an instance of bigotry. Before long "Big Dan's" was as much about ethnic prejudice as it was about rape, a conflict that resulted in pitting the Portuguese and their traditionalist views against the victim and antirape activists.

The case also brought up another issue that is important to this book: the printing of a rape victim's name. The use of the New Bedford victim's name became a huge source of contention in the press. Editorials and letters debated it, every argument was considered, and newspapers chose different solutions.

The New Bedford rape, therefore, is fascinating for several reasons. It evolved into a blatant example of the way women are regarded once they become rape victims; it revealed the inherent class prejudices of the press and the public; it exposed the raw nerves of downtrodden immigrants in America; and it put the press to an unusual test – a test of how to be fair in the light of violent feelings, extreme and opposing points of view, and vociferous criticism.

The case

The victim of the Big Dan's rape had been born and brought up in the North End of New Bedford. Abandoned by her mother in infancy, she was raised by her great-grandmother in a Portuguese-speaking household until she was five, when she moved to her grandparents' big house in New Bedford. Although she saw her mother occasionally, she never knew her father. The family lived primarily on welfare.

The girl spent her whole life in New Bedford. She attended local schools until she dropped out of high school because she was pregnant with a son, and then moved into an apartment with her boyfriend and had two more children. Employed intermittently, she continued to depend on welfare. She and her boyfriend fought constantly and ended up having what a neighbor called a "platonic relationship"; however, they kept on living together.

On March 6, 1983, the woman, by now twenty-one, celebrated her older daughter's third birthday with a small party. That evening, after putting her children to bed, she left her boyfriend to watch over them and went out to buy cigarettes. She walked to Big Dan's Tavern, a bar two blocks from her home, and once inside ordered a drink and chatted with the waitress, whom she knew. She stayed for a while, drinking and talking to people in the bar.

Some time later, as she told it, she was pushed to the floor by several men, her jeans were forcibly pulled off, and she was carried, struggling, crying and shouting for help, to the pool table at the back of the small bar. There she was raped, forced into oral sex, hit, held down, and molested by at least four men while others watched and perhaps cheered. No one tried to stop the assault and no one called the police.

After so many assaults she lost count, the woman managed to break free and run out of the door. Screaming and only half dressed, she ran into the street waving for help. A pick-up truck stopped and the men inside covered her and took her to the police station, where she explained what had happened. The police took her back to the bar, with her consent, where she identified some of her assailants, who were still hanging around drinking and, some said, boasting of the rape.

Four men were arrested on charges of aggravated rape – gang rape – and two others were arrested on charges of joint enterprise, which means encouraging an illegal act and doing nothing to stop it. The men were brought to trial in the nearby town of Fall River, Massachusetts.

The reporting

The Big Dan's case received meticulous attention from the local press for more than a year, from the beginning of March 1983, when the rape occurred, to April 1984, after the two tandem trials of the accused were over. The local papers I have examined are the New Bedford *Standard-Times*, which was the first paper to find the story; the *Portuguese Times*, a small, Portuguese-language weekly also located in New Bedford; the *Providence Journal*, the metropolitan newspaper of Rhode Island; the *Boston Herald*, a tabloid; and the *Boston Globe*. The reporters who covered the story for these papers were mostly men – the ratio was twenty-five men to ten women – but several women covered the trials virtually by themselves.

On the out-of-state newspapers, I looked at the *L.A. Times* and *The New York Times*, whose stories on the case were all by men; at *The Washington Post*, which gave the case a lot of attention and assigned only women to the story; and at *Newsweek*, which contributed its usual one page to the case, with no byline. On the whole, the national news relied on wire stories, also mainly written by men, which were often rewrites of the local reporters' stories.

Television was a prominent presence. A cable station covered the trial live, local television was all over the courtroom, and the national networks gave the case a great deal of attention before and during the trial. The all-pervasive presence of television contributed to making the media part of the story itself, which elicited its own set of reactions among the public. [. . .]

The press and the victim

During the early stages of reporting this case, before much was known about the victim or the circumstances of the crime, the press treated her with care. Sensitized to rape by the women's movement, and appalled by the reports of the cheering crowd in the bar, the papers refused to name her, even though her identity had been revealed on police records and in court. Several papers ran stories about rape trauma and the new rape shield laws, designed to protect a victim from having her sex life dragged through court in a trial. Columnists wrote many sympathetic pieces about rape victims and society's responsibility for the crime. In general, the first month's coverage revealed the relative enlightenment of the time, resisting the temptations of the rape narrative, treating rape as a societal rather than an individual problem, and attempting to recognize the victim's need for sympathy without blame.

One of the best of these background stories was "Understanding gang rape patterns," by *Boston Globe* writer Gary McMillan. McMillan referred to research by leading people in the field of sexual assault, particularly Menachim Amir's oft-quoted 1971 study of rape and Nicholas Groth's valuable work on sex offenders, to explain to the reader just how common gang rape is and the forms it usually takes. [. . .]

He also explained the legal aspects of prosecuting gang rapes, and ended,

> [T]he violence and sheer numbers involved in gang rapes spreads a sharp and strong miasma of fear among all women. As one 14-year-old girl in Easton said last week after watching a television program about gang rape, "Mommy, this means I have to be afraid all my life."
>
> (*Globe*, 4/11/83, p. 1.)

[. . .] The initial sympathy for the rape victim was allowed not only because of the enlightenment about rape at the time but also, ironically, because of the rape narrative. None of the rape myths had been pulled out to use against the victim yet, but the defendants, on the other hand, fit all the worst stereotypes about rapists. They were not married to the victim, [. . .] they were not rich, upper class, particularly handsome, or "nice" – the men were foreign, lower class, and sleazy (even Manuel Ferreira said so[1]) and as such, they were easy to perceive of and depict as criminals. Because the defendants fit the weird stranger myth, therefore, the victim was at first allowed her innocence, as a rather odd headline in the *Standard-Times* reflected: "After tragedy, 'she'll never be innocent again.' " [. . .]

---

[1] "Two of them should be in jail – they're terrible kids," Ferreira said to me in an interview.

The trials: opening day

The tandem trials opened on February 23, 1984 and lasted a little over a month. Nowhere was the impact of using the victim's name more apparent than in the opening story by Neil Downing of the *Providence Journal*.

> FALL RIVER, Mass. – A twenty-one-year-old mother of two was grabbed from behind as she left Big Dan's bar in New Bedford last March 6, and was sexually assaulted on a pool table while other patrons cheered her attackers, ignoring her cries for help . . .
>
> Veary and Asst. Dist. Atty. Robert J. Kane said that the woman, Maria A. Bianco, squirmed free and, naked from the waist down, ran into the street.
>
> (2/24/84 P-1.)[1]

After weeks of reading about the victim as an anonymous figure, the shock of seeing her name linked to a description of such brutality was strong enough, but that shock was exacerbated by Downing's choice of words. By using the phrase *squirmed free* rather than *struggled, escaped*, or *broke free*, he suggested an action that sounded not so desperate as intimate, a bit slimy, and decidedly sexual. [. . .] Also, by using the phrase *naked from the waist down*, Downing suggested something stripteaselike rather than terrifying.

The phrase *naked from the waist down* was first used by Levin of the *Standard-Times*. It was picked up by all the reporters on his newspaper during the first month after the crime, and again a year later during the trial, as well as by the *Portuguese Times* and the AP; however, there were other, less plurient ways of describing the scene. [. . .] Jonathan Kaufman of the *Boston Globe* managed to describe the same event without using the words *squirmed* or *naked from the waist down*:

> At one point, Veary said, the woman broke free and ran into the street wearing only a sock and a sweater. She stood in the middle of the street, a prosecution witness testified, and waved down a passing pick-up truck carrying three men.
>
> (2/24/84, p. 15.)

[. . .] Other reporters repeatedly described the victim in terms that would never be used for a man: *brunette, bubbly, hysterical*, and *unwed mother of two*. (Fathers are never described as "unwed," with all it implies about illegitimate children. Rather, they are described as "single fathers" if their parenthood is mentioned at all, indicating a sort of heroism.)

Karen Ellsworth, the other *Journal* reporter covering the case, spoke about why reporters sometimes choose the wrong words. "The nature of the newspaper business is that you don't have a lot of time to think about your choice of words," she said. "You'll use a word that, when you're writing the story, appears not to have any kind of connotation. It's only later that you stop and think about it." Perhaps reporters

---

[1] Not her real name. I have changed the victim's name, even though it is widely available now in records and news reports, because I have no wish to perpetuate the pain of the rape and its memory on her family – au.

could avoid this pitfall if they were less willing to appropriate the words of attorneys, who always have an ulterior design (the word "squirmed" originated in the mouth of Attorney Kane), were more aware of the implications of the words typically used to describe rape and sexual assault, and were more resistant to clichés in general. [. . .]

The victim exposed

As has been well documented, testifying in court is the most traumatic experience for a rape victim other than the rape itself. This is so not only because she has to face her assailants and endure cross-examination, which often makes her relive the assault and which questions her reputation, but because she becomes subject to scrutiny by the press.

The victim in Big Dan's had to testify twice, at the beginning of each of the tandem trials, and she had to do so standing up (there was no seat in the witness box) for a total of fifteen hours over three gruelling days in a row. While testifying, she faced all six defendants, a courtroom packed with people, constantly whirring television cameras, and a barrage of news reporters eager for a hot story.

To make things harder for her, this was the kind of rape trial in which the defense lawyers' only strategy was to discredit her. [. . .] Because there were so many witnesses to the fact that the men had been in the bar, and because the men had no alibis, the defendants' lawyers could not rely on misidentification as a defense. They therefore had only one strategy left – to prove that the woman had sex with the men willingly. [. . .]

At the beginning of the trials, when the victim took the stand, the coverage sounded sympathetic, if sensational, because she was telling her side of the story. Her account was powerful and had a profound effect on the jury and the public:

> "I could hear yelling, laughing, down near the end of the bar," she said,
> ". . . My head was hanging off the edge of the pool table . . . I was screaming,
> pleading, begging . . . One man held my head and pulled my hair. The more
> I screamed, the harder he pulled . . ."
> (*Washington Post*, 2/25/84, p. A3.)

Even though her words were strong, however, and invited sympathy, the press quickly found something to criticize: her calmness on the witness stand. Her lawyers were later quoted praising the victim for her self-control, but several of the trial reporters described her stance as "dispassionate" and "almost clinical," making her sound cold and tough, untroubled by what had happened. (The defense attorneys recognized this and later tried to turn it against her in their cross-examinations.) The press's reaction to her manner illustrated a paradox that rape experts have long pointed out: If a victim is calm in court, she is seen as not having suffered enough, which indicates she is not a genuine victim; if she is sobbing and frightened, she is seen as hysterical, unstable, and thus unreliable. By falling for this Catch 22, the press played into the hands of the defense lawyers.

Another subtle point that came up in the first testimony stories was that the victim was described, over and over again, as having left her children in bed while she went out to the bar. The fact that her boyfriend was at home with them was only mentioned in one story by one paper. This omission, unintentional as it probably was, gave the inaccurate impression that the victim was prepared to leave her small children unattended.

Of all the aspects of the early – and continuing – trial coverage, however, the one that most humiliated the victim was the explicit testimony, especially when it was coupled with her name.

The testimony in the courtroom had to be explicit because of the nature of the crime. Some of the men had been charged with aggravated rape, which meant under Massachusetts law that the prosecution had to prove actual sexual penetration; the other men had been charged with joint enterprise, which meant determining in detail what they had physically done. The court therefore had to hear about oral sodomy, about Vieira tickling Silva's rectum with a straw as Silva was raping the victim, about the sperm found in her vagina and on a defendant's underwear, and about other such graphic evidence.

The *Standard-Times* chose to cover all this with discretion. "We had a conversation to remind everybody about our policy with regard to profanity," recalled Ragsdale, the paper's editor. "The issue had to be extremely important for that profanity or vulgarism to find its way into the story." The *Providence Journal*, however, took the opposite stand: [. . .]

> Silva got on top of her. Neither had pants on. Pacheco said one of the pool players had his hand on her head, unzipped his pants, and tried to engage her in oral sex . . . Pacheco said Vieira then took a straw from the bar, walked over to the pool table and inserted it in Silva's rear end.
>
> (3/8/84, p. 8.)

> Raposo "denied having any involvement with the girl at first . . . then said he remembered holding the girl's legs and taking his penis out," Gormely said.
>
> (3/13/84, p. A4.)

Kukielski spoke about his paper's decision to be so graphic. "We were constantly torn between providing a full and uncensored report of a proceeding that people were watching in their living rooms [on cable television every day], and adhering to our normal standards about taste and references to sexual contact. It was a daily dilemma. . . . We weren't happy about writing these stories. We weren't happy about ruining people's breakfasts.

"Karen [Ellsworth] was a key player in the decision. She was fresh out of law school and she was a very strong advocate for using more anatomical detail than we were normally comfortable with. She was saying it was absolutely critical to judging the guilt or innocence of these people to have this information here."

Downing agreed with Ellsworth's reasoning. The problem with sanitizing rape reports, he said, is that you prevent the reader from understanding just what kind of crime rape is.

In many ways, Ellsworth and Downing's argument was valid. Graphic descriptions of sex crimes do force readers to realize their brutality, while sanitizing them does perpetuate the myth that rape is sex and does not hurt. However, the fact that the *Journal* used more explicit descriptions than any other paper, was one of the only papers to name the victim, and named her *against her will* changed the stakes. The reader was suddenly seeing Maria Bianco, by name, linked with images of her being raped and orally sodomized, screaming, crying, and "squirming." There can be no question that the result invaded her privacy, humiliated, and stigmatized her. [. . .]

The trial coverage

How well the defendants' claims succeeded in discrediting the victim in the eyes of the public was largely controlled by how each paper played them. To get an idea of the overall gist of the trial coverage, I took a look at the headlines during the first sixteen days of the trial.

The *Boston Herald*'s headlines added up to six slanted against the victim (for example, "HALF-NAKED WOMAN SMOKED POT: OFFICER TOLD"; "ALLEGED RAPE VICTIM 'AGREED TO MAKE LOVE' — LAWYER"; "SHE WAS 'POISONED WITH ALCOHOL')" and two in her favor ("THREAT TO KILL WITNESS TOLD AT RAPE TRIAL"; "PAIR CONFESSED RAPE ROLE: OFFICER") The two other headlines were mixed: "BARMAN: 'I SAW THE WHOLE THING' Witness recalls brutal rape of 'flirting' woman" (3/1/84, p. 4); "BARMAN UNSHAKEN: 'she was raped'. But small details don't match woman's version" (3/2/84, p. 2).

Among the other papers, the counts were not much more balanced. The *Providence Journal*'s headlines were more discreet than were the *Herald*'s and too unremarkable to be worth reproducing here, but I counted nine headlines in favor of the victim and three in favor of the defense — the only paper to have more headlines for her case than against it. The rest of the *Journal*'s headlines were neutral. The *Standard-Times* was even-handed, running six anti- and six provictim headlines. The *Boston Globe* was the most noncommittal in its wording, but it nevertheless ran only two headlines in the victim's favor and four against her. The *Washington Post*'s headlines were the most sensational after the *Herald*'s, and included four sympathetic to the victim and six against her. *The New York Times* ran two heads that made the victim look bad, and one that was favorable. The *Portuguese Times* and the *L.A. Times* ran only two headlines each, both slanted against the victim's case. In summary, thirty-one of the headlines contained statements detrimental to the victim and twenty-six reflected evidence supporting her story. This antivictim slant was further bolstered by the proliferation of stories about the hostility of the courtroom crowd. [. . .]

> BIG DAN'S COURTROOM CROWD PICKS HEROES
>
> "I'm for the guys more than the girl," said 19-year-old Ernie Santos of Fall River, a floor-sander. "I mean, what was she doing there in the first place? I think she was looking.". . .
>
> "I'm of Portuguese origin," said Louise Cariero, 20, of Fall River, "and a lot of our people feel the girl shouldn't have been in Big Dan's in the first place."
>
> (*Providence Journal*, 3/3/84, p. 5.)

This last story also quoted two people sympathizing with the victim, but the predominance of antivictim statements [. . .] revealed how little the people in that courtroom understood that rape is not sex, that women would no more "look for it" than they would look to be murdered, and that the behavior of a woman never excuses a rapist. As a *Washington Post* reporter put it: "At times during the Big Dan's rape case this week it was not clear who was on trial — the woman who claimed she was gang-raped in a New Bedford bar, or the six men charged with the crime."

(Ruth Marcus, 3/4/84, p. A2.)

The verdicts and the Portuguese protest

> TWO BIG DAN defendants were convicted yesterday of raping a 22-year-old mother of two on a barroom pooltable while customers cheered them on.
>
> (*Herald*, 3/18/84, p. 1.)

The jury in Vieira and Silva's trial had decided to believe the victim despite the slurs against her and despite the best efforts of a team of defense attorneys to discredit her. Furthermore, the jury opted for the most serious charge — aggravated rape.

A triumph, but a thin one, for the crowd outside the courtroom instantly exploded with fury — against the verdict, the jury, the district attorney, and, most of all, against the victim herself. The result was that the bulk of the stories, even in the light of the verdict, reflected the crowd's antagonism: "A man who identified himself as a friend of Vieira's hollered to reporters, 'The .... — she's the one that should go to jail." (*Herald*, 3/18/84, p. 6.) "'Why don't they bring that girl out in handcuffs!' someone shouted. 'Get her too!'" (*Standard-Times*, 3/18/84, p. 2.)

The protesters' objections boiled down to the issue that had permeated the case from the beginning: the victim versus the Portuguese.

Four days after Vieira and Silva were convicted, the verdicts in the trial of the remaining four were decided. The *Herald* announced the news with misplaced sympathy: "TEARS OF TWO RAPISTS" (3/23/84, p. 1). The verdict was split. Two of the men, Cordeiro and Raposo, were found guilty of aggravated rape. The other two, Jose and Virgilio Medeiros, the only defendants charged with joint enterprise, were acquitted. As reflected by the headline, the news of the verdicts was accompanied by a flood of sympathy for the defendants. Along with photographs of the two convicted men crying were stories in all the papers about the "shock and outrage" of the Portuguese community — not at what had been finally proved to have happened to the victim, who was, after all, a member of that community herself, but at what had been done to the defendants.

> A hero's welcome greeted Jose and Virgilio Medeiros as the two vindicated Big Dan's defendants bounded out of a Fall River courthouse as free men . . .
>
> Outside, cheers and applause erupted from the crowd as the innocent men ran to a waiting car with scores of reporters and cameramen behind them.
>
> (*Herald*, 3/23/84, p. 5.)

Virgilio Medeiros, who in his pretrial interview had described the victim crying and pleading with the men to leave her alone, now stood on the steps of the courthouse and said, "She led them on, there was no rape in that bar. No. Never."

And: "Everybody should be considered innocent because what happened wasn't a rape. The woman was the one who started everything."

On the night of the verdict, a gigantic demonstration erupted in support of the defendants: "8,000 march against 'bias' they say Big Dan's fueled." (*Providence Journal*, 3/24/84, p. A20.)

People marched carrying signs: "Where is Justice?" "Was She Willing?" "Justice Crucified. March 17, 1984." Others were quoted saying the jury had been biased by publicity and ethnic prejudice, that the judicial system had failed, and that it had all been the victim's fault:

> "If she had been home with her children this would not have happended."
> *(Providence Journal*, 3/23/84, p. A22.)
> "She is the one who deserves the prison sentence."
> *(Globe*, 3/24/84, p. 18.)
> "She should get punished too. If they raped her, she was the aggravator . . . I'm sorry to say it, but I think it was her." . . . "I am Portuguese and proud of it . . . I'm also a woman, but you don't see me getting raped." "They did nothing to her. Her rights are to be home with her two kids and to be a good mother. A Portuguese woman should be with her kids and that's it."
> *(Standard-Times*, 3/24/84, p. 3.).

[. . .]

Discussion

Even though the Big Dan's verdicts were hailed by the press as a triumph for feminists and proof that a woman "doesn't have to be a saint to get raped," as the *Boston Herald* put it, Maria Bianco should go down in history as one of the worst-treated rape victims of the decade. She was vilified by her community, which threatened her life and drove her out of town; and even though the press treated her well before the trials, she was so neglected during and after them that defense attorney smears were allowed to dominate newspaper pages without balance, and her enemies were able to grab headlines without a murmur in her defense.

The reasons Bianco attracted so much hostility are not hard to ascertain. [. . .] She knew the assailants (it was never clear whether she knew any of them before the rape, but she spent enough time with them in the bar to count in the public eye as knowing them – she certainly was not jumped by complete strangers); no weapon was used [. . .]; she was of the same race, class, and ethnic group as the assailants; she was young; she was attractive, and, above all, she deviated from the norm of a "good woman" by being alone in a bar full of men, drinking, when the attack occurred.

Any section of the public is liable to see these ingredients as discrediting a rape victim, as the defense lawyers knew when they relied upon them to undermine her story in court, but the Portuguese community took the victim-blaming to an extreme. The press at the time tried to analyze their hostility by quoting anthropologists and locals describing Portuguese culture as extremely traditionalist and machismo, but, as Ferreira said, those analyses only further infuriated the community, making it feel maligned and patronized. Sociologist Lynn Chancer, who studied the antivictim reaction of the local Portuguese women, supported that complaint by pointing out that a traditionalist view of women as belonging in their homes and to their men exists in many cultures, and criticizing the media for making it sound as if the attitude was exclusively Portuguese. Ferreira made the same point: "In American culture, too, if you see a woman go into a bar in a combat zone, what are you going to think about her?" Chancer also blamed the press for inflaming the ethnic issue by failing to mention that the victim, like her assailants, was of Portuguese descent.[. . .]

The flaw in the reporting of this case was not so much in ignoring the fact that the victim was Portuguese as in ignoring the chance to portray her as a human being rather than a symbol: victim to the feminists, vamp to the locals. [. . .] Once the defense attorneys and the suspects pulled out the rape myths to discredit the victim, the press fell in line and perpetuated those myths in the pages of its newspapers, enhancing them by the use of her name coupled with the graphic description of her sexual assault. [. . .]

Without Portuguese reporters or speakers, the local American papers were unable to portray the community in a nonstereotypical way, unable to find people who had not blindly turned against the victim, and unable to win the trust of the victim's family and friends in order to represent her side. The result was that the case polarized into the liberal American media versus the New Bedford Portuguese, which filled the local people with such a sense of injustice that they turned on the victim as a scapegoat. This was not entirely the press's fault, but it was certainly exacerbated by its failures.

In many ways, the press itself became as much a part of the Big Dan's story as did the victim and the defendants. By using the victim's name, by describing the trial with hitherto never-used explicitness, by profiling the defendants' community, and by running column after column expressing feminist views of rape and self-criticism, the press drew so much attention to itself that the community reacted as much to it as to the crime. As a result, the media came in for a lot of blame in postcase analyses, some of it undeserved, much of it well earned. [. . .]

Maria Bianco's treatment by her community was so blatantly unjust that it elicited widespread reaction after the case. Women's groups and feminists demonstrated and wrote about it for months following the trial. A sociologist conducted a study of why Bianco was so hated by her neighbors. Essayists and editorial writers analyzed the Portuguese hostility in magazines and newspapers. The bias against her instigated a re-examination of rules governing the media's access to trials. The use of her name inspired a governmental investigation into rape coverage. And, finally, the movie loosely based on the case, *The Accused*, portrayed the victim with much of the sympathy that had been so lacking in the press at the time of the case.

As a result, the Big Dan's case will not be forgotten. It revealed the raw underside of American society – the conflict between men and women, the suspicion of everyone toward victims, and the mutual hatred between settled Americans and those seen as foreign, lower-class, non-white, or "other" – and it revealed the way those elements can seduce and bias the press. [. . .]

References

"She remains a mystery," by Gayle Fee. *Boston Herald*, 2/29/84, p. 12. Fee's piece was the only profile of the victim to apper in the daily newspapers until her death.

"Requiem for a Rape Victim," by Carol Agus. *Newsday*, 12/30/86.

The only other local paper to devote a significant amount of space to the story was the *Fall River Herald*, but I did not analyse it bacause of difficulties locating clips and bacause it is a very small paper, of less significance to New Bedford residents than the *Standard-Times* or the *Portuguese Times*—au.

"To be made newsworthy, a provocative theme about personal moral competence will be typically bulit into the story." Jack Katz, "What Makes Crime 'News'?" In *Media, Culture & Society*, Vol. 9, 1987, pp. 47–75.

"Two Massachusetts rape laws make real difference," by Alan D. Sisitsky, *Boston Herald*, 3/24/83, p. 20. The *Standard-Times* also ran several back ground pieces on rape and the women's movement throughout the month, as did the *Boston Herald*.

See History chapter on the 1970s coverage of rape. Also, Gordon and Riger, *The Female Fear*, op cit.

Menachim Amir, *Patterns in Forcible Rape*, op cit.

A. Nicholas Groth, *Men Who Rape: The Psychology of the Offenter*, op cit.

Benedict, *Recovery*, op.cit., Chapter 4.

She spoke dispassionately, clinically, as if she were talking about someone else's ordeal." *Providence Journal*, 2/25/84, p. 1.

Hearld, 3/6/84, p.7; 3/14/84, p. 12; 3/16/84, p. 16; 3/9/84, p.10; 3/12/84, p. 9 respectively.

The quote was highlighted in bold print, as I've reproduced here—au.

Providence Journal, 3/23/84, p. 1.

Providence Journal, 3/29/84, p. 4.

Each paper gave a different estimate of the crowd. The numbers varied from 7,000 to 15,000.

Editorial in the *Boston Herald*, 3/23/84, p. 36:

> What the verdicts in the Big Dan's barroom rape cases . . . have said loudly and clearly is that a woman doesn't have to be a saint to be raped. And she doesn't have to be chaste as the day is long to have the right to say, "no."

The very fact that the *Herald* had to say this reveals that newspapers and the public grapple with the virgin–vamp dichotomy every time a rape case comes up.

"Women's Groups Protest Treatment of Big Dan's Victim." AP story in *Standard-Times*, 4/22/84, p. 6.

Lynn S. Chancer, "New Bedford, Massachusetts, March 6, 1983, March 22, 1984. The 'Before and After' of a Group Rape." *Gender & Society*, Vol. 1, No. 3, Sept. 1987, p. 252. Chancer, op cit., pp. 239–60.

Ellen Israel Rosen, "The New Bedford Rape Trial." *Dissent*, Vol. 92, 1985, pp. 207–12.

"Impact of Media Coverage on Rape Cases." U.S. Senate Judiciary Hearings J98 No. 112, Vol. 125.

The Accused, starring Jodie Foster, was far from an accurate portrayal of the actual Big Dan's case. The movie plot revolved around a legal question about joint enterprise that did not arise in the real cases, while ignoring the charges of aggravated rape.

Critical connections

Benedict's analysis is comprehensive in its consideration of key elements in the press treatment of the case: local vs. national coverage; representation of the victim, the trial coverage, the verdicts and the local response; the significance of class, race and gender in the reporting of the case; and the use of photographs. All receive a systematic analytical attention, resulting in the construction of a narrative case study that considers the story from beginning to end. Partly due to the emergence of online newspaper databases, detailed case study work is becoming increasingly rare as content analysis becomes more superficial and haphazard (Reading 9). Benedict's multi-layered study presents one example, or model, of how good case study work can be done.

The 'Big Dan's' Gang Rape case formed the basis of Jonathan Kaplin's Hollywood film *The Accused,* for which Jodie Foster won Best Actress in a Leading Role at the 1989 Academy Awards. In the transition from the Portuguese quarter of New Bedford, Massachusetts, to the Big Screen, the largely Portuguese cast of characters in the original event was converted into an almost exclusively white one for the movie. This deracialisation of an all-ethnic-minority cast for mainstream cinema audiences connects with McLaughlin's analysis of the *Daily Mail*'s deracialisation of the Lawrence family following the racist murder of Stephen Lawrence in 1993 (Reading 20). In both cases, racial difference appears to have been erased in order to more closely reflect the ethnicity of the principal target audience. It thus raises interesting questions about the ways in which notions of race and ethnicity, gender and class, innocence and respectability, presentation and marketability, interact in complex ways and cut across processes of mediatisation, potentially impacting at every stage from the street to the news report to the book to the screen.

Discussion questions

- Identify and discuss the research methods Benedict uses to analyse media coverage of the Big Dan's rape case.
- How does Benedict understand the media's portrayal of the central victim as simultaneously 'innocent' and of questionable 'respectability'?
- The victim and offenders in the Big Dan's rape case were nearly all Portuguese, yet the cast in the film *The Accused* is almost entirely white-American. Why do you think this is, and can any insight be gained from McLaughlin's (Reading 20) discussion of 'racialisation' and 'deracialisation' in the media representation of crime and criminal justice?

References

Cameron, D. and Frazer, E. (1987) *The Lust to Kill: A Feminist Investigation of Sexual Murder,* Cambridge: Polity Press.
Chancer, L. (2003) *High Profile Crimes: When Legal Cases Become Social Causes,* Chicago: University of Chicago Press.

Kitzinger, J. and Skidmore, P. (1995) 'Child Sexual Abuse and the Media', Summary Report to ESRC. Award no. R000233675. Report available from Glasgow Media Group.

Meyers, M. (1997) *News Coverage of Violence Against Women: Engendering Blame*, Thousand Oaks, London: Sage.

Soothill, K. and Walby, S. (1991) *Sex Crime in the News*, London: Routledge.

SECTION FOUR

Crime, entertainment and creativity

Introduction

S ECTION THREE FOCUSED specifically on news reporting of crime and criminal justice. This section widens the perspective to look at a broader range of cultural forms at the crime-media nexus. Of course, as stated in the Introduction to this reader and illustrated throughout Section One the extent of media penetration into the everyday means that virtually all issues of crime and control are to some extent mediatised. Virtually all, therefore, could theoretically be brought within the purview of media criminology. The aim in this section is to further explore the connections between crime, criminalisation and control, on the one hand, and media, mediatisation and representation on the other. From the crime novel, through film and television drama, to reality programming and the practice of graffiti writing, the readings included here collectively explore how crime and criminal justice are represented across a diversity of media, and how particular media and cultural practices can themselves be criminalised.

Tzvetan Todorov (1966) presents the classic structuralist analysis of detective fiction, focusing on three types of novel within the wider 'genre' – the 'whodunit', the 'thriller', and the 'suspense novel'. Robert Reiner (1994) offers a qualitative analysis of changing TV representations of the British police, exploring the dialectical relationship between fictional portrayals and the contemporaneous social, political and cultural contexts within which 'real world' policing was taking place. Mariana Valverde's (2006) investigation of US Cop dramas compares and contrasts the narrative conventions informing more traditional shows like *Law and Order*, newer 'reality' programming formats like *COPS*, and the phenomenally popular forensic policing model, exemplified by *CSI: Crime, Scene, Investigation*. Robert Reiner, this time with

Jessica Allen and Sonia Livingstone (2001), offers a longitudinal analysis of changing press and film representations of crime and criminal justice in the post-World War II period, that situates shifting representations of perpetrators and victims of crime, and key criminal justice institutions, within the wider theoretical context of the 'risk' society. Barry Langford (2005) draws from Todorov's genre analysis, developing in particular the notions of sub-genre and verisimilitude, to 'read' dramatic representations of gangsters and organised crime – from the 'heyday' movies of the 1930s, through the Godfather in 1970s, to Tarantino's postmodern pastiches of the 1990s and beyond – as a particular type of commentary on the prevailing socio-economic order. In a similar vein, Brian Jarvis (2007) situates the recently intensified popular fascination with serial killer film and literature within the context of a mass consumer culture that has emerged out of neo-liberal capitalist development. And in the final reading in this section, Jeff Ferrell (1996) presents a sociological and cultural analysis of graffiti writing. For Ferrell like many of the contributors in this Reader, a full appreciation of cultural forms must consider the organisation, practice, meaning and wider context within which those forms exist. Graffiti writing, therefore, is considered up close using ethnographic methods and a theoretical appreciation attuned to the interaction and excitement, control and resistance, the background and foreground factors that give it both purpose and meaning.

Tzvetan Todorov

THE TYPOLOGY OF DETECTIVE FICTION (1966)

Introduction and context

TZVETAN TODOROV is a literary theorist, originally born in Bulgaria, who played a key role in the development of structuralism as a forceful current in literary studies in France during the 1960s. 'The Typology of Detective Fiction' (1966), reproduced here in full, encapsulates the structuralist approach to classifying and making sense of large quantities of literary data. Todorov begins his discussion of detective fiction by locating the analysis within the context of genre and sub-genre (see also Readings 11 and 26 on film genres). Just like different genres of film have particular 'rules' of narrative development, so too do different genres of popular literature, for example romance, science fiction and in this case 'detective fiction'. Furthermore, the broad genre of 'detective fiction' contains within it further 'types' – or sub-genres – of story, which develop in accordance with their own, particular rules. The sub-genres of literary detective fiction that form the basis of Todorov's analysis are the 'whodunit', typified by Agatha Christie, the 'thriller', typified by Dashiell Hammett and Raymond Chandler, and the 'suspense novel', typified by William Irish and Patrick Quentin. Todorov thus compares and contrasts the (sometimes overlapping) rules governing the narrative development of these sub-genres of detective fiction in order to establish a structuralist framework within which the crime novel might be read critically as a literary device with its own internal logics and conventions, as well as being read for pleasure and distraction.

Detective fiction cannot be subdivided into kinds.
It merely offers historically different forms.
— Boileau and Narcejac, *Le Roman palicier*, 1964

If I use this observation as the epigraph to an article dealing precisely with 'kinds' of 'detective fiction,' it is not to emphasize my disagreement with the authors in question, but because their attitude is very widespread; hence it is the first thing we must confront. Detective fiction has nothing to do with this question: for nearly two centuries, there has been a powerful reaction in literary studies against the very notion of genre. We write either about literature in general or about a single work, and it is a tacit convention that to classify several works in a genre is to devalue them. There is a good historical explanation for this attitude: literary reflection of the classical period, which concerned genres more than works, also manifested a penalizing tendency – a work was judged poor if it did not sufficiently obey the rules of its genre. Hence such criticism sought not only to describe genres but also to prescribe them; the grid of genre preceded literary creation instead of following it.

The reaction was radical: the romantics and their present-day descendants have refused not only to conform to the rules of the genres (which was indeed their privilege) but also to recognize the very existence of such a notion. Hence the theory of genres has remained singularly undeveloped until very recently. Yet now there is a tendency to seek an intermediary between the too-general notion of literature and those individual objects which are works. The delay doubtless comes from the fact that typology is implied by the description of these individual works; yet this task of description is still far from having received satisfactory solutions. So long as we cannot describe the structure of works, we must be content to compare certain measurable elements, such as meter. Despite the immediate interest in an investigation of genres (as Albert Thibaudet remarked, such an investigation concerns the problem of universals), we cannot undertake it without first elaborating structural description: only the criticism of the classical period could permit itself to deduce genres from abstract logical schemas.

An additional difficulty besets the study of genres, one which has to do with the specific character of every esthetic norm. The major work creates, in a sense, a new genre and at the same time transgresses the previously valid rules of the genre. The genre of *The Charterhouse of Parma*, that is, the norm to which this novel refers, is not the French novel of the early nineteenth century; it is the genre 'Stendhalian novel' which is created by precisely this work and a few others. One might say that every great book establishes the existence of two genres, the reality of two norms: that of the genre it transgresses, which dominated the preceding literature, and that of the genre it creates.

Yet there is a happy realm where this dialectical contradiction between the work and its genre does not exist: that of popular literature. As a rule, the literary masterpiece does not enter any genre save perhaps its own; but the masterpiece of popular literature is precisely the book which best fits its genre. Detective fiction has its norms; to 'develop' them is also to disappoint them: to 'improve upon' detective fiction is to write 'literature,' not detective fiction. The whodunit par excellence is not the one which transgresses the rules of the genre, but the one which conforms to them: *No Orchids for Miss Blandish*[1] is an incarnation of its genre, not a transcendence. If we had properly described the genres of popular literature, there would no longer be an occasion to speak of its masterpieces. They are one and the same thing; the best

---

[1] Thriller by James Hadley Chase, first published in 1939. It is the subject of a famous essay by George Orwell, 'Raffles and Miss Blandish' (*Collected Essays, Journalism and Letters*, Vol. 3.)

novel will be the one about which there is nothing to say. This is a generally unnoticed phenomenon, whose consequences affect every esthetic category. We are today in the presence of a discrepancy between two essential manifestations; no longer is there one single esthetic norm in our society, but two; the same measurements do not apply to 'high' art and 'popular' art.

The articulation of genres within detective fiction therefore promises to be relatively easy. But we must begin with the description of 'kinds,' which also means with their delimitation. We shall take as our point of departure the classic detective fiction which reached its peak between the two world wars and is often called the whodunit. Several attempts have already been made to specify the rules of this genre (we shall return below to S. S. Van Dine's twenty rules); but the best general characterization I know is the one Butor gives in his own novel *Passing Time* (*L'Emploi du temps*). George Burton, the author of many murder mysteries, explains to the narrator that 'all detective fiction is based on two murders of which the first, committed by the murderer, is merely the occasion for the second, in which he is the victim of the pure and unpunishable murderer, the detective,' and that 'the narrative . . . superimposes two temporal series: the days of the investigation which begin with the crime, and the days of the drama which lead up to it.'

At the base of the whodunit we find a duality, and it is this duality which will guide our description. This novel contains not one but two stories: the story of the crime and the story of the investigation. In their purest form, these two stories have no point in common. Here are the first lines of a 'pure' whodunit:

> a small green index-card on which is typed:
>   Odel, Margaret.
> 184 W. Seventy-first Street. Murder: Strangled about 11 P.M. Apartment robbed. Jewels stolen. Body found by Amy Gibson, maid. [S. S. Van Dine, *The 'Canary' Murder Case*]

The first story, that of the crime, ends before the second begins. But what happens in the second? Not much. The characters of this second story, the story of the investigation, do not act, they learn. Nothing can happen to them: a rule of the genre postulates the detective's immunity. We cannot imagine Hercule Poirot or Philo Vance[2] threatened by some danger, attacked, wounded, even killed. The hundred and fifty pages which separate the discovery of the crime from the revelation of the killer are devoted to a slow apprenticeship: we examine clue after clue, lead after lead. The whodunit thus tends toward a purely geometric architecture: Agatha Christie's *Murder on the Orient Express*, for example, offers twelve suspects; the book consists of twelve chapters, and again twelve interrogations, a prologue, and an epilogue (that is, the discovery of the crime and the discovery of the killer).

This second story, the story of the investigation, thereby enjoys a particular status. It is no accident that it is often told by a friend of the detective, who explicitly acknowledges that he is writing a book; the second story consists, in fact, in explaining how this very book came to be written. The first story ignores the book completely,

---

[2] Hercule Poirot is the detective in many of Agatha Christie's novels, and Philo Vance is the detective in many of S. S. Van Dine's novels.

that is, it never confesses its literary nature (no author of detective fiction can permit himself to indicate directly the imaginary character of the story, as it happens in 'literature'). On the other hand, the second story is not only supposed to take the reality of the book into account, but it is precisely the story of that very book.

We might further characterize these two stories by saying that the first – the story of the crime – tells 'what really happened,' whereas the second – the story of the investigation – explains 'how the reader (or the narrator) has come to know about it.' But these definitions concern not only the two stories in detective fiction, but also two aspects of every literary work which the Russian Formalists isolated forty years ago. They distinguished, in fact, the *fable* (story) from the *subject* (plot)[3] of a narrative: the story is what has happened in life, the plot is the way the author presents it to us. The first notion corresponds to the reality evoked, to events similar to those which take place in our lives; the second, to the book itself, to the narrative, to the literary devices the author employs. In the story, there is no inversion in time, actions follow their natural order; in the plot, the author can present results before their causes, the end before the beginning. These two notions do not characterize two parts of the story or two different works, but two aspects of one and the same work; they are two points of view about the same thing. How does it happen then that detective fiction manages to make both of them present, to put them side by side?

To explain this paradox, we must first recall the special status of the two stories. The first, that of the crime, is in fact the story of an absence: its most accurate characteristic is that it cannot be immediately present in the book. In other words, the narrator cannot transmit directly the conversations of the characters who are implicated, nor describe their actions: to do so, he must necessarily employ the intermediary of another (or the same) character who will report, in the second story, the words heard or the actions observed. The status of the second story is, as we have seen, just as excessive; it is a story which has no importance in itself, which serves only as a mediator between the reader and the story of the crime. Theoreticians of detective fiction have always agreed that style, in this type of literature, must be perfectly transparent, imperceptible; the only requirement it obeys is to be simple, clear, direct. It has even been attempted – significantly – to suppress this second story altogether. One publisher put out real dossiers, consisting of police reports, interrogations, photographs, fingerprints, even locks of hair; these 'authentic' documents were to lead the reader to the discovery of the criminal (in case of failure, a sealed envelope, pasted on the last page, gave the answer to the puzzle: for example, the judge's verdict).

We are concerned then in the whodunit with two stories of which one is absent but real, the other present but insignificant. This presence and this absence explain the existence of the two in the continuity of the narrative. The first involves so many conventions and literary devices (which are in fact the 'plot' aspects of the narrative) that the author cannot leave them unexplained. These devices are, we may note, of essentially two types, temporal inversions and individual 'points of view': the tenor of each piece of information is determined by the person who transmits it, no observation

---

[3] This translation of the Russian Formalists' terms, *fabula* and *sjuzet*, is not entirely satisfactory, since 'story' and 'plot' are used loosely and sometimes interchangeably in much criticism of prose fiction. 'Discourse' is perhaps a more satisfactory rendering of *sjuzet*. [...]

exists without an observer; the author cannot, by definition, be omniscient as he was in the classical novel. The second story then appears as a place where all these devices are justified and 'naturalized': to give them a 'natural' quality, the author must explain that he is writing a book! And to keep this second story from becoming opaque, from casting a useless shadow on the first, the style is to be kept neutral and plain, to the point where it is rendered imperceptible.

Now let us examine another genre within detective fiction, the genre created in the United States just before and particularly after World War II, and which is published in France under the rubric '*série noire*' (the thriller); this kind of detective fiction fuses the two stories or, in other words, suppresses the first and vitalizes the second. We are no longer told about a crime anterior to the moment of the narrative; the narrative coincides with the action. No thriller is presented in the form of memoirs: there is no point reached where the narrator comprehends all past events, we do not even know if he will reach the end of the story alive. Prospection takes the place of retrospection.

There is no story to be guessed; and there is no mystery, in the sense that it was present in the whodunit. But the reader's interest is not thereby diminished; we realize here that two entirely different forms of interest exist. The first can be called *curiosity*; it proceeds from effect to cause: starting from a certain effect (a corpse and certain clues) we must find its cause (the culprit and his motive). The second form is *suspense*, and here the movement is from cause to effect: we are first shown the causes, the initial *données* (gangsters preparing a heist), and our interest is sustained by the expectation of what will happen, that is, certain effects (corpses, crimes, fights). This type of interest was inconceivable in the whodunit, for its chief characters (the detective and his friend the narrator) were, by definition, immunized: nothing could happen to them. The situation is reversed in the thriller: everything is possible, and the detective risks his health, if not his life.

I have presented the opposition between the whodunit and the thriller as an opposition between two stories and a single one; but this is a logical, not a historical classification. The thriller did not need to perform this specific transformation in order to appear on the scene. Unfortunately for logic, genres are not constituted in conformity with structural descriptions; a new genre is created around an element which was not obligatory in the old one: the two encode different elements. For this reason the poetics of classicism was wasting its time seeking a logical classification of genres. The contemporary thriller has been constituted not around a method of presentation but around the milieu represented, around specific characters and behavior; in other words, its constitutive character is in its themes. This is how it was described, in 1945, by Marcel Duhamel, its promoter in France: in it we find 'violence – in all its forms, and especially the most shameful – beatings, killings. . . . Immorality is as much at home here as noble feelings. . . . There is also love – preferably vile – violent passion, implacable hatred.' Indeed it is around these few constants that the thriller is constituted: violence, generally sordid crime, the amorality of the characters. Necessarily, too, the 'second story,' the one taking place in the present, occupies a central place. But the suppression of the first story is not an obligatory feature: the early authors of the thriller, Dashiell Hammett and Raymond Chandler, preserve the element of mystery; the important thing is that it now has a secondary function, subordinate and no longer central as in the whodunit.

This restriction in the milieu described also distinguishes the thriller from the adventure story, though this limit is not very distinct. We can see that the properties listed up to now – danger, pursuit, combat – are also to be found in an adventure story; yet the thriller keeps its autonomy. We must distinguish several reasons for this: the relative effacement of the adventure story and its replacement by the spy novel; then the thriller's tendency toward the marvelous and the exotic, which brings it closer on the one hand to the travel narrative, and on the other to contemporary science fiction; last, a tendency to description which remains entirely alien to the detective novel. The difference in the milieu and behavior described must be added to these other distinctions, and precisely this difference has permitted the thriller to be constituted as a genre.

One particularly dogmatic author of detective fiction, S. S. Van Dine, laid down, in 1928, twenty rules to which any self-respecting author of detective fiction must conform. These rules have been frequently reproduced since then (see for instance the book, already quoted from, by Boileau and Narcejac) and frequently contested. Since we are not concerned with prescribing procedures for the writer but with describing the genres of detective fiction, we may profitably consider these rules a moment. In their original form, they are quite prolix and may be readily summarized by the eight following points:

1. The novel must have at most one detective and one criminal, and at least one victim (a corpse).
2. The culprit must not be a professional criminal, must not be the detective, must kill for personal reasons.
3. Love has no place in detective fiction.
4. The culprit must have a certain importance:
    (a) in life: not be a butler or a chambermaid.
    (b) in the book: must be one of the main characters.
5. Everything must be explained rationally; the fantastic is not admitted.
6. There is no place for descriptions nor for psychological analyses.
7. With regard to information about the story, the following homology must be observed: 'author: reader = criminal: detective.'
8. Banal situations and solutions must be avoided (Van Dine lists ten).

If we compare this list with the description of the thriller, we will discover an interesting phenomenon. A portion of Van Dine's rules apparently refers to all detective fiction, another portion to the whodunit. This distribution coincides, curiously, with the field of application of the rules: those which concern the themes, the life represented (the 'first story'), are limited to the whodunit (rules 1–4a); those which refer to discourse, to the book (to the 'second story'), are equally valid for the thriller (rules 4b–7; rule 8 is of a much broader generality). Indeed in the thriller there is often more than one detective (Chester Himes's *For Love of Imabelle*) and more than one criminal (James Hadley Chase's *The Fast Buck*). The criminal is almost obliged to be a professional and does not kill for personal reasons ('the hired killer'); further, he is often a policeman. Love – 'preferably vile' – also has its place here. On the other hand, fantastic explanations, descriptions, and psychological analyses remain banished; the criminal must still be one of the main characters. As for rule 7, it has lost its pertinence with the disappearance of the double story. This proves that the development has chiefly affected the thematic part, and not the structure of the discourse itself (Van Dine does not note the necessity of mystery and consequently of the double story, doubtless considering this self-evident).

Certain apparently insignificant features can be codified in either type of detective fiction: a genre unites particularities located on different levels of generality. Hence the thriller, to which any accent on literary devices is alien, does not reserve its surprises for the last lines of the chapter; whereas the whodunit, which legalizes the literary convention by making it explicit in its 'second story,' will often terminate the chapter by a particular revelation ('You are the murderer,' Poirot says to the narrator of *The Murder of Roger Ackroyd*). Further, certain stylistic features in the thriller belong to it specifically. Descriptions are made without rhetoric, coldly, even if dreadful things are being described; one might say 'cynically' ('Joe was bleeding like a pig. Incredible that an old man could bleed so much,' Horace McCoy, *Kiss Tomorrow Goodbye*). The comparisons suggest a certain brutality (description of hands: 'I felt that if ever his hands got around my throat, they would make the blood gush out of my ears,' Chase, *You Never Know with Women*). It is enough to read such a passage to be sure one has a thriller in hand.

It is not surprising that between two such different forms there has developed a third, which combines their properties: the suspense novel. It keeps the mystery of the whodunit and also the two stories, that of the past and that of the present; but it refuses to reduce the second to a simple detection of the truth. As in the thriller, it is this second story which here occupies the central place. The reader is interested not only by what has happened but also by what will happen next; he wonders as much about the future as about the past. The two types of interest are thus united here – there is the curiosity to learn how past events are to be explained; and there is also the suspense: what will happen to the main characters? These characters enjoyed an immunity, it will be recalled, in the whodunit; here they constantly risk their lives. Mystery has a function different from the one it had in the whodunit; it is actually a point of departure, the main interest deriving from the second story, the one taking place in the present.

Historically, this form of detective fiction appeared at two moments: it served as transition between the whodunit and the thriller and it existed at the same time as the latter. To these two periods correspond two subtypes of the suspense novel. The first, which might be called 'the story of the vulnerable detective,' is mainly illustrated by the novels of Hammett and Chandler. Its chief feature is that the detective loses his immunity, gets beaten up, badly hurt, constantly risks his life, in short, he is integrated into the universe of the other characters, instead of being an independent observer as the reader is (we recall Van Dine's detective-as-reader analogy). These novels are habitually classified as thrillers because of the milieu they describe, but we see that their composition brings them closer to suspense novels.

The second type of suspense novel has in fact sought to get rid of the conventional milieu of professional crime and to return to the personal crime of the whodunit, though conforming to the new structure. From it has resulted a novel we might call 'the story of the suspect-as-detective.' In this case, a crime is committed in the first pages and all the evidence in the hands of the police points to a certain person (who is the main character). In order to prove his innocence, this person must himself find the real culprit, even if he risks his life in doing so. We might say that, in this case, this character is at the same time the detective, the culprit (in the eyes of the police), and the victim (potential victim of the real murderers). Many novels by William Irish, Patrick Quentin, and Charles Williams are constructed on this model.

It is quite difficult to say whether the forms we have just described correspond to the stages of an evolution or else can exist simultaneously. The fact that we can encounter several types by the same author, such as Arthur Conan Doyle or Maurice Leblanc, preceding the great flowering of detective fiction, would make us tend to the second solution, particularly since these three forms coexist today. But it is remarkable that the evolution of detective fiction in its broad outlines has followed precisely the succession of these forms. We might say that at a certain point detective fiction experiences as an unjustified burden the constraints of this or that genre and gets rid of them in order to constitute a new code. The rule of the genre is perceived as a constraint once it becomes pure form and is no longer justified by the structure of the whole. Hence in novels by Hammett and Chandler, mystery had become a pure pretext, and the thriller which succeeded the whodunit got rid of it, in order to elaborate a new form of interest, suspense, and to concentrate on the description of a milieu. The suspense novel, which appeared after the great years of the thriller, experienced this milieu as a useless attribute, and retained only the suspense itself. But it has been necessary at the same time to reinforce the plot and to re-establish the former mystery. Novels which have tried to do without both mystery and the milieu proper to the thriller – for example, Francis Iles's *Premeditations* and Patricia Highsmith's *The Talented Mr Ripley* – are too few to be considered a separate genre.

Here we reach a final question: what is to be done with the novels which do not fit our classification? It is no accident, it seems to me, that the reader habitually considers novels such as those I have just mentioned marginal to the genre, an intermediary form between detective fiction and the novel itself. Yet if this form (or some other) becomes the germ of a new genre of detective fiction, this will not in itself constitute an argument against the classification proposed; as I have already said, the new genre is not necessarily constituted by the negation of the main feature of the old, but from a different complex of properties, not by necessity logically harmonious with the first form.

Critical connections

There is a wealth of literature on the enduring popularity of the detective novel, and the structure and appeal of crime fiction more generally (Knight 2004; Priestman, 2003; Clarke, 2001). Tzvetan Todorov's 'The Typology of Detective Fiction' is included here because, like many of the readings in this collection, it is a defining example within its field. Crime fiction, and perhaps especially the detective novel, remains one of the most popular forms of media entertainment available today. Mandel's (1984) estimate two decades ago that more than 10,000 million copies of crime stories had been sold worldwide since 1945 can today be increased considerably. Agatha Christie novels alone have sold more than one billion copies, and up to one third of the fiction published in English belongs to the crime genre (Knight, 2004). Sutherland (2007), writing in *The Times* newspaper, noted the remarkable increase in the popularity of the detective novel in recent years, and in particular the new 'multinationalism' of crime writing which reflects the global breaking down of national boundaries (Dan Brown's (2003) stellar-selling *The Da Vinci Code* is a case in point). Given its apparently growing popularity, its clear prevalence in libraries and bookshops, and the fact that many if not most of the crime films we watch today began life as crime novels, this literary form clearly merits the critical attention of media criminology.

Considered alongside other readings in this collection, Todorov also illustrates the significance of genre across different media forms and formats. The excerpts by Steve Neale (Reading 11) and Barry Langford (Reading 26) make explicit use of genre analysis in their discussions of film studies research methodologies and critical readings of the gangster movie respectively. Both directly reference Todorov's contribution to the field. Brian Jarvis' Marxist and psychoanalytic treatment of the serial killer movie (Reading 27) is also grounded in a clear understanding of genre analysis.

Discussion questions

- What distinctive genre rules does Todorov identify for the 'whodunit', 'the thriller' and 'the suspense novel'?
- How many other sub-genres of detective fiction can you think of? What are their principal rules of narrative development and how do they differ structurally from those 'types' of detective fiction identified by Todorov?
- Can Todorov's method of analysis be used for any novel?

References

Clarke, J. (2001) 'The pleasures of crime: interrogating the detective story' in J.Muncie and E. McLaughlin (eds) *The Problem of Crime*, London, Sage.

Knight, S. (2004) *Crime Fiction 1800–2000*, Basingstoke, Palgrave.

Mandel, E. (1984), *Delightful Murder: A Social History of the Crime Story*, London: Pluto.

Priestman, M. (2003) *Cambridge Companion to Crime Fiction*, Cambridge: Cambridge University Press.

Sutherland, J. (2007) 'Hot on the Trail of Global Sleuths', *Times*, April 29 2007.

Robert Reiner

THE DIALECTICS OF DIXON:
THE CHANGING IMAGE OF THE TV COP
(1994)

Introduction and context

NEWS MEDIA ARE ORGANISATIONALLY and structurally oriented to exaggerate police effectiveness. The disproportionate focus on serious violent crimes (with which the police have the highest success rate), the detailed reporting of the trial and sentencing stages of criminal cases (which can only take place once the police have successfully arrested a suspect and the case has been brought to court), and the daily journalistic reliance on police press offices for a routine source of reportable crime information (often allowing the police to frame selected cases in their own terms), amplifies the percieved efficacy of the police. At a time of height-ened press adversarialism, the news media are frequently critical of police practice, and may condemn police ineffectiveness relating to particular cases (Reading 19), or even target individual (nearly always senior) officers for systematic and ongoing criti-cism. But the news media seldom if ever question the legitimacy of the wider institution itself. This favourable news representation of the police and policing has traditionally also been reflected in fictional representations, although, as Mariana Valverde illus-trates in Reading 24, in recent years the picture has become more blurred.

Robert Reiner's analysis of the *Changing Image of the TV Cop* offers an insight-ful sociological critique of shifting representations of British television crime busters in the post-war era. He argues that, though there have been countless television series featuring police officers in central roles, three in particular represent key 'moments' in a dialectical progression which situates the police as either carers or controllers and corresponds with a specific political imaginary of policing of post-war Britain. The thesis, represented by *Dixon of Dock Green*, presents the police primarily as carers in a low-crime consensual society. Its antithesis, *The Sweeney*, portrays the police primarily as controllers in a rising-crime, law and order society. And the synthesis, *The Bill*, represents police as both carers and controllers, situated within an altogether more complex and ambivalent imaginary of crime, control and social order.

There have been countless series on British TV featuring leading characters who are police officers. This huge array can, however, be summarised by three dominant moments each encapsulated by a hugely popular and mould-breaking example, carrying in its wake numerous more or less successful epigones in the same style. These are the moments of *Dixon of Dock Green, The Sweeney*, and *The Bill*. Linking these three distinct phases in the unfolding fictional representation of the police are some important series, which for all their particular significance, can be seen as transitional episodes in the transformation of the dominant image. *Z-Cars* (and its offshoots *Softly, Softly* and *Barlow*) was an extremely influential point in the transition from the image of policing conveyed by *Dixon* to the dramatically different *Sweeney*. Similarly, *The Gentle Touch* and *Juliet Bravo*, each highly regarded in its own right, represent the shift from *The Sweeney* to *The Bill*, which in ratings terms has proved to be the biggest blockbuster of them all. Each of these three moments represents a different balance between an image of the police as carers or controllers, and corresponds to different contexts in the politics of policing since the Second World War.

This can be captured as a dialectical progression. The thesis, represented by *Dixon*, presents the police primarily as carers, lightning rods for the postwar consensus climate. Its antithesis, *The Sweeney*, portrays the police primarily as controllers, heralding the upsurge of a tough law and order politics in the late 1970s. The synthesis, *The Bill*, suggests that care and control are interdependent, reinforcing each other. As one recent episode title put it, 'Force Is Part Of The Service'. Care is for control, and vice versa. [. . .] This corresponds to a phase in which the law and order policies of the early 1980s have been transcended by a more sophisticated synthesis in which conceptions of crime prevention and community policing have become dominant across the political spectrum (Reiner and Cross, 1991).

The thesis: Dixon

Dixon of Dock Green was a remarkable broadcasting phenomenon, and a momentously significant symbol for British policing, which still resonates powerfully today (Reiner, 1992, p. 761). Jack Warner's portrayal of the eponymous hero, PC George Dixon, has become the quintessential image of the traditional British bobby, and debates about the police still regularly provoke nostalgic calls for a return to the 'Dixon' style of policing, as if he had been a real person not a fictional character.

Dixon first appeared in the 1950 Ealing film *The Blue Lamp*, in which he was shot after twenty minutes, the rest of the story concerning the police chase for his killer (played by a young Dirk Bogarde). Jack Warner's portrayal of the kindly, avuncular bobby struck so deep a chord as the embodiment of the consensus mood of Britain in its finest hour (as the decade which began with the Battle of Britain gave way to the one opened by the Festival of Britain) that he was revived six years later for BBC TV. When the series began in 1956 Jack Warner was already over sixty years old, past the age when most chief constables, let alone patrolling constables, have long retired.

Yet the series (with Warner in the title role) lived on until 1976, beyond the period of the iconoclastic *Z-Cars* and well into the heyday of *The Sweeney*.

By that time Dixon and the cosy, communal, foot-patrol style of policing he personified seemed vastly anachronistic, at least in terms of TV heroics. What is hard to remember from the perspective of an age in which the Dixon series came increasingly to be seen as cosy and complacent, a model of policing as kindly community carers set in timeless aspic, was that it began life heralded as a new departure in realism. This is true of each new departure in the TV image of the police. TV police series have always adopted a realist style, incorporating evolving techniques to convey a feel of documentary authenticity. Thus the police procedurals which preceded *Dixon* emphasised that their stories came straight from the headlines or police files. *Dragnet* episodes always told us that the story they told was true: 'Only the names have been changed to protect the innocent.' The hero Sergeant Joe Friday's catch-phrase was 'just give me the facts, ma'am', conveying the concern with telling it like it is . . . or was supposed to be. The 1950s cinema series *Scotland Yard*, much revived on TV, opened with presenter Edgar Lustgarten – 'the world's foremost authority on crime and criminals' – reaching for a file inside the record room at the Yard, and beginning to read from it as the narrative began. The kitchen-sink style of *Dixon* was in its turn seen as a further deglamourising step towards verisimilitude, as were *Z-Cars* and *The Sweeney* with their iconoclastic puncturing of the goody-goody portrayal of *Dixon* and its progeny. *The Bill* for its part reaches new heights in the extent to which its producers emphasise the research incorporated in it, and the deliberate immersion of its writers, actors and creative personnel in the world of real policing, with attachments to police stations and the like (Lynch, 1992).

The author of *Dixon*, Ted Willis, like the writers of most subsequent series were to do, claimed to have delved deeply into the world of the real police through observation, and to be presenting a less glamorous image than other fiction. What Dixon debunked was the great detective myth of the TV sleuths of that time, conveyed in such series as *Colonel March of Scotland Yard* or *Dial 999*. *Dixon of Dock Green* was a novel departure in focusing on the comparatively humdrum routine of the foot-patrolling uniform constables and divisional CID of a local police station, not the serious crimes tackled by the elite squads that were the traditional grist of the TV cops-and-robbers mill.

Dixon featured typical working-class policemen who were part of an East End working-class community. They had family and personal connections with people outside the force, and were presented as more rounded personalities than the cerebral supersleuths. Above all, the series presented a much wider conception of the police role, dealing with a host of problems experienced by the local public, and not just crime. The crimes which did occur were ones with their roots in social problems, not an asocial and unexplained original capacity for sin. Even when dealing with the relatively petty crimes which formed his daily round, Dixon was as much a carer as a controller.

The image of police officers as carers rather than controllers persisted in *Z-Cars*, for all that the series was seen initially by many as a shocking new exercise in debunking the police image. The story has often been quoted of how the Chief Constable of Lancashire was so incensed by the portrayal of a PC in a row with his wife in the first episode that he immediately went to London to register a personal protest at the BBC (St Johnston, 1978, pp. 181–4). The iconoclasm of *Z-Cars* lay in its warts-and-all portrayal of the police as adults with personal weaknesses and defects, rather than the

Dixonesque superannuated boy scout image, as well as in its documentary visual style. It remained the case that the police were portrayed as working closely with local community problems of a complex kind, and that crime was seen as a product of social problems. As Laing puts it in discussing an episode concerning two twelve-year-old boys who engage in a spree of petty theft: 'Here the police . . . take on the role of the absent father – mixing authority and care . . . This view of the police as a paternalist institution recurs when, after John Watt has attempted to explain the boys' actions in terms of the "rotten world" they live in, Barlow comments that Watt "should have had three sons, since he would make a good father" . . . The idea of the police as the agency for restoring (or substituting for) broken family and community structures remained a recurring topic throughout the whole series' (Laing, 1991, p. 133).

Z-Cars is thus a transitional series between the Dixon and Sweeney eras. It retains the sense of police as carers, dealing with a complex array of community problems including crime as an aspect of these, rather than merely as repressive controllers of unequivocal evil. On the other hand it moves away from the one-dimensionally benevolent and virtuous portrayal of the police world. Individual officers are portrayed as fallible, and tensions and conflicts within the organisation are highlighted. As Troy Kennedy Martin, its first scriptwriter, put it: 'Z-Cars began as a reaction against Dixon' (Martin, 1978, p. 126), and it prefigures the subsequent developments of The Sweeney in its profanation of the police image. Nonetheless, with the perspective of hindsight, it is the conception of the police as carers not merely controllers, situated in a complexly structured community, that stands out.

The antithesis: The Sweeney

The image of the police as controllers rather than carers becomes paramount in the early 1970s with The Sweeney and its ilk (like The Professionals, Special Branch, Target, and Dempsey and Makepeace). As summed-up succinctly by one reference work, The Sweeney was 'a rough, tough, kick-'em-in-the-teeth crime series . . . with Detective Inspector Jack Regan and Detective Sergeant George Carter continuing to make life difficult for villains – two gangbusters from the Sweeney (underworld slang for the Flying Squad)' (Rogers, 1988, p. 534).

The depiction of the police world in The Sweeney was the Dixon image stood on its head. This was quite self-conscious, as the following passage from an early publicity article shows: 'He's not the sort of copper you'd ask for directions, not Jack Regan. Not as his super-charged Ford slews to a halt spraying gravel and burning tyre rubber like he owns shares in Pirelli. He's not the sort of copper you'd ask to find your dog. Not as the car door bursts open and he leans over it pointing a Police.38, so big it needs two hands to hold it. He's not the sort of copper you'd even ask for a warrant. Not as he grinds his knee into the pit of the villain's back as an added refinement to a half-nelson, spitting out: "The Sweeney! You're nicked!" But isn't he lovely?' (cited in Clarke, 1986, p. 219).

The Sweeney characterises the police as tough, relentless crusaders against crime. They are pitted against criminals who are not rooted in a broader community, nor presented in even a partly sympathetic light as the result of social problems. They are vicious and evil, 'villains' who must be fought and stamped out, and can only be combated successfully by police officers who are equally ruthless. To fight crime the police must themselves resort to tactics which appear to mirror those of their foes, using violence and guile for just ends.

The respectable public, naïve and sheltered from the urban jungles which the cop must control on their behalf, are squeamish and do not approve of the methods the police must use. The police organisation itself is a house divided. The uniform branches, depicted as plodding woodentops, are largely sheltered from the serious villainy which is *The Sweeney*'s stock-in-trade, and are incapable of comprehending or dealing with it. The organisational hierarchy are too concerned with public relations and are there to paint a sanitised gloss of correctness on the real street cops' shenanigans as they do the dirty work of suppressing villains. They collaborate with the politicians and lawyers who force the police to operate with 'one hand tied behind their backs' by due process of law restrictions. *The Sweeney* are thus doubly marginalised, from the community and their own bosses. They are driven into being a close-knit brotherhood of working partners, misunderstood by those whose interests they are seeking to protect in the only way possible. The image of the police in *The Sweeney* and its progeny is thus of the police officer as vigilante, breaking the rules of law to achieve true justice and protect a public unable or unwilling to countenance what is necessary for its own preservation.

Regan himself summed it up thus to his driver in a 1975 episode: 'I sometimes hate this bastard place. It's a bloody holiday camp for thieves and weirdos . . . all the rubbish. You age prematurely trying to sort some of them out. Try and protect the public and all they do is call you "fascist". You nail a villain and some ponced-up, pinstriped, Hampstead barrister screws it up like an old fag packet on a point of procedure and then pops off for a game of squash and a glass of Madeira . . . He's taking home thirty grand a year and we can just about afford ten days in Eastbourne and a second hand car . . . No, it is all bloody wrong my son' (cited in Clarke, 1986, p. 222).

The change in the police image conveyed by *The Sweeney* had two principal sources, one in the internal evolution of the crime film as a genre, the other in the developing politics of law and order. *The Sweeney* develops on British TV the characterisation of the cop as vigilante which had been pioneered in the late 1960s and early 1970s by a new, blue wave of American films which themselves reflected a somewhat similar conjuncture in law and order politics as Britain was to experience nearly a decade later (Reiner, 1978 and 1981). Stylistically and thematically the roots of *The Sweeney* are such films as *Dirty Harry* and *The French Connection*, and TV series like *Kojak* and *Starsky and Hutch*. The vigilante theme of *The Sweeney* also resonates with the advent of law and order as a major political issue, championed by the Conservatives and the police themselves in the build-up to Mrs Thatcher's election victory in 1979. The law and order campaigns of the late 1970s feature the same conception of crime as the vigilante cop shows on TV. Crime is the product of evil not social problems, and must be cracked down upon by the state, with the police as its thin blue line of defence which must be toughened and unleased (Hall *et al.*, 1978; Reiner, 1992a).

The main image of the police on TV in the late 1970s thus was as controllers not carers. However, the hidden dimension of this was a sort of care, and a continuation of the Dixon theme in one crucial respect. The fundamental motive of *The Sweeney* is concern for innocent victims, and a drive to care for them against the depredations of the villains who prey on them. It is this passion for true justice that legitimates bending what are seen as petty legal restrictions hampering the control of crime. As Charles Bronson, a doyen of American vigilante cop movies, voiced it in the 1983

10 To Midnight: 'Forget what's legal! Do what's right!' *The Sweeney* and the other vigilante cops are fundamentally as moral as Dixon, and their integrity is unimpeachable, even if they swear, drink, fornicate, and are insubordinate to their bosses. They may not be the boy scouts any longer (Clarke, 1986), but that is because they are fighting a tough war on behalf of vulnerable victims who cannot defend themselves. This hidden face of care by the vigilantes, prompting their control of villains, is made manifest in the synthesis of *Dixon* and *The Sweeney* which becomes the style of cop series in the 1980s, above all in *The Bill*.

The synthesis: *The Bill*

Starting in 1984, after a 1983 prototype 'Woodentop' in the Thames TV *Storyteller* series, *The Bill* was originally in the orthodox format of a weekly sixty-minute programme. In 1988 it changed to a pattern of twice-weekly half-hour shows (Lynch, 1992), and in 1993 to three shows a week. In ratings terms it is the most consistently popular of all TV police series in Britain, watched by over twelve million viewers for each episode (Mason, 1992, p. 2).

In essence *The Bill* is the soap opera of the police community and community policing, telling everyday tales of constabulary folk. In this it resembles *Dixon* and *Z-Cars*, being set in a working-class area, and featuring the whole gamut of policing roles, not merely the control of serious crime by elite CID units. However, the depiction of both public and police is much less cosy and incorporates some of the hard edges of *The Sweeney*. The CID are depicted as largely sharing the tough vigilante culture made familiar by *The Sweeny*, albeit tackling more mundane sorts of crime. However, their degree of alienation from their colleagues in uniform and the organisational hierarchy is less pronounced. They are fundamentally symbiotic parts of the division of policing labour, even though there is constant tension in style, culture and working practices.

Crime is also presented in a much more complex and ambivalent way, sometimes rooted in social problems and perpetrated by those needing care as much as control, sometimes the product of greed or brutality which seems beyond explanation and calling only for suppression. The twice-weekly format extended over many years, and latterly the thrice-weekly scheduling, has allowed the continuous introduction of themes reflecting the most recent developments in the policing world, from the impact of the Police and Criminal Evidence Act 1984 (PACE) to sector policing. These not only provide a sense of verisimilitude and topicality, but also allow the constant exploration of social issues like racism and sexism in the force which have never before been the subjects of primetime police series.

The continuing format also allows a much more pessimistic approach to the problems confronting the police. These are seldom wrapped up neatly at the end of the episode, but recur repeatedly in developing ways. They defy simple solutions, whether the boy scout decency of Dixon or the no-holds-barred, tough law and order of *The Sweeney*.

This synthesis of the caring and controlling elements of the police role has frequently been expressed explicitly in the series itself, most succinctly by a recent episode title: 'Force is Part of the Service.' The police provide the service of protecting the public by the appropriate use of legitimate force, although at the same time police forces perform a variety of non-forceful and simply helpful services to people in trouble.

The synthesis of care and control in the police image presented by *The Bill* was again the product both of developments in the cop show genre, and in law and order politics. The more complex demographics of police forces produced a whole wave of British shows featuring leading characters who were not white Anglo-Saxon Protestant males. The way was paved by female leads (*The Gentle Touch* and *Juliet Bravo*), and followed by ethnic minority police (from *The Chinese Detective* to *Sam Saturday*) and young novices (Rockcliffe's Babies). Growing awareness of the complexity of police organisations was reflected in series looking at policing from a management rather than street perspective (*Waterfront Beat, The Chief*). The nostalgic hunger for a return to the supposed golden days of Dixon-style community policing was reflected in such ultra-pacific series on predominantly service-style policing as *Specials* and *Heartbeat*. The sense of the world outside the police being much more messy, intractable and essentially anarchic than these cosy evocations of community was conveyed in an influential American series, *Hill Street Blues*, which in many ways paved the stylistic path for *The Bill*.

All these changes in the cop show genre echo developments in the politics of law and order. In the mid-1980s the Conservative government implicitly began a U-turn away from its reliance simply on a tough law and order approach, in the face of its apparent failure as manifested by record increases in recorded crime (Reiner and Cross, 1991). Crime prevention in which the public had to figure as key partners with the criminal justice professionals became central to policy. This was congruent with changes that had already begun to affect the police world internally, from the impact of the 1981 Scarman Report on the Brixton disorders to the 1983 application of the Financial Management Initiative on the police, which imposed a greater concern with the rational management of resources on the police hierarchy (Reiner, 1991). The politics of policing moved beyond the simple confrontation between tough law and order and liberal restraints on police power that was the stuff of *The Sweeney*.

The format and style of *The Bill* has become the ideal vehicle for the presentation and exploration of this much more complex sense of contradiction, ambivalence, messiness, and intractability as the very essence of the police world. The Janus-faced conception of police as carers and controllers simultaneously is presented as an uneasy synthesis, unlike the more straight forward foregrounding of only one aspect of the duality in *Dixon* and *The Sweeney*. However, in a fundamental way *The Bill* continues the most basic legitimating message of the earlier series. Whilst there may be bad apples in the organisation, and warts on even the most virtuous of the characters, the force as a whole performs a vital service, and does so with as much integrity and effectiveness as is humanly possible.

Conclusion: the Dixonian dialectic

This survey of the changing TV fictional presentation of the British police through an assessment of the three key phases in its evolution has suggested both flux and constancy. Changing exigencies both in the crime fiction genre and the politics of law and order outside the media have resulted in varying foregrounding of first a caring then a controlling face of the police. The synthesis of these two is apparent in *The Bill*, which currently dominates the genre.

Underneath the superficial flux is a constant underlying legitimating theme. The police, caring and controlling, perform a vital social function in the best possible way. They are a necessary evil, the moral street-sweepers of the urban jungles in which most people now live, symbolising the quixotic pursuit of order and security through their guardianship of the legitimate force which the state seeks to monopolise. As Raymond Chandler put it more expressively in *The Long Goodbye*, using the cops to control crime and other complex social problems is like taking aspirin to cure a brain tumour, but 'No way has yet been invented to say goodbye to them.'

Bibliography

Clarke, A. (1986) 'This is Not the Boy Scouts: Television Police Series and Definitions of Law and Order' in T. Bennett, C. Mercer and J. Woollacott (eds) *Popular Culture and Social Relations* (Milton Keynes: Open University Press).

Hall, S., Critcher, C., Jefferson, T., Clarke, J. and Roberts, B. (1978) 'The Social Production of News', in *Policing the Crisis: Mugging, the State and Law and Order* (London: Macmillan).

Laing, S. (1991) 'Banging in Some Reality: The Original "Z-Cars"' in J. Corner (ed.) *Popular Television in Britain: Studies in Cultural History* (London: British Film Institute).

Lynch, T. (1992) *The Bill: The Inside Story of British Television's Most Successful Police Series* (London: Boxtree).

Martin, T. K. (1978) 'Four of a Kind?' in H. R. F. Keating (ed.) *Crime Writers* (London: BBC).

Mason, P. (1992) *Reading the Bill: An Analysis of the Thames Television Police Drama* (Bristol University: Centre for Criminal Justice).

Reiner, R. (1978) 'The New Blue Films', *New Society*, 30.

Reiner, R. (1981) 'Keystone to Kojak: the Hollywood Cop' in P. Davies and B. Neve (eds) *Politics, Society and Cinema in America* (Manchester: Manchester University Press).

Reiner, R. (1991) *Chief Constables* (Oxford: Oxford University Press).

Reiner, R. (1992) 'Policing A Postmodern Society', *Modern Law Review*, 55, 6.

Reiner, R. (1992) *The Politics of the Police, 2nd edn* (Hemel Hempstead: Wheatsheaf).

Reiner, R. and Cross, M. (1991) (eds). *Beyond Law and Order* (London: Macmillan).

Rogers, D. (1988) *The ITV Encyclopedia of Adventure* (London: Boxtree).

St Johnston, E. (1978) *One Policeman's Story* (Chichester: Barry Rose).

Critical connections

Reiner's typological analysis of British television police drama is regularly invoked by media criminologists seeking to understand fictional portrayals of policing within a wider context of political change. Reiner's dialectic has been extended and updated by Leishman and Mason (2003), who identify defining cop dramas – thesis, antithesis and synthesis – since the 1980s, when the binary care-control axis that had shaped previous representations was complicated by the emergence of a more critical understanding of policing and the police. Reiner's significant contribution is the realisation that popular entertainment may often, by its very definition, be detached from reality, but it is rarely hermetically sealed off from contemporary political, cultural and moral sensibilities of society. Nor is police drama detached entirely from the structures of policing charged with the maintenance of order and public protection. Indeed, it is precisely through maintaining a sense of 'dramatic realism' that many police dramas 'work' for a contemporary television audience.

Discussion questions

- Explain and discuss Reiner's typology of television police drama.
- Draw up a list of recent police dramas and think about how they might be incorporated into Reiner's dialectical progression (see also Leishman and Mason, 2003). Do any of the series you have chosen represent a key 'moment' in the changing politics of policing?
- How useful would it be in an analysis like Reiner's to speak with the programme makers (see also Readings 8, 24 and 26)?

Reference

Leishman, F. and Mason, P. (2003) *Policing and the Media: Facts, Fictions and Factions*, Cullompton: Willan.

Mariana Valverde

FROM THE HARD-BOILED DETECTIVE TO THE PRE-CRIME UNIT (2006)

Introduction and context

M ARIANA VALVERDE BRINGS a postmodern sensibility to her exploration of US cop dramas, and transports us, via some more conventional dramas, into the 'hyperreal' world of the reality cop show. Here the boundaries between news, information and entertainment are at their most blurred and diffuse. In the hyperreal context of the 'reality' cop show, viewers (or rather participants) are imported 'into' the world of policing, where they can watch 'real' officers in action, 'experience' the thrill of the chase and arrest, and gain some sense of what it's 'actually like' to be a police officer. The narrative is stuttering and disjointed, the camera twitches and the focus blurs, the conversations are fragmented and inconclusive. But despite the interrupted and often confused nature of the programme's narrative development, Valverde suggests that the prevailing impressions of crime and disorder are unambiguous and concrete. What we are likely to find in the postmodern world of the reality cop show is the reification of existing conservative stereotypes – crime is a problem of a largely minority ethnic underclass, families are broken and unstructured, children are feckless and out of control, life in the projects is confused and chaotic – for this is what the cameras 'objectively' record.

Though invited to actively participate in the experience of policing the projects, the audience, Valverde suggests, is rendered entirely passive, completely dependent on the police to make sense of this fragmented and chaotic world. Of course, in the hyperreal world, nothing is as it seems, and the real policing we bear witness to is in fact a highly edited and often editorialised representation that corresponds to a particular imaginary of inner city urban crime and control. As such, it is inscribed with many of the same narratives of race, class and gender that characterise those cultural forms residing unselfconsciously on either side of the factual-entertainment divide – news and fiction.

On either side of the consideration of *COPS*, Valverde addresses the continuing success of two of those more conventional dramas referred to above – *Law & Order*, and *CSI: Crime Scene Investigation*.

The system as drama: *Law & Order*

The most common plot of cop films is the good cop's struggle against a corrupt or malfunctioning system. Because of this focus on the individual honest cop, in cop films, figures like judges and prosecutors usually appear only to delay or frustrate the progress of justice. The system is only presented from one point of view: and from the police point of view, prosecutors and judges undermine the work that has been done to apprehend the suspect (suspects, in the police view, being automatically criminals). By contrast, courtroom dramas and lawyer films, which also show the system from only one point of view, but one in another location, pay no attention to police work, or else feature it only as an obstacle (e.g. a bungled investigation).

The brilliance of the long-running series *Law & Order*, which shows no sign of exhaustion after 14 seasons and which has given rise to two spin-offs, is embedded in its distinctive half-and-half format. The cops are the main characters in the first half of each show. As a suspect is apprehended, the prosecutors then become the protagonists of the second half. This makes the show somewhat confusing to the uninitiated: accustomed to the single point of view of conventional narrative, the first-time viewer ends up spending the whole second half wondering what happened to the stars introduced in the first half. This unusual format, however, allows for endless variations on the theme of the conflicts between the two parts of the system, a conflict that is usually taken for granted and put in the background in both cop-centred films/TV series and in lawyer-focused representations. And after one has become familiar with the format, the show appears as much more interesting than other crime shows precisely because of the change in point of view at the half-hour mark.

The creator of the series, Dick Wolf, explains that the unusually complex structure, which necessitates having two sets of 'separate but equal' star actors, was the product of a certain business climate as much as an aesthetic or political choice. In the fascinating 2003 coffee-table book *Law & Order Crime Scenes*, featuring black-and-white artsy stills of the same crime scenes that were shown in colour and in moving images at the beginning of episodes, Wolf writes:

> The split-format structure of *Law & Order* was initially predicated on a business, not an artistic, idea. While producers incur a deficit in creating the original episodes, syndication is where the profit is made in television. It was therefore thought to be advantageous to have a product that could be sold either as a half-hour or a full-hour show. I was fishing for various possibilities to meet this demand and tossed around several ideas, among them, 'Day & Night' and 'Cops & Robbers'. But, ironically, when I hit upon 'Law & Order', I felt that I had come up with a series that would be creatively enhanced by the use of the split-format. (Wolf, 2003, p 8)

The show always opens with a crime – almost always graphically represented by a dead body – which quickly becomes the object of the New York homicide detective gaze.

The cops are shown linearly following up on clues and on witness statements, and going from one address (shown on the screen in black and white lettering, in Brecht-like style) to another. Their time is mainly spent interviewing witnesses and suspects. Physical clues are duly sent off to the forensics lab, but forensic work itself is rarely shown on the screen; the show follows the cops, not the biochemists.

The second half follows the more legalistic story of how prosecutors evaluate the evidence gathered by the cops and decide whether to lay a charge, and if so, what kind of charge. Sometimes the prosecutors' work has the effect of proving the cops wrong and forcing them to follow up avenues of inquiry that had been neglected earlier, a feature that, while undoubtedly reflective of 'real life', is rarely portrayed in mass-market representations of criminal justice. This complexity may be what explains the popularity of *Law & Order* among my academic colleagues.

While the cops always find a plausible suspect – otherwise the second half could not take place – the prosecutors are not always victorious. Occasionally the case unravels during the trial (though trials are not always shown, in keeping with the show's peculiar theory that the criminal justice system only has two consistent components). But more often, failure arises from the conflict between moral guilt and legal guilt. In one episode, the cops gathered evidence from the trash contained in a garbage bag left on the curb by a suspect, only to have the prosecutors inform them that since they only had a search warrant for the house, not the sidewalk or the garbage bag, this evidence was legally inadmissible. This meant that the prosecutors could only lay a lesser charge. And in a twist that is more typical of the early seasons of the programme than of recent, Republican-influenced content, the lesser charge turns out to be morally correct in the end, since the criminal in question turns out not to have been a typical criminal but rather a disinterested professional moved to violence by excessive zeal.

The show's half-and-half format has the highly political effect of formally precluding a third segment told from the standpoint of the defence. In contrast to lawyer films and books starring valiant defence counsel managing to obtain freedom for their (mainly innocent) clients (e.g. Scott Turow's novels), *Law & Order* completely excludes the defence bar. This is significant because it is symptomatic of a broader trend toward crime representations with conservative effects. During the years from Reagan to the second Bush administration, mainstream US crime television increasingly romanticized the capture and prosecution of villains. Occasionally, legal stories were told as tales of ordinary people managing to prevail over 'the system' and over powerful groups; but, significantly given the huge increase in harsh punishments and prison populations, the theme of the little guy up against an unjust system was generally explored in civil-law rather than criminal-law contexts (e.g. the extremely popular book and film *A Civil Action*). The criminal law and its enforcement, by contrast, became a field of dramatic events told almost wholly from the point of view of victims, cops and prosecutors. As critic Elayne Rapping puts it:

> What ever happened to the defense-attorney hero on television? Where are the Perry Masons? The TV versions of Atticus Finch, or the fictional-ized Clarence Darrow of *Inherit the Wind* and *Compulsion*? A one-time staple of TV series about crime and justice, this staunch advocate for the poor, the powerless, the unjustly accused has slowly receded from TV screens to be

replaced by heroic policemen and D.A.s [District Attorneys]. Even in pulp fiction and popular movies, it's the chasers and the prosecutors of the 'bad guy' criminals who, with certain exceptions that prove the rule, have long reigned supreme. Defense attorneys, more often than not, appear as sleazy, corrupt, and unscrupulous, tainted by some suspiciously radical political agenda, or, at best, as hopelessly inept – the strawman foils of those who represent 'true justice'. (Rapping, 2003, p 21)

Although *Law & Order* plots sometimes undermine the law-and-order ideology by showing that the criminal law cannot address fundamental social problems, nevertheless, two further points can be made to demonstrate the links between *Law & Order* and the rising tide of conservatism in the US throughout the 1980s and 1990s. First, what might seem like a small point. In the 2003 season, shot in 2002, the desks of every New York homicide cop sprouted US flags, as did many lapels owned by various male characters. In addition, the show's website was changed to show a background in which the show's trademark colours, blue and red (the show's title as shown on the opening screen is half red and half blue), acquire a distinctly nationalist dimension as the US flag emerges from the background and wafts in an invisible breeze. Murder is not a national or federal matter in the US, legally speaking: murderers are prosecuted by the people of the State of New York, not the Queen or the country. But the literal flag-waving has the effect of undermining this longstanding legal doctrine and suggesting to readers that local homicide detectives paid out of local property taxes labour not for their municipality but for the nation. Prosecutors, while less likely to sport flag lapel pins, rarely mention the criminal code of the State of New York, and are shown as all-purpose, national crime fighters.

The emergence of flags – signs put in the background, but which carry a heavy meaning in post-September 11 America – can be shown to be related to the fact, evident from content analysis alone, that over the years the prosecutors depicted in *Law & Order* have become more conservative. To quote Rapping again:

> Assistant [prosecutors] were first a race-conscious black male named Robinette and then a fairly liberal feminist, Claire Kincaid. Since then, each assistant, always an attractive white woman, has been increasingly less concerned with 'politically correct' morally troubling issues and more extreme in the pure pursuit of conviction at all costs . . . each successive woman has simply followed the tough-on-crime pattern now established by the series, with none of the ideological anguish typical of Robinette and Kincaid . . . (Rapping 2003, p 28)

The homicide side, for its part, has also changed over the years. The head white guy has here remained fairly constant, but his second in command – usually a man of colour – has changed. The Latino cop who held the role for the longest time was somewhat prone to violence, but usually only if subject to racial abuse. The current black cop, for his part, often beats up on suspects for no reason other than to subordinate them. That a high-class, artsy series with complex plots and excellent acting shows police brutality as a normal part of the job – rather than as a sign of the department's corruption, which is how it would have appeared in the 1970s – is perhaps a sign of the times. Criminals are evil, and the criminal justice system, while tough (the death penalty was reintroduced in New York State early in the life of the series), is sometimes powerless due to law's perpetual failures. What is conventionally regarded as falling within the sphere of 'torture' is never shown, and if shown would likely discredit the character engaging in it as well as the system. But when the black cop is shown throwing a chair at a suspect for no particular reason other than to vent his frustration at the whole population of youth gangs, no consequences follow, either for the cop or for the system. Repeatedly, the violent cop is merely told to 'cool it', and the plot goes on.

The normalization of police violence in the most popular police series on American television conveys a message on its own, quite apart from the messages about crime and justice contained in the plots. Showing police abuse of suspects going unpunished is perhaps not unrelated to the official US Government's response to the Iraqi war prisoner torture scandals. And needless to say, making the white characters (even when they are divorced alcoholics) appear as 'reasonable' by contrast to the violence-prone racial minority officers is also a powerful message of its own.

British television too has recently seen the rise of violence-prone police officers. Some of these are presented as the bent coppers in programmes featuring internal investigators as the heroes, in which case their tendency to violence is not normalized. But some of the tough-guy cops are romanticized, in series that seem designed specifically to lure viewers away from the much more violent offerings of US-made television shows and movies. The special undercover agents of *In Deep* are meant to be unusual – they are part of a small elite unit that infiltrates terrorist and organized crime groups, and the whole programme is based precisely on the fact that the world of the two tough-guy 'in deep' agents is totally removed from conventional crime fighting. But apart from the content, it is worth noting that the cinematographer of this show appears to have come straight from Hollywood – the camera often lingers on bloody faces and blown-up buildings, American-style, eschewing the much more restrained conventions of traditional British crime television. The popularity of programmes featuring armed special agents engaging in highly dangerous undercover work may be an indication of a certain normalization and indeed a glamorization of the violence committed by agents of British criminal justice, and perhaps also by British military personnel. The fatal shooting of an innocent Brazilian immigrant that took place in the London Tube after the July 2005 bombings would in a previous decade have looked to the British public like a scene from an American television programme. However, by 2005 scenes along those lines had already been featured in numerous British-made programmes featuring specialized law enforcement officers, such as bodyguards for foreign dignitaries and anti-terrorist specialists.

US-style violence has also been featured prominently in Ian Rankin's bestselling novels, whose protagonist is the Edinburgh homicide detective Inspector Rebus. The novels borrow heavily from the film noir aesthetic; they take place almost exclusively at night in anarchic, ugly, violence-ridden neighbourhoods. And Rebus's drinking habits rival those of characters played by Humphrey Bogart in the 1940s. Apart from these constant elements, there have been some significant shifts in the content. The first Rebus books were more concerned to convey a dark aesthetic, an Edinburgh whose existence tourists do not suspect; but later novels have featured increasingly graphic descriptions of violence – something not found in film noir, a genre in which there are numerous dead bodies but almost no blood. The old-fashioned, Holmes-like, almost purely intellectual skills of Ruth Rendell's Inspector Wexford and Colin Dexter's Inspector Morse, whose avuncular screen images functioned for years as messages reassuring (older, middle-class) British viewers that the world was fundamentally safe, seem to have given way to representations of police work that combine punches and kicks with a remarkable fondness for that mythical signifier of masculinity that British police have notoriously lacked, in art as in life, namely guns.

It is worth pausing for a moment to note that American cultural products that are exported around the world come to have different social implications, indeed different meanings, as they are transported and shown to different audiences – as they are placed in different contexts of consumption. Guns of course are normal in US police work, and are also worn by non-police state agents such as customs inspectors and immigration officers. Ordinary people also own handguns in huge numbers. But in the UK context guns have a different legal history and hence a different meaning. Just as whisky had a particular meaning in films and books written during or immediately after US Prohibition, so too semiotic elements that recur in crime films, such as guns, require specific analyses that take the specific location of the audience into account. Analyses of the 'translations' of US movies and television series that take place in countries that are also English-speaking and thus require no dubbing are, unfortunately, extremely scarce. And so we now turn to another US cultural product, one that as far as I know has not travelled very much outside of North America but which has given rise to a curious Canadian imitation that can be scrutinized to shed some light on these questions of the context of consumption, namely, the geographically specific meaning of signs used in representations of crime and of policing.

The return of the barbarian invasion: *COPS*

Police films are less popular today than they were in the 1970s and 1980s. In the world of film, the late 1990s and the early years of the twenty-first century were dominated by the craze for fantastical, quasi-historical mega-productions that is common to the success of *The Lord of the Rings*, the *Harry Potter* movies, and to the earlier *Star Wars* as well. On television, however, big-budget shows with large casts and all the latest computer-generated effects are not financially possible. And in any case, at the level of format, the small screen lends itself better to face-to-face interactions than to grand spectacles. Thus, audiences use television not so much to gain access to other worlds but rather to see the 'real' world (Ellis, 2000): to imaginatively explore the small-scale dramas of real life, be it the life of the family explored in soap operas or the life of the city explored in police series. Because police are usually represented as travelling back and forth across the social divides of class and race, the act of following the police around (with the help of the television camera) enables middle-class and respectable working-class viewers to explore, from the safety of the armchair, the seamy side of urban life. For all these reasons, police-centred television series are extremely popular, in the UK as in North America.

A series that first appeared on marginal channels and only in the daytime, *COPS*, has now become more mainstream, and is shown several times per day on different channels across North America. This is a 'reality' programme purporting to give the viewer a sense of what it is really like to be a police officer patrolling the streets of urban (and often suburban) America. Each episode runs for 22 minutes, half an hour with commercials, and is composed of several independent mini-episodes. It is thus well suited to channel-surfing and short attention spans.

A different police department is featured in each *COPS* show, so the characters change constantly. Continuity is provided by a standardized format, including the use of a hand-held video camera (always located right behind or beside the protagonist cop), and, last but not least, the theme song – a catchy reggae tune, 'Bad boy', played at the beginning as a series of disconnected shots follow one another on the screen. Sometimes the opening sequence features cops doing typical 'cop' things – putting handcuffs on youths, drawing their guns and crouching behind their cruisers expectantly, etc. But, remarkably, some of the opening sequences contain quite unrelated material that seems to have been selected for its curiosity or entertainment value rather than for any message it may convey about criminal justice. A high-speed boat moving across a harbour; a scantily clad black woman zooming along on roller blades; a surfer falling off the surfboard; and an officer engaged in the delicate task of grabbing a crocodile by the tail and putting it in a cage – these are just a few of the images that have appeared as part of the all-important opening sequence.

The combination of representations of policing with randomly collected scenes whose significance – or whose provenance – is never mentioned in the body of the programme has the effect of suggesting to the audience that this is not a serious documentary about police work, but a combination of amateur video footage of policing work and anything that might contribute to the entertainment of the audience. The theme song, which is extremely catchy, contributes to create an overall effect that one might describe as 'infotainment'. Sung with a Caribbean accent, the lyrics seem to empathize with the criminals and other low-life whose troubles are exploited by the show more than with the cops: 'Bad boy, bad boy, what'cha gonna do, what'cha gonna do when they come for you . . .' This song acquired a life of its own as it made it into the hit parade in 1993. Especially in the case of those opening sequences featuring roller bladers and crocodiles, not just 'bad boys', the powerful music combines with the images to suggest that we are in the world of fun and entertainment.

This fun-oriented opening, however, is rarely followed up in the body of the programme. Immediately after the opening sequence, we see a long shot of a city or town, with the name written out below – usually an unglamorous name like Indianapolis, not New York or Chicago – and we hear the incomprehensible but unmistakeable sounds of a dispatcher, usually a woman, calmly responding to emergency calls and organizing the response. The dispatcher's calm rational manner is misleading, however. Most of what follows consists of disconnected bits, through which respectable viewers sitting at home not only see life 'in the projects', among the underclasses, but are actually thrown into a semiotically confusing succession of badly lit video clips with noisy soundtracks that rarely amount to a coherent narrative.

Since the action is usually taking place at night, and the reality-TV format means there is no proper film lighting, it is literally impossible to really see what is going on. The visual confusion is compounded by the noises left in the soundtrack, among which it is often hard to distinguish any words other than those of the 'lead' cop, our guide to the underworld (Doyle, 1998). The inhabitants of the disordered world being policed appear to us as they appear to the largely white cops who brusquely enter their run-down apartments: unkempt and unintelligible. And due to the fact that the microphone goes with the police officers, the voices of those being policed are reduced to a babble of indistinct shouts and sentence fragments, even when the speakers are native English speakers and are not drunk or on drugs, which is probably a minority of situations.

It is important to note the marked political effects of 'technical' facts such as the location of the microphone. In class discussions in which I have asked students to reflect on film and television technical choices, I have learned that students are often quite informed about film conventions – lighting, cinematography, soundtrack – that are used in films and in big-budget television drama like *Law & Order*. When shown clips of *COPS* shows, however, students uniformly fail to note that the apparent artlessness of the home-movie reality-TV genre has its own formal conventions: conventions and technical features that have important political effects. Imagining that 'tricks' are only used in film and in professionally made television shows, they do not see that the fact that the camera goes with the cop from the cruiser into the apartment or house under investigation has the effect of presenting the 'underworld' as the cop sees it, that is, as a space of constant risk and potential danger. In the five years I have taught a course in which I ask them to analyse such footage, none of the students has realized, unaided, that the 'reality' soundtrack, full of unintelligible sounds, conveys a certain message about the world of crime precisely through the lack of coherent meaning (Doyle, 1998; Rapping, 2003).

The format of *COPS* episodes is as follows. A cop chosen to 'star' in the episode is introduced at the beginning – or rather, he introduces himself, for there is no narrator, in line with reality-TV conventions. 'He' is the operative word here; I watched 25 randomly selected episodes and none featured a woman cop except in secondary roles. The officer is immediately personalized and rendered sympathetic. 'I could have been a priest but I became a cop' is one man's story. Another one, obviously prompted (in a question later edited out) to highlight his race, tells us a long tale about having been one of the few well-behaved African-American kids in his neighbourhood. The tone is informal and wistful. As the cop reminisces, the video camera, located in the back seat of the cruiser, gives us a tight close-up and hence very sympathetic view of the archetypal 'cop on the beat'.

After a few minutes the biographical narrative is interrupted by a call from the dispatcher. The cop springs into action – which means, in this show as in real-life American policing, that he steps on the accelerator. The car then speeds along either to a particular address or in pursuit of a vehicle. If called to an address, the cops – who usually gather a couple of other cruisers along the way – pile out and get themselves organized to enter the house, guns drawn and shouting to one another in militaristic language.

The interiors shown on *COPS* are remarkable for their disorder. Beer bottles lie on the carpet, people who do not appear to form a 'normal' family emerge from the darkness (often into a space lit with an ordinary living room lamp unsuitable for filming), and broken fragments of conversation ensue. The people who appear are always poor, and usually Latino, black or generically 'ethnic'. Men wear undershirts and basketball tops. Women are scantily clad in bright polyester, usually overweight, and sometimes sporting curlers in their hair. Children are shown as being up very late at night.

That social and familial disorder is highly likely to have been compounded by the cops' entry – and that some of its features, such as the kids being out of bed, may have actually been caused by the cops' arrival, is not likely to occur to the audience, given that reality-TV is a genre that does not encourage, or even allow, examination of the social and political roots of what one sees. The visible disorder appears as the natural habitat of the disorderly, ill-dressed people one sees.

When the cops yell at the people in question and get only indistinct mumbles in reply, the dividing line between the forces of order and the uncivilized jungle is further underlined. The screen shows us rational, well-dressed, sober white men with well-trimmed haircuts trying to make sense of an inherently unintelligible world. And since watching the show inevitably enlists us too in the work of trying to decipher the sounds and the sights of a disorderly and confusing world – the semiotic work that seems to take up most of the cops' time – it takes an act of mental courage to avoid totally identifying with the cops.

The video camera often lingers painfully on the awkward speech and movements of suspects or witnesses who have clearly had too much to drink. Drinking is not an unusual behaviour for cops, of course, but since their leisure time is not represented on the show, what we see is that the disorderly classes are often drunk and incoherent, whereas the cops are always rational and sober.

Drugs too are shown as being normal in the environments being policed. Just about every car stopped is searched for drugs, and the rate of 'hits' is much higher on *COPS* than in real-life policing. One gets the impression that drugs must be everywhere even when the cops don't find them. And drug use contributes to the 'law-and-order' effect of the show because people who are caught having just consumed a mind-altering substance don't look very rational when filmed.[. . .] As our impatience to find out just what is going on grows, we the viewers come to empathize with the cops' own semiotic frustration: we are thus more likely to unwittingly adopt the cops' theories about disorder and crime.

Some of the people whose world is being invaded are clearly visible and identifiable – whether because they signed a consent form agreeing to be on television or whether a consent form was never brought to them, we don't know. Some of those apprehended by the police as suspects, however, have their faces technologically obscured. One imagines this protects their identity; but, given the general atmosphere of unintelligibility, the blurred face also adds to the general confusion.

Shots are sometimes heard, as well as other worrying noises – glass breaking, people running, etc. Rarely does the audience actually see what is going on, however. The lighting is simply inadequate, and there is only one video camera available, or so it seems. Thus, the audience is reduced to a purely passive state: in a mostly dark screen, we see a figure rapidly running in and out of the light, and we hear several noises that might indicate a crime being committed – but might also indicate someone running from the police. We thus cling to the communications among the police officers – the only ones we can hear clearly – for dear life. 'The subject is behind the house!', 'the subject is running down Thirteenth Street!'. . . and so forth.

At the end of the incident we are often still in the dark about who did what to whom and why. But as we climb back into the comforting space of the police cruiser, that haven of safety, we – the camera and the microphone, that is – finally have an opportunity to hear the real story. The cop introduced at the beginning now provides the narrative that interprets all of the chaotic detail just seen and heard, organizing it into a coherent story about crime and police, often with an explicit 'moral of the story'. We the viewers have just visited the 'scene' with the cops (even though the screen was mainly black for a good bit of time and the noises recorded were not obviously meaningful). Therefore we believe that from the comfort of our living room we have seen crime with our own eyes. We forget that we only know what is/was going on when the cop, seated at the wheel of the cruiser, finally interprets for us the alien world we have just visited. Needless to say, no microphone stays behind to record what the hapless inhabitants of the underworld think or say. [...]

The apotheosis of the forensic gaze: *CSI*

[...] While certain representations, such as gangster films, spend much time familiarizing audiences with particular villains, *COPS* is distinctive, among representations of cops and robbers, in that only the cops are individualized (the main cop by name, the others by police department). The 'robber' side of the old cops-and-robbers dialectic is represented not by individuals but by a demographic, a type – the type associated with the general social condition of 'disorder'. The vast majority of incidents to which the police are called do not amount to crimes that require detection – consisting mainly of domestic violence whose perpetrator is never in doubt or drug possession offences that only require routine searching of persons and vehicles to establish reasonable and probable cause. Criminals are never individualized for more than a few seconds; and neither are the crimes themselves. Unlike Sherlock Holmes, who is in some awe of his constant powerful enemy Professor Moriarty, these officers are not presented as in battle against a clever villain or in any way engaged in careful gathering of information to either charge specific criminals or to prevent crimes in the communities being policed. Prevention never enters their vocabulary, as if to tell the audience that nothing significant can be done to alter the future. The officers shown seem to think that their job is only to manage, temporarily, a series of unresolved or ambiguous situations whose common denominator is disorder.

Let us now turn to the tremendously successful forensic series *CSI: Crime Scene Investigation*. At first sight, this popular series does everything that is left undone in *COPS*. *CSI* – the most popular programme on American television in 2005 – is all about specific crimes and specific criminals, and the officers shown do use sophisticated knowledge. Interestingly, however, the criminals themselves are of little interest; and the victims and the witnesses are also given very short shrift. In general, people do not matter, either as criminals or as victims. Only the physical clues and the technical gadgets used to interpret those clues matter.

In keeping with this Sherlock Holmes approach, *CSI* shows virtually no uniformed officers. Even homicide detectives play a surprisingly secondary role. The central characters are those that in other shows (e.g. *Law & Order*) are placed behind the scenes and taken for granted: the technicians who examine the clues and the bodies. In real life, forensic technicians ('criminalists', as they are known in some parts of the US) simply turn over their test results, with minimal interpretation, to the homicide detectives. The detectives have other information, e.g. witness statements and existing police records. It is the homicide detectives (and sometimes their more specialized friends in the FBI) who are regarded in real life as being in the best position to generate a reliable account of the crime, having several kinds of evidence at their disposal (what is called 'triangulation' in social science research methods).

On *CSI*, however, the homicide detective has receded into the background completely. It is the forensic technicians, trained in applied biochemistry and in the use of tools like the microscope and the X-ray machine, who not only analyse the physical evidence but even reconstruct the crime, to the point of assigning guilt strictly from physical evidence. This is the Holmes theory of truth taken to the extreme – or, more accurately, it is the Holmes theory narrowed and impoverished. Holmes did not use only physical clues: as shown earlier, he also used a vast personal archive of variegated information about historical events, current affairs and so on. Holmes also spent much time reading up on previous criminal cases and used that information to analyse each new crime. The *CSI* technicians, by contrast, live only in the present, and they appear to have no information at all about the social world.

In one episode, the distraught father of a mentally ill young woman is revealed as the (unwitting) killer of his daughter – after one keen-eyed forensic technician, examining the woman's clothes closet, finds a recent stain on a dress that DNA analysis revealed to have been caused by the father's tears. What sort of relation the father might have had with his mentally ill daughter was not discussed at all. The devoted father's tears could have been a semiotically rich sign whose layers – love for the daughter, frustration about her outbursts during episodes of illness, anger at the lack of social supports, etc. – could have been explored to document the troubles afflicting families with special-needs children. But the social and psychological discourses that a programme like *Law & Order* would routinely include the depiction of a family tragedy were simply left aside. The salty water with the father's DNA was treated as a very simple signifier with only one (first-order) meaning, the forensic meaning.

To further the theory that truth is always, and exclusively, to be found in the physical traces left by a crime, the producers of *CSI* have developed some clever innovations in both photography and sound. As for visuals, *CSI* seems to have been the original site of a practice now used in a number of other crime shows including some British ones: shifting from shooting what the technician sees either with the naked eye or through a microscope or other machine, to an enhanced image that locates the body part or the knife fragment back in its original, just-before-the-crime condition. An example might help here. In one shot a technician is shown peering into a microscope. Immediately afterwards, the screen fills up completely with an image that one supposes is what the technician saw (though it was probably computer-enhanced): a bone with a jagged edge. The viewer is then taken back to the scene of the crime: and a miracle then takes place before the audience's eyes. The bit of jagged bone is transformed, through computer-enhanced photography, into a whole bone, which is in turn magically placed back inside the victim's body, with the body slowly resuscitated and shown as it was just before the fatal moment. The audience hitches a ride with the image as if on a magic carpet. We the audience bypass all human agency and are thus able to occupy God's own point of view.

In regard to the soundtrack, which is as cleverly innovative as the photograph as the image generated through the combined power of microscopes and computers performs its magic-carpet feat, we in the audience also hear plaintive sounds, somewhere between noise and music. The characters do not seem to hear them; the sounds are not presented as occurring in the lab. But the almost musical hissing and crackling is not mere background music; it is not like the doomsday music in a Hitchcock film, which reiterates the message being communicated both by the photographic format and by the plot or content. The sound is a sign in its own right. As the noise/music starts, one technician says to another: 'Let the bones whisper to you.' This underscores the point that the crackling heard by the audience is not mere studio orchestra work; it is, rather, the bones' own lines. Of course, it would provoke laughter and break all the codes of television drama to have the bones literally speak. But when the bones are given some lines of non-human speech, this does not come across as at all ridiculous, however implausible it may sound when an attempt is made (as I am doing now) to capture it in rational words and without images or sound effects. The overall impression at the point of consumption, the impression that the audience has, is that the bones do indeed hoarsely whisper the truth of the crime – and they do so not only to the technician but also to viewers directly. We know the true story of how the bone was broken even before the technician who is our guide has time to tell the story in words to his colleagues.

Thus we are lulled into believing that no interpretation or judgement is required, either on the part of detectives or on our part as an inquisitive audience. We are led to believe that the bones and other clues speak for themselves, literally, telling us in sound the same story that we also see in images as the pieces of the victim's body are taken back to their pre-crime state, resurrection-style, only to be immediately made to endure once again the trauma that caused the victim's death. The image of the clue (the broken bone) itself transports us, without any apparent human intervention, to the real (not deduced) crime. It then takes us briefly back to the pristine body before the crime – and then, as if switching from rewind to fast forward, it brings us back again to the present, to the body as clue.

The viewer is thus transported back in time – something that neither microscopes nor CAT scans can do, of course, but which conforms with the fundamental logic, the backward-reasoning logic, of any murder mystery or detective story. And the viewer feels as if he/she has seen the crime itself, with his/her own eyes. Who needs to hear Sherlock Holmes's long and tedious account of how he deduced what must have taken place? Who even needs a smart Sherlock Holmes actively using his brain as he peers through the magnifying glass to decide what is a clue and what is mere background? We are transported in time instantly and are thus able to see for ourselves the truth of the crime 'as it really happened', as the famous historian Otto Ranke said when describing the (impossible) ideal of history-writing.

References

Doyle, A. 'Cops: television policing as policing reality', in Cavender, G. and Fishman, M. (eds), *Entertaining Crime: Television Reality Programs*, 1998, New York: Aldine de Gruyter.

Ellis, J. *Seeing Things: Television in an Age of Uncertainty*, 2000, London: IB Touris Publishers.

Rapping, E. *Law and Justice as Seen on TV*, 2003, New York: New York University Press.

Wolf, D. *Law & Order Crime Scenes*, 2003, New York: Barnes & Noble.

Critical connections

Rather than simply analysing the content of television drama, Valverde's aim is to develop a wider understanding of different forms of cop show or variations within the genre – not only through relevant academic literatures, but also through close reference to professional critics and programme makers themselves. This type of ethnographic approach is particularly rare within sociological analyses considering representations of crime and criminal justice on television, partly because access to key players – writers, producers, directors – is so difficult to negotiate. The analysis of TV fiction and reality programming's blurring of the boundaries between the represented and the real picks up one of the central postmodern themes running throughout this Reader. First articulated by Jean Baudrillard (Reading 6) in his account of simulacra and simulation, the notion of hyperreality and 'death of the real' have been adopted by criminological researchers to varying degrees. Sheila Brown's (Reading 39) discussion of deviance in cyberspace takes this notion further, and Katja Franko Aas (Reading 40) draws heavily on Baudrillard's notion of simulation in her analysis of online and offline social governance.

Discussion questions

- To what extent can 'reality' police programmes like *COPS* be said to represent the 'reality' of policing?
- What particular qualities does *CSI: Crime Scene Investigation* possesses that makes it one of the most popular shows on American TV?
- Valverde identifies within a range of crime shows particular conventions of narrative development: how might these conventions be understood in terms of 'genre' and 'verisimilitude' (see also Readings 11, 22 and 26)?

Robert Reiner, Sonia Livingstone and Jessica Allen

CASINO CULTURE: MEDIA AND CRIME IN A WINNER–LOSER SOCIETY (2001)

Introduction and context

REINER *ET AL.* (2001) conduct a longitudinal analysis exploring the changing content and context of crime and criminal justice in news and entertainment media between 1945 and 1991. They explore film, television and the British press, locating their discussion within the context of the 'risk society' (Beck, 1992). Fundamentally, the 'risk society' thesis suggests that the transition from modernity to late- or postmodernity has been characterised by a shift away from the focus on economic inequality toward the nature, patterning and control of 'risk'. Whereas modernity was characterised by the positive problem of acquiring 'goods' (income, education, housing and health), the 'risk society' is characterised by the negative problem of avoiding 'bads' (global warming, AIDS, pollution ... and crime) (see also Mythen and Walklate, Reading 41). In the unequal society, the distribution of 'goods' could be broadly understood in terms of class. In the unsafe or 'risk' society, 'bads' are global and affect everyone more or less equally, regardless of class position. Politics has been reconfigured within this new environment, and political communication focuses less on delivering us our dreams and more on protecting us from our nightmares (Curtis, 2004).

Reiner *et al.* (2001) employ a mix of quantitative and qualitative research methods, first to identify trends and patterns and then to explore them in greater depth. Both news and fictional representations of offenders changed relatively little throughout their study, though they have become less sympathetic towards the structural influences on criminality and more condemnatory of what is perceived as individual evil. Whilst portrayals of the criminal justice system remain supportive overall, they have nonetheless become more complex and critical, paying greater attention, for example, to police ineffectiveness, corruption within the criminal justice system, and conflict between criminal justice institutions. The most significant change relates to representations of the crime victim, who has 'moved from a shadowy and purely functional role in crime narratives to a pivotal position. Their suffering increasingly constitutes the subject position or the *raison d'être* of the story' (Reiner *et al.*, 2000: 187). The increasing centrality of crime victims in the media reflects the 'discovery', growing concern about and subsequent politicisation of the victim within criminal justice systems (and criminology) throughout the 1980s (Davies *et al.* 2007).

Introduction: from riskophobia to riskophilia – the coming of casino culture

[. . .] One of the most influential theorizations of the current stage of social development (which has become increasingly applied to issues of crime and justice) is the concept of the 'risk society'. [. . .] For all the proliferation of risk discourses, inside and outside the academy, there is much ambiguity about what is involved. The pioneering analyses of 'risk society' (notably Beck, 1992) do not refer to issues of crime or disorder, leaving even more interpretive latitude for those who seek to apply the concept to criminology and criminal justice. There is a particular ambiguity about how far the notion of 'risk society' implies a change in the extent or nature of risk, as distinct from new cultural sensibilities and techniques of seeking to achieve security.

With regard to the kinds of risks on which Beck concentrates (physical dangers of various kinds such as environmental and food hazards) it is implausible to see them as more threatening in some absolute sense than the dangers of 'class society' or earlier social formations. Rather the point is that they are 'manufactured' as opposed to 'external' risks (Giddens, 1998: 27–8). In addition one of Beck's central points is that in 'risk society' the threats are global and face everyone more or less equally. Although there may be attempts by the wealthy and powerful to gain positions of advantage in the 'distribution of bads' these are largely futile.

None of these features of the seminal 'risk society' analyses apply straightforwardly to crime and criminal justice. Arguably there *is* in an absolute sense more danger of criminal victimization now than in earlier stages of modernity (although fear of crime is often seen as being disproportionate to 'objective' measures of risk). Crime has always been a 'manufactured' rather than 'external' risk, in that its incidence is socially constructed – although a key feature of popular and media conceptions is the criminal as 'outsider'. Although we do know from victimization surveys that crime disproportionately hits the more vulnerable sections of the population, it nonetheless is a threat that faces all social strata, even if more powerful or affluent groups do increasingly seek to buy more adequate provisions for security.

The concept of 'risk society' connotes not only a shift in the nature of risk, but also an alteration in cultural sensibilities, and above all, in strategies for dealing with risk. [. . .] Here the analysis has parallels with other influential conceptualizations of the contemporary period, such as theories of postmodernity and neo-liberalism.

Perhaps the key themes are the decline of the grand narrative of progress – the hallmark of modernity – and the 'death of the social' (Rose, 1996; Stenson, 1998). Problems are not seen as having fundamental causes that can be ameliorated by collective policy. Rather they are regarded as either the product of chance or of individual action. The state and its agencies are problems not solutions. Remedies cannot be found in social policy but by changing the behaviour of the people responsible, and by individual self-help strategies such as insurance or personal protection. Problems and solutions are demoralized, de-mystified, secularized. Events are judged problematic not in terms of absolute moral codes but because they risk causing harm to us, or to those we identify or at least empathize with. Actions are good not because they embody virtue but because they work.

Individuals are held responsible for their fates, in a 'winner–loser culture' (James, 1995). In an increasingly deregulated global market place, where there is a continuous proliferation of new millionaires and new paupers, the stakes are ever higher. The National Lottery is the quintessence of this new casino culture. Instead of the cradle to grave security of a welfare state the ideal is winner takes all, and the compensation for the substantial risk of losing is the scintilla of hope of being that winner. Some thirty years ago when he constructed his magisterial theory of justice (as what has proved to be an intellectual Custer's Last Stand defence of the welfare state) John Rawls could still assume with some plausibility that people were risk averse (Rawls, 1973: 152–61). This riskophobic culture has clearly been replaced by a riskophiliac one. The media play a pivotal role in reproducing this, celebrating the winners as celebrities and devaluing any styles of life other than spectacular consumerism.

In relation to crime and criminal justice this is reflected in many changes of the last quarter of the twentieth century. The optimistic paradigm that crime could and would be conquered by social progress and rehabilitation of individual offenders, which dominated policy from the late nineteenth century until the 1970s (Garland, 1985, 2000), has been eclipsed by a combination of more pragmatic and more punitive responses. This has been underlined by an aggressive analytic 'know-nothingism' epitomized above all by James Q. Wilson's scornful dismissal of the idea of social 'root causes' of crime in favour of a tough administrative realism. The 'rehabilitative ideal' has been replaced by incapacitation, general deterrence and revenge as the purposes of penal policy.

Criminals now are to be condemned and contained, not understood and changed. 'Tough on the causes of crime' means a variety of what David Garland has dubbed 'criminologies of everyday life': pragmatic routines to minimize opportunities for offending such as situational crime prevention and targetting 'hot spots' (Garland, 1996). Without a social dimension, individual target-hardening becomes a burgle-my-neighbour tactic; problem-oriented policing becomes problem-suppressing policing. The police are no longer custodians and symbols of public tranquillity and virtue, but compete in a commercialized marketplace for security with other (mainly private) suppliers (South, 1997; Johnston, 2000). Customers (private and governmental) choose the best deals from a 'pick'n'mix' policing bazaar (Reiner, 1997a: 1038–9). Crime becomes a practical hazard not a moral threat. The criminal justice system operates increasingly in actuarial terms of seeking to calculate and minimize risks pragmatically rather than achieving broader ideals of justice (Feeley and Simon, 1994). [. . .]

This chapter attempts to assess the role of mass media representations of crime and criminal justice in relation to the above changes. It does so by considering the implications of our historical study of mass media representations of crime and criminal justice since the Second World War. [. . .]

Research methods

[. . .]

The historical content analyses

The cinema research combined a generic analysis of all films released in Britain since 1945 (which included an increasing proportion of US films over the period), and detailed quantitative and qualitative content analyses of box-office hits. The latter were chosen as approximating the most influential films of the period. For television, we focused on fictional crime series. The ephemeral character of television news presents insuperable problems of non-availability for the study of long-term changes in content. [. . .]

What counts as 'crime' is, of course, subject to enormous definitional and conceptual debate and difficulties. For the purposes of this research a straightforward legal positivist definition was adopted: we took a 'crime' in a media narrative to be any act which appeared to violate English criminal law (at the time of the story).

In the quantitative analyses of our data we adopted a three-stage periodization: 1955–64; 65–79; and 1980–91. Clearly any single year cut-off points are fairly arbitrary. However, this broad three-fold division corresponds to the picture given by most histories of the period since the end of the Second World War. The first period is one of post-war recovery, merging into what is usually seen as an era of unprecedented mass affluence, consumerism, and political and social consensus. The middle period – the 'sixties' – sees the continuation of mass affluence and consumerism. However, it was widely experienced as a time of conflict, change, and questioning of traditional patterns of morality, authority, sexuality, and relationships between generations and ethnic groups. The third period sees the attempts by the Reagan and Thatcher governments to combine a return to earlier moral certainties with neo-liberal economic policies. In the end the latter tended to undermine the former, although 'culture wars' about morality, gender and family continue to rage. What became increasingly clear was that there had occurred a profound break in social and economic development during the 1970s, whether this is interpreted primarily in terms of late or postmodernity, risk society, globalization or other competing theorizations. We began the research with this rough periodization in mind, but translated it into the precise three periods we used for the quantitative analysis after this appeared to fit the emerging data most coherently.

Film   The film study was based on two different samples. A random 10 % sample of all films released in Britain since 1945 was drawn from a source which also provided synopses of these (*Film Review* which has been published annually since 1944). This sample was coded by genre to calculate the changing proportion of crime films (i.e. with narratives centred on the commission and/or investigation of a crime), and the extent to which there were significant representations of crime in other films. A smaller sample of 84 films was drawn randomly from the 196 crime movies since

1945 that had been listed amongst the top box-office hits in Britain. These were viewed and analysed in detail to assess qualitative changes. [. . .]

Television   The television study examined all the top twenty television programmes for every year since 1955 (when audience ratings first became available). These were coded according to genre to see the changing proportions which were focused on crime or criminal justice.

Audience reception of crime media

Historical study of how audiences interpret mass media representations of crime and criminal justice clearly raises profound methodological difficulties. Our project combined methods from oral history with audience reception methods, using homogeneous focus groups to interpret specific media contents. The key dimension of analysis was age, although we also considered gender, ethnicity and class. Audience age indexes two phenomena: position in the life course and generation.

Selected examples of images and texts were used to stimulate focus group discussion of the media in relation to crime, social change, and notions of authority and responsibility. After a pilot group discussion, sixteen focus groups (of approximately 20, 40, 60, and 80 years of age, each separated by gender and into two rough class groupings)were recruited from seven locations in the south-east of England (covering urban, suburban areas). Ninety-six people were interviewed in all.

The changing content of media representations of crime

Crime narratives and representations are, and always have been, a prominent part of the content of all mass media. Our study attempts to assess the long-term trends in crime content since the Second World War. For the cinema we measured the proportion of all narratives which were primarily crime stories. We also estimated the proportion that had significant crime content, even if not primarily focused on crime. The absence of change in the quantity of crime represented would not falsify any claims about possible relationships between trends in media content and developments in crime and criminal justice. Nonetheless a significant increase or decrease would be of considerable interest in examining the validity of the different discourses about the media/crime link. For example, an increase in crime stories might be seen as related to the rise of crime risk discourse.

In our random sample of cinema films there did not appear to be any significant pattern of change in the extent of representation of crime. There is no clear trend for the proportion of crime films to either rise or fall, although there are many sharp fluctuations in individual years around this basic steady state (Allen, Livingstone and Reiner, 1997). Crime has clearly been a significant concern of the cinema throughout the post-war period (and probably before that as well). In most years around 20 per cent of all films released are crime films.

[. . .] Changes in levels and patterns of offending, or of fear of crime, cannot be attributed to a sheer quantitative increase in crime content in the media. [. . .] Changes in the way that crime narratives are constructed are more significant than their sheer quantity.

Media crime patterns

Our analysis of cinema films distinguished three types of crime in terms of their function within the narrative (Allen, Livingstone and Reiner, 1998). Adapting Hitchcock's terminology for the object that is pursued in a story, we call the crime providing the primary focus or motive for a story the 'McGuffin'. 'Consequential' crimes are those which are necessary adjuncts of this, either before or after (for example in order to escape capture). 'Contextual' crimes are those which are represented in the narrative but are not related to the 'McGuffin' (for example the bank robbery Clint Eastwood encounters while munching a hamburger in *Dirty Harry*).

Throughout the period 1945–91 the most frequent 'McGuffin' was homicide, but to a slightly diminishing extent: in 50% of crime films between 1945–64; 35% for 1965–79; 45% 1980–91. Property crime 'McGuffins' virtually disappeared: 32% of films 1945–64; 20% 1965–79; only 5% 1980–91. Sex-related 'McGuffins' (e.g. rape or prostitution) have become more frequent, although still rare: 3% 1945–64; 10% 1965–79; 15% 1980–91. Drugs have shown a curvilinear pattern: 2% 1945–64; 10% 1965–79; 5% 1980–91.

The extent of violence depicted in the presentation of the 'McGuffin' has increased considerably. The proportion of films in which it was associated with significant pain rose from 2% 1945–64; 20% 1965–79; to 40% 1980–91. This has consequences for the typical representation of offenders, victims, police and the criminal justice system.

The representation of consequential crimes has changed even more markedly. Between 1945–64 14% of films depicted no consequential crimes, 43% showed one, and 43% featured multiple consequential crimes. After that there are hardly any films without consequential crimes, and over 80% feature multiple offences of this kind. The extent of violence depicted in these crimes has also multiplied considerably. Whereas between 1945–64 74% of films had consequential crimes involving little or no violence, and only 5% featured significant levels of violence, by 1980–91 these proportions had changed to 16% and 47% respectively.

The representation of contextual crimes is the most striking change. Contextual crimes have proliferated, connoting a society pervaded by generalized crime risks. Between 1945–64 32% of films had no contextual offending at all, 9% showed just one contextual crime, and 59% had multiple crimes of this type. By 1980–91 only 15% of films showed no contextual crimes, and 80% featured multiple offences unrelated to the central narrative. An increasing proportion of contextual offences are violent and/or sex- and drug-related, and a diminishing proportion are property offences (as with the 'McGuffin' crimes). The extent of violence portrayed in these offences has increased. In 1945–64 90% had no or only minor violence, by 1980–91 these proportions had changed to 29% and 65% respectively.

Overall then our findings show that although murder has always been the most common 'McGuffin' crime in films, there is over our period a diminishing proportion featuring property crime, and an increase in the representation of violent crimes of all kinds. The extent of violence inflicted in these offences has sharply increased. The large rise in the depiction of consequential and especially contextual offences implies a picture of a society much more threatened by all pervasive risks of violent crime. [. . .]

This means that the standard research finding that the media over-report violent and sexual offences disproportionately (Reiner, 1997b: 199–203) requires some qualification. This has indeed been true throughout the post-war period, but the extent of the imbalance has increased markedly. [. . .]

Criminal justice

The representation of the criminal justice system and its agents has changed in substantial ways. However, on most dimensions the representation of criminal justice alters in a curvilinear pattern. Variables are at their highest or lowest in the middle years (1964–79) of our period.

The cinema research shows an increasing prevalence of criminal justice agents as heroes (or at any rate the central protagonists) of narratives, although this is subject to something of a U-shaped pattern. The key aspect is the rise (and partial fall) of police heroes. The police are the protagonists of only 9% of films between 1945–64, but 50% of those between 1965–79, and 40% of those between 1980–91. There was a continuous decline in amateur investigator heroes: 36% 1945–64; 5% 1965–79; none 1980–91. Victim-related protagonists clearly increased, but also in a curvilinear pattern: 13% in 1945–64; none 1965–79; 25% 1980–91. Overall there is a clear decline of amateur sleuths in favour of criminal justice professionals, especially the police, and an increase in victim or victim-related heroes. The police predominance is especially marked in the middle period, although substantial more recently as well. The rise of police protagonists is structurally related to the representation of crime risks as all pervasive, and hence requiring a bureaucratic organization of professionals to contend with it.

Overall the representation of police protagonists has become less positive over time, although there is a clear curvilinear pattern. Critical and negative images are most common in the period 1964–79, although they are more frequent in 1980–91 than 1945–64. This applies both to the success and the integrity of the police protagonists.

The police and criminal justice system are portrayed as slightly less successful over time. Throughout the period the overwhelming majority of movie crimes are cleared-up. However, there is a marked change in how this is achieved. In the first period 1945–64 the most common method of clear-up is that the offender is brought to justice: 39%. In the two later periods this becomes very infrequent (15% 1965–79, 10% 1980–91). The most frequent method of clear-up becomes the killing of the offender – in 35% of films 1965–91.

The police come to be represented more frequently as vigilantes than as enforcers of the law. In 89% of films between 1945–64 the police remain within the parameters of due process of law in their methods, but they break these in 80% of films between 1965–79, and 67% from 1980–91. The police are also shown as more likely to use force, both reasonable and excessive force. Between 1945–64 the police protagonists are not shown using force in 54% of films, and in 40% the force used is reasonable and proportionate (e.g. minimal self-defence). Only in 3% of films were they shown using excessive force. But this is shown in 44% of films from 1965–79, and 25% from 1980–91.

The police protagonists are represented as entirely honest in personal terms in 89% of films between 1945–64; but only in 67% between 1965–79, and 77% 1980–91. In no films in the early period are they shown as seriously corrupt, but they are in 13% of films 1965–79, and 15% 1980–91. They are shown as engaged in petty corruption in 11% of 1945–64 films; 20% between 1965–79, and 8% between 1980–91. They are also represented as increasingly personally deviant (in terms of such matters as excessive drinking, swearing, and extra-marital sexual activity).

The criminal justice system is also portrayed as more divided internally. Conflict within police organizations features in only 15% of films 1945–64, but 79% from 1965 to 1979, and 56% 1980–91. Conflict between criminal justice organizations, such as the police and the courts, also becomes more frequent. It is represented in only 20% of films 1945–64, but 70% from 1965–91. Police officers themselves become more internally divided: conflict between buddies occurs in only 9% of films 1945–64, but over 50% thereafter. [. . .]

Criminals

We have not uncovered any significant trends in the portrait of the personal characteristics of offenders. Throughout the period they are predominantly middle-aged or older (though there is a small tendency to portray young offenders more frequently), white (although the proportion of ethnic minority offenders is increasing slightly) [. . .], and male (confirming earlier studies). One way our findings challenge previous content analyses is that we find that only a minority of stories feature middle or upper-class offenders. This does not change significantly over time.

Criminals are overwhelmingly portrayed unsympathetically throughout the period. [. . .] There is little change, and what there is suggests an increasingly unfavourable image of offenders. For example, they are shown using excessive or sadistic force in an increasing proportion of films (80% between 1980–91 as compared to 50% 1945–64). They are portrayed as committing crimes because of external causal pressure in a decreasing minority of films (30% 1945–64; around 15% thereafter). Increasingly they are represented as purely evil and enjoying their offending (from around 60% 1945–64 to 85% 1980–91). Films in which some sympathy is shown for offenders have declined over time: 40% 1945–64; 20% 1965–79; 15% 1980–91.

This predominantly (and slightly increasingly) unfavourable portrayal of offenders goes against the claim that crime has been stimulated by more sympathetic media representations. However, crime is represented as increasingly rewarding. In 91% of films between 1945–64 'crime does not pay' in that the offenders are unsuccessful and/or apprehended. After 1965 this is only true in 80% of the stories – although this still suggests an overwhelming message about the folly of offending (especially in the light of the low and diminishing clear-up rates found in official statistics).

Victims

Probably the clearest and most significant changes we have found are in the representation of victims. Victims have moved from a shadowy and purely functional role in crime narratives to a pivotal position. Their suffering increasingly constitutes the subject position or the *raison d'être* of the story (mirroring the 'discovery' of, and increasing concern about, victims in criminal justice systems around the world – cf. Rock, 1990; Zedner, 1997). In the film sample, no concern is evinced for the plight of the victim in 45% of cases 1945–64; 35% 1965–79; but only 11% 1980–91. Victimization is shown as having traumatic consequences in 74% of films between 1980–91, 40% 1965–79, but only 25% 1945–64. Victims are increasingly represented as the protagonists of films, that is to say as the principal subject position. They are protagonists in 56% of the films where they are presented as characters at all as (opposed to corpses or case files) between 1980–91, but only 26% 1965–79, and 16% 1945–64. [. . .]

Conclusion: from morality tales to calculated risks

The media representation of crime since the Second World War exhibits a clear peri-odization in terms of three ideal-type narrative structures. The first post-war decade is a period of consensus and social harmony in representations of criminal justice. Crime stories [. . .] present an image of society as based largely on shared values and a clear yet accepted hierarchy of status and authority. Crime was as defined by Durkheim: it united all healthy consciences to condemn and extirpate it. Criminals were normally brought to justice: crime did not pay. The forces of law always got their man. The criminal justice system was almost invariably represented as righteous, dedicated, and efficient.

During the mid-1960s the dominant mode of representation of crime and justice shifts discernibly. The values and integrity of authority come to be questioned increasingly. Doubts about the justice and effectiveness of criminal justice proliferate. Increasing prominence is given to conflict: between ethnic groups, men and women, social classes, even within the criminal justice system itself. Whilst street-cops more frequently feature as protagonists, they are often morally tarnished if not outright corrupt. However, the increasing criticism of the social order and criminal justice is from a standpoint of reform, the advocacy of preferable alternatives.

Since the late 1970s another shift is discernible, the advent of what could be called a post-critical era. Stories are increasingly bifurcated between counter-critical ones, which seek to return as far as possible to the values of consensus, and those which represent a hopelessly disordered beyond-good-and-evil world, characterized by a Hobbesian war of all against all. It is this division of narratives which accounts for the curvilinear pattern of many variables: there is some attempt to restore the values of the past, challenged by those which portray the exacerbation of the conflicts of the middle period.

Underneath the shifts in the mode of representation of concrete aspects of crime and justice, however, can be discerned a more fundamental shift in discourse. [. . .] This echoes the themes of the 'risk society' discourse outlined earlier. There is a demys-tification of authority and law, a change in the conceptualization of criminal justice from sacred to secular. Pragmatism and contingency push out moralistic certainties.

The marked changes in the representation of victims are the clearest emblem of the new risk discourse in popular cultural conceptions of crime. Crime moves from being something that must be opposed and controlled *ipso facto* – because the law defines it thus – to a contested category. Crime *may* be wrong, but this is a pragmatic issue, turning on the risk of harm to individual victims that audiences sympathize or empathize with, not from the authority of the law itself. The moral status of charac-ters in a story [. . .] is no longer ascribed by their formal legal role. It has to be established from scratch in each narrative, and turns on who causes serious suffering to the vic-tims occupying the subject position. Increasingly the latter may be the legally defined offenders, represented as victimized by a criminal injustice system.

However, the majority of narratives continue to work to justify ultimately the criminal justice viewpoint, although this has to be achieved by demonstrating particular harm to identifiable individual victims. In this sense the media both continue to repro-duce a more complex and brittle order, and to function as sources of social control. Above all they reflect the increasing individualism of a less deferential and more desubordinate culture. Media narratives traditionally performed the ideological work of reconciling tensions between the values of individualism and community, suggesting a dynamic interdependence between them. Plots rescued individualism from tipping over into egoism as regularly as their rugged individualist heroes came in the end to act as saviours of social order (Bellah *et al.*, 1996: 144—7). In the risk discourse which has come to prevail, however, heroes are merely the fittest individuals in a struggle for self-preservation.

References

Allen, J., Livingstone, S. and Reiner, R. (1997) 'The Changing Generic Location of Crime in Film: A Content Analysis of Film Synopses', *Journal of Communication* 47:89–101.

Allen, J., Livingstone, S. and Reiner, R. (1998) 'True Lies: Changing Images of Crime in British Postwar Cinema'. *European Journal of Communication* 13: 53–75.

Beck, U. (1992) *Risk Society*. London: Sage.

Bellah, R., Madsen, R., Sullivan, W., Swidler, A. and Tipton, S. (1996) *Habits of the Heart*, second edition. Berkeley: University of California Press.

Feeley, M. and Simon, J. (1994) 'Actuarial Justice: the Emerging New Criminal Law' in D. Nelken (ed.) *The Futures of Criminology*, pp.173–201. London: Sage.

Garland, D. (1985) *Punishment and Welfare*. Aldershot: Gower.

Garland, D. (1996) 'The Limits of the Sovereign State: Strategies of Crime Control in Contemporary Society'. *British Journal of Criminology* 36: 1–27.

Garland, D. (2000) "The Culture of a High-Crime Society'. *British Journal of Criminology* (forthcoming).

Giddens, A. (1998) 'Risk Society: the Context of British Politics' in J. Franklin (ed.) *The Politics of Risk Society*. Cambridge: Polity.

James, O. (1995) *Juvenile Violence in a Winner—Loser Culture*. London: Free Association Books.

Johnston, L. (2000) *Policing Britain*. London: Longman.

Rawls, J. (1973) *A Theory of Justice*. Oxford: Oxford University Press.

Reiner, R. (1997a) 'Policing and the Police' in M. Maguire, R. Morgan and R. Reiner (eds) *The Oxford Handbook of Criminology*. Oxford: Oxford University Press.

Reiner, R. (1997b) 'Media Made Criminality' in *The Oxford Handbook of Criminology*, edited by M. Maguire, R. Morgan and R. Reiner, pp. 189–231. Oxford: Oxford University Press.

Rock, P. (1990) *Helping Victims of Crime*. Oxford: Oxford University Press.

Rose, N. (1996) 'The Death of the Social?', *Economy and Society*, 25: 321–56.

South, N. (1997) 'Control, Crime and "End of Century" Criminology' in Francis, P., Davies, P. and Jupp, V. (eds.) *Policing Futures*. London: Macmillan.

Stenson, K. (1998) 'Beyond Histories of the Present', *Economy and Society* 29: 333–52.

Zedner, L. (1997) 'Victims' in *The Oxford Handbook of Criminology*, edited by M. Maguire, R. Morgan and R. Reiner, pp.577–612. Oxford: Oxford University Press.

Critical connections

Whilst the sympathetic portrayal of crime victims may have increased enormously in recent years, media representations of victims remain highly selective and unrepresentative (Greer, 2007; Chermak, 1995). There exists a complex and at times unpredictable 'hierarchy of victimhood' – influenced but not determined in any straightforward sense by the social divisions of race, class, gender, age and sexuality – that determines which crime victims come within the horizon of media visibility and which do not. While there is no simple formula for predicting media interest in and portrayal of crime victims, notions of 'innocence' and (middle-class) 'respectability' are certainly of key significance (Greer, 2007). As McLaughlin demonstrates in Reading 20, Stephen Lawrence ultimately became an iconic victim following his murder, *despite* his racial minority status, *because* he could be portrayed as completely innocent, the victim of racist thugs whose violence also assaulted the moral values of Middle England. Benedict's analysis of the reporting of the 'Big Dan's' gang rape (Reading 21) similarly highlights the complexity of media narratives, illustrating how victims – perhaps especially in cases of rape and sexual assault – can be portrayed as 'innocent' whilst at the same time having their 'respectability' called into question. The deracialised film interpretation of the case deals with some of these complexities, but starts by locating the victim within a context of unequivocal innocence. That similar trends were found across news and entertainment media formats reinforces the point that media representations do not exist within a political and cultural vacuum, nor are they hermetically sealed off from the wider society. Rather, they are a product of society and derive directly from it.

Discussion questions

- Reiner *et al.* find that victims have become the central focus in a growing number of crime stories. Drawing from Readings 4 and 10, conduct a brief content analysis of crime news *photographs* to see if this finding bears out.
- What evidence can you find in newspaper reporting for the 'politicisation' of crime and criminal justice in a 'risk society'?
- How would you describe the portrayal of victims, offenders and the criminal justice system in the news reports you are looking at?

References

Beck, U. (1992) *Risk Society: Towards a New Modernity*, London: Sage.

Chermak, S. (1995) *Victims in the News*: *Crime and the American News Media*, Boulder, CO: Westview Press.

Curtis, A. (2004) T*he Power of Nightmares: The Rise of the Politics of Fear*, British Broadcasting Corporation.

Davies, P., Francis, P. and Greer., C. (eds) (2007) *Victims, Crime and Society*, London: Sage.

Greer, C. (2007) 'News Media, Victims and Crime', in P. Davies, P. Francis, C. Greer (eds) *Victims, Crime and Society*, London: Sage.

Barry Langford

THE GANGSTER FILM: GENRE AND SOCIETY (2005)

Introduction and context

T RACING THE DEVELOPMENT of the gangster film from the 1930s 'heyday' to the postmodern pastiches of Tarantino's *Reservoir Dogs* (1992) and *Pulp Fiction* (1994) and the knowingly ironic *The Sopranos*, Barry Langford illustrates how the changing image of the gangster can be read as a critique of the dominant socio-economic order. The gangster can be thought of as the 'urban cowboy' of cinema, and gangster movies as articulating a particular view of the metropolitan experience. At the heart of the American gangster movie's appeal, Langford suggests, is the ambivalent position the main protagonists hold with respect to morality, ethnicity, class and the American way. In pre-Second World War renditions, the gangster is simultaneously the embodiment of capitalist entrepreneurialism and individual achievement, a figure of identification for marginalised ethnic communities, a commentary on the meaning of 'family' in a capitalist society, and an anti-heroic critique of mainstream American values. Despite the traditional path of the main protagonist, emerging 'from obscurity to wealth and power, only to end in inevitable downfall and defeat', the message that 'crime does not pay' is often muddied by a wider acknowledgement or appreciation of the structural and cultural conditions that might drive, even encourage, 'gangsterism'. Post-classical representations of the gangster depict a more cynical and frustrated protagonist. Gangsters are less exceptional and more disillusioned. They are involved in the everyday 'business' of organised crime, and characters nostalgically contrast the present (corporate, impersonal, 'corrupt') with an altogether more romanticised vision of the past. The ethnic compartmentalisation and homogenisation that characterised earlier gangster movies gives way to an ethnic pluralisation in later representations, and organised crime spreads not only across media, from cinema to television, but also across communities. The African-American gangster film is very much a product of the 1990s, and offers a starkly contrasting interpretation of the American Dream from that invoked in the pre-War genre classics.

Los Angeles, 1994. Professional hitmen Vincent Vega and Jules Winfield, returning from another successful assignment, have to deal with an unexpected problem: engaged in an animated discussion of chance and fate, Vincent unintentionally proves a point by accidentally discharging his pistol and killing their associate Marvin – more exactly, he splatters his brains copiously over the back seat and windows of their Lincoln Continental. Understandably apprehensive of the unwelcome attention their sanguinary state might draw should they continue cruising the LA freeway, Jules arranges an emergency pitstop at his friend Jimmie's place. The cool welcome Jimmie gives them has nothing to do with any moral revulsion or even physical squeamishness about murder and bloodshed, and everything to do with his apprehensions at how his wife – a night-shift nurse, entirely innocent of Jimmie's underworld connections – will respond upon her imminent return: 'if she comes home and sees a bunch of gangsters doing a bunch of gangster shit, she's going to flip'.

In this celebrated (or notorious) sequence from his breakthrough hit *Pulp Fiction* (1994), Quentin Tarantino's characteristically memorable summation of his (deliberately) two-dimensional criminals and their milieu as 'gangster shit' reveals a good deal about the place the gangster genre occupies in contemporary Hollywood film. In the first place, we are referred to an instantly recognisable and moreover highly stylised and codified world. We, Jules and Jimmie's wife all know 'gangster shit' when we see it. This familiarity is accentuated, flattened out comic-book style, and pushed to a parodic extreme by Tarantino, recasting the gangster's traditional interest in self-expression through personal cool and sartorial style as an ironic mod uniformity: Vincent and Marcellus inherit from the crew in Tarantino's debut film *Reservoir Dogs* (1991) a parodic underworld 'uniform' of black suits, white shirts and skinny black ties, in homage to the early 1960s style of the contract killers played by Lee Marvin and Clu Galager in *The Killers* (1964), among others. This retro intertextual styling immediately announces these gangsters' distance from 'real' crime and their imbrication in an elaborate, hermetic world of their own (it also makes the Hawaiian beach gear in which they begin and end the film still more richly incongruous) (see Bruzzi, 1997: 67–94).

Tarantino's version of gangsterdom may be by some distance the most highly stylised and reflexive in contemporary US cinema, but the invocation of a codified, self-consciously ritualised fictive universe is common to many other films of the 1990s and 2000s. In *Things to Do in Denver When You're Dead* (1995), the sharp suit and slick moves of doomed gangster Jimmy 'the Saint' instantly out him as a gangster to the society girl he dreams of romancing. Michael Mann's gangster films push to a hermetic extreme a 'professionalising' tendency built into the genre from its emergence in the early 1930s, excluding the ordinary public almost entirely from their elaborate cops-and-robbers (and killers) arabesques: in *Thief* (1981), *Heat* (1995) and *Collateral* (2004), theft and murder are largely impersonal affairs in which individual interaction is simply a means to work through obscure principles and opaque codes; wealth is not the object of crime as a means to personal enrichment but a virtually abstract entity that provides a notional stake for the essential contest between pursuer and quarry. In many ways the knowing, stagy tenor in which such narratives unfold recalls the Italian 'Spaghetti Westerns' of the 1960s and early 1970s – it is no coincidence that Sergio

Leone is a major influence on, and is frequently alluded to by, both Tarantino (particularly in *Kill Bill, Vol. 1*, 2003) and other contemporary gangster *auteurs* such as John Woo (notably *A Better Tomorrow*, Hong Kong 1988).

Contemporary gangster films often make the audience's assumed familiarity with gangster film codes and conventions a source of knowing humour, such as Marlon Brando's impersonation of his own famous Godfather character – a kind of 'Corleone drag' – in *The Freshman* (1990), or similar comic turns by actors with established Mob personae such as Joe Pesci (*My Cousin Vinny*, 1992) and James Caan (*Honeymoon in Vegas*, 1992; *Mickey Blue Eyes*, 1999). Although the comic stylisation in the successful HBO TV series *The Sopranos* (1998–) is less broad, the series still takes as a given the post-classical gangster's inevitable refraction through the archaeology of the genre; reflexivity and intertextuality here are less stylistic flourishes than naturalised facts of Mob life, as Tony Soprano and his suburban crew constantly invoke – albeit they reliably fail to live up to – the heroic models of their screen favourites, above all the *Godfather* trilogy (1972, 1974, 1991). In fact, *The Sopranos'* central conceit – that a contemporary organised crime boss is liable to find the challenges of modern American suburban life as taxing, and harder to resolve, than the traditional Mafia business of murder and extortion – is comprehensible and enjoyable largely because the audience are assumed to be familiar with the generic norms and how *The Sopranos* plays with them (see Creeber, 2002; Nochimson, 2003–4).

Our gangsters, ourselves: crime, America and modernity

As these examples help demonstrate, the gangster has become a highly visible figure in contemporary cinema. Indeed, while recent decades have seen Hollywood's other classical genre protagonists (the cowboy, the song-and-dance man, the private eye) suffer a fairly steady decline, the gangster has gone from strength to strength. Since *The Godfather* launched a major generic revival in the early 1970s, the genre's popularity has grown, to the point where the gangster can fairly claim to stand alongside the Western hero as a globally recognisable American cultural emblem (albeit a much more ambivalent and controversial one). As Neale (2000: 77f.) notes, the film gangster like the Western hero has often been discussed in socially symptomatic terms; in fact, the gangster is frequently received as the Westerner's urban mirror image, enacting the conflicts and complexities of an emergent urban modern imaginary as the cowboy enacts those of a residual agrarian myth.[1] Like the Westerner, the gangster and his values have been embedded in a fairly stable thematic and iconographie universe established and consolidated through decades of reiteration and revision, and a certain masculine style and the elaboration of a code of behaviour through acts of decisive violence are central concerns in both genres. A number of writers draw parallels between the two genres: McCarty (1993: xii) describes the gangster film as 'the modern continuation of the Western – a story the Western had grown too old to tell.' Direct narrative translations from one genre to the other, however, though not unknown, are infrequent – *The Oklahoma Kid* (1939) is a straightforward transposition of the Warner's gangster model to the frontier, complete with Cagney and Bogart, during a transitional period for both genres; *Last Man Standing* (1996) relocates *A Fistful of Dollars* (1964; itself a Western remake of Akira Kurosawa's samurai film *Yojimbo*, Japan 1962) to a Depression-era gangster milieu. The rarity of these generic exchanges may point to some more fundamental divergences.

In the first place, during the classical Hollywood period the gangster featured far less frequently *as protagonist* than the cowboy or gunfighter. The sensational success of the first wave of sound-era gangster films in the early 1930s fired a (largely synthetic) moral panic that has been widely covered by genre historians (see Rosow, 1978: 156–71; Maltby, 1995b; Munby, 1999: 93–110) and whose outcome was the announcement in 1935 by the Production Code Administration of a moratorium on Hollywood gangster film production. In fact, the gangster cycle may have run its commercial course by 1935, and since the Production Code – an enforceable reality from 1934 – was going to make the sympathetic or even balanced depiction of any kind of professional criminal very difficult if not impossible, the studios may have felt the sacrifice of the gangster film well worth the public relations benefits it secured. The upshot in any event was that after 1935 gangsters became heavies – antagonists to such 'official' heroes as police detectives, FBI agents and T-Men (Treasury Agents), or the balefully anti-social presence that ensured that an 'outlaw hero' like the private eye, however often at odds with official law enforcement, nonetheless remained visibly on the side of the angels (see Ray, 1985: 59–66). Often enough, the same actors who had risen to stardom in the first wave of gangster films, like James Cagney and Edward G. Robinson, now represented the forces of law and order (frequently with fairly minimal retooling of their screen personae). As early as 1939, the traditional racketeering, bootlegging mobster had already become something of a nostalgic figure: Cagney laments in *The Roaring Twenties* (1939) that 'all the A-1 guys are gone or in Alcatraz . . . all that's left are soda jerks and jitterbugs'. Films focusing once again not on heroic gangbusters and undercover agents but on the career criminal himself and his organisation became possible only with the gradual relaxation of the Code during the 1950s and its final abolition in 1966. *The Godfather* –by no means the only Mafia chronicle of the late 1960s and early 1970s, though by far the most successful – combined a careful sense of prior genre history with a new emphasis on the intricate, hermetic inner world of the Mafia, and its scale and seriousness as well as its huge popularity established new and durable parameters for the genre.

Westerns and gangster films share a defining ambivalence with which they engage the values of settled civilisation. However, where the Western typically offers the spectator a subject position *outside* community from which to measure its gains and losses, the gangster's story unfolds for better or worse wholly within the domain of a highly developed and above all urban culture. In fact, just as the Western works through issues around the closing of the historical frontier, the gangster genre answers to the metropolitan experience of rapid, large-scale urbanisation. Both distil material history into a set of narrative paradigms, character types and typical settings that reshape historical experience into meaningful aesthetic form. The gangster is the man of the city as the cowboy is the man of the frontier.

In terms of genre history, the same endemic critical selectivity we have already seen at work upon the Western and musical canons has in this case ensured that the received version of the 'classic' gangster film and its iconic protagonist in the most influential and widely-read accounts has been derived from an extraordinarily small number of films. According to Schatz (1981: 86–95) 'the narrative formula seemed to spring from nowhere in the early 1930s', when effectively just three films make up 'possibly the briefest classic period of any Hollywood genre'. These films – *The Public Enemy* (1930), *Little Caesar* (1931) and *Scarface* (1932), the first two at Warner Bros., the last independently produced by Howard Hughes – have hugely over-shadowed both their predecessors in the silent and very early sound eras and all but a few later gangster films until the gangster revival launched by *The Godfather*. Hardy (1998: 304–12) directly contradicts Schatz's account of the genre's origins, stating that 'the genre did not spring to life fully formed', but while extending the gangster film's prehistory back into the late silent period and *Underworld* (1927, scripted by Ben Hecht, who also wrote the screenplay for *Scarface*, also cited, though not discussed, by Schatz), he too takes the canonical 1930s trio as generically definitive. Shadoian (2003: 32–61) declares that 'the flurry of early thirties gangster films laid down the bases for future developments', but discusses only *Little Caesar* and *The Public Enemy* and otherwise refers in his section on 'the Golden Age' of the 1930s only to *Scarface* and one other 1930s gangster film, the comedy *The Little Giant* (1933), which is cited in passing to exemplify the ways in which (exactly twelve months after the release of *Scarface*, 'the ultimate expression of the genre's early phase[2]') the Hollywood gangster had become 'a domesticated creature . . . an anachronism . . . the stuff of legend more than fact' (p. 31). However, Rosow (1978: 120–210) lists at least nine other directly contemporaneous gangster films of the late 1920s and early 1930s.

In fact, Hardy, Schatz and even Shadoian do all make reference to one very much earlier film about urban criminal gangs, D. W. Griffith's *The Musketeers of Pig Alley* (1912), but none of them explore either the intervening two decades or the possible relationship between the (early/late) silent-era gangster and his more celebrated successors. Shadoian's view that after Griffith the gangster film 'struggled in unfertilised soil through to the end of the twenties' (p. 29) seems to be the majority opinion. However, Grieveson (2005 forthcoming) discusses a range of more than thirty silent gangster films dating back as early as 1906, of which *Regeneration* (1915) – described by its director Raoul Walsh as 'the first full-length gangster picture ever made' – is perhaps the best-known. While some of these films, such as the series of films in the mid-1910s on white slave rings (notably *Traffic in Souls*, 1913) and another, slightly later series about Chinatown and 'Tong' gangs, seem remote from the concerns of later gangster films, others have quite clear connections: for example, the films dealing with the Italian 'Black Hand' (in *The Godfather, Part II*, the predatory Don Fanucci, the young Vito Corleone's first 'hit', is identified as a member of the Black Hand).[3] This genre archaeology is of more than narrowly academic interest since it bears directly not only on the standard accounts of genre conventions but also on the ways in which the gangster film has most often been historically located.

Numerous studies of the genre, including the three cited above, take it as axiomatic that the seminal gangster films are directly contemporary with the phenomenon they depict. The banner newspaper headlines screaming of mob warfare that spiral dizzily out of the screen, an instant genre cliché (nostalgically invoked in *The Godfather*'s 'mattresses' montage), are taken as metonymic of the gangster film's own determined topicality. Organised crime had of course rocketed, and hence come to national prominence, during America's extraordinary and wholly unsuccessful experiment with Prohibition from 1919 to 1933 (although as Ruth (1996: 45) points out, both as criminological fact and as a public figure the gangster 'predated his bootlegger incarnation'). The unremarkable desire to have a drink set millions of otherwise law-abiding citizens on the wrong side of the law; quenching their thirsts required the establishment of regional networks of illegal production, distribution and sale of alcohol, an immensely profitable if risky business that won huge fortunes and in a few cases – most notably Chicago's Al Capone, the original 'Scarface' – nationwide notoriety, aided and abetted by a sensation-hungry press.

As clearly relevant as Prohibition-era gangsters were to the 1930s gangster cycle, however – Rosow (1978: 201–10) incidentally identifies not *Little Caesar* but *The Doorway to Hell* (1930) as the first film based on Al Capone and a strong influence on the better-known later films – if the gangster is truly to be identified with the Prohibition-era mobster one might ask why such evidently topical and compelling material only found its way onto movie screens very shortly before the Volsted Act was repealed in 1933. Schatz (1981: 85) and others argue that the gangster film had to await the coming of sound (in 1927) for the soundtrack of gangland – 'gunshots, screams, screeching tires' and also a specific style of fast-paced, hard-boiled dialogue – to bring the gangster and his urban milieu fully to life.[4] However, what Grieveson and other scholars of early cinema's relationship to urban modernity demonstrate is that throughout the silent era – in US political terms roughly congruent with the Progressive period – there was a well-established discourse that comprehended crime and vice in America's burgeoning metropolises (above all New York and Chicago) in terms of social hygiene and reform (see Grieveson, 1997, 2005 forthcoming; Gunning, (1997), and that the silent-era gangster was more likely to be conceived in these terms than in the quasi-Nietzschean mode often identified with the 1930s film gangster (Rosow, 1978: 67 also notes that gangster films first appeared 'in the context of Progressive documentary realism'). In other words, the silent gangster film used a different, rather than simply an inadequate, 'language' to articulate the experience of urban modernity.

The emphasis on social environmental factors in the production of criminality and the associated conviction in the efficacy of reform, meant that one of the dominant themes of silent-era gangster films was the concept of personal redemption from a life of crime (such conversion narratives also dominated the Victorian and early-twentieth-century stage melodramas that provided early film-makers with many of their drama-turgic models). The striking absence of any suggestion of remorse or efforts at restitution from the protagonists of the early 1930s films who – with the possible and limited exception of Tom Powers in *The Public Enemy* – go wholly unrepentant to their violent ends is often cited as a decisive break and an indication of the classic gangster's breakout into modernity from the residual Victorianism of the silent era. In fact, the reintroduction of such moralistic motifs into later 1930s gangster films, both pre-moratorium (*Manhattan Melodrama*, 1934, whose gangster protagonist Blackie (Clark Gable) virtually lobbies his best friend the DA to send him to the chair) and after (*Dead End*, 1936, with its slum setting and strong elements of social critique, and *Angels With Dirty Faces*, 1938, whose gangster anti-hero (Cagney) feigns cowardly breakdown on his way to the gas chamber to save the next generation of street kids from wanting to emulate him) is often cited as evidence of their generic inauthen-ticity and the gangster film's general decline after *Scarface*. However, if the 1930–32 classics are not regarded as the gangster film's originary moment but located in a longer generic history, it is if anything the repentance theme that starts to look like the main-stream generic tradition and the titanic *Scarface*-style individualist the exception.

Given for example that the genre has influentially been read as an allegory of both the allure and the potentially catastrophic consequences of untrammelled individualism, it may be no accident that the gangster film thrives in the early years of the Depression, in the immediate aftershock of the Wall Street Crash of October 1929. The traumatic collapse of the 1920s boom – fuelled by wild stock-market speculation rather than industrial expansion – not only undermined the triumphal capitalism of the Coolidge and Hoover eras, but called into question the very premises of the American social and economic system. In the years before more positive, pro-social models of responding to the crisis emerged under Roosevelt's New Deal, the screen gangster violently articulated the disturbing possibility that the quintessentially American values encapsulated in the 'Horatio Alger myth' – the poor boy who makes good through his own determination, hard work, dedication to achieving his goals and so forth – might actually prove destructive, both to himself and to the wider society, if left uncurbed. The gangster shares the Alger myth's attractive qualities of vitality, vigour and determination; but he also exposes their dark underbelly: recklessness, selfishness, sadism and an ultimately self-defeating spiral of violent self-assertion. Thus the gangster film typically stands in an at least implicitly critical relationship to the society it depicts. In Robert Warshow's ([1948] 1975a) influential argument, to the (American) audience the gangster is an exemplary and admonitory figure of fatally overreaching ambition, yet one who also bespeaks some uneasy truths about American capitalism. This critical dimension to the gangster film may be qualified by the perception that the gangster's typical narrative trajectory – from obscurity to wealth and power, only to end in inevitable downfall and defeat – is constructed to underpin a simplistic moral that 'crime does not pay'. As Munby points out, however, the intense controversy culminating in the Hays' Office 'moratorium' implies at the very least that such a message, even if intended, was not wholly or satisfactorily transparent to contemporary Establishment viewers of 1930s gangster films. On the contrary, elite opinion in this period was persistently exercised at the prospect that the glamorous portrayal of Mob life in these films – notwithstanding the gangster's inevitable bloody doom – would attract impressionable urban youths towards a life of crime rather than deter them from it (see also Springhall, 1998).

Munby and other commentators also suggest, however, that elite deprecation of the gangster film was in fact less a reflection of real anxiety about these films' role in encouraging an upsurge in violent racketeering than a focal point for a deeper nativist hostility to the growing visibility and political and economic power of new ethnic groups in the early-twentieth-century United States, directed at Catholics in general and Italian-Americans in particular. The Depression-era gangsters might thus serve as cautionary fables not only of individualism rampant, heedless of social constraints, but also of the dangers of ethnic particularism versus assimilation. Portraying Italian- (as in *Little Caesar* and *Scarface*) or Irish- (as in *The Public Enemy*) Americans as gangsters might seem to serve such xenophobic ideologies rather well. (The scenes of public outrage at gangland excesses in *Scarface* – interpolated just prior to release over director Howard Hawks's protests and without his cooperation – include a reference to the gangsters as 'not even citizens!' suggesting that one part of the gangster film's agenda is to render criminal violence 'unAmerican'.) Unsurprisingly, prominent Italian-Americans like New York Mayor Fiorella La Guardia quickly denounced such characters as Rico (in *Little Caesar*) as defamatory. (Vigorous protests accompanied the production and release of *The Godfather*, and have themselves become the object of satire in *The Sopranos*.)

On the other hand, by implying that American society, far from welcoming the 'huddled [immigrant] masses' into the mainstream culture, relegated ethnic minorities to the economic margins where asocial activities offered in effect the only escape route from poverty and social exclusion, the gangster film could be read as a corrosive critique of hegemonic American values. And, endowed with so much more vigour, wit and charisma than the ossified forces of established authority (criminal or legal) he opposes and overcomes, the gangster provides a powerful – and a transgressive – figure of identification for the ethnic, urban constituency he represents.

Alongside ethnicity, as an urban form dealing with responses to deprivation in a highly materialistic culture, the gangster film also inevitably sheds light on a greater unmentionable, not only in Hollywood but in American society generally: class. While the 'official' American ideology – including the Turnerian myth of the frontier – stigmatised class societies and class struggle as 'Old World' evils that had been purged from the idealised American commonwealth, the growth of labour unions and such political movements as Populism meant that class conflict was in fact at its most intense in American society in the years immediately before and after the First World War. Lulled by the briefly shared prosperity of the 1920s, the onset of the Depression saw the spectre of class conflict return with a vengeance (see Parrish, 1992: 405 21). As with ethnicity, the gangster ambivalently enacts some of the brutal realities of class in modern America, both exposing and falling victim to the exigencies of class struggle. In fact, the gangster might be seen as an exemplary subject of ideological misrecognition: Tony Camonte in *Scarface* mistakes the advertising slogan 'the world is yours' as a personal message and sets out to act upon it. Established at the outset of the narrative as belonging to a lower professional and social order than his boss or patron, the gangster devotes his ferocious energies not to assaulting or over-turning this social and economic hierarchy, but to triumphing within it by a more ruthless exploitation of its values than anyone else. Far from being disaffected or alienated from the system, the gangster displays an extreme degree of investment in it. As Edward Mitchell (1976) argues, he wholeheartedly adopts the logic of the key elements of early-twentieth-century American ideology that underpinned the existing distribution of resources – a secularised Puritanism (whose concept of the 'elect' could be adapted to underpin the notion of a heroic 'man of destiny', fated to triumph where others fail) and Social Darwinism (where the neutral processes of natural selection were recast as 'the survival of the fittest' and used to justify the vicious dog-eat-dog contest of laissez-faire capitalism). The gangster's progress up the professional ladder is accompanied by the traditional trappings of self-improvement – not only fine clothes, fast cars and the woman of his dreams, but a self-conscious cultivation of taste (Tony Camonte attends a performance of Somerset Maugham's *Rain*, 'a serious show'; Bugs Raymond (Edward G. Robinson) in the gangster comedy *The Little Giant* studies Plato and acquires abstract modern art). Yet his gutter origins ultimately betray him, both to the audience and to his peers: Poppy finds Tony's apartment 'gaudy', the Corleones endure WASP jibes at their 'guinea charm' and 'silk suits'; Noodles in *Once Upon a Time in America* finally accepts his lost love Deborah's insight that 'he'll always be a two-bit punk'. In fact, it is the gangster's deracination that finally dooms him: his investment in ascending the ladder of class compels him to adopt an alien identity and attenuates the powerful energies of self-assertion that have taken him this far.

A Marxist reading of the genre would stress this notion of self-alienation as an ineradicable function of capitalism, and might point to the corruption of the family, a repeated motif in gangster films since the 1930s, as a key marker. According to Marx and his collaborator Friedrich Engels, the cultural privileging of the 'Holy Family' under bourgeois society is a characteristic ideological ruse – diverting the worker's valid aspirations towards self-realisation in a politically harmless direction (which is also economically necessary to replenish the workforce) while offering him a petty tyranny of his own (over his wife and children) to assuage the misery of his own class oppression. The family unit thus becomes a grim parodic miniature of the unjust and twisted power relations that typify bourgeois capitalism as a whole. However, this implies that the inherently unstable contradictions of class society – and their potential for catastrophic implosion – might also be encountered in the family. From such a perspective, the gangster's characteristic obsession with preserving 'his' family, which nonetheless leads ineluctably to its destruction, becomes enormously revealing. In *Scarface*, Tony Camonte's incestuous bond with his sister Cesca, which drives him to murder her husband, becomes a lover's pact that sees them die side by side in a hail of police bullets. Michael Corleone insists throughout *The Godfather, Part II* that his criminal enterprises, like his father's, are all intended for 'the good of the family'; but as his power crests his family is progressively decimated, and he is himself either directly responsible for, or implicated in, the deaths of his brother-in-law, his brother and his daughter (and his unborn child, aborted by his wife Kay in revulsion against the 'evil' Michael has wrought). His uncomprehending mother reassures him that 'you can never lose your family', but Michael realises that 'times have changed'. Michael's blind pursuit of power, ostensibly in the name of the family, unleashes uncontainable forces that must ultimately destroy it, perfectly encapsulating the Marxist insight that the 'protected' familial realm cannot finally be protected from the atomising forces of the very capitalism that claims to preserve it. In *Force of Evil* (1947) Mob lawyer Joe Morse's involvement with ruthless racketeer Tucker leads indirectly but inexorably to his brother Leo's murder; *The Godfather, Part II* ends with Michael himself ordering the murder of his brother Fredo.

The centrality of the family to the gangster seems at first glance paradoxical: for if anything the gangster is identified with the catastrophic apotheosis of the overweening, even imperial self. The gangster film is in fact the only major genre to be named after its protagonist. Yet as the very word implies, the gangster's apparently hypertrophic individualism is itself only skin-deep and ultimately vulnerable: unlike the Westerner the gangster – an *organised* criminal – is heavily reliant on others not only for his power but for his identity. For all that his story apparently enacts wild self-assertion and radical self-fashioning, from another perspective it becomes apparent that the gangster's selfhood is really constructed through the group. *Goodfellas* (1989) opens with the bald statement in voiceover: 'All my life I always wanted to be a gangster', but the remainder of the film works through with brutal thoroughness the mutually contradictory thrust of the desire on the one hand to belong, and by belonging to confirm an apparently secure selfhood (knowing what one wants and acting to achieve it) versus on the other the inherent logic of violence that will inevitably end up making victims of the gang's own members and reducing the gangster himself to a state of paranoid uncertainty.[5]

Warshow's sense of the gangster as throwing into relief the values of mainstream America is captured in the gangster's ambivalent relationship to his 'family' (the gang *or* his actual blood relations), which may express the profoundly ambiguous place of community in a society that supremely valorises the individual at the expense of the collective. Typically, the gang itself is both indispensable and a burden, even a threat, to the gangster: he needs the support of his soldiers, and it is by his ascent from the ranks that his self-assertion is measured; yet the gangster knows only too well how dangerous it is to rely on any ties, even those of blood. Not only the outright treachery, but the simple unreliability of one's associates, is a repeated trope of the genre: Fredo Corleone's weakness and resentment make him an unwitting accomplice to an attempt on his brother Michael's life in *The Godfather, Part II* (in the first *Godfather* it is Fredo who is driving his father, and who fails to draw his own gun, when the Don is shot down in the street); Carlito spends most of *Carlito's Way* (1993) trying, and failing, to extricate himself from the toils of his attorney Dave Kleinfeld's greed and recklessness. The gangster film implicitly ironises its subject inasmuch as it stresses the self-sufficient individual the gangster desires to be and insists he is, yet – precisely because he is a *gangster* – he can never become.

This performative contradiction of radical autonomy and dependency can also be read in psychoanalytic terms: the gangster's riotous self-assertion, whether expressed through the violence he inflicts on others or through his characteristic ostentatious displays of wealth and power (clothes, cars, guns, women), literally embodies Lacan's notion of the 'gaze of the Other'. The gangster conceives of himself as self-authored/authorised, in thrall to no one – in fact, as classically in Tony Camonte's ruthless rise to power in *Scarface*, being in the power of, or reliant on, others is intolerable to him. Yet as Lacan's account of the subject's constitution through entry into the Symbolic order (paradigmatically language, but by extension all of the social structures through which the individual is socialised) makes clear, individuality is a function of relationality: identity is confirmed only by its constitution in the regard of an Other. Refusal to register the role of others/the Other in limning the subject's selfhood is at best regressive infantile fantasy, at worst psychotic. Elements of both tendencies are present in the classic 1930s gangsters; as the genre takes on *noir* shadings in the postwar period, in the mother-fixated sociopath Cody Jarrett (James Cagney) in *White Heat* (1949), both are wholly uncontained and violently acted out.

In this section we have touched on several themes that have structured gangster films since the silent era, including individualism and the 'American Dream', selfhood and subjectivity, masculinity, urbanism, the family, class and ethnicity. All of these were very much 'live' categories in the cultural discourses of pre-Second World War America. Following the 1935 moratorium, the gangster was displaced by the pro-social 'official' hero – the police detective, Treasury or FBI agent – in the later 1930s and by the early 1940s had become a nostalgic figure. During the war years even gangsters (on-screen at least) placed their patriotic duty before their private gain (see Young, 2000). Throughout the 1950s, in such films as *The Big Heat* (1953), *The Big Combo* and *The Phoenix City Story* (both 1955), gangsters featured as increasingly impersonal antagonists – quasi-corporate crime syndicates that, like the pods in *Invasion of the Body Snatchers* (1955), mirrored contemporary anxieties about both Communism and the domestic culture of conformity – to 'official' heroes whose own motives and methods became increasingly questionable. Mason (2002: 97–119) sees the films of this period as preoccupied with conspiracy and the systemic failures of 'straight' society to protect and enable masculine individuality, consequently provoking that individuality to take on ever more stressful and 'illegitimate' forms.

Other major genres suffered far more from Old Hollywood's terminal crisis than the gangster film, which was neither ideologically central to the outgoing system (like the Western) nor directly implicated economically in its collapse (like the failed musicals of the late 1960s). The Production Code's abolition in 1966 and its replacement in 1968 by a national ratings system also meant that the remaining inhibitions on content – massively attenuated by the mid-1960s, but still with some force to the extent that exhibitors were attached to the Code Seal of Approval – were no longer a problem. The remainder of this chapter will look in more detail at the ways that since the return of the gangster as protagonist in *Bonnie and Clyde* (1967) and *The Godfather*, the thematic preoccupations of the 1930s gangster cycle have been renewed, reviewed and extended, in a period marked in the gangster film as in other traditional genres by an intense self-consciousness concerning generic traditions and the uses of genre revisionism.

The gangster revival

The Godfather – whose success was a major factor driving Hollywood's early 1970s nostalgia boom – established an enduring popularity for the 'retro' gangster film, often lavishly mounted prestige vehicles, sometimes on an epic scale, dramatising the halcyon years of the pre-Second World War Mob: examples include, in addition to *Godfathers II* and *III, Lepke* (1975), *Lucky Lady* (1976), *F*I*S*T* (1978), *Once Upon a Time in America, The Untouchables* (1987), *Miller's Crossing* (1990), *Billy Bathgate* (1991), *Bugsy* (1992) and *The Road to Perdition* (2001). Grandiose thematic pretensions, generally aspiring to statements about the (lost) American Dream, alongside the self-conscious rendering of the gangster as a quintessential American figure, are notable features inherited by many of these films from Coppola's saga (which opens with the line 'I believe in America' – spoken symbolically enough by an undertaker), as is a Stygian visual register aping Gordon Willis's atmospheric photography for the first two films and intended to communicate the murky moral universe inhabited by the characters. Most retro Mob films focus on the trials of leadership and several advertise the parallels between the objectives and the methods of organised crime and those of 'legitimate' corporate business. This marks a subtle yet clear ideological shift in the presentation of the generic material. In post-classical Hollywood the gangster becomes less of an exceptional and cautionary figure, and increasingly representative of the frustration and disillusion that have terminally corroded the promise of America. Exploitative, ruthless organised crime itself is represented – most famously in *The Godfather* – as not a caricature but simply the unmasked truth of 'straight' contemporary American society, in all its relentless dehumanisation. Rumours about Mafia implication in the assassination of President Kennedy in 1963 had gained wide circulation by the start of the 1970s, and with ongoing revelations about criminality at the highest political levels, culminating in 1973 with former White House Counsel John Dean's dramatic refusal to reassure the Watergate enquiry that the Nixon White House's 'dirty tricks' would stop even at murder, the gangster film seemed all too apposite a vehicle for allegorising power relations in contemporary America.

Several post-classical gangster films, including *The Godfather, Part II, Bugsy* and *Things to Do in Denver When You're Dead*, re- (and dis)locate the gangster away from his natural dense urban milieu into the Western wilderness, ironically observing the incongruities that result; 'old-school' veterans such as Frankie Pentangeli in *Godfather II* and Joe Hess, the narrator of *Things to Do in Denver*, nostalgically figure the lost verities of the gangster's urban origins and invoke integrated ethnic communities dissipated by suburban dispersal. With the virtual absence of any visible or effective structures of law enforcement in many of these films, the identificatory conflictual locus reorients itself around the clash between an 'old-school' criminal – characterised by loyalty to crew, (some) regard for human life and rugged individualism – and an impersonal, quasi-corporate criminal organisation. The anti-heroic version of the American Dream embodied by the classic individualist gangster seems to dissipate alongside the decline of its 'official' counterpart in mainstream society; thus the old-style gangster becomes a nostalgically heroicised figure standing in opposition to a machine-like bureaucracy whose ruthlessness is intensified, rather than diminished, by its depersonalisation. This sub-genre is foreshadowed in both some prewar gangster films like *The Roaring Twenties* and *High Sierra* (1941) – compare Carlito Brigante's (Al Pacino) characterisation of the contemporary scene where 'there ain't no rackets . . . just a bunch of cowboys ripping each other off' with Eddie Bartlett's swipe at 'soda jerks and jitterbugs' in *The Roaring Twenties*, quoted above – and postwar *noir* gangster films like *Force of Evil* and *The Gangster* (1949). However, its paradigmatic film is *Point Blank* (1967), whose dream-like narrative sees the betrayed Walker, in single-minded pursuit of the loot stolen from him, frustrated and suspended – 'on hold' – in an endless series of stonewalling referrals to higher authority. The obsessive simplicity of Walker's quest for 'his' money is repeatedly characterised by the 'suits' he has to deal with as a relic of an older, obsolete way of doing business. *Point Blank* is narrated as a series of stylised vignettes whose frequently unplaceable, dream-like quality opens the possibility that the entire film is the dying Walker's *Pincher Martin*-like fantasy of revenge as he bleeds out on the floor of Alcatraz, and links the film strongly to the oneiric strain in *film noir*. More prosaic accounts of mavericks outwitting sclerotic corporate crime in the same period include *Charley Varrick* ('the last of the independents') and *The Outfit* (both 1973).

Alongside mythic and nostalgia narratives, another strand in the post-classical gangster film has been a series of films focusing not on titanic kingpins but on lower-level gangsters: 'wiseguys', 'soldiers' and day-to-day villains who aspire not to the Presidency but to more modest degrees of comfort and status. In this mode, Martin Scorsese's *Mean Streets* (1973), a portrayal of a group of Italian-American petty hoods critically lauded but little seen on its original release, has proved enormously influential. Scorsese's own distinctive style, refined in *Goodfellas* and *Casino* (1995), combines an intense naturalism of setting and performance with a highly demonstrative and intensely aestheticised visual style, resulting in an almost hallucinatory and yet also hyper-real penetration of his characters and their milieu. *Atlantic City* (1981), *State of Grace* (1990), *Donnie Brasco* (1997) as well as *The Sopranos* and the comedies *Mad Dog and Glory* (1989) and *The Whole Nine Yards* (2000) wholly or in part explored terrain opened up by *Mean Streets* (itself strongly influenced by Pasolini's *Accatone*, 1960), though lacking Scorsese's kinetic, visionary style.

The focus on urban small-timers in some cases – such as *Donnie Brasco* – imparts to the mainstream urban gangster film some of the fatalism traditionally associated with its rural variant. Films relating the exploits of Depression-era outlaws from *Machine Gun Kelly* (1958) to *Bloody Mama* (1971) and *Thieves Like Us* (1974) emphasise the roots of their protagonists' turn to crime in dispossession, deracination and despair, and offer fewer corrective alternative models (the priest, the crusading journalist) than their urban counterparts. The most famous rural gangster film, *Bonnie and Clyde* (1967), identifies its highly glamorised couple explicitly with Dustbowl victims of economic banditry – at one point, Clyde hands his gun to an unhoused farmer (and his Black farmworker) to take cathartic potshots at their former small-holding, now foreclosed on by the bank – as well as more loosely with the youth counterculture then adopting a more militant stance in relation to the straight Establishment. While both rural and urban gangsters are typically doomed, rural gangsters seem to enjoy few of the glamorous fruits – the penthouse apartments, sleek automobiles and designer clothes – of their urban colleagues: their pickings are slimmer, their lives more fugitive and itinerant. The rural gang closely resembles a family horde like the James Gang or the Daltons and is correspondingly small-scale, lacking the hierarchical, crypto-corporate aspect of the urban crime Syndicate. Whereas the urban gangster film has usually, as we have seen, been constructed in mythic polarity to the Western, there are strong links between the rural gangster film, some film versions of the Jesse James and Billy the Kid myths (notably *Billy the Kid*, 1930, *Pat Garrett and Billy the Kid*, 1973, and *Jesse James*, 1939), and the outlaw tradi-tion that Eric Hobsbawm terms 'social banditry'. Another traditional syntactic feature of the Western to migrate to the contemporary gangster film is the dream of escaping 'across the border', which features in *Carlito's Way* and the Tarantino-scripted *True Romance* (1994): these films play off the established post-*Godfather* concept of organ-ised crime as the image of a universally oppressive and destructive social reality and suggest that whereas for the classic gangster fantasies of self-advancement and fulfil-ment were sustainable and even (however briefly) realisable within society, these are today only achievable in an imaginary 'elsewhere'.

The most obvious innovation in the gangster film in recent years is the incorporation of the African-American experience into the classic ethnic gangster paradigm, with films like *Boyz N the Hood* (1990) and *Dead Presidents* (1995) faithfully translating classic models like *Dead End* and *The Roaring Twenties* to the modern urban ghetto. Other films, however – notably *Menace II Society* (1993) – evince a nihilistic despair at odds with all but the most dyspeptically revisionist New Hollywood white gangster films. As Munby (1999: 225–6) and Mason (2002: 154–7) argue, these differences can be attributed to the irrelevance of the mythology of the American Dream to Black Americans – upon whose exclusion from the possibility of 'Americanisation' and *embourgeoisement* the Dream is in fact partly predicated. A controversy virtually identical to that surrounding the 1930s gangster cycle erupted around the African-American themed gangster ('gangsta') films of the early 1990s, with both White elite opinion-formers and Black religious and political leaders inveighing virtually unanimously against the high body-counts and apparent glorification of inner-city drug lords in such films as *New Jack City* (1991) and *Menace II Society*. Both box-office returns and accounts of audience response in African-American neighbourhoods, by contrast, suggested that some Black audiences found in the larger-than-life protagonists figures of these films precisely the kind of militant empowerment their critics so feared (see Munby, 1999: 225f.).

Beyond Hollywood

Most national cinemas – other than those, such as the Soviet-era Eastern Bloc, for whom domestic crime was an ideological impossibility – have produced their indigenous variants of the gangster genre, with particularly strong indigenous gangster traditions in Britain and France. Few, however, have used the figure of the gangster himself in the culturally and socially paradigmatic manner of his American incarnation. A notable exception to this rule is Harold Shand (Bob Hoskins), the London gangland boss in *The Long Good Friday* (GB 1980), whose plans to internationalise his operations by a link-up to the US Mafia and to diversify into property development are depicted as a cautionary Thatcherite fable. Harold's plans are ironically undone by the return of a political and colonial repressed, the Troubles in Northern Ireland; Swain (1998: 2) argues that Harold's 'railings against an unseen and unknown enemy (which turns out to be the IRA) are suggestive of a generic as well as political anxiety,' and the film indeed suggests that Harold's aspirations to leave his roots behind (he lives on a boat) and become a player on the global gangster stage are doomed by his (and Britain's) bloody unfinished business at home.

Whereas the American screen gangster takes paradigmatic shape early on in the genre's history, the British gangster mutates through several guises, from the postwar 'spiv' cycle, including *They Made Me a Fugitive, Brighton Rock* (both GB 1947), *It Always Rains on Sundays* and *The Noose* (both GB 1948: see Murphy, 1989: 146–67) through Stanley Baker's Americanised crime boss in *The Criminal* (GB 1960). However, arguably it is only with the emergence of the Kray Brothers as mythic gangland archetypes that the British gangster film acquires its defining semantic element, the 'Firm'. British gangster films of the early 1970s such as *Villain* and *Get Carter* (both GB 1971) as well as *Performance* (GB 1970) clearly invoke the Kray myth, which becomes an increasingly nostalgic informing presence in later gangster films including *The Long Good Friday, The Hit* (1984), *Gangster No.1* and *Sexy Beast* (both GB 2000), as well as the US-made *The Limey* (2001). (Several of these, as Steve Chibnall (2001: 281–91) notes, adopt revenge motifs from Jacobean tragedy.) The late 1990s saw a cycle of semi-comic gangster films (including *Lock, Stock, and Two Smoking Barrels*, GB 1998, and *Snatch*, GB 2000) whose casual violence and macho posturings have been connected by Chibnall with the concomitant rise of 'lad culture' in the UK (see also Murphy and Chibnall, 1999).

Bruzzi (1995: 26) compares the American and French genres in terms of the gangster's personal style, arguing that whereas classic American gangster films are characterised by frenetic action and fast talking, their French counterparts are quiet and exaggeratedly slow, and despite their generic similarities, 'the French and American films have always diverged on the level of tone. Though the gangster film may come more naturally to Americans, the French do it with more style.'

In non-western cinemas, Keiko McDonald (1992) explores the long-running popularity of the Japanese *Yakuza* film since the 1930s as an example of a genre, like the Western, that over its long lifespan directly reflects changing Japanese social consciousness. Perry Farrell's *The Harder They Come* (Jamaica, 1972), set in the slums of Kingston, renovates tropes from both the urban (*Regeneration, Little Caesar*) and the rural (*Bonnie and Clyde*) US gangster film and demonstrates how the phenomenon of 'uneven development' permits categories originating in Depression America to translate themselves readily into the terms of other cultures undergoing comparable socio-economic upheaval.

Notes

1. The concept of 'residual' and 'emergent' ideologies is from Raymond Williams ([1973] 1980: 40–2)
2. *Scarface* was released on 9 April 1932; *The Little Giant* premiered on 14 April 1933.
3. *Gangs of New York* (2003), loosely based on Herbert Asbury's (1927) popular history of the same title, returns to an even earlier (Civil War) period of New York gang warfare.
4. '[*Alibi*] has the speed and the sinister staccato sound quality of a machine gun' (Screenland reviewer quoted in Rosow, 1978: 133).
5. *Goodfellas* encapsulates this double bind in a montage that choreographs an endless series of gang slayings – motivated not by betrayal but by the fear of betrayal – to the plangent play-out of Eric Clapton's 'Layla', one of rock's most urgent statements of desire.

References

Bruzzi, S. (1995) 'Style and the Hood: Gangsters, American and French Style', *Sight & Sound*, 5 (November): 26–7

Bruzzi, S. (1997) *Undressing Cinema: Clothing and Identity in the Movies*. London: Routledge.

Chibnall,S. (2001) 'Travels in Ladland: The British Gangster Film Cycle, 1998–2001', in Murphy, R. (ed.) (2001) *The British Cinema Book*, 2nd edn. London: BFI, pp. 281–91.

Creeber, G. (2002) '"TV Ruined the Movies": Television, Tarantino, and the Intimate World of *The Sopranos*', in Lavery, D. (ed.) (2002) *This Thing of Ours: Investigating The Sopranos*. London: Wallflower, pp. 124–34.

Grieveson, L. (1997) 'Policing the Cinema: Traffic in Souls at Ellis Island, 1913', *Screen*, 38.2: 139–71

Grieveson, L. (2005 forthcoming) 'Gangsters and Governance in the Silent Era', in Grieveson, L. et al. (eds) (2005 forthcoming) *Mob Culture: Hidden Histories of American Gangster Film*. Oxford: Berg.

Gunning, T. (1997) 'From the Kaleidoscope to the X-Ray: Urban Spectatorship, Poe, Benjamin, and *Traffic in Souls* (1913)', *Wide Angle*, 19.4: 25–61.

Hardy, P. (ed.) (1988) *Gangsters: The Aurum Film Encyclopedia*. London: Aurum Press.

Maltby, R. (1995b) 'Tragic Heroes? A1 Capone and the Spectacle of Criminality, 1947–1931', in Benson, J. et al. (1995), *Screening the Past: The Sixth Australian History and Film Conference*. Melbourne: Le Trobe University Press.

Mason, F. (2002) *American Gangsters Cinema: From* Little Caesar *to* Pulp Fiction. London: Palgrave.

McDonald, K. I. (1992) 'The *Yakuza* Film: An Introduction', in Nolletti, A., Jr and Desser, D. (eds) (1992) *Reframing Japanese Cinema: Authorship, Genre, History*. Bloomington, IN: Indian University Press.

Mitchell, E. (1976) 'Apes and Essences: Some Sources of Significance in the American Gangster Film', *Wide Angle*, 1.1: 22–9.

Munby, J. (1999) *Public Enemies, Public Heros: Screening the Gangster* from Little Caesar *to* Touch of Evil. Chicago: University of Chicago Press.

Murphy, R. (1989) *Realism and Tinsel: Cinema: and Society in Britain, 1939–1948*. London: Roultedge.

Murphy, R. and Chibnall, S. (eds) (1999) *British Crime Cinema*. London: Roultedge.

Neale, S. (2000) *Genre and Hollywood*. London: Routledge.

Nochimson, M. P. (2003–4) 'Waddaya Looking at? Re-Reading the Gangster Genre Through *The Sopranos*', *Film Quarterly*, 56.2: 2–13.

Parrish. M. E. (1992) *Anxious Decades: America In Prosperity and Depression, 1920–1941*: New York: W. W. Norton.

Ray, R. H. (1985) *A Certain Tendency of the Hollywood Cinema*. Princeton, NJ: Princeton University Press.

Rosow, E. (1978) *Born to Lose: The Gangster Film in America*. New York: Oxford University press.

Ruth, D. (1996) *Inventing the Public Enemy: The Gangster in American Culture*, 1918–1934. Chicago: University of Chicago Press

Schatz, T. (1981) *Hollywood Genres: Formulas, Filmmaking and the Studio System*. New York: Random House.

Shadoian, J. (2003) *Dreams and Dead Ends: The American Gangster Film*, 2nd edn. New York: Oxford University Press.

Springhall, J. (1998) 'Censoring Hollywood: Youth, Moral Panic and Crime/Gangster Movies of the 1930s', *Journal of Popular Culture*, 32.3: 135–54.

Warshow, R. (1948) (1975ab) 'The Gangster as Tragic Hero', in *The Immediate Experience: Movies, Comics, Theatre and Other Aspects of Popular Culture*. New York: Atheneum, pp. 127–33.

Williams, R. (1973) (1980) 'Base and Superstructure in Marxist Cultural Theory', in *Problems in Materialism and Culture*. London: Verso, pp. 31–49.

Young, N. (2000) "We May Be Rats, Crooks and Murderers, but We're Americans: Controlling the Hollywoood Gangster Protagonist during Early World War II", *Irish Journal of American Studies*, 9: 112–28.

Critical connections

Langford's analysis employs a number of the concepts discussed by Steve Neale (Reading 11), and Tsvetan Todorov (Reading 22) – notions of genre, sub-genre, and verisimilitude – to demonstrate how media criminologists can borrow from film studies to get below the surface content of media representations and conduct deeper intertextual analyses sensitised to the inner workings of film, as well as the wider socio-political contexts out of which they emerge. Brian Jarvis too employs notions of genre and sub-genre to explore the 'big business' of Serial Killer movies in Reading 27. Taken together, these readings offer a grounding in the basic concepts of genre and genre analysis, and present some clear and accessible examples of how notions of genre and sub-genre can be used critically to 'read' culturally expressive texts like film, television and literature.

Discussion questions

- In what ways can the gangster movie be 'read' as a critique of the dominant socio-economic order in a capitalist society?
- What sub-genres of gangster movie are there, and what makes them distinct?
- Compare and contrast the portrayal of gangsters and organised crime in the 1930s 'heyday' films with the Sopranos.

Brian Jarvis

MONSTERS INC.: SERIAL KILLERS AND CONSUMER CULTURE (2007)

Introduction and context

B RIAN JARVIS PRESENTS a highly original analysis of the place of serial killer fiction and film in mass consumer culture. The fascination with serial killers and serial killer memorabilia now constitutes a global market in which people can buy and sell everything 'from serial killer art (paintings, drawings, sculpture, letters, poetry), to body parts (a lock of hair or nail clippings), from crime scene materials to kitsch merchandising that includes serial killer T-Shirts, calendars, trading cards, board games, Halloween masks and even action figures of "superstars" like Ted Bundy, Jeffrey Dahmer and John Wayne Gacy' (Jarvis, 2007: 327). Whilst such a seemingly morbid and tasteless fascination may seem the preserve of a rather macabre deviant minority, Jarvis insists it is in fact merely the hardcore version of a mainstream obsession with serial killers. Brett Easton Ellis and Mary Harron's *American Psycho* (1991 and 2000), Thomas Harris' Hannibal Lecter novels and their film adaptations, and David Finchers *Se7en* (1995) all provide examples, it is suggested, of the connections between the 'normal' desires created by contemporary consumer culture and the practices of monstrous violence that define the serial killer industry. Drawing from Marxist, psychoanalytic and postmodern theory, Jarvis argues that the current fascination with serial killers and killing can be understood in terms of its explicit and implicit parallels with serial consumption in late modern capitalist culture.

Just do it: killers, consumers and violence

[. . .] One of the most conspicuous commonplaces in the popular discourses of serial killing concerns the terrifying *normality* of the murderer. Rather than appearing monstrously different, the serial killer displays a likeness that disturbs the dominant culture. The violence of consumerism is similarly hidden beneath a façade of healthy normality. The glossy phantasmagoria of youth and beauty, freedom and pleasure, obscures widespread devastation and suffering. Etymology is instructive in this regard: to 'consume' is to devour and destroy, to waste and obliterate. With this definition in mind, Baudrillard (1998: 43) has traced a provocative genealogy between contemporary capitalism and tribal potlatch: 'consumerism may go so far as *consumation*, pure and simple destruction'. The *consumation* of contemporary consumer capitalism assumes multiple forms: pollution, waste and the ravaging of non-renewable resources, bio-diversity and endangered species; the slaughter of animals for food, clothing and medicine; countless acts of violence against the consumer's body that range from spectacular accidents to slow tortures and poisonings. At the national level the consumer economy produces radical inequalities that encourage violent crime. At the international level, consumer capitalism depends heavily on a 'new slavery' for millions in the developing world who are incarcerated in dangerous factories and sweatshops and subjected to the repetitive violence of Fordist production. [. . .]

The violence of consumerism is structural and universal rather than being an incidental and localized side effect of the system. For many in the over-developed world this violence remains largely unseen, or, when visible, apparently unconnected to consumerism. In cultural representations of the serial killer, however, consumerism and violence are often extravagantly integrated. In fact, the leading 'brand names' in the genre are typically depicted as *über*-consumers. In Bret Easton Ellis's *American Psycho* (1991), the eponymous Patrick Bateman embodies a merger between ultra-violence and compulsive consumerism. A catalogue of obscene and barbaric atrocities (serial murder, rape and torture) is interwoven with endless shopping lists of designer clothes and fashionable furniture, beauty products and audiovisual equipment, videos and CDs alongside multiple purchases at restaurants, gyms, health spas, concerts and clubs. As James Annesley (1998: 16) notes, 'In *American Psycho* the word "consume" is used in all of its possible meanings: purchasing, eating and destroying'. Each brand of consumption is described in the same flat, affectless tone to underscore Bateman's perception of everything in the world as a series of consumables arranged for his delectation.

Patrick Bateman thus represents a gothic projection of consumer pathology. In this respect, although his name echoes Norman Bates from Hitchcock's *Psycho*, Bateman can be seen as a Yuppie analogue to the aristocratic Hannibal Lecter. Both killers coolly collect and consume body parts and can boast an intimate familiarity with fashionable commodities. In *Silence of the Lambs*, *Red Dragon* and *Hannibal*, Lecter offers a connoisseur's commentary on designer suits and Gucci shoes (a present for Clarice), handbags, perfume and aftershave. Lecter himself has become a voguish icon in millennial popular culture although his name alludes to mid-19th-century French verse. Baudelaire's 'Au Lecteur' (1998: 5) concludes with the following apostrophe:

> Tu le connais, lecteur, ce monstre délicat,
> Hypocrite lecteur, – mon semblable, – mon frère!

[You know him, reader, that fastidious monster,
You hypocritical reader, – my double, – my brother!]

If we follow Harris's allusion, Lecter can be read, like Bateman, as the dark double of the monstrous consumer. Serial killers' perverse charisma might be attributed in part to their function as allegorical embodiments of consumer drives and desires. According to this reading, the serial killer's cannibalism is less a barbaric transgression of the norm and more a Nietzschean distillation of reification (in its simplest terms the tendency, central to consumerism, to treat people as objects and objects as people).

In *Silence of the Lambs*, the casting of serial killer as predatory *über*-consumer is underscored by animal and insect imagery. Clarice Starling is haunted by traumatic childhood memories of witnessing the hidden violence of animal slaughter. Dr Lecter diagnoses her devotion to the law as an attempt to silence the 'screaming of the lambs'. Perhaps Lecter's cannibalism might be diagnosed as an alternate response to that 'screaming', one which reverses power relations by putting consumers on the menu. Alongside the lambs, moths are a second key symbol that hint at the widespread though often invisible violence of consumerism:

> *Some [moths] are [destructive], a lot are, but they live in all kinds of ways. Just*
> *like we do . . . The old definition of moth was 'anything that gradually, silently*
> *eats, consumes, or wastes any other thing.' It was a verb for destruction too . . . Is*
> *this what you do all the time – hunt Buffalo Bill? . . . Do you ever go out for*
> *cheeseburgers and beer or the amusing house wine? (Harris, 1990: 102)*

The second serial killer in *Silence of the Lambs* is similarly doubled with the consumer and associated with animal imagery. While Lecter hunts for food, the predatory Buffalo Bill hunts for clothing. After the chase, Buffalo Bill deprives his prey of subjectivity and treats them like livestock: victims are penned, fed and then flayed for their skins. The nickname given to Jame Gumb by the media is suggestive. As a professional hunter, Buffalo Bill Cody was one of those responsible for reducing the bison population in North America from approximately 60 million to around 300 by 1893. After the near extinction of his prey, Buffalo Bill moved from animal slaughter to entertainment with his travelling 'Wild West' show. Thomas Harris's 'Buffalo Bill', with his own serial killer trade marks, combines an identical mixture of hunting, slaughter and flaying with spectacle and entertainment. Buffallo Bill, alongside Francis Dolarhyde (the name of the killer in Harris's *Red Dragon* again links money, skins and a doppelganger monster, Stevenson's Mr Hyde) and above all the iconic Hannibal Lecter, have established Harris as a brand market leader in the commodification of serial killing.

The roots of the *brand* – the repeated logo or symbol that identifies a product – lie in cattle ranching. At the first crime scene in David Fincher's *Se7en*, a morbidly obese murder victim is discovered after being forced to eat himself to death. (This MO is repeated in Brett Leonard's *Feed* (2005) when a serial killer force-feeds obese women and broadcasts their demise on the Internet.) When the detectives in *Se7en* investigate the crime scene they discover the word 'Gluttony' scrawled in grease behind the victim's refrigerator beside a neat pile of cans with the 'Campbell's Soup' brand clearly visible. The repetition of the Campbell's brand of course alludes to Warhol's series of paintings on the subject of consumer seriality. If, like the detectives in *Se7en*, we are prepared to 'look behind' objects in serial killer texts we may discover further clues to the hidden violence of serial consumerism.

Discover a new you: killers, consumers and the dream of 'becoming'

> *His product should already have changed its skin and stripped off its original form*
> *. . . a capitalist in larval form . . . His emergence as a butterfly must, and yet must*
> *not, take place in the sphere of circulation. (Marx, 1990:204, 269)*

Although the serial killer in David Fincher's *Se7en* justifies his murders with pseudo-religious rhetoric, the victims he chooses also exemplify some of the capital vices and anxieties exploited by consumerism: the 'Gluttony' victim is guilty of over-eating; the 'Pride' victim is a fashion model guilty of acute narcissism; the 'Sloth' victim, according to Richard Dyer (1999: 40), is a case study in the dangers of under-exercising; the 'Lust' victim embodies a hardcore version of mainstream desires and fetishes. By foregrounding 'sins' that are central to consumerism and by naming the murderer 'John Doe', *Se7en* hints at the hyper-normality of serial killer pathology. Key aspects of consumer sensibility intersect with the trademark features of serial killer psychology: anxious and aggressive narcissism, the compulsive collection of fetish objects and fantasies of self-transformation.

In *Silence of the Lambs*, the epiphanic moment in Starling's search for Jame Gumb comes in the bedroom of the killer's first victim: Frederika Bimmel. As a point of view (POV) shot surveys the dead woman's possessions the spectator sees the following: a romantic novel (entitled *Silken Threads*) beside a diet book, wallpaper with a butter-fly motif, a tailor's dummy and paper diamonds in the closet. Starling intuitively connects the paper diamonds to the cuts made by Gumb in the bodies of his victims. The spectator, however, might make additional connections. Demme's *mise-en-scène* offers a symbolic suturing of the normal girl's bedroom and the serial killer's lair. Both spaces house dreams of romantic metamorphosis driven by self-dissatisfaction: the moths in Gumb's basement are linked to the *Silken Threads* and butterflies in Bimmel's bedroom while the diet book suggests the young woman shared the serial killer's anxiety about body image. Clarice Starling, the young woman figuratively donning the traditional male garb of law enforcement (a woman trying to make it in a man's world), is perhaps too preoccupied with tracking down a man who wants to wear a 'woman suit' to pursue these leads. *Silence of the Lambs* extravagantly foregrounds the importance of gender to subject formation. At the start of the film we are introduced to Clarice Starling in androgynous sweaty sportswear while training on an obstacle course. When the spectator subsequently arrives at the serial killer's house, we see Jame Gumb sewing, pampering his poodle and parading before the camera like a catwalk model.

Jame may be symbolically feminized, but in Demme's film, as in Harris's novels, *Se7en*, *American Psycho* and the vast majority of serial killer texts, the murderer is bio-logically male. There are variations in the statistics (roughly between 88–95%), but the vast majority of serial killers are male (Vronsky, 2004). From a feminist perspective it could be argued that serial killing is not so much a radical departure from normal codes of civilized behaviour as it is an intensification of hegemonic masculine ideals.

For the serial killer the murder is a means to an end and that end intersects in places with socially sanctioned definitions of masculine identity in institutions such as the military, many working places and the sports industry. The serial killer is driven by the desire to achieve mastery, virility and control: his objective is to dominate and possess the body and the mind of his victims. According to the binary logic of patriarchy, the killer/victim dyad produces a polarization of gender norms: the killer embodies an *über*-masculinity while the victim who is dominated, opened and entered personifies a hyper-femininity (irrespective of biology). The gendered power relations of serial homicide climax but do not end with the act of murder. Post-mortem the murderer will often take fetish objects from his victim. These totems function as testimony to his continuing domination of a dead body which exhibits an extreme form of the passivity which patriarchy seeks to assign to the feminine.

While serial killing is both literally and symbolically a male affair, the paradigmatic consumer is of course female. According to patriarchal folklore men are the primary producers and unenthusiastic shoppers while most women are devoted consumers and typically figure in the family as the person with overall responsibility for decision making with regard to most domestic purchases. Brett Leonard's *Feed* (2005) might be mentioned here as a particularly pure example of this stereotypical dichotomy between the male serial murderer and the female consumer (the victims in the film are 'Gainers' who are fed to death). However, since the 1980s and throughout the period which has seen a dramatic rise in serial killer art, the consumer sphere has witnessed a withering of gender polarities. From the late 19th and for much of the 20th century, women were the primary target of advertising, particularly in the fields of beauty and fashion. The female consumer was relentlessly bombarded by images and messages in magazines, on billboards, and then through radio, cinema and TV, that encouraged physical self-obsession. Beneath the patina of positivity, this bombardment aimed to promote an anxious policing of the female body – how the body looked and felt, what went over, into and came out of it. The covert imperative of this advertising was to manufacture that sense of inadequacy and self-dissatisfaction which is the essential psychological prerequisite for luxury purchases. Since the 1980s, the beauty and fashion industries, recognizing the potential of a relatively untapped market, began to target the male consumer in a similar manner. Subsequently, there has been a massive worldwide increase in sales of male fashion accessories, cosmetics and related products.

In the context of this erosion of gender polarities within consumer culture, it is noticeable that representations of the serial killer often involve androgyny and gender crisis. The killer is typically feminized by association with consumer subjectivity. He is obsessed with different forms of consumption and collecting and driven by dreams of 'becoming' (the key phrase in Harris' *Red Dragon*), of radically refiguring his appearance and thus his identity. The killer's violence might be read both as complicity with and rebellion against feminization through a reassertion of primitive masculinity. According to Baudrillard (1996: 69), in consumer culture there is a 'general tendency to feminize objects . . . All objects . . . become women in order to be bought'. The feminization of the commodity is structurally integrated with the commodification of the feminine and the serial killer aims to assert mastery over both spheres. The violence of serial homicide might even be diagnosed as a nostalgic mode of *production* (of corpses and fetish objects) for the anxious male subject.

In *Silence of the Lambs*, Lecter offers the following diagnosis of Gumb's pathology: 'He's tried to be a lot of things . . . [But] *he's not anything, really, just a sort of total lack that he wants to fill*' (Harris, 1990: 159, 165). The killer is driven by a profound sense of lack to 'covet' (Lecter's term) what he sees everyday and then to hunt for the new skin that would enable a radical self-transformation. In this respect Gumb constitutes a psychotic off-shoot of normal consumer psychology: his violent response to lack is deviant, but the desires which move him are mainstream. Gumb succumbs to mass media fantasy and advertising which have trained him to feel incomplete and anxious while promising magical metamorphoses on consumption of the ideal (feminized) commodity. The dreams of the serial killer and the serial consumer converge: reinventing the seif through bodily transformation and transcendence. Buffalo Bill, we might say, is merely fleshing out the advertising fantasy of a 'new you'. This is the same dream of 'becoming' pursued by Francis Dollarhyde in *Red Dragon/Manhunter*. It is also the dream of Patrick Bateman, known by his acquaintances as '*total GQ*' (Ellis, 1991: 90) but who, like Jame Gumb, experiences himself as 'total lack': 'There is an idea of a Patrick Bateman; some kind of abstraction. But there is no real me: only an entity, something illusory . . . I simply am not there' (pp. 376–7). Bateman attempts to fill the void with an endless procession of commodities and logos: designer clothes and cuisine, male grooming products and technological gadgets, Versace, Manolo Blahnik, Giorgio Armani. Bateman is a cut-up (like his victims) of commodity signs. He talks in the language of advertising and incessantly imagines himself in commercials, sit-coms, chat shows, action movies and porn films. Bateman's ultra-violence gives physical expression to the acute feelings of anxiety and incompletion which accompany the consumer society's unachievable fantasy of perfect bodies living perfect lives. [. . .]

In his critique of the French arcades, the first cathedrals of consumer capital and forerunners of the department store and mall, Benjamin (1999: 62–3) argued that

> *fashion stands in opposition to the organic. It couples the living body to the inorganic world. To the living, it defends the rights of the corpse . . . fashion has opened the business of dialectical exchange between women and ware — between carnal pleasure and corpse . . . For fashion was never anything other than the parody of the motley cadaver, provocation of death through the woman.*

Exquisite corpse: killers, consumers and mannequins

> *The sexual impulse-excitations are exceptionally plastic. (Freud, 1981: 389)*

According to Benjamin (1999), a key fetish object in the phantasmagorical arcades was the mannequin:

> *the fashion mannequin is a token from the realm of the dead . . . the model for imitation . . . Just as the much-admired mannequin has detachable parts, so fashion encourages the fetishist fragmentation of the living body . . . the woman mimics the mannequin and enters history as a dead object. (p. 78)*

One of Benjamin's German contemporaries, Hans Bellmer, explored the deathly sensuality of the mannequin through the lens of surrealist photography. Eroticized dolls were dressed in veils and underwear or covered in flowers. The mannequin was shot both as whole and dismembered, sometimes posed coyly and at other times torturously convoluted and bound in a perverse meeting of the shop window and the S&M dungeon.

In the 1980s and 1990s, the photographer Cindy Sherman developed a more explicit and grisly mode of mannequin pornography. In her 'Disaster', 'Fairy Tale' and 'Sex' series, Sherman deploys dolls and prosthetic body parts in tableau that combine eroticism, violence and abjection. Sherman's photographs recall Lacan's (1989) work on 'images of the fragmented body':

> These are the images of castration, mutilation, dismemberment, dislocation, evisceration, devouring, bursting open of the body . . . One has only to listen to children aged between two and five playing, alone or together, to know that the pulling off of the head and the ripping open of the belly are themes that occur spontaneously to their imagination, and that this is corroborated by the experience of the doll torn to pieces. (p. 179)

Images of the deconstructed body are everywhere in the infantile fantasies of consumer culture: perfect legs, perfect breasts, perfect hair, perfect teeth, bodies endlessly dismembered in the ceaseless strafing of advertising imagery. Sherman's photography foregrounds the rhetoric of advertising: the dissection of the body by fashion, fitness and beauty industries into fragmentary fetishes. At the same time these images stage a spectacular return of the repressed for those anxieties (about filth, aging, illness and death) covertly fuelled by consumerism's representational regime.

In 1997, Sherman attempted to import her 'imagos of the fragmented body' into the mainstream in the film *Office Killer*. Dorine Douglas, a female serial killer, murders her co-workers at *Constant Consumer* magazine and takes the corpses home to her cellar where she plays with them as life-size dolls. Douglas's hobby echoes Jeffrey Dahmer's confession that his 'experimentation' with the human form began with the theft of a mannequin from a store: 'I just went through various sexual fantasies with it, pretending it was a real person, pretending that I was having sex with it, masturbating, and undressing it' (cited in Tithecott, 1999: 46). The mannequin enjoys a peculiar prominence in serial killer texts. In *Maniac* (1980), Frank Zito scalps his victims and places his trophies on the fashion mannequins that decorate his apartment. In Demme's *Silence of the Lambs*, Benjamin Raspail's decapitated head is placed on a shop dummy and mannequins are conspicuous in Jame Gumb's garment sweatshop. Similarly, in *Ed Gein* (2000), the eponymous killer's 'woman suit' is draped over a mannequin in his workshop. The climactic scenes in the serial killer road movie *Kalifornia* (1993) take place in mock suburban dwellings (part of a nuclear test site) occupied exclusively by mannequins. In *House of Wax* (2005) the serial killer transforms his victims into living dolls by encasing them in wax and a similar MO is evident in *The Cell* where the killer bleaches his female victims' bodies in imitation of the dolls he played with as a child.

Although mannequins are less conspicuous in Ellis's *American Psycho* (1991) than in *Glamorama* (in which they function as a key motif signifying the millennial merger of fashion with terrorism), they still perform a crucial symbolic function. Mannequins epitomize the ideal of 1980s body fascism: tall, youthful, slim, impervious to wrinkles, scars and blemishes, untouched by illness and aging. Bateman's obsession with the designer clothing worn by others in his social circle underlines their status (and his own) as mobile mannequins. Bateman's fetishistic fascination with '*hard bodies*' – both the muscular torso built in the gym and the stiff and frozen body parts he collects – similarly attests to the prevalence of a mannequin ideal in contemporary consumer culture. In ironic affirmation of this aesthetic, the film adaptation of Ellis's novel was accompanied by the marketing of an 'American Psycho Action Figure' – an 18 inch mini-mannequin equipped with fake Armani suit and knife.

In pursuit of the hegemonic fantasy of the *hard body*, in the gym and in his daily fitness regime, Bateman remorselessly punishes himself. The *über*-consumer is narcissistically fixated on his abdominal muscles, his face, his skin tone, how his body is adorned, what goes into it (dietary obsessions) and comes out (especially blood). The violence that Bateman inflicts on his victims appears as an extension of his own masochistic self-objectification:

> *Shirtless, I scrutinize my image in the mirror above the sinks in the locker room at Xclusive. My arm muscles burn, my stomach is as taut as possible, my chest steel, pectorals granite hard, my eyes white as ice. In my locker in the locker room at Xclusive lie three vaginas I recently sliced out of various women I've attacked in the past week. Two are washed off, one isn't. There's a barrette clipped to one of them, a blue ribbon from Hermès tied around my favourite.* (Ellis, 1991: 370)

In Bateman's locker we witness the gender confusion of the male killer and the latent violence of consumer body culture writ large. Bateman's attempt to transform himself into an anthropomorphized phallus is partly offset by the accessories (a hair clasp and ribbon) and pathologies gendered 'feminine' by patriarchy (vanity and masochism). According to Baudrillard (1998: 129), consumers are ultimately encouraged to *consume* themselves: 'in the consumer package, there is one object finer, more precious and more dazzling than any other . . . That object is the BODY'. For Patrick Bateman, serial killing is a mode of *extreme make-over*: a refashioning of bodies, including his own, into trophies. In Demme's *Se7en*, John Doe's body terrorism (force-feeding a fat man, cutting off a female model's nose) mirrors, albeit in grotesque distortions, the mania of millennial consumer society. Similarly, the serial killers in Thomas Harris are fixated on bodily transformation: Buffalo Bill attempts to put himself inside a new body while Lecter puts others' bodies inside himself. The horrific practices of these fictional killers find their everyday analogue in the slow serial torture of the consumer's body by capital: the injections and invasions of cosmetic surgery, the poisonings, pollutions and detoxifications, the over-consumption and dieting, the leisure rituals and compulsive exercise.

In an early scene from Mary Harron's adaptation of *American Psycho* we witness Patrick Bateman's morning exercise and beauty regime: crunches and push-ups are followed by 'deep-pore cleanser lotion . . . water-activated gel cleanser . . . honey-almond body scrub'. As Bateman admires himself in the bathroom mirror his face is sheathed in a 'herbal mint facial masque' that lends the skin a mannequin sheen. When Bateman peels off his synthetic second skin the gesture echoes the gothic facials practised in *Silence of the Lambs*. Lecter, who, at their first meeting, identifies Clarice by her skin cream, escapes his captors by performing an improvised plastic surgery – he removes a guard's face and places it over his own. This act is the prelude to a subsequent 'official' plastic surgery performed to disguise his identity. Jame Gumb's needlepoint with human flesh might be traced back to Norman Bates's taxidermy. Robert Bloch's *Psycho* (1959) (the inspiration for Hitchcock's movie) was loosely based on Ed Gein's flaying and preserving of human flesh. Gein's ghost also haunts the exploits of the Sawyer family in the series of *Texas Chainsaw* films: throughout the original (1973), the sequels (1986, 1990), the *Next Generation* (1994), the remake (2003), and the *Beginning* (2006) flesh is flayed, cut, tanned, sewed, worn, displayed and consumed. Mark Seltzer (1998) has noted the prevalence of 'skin games' in serial killer cinema and fiction. Beneath these 'games' we might catch glimpses of a profound skin dis-ease promoted by the mannequin aesthetics of the beauty industry. As Judith Halberstam (1995: 163) has commented, 'We wear modern monsters like skin, they are us, they are on us and in us'.

Obey your thirst: compulsive seriality

> The circulation of money is the constant and monotonous repetition of the same process . . . the endless series . . . the series of its [the commodity's] representations never comes to an end. (Marx, 1990: 156, 210–11)

> The structure of repetition which is the economy of death. (Blau, 1987: 70)

Baudrillard (1998) proposes that the models and mannequins conspicuous in consumer culture are 'simultaneously [a] negation of the flesh and the exaltation of fashion' (p. 141). Conversely, it might be argued that contemporary consumerism entails a massive extension and eroticization of epidermises. The bioeconomics of consumerism involves ceaseless and intimate miscegenation between capital, commodity and the corporeal. This results in both an objectification of the body and a somatization of the commodity. In his *Critique of Commodity Aesthetics*, Haug (1986) explores 'the generalized sexualization of commodities . . . the commodity's skin and body' as it penetrates the 'pores of human sensuality' (pp. 42, 76). The passion for commodities, their pursuit and possession by consumers might be diagnosed as a socially-sanctioned fetishism. The collection of shoes and the collection of human feet of course involve radically different fetishistic (not to mention ethical) intensities, but these activities share psychodynamic similarities.

For Baudrillard (1996: 87) there is a 'manifest connection between collecting and sexuality . . . it constitutes a regression to the anal stage, which is characterized by accumulation, orderliness, aggressive retention'. Case studies suggest that serial killers are often devoted collectors (see Vronsky, 2004). Their histories typically begin with killing and collecting dead animals and when they progress to human prey the murder is accompanied by the taking of a trophy. In *Collectors*, Julian Hobbs (2000) offers an uncomfortable analogy between this trophy-taking, the hoarding practised by the cult followers of serial killers and the collection of images by the documentary film-maker. This practice is similarly conspicuous in fictional representations of the serial killer from Norman Bates's collection of stuffed birds, to his namesake, Patrick Bateman, who compulsively collects (and seemingly without distinction) clothes, gadgets, music CDs, body parts and serial killer biographies: 'Bateman reads these biographies all the time: Ted Bundy and Son of Sam and *Fatal Vision* and Charlie Manson. All of them' (Ellis, 1991: 92). In *Silence of the Lambs*, Gumb collects flayed flesh while the more refined (at least while incarcerated) Lecter 'collect[s] church collapses, recreationally' alongside fine art prints (Harris, 1990: 21). The killer in *Kiss the Girls* (1997), like Jame Gumb, collects his victims and hoards them underground. Similarly, in *The Cell*, the killer locks his victims in underground storage before using them to build a collection of human dolls. Although the killer in *The Bone Collector* is only interested in accumulating skeletal fragments, his activities similarly require *subterranean* investigations. Digging beneath the psychological surface of the collector and his system of sequestered objects', Baudrillard (1996) detects a 'powerful anal-sadistic impulse':

> The system may even enter a destructive phase, implying the self-destruction of the subject. Maurice Rheims evokes the ritualised 'execution' of objects – a kind of suicide based on the impossibility of ever circumscribing death. It is not rare . . . for the subject eventually to destroy the sequestered object or being out of a feeling that he can never completely rid himself of the adversity of the world, and of his own sexuality. (pp. 98–9)

Irrespective of the object, 'what you really collect is always yourself' (Baudrillard, 1996: 91). Serial killing, like consumerism, is driven by a sense of lack. Psychological profiles of serial killers typically diagnose the cause of the subject's compulsive behaviour as a profound sense of incompletion (see Seltzer, 1998). Although of a different order, comparable dynamics are evident in what Haug (1986) calls the 'commodity-craving' of consumer sensibility. Estimates vary (from 1 to 25%) but an increasing number of studies agree that compulsive shopping is a recognizable and burgeoning problem (Hartson and Koran, 2002). *American Psycho* offers an extended parallelism between compulsive consumerism and compulsive violence. Attempting to describe the sensations he experiences after his first documented attack Bateman relies on consumerist tropes:

> I feel ravenous, pumped up, as if I'd just worked out . . . or just embraced the first line of cocaine, inhaled the first puff of a fine cigar, sipped the first glass of Cristal. I'm starving and need something to eat. (Ellis, 1991: 132)

Ellis juxtaposes exhaustive catalogues of commodities with exhaustive catalogues of sexual violence and proposes that the frenzy of consumer desire climaxes, for Bateman, not with fulfilment, but increasing boredom and acute anxiety. In *Serial Killers*, Mark Seltzer (1998: 64) proposes that

> The question of serial killing cannot be separated from the general forms of seriality, collection and counting conspicuous in consumer society . . . and the forms of fetishism – the collecting of things and representations, persons and person-things like bodies – that traverse it.

Every aspect of Bateman's existence is structured by the compulsively circular logics of capitalist reproduction. Bateman (Norman Bates's yuppie double) has seen the film *Body Double* 37 times. When he is not watching *Body Double* over and over, Bateman compulsively consumes other examples of serialized mass culture: daily episodes and reruns of *The Patty Winters Show* (a parodic double of the *Oprah Winfrey Show*); restaurant reviews and fashion tips in weekly magazines; crime stories in the newspapers and on TV, endlessly repeated video footage of plane crashes. On a shopping expedition, Bateman finds himself mesmerized while 'looking at the rows, the endless rows of ties' (Ellis, 1991: 296). On the run from the police he is similarly paralysed by rows of luxury cars (BMW 3, 5, 7 series, Jaguar, Lexus) and thus unable to choose a getaway vehicle. Bateman collects clothes in series (matching suits, shirts, shoes), beauty products, music CDs, varieties of mineral water, recipes and menus. Despite the advertising promises of unique purchases that offer instant fulfilment, there are no *singular* only *serial* objects in consumer society and 'each commodity fills one gap while opening up another: each commodity and sale entails a further one' (Haug, 1986:91).

The pullulation of serial objects is accompanied by the expansion of serialized spaces. Throughout *American Psycho*, Bateman is continually lost and unable to distinguish between identical office buildings, restaurants, nightclubs and apartment buildings. This confusing interchangeability extends to people. Although clothing is instantly recognizable (everyone identifies everyone else by labels) people repeatedly misidentify each other. Thus, *American Psycho* underscores Jeffrey Nealon's (1998: 112) disturbing contention that, in contemporary consumer society, 'identity, for both commodity and human, is an effect rather than a cause of serial iteration'. The killer in *Se7en*, the anonymously named John Doe, attempts to build a distinctive identity by performing a series of grisly murders. At the first crime scene, as noted earlier, Doe's arrangement of Campbell's soup cans clearly alludes to Warhol's work on the seriality and compulsive repetition of consumerism. *Manhunter* (1986), the first of the Hannibal Lecter films, makes a similar point in more comic fashion. A shot-reverse-shot sequence in a supermarket is littered with glaring continuity errors as father and son remain motionless while the products lined up in neat rows on the shelves behind them change (and the sequence ends with the detective framed by the *cereals* aisle). In *Manhunter*, Dollarhyde's repetitive violence is partly inspired by Hannibal Lecter. This repetition is repeated in *Red Dragon*, the remake of *Manhunter*. Serial killers are often copycats and serial killer cinema repeats this trait: in *Copycat* the killer repeats famous murders and in *Virtuosity* a virtual criminal is manufactured from a serial killer database. Serial killer films themselves become series, spawning sequel after sequel. Although these narratives typically conclude with the murder of the killer, the audience is reassured that he will return in a vicious circle that begs the question: *can seriality itself be killed?* [. . .]

References

Annesley, James (1998) *Blank Fictions: Consumerism, Culture and the Contemporary American Novel*. London: Pluto.

Baudelaire, Charles (1998) *The Flowers of Evil*. Oxford: Oxford World's Classics.

Baudrillard, Jean (1996) *The System of Objects*. London: Verso.

Baudrillard, Jean (1998) *The Consumer Society: Myths and Structures*. London: SAGE Publications.

Benjamin, Walter (1999) *The Arcades Project*. Cambridge, MA: Harvard University Press.

Blau, Herbert (1987) *The Eye of the Prey: Subversions of the Postmodern*. Bloomington, IN: Indiana University Press.

Dyer, Richard (1999) *Se7en*. London: BFI.

Easton Ellis, Bret (1991) *American Psycho*. London: Picador.

Freud, Sigmund (1981) *Introductory Lectures on Psychoanalysis*. Harmondsworth: Penguin.

Halberstam, Judith (1995) *Skin Shows: Gothic Horror and the Technology of Monsters*. Durham, NC: Duke University Press.

Harris, Thomas (1990) *Silence of the Lambs*. London: Mandarin.

Hartson, H. J. and Koran, L. M (2002) 'Impulsive Behaviour in a Consumer Culture', *International Journal of Psychiatry in Clinical Practice* 6(2): 65–8.

Haug, W. F. (1986) *Critique of Commodity Aesthetics: Appearance, Advertising and Sexuality in Capitalist Society*. Cambridge: Polity.

Hobbs, Julian (2000) *Collectors*. Abject Films.

Lacan, Jacques (1989) *Ecrits: A Selection*. London: Routledge.

Marx, Karl (1990) *Capital: Volume 1*. London: Penguin.

Nealon, Jeffrey T. (1998) *Alterity Politics: Ethics and Performative Subjectivity*. Durham, NC: Duke University Press.

Seltzer, Mark (1998) *Serial Killers: Death and Life in America's Wound Culture*. London: Routledge.

Tithecott, Richard (1999) *Of Men and Monsters: Jeffrey Dahmer and the Construction of the Serial Killer*. Madison, WI: University of Wisconsin Press.

Vronsky, Peter (2004) *Serial Killers: The Methods and Madness of Monsters*. New York: Berkley Books.

Critical connections

The popular fascination with serial killers and serial killing exists as only one manifestation of the much wider late modern obsession with death, violence and gore. The long-running and enormously popular US crime show *CSI: Crime Scene Investigation*, for example, which provides a focus for Mariana's Valverde's analysis in Reading 24, is extremely graphic in its presentation of violence as entertainment. And with the prevalence of cable TV, this show airs every day. Fatal injuries – shootings, stabbings, burnings – are reconstructed in slow motion and extreme close-up, blood spatter patterns are expertly 'read', suspects identified, killers caught, and crimes invariably solved. At the same time as satisfying the public thirst for mediated violence, *CSI* and its many spin offs and imitators serve other ends by combining 'the traditions of the crime genre with a new forensic realism to fuse the police and science with a convergent moral authority' (Cavender and Deutsch, 2007: 68). Thus, despite its clever innovations in sound and vision, as Valverde points out (Reading 24), *CSI* retains a classic narrative moral closure – the police are the good guys, and the good guys generally win – common to nearly all crime stories, including most serial killer movies.

Jarvis' analysis of serial killer movies is informed by Literature and Film studies and psychoanalytic theory, as well as a firm grasp of criminological perspectives. *Monsters Inc.* thus neatly illustrates the usefulness of adopting an interdisciplinary approach which draws from outside the often narrow boundaries of mainstream criminology. This interdisciplinary approach is echoed in readings throughout this book – see, for example, Mariana Valverde's examination of police drama and reality police programming (Reading 24), Sheila Brown's exploration of cybercrime (Reading 39), and Jeff Ferrell's analysis of hip-hop graffiti culture (Reading 28).

Discussion questions

- Why is serial-killer film and literature so popular today?
- How might the serial killer be understood as a product of modernity?
- How might we go about characterising differences between portrayals of extreme legitimate and illegitimate violence?

Reference

Cavender, G, and Deutsch. S. (2007) 'CSI and Moral authority: The Police and Science', in *Crime, Media, Culture*, 3, 1: 67–81.

Jeff Ferrell

CRIMES OF STYLE (1996)

Introduction and context

THE CRIME AND MEDIA nexus embraces a wide diversity of activities and behaviours, many of which lie outside the mainstream realms of news production and entertainment programming. As one illustration of this diversity, Jeff Ferrell, the originator and still the leading light of cultural criminology, develops a theoretically rich critique of the criminalisation of graffiti artists and the cultural practice of 'doing graffiti'. Ferrell engages in a rich, liquid ethnography (Ferrell *et al.* 2008) of the subcultural organisation, meaning and practice of graffiti writing. In keeping with the ethos adopted throughout this Reader, he insists that this 'crime of style' cannot be understood simply as an outsider looking in. Rather, it must be explored in terms of the details of its practice, its interactional processes, its internal and external politics and its rooting in the wider aesthetics and thrill of transgression.

As Ferrell (1999) notes elsewhere, 'Building on Katz's wide ranging exploration of the sensually seductive "foreground" of criminality, cultural criminologists ... have utilized *verstehen*-oriented methodologies to document the experiences of "edge-work" and "the adrenalin rush" – immediate, incandescent integrations of risk, danger and skill – that shape participation and membership in deviant and criminal subcultures' (see also Reading 17). Here, then, graffiti is theorised in terms of the dialectic between the structures and situations of crime, between the background political economy of criminality and the foreground aesthetics and meanings of criminal transgression. Cultural criminology is thus underpinned by classic symbolic interactionism, subcultural theory and phenomenology. But it also brings with it a postmodern sensibility attuned to the mediatisation of everyday life, the fluidity of contemporary identities, the shift to a mass consumer society, and the ontological uncertainties that define the contemporary condition.

Figure 28.1 Graffiti wall, Amsterdam, the Netherlands.
Source: Jeff Ferrell

Crimes of style: graffiti writing

> Shoplifters of the world, unite and take over.
>
> The Smiths (1987)

Earlier chapters have explored with some care the subcultural organization of graffiti writing – as manifest in crews, tags, and walls of fame – and the social dynamics of activities like tagging, piecing, going over, and dissin'. Often, these subcultural activities have been examined in fine detail, with accounts of subtle variations in tag names, or the particularities of spray paint. This ethnography of graffiti writing was in turn based on Becker's (1963) and Polsky's (1969) general contention that an understanding of behavior labeled as deviant or criminal must evolve from a close examination of its actual practice. But is it really necessary to know what brand of spray paint graffiti writers prefer, or how they negotiate the design of an illegal piece? Beyond some sort of voyeuristic pleasure, why do such details matter?

To begin with, these details matter because they constitute the experiential setting of deviance and criminality, the immediate, interactional dynamic through which criminals construct crime. Taken as a whole, such details begin to get at the daily experience of crime, at the rhythmic nuances of criminal acts and interactions. If we set out to study crime as a social event, rather than a derivative analytic category; to pay attention to crime as a lived, socially constructed experience, rather than a statistical residue, its subtleties must be taken into account. As a statistical aggregate, or as the product of background variables, crime carries the clean lines of abstraction; as a social event, it takes on the textures and nuances of human interaction.

It is out of this "interactionist" view of deviance and crime, of course, that Becker and Polsky originally made their injunctions, and within this view that "intensive field observation" (Becker, 1963: 193) of crime's social details matters.[1] Recent developments in criminology have taken this sense of crime as interaction a further step, and reemphasized the importance of situational detail. Katz (1988: 312, 317) argues that only through awareness and analysis of the phenomenological foreground of criminality, of the intricacies of its "lived sensuality," can we understand the "moral and sensual attractions in doing evil," and thus the nature of criminality itself. Because of this, he pays close attention to the badass' "bump" and "whatchulookinat?" ploys, the homeboy's ritually white undershirt, and other phenomena which allow him "to follow in detail the lived contours of crime." Katz thus blends the phenomenologist's precise attention to situational detail with the interactionist's concern for the situation's social negotiation and construction. In so doing, he demonstrates that the meaning of crime develops not only out of long-term interactions and criminal "careers," but out of the precise details of particular criminal events.

The details of the Denver graffiti scene show that writers construct graffiti and its meaning out of this blend of subcultural history and situational immediacy. A night's tagging certainly evolves out of prior tagging experiences, networks of friendship among the writers, and technical and aesthetic expertise developed over the course of writers' careers; but it also takes shape and meaning within the immediate contingencies of boredom, missed phone calls or bus connections, passing cars and pedestrians, and well or poorly-lit alleys. Piecing likewise incorporates shared aesthetic resources, and a certain degree of planning; but particular incidents of piecing also evolve from immediate issues of interpersonal conflict or cooperation, outsider interruptions, dwindling paint or beer supplies, and even changes in the weather. They thus become meaningful for the writers not as moments of generic graffiti writing, but in the immediacy of distinctly shared experience. As with other criminal acts, the meaning of graffiti writing is embedded in the details of its execution.

The social and situational details of graffiti writing matter for a second reason, as well. [. . .] [T]his experiential foreground incorporates also the practical aesthetics of graffiti writing. The organization of graffiti writing around the aesthetic concerns of the writers, around matters of style, is no abstract, formal exercise. Instead, it is a collective enterprise negotiated in the emergence of tags and subcultural identities, in informal sanctions against "trash paint" and "biting," in collaborative piecebook designs and "art sessions," and in the interplay of status and style manifested in "going over" and "dissin'." This essential characteristic of graffiti writing – that it is a "crime of style" – cannot be understood without paying close attention to its particulars, to the actual practice of "doing graffiti." As Becker (1963: 190) argues,

> we often turn collective activity – people doing things together – into abstract nouns whose connection to people doing things together is tenuous. We then typically lose interest in the more mundane things people are actually doing. We ignore what we see because it is not abstract, and chase after the invisible "forces" and "conditions" we have learned to think sociology is all about.

Graffiti writing is not an abstraction driven by the concept of Style, or the force of Aesthetics; it is collective activity constructed out of the practical aesthetics of its writers.[2]

A close examination of graffiti writing, then, reveals it to be a crime of style, grounded in the shared aesthetic resources of the writers. What, though, of other deviant or criminal acts? Would similar attention to detail expose aesthetic or stylistic elements in other less overtly "arty" forms of criminality? Research in a variety of areas shows that it would. Working within the traditions of British cultural studies and the "new criminology," Hall and Jefferson (1976), Hebdige (1979), Cosgrove (1984) and others have demonstrated that nuances of style and meaning lie at the very heart of individual and collective crime and deviance, and have sketched an aesthetics of deviance and criminality from the experiences of zoot suiters, skinheads, rude boys, and drug users. Drawing on these and a plethora of other sources, Katz (1988) has located this aesthetics of crime firmly in the lived experience of criminal events.

Katz, for example, examines the "ways of the badass" – that is, the ways in which young men construct tough, alien identities. Focusing on the interplay of social status, personal identity and style, and the symbolism of the badass, Katz (1988: 88, 90) considers dark sunglasses, guttural noises, the "ghetto bop and the barrio stroll," tattoos, and other stylistic strategies which together form an "alternative deviant culture." He in turn examines specific manifestations: the "coherent deviant [a]esthetic" of the Mexican-American cholo and the British (and later U.S.) punk; the youth gang's ritualized affection for weapons; the "bump" and other stylized devices of aggression.

In this discussion – as in his discussions of "street elite" style, ritualized Black street talk, and symbolic violence – Katz, like the British new criminologists, grounds the meaning of deviance and criminality in the style of its practice. The black leather jacket and the zoot suit, the cholo's closing "Shaa-haa" and the young black's opening "shit" (see Katz, 1988: 83–87) – these are not mere "affectations" added to deviant projects and identities, but the building blocks of crime and deviance as they are lived and experienced. To speak, then, of the "culture of violence" or the "culture of crime" is to talk not only about background factors which perpetuate violence or crime, but about the style and symbolism – the aesthetic texture – of its foreground.

Katz's inquiry into urban adolescent "gangs" – "street elites" – locates this aesthetic of crime within patterns of social class, ethnicity, authority, and age. Katz (1988: 120, 151, 114, 145) demonstrates not only how these groups "style themselves as elites," follow "[a]esthetic leadership," and battle for "symbolic rewards," but how these styles of deviance and crime develop out of the lived experience of inner city adolescence. Thus, Katz argues, "homeboys" and other low income, minority street elites ritually celebrate their neighborhood ties, where middle income, white adolescents attempt symbolically to conceal or destroy their origins. And, when street elites encounter the "mundane authority" of the school, they can draw on the collective power of the group not only to opppose that authority, but to transcend it symbolically.

Here, as in Cosgrove's (1984) study of zoot suiters and "style warfare," and Hall and Jefferson's (1976) collected studies on "resistance through rituals," we begin to see a third sort of significance to the detailed, experiential foreground of crime and deviance. The foreground is political; a dynamic of power and authority is embedded in the meaning and style of the criminal experience. The methods and epistemologies of positivist or "structural" criminologies – the dislocated number sets which cross-match crime's background factors in an attempt to measure criminality "objectively" – obscure, therefore, not only the interactional process through which crime is constructed, but its political content as well. To ignore the foreground of criminality in favor of an analysis of political or economic structures is, ironically, to miss the very meaning of these structures in the reality of crime.

If we understand political/economic domination and inequality to be causes, or at least primary contexts, of crime, we can also understand that these are mediated and expressed through the situational dynamics, the symbolism and style, of criminal events. To speak of a criminal "event," then, is to talk about the acts and actions of the criminal, the unfolding interactional dynamics of the crime (both between the "criminals," and among the criminals and victims), and the patterns of inequality and injustice embedded in the thoughts, words, and actions of those involved. In a criminal event, as in other moments of everyday life, structures of authority, social class and ethnicity intertwine with situational decisions, personal style, and symbolic references. Thus, while we cannot make sense of crime without analyzing structures of inequality, we cannot make sense of crime *only* by analyzing these structures, either. The meaning and aesthetics of criminal events interlock with the political economy of criminality.[3]

Youthful adventures in crime – vandalism, theft, and especially shoplifting – exemplify these interconnections. Certainly shoplifting has to do with the creation of needs, the structuring of consumption, and the commodification of desire under late capitalism. Yet these societal processes alone cannot explain the particular, situational dynamic of shoplifting. The event of shoplifting has a "magical" (Katz, 1988: 54) and seductive quality about it that develops independently of any overt need on the part of the shoplifter for the shoplifted items. For the shoplifter, the event unfolds as a sort of thrilling and sensually gratifying game, a dramatic and illicit adventure. This magically seductive adventure is, of course, tangled up with the illicit acquisition of late capitalist consumer goods; but it is tangled in a particular way that can be neither known nor predicted from afar. Our understanding of both crime and capitalism is thus enriched by paying attention to the particular contours of shoplifting. Shoplifting explains capitalism in the same way that capitalism explains shoplifting.[4]

Graffiti writing likewise embodies the dialectic between structures and situations of crime. The writing of graffiti in Denver and elsewhere unfolds within systems of legal and economic domination, systems which guarantee unequal access to private property and cultural resources. [. . .] [T]hese systems are in turn utilized and managed by moral entrepreneurs who expand political/economic domination by further criminalizing graffiti writing. But while these factors set the context for graffiti writing, they do not define the writing itself. They alone cannot explain the subtle ways in which writers appropriate and subvert pop culture imagery, and draw on hip hop culture – itself an elegant and elaborate response to political/economic and ethnic domination. They cannot predict the "adrenalin rush" that graffiti's illegality generates for its writers, or the many ways in which criminalization in fact amplifies and reconstructs the writing of graffiti. These details of graffiti writing – these intersections of politics and interpersonal style, of criminalization and criminal event – can only be explained from inside the writing itself.

The political character of criminal events in turn forces us to question conventional distinctions between crime and resistance, to muddy the boundaries between unconscious response and conscious insubordination. As we coordinate the phenomenological stare with the critical gaze of anarchism (and other progressive social theories), we are compelled to re-examine the experience of crime as lived by its participants. And as we do, we may begin to see differently all sorts of sensually appealing, if politically "unsophisticated," criminal events: vandalism, shoplifting, graffiti writing, and the like. Until we understand the meaning of these events for their perpetrators, we would be hard pressed to dismiss them as without political content, or the possibilities of resistance.[5]

Does this imply that every broken window, every leather-jacketed street fighter spitting teeth and blood, every scooped-out liquor store cash register – every Krylon-tagged alley wall – signifies an act of politically conscious resistance? Absolutely not, and maybe yes. Our answer depends, at least in part, on what we mean by "conscious." The logic of such criminal events is partly situational; understandings and meanings of the event blossom within its interactional boundaries. The question thus becomes, not "Is this crime or resistance?" but "In what ways might the participants in this event be conscious of, and resistant to, the contradictions in which they are caught?" Whatever the answer, two things seem certain. The first is that we must take the time to pay attention to what people are actually doing when they are sticking up liquor stores, shoplifting shoes, or spraying graffiti. The second is that political-economic structures – and thus power, control, subordination, and insubordination – are embedded in these events as surely as in governmental scandals or labor strikes.[6]

When we look at graffiti writing in this way, we find its many nuances pointing toward an interesting conclusion: the politics of graffiti writing are those of anarchism. The adrenalin rush of graffiti writing – the moment of illicit pleasure that emerges from the intersection of creativity and illegality – signifies a resistance to authority, a resistance experienced as much in the pit of the stomach as in the head. Guerin (1970: 13) asserts that "anarchism can be described first and foremost as a visceral revolt," and graffiti writing certainly constitutes visceral resistance to the constraints of private property, law, and corporate art. Engaging in "direct action" against these authorities, graffiti writers together celebrate their insubordination in spray paint and marker, and in the pleasure and excitement of doing graffiti. And this forbidden pleasure in turn reveals as much about authority, and resistance to it, as the moments of intellectual clarity gained from a close reading of *The German Ideology* or *The Conquest of Bread*.[7]

That the pleasures of graffiti writing result not only from its illegality, but from the collective creativity of the writers, confirms its meaning as a form of anarchist resistance. Working together, graffiti writers construct an alternative, street-wise aesthetic that subverts the pre-packaged imagery of the culture industry and city hall. Playing with their own images and designs, appropriating and reconfiguring pop culture icons, they engage in a process of cultural resistance enlivened by beauty and style. If Goldman taught us that a revolution without dancing is not worth attending, graffiti writing confirms that resistance without creativity – resistance as a sort of analytic, intellectualized machinery of opposition – may not be worth the trouble. Without the spark of playful creativity, resistance becomes another drudgery, reproducing in its seriousness the structures of authority it seeks to undermine. The imaginative play of graffiti writing and other anarchist enterprises defines their existence outside the usual boundaries of intellectual and emotional control.[8]

As with more violent forms of anarchist resistance, graffiti writing is also notable for the sudden and mysterious manner in which it appears. If graffiti writing escapes the uninspired seriousness of conventional politics, it escapes the scheduled tyranny of deadlines and datebooks as well. This detail of graffiti writing – that writers do graffiti in the middle of the night, when and if they feel like it – carries two sorts of political meaning. It pulls the writers outside the world of daily work, insures that graffiti writing will not itself become a sort of routinized labor, and thus further

Figure 28.2 Graffiti writers at work, Denver, Colorado, USA.
Source: Jeff Ferrell

Figure 28.3 Graffiti piece, Berlin, Germany.
Source: Jeff Ferrell

locates graffiti writing outside conventional channels of authority and control.[9] This spontaneity also contributes to the threat which graffiti writing poses to those in authority. Denver City Council President Cathy Donahue complained to the Metro Wide Graffiti Summit:

> It is illegal to deface somebody's property, but the problem became that no one ever sees them. And people have tried to catch.. . . I've seen acres of graffiti and I have never, ever seen anybody put it on.

Her comments of course recall the lamentations of other authorities faced with episodes of "undisciplined" guerrilla warfare and popular insurgency, as well they might. As a form of aesthetic guerrilla warfare, graffiti writing resembles the resistance waged by Makhno and his anarchist fighters during and after the Russian revolution:

> When cornered, the Makhnovists would bury their weapons, make their way singly back to their villages, and take up work in the fields, awaiting the next signal to unearth a new cache of arms and spring up again in an unexpected quarter (Avrich, 1973: 23).

Any characterization of graffiti writing as "guerrilla warfare," though, must be balanced against another essential detail of its production: its vulnerability. As seen previously, anti-graffiti entrepreneurs take care to portray graffiti writers as forcing their tags and pieces on defenseless victims in a series of violent assaults. The lived experience of graffiti writing, though, shows this assertion to be false in two ways. First, graffiti writers paint not on people, but on property; if their painting embodies disrespect, it is not for individuals, but for the sanctity of private (and "public") walls and fences. Only in a social order that systematically confuses persons and property could moral entrepreneurs hope to confuse graffiti writing with assault. Second, when faced with graffiti on their property, the majority of home owners – and certainly large corporations and the city – have ample ability to erase the offending images and symbols. With access to financial and technological resources far greater than those of the writers, property owners can wipe out in minutes graffiti that may have taken hours to produce.[10]

Rather than forcing their art on helpless victims, then, graffiti writers in fact produce art in and of the urban community. This graffiti art is vulnerable to direct public response in ways that city-administered "public" art is not; and its images intrude on the public with far less impunity than those of the television commercial and the roadside billboard. In fact, unlike the administrators of commercial and "public" art, graffiti writers make no claims as to protecting, preserving, or profiting from their public art. They own and control their throw-ups and pieces less than they simply expose them to public appreciation (or condemnation). As Eye Six says,

> In that respect, it's probably the dumbest crime you can get involved in. Not only are you in danger of getting thrown in jail and getting fined and such, you don't get any money out of it at all (in Ferrell, 1990a: 10).[11]

Because of this, conflicts over graffiti writing are susceptible to the sort of direct, street-level resolution essential to anarchist social relations. Conflicts among the writers themselves are played out in the dynamics of dissin' and going over.

Property owners and the city can resort to the censorship of the sandblaster – with, of course, the possiblity that the writers will return to paint again the clean wall. And, as has happened in Denver, this interplay may eventually result in some agreement or compromise between writers and property owners. While these are not perfectly harmonious processes of community negotiation – partly because they originate in inequalities of privilege and power – they can at least keep the resolution of conflict in the hands of the participants, and outside the authoritarian entanglements of the law. Significantly, the vulnerability of graffiti writing to these direct processes is mirrored in other forms of street art and entertainment. Noting the "eccentric, anarchistic nature of the busker," Parks (1990: 8) argues,

> minstrel buskers remain public property. They are accountable daily to the people. They are naked, vulnerable, and open to judgement every time out....This closeness to hand-to-mouth existence is what expunges the tyranny of the pop show and by example strengthens resistance to it.[12]

The contrast between graffiti art and the "art" of the corporation and the government, and the link between graffiti writing, busking, and other forms of anarchist entertainment, both point to a final dimension of graffiti writing as anarchist resistance. Graffiti writing breaks the hegemonic hold of corporate/governmental style over the urban environment and the situations of daily life. As a form of aesthetic sabotage, it interrupts the pleasant, efficient uniformity of "planned" urban space and predictable urban living. For the writers, graffiti disrupts the lived experience of mass culture, the passivity of mediated consumption. As Eye Six says,

> Your average person is just subservient to whatever is thrown up. Whatever building is built, whatever billboard is put up – whatever. They just sit on their asses; they pretty much go with the flow like all sheep do.....At least we act on our feelings. We don't just sit around and doodle in our houses, we go out and get paint (in Ferrell, 1990a: 10).

For the commuter and the office worker, graffiti provides a series of mysterious, ambiguous images – and some of the few available public images not bought and paid for by corporate art programs, city governments, or NEA grants. As will be seen shortly, graffiti resists not only authority, but the aesthetics of authority as well.[13]

Graffiti writing thus constitutes a sort of anarchist resistance to cultural domination, a streetwise counterpoint to the increasing authority of corporate advertisers and city governments over the environments of daily life. Developed not out of particular intellectual traditions or political programs, but from the direct, collective action of young writers, graffiti writing tears at the boundaries of mass culture. As they piece and tag together, graffiti writers carve a bit of cultural space from the enforced monotony of the urban environment.

Like the more general understanding of graffiti writing, this appreciation of graffiti writing as resistance rests on a sociological perspective. Such a perspective highlights the collective construction of graffiti writing's political effects, the interplay between graffiti writers, home owners, commuters, and others sharing the urban environment. It focuses less on the psycho-pathological motivations of individual writers than on the shared experience of graffiti writing, the situationally negotiated meaning of adrenalin rushes, alternative aesthetics, and nighttime adventures. And, as above, it pays attention to the political dynamics of criminal events, even when such dynamics appear at first glance not to be known to or articulated by the individuals involved.

Moreover, what would it mean to talk about the political motivations of individual writers? Must an intellectually refined political sense be present (and spoken) to categorize a writer's graffiti as political, or simply an unwillingness to play by the rules, a sense of free floating outside the authority of conventional culture? Eye Six, for example, points out that he is "not into . . . political murals," and adds that "when I'm doing a mural, I try and keep my own personality out of it, in terms of politics." Indeed, his pieces seldom if ever include conventional political imagery. Yet, as just seen, he has a keen sense of cultural domination and subservience, and an apprecia-tion of graffiti as direct action, as well: "When you're doing graffiti, you choose your own vision, you choose your own location, you don't ask anybody's permission, you don't expect any monetary reward, you go in the hole and do your deal" (in Ferrell, 1990a: 10). For Eye Six and other writers, politics may or may not have meaning at the level of mayoral elections or social "issues," as narrowly defined; but it certainly develops out of the praxis of lived experience and aesthetic orientation.[14]

Can we therefore conclude that graffiti writing constitutes an ideal act of anar-chist resistance? Probably not, in that graffiti writing is beset by interpersonal con-flicts, limited awareness of broader issues, a good bit of heavy drinking, and other "flaws." But if "flawed" means caught within a web of contradictions, and not fully real-ized, then all resistance is flawed, as is all praxis, and all anarchy. To dismiss graffiti writing – and similarly, hip hop music and culture – as "flawed" is not only to buy into elitist, intellectualized assumptions about culture and cultural change, but to throw away the lived experience of resistance. And if indeed graffiti writing is a flawed act of resistance, it is surely no more flawed than peace marches which file along permitted routes while singing the songs of million dollar rock idols, or political campaigns which will, at best, elect "progressives" into a representational system of compromise and corruption.

Appreciating graffiti writing as a form of anarchist resistance, then, does not require romanticizing the process of doing graffiti, nor ignoring graffiti's social and cultural limitations. In fact, a sense of graffiti writing as resistance develops from quite the opposite direction: from closely examining the lived details of its production. And when we pay attention to the actualities of graffiti writing, we discover not only these political qualities, but a comparative perspective as well. In many ways, graffiti writing in the cities of the United States resembles that which develops out of Third World political struggles. Although certainly operating in different social and cultural environments, both constitute direct responses to the authoritarian domination of daily life. Both are inherently political acts, in terms of their own internal politics of resistance, and their politicization by those in power. And both engage power in the arena of style, and thus confront the aesthetics of authority.[15]

Notes

1.   Becker (1963: 181) prefers "interactionist theory of deviance" to "labelling theory." and rightly so. Good, basic interactionist sociology lays the foundation for this sort (and any sort) of criminology.

2. Or, as Clake (1976: 179–180) says, "What must also be stressed is the specificity of each style. This means sensitivity not merely to the objective variations in each style... but also to the different material and cultural conditions under which the styles are generated." My thanks also to H. Stith Bennett for his insights as to the concrete nature of "people doing things together."

3. As already seen in the case of graffiti writing, crime is, of course, also directly political in the sense of being defined constructed by agents of the state, moral entrepreneurs, and other authorities, in their own interest.

4. The Smiths (1987) sing, "Shoplifters of the world, unite and take over." Whatever they mean by this, we might mean the following: Shoplifting embodies both an immersion in commodity culture, and a misshapen but powerful resistance to its rules. But what if everyone shoplifted? Indeed—to what extent would that constitute a united takeover of capitalism? This sort of analysis thus moves beyond Merton to consider the *rebellious politics* of deviant or criminal "innovation." See also Jane's Addiction, "Been Caught Strealing," 1990.

5. For more on notions of crime and resistance, see, for example, Scott, 1990; Sholle, 1990; Atlanta and Alexander, 1989; Hebdige, 1979; and Hall and Jefferson, 1976.

6. As the left realists would remind us, this also means paying close attention to the actual, lived effects of those events on their victims. As we do so, though, we must distinguish between crimes against corporations and the state—shoplifting from chain stores, spraying graffiti on "public" property—and crimes which further Victimize women, the poor, and other relatively powerless groups. Again, paying attention to the nuances of distinct criminal events—rather than, for example, lumping all acts of theft together—is critical. For more on the situated rationally of criminal events, see Katz, 1988.

7. See Lyng (1990) on the social psychology of various "edgework" experiences not unlike the graffiti writer's adrenalin rush.

8. See Hebdige, 1979; Atlanta and Alexander, 1989; Ferrel, 1991. Interestingly, in a discussion of people's remaking of mass culture into popular culture, Fiske (1991: 5-6) agues similarly that

> One has to look for the origins of evasion or resistance in the specific social circumstances of those who do this remaking .... The main gain is pleasure and a sense of self-control, or at least control over some of the conditions of one's existence.... Popular pleasures are socially located and organized by the subordinate.... Popular pleasures are often much more located in the body, in the physical, they are much more vulgar.

And as Hebdige (1988: 19, 34) wires in regard to youth cultures,

> I want to challenge the distinction between "pleasure" and "politics"... and to pose instead another concept: the politics of pleasure.... "Politics" and "pleasure," crime and resistance, transgression and carnival are meshed and confounded.

9. This distaste for scheduling also creates problems in writers' doing "signpainting" for others. Becker (1963: 97, 117) likewise notes jazz musicians' noctural schedules as contributing to their deviant careers. See also Melbin (1987) on the conflicts between "nighttimers" and "daytimers."

10. Neighborhood anti-graffiti activists proudly announced to the 1990 Metro Wide Graffiti Summit that, with newly available equipment, they could remove graffiti far faster than writers could put it up. As *The Denver Post* reported:

> Ray Krupa, a resident of the Barnum neighborhood in west Denver, said he has taken it upon himself to wage a one-man war on graffiti in his area. Last year, he embarked on a cleanup of a 110 square-block area.... "I'm more efficient than the graffiti taggers," Krupa explained. "I have a truck and a big roller. They're on foot and have a spray can. I can wipe out 20 hours of their tagging in three or four hours" (in Gottlieb, 1990: 6B).

11. Graffiti that comes in off streets to be co-opted into conventional art worlds suffers not only from the loss of its street vitality, then, but also from becoming an individually owned commodity to be sold for a profit. See Sanders (1989: 149–163) on the similarities between the artistic legitimation of graffiti writing and tattooing.
Chalfant and Prigoff (1987: 10) also note the irony of gaffiti's "imposition" on others in their discussion of "3D," a British graffiti writer:

> To the objection that writers are forcing their art on a public that has had no say in the matter, 3D answers that people are quite powerless in any case to do anything about the esthetics of their surroundings: "In the city you don't get any say in what they build. You get some architect that does crappy glass buildings or gray buildings. No one comes up and says, 'We're building this, do you like it? Here's the drawings, we'll take a poll.' so why should I have to explain what I do? I live in the city, I am a citizen."

12. Under a section on "Social conditions conducive to anarchy and justice," Tifft (1979:399) notes: "We continue to break barriers and to be committed to risk and vulnerability." The notion of the anarchist as a "ragged clown" captures not only the humor of anarchism, but this vulnerability as well.
13. On the corporate control of "public" environments, see Schiller, 1989.
14. Pink, a female graffiti writer in New York City, says, "Graffiti means 'I'm here'.... People think ghetto children should be seen and not heard, that we're supposed to be born and die in the ghetto. They want to snub us, but they can't" (in Mizrahi, 1981:20; see Atlanta and Alexander, 1989: 167–168).
15. On Third World graffiti, see, for example, Cortazar, 1983; Chaffee, 1989; Sheesley and Bragg, 1991. See also Bushnell (1990) on Moscow graffiti, and Posener's (1982) excellent photographic essay on politically progressive graffiti in Great Britain. Comparisons of First World and Third World graffiti also recall the sharp similarities between internal and external colonialism. Thus, as before, the politics of graffiti writing transcends a narrow conception of individual motivation; the social meanings of "intentionally" political Third World graffiti and "unintentionally' political Third World graffiti and "unintentionally" political First World graffiti overlap in the lived Politics of authority and insubordination.

References

Atlanta and Alexander (1989). "Wild Style: Graffiti Painting." In Angela McRobbie, ed., *Zoot Suits and Second-Hand Dresses*. Houndmills, U.K: Macmillan, 156–168.

Avrich, Paul, (ed.) (1973). *The Anarchists in the Russian Revolution*. Ithaca, N.Y.: Cornell University Press.

Becker, Howard S. (1963). *Outsiders: Studies in the Sociology of Deviance*. New York: Free Press.

Bushnell, John (1990). *Moscow Graffiti: Language and Subculture*. Boston: Unwin Hyman.

Chaffee, Lyman (1989). "Political Graffiti and Wall Painting in Greater Buenos Aires: An Alternative Communication System." *Studies in Latin American Popular Culture* 8: 37–60.

Chalfant, Henry and James Prigoff (1987). *Spraycan Art*. London: Thames and Hudson.

Clarke, John (1976). "Style." In Stuart Hall and Tony Jefferson, eds., *Resistance Through Rituals: Youth Subcultures in Post-War Britain*. London: Hutchinson, 175–191.

Cortazar, Julio (1983). "Graffiti." In *We Love Glenda So Much and Other Tales*. New York: A. Knopf, 33–38.

Cosgrove, Stuart (1984). "The Zoot-Suit and Style Warfare." *Radical America* 18: 38–51.

Ferrell, Jeff (1990a) "Bomber's Confidential: Interview with Eye Six and Rasta 68." (Part Two). *Clot* 1: 10–11.

Ferrell, Jeff (1991). "The Brotherhood of Timber Workers and the Culture of Conflict." *Journal of Folklore Research* 28: 163–177.

Fiske, John (1991). "An Interview with John Fiske." *Border/Lines* 20/21: 4–7.

Gottlieb, Alan (1990). "City leaders vow to persevere in battle against graffiti." *The Denver Post* (May 12): 6B.

Guerin, Daniel (1970) *Anarchism*. New York: Monthly Review Press.

Hall, Stuart and Tony Jefferson, (eds) (1976) *Resistance through Rituals: Youth Subcultures in Post-War Britain*. London: Hutchinson.

Hebdige, Dick (1979) *Subculture: The Meaning of Style*. London: Methuen.

Katz, Jack (1988) *Seductions of Crime: Moral and Sensual Attractions in Doing Evil*. New York: Basic Books.

Lyng, Stephen (1990). "Edgework: A Social Psychological Analysis of Voluntary Risk Taking." *American Journal of Sociology* 95: 851–886.

Melbin, Murray (1987). *Night as Frontier*. New York: Free Press.

Mizrahi, Marilyn (1981). "Up from the Subway." *In These Times* (October 21–27): 19–20.

Parks, Ron (1990) "Busking." *Border/Lines* 19: 7–8.

Polsky, Ned (1969) *Hustlers, Beats and Others*. Garden City, N.Y.: Doubleday.

Posener, Jill (1982). *Spray It Loud*. London: Pandora Press.

Scott, James (1990). *Domination and the Arts of Resistance*. New Haven: Yale.

Sheesley, Joel and Wayne Bragg (1991). *Sandino in the Steets*, Bloomington: Indiana University Press.

Sholle, David (1990). "Resistance: Pinning Down a Wandering Concept in Cultural Studies Discourse." *Journal of Urban and Cultural Studies* 1:87–105.

Critical connections

Media and mediatisation are integral to understanding criminal cultures and cultures of criminalisation. Particular media forms – mass media, news conferences, political press releases – can be instrumental in the processes through which other media forms – the products of artists, musicians, film makers – are delegitimised, marginalised or criminalised. This spiralling process of mediatised claim and counter-claim creates a 'complex hall of mirrors', generating not only images, but images of images, as 'culture wars' are fought over the linkages between signs and symbols, lifestyles and legitimacy, what is culture and what is crime.

Though the interests of cultural criminology are expansive and its proponents have tackled everything from dumpster diving (Ferrell, 2006) to the war on terror and the 'sins of Abu Ghraib' (Hamm, 2007), the perspective is not without its critics. Some have argued that cultural criminology's focus on 'the allegedly plural and transgressive sub-cultural foreground of criminality has drawn our attention away from the restrictive and constitutive politico-cultural power that the mutating "deep structure" of capitalism wields over contemporary social life' (Hall and Winlow, 2006: 82). Cultural criminologists respond by insisting that the orientation towards the cultural is less a turn 'away from a materialist analysis of capitalism as towards a fuller analysis of power, domination, and crime ... [P]ower, conflict, and crime can configure themselves in any number of ways, with capitalism and its crimes but one among them' (Ferrell, 2006: 92). The debate continues, and can only be good for the development of reflexive, critical criminology at a time when administrative, ahistorical and anti-sociological 'criminologies of everyday life' (Garland, 2001) have secured such a tight grasp on the criminological mainstream and policy agenda.

Discussion questions

- How can graffiti be conceived as a form of cultural and political resistance?
- In what ways are subcultural styles and practices repackaged for mass consumption in a market society?
- Cultural criminology insists that both the 'background' political economy of criminality and the 'foreground' aesthetics, emotions and meanings of criminal transgression should constitute the object of criminological enquiry. Discuss this claim with respect to different forms of deviance and 'criminality'.

References

Ferrell, J. (2006) *Empire of Scrounge: Inside the Urban Underground of Dumpster Driving, Trash Picking, and Street Scavenging*, New York: New York University Press.

Ferrell, J. (2007) 'For a ruthless cultural criticism of everything existing' in *Crime, Media, Culture: An International Journal*, 3: 1, 91–100.

Ferrell, J. (1999) 'Cultural criminology' in E. McLaughlin et al (eds) (2003) *Criminological Perspectives; Essential Readings*, London: Sage.

Ferrell, J., Hayward, K. and Young, J. (2008) *Cultural Criminology: An Invitation*, London: Sage.

Garland, D. (2001) *The Culture of Control*, Oxford: Oxford University Press.

Hall, S. and Winlow, S. (2007) Cultural criminology and primitive accumulation: A formal introduction for two strangers who should really become more intimate, in *Crime, Media, Culture; An International Journal*, 3, 1: 82–90

Hamm, M. (2007) 'High Crimes and Misdemeanors: George Bush and the Sins of Abu Ghraib', in *Crime, Media, Culture: An International Journal*, 3, 3,: 259–284.

SECTION FIVE

Effects, influence and moral panic

Introduction

CONCERNS ABOUT THE IMPACT of media images on individuals and society at large are as old as media themselves. One of the most striking commonalities across the now vast literature on media influence is the assertion, and frequently just the assumption, that the media are primarily damaging or detrimental to society. The pro-social impact of media has been much less researched. Three principal areas of research interest are the 'effects' of media violence on human behaviour, the impact of media images of crime and deviance on fear of crime, and the role of media in the production of moral panics.

Concerns about media influence have taken different forms depending on their ideological underpinnings. For the traditional right, the concern has been that media representations – nearly always popular cultural rather than news-related – glamorise violence and criminality and, in so doing, increase the likelihood that media consumers will engage in violent or criminal behaviour themselves. On the left, the concern has been that media images of crime and violence increase fear of crime (FOC). Since a fearful public is allegedly more malleable and open to political persuasion, the suggestion is that FOC, and in its particularly acute form 'moral panic', forms one part of the shift toward an authoritarian state by legitimating the introduction of more punitive law and order policies or national security measures, crucially with the consent of the people. Moral panics – intense, media-fuelled bursts of collective concern or outrage directed against particular 'folk devils' – have been researched and written about so much that the term has moved into common parlance and is today routinely deployed by journalists and politicians when commenting on matters of crime and disorder (Altheide, 2009).

The readings selected for inclusion in this section of the book comprise the seminal research statements in each field – media effects, fear of crime and moral panic – each of which has generated scores if not hundreds of attempts to replicate, confirm, challenge or debunk the original findings. For each original research statement there is a critical answer. Thus Albert Bandura and colleagues' (1963) classic research on mediated violence and imitative learning – the paradigmatic example of media–violence research – should be read alongside David Gauntlett's (2001) critique of the 'effects industry' that emerged in its wake. Barker and Petley (2001) echo many of Gauntlett's criticisms in their discussion of how media-violence research *should* be conducted. Gerbner and Gross's (1976) largely quantitative research led them to assert in the 1970s that heavy television viewing cultivates fear and anxiety, and an overriding view of the world as 'mean and scary'. Ditton *et al.*'s (2004) more recent research prioritises a qualitative approach to understanding media and fear of crime which, they claim, can better account for the variable meanings that media violence may hold for different consumers in different contexts, depending on myriad factors including class, rage, gender, age, and personal experience. Stanley Cohen's (1972, 2002) classic sociological development of the concept of 'moral panic' – in this analysis around particular youth cultures in 1960s Britain – laid the foundations for countless adaptations and applications across a vast array of settings. Whilst fully acknowledging the importance of this original statement, however, McRobbie and Thornton (1995) argue that some 30 years later the concept needs to be rethought within the context of multi-mediated societies.

References

Altheide, D. (2009) 'Moral Panic: From Sociological Concept to Public Discourse', in *Crime, Media, Culture: An International Journal*, 5, 1:79–99.

Albert Bandura, Dorothea Ross and Sheila Ross

IMITATION OF FILM-MEDIATED AGGRESSIVE MODELS (1963)

Introduction and context

'**I**MITATION OF FILM-MEDIATED AGGRESSIVE MODELS' describes research conducted by Albert Bandura and colleagues at Stanford University, California, in the 1960s. Given its focus on imitative learning, it is ironic that the study has itself spawned hundreds of imitations, and now represents the archetype for laboratory-based media 'effects' research. Subjects are exposed to a violent stimulus, to which a control group is not exposed, and then subsequent behaviour is observed in order to measure the degree of media 'effect'. This stimulus-response design has been amended and adapted over several decades by scores of researchers to cater for variations in age, gender and class, exposure to different forms of violence, with different repercussions (rewarded or punished, for example), and over different periods of time. But the fundamental proposition has remained largely unaltered: there is a direct causal connection between exposure to media violence and subsequent aggressive or violent behaviour, and that connection can be (quantitatively) evidenced through the application of scientific method. Yet despite a huge number of research studies, the media effects debate remains unresolved and the cumulative body of 'evidence' is highly equivocal (Livingstone, 1996). This is partly, as Robert Reiner points out, because 'the armoury of possible research techniques for assessing directly the effects of media images on crime is sparse and suffers from evident and long-recognized limitations' (2007: 318).

Most of the research on the possible effects of film-mediated stimulation upon subsequent aggressive behavior has focused primarily on the drive reducing function of fantasy. While the experimental evidence for the catharsis or drive reduction theory is equivocal (Albert, 1957; Berkowitz, 1962; Emery, 1959; Feshbach, 1955, 1958; Kenny, 1952; Lövaas, 1961; Siegel, 1956), the modeling influence of pictorial stimuli has received little research attention.

A recent incident (San Francisco Chronicle, 1961) in which a boy was seri-ously knifed during a re-enactment of a switchblade knife fight the boys had seen the previous evening on a televised rerun of the James Dean movie, *Rebel Without a Cause*, is a dra-matic illustration of the possible imitative influence of film stimulation. Indeed, anec-dotal data suggest that portrayal of aggression through pictorial media may be more influential in shaping the form aggression will take when a person is instigated on later occasions, than in altering the level of instigation to aggression. [. . .]

The present study sought to determine the extent to which film-mediated aggressive models may serve as an important source of imitative behavior.

Aggressive models can be ordered on a reality-fictional stimulus dimension with real-life models located at the reality end of the continuum, nonhuman cartoon characters at the fictional end, and films portraying human models occupying an intermediate position. It was predicted, on the basis of saliency and similarity of cues, that the more remote the model was from reality, the weaker would be the tendency for subjects to imitate the behavior of the model.

Of the various interpretations of imitative learning, the sensory feedback theory of imitation recently proposed by Mowrer (1960) is elaborated in greatest detail. According to this theory, if certain responses have been repeatedly positively rein-forced, proprioceptive stimuli associated with these responses acquire secondary reinforcing properties and thus the individual is predisposed to perform the behavior for the positive feedback. Similarly, if responses have been negatively reinforced, response correlated stimuli acquire the capacity to arouse anxiety which, in turn, inhibit the occurrence of the negatively valenced behavior. On the basis of these con-siderations, it was predicted subjects who manifest high aggression anxiety would perform significantly less imitative and nonimitative aggression than subjects who display little anxiety over aggression. Since aggression is generally considered female inappropriate behavior, and therefore likely to be negatively reinforced in girls (Sears, Maccoby, & Levin, 1957), it was also predicted that male subjects would be more imitative of aggression than females.

To the extent that observation of adults displaying aggression conveys a certain degree of permissiveness for aggressive behavior, it may be assumed that such expo-sure not only facilitates the learning of new aggressive responses but also weakens competing inhibitory responses in subjects and thereby increases the probability of occurrence of previously learned patterns of aggression. It was predicted, therefore, that subjects who observed aggressive models would display significantly more aggres-sion when subsequently frustrated than subjects who were equally frustrated but who had no prior exposure to models exhibiting aggression.

Method

Subjects

The subjects were 48 boys and 48 girls enrolled in the Stanford University Nursery School. They ranged in age from 35 to 69 months, with a mean age of 52 months.

Two adults, a male and a female, served in the role of models both in the real-life and the human film-aggression condition, and one female experimenter conducted the study for all 96 children.

General procedure

Subjects were divided into three experimental groups and one control group of 24 subjects each. One group of experimental subjects observed real-life aggressive models, a second group observed these same models portraying aggression on film, while a third group viewed a film depicting an aggressive cartoon character. The experimental groups were further subdivided into male and female subjects so that half the subjects in the two conditions involving human models were exposed to same-sex models, while the remaining subjects viewed models of the opposite sex.

Following the exposure experience, subjects were tested for the amount of imitative and nonimitative aggression in a different experimental setting in the absence of the models.

The control group subjects had no exposure to the aggressive models and were tested only in the generalization situation.

Subjects in the experimental and control groups were matched individually on the basis of ratings of their aggressive behavior in social interactions in the nursery school. The experimenter and a nursery school teacher rated the subjects on four five-point rating scales which measured the extent to which subjects displayed physical aggression, verbal aggression, aggression toward inanimate objects, and aggression inhibition. The latter scale, which dealt with the subjects' tendency to inhibit aggressive reactions in the face of high instigation, provided the measure of aggression anxiety. Seventy-one percent of the subjects were rated independently by both judges so as to permit an assessment of interrater agreement. The reliability of the composite aggression score, estimated by means of the Pearson product-moment correlation, was . 80.

Data for subjects in the real-life aggression condition and in the control group were collected as part of a previous experiment (Bandura et al., 1961). Since the procedure is described in detail in the earlier report, only a brief description of it will be presented here.

Experimental conditions

Subjects in the Real-Life Aggressive condition were brought individually by the experimenter to the experimental room and the model, who was in the hallway outside the room, was invited by the experimenter to come and join in the game. The subject was then escorted to one corner of the room and seated at a small table which contained potato prints, multicolor picture stickers, and colored paper. After demonstrating how the subject could design pictures with the materials provided, the experimenter escorted the model to the opposite corner of the room which contained a small table and chair, a tinker toy set, a mallet, and a 5-foot inflated Bobo doll. The experimenter explained that this was the model's play area and after the model was seated, the experimenter left the experimental room.

The model began the session by assembling the tinker toys but after approximately a minute had elapsed, the model turned to the Bobo doll and spent the remainder of the period aggressing toward it with highly novel responses which are unlikely to be performed by children independently of the observation of the model's behavior. Thus, in addition to punching the Bobo doll, the model exhibited the following distinctive aggressive acts which were to be scored as imitative responses:

The model sat on the Bobo doll and punched it repeatedly in the nose.

The model then raised the Bobo doll and pommeled it on the head with a mallet.

Following the mallet aggression, the model tossed the doll up in the air aggressively and kicked it about the room. This sequence of physically aggressive acts was repeated approximately three times, interspersed with verbally aggressive responses such as, "Sock him in the nose . . .," "Hit him down . . .," "Throw him in the air . . .," "Kick him . . .," and "Pow."

Subjects in the Human Film-Aggression condition were brought by the experimenter to the semi-darkened experimental room, introduced to the picture materials, and informed that while the subjects worked on potato prints, a movie would be shown on a screen, positioned approximately 6 feet from the subject's table. The movie projector was located in a distant corner of the room and was screened from the subject's view by large wooden panels.

The color movie and a tape recording of the sound track was begun by a male projectionist as soon as the experimenter left the experimental room and was shown for a duration of 10 minutes. The models in the film presentations were the same adult males and females who participated in the Real-Life condition of the experiment. Similarly, the aggressive behavior they portrayed in the film was identical with their real-life performances.

For subjects in the Cartoon Film-Aggression condition, after seating the subject at the table with the picture construction material, the experimenter walked over to a television console approximately 3 feet in front of the subject's table, remarked, "I guess I'll turn on the color TV," and ostensibly tuned in a cartoon program. The experimenter then left the experimental room. The cartoon was shown on a glass lens screen in the television set by means of a rear projection arrangement screened from the subject's view by large panels.

The sequence of aggressive acts in the cartoon was performed by the female model costumed as a black cat similar to the many cartoon cats. In order to heighten the level of irreality of the cartoon, the floor area was covered with artificial grass and the walls forming the backdrop were adorned with brightly colored trees, birds, and butterflies creating a fantasyland setting. The cartoon began with a close-up of a stage on which the curtains were slowly drawn revealing a picture of a cartoon cat along with the title, *Herman the Cat*. The remainder of the film showed the cat pommeling the Bobo doll on the head with a mallet, sitting on the doll and punching it in the nose, tossing the doll in the air, and kicking it about the room in a manner identical with the performance in the other experimental conditions except that the cat's movements were characteristically feline. To induce further a cartoon set, the program was introduced and concluded with appropriate cartoon music, and the cat's verbal aggression was repeated in a high-pitched, animated voice.

In both film conditions, at the conclusion of the movie the experimenter entered the room and then escorted the subject to the test room.

Aggression instigation

In order to differentiate clearly the exposure and test situations subjects were tested for the amount of imitative learning in a different experiment: a room which was set off from the main nursery school building.

The degree to which a child has learned aggressive patterns of behavior through imitation becomes most evident when the child is instigated to aggression on later occasions. Thus, for example, the effects of viewing the movie, *Rebel Without a Cause,* were not evident until the boys were instigated to aggression the following day, at which time they re-enacted the televised switchblade knife fight in considerable detail. For this reason, the children in the experiment, both those in the control group and those who were exposed to the aggressive models, were mildly frustrated before they were brought to the test room.

Following the exposure experience, the experimenter brought the subject to an anteroom which contained a varied array of highly attractive toys. The experimenter explained that the toys were for the subject to play with, but, as soon as the subject became sufficiently involved with the play material, the experimenter remarked that these were her very best toys, that she did not let just anyone play with them, and that she had decided to reserve these toys for some other children. However, the subject could play with any of the toys in the next room. The experimenter and the subject then entered the adjoining experimental room.

It was necessary for the experimenter to remain in the room during the experimental session; otherwise, a number of the children would either refuse to remain alone or would leave before the termination of the session. In order to minimize any influence her presence might have on the subject's behavior, the experimenter remained as inconspicuous as possible by busying herself with paper work at a desk in the far corner of the room and avoiding any interaction with the child.

Test for delayed imitation

The experimental room contained a variety of toys, some of which could be used in imitative or nonimitative aggression, and others which tended to elicit predominantly nonaggressive forms of behavior. The aggressive toys included a 3-foot Bobo doll, a mallet and peg board, two dart guns, and a tether ball with a face painted on it which hung from the ceiling. The nonaggressive toys, on the other hand, included a tea set, crayons and coloring paper, a ball, two dolls, three bears, cars and trucks, and plastic farm animals.

In order to eliminate any variation in behavior due to mere placement of the toys in the room, the play material was arranged in a fixed order for each of the sessions.

The subject spent 20 minutes in the experimental room during which time his behavior was rated in terms of predetermined response categories by judges who observed the session through a one-way mirror in an adjoining observation room. The 20-minute session was divided in 5-second intervals by means of an electric interval timer, thus yielding a total number of 240 response units for each subject.

The male model scored the experimental sessions for all subjects. In order to provide an estimate of interjudge agreement, the performances of 40% of the subjects were scored independently by a second observer. The responses scored involved highly specific concrete classes of behavior, and yielded high interscorer reliabilities, the product-moment coefficients being in the .90s.

Response measures

The following response measures were obtained:

Imitative aggression. This category included acts of striking the Bobo doll with the mallet, sitting on the doll and punching it in the nose, kicking the doll, tossing it in the air, and the verbally aggressive responses, "Sock him," "Hit him down," "Kick him," "Throw him in the air," and "Pow."

Partially imitative responses. A number of subjects imitated the essential components of the model's behavior but did not perform the complete act, or they directed the imitative aggressive response to some object other than the Bobo doll. Two responses of this type were scored and were interpreted as partially imitative behavior:

Mallet aggression. The subject strikes objects other than the Bobo doll aggressively with the mallet.

Sits on Bobo doll. The subject lays the Bobo doll on its side and sits on it, but does not aggress toward it.

Nonimitative aggression. This category included acts of punching, slapping, or pushing the doll, physically aggressive acts directed toward objects other than the Bobo doll, and any hostile remarks except for those in the verbal imitation category; for example, "Shoot the Bobo," "Cut him," "Stupid ball," "Knock over people," "Horses fighting, biting."

Aggressive gun play. The subject shoots darts or aims the guns and fires imaginary shots at objects in the room.

Ratings were also made of the number of behavior units in which subjects played nonaggressively or sat quietly and did not play with any of the material at all.

Results

The mean imitative and nonimitative aggression scores for subjects in the various experimental and control groups are presented in Table 1. [. . .]

Total aggression

The mean total aggression scores for subjects in the real-life, human film, cartoon film, and the control groups are 83, 92, 99, and 54, respectively [. . .] confirming the prediction that exposure of subjects to aggressive models increases the probability that subjects will respond aggressively when instigated on later occasions. [. . .] [S]ubjects who viewed the real-life models and the film-mediated models do not differ from each other in total aggressiveness but all three experimental groups expressed significantly more aggressive behavior than the control subjects (Table 2).

Table 1 Mean aggression scores for subgroups of experimental and control subjects

| Response category | Experimental groups | | | | | |
| | Real-life aggressive | | Human film-aggressive | | Cartoon film-aggressive | |
	F Model	M Model	F Model	M Model		Control group
Total aggression						
Girls	65.8	57.3	87.0	79.5	80.9	36.4
Boys	76.8	131.8	114.5	85.0	117.2	72.2
Imitative aggression						
Girls	19.2	9.2	10.0	8.0	7.8	1.8
Boys	18.4	38.4	34.3	13.3	16.2	3.9
Mallet aggression						
Girls	17.2	18.7	49.2	19.5	36.8	13.1
Boys	15.5	28.8	20.5	16.3	12.5	13.5
Sits on Bobo doll[a]						
Girls	10.4	5.6	10.3	4.5	15.3	3.3
Boys	1.3	0.7	7.7	0.0	5.6	0.6
Nonimitative aggression						
Girls	27.6	24.9	24.0	34.3	27.5	17.8
Boys	35.5	48.6	46.8	31.8	71.8	40.4
Aggressive gun play						
Girls	1.8	4.5	3.8	17.6	8.8	3.7
Boys	7.3	15.9	12.8	23.7	16.6	14.3

[a] This response category was not included in the total aggression score.

Imitative aggressive responses

[. . .] [S]ubjects who observed the real-life models and the film-mediated models, relative to subjects in the control group, performed considerably more imitative physical and verbal aggression (Table 2).

Illustrations of the extent to which some of the subjects became virtually "carbon copies" of their models in aggressive behavior are presented in Figure 29.1. The top frame shows the female model performing the four novel aggressive responses; the lower frames depict a male and a female subject reproducing the behavior of the female model they had observed earlier on film. [. . .]

Table 2 Significance of the differences between experimental and control groups in the expression of aggression

Response category	x_r^2	P	Comparison of treatment conditions[a]					
			Live vs. Film	Live vs. Cartoon	Film vs. Cartoon	Live vs. Control	Film vs. Control	Cartoon vs. Control
			P	P	P	P	P	P
Total aggression	9.06	<.05	ns	ns	ns	<.01	<.01	<.005
Imitative aggression	23.88	<.001	ns	<.05	ns	<.001	<.001	<.005
Partialimitation								
Mallet aggression	7.36	.10>p>.05						
Sits on Bobo doll	8.05	<.05	ns	ns	ns	ns	<.05	<.005
Nonimitative aggression	7.28	.10>p>.05						
Aggressive gun play	8.06	<.05	<.01[b]	ns	ns	ns	<.05	ns

[a] The probability values are based on the Wilcoxon test.
[b] This probability value is based on a two-tailed test of significance.

Indeed, the available data suggest that, of the three experimental conditions, exposure to humans on film portraying aggression was the most influential in eliciting and shaping aggressive behavior. Subjects in this condition, in relation to the control subjects, exhibited more total aggression, more imitative aggression, more partially imitative behavior, such as sitting on the Bobo doll and mallet aggression, and they engaged in significantly more aggressive gun play. In addition, they performed significantly more aggressive gun play than did subjects who were exposed to the real-life aggressive models (Table 2).

Influence of sex of model and sex of child

[. . .] Sex of subjects had a highly significant effect on both the learning and the performance of aggression. Boys, in relation to girls exhibited significantly more total aggression ($t = 2.69, p <.01$), more imitative aggression ($t = 2.82, p <.005$), more aggressive gun play ($z = 3.38, p <.001$), and more nonimitative aggressive behavior ($t = 2.98, p <.005$). Girls, on the other hand, were more inclined than boys to sit on the Bobo doll but refrained from punching it ($z = 3.47, p <.001$).

The analyses also disclosed some influences of the sex of the model. Subjects exposed to the male model, as compared to the female model, expressed significantly more aggressive gun play ($z = 2.83, p <.005$). The most marked differences in aggressive gun play ($U = 9.5, p <.001$), however, were found between girls exposed to the female model ($M = 2.9$) and males who observed the male model ($M = 19.8$). [. . .]

These findings [. . .] provide further support for the view that the influence of models in promoting social learning is determined, in part, by the sex appropriateness of the model's behavior (Bandura et al., 1961). [. . .]

Figure 29.1 Photographs from the film, *Social Learning of Aggression through Imitation of Aggressive Models*.

Discussion

The results of the present study provide strong evidence that exposure to filmed aggression heightens aggressive reactions in children. Subjects who viewed the aggressive human and cartoon models on film exhibited nearly twice as much aggression than did subjects in the control group who were not exposed to the aggressive film content.

In the experimental design typically employed for testing the possible cathartic function of vicarious aggression, subjects are first frustrated, then provided with an opportunity to view an aggressive film following which their overt or fantasy aggression is measured. While this procedure yields some information on the immediate influence of film-mediated aggression, the full effects of such exposure may not be revealed until subjects are instigated to aggression on a later occasion. Thus, the present study, and one recently reported by Lövaas (1961), both utilizing a design in which subjects first observed filmed aggression and then were frustrated, clearly reveal that observation of models portraying aggression on film substantially increases rather than decreases the probability of aggressive reactions to subsequent frustrations.

Filmed aggression, not only facilitated the expression of aggression, but also effectively shaped the form of the subjects' aggressive behavior. The finding that children modeled their behavior to some extent after the film characters suggests that pictorial mass media, particularly television, may serve as an important source of social behavior. [. . .]

The view that the social learning of aggression through exposure to aggressive film content is confined to deviant children (Schramm, Lyle, & Parker, 1961), finds little support in our data. The children who participated in the experiment are by no means a deviant sample, nevertheless, 88% of the subjects in the Real-Life and in the Human Film condition, and 79% of the subjects in the Cartoon Film condition, exhibited varying degrees of imitative aggression. In assessing the possible influence of televised stimulation on viewers' behavior, however, it is important to distinguish between learning and overt performance. Although the results of the present experiment demonstrate that the vast majority of children *learn* patterns of social behavior through pictorial stimulation, nevertheless, informal observation suggests that children do not, as a rule, *perform* indiscriminately the behavior of televised charac-ters, even those they regard as highly attractive models. The replies of parents whose children participated in the present study to an open-end questionnaire item con-cerning their handling of imitative behavior suggest that this may be in part a function of negative reinforcement, as most parents were quick to discourage their children's overt imitation of television characters by prohibiting certain programs or by labeling the imitative behavior in a disapproving manner. From our knowledge of the effects of punishment on behavior, the responses in question would be expected to retain their original strength and could reappear on later occasions in the presence of appropriate eliciting stimuli, particularly if instigation is high, the instruments for aggression are available, and the threat of noxious consequences is reduced. [. . .]

A question may be raised as to whether the aggressive acts studied in the present experiment constitute "genuine" aggressive responses. Aggression is typically defined as behavior, the goal or intent of which is injury to a person, or destruction of an object (Bandura & Walters, 1959; Dollard, Doob, Miller, Mowrer, & Sears, 1939; Sears, Maccoby, & Levin, 1957). Since intentionality is not a property of behavior but primarily an inference concerning antecedent events, the categorization of an act as "aggressive" involves a consideration of both stimulus and mediating or terminal response events.

According to a social learning theory of aggression recently proposed by Bandura and Walters (in press), most of the responses utilized to hurt or to injure others (for example, striking, kicking, and other responses of high magnitude), are probably learned for prosocial purposes under nonfrustration conditions. Since frustration generally elicits responses of high magnitude, the latter classes of responses, once acquired, may be called out in social interactions for the purpose of injuring others. On the basis of this theory it would be predicted that the aggressive responses acquired imitatively, while not necessarily mediating aggressive goals in the experi-mental situation, would be utilized to serve such purposes in other social settings with higher frequency by children in the experimental conditions than by children in the control group.

The present study involved primarily vicarious or empathic learning (Mowrer, 1960) in that subjects acquired a relatively complex repertoire of aggressive responses by the mere sight of a model's behavior. It has been generally assumed that the neces-sary conditions for the occurrence of such learning is that the model perform certain responses followed by positive reinforcement to the model (Hill, 1960; Mowrer, 1960). According to this theory, to the extent that the observer experiences the model's reinforcement vicariously, the observer will be prone to reproduce the model's behavior. While there is some evidence from experiments involving both human (Lewis & Duncan, 1958; McBrearty, Marston, & Kanfer, 1961; Sechrest, 1961) and animal subjects (Darby & Riopelle, 1959; Warden, Fjeld, & Koch, 1940), that vicarious reinforcement may in fact increase the probability of the behavior in question, it is apparent from the results of the experiment reported in this paper that a good deal of human imitative learning can occur without any reinforcers delivered either to the model or to the observer. [. . .]

References

Albert, R. S. The role of mass media and the effect of aggressive film content upon children's aggressive responses and identification choices. *Genet. Psychol. Monogr.*, 1957, 55, 221–285.

Bandura, A., & Walters, R. H. *Adolescent aggression.* New York: Ronald, 1959.

Bandura, A., & Walters, R. H. *The social learning of deviant behavior: A behavioristic approach to socialization.* New York: Holt, Rinehart, & Winston, in press.

Banduta, A., Ross, Dorothea & Ross, Sheela A. Transmission of aggression through imitation of aggressive models. *J. Abnorm. Soc. Psychol.*, 1961, 63, 575–583.

Berkowitz, L. *Aggression: A social psychological analysis.* New York: McGraw-Hill, 1962.

Darby, C. L, & Riopelle, A. J. Observational learning in the Rhesus monkey. *J. comp. physiol. Psychol.*, 1959, 52, 94–98.

Dollard, J., Doob, L. W., Miller, N. E., Mowrer, O. H., & Sears, R. R. *Frustration and aggression.* New Haven: Yale Univer. Press, 1939.

Emery, F. E. Psychological effects of the Western film: A study in television viewing: II. The experimental study. *Hum. Relat.*, 1959, 12, 215–232.

Feshbach, S. The drive-reducing function of fantasy behavior. *J. abnorm. soc. Psychol.*, 1955, 50, 3–11.

Feshbach, S. The stimulating versus cathartic effects of a vicarious aggressive activity. Paper read at the Eastern Psychological Association, 1958.

Hill, W. F. Learning theory and the acquisition of values. *Psychol. Rev.*, 1960, 67, 317–331.

Kenny, D. T. An experimental test of the catharsis theory of aggression. Unpublished doctoral dissertation, University of Washington, 1952.

Lewis, D. J., & Duncan, C. P. Vicarious experience and partial reinforcement. *J. abnorm. soc. Psychol.*, 1958, 57, 321–326.

Lövaas, O. J. Effect of exposure to symbolic aggression on aggressive behavior. *Child Develpm.*, 1961, 32, 37–44.

McBrearty, J. F., Marston, A. R., & Kanfer, F. H. Conditioning a verbal operant in a group setting: Direct vs. vicarious reinforcement. *Amer. Psychologist*, 1961, 16, 425. (Abstract)

Mowrer, O. H. *Learning theory and the symbolic processes.* New York: Wiley, 1960.

San Francisco Chronicle. "James Dean" knifing in South City. *San Francisco Chron.*, March 1, 1961, 6.

Schramm, W., Lyle, J., & Parker, E. B. *Television in the lives of our children.* Stanford: Stanford Univer. Press, 1961.

Sears, R. R., Maccoby, Eleanor E., & Levin, H. *Patterns of child rearing.* Evanston: Row, Peterson, 1957.

Sechrest, L. Vicarious reinforcement of responses. *Amer. Psychologist*, 1961, 16, 356. (Abstract)

Siegel, Alberta E. Film-mediated fantasy aggression and strength of aggressive drive. *Child Develpm.*, 1956, 27, 365–378.

Warden, C. J., Fjeld, H. A., & Koch, A. M. Imitative behavior in cebus and Rhesus monkeys. *J. genet. Psychol.*, 1940, 56, 311–322.

Critical connections

The behavioural effects tradition, typified in Bandura *et al.*'s (1963) research, has been subject to punishing criticism from a wide range of researchers representing a diversity of methodological and theoretical positions. Many of the most forceful criticisms are outlined by David Gauntlett in this Reader (Reading 30), and need not be elaborated in detail here. One key point, however, is that effects research contains at least an implicit suggestion that people are passive recipients of media messages, and that this passivity in part accounts for their susceptibility to media influence. This view of a simple and mechanical determinism ignores the crucial issue of human reflexivity and, as such, it runs directly counter to more holistic qualitative analyses, including both Stuart Hall's classic Encoding–Decoding model (1980), and the recent audience research by Jenny Kitzinger (2004) (Readings 4 and 13 respectively). The aim in these studies is not to deny or dismiss the possibility of direct media influence, but to conceptualise and understand media reception as an interactive or dialectical social process shaped by a host of structural and cultural variables. Behavioural effects research tends to ignore wider structural and cultural factors, looking instead for a pure and isolated media effect.

Discussion questions

●   What is the central premise of imitative social learning?
●   Is it possible to identify particular types of person who might be more or less susceptible to media influence?
●   To what extent are you influenced by violence in the media, and do different forms of media violence influence or affect you in different ways?

References

Livingstone, S. (1996) 'On the Continuing Problem of Media Effects', in J. Curran and M. Gurevitch (eds) *Mass Media and Society*. London: Arnold.

Reiner, R. (2007) 'Media Made Criminality: The representation of crime in the mass media', in M. Maguire, R. Morgan and R. Reiner (eds) *The Oxford Handbook of Criminology* (4th edn). Oxford: Oxford University Press.

David Gauntlett

THE WORRYING INFLUENCE OF 'MEDIA EFFECTS' STUDIES (2001)

Introduction and context

O NE OF THE MOST cogent general critiques of effects research is presented by David Gauntlett in 'The Worrying Influence of Media Effects Studies'. Gauntlett seeks to deconstruct the media effects industry by identifying the commonalities across a range of studies, rather than picking on any one study in particular. This approach is especially helpful within the context of this book, since it provides readers with an 'evaluative check list' of sorts which can be applied to any media effects research studies they may come across – including some of those excerpted in these pages. Gauntlett's criticisms of media effects studies are not of a superficial nature. Rather, they raise fundamental questions about the validity and appropriateness of the theories, methods, concepts and – in many cases – the moral politics that have traditionally underpinned much 'effects' research.

Ten things wrong with the 'effects model'

This analysis contains very few references to specific studies because these arguments apply to *so many* studies. The author hopes that the intelligent student of media effects studies will apply these ideas to whatever research they read about elsewhere. The book *Moving Experiences* (Gauntlett, 1995) was a close examination of numerous individual studies; the criticisms below are deliberately much more general.[1]

The effects model tackles social problems 'backwards'

To understand the causes of violence, or other human behaviour, research should logically begin with the people who engage in those actions. By studying what motivates and prompts their behaviour, by understanding their background and their goals, we might hope to be able to explain the roots of such acts.

Media effects researchers, however, have typically started at the wrong end of this question: informed only by speculation (and, often, a certain disregard for both young people and popular media), they begin with the idea that the media is to blame, and then try to make links back to the world of actual violence. This 'backwards' approach to a perceived problem makes little sense. To illustrate this point by way of a different example: if it had been suggested that the most successful entrepreneurs were people who had listened to a great deal of classical music when younger, the first step in any investigation of a causal link would be to interview a number of successful entrepreneurs and ask them whether they had heard much classical music and, if so, whether (and how) they felt it had affected their development. Only then, if this provided encouraging results, would we proceed to the second stage, which would be focused upon classical music itself: for example, we might try to identify 'inspirational' chords or harmonies and engage in studies which explored how people seemed to be affected by the music. The problem with much media effects research, however, is that researchers have jumped straight to the second stage – investigating the media and its possible 'effects' – without even bothering with the first one, namely checking whether any notable suspects have in fact been affected.

To understand violent people, I recommend studying violent people. [...]

In [a] well-designed piece of research [...], Hagell and Newburn (1994) studied 78 teenage offenders (who had histories of violence and other serious offences), and compared them with a group of over 500 non-offending young people of the same age. They found that the young offenders, when not incarcerated, actually watched *less* television and video than their other teenage counterparts, and even had less access to the technology in the first place. They were found to have no particular interest in specifically violent programmes, and either enjoyed the same material as non-offending teenagers or were simply uninterested in it. In particular, most of the young offenders were simply not sufficiently engaged with television to be able to answer a question about identifying with television characters, which they generally seemed to think would be a pretty stupid thing to do anyway. [...]

The effects model treats children as inadequate

Much of the discourse about children and the media positions children as potential victims, and as little else. Furthermore, media effects research usually employs methods which will not allow children to challenge this assumption. The studies give no voice to young people and no opportunity for them to demonstrate their independence, intelligence or free will. The hundreds of shallow quantitative studies, often conducted by 'psychologists', have often been little more than traps for their subjects. The methods used – most obviously in numerous misguided laboratory and field experiments – allow, paradoxically, no scope for developing any psychological insights. The young participants may or may not fall into the trap of giving the response which is then read as evidence of a media effect, but, since the researchers record only this binary result, the subjects are unable to provide their observers with any evidence at all of their skills or critical abilities. In addition, whilst the responses of children in experiments are generally interpreted as being unique to this age group, comparison studies of adults are rarely performed. The researchers, we have to presume, are simply not bothered by such matters.

Research which has sought to establish what children can and do understand about the media have exposed the deficiencies of previous research. Such projects have shown that children can and do talk intelligently, and indeed cynically, about the media (Buckingham, 1993, 1996), and that children as young as seven can make thoughtful, critical and 'media literate' video productions themselves (Gauntlett, 1997).

Assumptions within the effects model are characterised by barely-concealed conservative ideology

Media effects research is good news for conservatives and right-wing 'moralists'. Whilst not all of the researchers engaged in effects research have a particular interest in advancing right-wing and moralistic causes, that is nevertheless their definite function, since the studies heavily reinforce the idea that violence in society can be explained by looking to the media.

Conservatives have traditionally liked to blame popular culture for the ailments of society, not only because they fear new and innovative forms of media, but also because it allows them to divert attention away from other and, for them, more awkward social questions such as levels of welfare provision and (in the States) the easy availability of guns.

Media effects researchers often talk about the *amount* of violence in the media, encouraging the view that it is not important to consider the *meaning* of the scenes involving violence which appear on screen. Again, this makes life easy for people who wish to turn public attention away from the real social causes of violence and to blame the media instead.

Critics of screen violence often reveal themselves to be worried about the challenges to the status quo which they feel that some violent movies present (even though most European and many American film critics see most popular films as being ridiculously status quo-friendly). For example, Michael Medved, author of the successful *Hollywood vs. America: Popular Culture and the War on Traditional Values* (1992) finds worrying and potentially influential displays of 'disrespect for authority' and 'anti-patriotic attitudes' in films like *Top Gun* – a movie which many other commentators find embarrassingly jingoistic. This opportunistic mixing of concerns about the media roots of violence with a political critique of the content of violent films represents a particularly distasteful trend in 'social concern' commentary. Media effects studies and TV violence content analyses help only to sustain such an approach by maintaining the notion that 'antisocial behaviour' is an objective category which can be measured, which is common to numerous programmes, and which will negatively affect those children who see it portrayed on screen.

The effects model inadequately defines its own objects of study

Media effects studies are usually extremely undiscriminating about how they identify worrying bits of media content, or subsequent behaviour by viewers. An act of 'violence', for example, might be smashing cages to set animals free or using force to disable a nuclear-armed plane. It might be kicking a chair in frustration or a cruel and horrible murder. In many studies, 'verbal aggression' is included as a form of aggression, which means that studies which are interpreted by most people as being about the representation of physical violence may actually be more concerned with the use of swear words. Once processed by effects research, all of these various depictions or actions simply emerge as a 'level of aggression', but without a more selective and discriminating way of compiling these numbers, the results can be at best deceptive and at worst virtually meaningless. [. . .]

The effects model is often based on artificial studies

Since careful sociological studies of media influences require considerable amounts of time and money, they are heavily outnumbered by simpler studies which often put their subjects into artificial and contrived situations (but then pretend that they are studying the everyday world). Laboratory and field experiments involve forcing participants to watch a particular programme or set of programmes which they would not have chosen if left to their own devices and – just as artificially – observing them in a particular setting afterwards. In these settings, the behaviour of the children towards an inanimate object is often taken to represent how they would behave towards a real person. Furthermore, this all rests on the mistaken belief that children's behaviour will not be affected by the fact that they know that they are being manipulated, tested and/or observed. (Studies by researchers such as Borden (1975) have shown that this is quite erroneous: participation in an experiment, and even the appearance of the adults involved in the study, can radically affect children's behaviour.)

The effects model is often based on studies with misapplied methodology

Many of the studies which do not rely on the experimental method, and so may evade the flaws mentioned above, fall down instead by wrongly applying a methodological procedure or by drawing inappropriate conclusions from particular methods. For example, the widely-cited longitudinal panel study[2] by Huesmann et al. (Lefkowitz et al., 1972, 1977) has been slated, less famously, for failing to keep to the proper procedures, such as assessing aggressivity or levels of TV viewing with the same measures at different times, procedures which are obviously necessary if the study's statistical findings are to have any validity (Chaffee, 1972; Kenny, 1972). The same researchers have also failed to account adequately for the fact that the findings of this study and of another of their own (Huesmann et al., 1984) completely contradict each other, with the former concluding that the media has a marginal effect on boys but no effect on girls, and the latter arguing the exact opposite! They also seem to ignore the fact that their own follow-up of their original set of subjects twenty-two years later suggested that a number of biological, developmental and environmental factors contributed to levels of aggression, whilst the media was not even mentioned (Huesmann et al., 1984a). These astounding inconsistencies, unapologetically presented by perhaps the best-known researchers in this area, must surely be cause for considerable unease about the effects model. More careful use of similar methods, as in the three-year panel study involving over 3,000 young people conducted by Milavsky *et al.* (1982a, 1982b), has indicated only that significant media effects are not to be found.

Perhaps the most frequent and misleading abuse of research methodology occurs when studies which are simply *unable* to show that one thing causes another are treated as if they have done so. Such is the case with correlation studies, which can easily find that a particular personality type is also the kind of person who enjoys certain kinds of media – for example, that violent people like to watch 'violent films' – but are quite unable to show that media use has *produced* that character. Nevertheless, psychologists such as Van Evra (1990) and, as we have seen, Browne and Pennell (1998) and Browne (1999) have assumed that this is probably the case. There is a logical coherence to the idea that children whose behaviour is antisocial and disruptive will also have a greater interest in the more violent and noisy television programmes, whereas the idea that their behaviour is a *consequence* of these programmes lacks both rational consistency and empirical support.

The effects model is selective in its criticisms of media depictions of violence

As suggested earlier, effects studies may involve distinctly ideological interpretations of what constitutes 'antisocial' action. Furthermore, researchers tend to refer only to violence in *fictional* TV programmes and films. Violence shown in news and factual programming is generally exempt from researchers' criticisms – although they typically fail to account for this. The point here, of course, is not to argue for serious coverage of serious violent events to be subjected to the same simplistic, blinkered criticisms that are aimed at fictional portrayals. However, there is a substantial problem with an approach which suggests that on-screen violence is bad if it does not extend this to cover news and factual violence, which is often cruel and has no visible negative consequences for the perpetrator. That it is mainly popular fictional programmes which are singled out for criticism suggests (again) that many researchers have in fact an ideological objection to this particular area of television, and that their concerns about violence in this area are but an aspect of their negative attitude towards popular television forms in general.

The effects model assumes superiority to the 'masses'

An obvious point which can be made about all media effects studies is that whilst the researchers consider that other people might be affected by media content, they assume that their own approach is objective and that the media will have no effect on *them*. In fact, surveys show that almost everybody feels this way: whilst varying percentages of the population say they are concerned about media effects on others, almost nobody says that they have ever been affected *themselves*. Sometimes the researchers excuse their approach by saying that they are mature adults, whereas their concerns lie with *children*, but, as already noted, one of the many flaws of the effects model is that it treats children as inadequate. In cases in which this is not possible, because the researchers have used young adults in their study, it is traditional to invoke the menacing spectre of the unruly 'Other' (the undiscriminating 'heavy viewer', the 'uneducated', the working class, and so on) as the victim of 'effects', thus allowing the researchers over-enthusiastically to interpret their weak or flawed data in such a way as to suggest that somebody other than them will be negatively affected by the media.

The effects model makes no attempt to understand meanings of the media

A further fundamental flaw, already hinted at above, is that the effects model necessarily rests on a base of reductive assumptions about and unjustified stereotypes of media content. To assert that, say, 'media violence' will bring about negative consequences is not only to presume that depictions of violence in the media always promote antisocial behaviour, and that such a category actually exists and makes sense, but it also assumes that whatever medium is being studied by the researchers holds a singular message which will be carried unproblematically to the audience. The effects model, therefore, performs the double deception of presuming (a) that the media presents one singular and clear-cut 'message', and (b) that the proponents of the effects model are in a position to identify just what that message is.

The assumption that similar acts of violence in different programmes or films will all have the same power and 'message' ignores the all-important *meanings* of media content: for example, seeing a woman cut in two in a violent thriller would be quite different to seeing Darth Maul chopped in half at the climax of *Star Wars: The Phantom Menace* (1999). Equally seriously, different viewers will respond to the *same* scene quite differently (some people will be delighted when Obi-Wan slices Darth Maul, others will be disappointed, others will wish that Queen Amidala had killed him, and so on), In-depth qualitative studies have, entirely unsurprisingly, given strong support to the view that media audiences routinely arrive at their own, often heterogeneous, interpretations of everyday media texts (see for example Buckingham, 1993, 1996; Hill, 1997; Gauntlett and Hill, 1999; Schlesinger *et al.*, 1992; Gray, 1992; Palmer, 1986). The effects model can really only make sense to people who consider popular entertainment to be a set of very basic propaganda messages flashed at the audience in the simplest possible terms.

The effects model is not grounded in theory

How does seeing an action depicted by the media translate into a motive which actually prompts an individual to behave in the same way? The lack of convincing explanations (let alone anything which we could call a 'theory') of how this process might occur is perhaps the most important and worrying problem with effects research. There is the idea that violence is 'glamorised' in some films and TV shows, which sometimes seems relevant; however, the more horrifyingly violent a production is, the less the violence tends to be glamorised. On these terms, effects researchers' arguments that children must be protected from the most violent media depictions, doesn't quite make sense. As with the model as a whole, it just isn't subtle enough.

Even in the case of a film in which serious violence looks rather stylish, such as in the virtual reality world of *The Matrix* (1999), there is no good explanation of why anyone would simply copy those actions; and we do *need* an explanation if the effects hypothesis is to rise above the status of 'not very convincing suggestion'.

This lack of firm theory has led to the effects model basing itself on the variety of assumptions outlined above – that the media (rather than people) is an unproblematic starting-point for research; that children are unable to 'cope' with the media; that the categories of 'violence' or 'antisocial behaviour' are clear-cut and self-evident; that the model's predictions can be verified by scientific research; that screen fictions are of concern, whilst news pictures are not; that researchers have the unique capacity to observe and classify social behaviour and its meanings, but that those researchers themselves need not attend to the various possible meanings which media content may have for its audiences. Each of these very substantial problems has its roots in the failure of media effects commentators to found their model in any coherent theory at all.

So is media effects research finished?

Depressingly, the media effects model remains quite popular. [. . .] It could be said that there is little point in trying to question the methodology of those people working within the effects model, because, by our own definition of that work, they are much more concerned with creating an illusion of empiricism to support their prejudged conclusions than in designing methodologically sound research. In other words, they're not going to stop. The solution must be two-fold: to raise awareness of the flaws in that research in the hope that this will make it more difficult for the press to report their findings uncritically and, perhaps more importantly, to produce new kinds of research which will tell us more subtle and interesting things about possible media influences than anything which the effects researchers can provide.

In conclusion, it is both bemusing and somewhat frightening to note the numbers of psychologists (and others) who conduct research according to prescribed recipes, despite the many well-known flaws with those procedures, when it is in fact so easy to imagine alternative research methods and processes. For example, I usefully tried out a method which encouraged children to make videos *themselves* as a way of exploring what they had got from the mass media (Gauntlett, 1997), and nor is it exactly hard to think of different and probably superior alternative methods – see also, for example, Philo (1990, 1996). The discourses about 'media effects' from politicians and the popular press are already quite laughably simplistic enough: academics shouldn't encourage them in their delusions.

Notes

1.   For a previous discussion of this topic, see also Gauntlett (1998).
2.   A longitudinal panel study is one in which the same group of people (the panel) is surveyed and/or observed at a number of points over a period of time.

References

Borden, Richard J. (1975), 'Witnessed aggression: influence of an observer's sex and values on aggressive responding', in *Journal of Personality and Social Psychology*, 31: 3, pp. 567–73.

Browne, Kevin (1999), 'Violence in the media causes crime: myth or reality', Inaugural Lecture, 3 June 1999, University of Birmingham.

Browne, Kevin and Pennell, Amanda (1998), 'Effects of video violence on young offenders', *Home Office Research and Statistics Directorate Research Findings*, No. 65.

Buckingham, David (1993), *Children Talking Television: The Making of Television Literacy*, London: Falmer Press.

Buckingham, David (1996), *Moving Images: Understanding Children's Emotional Responses to Television*, Manchester: Manchester University Press.

Chaffee, Steven H. (1972), 'Television and adolescent aggressiveness (overview)', in Comstock, George A., and Rubenstein, Eli A., eds, *Television and Social Behaviour. Reports and Papers, Volume III: Television and Adolescent Aggressiveness*, National Institute of Mental Health, Maryland.

Gauntlett, David (1995), *Moving Experiences: Understanding Television's Influences and Effects*, London: John Libbey.

Gauntlett, David (1997), *Video Critical: Children, the Environment and Media Power*, Luton: John Libbey Media.

Gauntlett, David (1998), 'Ten things wrong with the "effects model"', in Dickinson, Roger, Harindranath, Ramaswani, and Linne, Olga, eds, *Approaches to Audiences*, London: Edward Arnold, pp. 120–30.

Gauntlett, David, and Hill, Annette (1999), *TV Living: Television, Culture and Everyday Life*, London: Routledge.

Gray, Ann (1992), *Video Playtime: The Gendering of a Leisure Technology*, London: Routledge.

Hagell, Ann and Newburn, Tim (1994), *Young Offenders and the Media: Viewing Habits and Preferences*, London: Policy Studies Institute.

Hill, Annette (1997), *Shocking Entertainment: Viewer Response to Violent Movies*, Luton: John Libbey Media.

Huesmann, L. Rowell, Eron, Leonard D., Lefkowitz, Monroe M. and Walder, Leopold O. (1984a), 'Stability of aggression over time and generations', in *Developmental Psychology*, 20:6, pp. 1120–34.

Kenny, David A. (1972), 'Two comments on cross-lagged correlation: threats to the internal validity of cross-lagged panel inference as related to "Television violence and child aggression: a follow-up study",' in Comstock and Rubenstein, eds, *Television and Social Behavior: Reports and Papers, Volume III: Television and Adolescent Aggressiveness*, Maryland: National Institute of Mental Health.

Lefkowitz, Monroe M., Eron, Leonard D., Walder, Leopold O. and Huesmann, L. Rowell (1972), 'Television violence and child aggression: a follow-up study', in Comstock, George A. and Rubenstein, Eli A., eds, *Television and Social Behavior: Reports and Papers, Volume III: Television and Adolescent Aggressiveness*, Maryland: National Institute of Mental Health.

Lefkowitz, Monroe M., Eron, Leonard D., Walder, Leopold O. and Huesmann, L. Rowell (1977), *Growing Up To Be Violent: A Longitudinal Study of the Development of Aggression*, New York: Pergamon Press.

Medved, Michael (1992), *Hollywood vs. America: Popular Culture and the War on Traditional Values*, London: HarperCollins.

Milavsky, J. Ronald, Kessler, Ronald C., Stipp, Horst and Rubens, William S. (1982a), *Television and Aggression: A Panel Study*, New York: Academic Press.

Milavsky, J. Ronald, Kessler, Ronald, Stipp, Horst and Rubens, William S. (1982b), 'Television and aggression: results of a panel study', in Pearl, David, Bouthilet, Lorraine and Lazar, Joyce, eds, *Television and Behavior: Ten Years of Scientific Progress and Implications for the Eighties, Volume 2: Technical Reviews*, Maryland: National Institute of Mental Health.

Palmer, Patricia (1986), *The Lively Audience: A Study of Children Around the TV Set*, Sydney: Allen and Unwin.

Philo, Greg (1990), *Seeing and Believing: The Influence of Television*, London: Routledge.

Philo, Greg (ed.) (1996), *Media and Mental Distress*, London: Longman.

Schlesinger, Philip, Dobash, R. Emerson, Dobash, Russell P. and Weaver, C. Kay (1992), *Women Viewing Violence*, London: British Film Institute.

Van Evra, Judith (1990), *Television and Child Development*, Hillsdale, New Jersey: Lawrence Erlbaum Associates.

Critical connections

Despite serious and well-known methodological, conceptual and theoretical limitations, and the lack of sustained evidence regarding media effects, the insistence on a straightforward causal connection between media consumption and criminal behaviour remains common currency among politicians and moral conservatives. Following the murder of toddler James Bulger by two ten-year-olds in 1993, the film *Child's Play III*, and other 'video nasties', were identified (spuriously as it turned out) as a likely cause (Barker, 2001). When two teenagers fatally shot 12 classmates and one teacher and injured 21 others in Columbine in 1999, before shooting themselves, the music of Marilyn Manson, the Hollywood film *The Basketball Diaries*, and violent computer games were all identified as causal factors (Muzzatti, 2003). In the midst of an apparent spate of fatal shootings involving black youth in Birmingham, England, in 2003, then Home Secretary David Blunkett squarely blamed the media, insisting that rap music had 'created a culture where killing is almost a fashion accessory' (Mueller, 2003).

Such claims may be asserted because this is what the claims-makers genuinely believe to be true. At times, however, they undoubtedly arise from a sense of frustration, even helplessness, and the need for a scapegoat: it is much easier to blame the media for violence than it is to deal with the more intractable problems of gross structural inequality, increasing relative deprivation and youth alienation in mass consumer culture. Thus, with or without convincing evidence, claims that the media cause crime will persist because they serve particular social and political functions.

Discussion questions

• Effects research tends to focus on the impact of fictional portrayals of violence, particularly in film. What link might there be between property crimes and the advertising industry in a consumer society?

- There have been literally hundreds of research investigations into the effects of media violence on society, yet the research evidence remains inconsistent are equivocal? Why is this?
- Despite a clear lack of consistent or conclusive research 'evidence', politicians and moral campaigners continue to 'blame' the media for acts of crime and violence in society because to do so serves particular political ends. Evaluate this contention.

References

Barker, M. (2001) 'The Newson Report: A Case Study in Common Sense', in M. Barker and J. Petley (eds) (2001) *Ill Effects: The Media/Violence Debate* (2nd edn). London: Routledge.

Mueller, A. (2003) 'Rock in the Dock', the *Guardian*, 18th January, available at http://arts.guardian.co.uk/features/story/0,,876979,00.html.

Muzzatti, S. (2003) 'Criminalizing Marginality and Resistance: Marilyn Manson, Columbine and Cultural Criminology', paper presented at the American Society of Criminology Conference, Denver, Colorado, November 2003.

Martin Barker and Julian Petley

FROM BAD RESEARCH TO GOOD – A GUIDE FOR THE PERPLEXED (2001)

Introduction and context

IN THE INTRODUCTION TO *Ill effects: The Media/Violence Debate*, Martin Barker and Julian Petley (2001) state their position unequivocally. It is worth stating this position in detail (Barker and Petley, 2001: 1–2):

> The claims about the possible 'effects of violent media' are not just false, they range from the daft to the mischievous. The reason for this is that those who insistently make these claims are asking the wrong question . . . The central reason, then, why the insistent question is so wrong is because *there is no such thing as 'violence' in the media which can have harmful – or beneficial – effects*. Of course, different kinds of media use different kinds of 'violence' for many different purposes – just as they use music, colour, stock characters, deep-focus photography, rhythmic editing and scenes from the countryside, among many others. But in exactly the same way as it is daft to ask 'what are the effects of rhythmic editing or the use of countryside scenes?' without at the same time asking where, when, and in what context these are used, so, we insist, it is stupid simply to ask 'what are the effects of violence?'

Of course, saying a particular piece of research is bad is one thing. Identifying precisely how and why it is bad, and then going on to contrast it with 'good' research, is something else. The clear demonstration that good research on media, violence and audiences can be done, if conducted in accordance with the sufficiently rigorous concepts, theories and methods, is the main objective in Barker and Petley's (2001) chapter excerpted here. Attempts to count 'violence' and measure media 'effects' on a supposedly monolithic 'audience' within a purely quantitative framework, they main-tain, are doomed to failure. However, drawing on the work of qualitative audience researchers, including Jenny Kitzinger (see also Reading 13) and David Gauntlett (see also Reading 30), Barker and Petley demonstrate that it is possible to explore the 'meaning' that different forms of media violence may hold for different audiences in different contexts.

Undoing the category 'violence'

We begin at the heart of the beast. A small but growing number of studies has begun to question the status of that central term 'violence', each in different ways showing that for real viewers, as against 'effects' researchers and moral campaigners, 'violence' is not some singular 'thing' which might grow cumulatively like poison inside people.

One of the earliest studies to explore the dimensions of 'violence' was Schlesinger *et al*.'s *Women Viewing Violence* (1992), which was undertaken for the Broadcasting Standards Council. The research focused on women's responses to four very different kinds of programme. One was *Crimewatch UK*, the BBC programme in which viewers are invited to call in with information to help solve current cases, focusing on an episode dealing with the rape and murder of a young hitchhiker. Second was *EastEnders*, the popular soap opera, and in particular a story-line about domestic violence. Third was a hard-hitting drama, *Closing Ranks*, also dealing directly with violence in the home, this time centred on a policeman's family. Finally, the 1989 feature film *The Accused*, which explored the difficulties of proving rape in a case in which men claimed that a woman had been behaving provocatively; the film ends by showing the rape. Schlesinger *et al*.'s research is particularly useful for the range of women interviewed, and its mix of research methods. They recruited women across a wide range of class, age and ethnic backgrounds, and distinguished those with and without personal experience of violence. Their research combined questionnaires giving a picture of the social posi-tions of their respondents, and close interviewing of the women in order to gain access to the detailed patterns of their responses.

Their findings reveal many things. They show, for instance, that for many women there is an important distinction between finding something *disturbing* and nonethe-less *wanting it to be shown*. The responses to *EastEnders* proved complicated, in that the violence involved a white man and a black woman, and the black women in the research tended to assess the events in terms of their *racial* significance rather than in terms of domestic violence. Again, in the responses to the *Crimewatch* hitchhiker story, wider cultural attitudes concerning women going out on their own cut across wom-en's assessment of the programme. *The Accused* aroused strong feelings across almost all participants, with close identification with Jodie Foster's victim-character. But only in a few cases, did these strong feelings result in demands for censorship. Rather, it brought forth discussion of 'men' as viewers, and of what might be done to control their ways of watching programmes containing violence against women. Here is perhaps their most important conclusion:

> The issue is not whether depictions of violence increase the likelihood
> of similar violence among potential perpetrators, but the feelings and

reactions that it creates among those who are the actual or potential victims of violence. Are women likely to feel more vulnerable, less safe or less valued members of our society if, as a category, they are with some frequency depicted as those who are subjected to abuse? If so, the portrayal of violence against women may be seen as negative, even if women viewers have never experienced such violence and/or its likelihood is not increased.

(Schlesinger et al., 1992: 170)

These are not comfortable findings, and they challenge us all to a proper democratic debate about these issues. But comfortable or not, they change the terms in which that debate will need to take place. For it is not the sheer fact of the presence of violence that is the issue: it is its purpose and meanings, both within individual media items and the wider circuits and currents of feelings and ideas that accompany it, that have to be examined.

In 1998 Schlesinger et al. followed up this first investigation with a study of the ways in which groups of men perceived, understood and judged different kinds of media violence. They recognise that they are explicitly challenging the traditional 'effects' agenda: '[T]he present study, like its predecessor, is not a simplistic "effects" or "no effects" piece of research. Both studies represent attempts to move the research agenda away from this narrow debate onto more productive and relevant ground' (1998: 4).

The study used 88 men aged between 18 and 75, with a deliberate mix of class, ethnic memberships and sexual preferences, and showed them various combinations of: an episode of EastEnders featuring alcoholism leading to domestic violence; Trip Trap, a quality TV drama addressing issues of sexual violence; a documentary about street fighting; and two Hollywood box office successes, Basic Instinct and Under Siege. There was as much variety in the specific responses as there had been among their women interviewees, but even more strongly than the women, the men's perceptions and judgements of violent media were based on the rules and standards of the groups and communities to which they belonged. So, the street-fighting was judged 'ordinary' and in fact exciting by those men whose lives included the kinds of relationships and risks that fairly easily lead to such fights.

But even more strongly than in the case of the women, a line was drawn between 'realistic' violence – which could make you stop and think – and 'unrealistic' violence such as the two Hollywood films. These were assessed not against 'life' but against other movies – their meaning for men such as these was in terms of a world of entertainment.

Yet again, therefore, research that listens to the operative ideas of people, rather than encasing them in psychologistic language, finds people always responding to 'violent media' through their social and historical worlds, through shared understandings, and with (whether we like or approve of them or not) complicated moral codes.[1]

Finally, in this section, we want to draw attention to Defining Violence (1999), by David Morrison. This research, which was commissioned by all the major broadcasters and carried out at Leeds University, set out to discover 'the subjective meaning of violence. How, in other words, did people classify acts as violent and other acts, although ostensibly violent, as not really violent? Did people, furthermore, have a common definition of violence, or were there many different definitions?'

(1999: vii). To answer these questions, the researchers recruited a wide range of people who might be expected to have different experiences of and attitudes to violence both in real life and on screen: policemen; young men and women drawn from cultural groups familiar with violence; women who had a heightened fear, but no personal experience, of violence; women with small children; men with small children, and so on. The groups were shown a wide variety of visual material and, in a significant methodological move, were given the chance during discussions actually to re-edit the footage as a means of clarifying what they meant by 'violence'.

What the research showed was that it is not particular acts which make a pro-gramme seem violent, but the context in which they occur, a finding which clearly backs up the work of Schlesinger *et al.* (1992, 1998). The Leeds researchers were able to distinguish several different kinds of fictional screen violence:

> *Playful violence* is clearly acted violence, and is seen as unreal. The violence looks staged, and has little significance beyond its entertainment value. It is invariably seen as violence with a little v. A lot of violent action may be involved, but it is not graphic and does not assault the sensibilities.

> *Depicted violence* is violence that is characterised by 'realism'. It attempts to depict violence as it would appear in real life. It often includes close-up shots of injury, and is very graphic. This can indeed assault the sensibilities, and is invariably defined as violence with a big V.

> *Authentic violence* is violence set in a world that the viewer can recognise. A classic case would be domestic violence. Violence in a pub or shopping precinct might be other examples. It is closer to the life of the viewer than other forms of violence. It might be seen as violence with a little v, depending on how the scene is played, although it does have the potential to be big V, and even massive V. In other words, it has the possibility of assaulting the senses very strongly indeed.
>
> (Morrison, 1999: 4-5)

These categories helped them to determine how their group members distinguished between violent scenes, but they still left a central question: what causes something to be perceived as violent? Group discussions revealed two determining factors: the *nature and quality* of the violence portrayed, which is a moral factor, and the *way in which* it was portrayed, which is an aesthetic one. The elements which make up the first factor the researchers called the *primary definers* of violence, those which contribute to the second factor the *secondary definers*. Together these determine the definition of violence. The primary definers are 'drawn from real life, and what is deemed violent on screen is the same as what is deemed violent in real life. An act is defined as violent in real life if it breaks a recognised and mutually agreed code of conduct' (ibid.: 6). Thus, for example, for some groups a punch thrown in a pub is not judged to be violent in any serious sense, whereas 'glassing' somebody in the same situation would universally be regarded as a violent act. The researchers also found that the most prevalent general rule seems to be that behaviour which is judged to be appropriate, fair and justified – even when overtly violent – is not usually seen to be seriously or 'really' violent.

Once the primary definers have come into play, the secondary ones establish and grade the *degree* of violence perceived by the viewer:

> The secondary definers categorise a scene of violence if it looks 'real' – as the viewer imagines it would if witnessed in real life. Close-up shots of an injury, and splattering blood, both make violence look 'real'. So does the manner in which an injury is delivered, and how it is portrayed. Each of these elements helps to produce a greater sense of violence once the primary definers have established the scene to be violent in the first place.
>
> (ibid.: 7)

From their work with these groups, the researchers finally arrived at the following definition of violence:

> Screen violence is any act that is seen or unequivocally signalled which would be considered an act of violence in real life, because the violence was considered unjustified either in the degree or nature of the force used, or that the injured party was undeserving of the violence. The degree of violence is defined by how realistic the violence is considered to be, and made even stronger if the violence inflicted is considered unfair.
>
> (ibid.: 9)

This is valuable research with a great deal to teach, but here we simply draw attention to one of their central propositions, namely that in order to understand the meaning of 'violence' in the media, you have to understand the moral codes that different audiences bring to bear as they watch.

Positive pleasures

One central problem of the 'effects' tradition is its treatment of those who dare to enjoy or even admit to being users of the kinds of materials condemned by the moral campaigners. Because the materials (films, videos, games, whatever) are 'known' to be harmful, their audiences *must* be at best blind, at worst already thoroughly corrupted. So the only question, in truth, that 'effects' research knows to ask is: what signs are there that audiences for 'harmful media' have been adversely affected? Again, this is a question that the new qualitative research has sought to supplant. A few, too few, studies have done so by learning how to listen to the real enthusiasts, and in doing so have come up with some real surprises.[2]

One limitation of Schlesinger *et al.*'s first study was that many of its women respondents would not normally have watched, or certainly not watched with enjoyment, some of the materials about which they were asked to comment. In this, in fact, the research fits a little too comfortably with a stereotypical image that 'violent programming' is enjoyed only by men, not women.[3] Annette Hill's (1997) research has begun to unpick this. Hill's study investigates in detail the kinds of pleasure that both men and women have taken in the crop of films that, post-Tarantino and *Pulp Fiction*, have generally been regarded by the media as upping the stakes in 'levels of violence'. Most interestingly, Hill found a great deal of overlap between the responses of male and female fans of these films. For both, the most important element in the films was not the violence *per se* but the ways in which they found them mentally challenging and boundary-testing. According to Hill, consumers of violent movies possess 'portfolios of interpretation', a concept which she uses to catch hold of the ways people become *experienced* and *knowledgeable* in their ways of understanding violent movies. These 'portfolios' include:

- a conscious awareness that violent movies test viewers in various ways;
- anticipation and preparation as an essential aspect of the enjoyment of viewing violent movies;
- building relationships and engaging with certain screen characters, whilst establishing a safe distance from others;
- bringing into play a variety of methods to self-censor violence;
- utilising violent images as a means of testing personal boundaries and as a safe way (within a clearly fictional setting) of interpreting and thinking about violence;
- actively differentiating between real-life violence and fictional violence.

Hill also draws attention to the fact that the process of viewing violent films is very much a social activity, arguing that 'part of the enjoyment of viewing violence is to monitor audience reactions, as the films themselves provoke reaction. Individual response is part of a much wider awareness of the variety of responses available to consumers of violent movies' (Hill, 1997: 105–6).

Understanding how its actual audiences respond to a film all too easily dismissed as simply 'violent' was part of a project into the reception of action-adventure movies by Martin Barker and Kate Brooks (1998). In particular, they were interested in the ways in which fans talked about how they used and enjoyed the film, which led them to analyse what they called the fans' 'vocabularies of involvement and pleasure'. These revealed a series of practices of pleasure which included: physical satisfaction; being part of a crowd; creating imaginative worlds; game-playing and role-playing; taking risks; rule-breaking and defying convention; confirming membership of communities of response; and critical appreciation. A key point about these practices of pleasure is that they all

> involve some kind of preparation, and therefore have a pattern of involvement which extends beyond the moments of pleasure, on which in significant ways the pleasures depend. Crudely, there are things we have to do, and to know, and to prepare for in advance if any of these pleasures are to be gained.
>
> (Barker and Brooks, 1998:145)

In relation to their target film *Judge Dredd*, Barker and Brooks identified a number of distinct patterns of expectation revealed by their interviewees, each expressing in its own 'language' a particular relation to the film and cinema-going, and providing a basis for distinct ways of being involved. According to Barker and Brooks, each vocabulary of involvement and pleasure represents a culturally-generated SPACE (standing for Site for the production of Active Cinematic Experiences) into which an individual can move. There were six such SPACES:

- The Action-Adventure SPACE, for those aiming to become involved in the film at a sensuous, physical level, treating it as a roller-coaster experience.
- The Future-Fantastic SPACE, for those anticipating a physical experience too, but also getting ready to respond to spectacular technologies and demonstrations of new cinematic skills.
- The 2000 AD-Follower SPACE, for those already familiar with the Judge Dredd world and who are hoping to see a huge character made as big and as public as he deserves and requires.
- The Film-Follower SPACE, for those committed to cinema as a medium and wanting the film to contribute to some aspect of 'cinematic magic'.
- The Stallone-Follower SPACE, for those wanting to see what the film adds to Stallone's career and his screen persona.
- The Culture-Belonging SPACE, for those who choose to raid a film for information, jokes, stories, catch-phrases which can contribute to their on-going membership of local groups.

Barker and Brooks are particularly interested in those respondents who combine two SPACES: Action-Adventure and Future-Fantastic. What they point to is an intriguing parallel between the filmic pleasures sought by young working class audiences – just the kind of young males who feature strongly in scares about 'dangerous' media – and the world view of those early Utopians, the medieval Chiliasts described by Karl Mannheim in *Ideology and Utopia* (1960). The Chiliasts, who tended to be drawn from the 'oppressed strata of society', sought their Utopia not in some far distant future, rather:

> The Chiliast expects a union with the immediate present. Hence he is not preoccupied in his daily life with optimistic hopes for the future romantic reminiscences . . . He is not actually concerned with the millennium that is to come; what is important for him is that it has happened here and now, and that it arose from mundane existence, as a sudden swing over into another kind of existence.
>
> (Mannheim, 1960: 195)

In other words, what Chiliasm offered was a way of experiencing *in the present* the qualities of a transformed world, a process in which 'spiritual fermentation and physical excitement' (ibid.: 192) played its part and in which 'sensual experience is present in all its robustness' (ibid.: 194). In short: 'for the real Chiliast, the present becomes the breach through which what was previously inward bursts out suddenly, takes hold of the outer world and transforms it' (ibid.: 193).

The parallels with action movie fans' love of cinema's sensuous qualities, its orgiastic excess and its possibilities for envisioning other worlds are thought-provoking. Furthermore, just as Mannheim points out that 'the utopian vision aroused a contrary vision' (ibid.: 192), so action films such as *Judge Dredd* have been misrepresented and condemned as 'gratuitously violent' and so on. Barker and Brooks are at pains not to over-emphasise the parallel, but at the same time they do insist that it is a significant and meaningful one:

> To understand their participation in this way is not to romanticise their love of film as some kind of political opposition. It is simply to consider the particular ways in which their love of Action films is embroidered into the rest of their lives, and to see in it the incipient signs of an awareness of disjunctions: between present and future, between the celebration and the dread of the impact of technology in and on their lives; between heroic rescue of the world and the oppressiveness of 'heroes'; between the wealth that is possible, that is put daily on display in front of them, and the actual lot of 'the common people'. And that, paradoxically, means that the other world which can be glimpsed is not pretty. It is not the 'peaceful, other' world of the hippies. It can only operate as a utopia by simultaneously celebrating and excoriating the dumb brutalities of new technologies, their business lords and their oppressive systems.
>
> (Barker and Brooks, 1998: 290–1)

If they are right, the significance of Barker and Brooks' findings is that what is condemned as 'gratuitous' and 'immoral' is actually experienced by its key fans as *political*. [. . .]

Children and the media

At the heart of the 'effects' tradition stands the figure of the 'child': innocent, vulnerable, corruptible. A small but growing group of researchers have undertaken the difficult task of learning how to investigate children's own views and understandings of the media. The results have been distinctly productive. [. . .]

Some of the most valuable work on children and television to have emerged in recent years has been carried out by David Buckingham, most notably in *Children Talking Television* (1993) and *Moving Images* (1996). Buckingham's work is concerned not with television's 'effects' in the conventional sense of the term, but rather with how children and young people actually perceive, define and understand television programmes. His research brief has been wide. [. . .] In particular he has become concerned with the ways in which children become citizens of their society (see Buckingham (2000)), and the role of the media in these processes. As Buckingham points out, one of the many problems of traditional research into children's relationship with television is that 'it has paid very little attention to the diverse ways in which they make sense of what they watch; to the kinds of knowledge they bring to television, and the critical skills they develop in relation to it; or to the social contexts in which the medium is used and talked about' (1996: 7). Buckingham's focus, on the other hand, is precisely upon the development of television literacy in children. His own qualitative researches lead him to this conclusion:

> Children respond to and make sense of television in the light of what they know about its formal codes and conventions, about genre and narrative,

and about the production process. In these respects, they are much more active and sophisticated users of the medium than they are often assumed to be.

(1996: 7)

Buckingham's work is too wide to be adequately summarised here, but among his more specific conclusions are the following:

- most parents and children challenged the view that television on its own was a sufficient cause of violent behaviour. Parents were more likely to express concern about the possible 'effects' of television on other people's children than on their own, whilst the children themselves displaced such concerns onto younger children. Parents were more concerned that their children might be frightened or traumatised by violence on television than that they might try to imitate it;
- children had negative responses, such as fright, disgust, sadness or worry, not only to the more predictable genres such as horror, but also to a surprisingly wide and apparently innocuous range of programmes, including those specifically aimed at children. Negative responses are common amongst children, though they are rarely severe or long-lasting;
- children clearly distinguished between factual and fictional material on television, and found it easier to distance themselves from the latter than from the former. However, even where factual material, such as news coverage of wars and disasters, was described as upsetting it was also regarded by many as being important to watch, in that it provided necessary information about the real world;
- the main concern of children who watched horror films or true crime programmes was that they might become victims of violence. There was little sense of vicarious 'identification' with the monster or the perpetrator of violence;
- children had a wide range of strategies to protect themselves from or deal with negative responses. These ran the gamut from partial or total avoidance of potentially upsetting programmes to actively denying their reality status ('it's only a movie');
- children who watched fictional violence might become habituated to watching more fictional violence, but this did not 'desensitise' their perceptions of real-life violence, whether mediated by television or not.

Buckingham's work on children as media audiences is among the very best, in our view. He has shown with commendable clarity how research on children and the media should be conducted. And his work challenges in detail many of the assumptions that underpin the 'figure' of the child which is so essential to media moral scares. But it does much more than this. It shows the ways in which even young children are already making complex moral decisions about what they should watch, and for whom particular kinds of materials are appropriate. It also shows that children themselves know about, and indeed are influenced by, those scares – a point of greater weight than has so far been acknowledged.[4]

Symbolic politics

[T]here is a strong tendency for press, politicians and pundits to 'name' something as 'violence', to judge it in simplistic moral terms, and thus to warrant searches for simple 'causes' (such as 'violent media') of events which happen for a whole variety of complex social and political reasons. An important example of just this kind is explored in Darnell Hunt's (1997) study of responses to the television coverage of the 1992 Los Angeles 'riots', which followed the initial Not Guilty verdict for the police who had been filmed beating up black motorist Rodney King. [. . .] Hunt investigated the responses to the television coverage of white, Latino and black LA viewers, and shows the different ways in which these audiences understood the events, the key players, and the 'violent acts' committed according not simply to their 'colour' but to their sense of the communities to which they belong.

Hunt argues that people responded to the TV coverage in the light of their 'raced subjectivity', that is, their sense of who they are and what groups they belong to in the wider world. This strongly affected not only their responses to the particular coverage, but also their wider sense of which media and which spokespeople they will trust. But perhaps most interestingly for our purposes, Hunt uncovered the way people acknowledged or denied a 'racial' component:

> When one surveys intergroup patterns . . . evidence begins to mount for what I have referred to as 'raced ways of seeing'. Black-raced and Latino-raced study groups were quite animated during the screening of the KTTV text, while white-raced study groups watched quietly. For black-raced informants, in particular, raced subjectivity was clearly an important lens through which the events and the text were viewed . . . [W]hile white-raced and Latino-raced informants were *less* likely than their black-raced counterparts to talk about themselves in raced terms, they were *more* likely than black-raced informants to condemn the looting and fires and to support the arrests.
>
> (Hunt, 1997: 141)

Hunt is arguing that *everyone* responded via their sense of their 'racial' community, but that this was most clearly *acknowledged* in the case of black viewers. For white and Latino viewers, in ducking this, represented their responses through the seemingly 'neutral' categories of 'violence' and 'law and order'. The echoes for our own experiences of attitudes towards 'violence' are clear and audible.

In this connection, it is also worth considering the research reported in an essay by John Gabriel (1996), who explored the ways in which the film *Falling Down* was received in Britain. [. . .] Gabriel starts by recognising the complicated meanings of this film, which tracks a white middle class defence worker (played by Michael Douglas), known mainly through his car plates 'tag', D-Fens, who, finding his world going to pieces as he loses his job and is mugged and cheated by various ethnic groups, fights back violently, and is eventually killed. When the film was released in America, a series of press stories reported that white male audiences had cheered on Douglas' character, apparently identifying with his assertion that 'whiteness' has become minority in contemporary America.

Gabriel explores in detail the responses of 16 viewers, of whom a number were non-white. He found some real complexities in their responses, based on people at times giving and at others withholding their assent to his actions and values. So, his black interviewees could join in and cheer when D-Fens confronts, as they felt on the basis of class, some rich golfers who seek to exclude him. But when he faces down a group of Latino muggers, they recognise a racist potential in him which leads them to distance themselves from him. So, although Gabriel's reading of the film indicates that it is centrally organised around ideas of 'whiteness', he concludes that 'whiteness' is not a singular thing, but something conveyed and understood in complicated ways:

> Ironically, D-Fens was arguably at his most popular with his audience not in the Korean shop or the wasteland with the Latino gang members, but on the golf course when he confronted another version of white masculinity. In this scene, the golfers were more conspicuously white than D-Fens himself, not just because their whiter-than-white outfits outshone D-Fens' battle-dress, but also because their whiteness was associated with the affluence and exclusivity of the golf-course setting.
>
> (Gabriel, 1996: 150)

But D-Fens' seeming racism could be 'written out' by audiences who could see him as flawed and driven to extremes by his frustrations – and who could thus see his death as redeeming him. [. . .] Gabriel reveals complexities of both attention and symbolic response which can be grasped only by methods of research which hear their audiences in complex ways. Both pieces of research, crucially, remind us that 'violence' too easily becomes a coded term hiding all sorts of political factors and preferences. [. . .]

'Effects' and beyond

It should by now be abundantly clear that a good deal of work on how audiences respond to media portrayals of violence of one kind or another has moved far beyond the crudities of the 'effects' paradigm. However, as David Buckingham points out:

> There are, of course, other effects which have been addressed within media research – effects which might broadly be termed 'ideological'. For example, the extensive debates about media representations of women or of ethnic minority groups are clearly premised on assumptions about their potential influence on public attitudes.
>
> (Buckingham, 1996: 310)

We agree. Anyone with half an eye on the recent *News of the World* campaign to 'name and shame' paedophiles couldn't help but see real 'effects' of media output. Vigilantism, attacks on innocent people, at times escalating to near-riots: all fed by the ways in which the media, and especially the tabloid press, covered the murder of Sarah Payne, 'informed' their readers and gave vent to the most brutish of feelings in their editorial columns. But the example is apposite. No one 'copied'. No direct 'message' was involved. There was no 'cumulative' influence. The issue of *how* the media can be influential must now move centre-stage. The trouble is, the word 'effects' has come to be burdened with such a mighty load of negative, judgmental and censorious connotations that we need virtually a new language in order to delineate the impacts which Buckingham rightly calls 'ideological'.

Some particularly useful work in this area has emerged from the Glasgow University Media Group, and we highlight two studies in particular. The first is *Seeing and Believing* (1990) by Greg Philo, which is based on a study of responses to television coverage of the 1984–5 coal dispute. Here, foreshadowing the study by Morrison (1999) described earlier, groups of people were asked not simply to comment on the news broadcasts which the researchers showed them, but also to write their own. As Philo explains:

> This would show what they thought the content of the news to be on a given issue. It might then be possible to compare this with what they actually believed to be true and to examine why they either accepted or rejected the media account. The approach made members of the public temporarily into journalists and became the basis for the study.
>
> (1990: 8)

Philo was interested in the differences within the audience (including gender, regional location, class position, political culture and so on), and the consequences these might have for the way in which information from the media is received. Investigation of the complex interactions of media messages and their readers thus enabled the researchers to investigate 'long-term processes of belief, understanding and memory'.

What the researchers found was that in many cases there were 'extraordinary similarities' between the actual news programmes which their groups had watched and the news reports which they themselves subsequently wrote. In particular the groups tended strongly to reproduce the themes of the 'drift back to work' and of 'escalating violence' (especially by striking miners) which so heavily dominated media coverage of the dispute. To quote Philo: 'it was remarkable how closely some of the group stories reflected not only the thematic content of the news but also the structure of actual headlines. One of the surprises in this research was the clarity with which the groups were able to reproduce themes from the news. It also surprised group members' (ibid.: 260).

The researchers also found remarkable the number of people who believed that the violent images of picketing which they saw on television accurately represented the everyday reality of picketing during the dispute. In all, 54 per cent of the general sample believed that the picketing was mostly violent, and the source for these beliefs was overwhelmingly given as the media, with the emphasis on television because of its immediate quality. However, Philo warns:

> It would be wrong to see people as being totally dependent on such messages, as if they were simply empty vessels which are being filled up

by *News at Ten*. To accept and believe what is seen on television is as much
a cultural act as the rejection of it. Both acceptance and rejection are
conditioned by our beliefs, history and experience.

(ibid.: 260)

What emerged here was that beliefs about how much violence occurred on picket
lines, and about how accurately television reflected actual daily life on the lines,
differed greatly according to how much specialist knowledge and direct experience of
the strike group members possessed. In short, the more knowledge they possessed
the less likely they were to believe that the picketing was mostly violent and
that the television pictures of violence accurately represented the daily reality of
the strike. But perhaps the most interesting finding came from a 'wild card' in the
research. Respondents had been given a set of stills from news broadcasts which they
were asked to put in order and then to write an accompanying news commentary.
Among the stills was a shot of a gun (in fact, from a news item about a working
miner threatening to defend himself). Such was the force of the news 'template' of
picket line violence that even those who were most suspicious of the television
coverage tended to associate the gun with the strikers or with 'militant outsiders'.
Either way, even a year after the events, critics of the coverage and supporters of the
striking miners still had to *defend themselves* against the perceived force of the news'
claims. [. . .]

The great strength of the recent rise of qualitative media audience research has
been in the impetus which it has given to replacing figures of 'the audience' with
detailed pictures of different kinds of audiences. This research, utilising increasingly
sophisticated methodology, works from how those audiences themselves talk about
or in other ways express their feelings about, responses to and relationships with
different media.

This kind of research is not easy to conduct, but its findings are like gold dust
amid the false glint of 'effects' findings (where, we are tempted to say, the brightest
glitter comes from the tempting spectacle of seemingly wide open coffers of public
money poured for over seventy years into asking stupid questions in unanswer-
able ways). We badly need more such research, because now we are beginning to
understand a number of important processes in the ways that the media can persuade
particular groups of readers and viewers under particular circumstances. [. . .]

Notes

1.   An interesting small test. Schlesinger *et al.* (1998) include the following sentence
      from one man, reporting his feelings about films such as *Under Siege*: 'you do
      desensitise from it . . . 'cos you know it's not real'. The complexities of categorisa-
      tion, self-evaluation and recognition of social discourses indicated in this one
      sentence are beyond understanding by the crudities of traditional psychological
      theory.
2.   There is, of course, a substantial and important body of work on fans of other kinds
      of material, most famously on science fiction fans (see, for instance, Tulloch
      and Jenkins (1995)). Only more rarely have researchers examined fans of more

controversial materials. For instance we still await, as far as we know, a single published study of horror fans.

3.   Aside from the studies of audiences we are reporting on here, there is an altogether other kind of work which is still interesting and useful. This is a kind of advanced 'textual' work carried out in the cultural studies tradition. Essentially, it asks the question: what kinds of use do things such as horror films, or slasher movies, *allow* or support? Are the films constructed in such a way as to allow or sustain sympathy with the aggressors, for instance? Carol Clover's (1992) justly well-known study of slasher movies is a prime example of this kind of work, where she demonstrates the narrative significance of the 'final girl' who so often defeats the monstrous assailant. More recently Isabel Pinedo (1997) has looked in particular at the possibilities for female (including her own) pleasure generated by the way horror movies are constructed. Particularly worthy of note in this respect is Brigid Cherry's essay in Stokes and Maltby (1999) which usefully challenges the notion that 'horror' is a genre for young males. Cherry crosses the line between textual work and audience studies. First, she gathers together overwhelming quantitative evidence to show that women, and in particular young women, have long been among the prime audiences for horror films, and take great pleasure in them (as against being 'dragged along' by boyfriends). She then interviewed a number of women in order to find out just what those pleasures actually are. What she reveals is that women fans are critical and selective, and that many contemporary young women reject the older 'screamer' representation of women in horror films as sexist. As ever, the category 'horror' therefore contains good and bad examples, from their point of view ('boring and predictable' films being scorned). Furthermore, in recent films they frequently delight in the sexual possibilities raised by the figure of the vampire, an involvement which Cherry calls a 'subversive affinity' with the monsters who threaten the women in the films (along with a pleasure in the gothic romanticisation of the past carried by costume and setting). At the same time, the small but significant crop of recent films with strong female leads (the *Alien* series being the most obvious example) has offered, for some women, a more straightforward involvement in the pleasures of horror.

4.   A forthcoming book (Wallflower Press, 2001) by Barker *et al.* will report on the findings of a research project into the reception in Britain of David Cronenberg's *Crash*. The research demonstrates the powerful, misleading, and intrusive effects of the campaign against the film on viewers who mainly 'wanted to see for themselves' what the film was like.

References

Barker, Martin and Kate Brooks (1998), *Knowing Audiences: Judge Dredd, Its Friends, Fans and Foes*, Luton: University of Luton Press.

Barker, Martin, Jane Arthurs and Ramaswami Harindranath (forthcoming 2001), *The 'Crash' Controversy,* London: Wallflower Press.

Buckingham, David (1993), *Children Talking Television: the Making of Television Literacy*, London: Falmer Press.

Buckingham, David (1996), *Moving Images: Understanding Children's Emotional Responses to Television*, Manchester: Manchester University Press.

Buckingham, David (2000), *The Making of Citizens:Young People, News and Politics,* London: Routledge.

Cherry, Brigid (1999), 'Refusing to refuse to look; female viewers of the horror film', in Stokes, Melvyn and Richard Maltby, eds, *Identifying Hollywood's Audiences: Cultural Identity and the Movies*, London: British Film Institute.

Clover, Carol J. (1992), *Men, Women and Chainsaws: Gender in the Modern Horror Film*, London: B.F.I..

Gabriel, John (1996), 'What do you do when minority means you? *Falling Down* and the construction of "whiteness"', *Screen*, 37:2, 129–51.

Glasgow University Media Group, John Eldridge (ed.) (1993), *Getting the Message: News, Truth and Power*, London; Routledge.

Glasgow University Media Group, Greg Philo (ed.) (1999), *Message Received*, Harlow: Addison Wesley Longman.

Hill, Annette (1997), *Shocking Entertainment: Viewer Response to Violent Movies*, Luton: University of Luton Press.

Hunt, Darnell M. (1997), *Screening the Los Angeles 'Riots'*, New York: Cambridge University Press.

Mannheim, Karl (1960), *Ideology and Utopia*, London: Routledge and Kegan Paul.

Morrison, David E. (1999), *Defining Violence: The Search for Understanding*, Luton: University of Luton Press.

Philo, Greg (1990), *Seeing and Believing: The Influence of Television*, London: Routledge.

Pinedo, Isabel Cristina (1997), *Recreational Terror: Women and the Pleasures of Horror Film Viewing*, NY: SUNY Press.

Schlesinger, Philip, R. Emerson Dobash, Russell P. Dobash and Kay C. Weaver (1992), *Women Viewing Violence*, London: British Film Institute (in association with the Broadcasting Standards Council).

Schlesinger, Philip, Richard Haynes, Raymond Boyle, Brian McNair, R. Emerson Dobash and Russell P. Dobash (1998), *Men Viewing Violence*, London: Broadcasting Standards Council

Tulloch, John and Henry Jenkins (1995), *Science Fiction Audiences: Watching* Doctor Who and Star Trek, London: Routledge.

Critical connections

There are within media criminology early stirrings of a renewed interest in engaging with media audiences. Robert Reiner *et al.'s* research on changing media representations of crime and criminal justice in the post-Second World War era (Reading 25) incorporated focus groups with media audiences to explore the meaning of (frequently violent) images in news, television and film. One of the study's greatest strengths was its interdisciplinary nature: the audience research was led by Sonia Livingstone, a Professor of Social Psychology in a Department of Communications. My own research with Eugene McLaughlin (see also Reading 20) on 'murder news' similarly incorporates qualitative focus group work to explore what media consumers do with murder news, and what murder news does to them. And Stanley Cohen, whose work on the sociology of social reaction has spanned several decades (Reading 34), is engaged in audience research with psychologists at Birkbeck College, University of London, to explore how people receive and interpret Amnesty International campaigns about global atrocities and suffering. These researches, all qualitative in nature and all focused around various forms of focus group interaction, employ many of the techniques described by Barker and Petley, and Kitzinger (in Reading 13), and seek to develop a more in depth understanding of the complex processes through which people access, consume, interpret and react to media images in their everyday lives.

Discussion questions

- Why is the term 'media violence' so problematic?
- Can emotional reactions to media images be measured quantitatively (see also Readings 29 and 30)?
- What, according to Barker and Petley, constitutes 'good' research on media influence?

George Gerbner and Larry Gross

LIVING WITH TELEVISION: THE VIOLENCE PROFILE (1976)

Introduction and context

T HE MOST WELL-KNOWN AND WIDELY CITED body of literature relating to media and fear of crime is the cultivation research conducted by George Gerbner and colleagues. This research developed over several decades, but it is one of the first two highly influential articles, which laid the foundations for dozens of subsequent studies, that is reproduced here. In it, George Gerber and Larry Gross (1976) set out their original statement that television is society's chief mechanism of 'enculturation', and that the primary impact of media is to reinforce, not challenge, established author-ity. Critical of the stimulus-response format (see Reading 28), Gerbner and Gross insist that media influence is cumulative, over time 'cultivating' within individuals a particular world view. Their study adopts a large-scale quantitative methodology incorporating content analysis of complete television schedules in major US cities, and survey ques-tionnaires to assess the correlation between the viewing of television violence and beliefs on matters of politics, public safety and social order. Because television overstates both the seriousness and risk of criminal victimisation, portraying the world as 'mean and scary', heavy viewing is said to cultivate higher fear of crime. Fearful citizens, it is argued, tend to be depoliticised, more dependent on established authority, more punitive, and more likely to acquiesce to authoritarian measures of control.

We begin with the assertion that television is the central cultural arm of American society. It is an agency of the established order and as such serves primarily to extend and maintain, rather than to alter, threaten, or weaken conventional conceptions, beliefs, and behaviors. Its chief cultural function is to spread and stabilize social patterns, to cultivate not change but resistance to change. Television is a medium of the socialization of most people into standardized roles and behaviors. Its function is, in a word, enculturation.

The substance of the consciousness cultivated by TV is not so much specific attitudes and opinions as more basic assumptions about the "facts" of life and standards of judgment on which conclusions are based. The purpose of the Cultural Indicators project is to identify and track these premises and the conclusions they might cultivate across TV's diverse publics.

We shall make a case for studying television as a force for enculturation rather than as a selectively used medium of separate "entertainment" and "information" functions. First, we shall suggest that the essential differences between television and other media are more crucial than the similarities. Second, we will show why traditional research designs are inadequate for the study of television effects and suggest more appropriate methods. Third, we will sketch the pattern of evidence emerging from our studies indicating that "living" in the world of television cultivates conceptions of its own conventionalized "reality."

The reach, scope, ritualization, organic connectedness, and non-selective use of mainstream television makes it different from other media of mass communications

TV penetrates every home in the land. Its seasonal, cyclical, and perpetual patterns of organically related fact and fiction (all woven into an entertainment fabric producing publics of consumers for sale to advertisers) again encompass essential elements of art, science, technology, statecraft, and public (as well as most family) story-telling. The information-poor (children and less educated adults) are again the entertainment-rich held in thrall by the myths and legends of a new electronic priesthood.

If you were born before, say, 1950, television came into your life after the formative years as just another medium. Even if you are now an "addict," it will be difficult for you to comprehend the transformations it has wrought. Could you, as a twelve-year-old, have contemplated spending an average of six hours *a day* at the local movie house? Not only would most parents not have permitted such behavior but most children would not have imagined the possibility. Yet, in our sample of children, nearly half the twelve-year-olds watch at least six hours of television every day.

Unlike print, television does not require literacy. Unlike the movies, television is "free" (supported by a privately imposed tax on all goods), and it is always running. Unlike radio, television can show as well as tell. Unlike the theater, concerts, movies, and even churches, television does not require mobility. It comes into the home and reaches individuals directly. With its virtually unlimited access from cradle to grave, television both precedes reading and, increasingly, preempts it.

Television is the first centralized cultural influence to permeate both the initial and the final years of life – as well as the years between. Most infants are exposed to television long before reading. By the time a child reaches school, television will have occupied more time than would be spent in a college classroom. At the other end of the lifelong curriculum, television is there to keep the elderly company when all else fails.

All societies have evolved ways of explaining the world to themselves and to their children. Socially constructed "reality" gives a coherent picture of what exists, what is important, what is related to what, and what is right. The constant cultivation of such "realities" is the task of mainstream rituals and mythologies. They legitimize action along socially functional and conventionally acceptable lines.

The social, political, and economic integration of modern industrial society has created a system in which few communities, if any, can maintain an independent integrity. We are parts of a Leviathan and its nervous system is telecommunications. Publicly shared knowledge of the "wide world" is what this nervous system transmits to us.

Television is the chief common ground among the different groups that make up a large and heterogeneous national community. No national achievement, celebration, or mourning seems real until it is confirmed and shared on television.

Never before have all classes and groups (as well as ages) shared so much of the same culture and the same perspectives while having so little to do with their creation. Representation in the world of television gives an idea, a cause, a group its sense of public identity, importance, and relevance. No movement can get going without some visibility in that world or long withstand television's power to discredit, insulate, or undercut. Other media, used selectively and by special interests or cultural elites, cultivate partial and parochial outlooks. Television spreads the same images and messages to all from penthouse to tenement. TV is the new (and only) culture of those who expose themselves to information only when it comes as "entertainment." Entertainment is the most broadly effective educational fare in any culture.

All major networks serving the same social system depend on the same markets and programming formulas. That may be one reason why, unlike other media, television is used non-selectively; it just doesn't matter that much. With the exception of national events and some "specials," the total viewing audience is fairly stable regardless of what is on. Individual tastes and program preferences are less important in determining viewing patterns than is the time a program is on. The nearly universal, non-selective, and habitual use of television fits the ritualistic pattern of its programming. You watch television as you might attend a church service, except that most people watch television more religiously.

Constitutional guarantees shield the prerogatives of ownership. Technological imperatives of electronics have changed modern governance more than Constitutional amendments and court decisions. Television, the flagship of industrial mass culture, now rivals ancient religions as a purveyor of organic patterns of symbols – news and other entertainment – that animate national and even global communities' senses of reality and value.

These considerations led us to question many of the more common arguments raised in discussions of television's effects

An important example is the concern over the consequences of violence on television. The invention and development of technologies which permit the production and dissemination of mass mediated fictional images across class lines seems invariably to raise in the minds of the established classes the specter of subversion, corruption and unrest being encouraged among the various lower orders – poor people, ethnic and racial minorities, children and women. The specter arises when it seems that the lower orders may presume to imitate – if not to replace – their betters. Whether the suspect and controversial media are newspapers, novels, and theater, as in the nineteenth century, or movies, radio, comic books, and television as in the twentieth, concern tends to focus on the possibilities of disruption that threaten the established norms of belief, behavior, and morality.

In our view, however, that concern has become anachronistic. Once the industrial order has legitimized its rule, the primary function of its cultural arm becomes the reiteration of that legitimacy and the maintenance of established power and authority. The rules of the games and the morality of its goals can best be demonstrated by dramatic stories of their symbolic violations. The intended lessons are generally effective and the social order is only rarely and peripherally threatened. The *system* is the message and, as our politicians like to say, the system works. Our question is, in fact, whether it may not work too well in cultivating uniform assumptions, exploitable fears, acquiescence to power, and resistance to meaningful change.

Therefore, in contrast to the more usual statement of the problem, we do not believe that the only critical correlate of television violence is to be found in the stimulation of occasional individual aggression. The consequences of living in a symbolic world ruled largely by violence may be much more far-reaching. Preparation for large-scale organized violence requires the cultivation of fear and acquiescence to power. TV violence is a dramatic demonstration of power which communicates much about social norms and relationships, about goals and means, about winners and losers, about the risks of life and the price for transgressions of society's rules. Violence laden drama shows who gets away with what, when, why, how and against whom. "Real world" *victims* as well as violents may have to learn their roles. Fear – that historic instrument of social control – may be an even more critical residue of a show of violence than aggression. Expectation of violence or passivity in the face of injustice may be consequences of even greater social concern. We shall return to this theme with data from our studies.

The realism of TV fiction hides its synthetic and functionally selective nature

[...] The world of television drama is a mixture of truth and falsehood, of accuracy and distortion. It is not the true world but an extension of the standardized images which we have been taught since childhood. The audience for which the message of television is primarily intended (recall that an audience of about 20 million viewers is necessary for a program's survival) is the great majority of middle-class citizens for whom America is a democracy (our leaders act in accordance with the desires of the people), for whom our economy is free, and for whom God is alive, white, and male.

The implications for research are far-reaching and call into question essential aspects of the research paradigm stemming from historic pressures for behavior manipulation and marketing efficacy

They suggest a model based on the concept of broad enculturation rather than of narrow changes in opinion or behavior. Instead of asking what communication "variables" might propagate what kinds of individual behavior changes, we want to know what types of common consciousness whole systems of messages might cultivate.

This is less like asking about preconceived fears and hopes and more like asking about the "effects" of Christianity on one's view of the world or – as the Chinese *had* asked – of Confucianism on public morality. To answer such questions, we must review and revise some conventional articles of faith about research strategy.

First, we cannot presume consequences without the prior investigation of content, as the conventional research paradigm tends to do. Nor can the content be limited to isolated elements (e.g., news, commercials, specific programs), taken out of the total context, or to individual viewer selections. The "world" of television is an organic system of stories and images. Only system-wide analysis of messages can reveal the symbolic world which structures common assumptions and definitions for the generations born into it and provides bases for interaction (though not necessarily of agreement) among large and heterogeneous communities. The system *as a whole* plays a major role in setting the agenda of issues to agree or disagree about; it shapes the most pervasive norms and cultivates the dominant perspectives of society.

Another conventional research assumption is that the experiment is the most powerful method, and that change (in attitudes, opinions, likes–dislikes, etc., toward or conveyed by "variable X") is the most significant outcome to measure. In the ideal experiment, you expose a group to X and assess salient aspects of the state of the receivers before and after exposure, comparing the change, if any, to data obtained from a control group (identical in all relevant ways to the experimental group) who have not received X. No change or no difference means no effect.

When X is television, however, we must turn this paradigm around: stability may be *the* significant outcome of the sum total of the play of many variables. If nearly everyone "lives" to some extent in the world of television, clearly we cannot find unexposed groups who would be identical in all important respects to the viewers. We cannot isolate television from the mainstream of modern culture because it *is* the mainstream. We cannot look for change as the most significant accomplishment of the chief arm of established culture if its main social function is to maintain, reinforce, and exploit rather than to undermine or alter conventional conceptions, beliefs, and behaviors. On the contrary, the relative ineffectiveness of isolated campaigns may itself be testimony to the power of mainstream communications.

Neither can we assume that TV cultivates conceptions easily distinguishable from those of other major entertainment media. (But we cannot emphasize too strongly the historically novel role of television in standardizing and sharing with all as the common norm what had before been more parochial, local, and selective cultural patterns.) We assume, therefore, that TV's standardizing and legitimizing influence comes largely from its ability to streamline, amplify, ritualize, and spread into hitherto isolated or protected subcultures, homes, nooks, and crannies of the land the conventional capsules of mass produced information and entertainment.

Another popular research technique which is inappropriate is the experimental or quasi-experimental test of the consequences of exposure to one particular type of television programming

Much of the research on media violence, for example, has focused on the observation and measurement of behavior which occurs after a viewer has seen a particular program or even isolated scenes from programs. All such studies, no matter how clean the design and clear the results, are of limited value because they ignore a fundamental fact: the world of TV drama consists of a complex and integrated system of characters, events, actions, and relationships whose effects cannot be measured with regard to any single element or program seen in isolation.

How should, then, the effects of television be conceptualized and studied?

We believe that the key to the answer rests in a search for those assumptions about the "facts" of life and society that television cultivates in its more faithful viewers. That search requires two different methods of research. The relationship between the two is one of the special characteristics of the Cultural Indicators approach.[1]

The first method of research is the periodic analysis of large and representative aggregates of television output (rather than individual segments) as the system of messages to which total communities are exposed. The purpose of message system analysis is to establish composition and structure of the symbolic world. We have begun that analysis with the most ubiquitous, translucent, and instructive part of television (or any cultural) fare, the dramatic programs (series, cartoons, movies on television) that populate and animate for most viewers the heartland of the symbolic world. Instead of guessing or assuming the contours and dynamics of that world, message system analysis maps its geography, demography, thematic and action structure, time and space dimensions, personality profiles, occupations, and fates. Message system analysis yields the gross but clear terms of location, action, and characterization discharged into the mainstream of community consciousness. Aggregate viewer interpretation and response starts with these common terms of basic exposure.

The second step of the research is to determine what, if anything, viewers absorb from living in the world of television. Cultivation analysis, as we call that method, inquires into the assumptions television cultivates about the facts, norms, and values of society. Here we turn the findings of message system analysis about the fantasy land of television into questions about social reality. To each of these questions there is a "television answer," which is like the way things appear in the world of television, and another and different answer which is biased in the opposite direction, closer to the way things are in the observable world. We ask these questions of samples of adults and children. All responses are related to television exposure, other media habits, and demographic characteristics. We then compare the response of light and heavy viewers controlling for sex, age, education, and other characteristics. The margin of heavy viewers over light viewers giving the "television answers" within and across groups is the "cultivation differential" indicating conceptions about social reality that viewing tends to cultivate.

Our analysis looks at the contribution of TV drama to viewer conceptions in conjunction with such other sources of knowledge as education and news. The analysis is intended to illuminate the complementary as well as the divergent roles of these sources of facts, images, beliefs, and values in the cultivation of assumptions about reality.

---

[1] For a more detailed description of the conceptual framework for this research see "Cultural Indicators: The Third Voice" (1).

We shall now sketch some general features of the world of network television drama, and then report the latest findings about violence in that world

As any mythical world, television presents a selective and functional system of messages. Its time, space, and motion – even its "accidents" – follow laws of dramatic convention and social utility. Its people are not born but are created to depict social types, causes, powers, and fates. The economics of the assembly line and the require-ment of wide acceptability assure general adherence to common notions of justice and fair play, clear-cut characterizations, tested plot lines, and proven formulas for resolving all issues.

Representation in the fictional world signifies social existence; absence means symbolic annihilation. Being buffeted by events and victimized by people denotes social impotence; ability to wrest events about, to act freely, boldly, and effectively is a mark of dramatic importance and social power. Values and forces come into play through characterizations; good is a certain type of attractiveness, evil is a personality defect, and right is the might that wins. Plots weave a thread of causality into the fabric of dramatic ritual, as stock characters act out familiar parts and confirm preferred notions of what's what, who's who, and who counts for what. The issue is rarely in doubt; the action is typically a game of social typing, group identification, skill, and power.

Many times a day, seven days a week, the dramatic pattern defines situations and cultivates premises about society, people, and issues. Casting the symbolic world thus has a meaning of its own: the lion's share of representation goes to the types that dominate the social order. About three-quarters of all leading characters are male, American, middle- and upper-class, and in the prime of life. Symbolic independence requires freedom relatively uninhabited by real-life constraints. Less fully represented are those lower in the domestic and global power hierarchy and characters involved in familiar social contexts, human dependencies, and other situations that impose the real-life burdens of human relationships and obligations upon freewheeling activity.

Women typically represent romantic or family interest, close human contact, love. Males can act in nearly any role, but rare is the female part that does not involve at least the suggestion of sex. While only one in three male leads is shown as intending to or ever having been married, two of every three females are married or expect to marry in the story. Female "specialties" limit the proportion of TV's women to about one-fourth of the total population.

Nearly half of all females are concentrated in the most sexually eligible young adult population, to which only one-fifth of males are assigned; women are also dispro-portionately represented among the very young and old. Children, adolescents, and old people together account for less than 15 percent of the total fictional population.

Approximately five in ten characters can be unambiguously identified as gainfully employed. Of these, three are proprietors, managers, and professionals. The fourth comes from the ranks of labor – including all those employed in factories, farms, offices, shops, stores, mining, transportation, service stations, restaurants, and house-holds, and working in unskilled, skilled, clerical, sales, and domestic service capaci-ties. The fifth serves to enforce the law or preserve the peace on behalf of public or private clients.

Types of activity – paid and unpaid – also reflect dramatic and social purposes. Six in ten characters are engaged in discernible occupational activity and can be roughly divided into three groups of two each. The first group represents the world of legitimate private business, industry, agriculture, finance, etc. The second group is engaged in activity related to art, science, religion, health, education, and welfare, as professionals, amateurs, patients, students, or clients. The third makes up the forces of official or semiofficial authority and the army of criminals, outlaws, spies, and other enemies arrayed against them. One in every four leading characters acts out a drama of some sort of transgression and its suppression at home and abroad.

Violence plays a key role in such a world. It is the simplest and cheapest dramatic means available to demonstrate the rules of the game of power. In real life much violence is subtle, slow, circumstantial, invisible, even impersonal. Encounters with physical violence in real life are rare, more sickening than thrilling. But in the symbolic world, overt physical motion makes dramatically visible that which in the real world is usually hidden. Symbolic violence, as any show of force, typically does the job of real violence more cheaply and, of course, entertainingly.

Geared for independent action in loosely-knit and often remote social contexts, half of all characters are free to engage in violence. One-fifth "specialize" in violence as law breakers or law enforcers. Violence on television, unlike in real-life, rarely stems from close personal relationships. Most of it is between strangers, set up to drive home lessons of social typing. Violence is often just a specialty – a skill, a craft, an efficient means to test the norms of and settle any challenge to the existing structure of power.

The Violence Profile is a set of indicators tracing aspects of the television world and of conceptions of social reality they tend to cultivate in the minds of viewers

Four specific types of indicators have been developed. Three come from message system analysis: (1) the context of programming trends against which any aspect of the world of television can be seen; (2) several specific measures of violence given separately and also combined in the Violence Index; and (3) structural characteristics of the dramatic world indicating social relationships depicted in it (in the present report, "risk ratios"). The fourth type of indicator comes from cultivation analysis and will be shown in this report as the "cultivation differential." Although the Violence Profile is the most developed, the Cultural Indicators project is constructing similar profiles of other aspects and relationships of the media world. [...]

Three sets of violence measures have been computed from the direct observational data of the message system analysis. They show the percent of programs with any violence at all, the frequency and rate of violent episodes, and the number of roles calling for characterizations as violents, victims, or both. These measures are called *prevalence*, *rate*, and *role*, respectively. Each is given separately in all the tabulations that follow.

For ease of illustration and comparison, the three types of measures are also combined to form the Violence Index. The Index itself is not a statistical finding but serves as a convenient illustrator of trends and facilitates gross comparisons. The Index is obtained by adding measures of prevalence, rates (doubled to raise their relatively low numerical value) and roles. The formula can be seen on Tables 1 through 4.

Before presenting the trends indicated by the measures just discussed, let us glance at the first indicator, that of program mix. "Action" programs contribute most violence to the world of television drama. Figure 1 shows that such programs comprise more than half of all prime-time and weekend daytime programming, and their proportion of the total has not changed much in recent years. In fact, while general (non-cartoon) crime and adventure plays dropped from their 1974 high of 62 percent to 54 percent in 1975, cartoon crime and adventure rose in the same period from 47 percent to 66 percent of all cartoons.

These programming trends foreshadow the violence findings that follow. We can summarize them by noting that there has been *no significant reduction in the overall Violence Index despite some fluctuations in the specific measures and a definite drop in "family hour" violence, especially on CBS, in the current season.* The "family hour" decline has been matched by a sharp increase in violence during children's (weekend daytime) programming in the current season and by an even larger two-year rise in violence after 9 p.m. EST. [...]

The indicators reflected in the Violence Index are clear manifestations of what network programmers actually do as compared to what they say or intend to do. Network executives and their censorship ("Standards and Practices") offices maintain close control over the assembly line production process that results in the particular program mix of a season (2). While our data permit many specific qualifications to any generalization that might be made, it is safe to say that network policy seems to have responded in narrow terms, when at all, to very specific pressure, and only while the heat was on. After nine years of investigations, hearings, and commissions (or since we

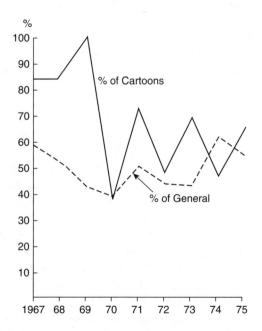

Figure 1 "Action" (crime, western, adventure) programs as percent of cartoon and of other (general) programs analyzed

have been tracking violence on television), eight out of every ten programs (nine out of every ten weekend children's hour programs) still contain some violence. The overall rate of violent episodes, 8 per hour, is, if anything, higher than at any time since 1969. (The violence saturation of weekend children's programs declined from the 1969 high but increased from its 1974 low to 16 per hour, double that of overall programming, as can be seen on Table 4.) Between six and seven out of every ten leading characters (eight and nine for children) are still involved in some violence. Between one and two out of every ten are still involved in killing. Reductions have been achieved in the portrayal of on-screen killers (especially during weekend children's hours) and in "family hour" violence (especially by CBS), but, as we have noted, a sharp rise in late evening and general children's violence has canceled out any overall gains from the latter.

It is clear, at least to us, that deeply rooted sociocultural forces, rather than just obstinacy or profit-seeking, are at work. We have suggested earlier in this article, and have also developed elsewhere (3, 4), that symbolic violence is a demonstration of power and an instrument of social control serving, on the whole, to reinforce and preserve the existing social order, even if at an ever increasing price in terms of pervasive fear and mistrust and of selective aggressiveness. That maintenance mechanism seems to work through cultivating a sense of danger, a differential calculus of the risks of life in different groups in the population. The Violence Profile is beginning to yield indicators of such a mechanism, and thereby also of basic structural and cultivation characteristics of television programming.

The structural characteristics of television drama are not easily controlled. They reflect basic cultural assumptions that make a show "entertaining" – i.e., smoothly and pleasingly fitting dominant notions (and prejudices) about social relations and thus demonstrating conventional notions of morality and power.

The most elementary – and telling – relationship involved in violent action is that of violent and victim. The pattern of those who inflict and those who suffer violence (or both) provides a differential calculus of hazards and opportunities for different groups of people in the "world" of television drama. Table 5[2] presents a summary of the scores of involvement and what we call risk ratios. The character score is the roles component (CS) of the Violence Index; it is the percent of all characters involved in any violence plus the percent involved in any killing. The violent–victim and killer–killed (risk) ratio are obtained by dividing violents and victims, or killers and killed within each group. The plus sign means more violents or killers in the group; the minus sign means more victims (hurt) or killed.

We see that the 1967–75 totals show 1.19 male and 1.32 female victims for every violent male and female. Even more striking are the differential risks or fatal victimization. There were nearly two male killers for every male killed; however, for every female killer one woman was killed.

Table 5 also shows the differential risks of involvement and victimization attributed to other groups, projecting assumptions about social and power relations. Old men, married men, lower class, foreign, and nonwhite males were most likely to get killed rather than to inflict lethal injury. "Good guys" were of course most likely to be the killers.

Among females, more vulnerable than men in most categories, both young and old women as well as unmarried, lower class, foreign, and nonwhite women bore

[2] All tables appear after Critical connections on pp. 434–441.

especially heavy burdens of relative victimization. Old, poor, and black women were shown *only* as killed and never as killers. Interestingly, "good" women, unlike "good" men, had no lethal power, but "bad" women were even more lethal than "bad" men. The victimization of the "good" woman is often the curtain-raiser that provokes the hero to righteous "action."

The pattern of relative victimization is remarkably stable from year to year. It demonstrates an invidious (but socially functional) sense of risk and power. We do not yet know whether it also cultivates a corresponding hierarchy of fear and aggression. But we do have evidence to suggest that television viewing cultivates a general sense of danger and mistrust. That evidence comes from the fourth and final element of the Violence Profile, the component we call the cultivation differential.

The cultivation differential comes, of course, from the cultivation analysis part of the Cultural Indicators research approach

It highlights differences in conception of relevant aspects of social reality that television viewing tends to cultivate in heavy viewers compared to light viewers. The strategy is obviously most appropriate to those propositions in which television might cultivate conceptions that measurably deviate from those coming from other sources. Furthermore, the independent contributions of television are likely to be most powerful in cultivating assumptions about which there is little opportunity to learn first-hand, and which are not strongly anchored in other established beliefs and ideologies

The obvious objection arises that light and heavy viewers are different prior to – and aside from – television. Factors other than television may account for the difference.

The point is well taken. We have found, as have others, that heavy viewing is part and parcel of a complex syndrome which also includes lower education, lower mobility, lower aspirations, higher anxieties, and other class, age, and sex related characteristics. We assume, indeed, that viewing helps to hold together and cultivate elements of that syndrome. But it does more than that. Television viewing also makes a separate and independent contribution to the "biasing" of conceptions of social reality within most age, sex, educational, and other groupings, including those presumably most "immune" to its effects.

Our study of TV's contribution to notions of social reality proceeds by various methods, each comparing responses of heavy and light viewers, with other character-istics held constant. Of the different methods used in cultivation analysis, only adult survey results are included in this report; the others are still in the process of development and summarization. These surveys were executed by commercial survey research organizations. For details of sampling, etc., the reader is referred to the Technical Report (5).

To probe in the direction of the pattern suggested by our message analysis, we obtained responses to questions about facts of life that relate to law enforcement, trust, and a sense of danger. Figure 2 presents the results of the first question asking what proportion of people are employed in law enforcement. The "television answer" (slanted in the direction of the world of television) was five percent. The alternative answer (more in the direction of reality) was one percent.

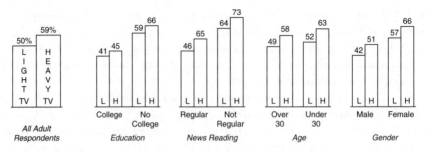

Figure 2 Percent giving the "television answer" to a question about the proportion of people employed in law enforcement

As Figure 2 shows, the heavy viewers (those viewing an average of four hours a day or more) were always more likely to give the television answer than the light viewers (those viewing an average of two hours a day or less). Figure 3 shows similar results for the question "Can most people be trusted?" and Figure 4 for the question "During any given week, what are your chances of being involved in some type of violence?" One in ten (the "television answer") or one in a hundred?

Let us take education as probably the best index of a complex of social circumstances that provide alternative informational and cultural opportunities. Those of our respondents who have had some college education are less likely to choose the "television answer" than those who have had none. But *within* each group, television viewing "biases" conceptions in the direction of the "facts" it presents. When we compared light and heavy viewers within the "college" and the "no college" groups, we got

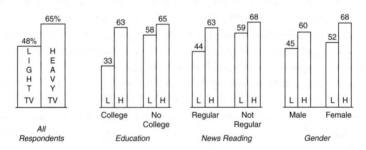

Figure 3 Percent responding "Can't be too careful" to the question "Can most people be trusted?"

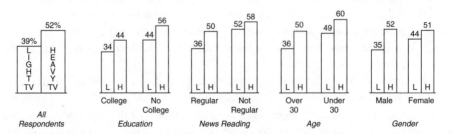

Figure 4 Percent giving the "television answer" (exaggerating) their own chances of being involved in violence

a typical step-wise pattern of the percentage of "television answers." Regular reading of newspapers makes a similar difference.

Both college education and regular newspaper reading seem to reduce the percentage of "television answers," but heavy viewing boosts it within both groups. This appears to be the general pattern of TV's ability to cultivate its own "reality."

An exaggerated impression of the actual number of law enforcement workers seems to be a consequence of viewing television. Of greater concern, however, would be the cultivation of a concomitantly exaggerated demand for their services. The world of television drama is, above all, a violent one in which more than half of all characters are involved in some violence, at least one-tenth in some killing, and in which over three-fourths of prime-time hours contain some violence. As we have suggested, the cultivation of fear and a sense of danger may well be a prime residue of the show of violence.

Questions about feelings of trust and safety may be used to test that suggestion. The National Opinion Research Corporation's 1975 General Social Survey asked "Can most people be trusted?" Living in the world of television seems to strengthen the conclusion that they cannot. Heavy viewers chose the answer "Can't be too careful" in significantly greater proportions than did light viewers in the same groups, as shown in Figure 3. Those who do not read newspapers regularly have a high level of mistrust regardless of TV viewing. But, not surprisingly, women are the most likely to absorb the message of distrust.

Focusing directly on violence, we asked a national sample of adults about people's chances of being involved in violence in any given week. Figure 4 shows the patterns of overestimations in line with television's view of the world. It may explain why in recent surveys, such as the Detroit study conducted by the Institute of Social Research (6), respondents' estimates of danger in their neighborhoods had little to do with crime statistics or even with their own personal experience. The pattern of our findings suggests that television and other media exposure may be as important as demographic and other experiential factors in explaining why people view the world as they do.

Television certainly appears to condition the view of the generation that knew no world without it. All the figures show that the "under 30" respondents exhibit consistently higher levels of "television responses," despite the fact that they tend to be better educated than the "over 30" respondents. We may all live in a dangerous world, but young people (including children tested but not reported on here), the less educated, women, and heavy viewers within all these groups sense greater danger than light viewers in the same groups. College education (and its social correlates) may counter the television view, but heavy exposure to TV will counteract that too.

Fear is a universal emotion and easy to exploit. Symbolic violence may be the cheapest way to cultivate it effectively. Raw violence is, in comparison, risky and costly, resorted to when symbolic means fail. Ritualized displays of any violence (such as in crime and disaster news, as well as in mass-produced drama) may cultivate exaggerated assumptions about the extent of threat and danger in the world and lead to demands for protection.

What is the net result? A heightened sense of risk and insecurity (different for groups of varying power) is more likely to increase acquiescence to and dependence upon established authority, and to legitimize its use of force, than it is to threaten the social order through occasional non-legitimized imitations. Risky for their perpetrators and costly for their victims, media-incited criminal violence may be a price industrial cultures extract from some citizens for the general pacification of most others.

As with violence, so with other aspects of social reality we are investigating, TV appears to cultivate assumptions that fit its socially functional myths. Our chief instrument of enculturation and social control, television may function as the established religion of the industrial order, relating to governance as the church did to the state in earlier times.

References

1. Gerbner, George. "Cultural Indicators: The Third Voice." In *Communications Technology and Social Policy.* New York: John Wiley and Sons, 1973.
2. Gerbner, George, Larry Gross, and William H. Melody. *Communications Technology and Social Policy.* New York: John Wiley and Sons, 1973.
3. Gerbner, George. "Scenario for Violence." *Human Behavior,* October 1975.
4. Gerbner, George, and Larry Gross. "The Scary World of Television," *Psychology Today,* April 1976.
5. Gerbner, George, and Larry Gross, with the assistance of Michael F. Eleey, Suzanne K. Fox, Marilyn Jackson-Beeck, and Nancy Signorielli. "Violence Profile No. 7: A Technical Report." Annenberg School of Communications, 1976.
6. "Personal Safety a Major Concern: Public Perceptions of Quality of Life in Metropolitan Detroit Examined in ISR Study." *ISR Newsletter,* Winter 1976, p. 4.

Critical connections

While supported in some studies (Hawkins and Pingree, 1980; Morgan, 1983), researchers outside the US have generally failed to replicate the cultivation effect (Gunter, 1987; Cumberbatch, 1989). Furthermore, a number of empirical and theoretical weaknesses have been identified (many of these are discussed by Ditton *et al.* in Reading 33). Despite such criticisms, the fundamental claim underpinning cultivation research – that particular forms of distorted and distorting media communication can generate widespread anxiety, greater demands for protection, and the tacit acceptance of authoritarian governance – shares much wider support across a diversity of research positions. This view is explicit in Hall *et al.*'s (1978) *Policing the Crisis* (Reading 18), where it is inflected through a Gramscian reading of the state's repressive response to a 'crisis in hegemony'. And it forms a central argument in Mythen and Walklate's (2006) *Communicating the Terrorist Risk* (Reading 41), where it is articulated in terms of the state 'harnessing a culture of fear' in the 'risk society' in order to legitimate tough anti-terror legislation and the construction of the non-white 'terroristic other'. Thus the greatest problems with cultivation analysis do not derive from the validity of its central concerns. Most problematic is the imprecise articulation and application of these concerns within a quantitative research framework, and the weakness of the methodology employed to assess or 'measure' the impact of television.

For Gerbner and Gross, the introduction of television – the 'electronic priesthood' – shaped individual consciousness and social organisation in a manner which the previously dominant mode of communication – print culture – never could. 'Television, the flagship of industrial mass culture, now rivals ancient religions as a purveyor of organic patterns of symbols – news and other entertainment – that animate national and even global communities' sense of reality and value' (Gerbner and Gross, 1976: 177). Marshall McLuhan (Reading 2) viewed the introduction of television in broadly positive terms and saw it potentially as part of a process of 're-tribalisation', a key element in the wider electronic mode of communication that could overcome the individualism and nationalism promoted by print culture. Gerbner and Gross, in contrast, are concerned primarily with the deleterious effects of television, which they see as creating passive, depoliticised and fearful consumers, overly-dependent on established authority and socialised into dominant power relations of gender, race and class.

Discussion questions

- Outline and discuss the central tenets of Gerbner and Gross's cultivation thesis.
- Why, despite using the same or similar methodological approaches, do you think other researchers have found it so difficult to replicate Gerbner and Gross's findings?
- Is it reasonable in an age of media proliferation (Readings 5, 6 and 7) to maintain that television is society's chief mechanism of 'enculturation'?

References

Cumberbatch, G. (1989) 'Violence in the Media: The Research Evidence', in G. Cumberbatch and D. Howitt (eds) *A Measure of Uncertainty: the Effects of the Mass Media*. London: John Libbey.

Gunter, B. (1987) *Television and the Fear of Crime*. London: John Libbey.

Hawkins, R. and Pingree, S. (1980) 'Some Processes in the Cultivation Effect', in *Communication Research, 7*, 2: 193–226.

Morgan, M. (1983) 'Symbolic Victimisation and Real World Fear', in *Human Communication Research, 9*, 2: 146–57.

Table 1 Violence measures for all programs in sample

		1967	1968	1969	1970	1971	1972	1973	1974	1975	TOTAL
SAMPLES (100%)		N	N	N	N	N	N	N	N	N	N
	Programs (plays) analyzed	96	87	121	111	103	100	99	96	111	924
	Program hours analyzed	62.0	58.5	71.8	67.2	70.3	72.0	75.2	76.0	77.3	630.2
	Leading characters analyzed	240	215	377	196	252	300	359	346	364	2649
PREVALENCE		%	%	%	%	%	%	%	%	%	%
(%P)	Programs containing violence	81.3	81.6	83.5	77.5	80.6	79.0	72.7	83.3	78.4	79.8
	Program hours containing violence	83.2	87.0	83.2	78.3	87.2	84.2	79.7	86.8	83.0	83.6
RATE		N	N	N	N	N	N	N	N	N	N
	Number of violent episodes	478	394	630	498	483	539	524	522	626	4694
(R/P)	Rate per all programs (plays)	5.0	4.5	5.2	4.5	4.7	5.4	5.3	5.4	5.6	5.1
(R/H)	Rate per all hours	7.7	6.7	8.8	7.4	6.9	7.5	7.0	6.9	8.1	7.4
	Duration of violent episodes (hrs)	—	—	—	—	—	—	3.2	3.8	3.6	10.6
ROLES (% OF LEADING CHARACTERS)		%	%	%	%	%	%	%	%	%	%
	Violents (committing violence)	55.8	49.3	48.5	52.0	46.0	39.3	34.5	40.8	43.1	44.6
	Victims (subjected to violence)	64.6	55.8	58.9	56.6	50.8	49.7	48.2	51.2	53.8	54.0
(%V)	Any involvement in violence	73.3	65.1	66.3	62.8	61.5	58.3	55.7	60.7	64.8	62.9
	Killers (committing fatal violence)	12.5	10.7	3.7	6.6	8.7	7.7	5.8	9.8	6.3	7.7
	Killed (victims of lethal violence)	7.1	3.7	2.1	4.6	3.2	4.7	3.3	5.8	3.8	4.2
(%K)	Any involvement in killing	18.7	11.6	5.6	8.7	9.9	9.7	7.5	13.6	9.1	10.2
INDICATORS OF VIOLENCE											
	Program Score: PS = (%P) + 2(R/P) + 2(R/H)	106.6	104.1	111.4	101.3	103.7	104.8	97.3	107.9	105.8	104.8
	Character V-Score: CS = (%V) + (%K)	92.1	76.7	71.9	71.4	71.4	68.0	63.2	74.3	73.9	73.0
	Violence Index: VI = PS + CS	198.7	180.9	183.3	172.7	175.1	172.8	160.5	182.2	179.7	177.8

Table 2 Violence measures for family hour only

	1967	1968	1969	1970	1971	1972	1973	1974	1975	TOTAL
SAMPLES (100%)	N	N	N	N	N	N	N	N	N	N
Programs (plays) analyzed	38	36	38	35	28	27	32	29	31	294
Program hours analyzed	30.0	27.0	27.3	26.0	25.0	23.5	29.0	27.0	21.5	236.3
Leading characters analyzed	103	102	130	76	78	98	110	109	105	911
PREVALENCE	%	%	%	%	%	%	%	%	%	%
(%P) Programs containing violence	78.9	75.0	63.2	57.1	75.0	74.1	56.3	69.0	51.6	66.7
Program hours containing violence	86.7	83.3	74.3	67.3	86.0	85.1	70.7	77.8	60.5	77.1
RATE	N	N	N	N	N	N	N	N	N	N
Number of violent episodes	240	123	122	86	110	122	147	108	77	1135
(R/P) Rate per all programs (plays)	6.3	3.4	3.2	2.5	3.9	4.5	4.6	3.7	2.5	3.9
(R/H) Rate per all hours	8.0	4.6	4.5	3.3	4.4	5.2	5.1	4.0	3.6	4.8
Duration of violent episodes (hrs)	—	—	—	—	—	—	0.9	1.0	0.5	2.4
ROLES (% OF LEADING CHARACTERS)	%	%	%	%	%	%	%	%	%	%
Violents (committing violence)	58.3	39.2	36.2	32.9	37.2	37.8	29.1	29.4	16.2	35.0
Victims (subjected to violence)	68.9	46.1	40.8	39.5	38.5	40.8	33.6	36.7	27.6	41.4

(Continued)

Table 2 Violence measures for family hour only—cont'd

	1967	1968	1969	1970	1971	1972	1973	1974	1975	TOTAL
(%V) Any involvement in violence	75.7	56.9	49.2	40.8	50.0	50.0	40.9	45.0	36.2	49.5
Killers (committing fatal violence)	22.3	10.8	6.2	3.9	9.0	4.1	6.4	12.8	1.0	8.6
Killed (victims of lethal violence)	7.8	4.9	3.1	1.3	2.6	3.1	4.5	7.3	0.0	4.0
(%K) Any involvement in killing	28.2	12.7	9.2	3.9	10.3	5.1	10.0	16.5	1.0	11.0

INDICATORS OF VIOLENCE

	1967	1968	1969	1970	1971	1972	1973	1974	1975	TOTAL
Program Score: PS = (%P) + 2(R/P) + 2(R/H)	107.6	90.9	78.5	68.7	91.7	93.5	75.6	84.4	63.7	84.0
Character V-Score: CS = (%V) + (%K)	103.9	69.6	58.5	44.7	60.3	55.1	50.9	61.5	37.1	60.5
Violence Index: VI = PS + CS	211.5	160.6	137.0	113.4	151.9	148.6	126.5	145.9	100.9	144.5

Table 3 Violence measures for late evening (9–11 p.m. EST)

	1967	1968	1969	1970	1971	1972	1973	1974	1975	TOTAL
SAMPLES (100%)	N	N	N	N	N	N	N	N	N	N
Programs (plays) analyzed	26	21	26	26	34	33	30	29	35	260
Program hours analyzed	25.0	24.0	30.5	28.0	30.3	33.0	27.5	33.0	39.5	270.7
Leading characters analyzed	75	60	88	56	91	119	104	115	133	841
PREVALENCE	%	%	%	%	%	%	%	%	%	%
(%P) Programs containing violence	69.2	76.2	80.8	69.2	76.5	69.7	63.3	86.2	85.7	75.4
Program hours containing violence	76.0	89.6	84.4	80.4	87.6	79.8	79.1	92.4	92.4	85.1
RATE	N	N	N	N	N	N	N	N	N	N
Number of violent episodes	87	99	110	116	129	172	130	220	284	1347
(R/P) Rate per all programs (plays)	3.3	4.7	4.2	4.5	3.8	5.2	4.3	7.6	8.1	5.2
(R/H) Rate per all hours	3.5	4.1	3.6	4.1	4.3	5.2	4.7	6.7	7.2	5.0
Duration of violent episodes (hrs)	–	–	–	–	–	–	1.3	1.8	1.9	5.0
ROLES (% OF LEADING CHARACTERS)	%	%	%	%	%	%	%	%	%	%
Violents (committing violence)	38.7	55.0	34.1	46.4	44.0	37.8	32.7	56.5	51.1	44.0
Victims (subjected to violence)	42.7	55.0	44.3	50.0	48.4	45.4	36.5	61.7	59.4	49.7
(%V) Any involvement in violence	56.0	68.3	52.3	57.1	59.3	55.5	41.3	71.3	68.4	59.1
Killers (committing fatal violence)	5.3	16.7	5.7	14.3	15.4	16.0	12.5	16.5	16.5	13.6
Killed (victims of lethal violence)	4.0	5.0	2.3	12.5	5.5	8.4	6.7	10.4	9.8	7.4
(%K) Any involvement in killing	9.3	16.7	6.8	21.4	17.6	19.3	14.4	24.3	23.3	17.6
INDICATORS OF VIOLENCE										
Program Score: PS=(%P)+2(R/H) +2(R/H)	82.9	93.9	96.4	86.4	92.6	90.5	81.5	114.7	116.3	95.7
Character V-Score: CS = (%V) + (%K)	65.3	85.0	59.1	78.6	76.9	74.8	55.8	95.7	91.7	76.7
Violence Index: VI = PS + CS	148.2	178.9	155.5	165.0	169.5	165.3	137.2	210.4	208.1	172.4

Table 4 Violence measures for weekend daytime (children's) hours

	1967	1968	1969	1970	1971	1972	1973	1974	1975	TOTAL
SAMPLES (100%)	N	N	N	N	N	N	N	N	N	N
Programs (plays) analyzed	32	30	57	50	41	40	37	38	45	370
Program hours analyzed	7.0	7.5	14.0	13.2	15.0	15.5	18.7	16.0	16.3	123.2
Leading characters analyzed	62	53	159	64	83	83	145	122	126	897
PREVALENCE	%	%	%	%	%	%	%	%	%	%
(%P) Programs containing violence	93.8	93.3	98.2	96.0	87.8	90.0	94.6	92.1	91.1	93.2
Program hours containing violence	94.0	92.2	97.6	95.6	88.5	92.3	94.6	90.6	89.8	92.7
RATE	N	N	N	N	N	N	N	N	N	N
Number of violent episodes	151	172	398	296	244	245	247	194	265	2212
(R/P) Rate per all programs (plays)	4.7	5.7	7.0	5.9	6.0	6.1	6.7	5.1	5.9	6.0
(R/H) Rate per all hours	21.6	22.9	28.4	22.5	16.2	15.8	13.2	12.1	16.2	18.0
Duration of violent episodes (hrs)	–	–	–	–	–	–	1.0	0.9	1.2	3.2
ROLES (% OF LEADING CHARACTERS)	%	%	%	%	%	%	%	%	%	%
Violents (committing violence)	72.6	62.3	66.7	79.7	56.6	43.4	40.0	36.1	57.1	54.8
Victims (subjected to violence)	83.9	75.5	81.8	82.8	65.1	66.3	67.6	54.1	69.8	70.9

(%V)	Any involvement in violence	90.3	77.4	88.1	93.8	74.7	72.3	77.2	64.8	84.9	79.9
	Killers (committing fatal violence)	4.8	3.8	0.6	3.1	1.2	0.0	0.7	0.8	0.0	1.2
	Killed (victims of lethal violence)	9.7	0.0	1.3	1.6	1.2	1.2	0.0	0.0	0.8	1.3
(%K)	Any involvement in killing	14.5	3.8	1.9	3.1	1.2	1.2	0.7	0.8	0.8	2.3

INDICATORS OF VIOLENCE

Program Score: PS = (%P) + 2(R/P) + 2(R/H)	146.3	150.7	169.1	152.8	132.2	133.9	134.4	126.6	135.3	141.1
Character V-Score: CS = (%V) + (%K)	104.8	81.1	89.9	96.9	76.9	73.5	77.9	65.6	85.7	82.3
Violence Index: VI = PS + CS	251.2	231.8	259.0	249.7	208.1	207.4	212.3	192.1	221.1	223.4

Table 5 Risk ratios for all programs studied 1967–75

Groups	Male Characters				Female Characters			
	N	Character score	Violent-victim ratio	Killer-killed ratio	N	Character score	Violent-victim ratio	Killer-killed ratio
All characters	2010	80.0	−1.19	+1.97	605	48.9	−1.32	1.00
Social age								
Children-adolescents	188	64.9	−1.83	+0.00	77	46.8	−1.39	0.00*
Young adults	431	81.2	−1.21	+3.07	209	59.8	−1.67	+1.29
Settled adults	1068	80.8	−1.15	+1.98	267	37.8	1.00	1.00
Old	81	58.0	+1.03	−2.00	22	50.0	−2.25	−0.00*
Marital status								
Not married	1133	83.6	−1.16	+2.24	306	57.2	−1.51	−1.43
Married	462	66.9	−1.33	+1.57	252	39.3	−1.11	+1.40
Class								
Clearly upper	196	87.2	−1.28	+1.15	70	52.9	−1.64	+1.33
Mixed; indeterminate	1744	78.7	−1.19	+2.36	517	48.2	−1.26	1.00
Clearly lower	70	91.4	−1.11	−1.33	18	55.6	−2.67	−0.00*

Nationality								
U.S.	1505	75.0	-1.19	+2.39	503	46.1	-1.39	-1.08
Other	276	96.7	-1.22	+1.13	66	60.6	-1.55	+3.00
Race								
White	1533	77.6	-1.20	+2.12	541	49.9	-1.29	+1.07
Other	264	83.3	-1.27	+1.33	50	38.0	-2.43	-0.00*
*Character type***								
"Good" (heroes)	928	69.3	-1.26	+3.47	314	43.3	-1.56	-6.00
Mixed type	432	71.1	-1.31	+1.09	156	43.6	-1.37	1.00
"Bad" (villains)	291	114.1	-1.03	+1.80	41	82.9	+1.14	+2.00

*Group has neither violents nor victims. If 0.00 is preceded by a sign, group has either no violents or no victims; +0.00 means only violent(s) but no victims(s); -0.00 means only victim(s) but no violent(s).

**This classification was introduced in 1969.

Note: Character score is the percent of characters involved in any violence plus the percent involved in any killing. V-v ratio is of violents (+) and victims (−). K-k ratio is of killers (+) and killed (−).

Jason Ditton, Derek Chadee, Stephen Farrall, Elisabeth Gilchrist and Jon Bannister

FROM IMITATION TO INTIMIDATION: A NOTE ON THE CURIOUS AND CHANGING RELATIONSHIP BETWEEN THE MEDIA, CRIME AND FEAR OF CRIME (2004)

Introduction and context

DITTON *ET AL*. begin 'From Imitation to Intimidation' with a review of the existing research on media and fear of crime, concluding that the findings are, at best, scattered and vague. They note that, of a total of 73 substantive attempts to establish a connection between media consumption and fear of crime, only 27 per cent of studies find a positive relationship, while 73 per cent do not. Yet, as Sacco (1982:476) has noted, the suggestion that there exists a direct causal connection between mass media and perceptions of crime retains a certain intuitive appeal:

> In general, this position seems to follow logically from the three widely accepted assumptions upon which it is based. First, since most people do not have direct personal experience with serious crime, the major source of public thought and feeling regarding crime must be vicarious in nature. Second, the mass media of communication are information sources to which the members of modern society widely attend. Finally, as a number of researchers have documented, contemporary . . . media contain a substantial proportion of crime-related news and information content.

Ditton *et al.* suggest that one reason why an actual relationship between media consumption and fear of crime has been convincingly evidenced so infrequently may have much to do with the methodological approach adopted and the questions asked. Thus they approach the problem in a manner that seeks to overcome the weaknesses inherent in much previous research. Their significant contribution is the combination of quantitative and qualitative research methods in the exploration of media consumption and fear of crime. The quantitative part of the analysis, they reveal, in line with much of the quantitative research in this area, yields little in the way of significant results (see also Greer, 2009; Reiner, 2007). It is through the qualitative assessment of how people actively use media, and what 'meaning' they take from or apply to the crime content they consume, that the more nuanced appreciation of media 'influence' is derived.

"It is not easy to make people afraid" (Altheide 2002:59).

Although generally bedevilled by differing definitions of what constitutes crime and how it should be measured, it has been broadly established that crime constitutes a relatively constant, although not particularly large, percentage of newspaper, television and radio news. It has also been shown that the selection reported tends to be sensational rather than mundane. A review of the research studies that suggest these generalizations can be found in Chadee and Ditton (forthcoming). It has also become commonplace to assert that since so few people are crime victims,[1] then the comparatively large levels of survey-discovered fear of crime must inevitably be related to media consumption. An historic problem has been, surprisingly, the difficulty in establishing this relationship.

The media and fear

Although the dominant current attitude towards the relationship between the media and crime is of the former's causing fear of the latter, it wasn't always so. As Morgan (1983: 146) has pointed out, prior to the path-breaking work of George Gerbner and his associates (Gerbner *et al.* 1976, 1979, 1980), most research attention in the field was oriented to connecting the media to viewers' aggression (i.e. as potential offenders) rather than to their anxieties (i.e. as potential victims).[2]

Two particularly influential pieces (Gerbner and Gross 1976; Gerbner *et al.* 1979) established the position that frequent viewers of television were more likely to believe that they might become crime victims – particularly of violence – than light television viewers. Gerbner's approach to research currently appears distinctly amateurish, but findings were simply expressed, and they blended well with then current concerns about the amount of violence on American television. So much so, in fact, that another study published in the same year (Teeven and Hartnagel 1976), but which found only weak or non-existent relationships between exposure to televised violence and perceptions of the crime rate, and concluded 'there appears to be little relationship between television violence as objectively measured on favourite shows and either perceptions of crime or reactions to crime' (*ibid.*: 346), cheerfully could be ignored.

Gerbner's opus was also almost immediately challenged by Doob and Macdonald (1979), who attempted to replicate the original findings. They found that 'when the effect of neighborhood is removed, the "effect" of television is reduced to almost nothing' (*ibid.*: 175). Further, when sample demographics were entered in stepwise regression, 'the media questions had no significant predictive value. Most relevant to the Gerbner results is of course the lack of importance of total television viewing when it first entered the equation' (*ibid.*: 176).[3] Later, Hughes (1980) re-examined Gerbner's own data, including additional variables, and using multivariate rather than univariate analysis. He concluded (*ibid.*: 295) that Gerbner's

> . . . hypothesis concerning television watching and the perception of environmental menace, reverses direction after controls, and while this relationship is not statistically significant, it suggests that those who watch television heavily are *less* likely to be afraid of walking alone at night in their neighborhoods.

Hirsch (1980) also concluded that Gerbner's claimed relationships disappear with the introduction of appropriate statistical controls and their application simultaneously rather than sequentially. Later still (Hirsch 1981), he also re-examined Gerbner's data and, after, stated that Gerbner's hypotheses were so broad as to be irrefutable (and, thus, untestable), and the correlations were nevertheless so weak that a respondent's star sign was a more powerful predictor of fear than was even heavy viewing: 'Zodiac sign, while not consistently strong in showing the power of television to influence viewers' attitudes, remains an important indicator. It is very significantly associated (χ^2, 0.01) with the number of hours viewed by the respondents in the NORC sample' (*ibid.*: 31). A footnote at this point in his text suggests that 'Respondents under the signs of Cancer, Leo, and Virgo are significantly more likely to fall into the category of heavy viewers'.

In response to these and earlier criticisms, Gerbner *et al.* (1980) introduced new concepts of 'mainstreaming' and 'resonance', but these theoretical patches are not entirely convincing. Both Wober (1978) and Wober and Gunter (1982) attempted to replicate Gerbner in the United Kingdom, but failed in both attempts, although their approach differed methodologically from that of Gerbner and his associates. Wober and Gunter concentrated on type of programming rather than on total hours watched, and introduced pre-existing personality factors to explain inconsistencies in the relationship between crime viewing and crime fear.[4] At around the same time, Zillman (1980: 159) was to say of the Gerbner work that their

> . . . interpretation not only lacks validity in a technical sense, but it also seems to be at variance with basic psychological considerations. If exposure to transgression-laden suspenseful drama produces acute anxieties, the viewer should shun such dramatic fare. He or she should avoid repeating the adverse experience, and this avoidance should convert the heavy viewer into a light viewer. . . . It appears that the findings reported by Gerbner and Gross are equally (if not more) consistent with the alternative causal possibility: Anxiety may foster heavy viewing of programs that

feature suspenseful drama. Unlike the Gerbner–Gross proposal, such an expectation is not based on the consideration of fear-inducing stimuli alone, but on the suspense-resolution unity instead.

Of later attempts to establish a positive relationship between television viewing and fear of crime – there is, inevitably, no consistency in sampling size or selection method, and considerable variance in choice of measure of both independent and dependent variables – some have managed to establish some sort of relationship (Morgan 1983; O'Keefe and Reid-Nash 1987; Gebotys et al. 1988; Sparks and Ogles 1990; Bazargan 1994; Haghighi and Sorensen 1996; Chiricos et al. 1997, 2000; Lane and Meeker 2003), and others have failed (Gomme 1986; Sacco 1982; Skogan and Maxfield 1981; O'Keefe 1984). Of those that succeeded, Morgan (1983) failed to control for prior victimization, and O'Keefe and Reid-Nash (1987), Gebotys et al. (1988), Sparks and Ogles (1990), Bazargan (1994) and Chiricos et al. (1997) only managed to establish a relationship at the $p < 0.05$ level.[5] To claim a positive relationship at this level of statistical significance is essentially arbitrary, particularly for large samples, or for small samples which are not purely random ones. Finally, Haghighi and Sorensen (1996) claim a relationship, but close inspection of their data suggests (Table 2) that the 'effect' is noticeably curvilinear for degree of local media attention to violent crime; is significant for only three of seven offence groups for watching television crime shows; and significant for only two of seven offence groups for total television hours watched (in one case, low viewers were more worried; in the other, the highest viewers were the least worried).

The same critical approach to studies of the relationship between newspaper reading and the fear of crime leads broadly to the same conclusion. Some have found a positive relationship (Jaehnig et al. 1981; Gordon and Heath 1981; Heath 1984; Gebotys et al. 1988; Liska and Baccaglini 1990; Winkel and Vrij 1990; Williams and Dickinson 1993; Haghighi and Sorensen 1996; Lane and Meeker 2003) and some have not (Sacco 1982; Skogan and Maxfield 1981; Gomme 1986; O'Keefe and Reid-Nash 1987; Bazargan 1994; Perkins and Taylor 1996; Chiricos et al. 1997). Of those that succeeded, Jaehnig et al. (1981) only found a broad rank ordering within a tiny sample, and Heath (1984), Gebotys et al. (1988) and Williams and Dickinson (1993) only managed to establish a relationship at the $p < 0.05$ level. Williams and Dickinson (1993) is, in addition, a good example of poor research strategy: two questionnaires were sent to each of 500 households, with a resulting 29 per cent response rate. Analysis was univariate, and effects were not controlled for the influence of other variables, even for such important ones as gender. Liska and Baccaglini (1990) only found a strong positive relationship (at 0.59) for the initial report of a local homicide in the first 15 pages of a local newspaper; Lane and Meeker (2003) found a positive effect for whites, but not for Latinos (the reverse of what they found for race and television viewing frequency); and Gordon and Heath's (1981) results turn out to be, on close inspection, not quite as conclusive as at first sight. They conducted research in three American cities, and conclude 'in all three cities, readers of the newspaper that devotes the largest proportion of its news-hole to crime exhibit higher levels of fear of crime than do readers of other papers in those cities . . .' but 'In Chicago, residents who read no newspaper exhibit more fear of crime than do readers of either of the newspapers analysed. In Philadelphia, residents who read no newspaper exhibit less fear of crime than do readers of any of the city's newspapers, and in San Francisco, nonreaders exhibit more fear than do readers of one of the papers and less fear than readers of the other paper' (*ibid.*: 246).

One recent review (Eschholz 1997) has carefully detailed the research evidence, from which it can be deduced that of 14 studies of the effects of newspaper consumption on fear of crime, and 25 studies of the effects of television consumption on fear of crime, a total of 73 attempts to discover a general relationship have been made. Of these, 30 (41 per cent) discovered a positive relationship, and 43 (59 per cent) did not. If simple broad rank order effects and those with significance levels of only $p < 0.05$ are discounted, then only 20 (27 per cent) discovered a positive relationship, and 53 (73 per cent) did not.[6]

However, there are a number of reasons why it would be premature to dismiss the media from having any role in shaping people's views about crime. First, although it was at one time suspected that the causal relationship between media consumption and fear of crime might be the opposite of that commonly hypothesized (i.e. that scared people stay indoors and watch more television, Gunter 1987: 33; Zillman 1980: 159), it is now accepted, from consideration of non-locally generated fear and from longitudinal study, that it is the media which cause whatever fear is discovered (Heath and Petraitis 1987: 122; O'Keefe and Reid-Nash 1987).

Secondly, the absence of significant fear effects following the consumption of television drama in particular may well be accounted for by the reassuring rather than frightening nature of drama content (Sparks 1992). As Gunter (1987: 96) puts it, 'if television has a lesson to teach the world, it is equally or more likely to be that the world is a just and safe place than that it is a dangerous one'. Zillman (1980: 160), Tamborini *et al.* (1984: 495) and Weaver and Wakshlag (1986: 154) go even further, and suggest that the anxious may even seek out violent televised drama in order to relieve anxiety. Related to this, Lamneck (1991: 651) suggests that there is little reason to believe that newspaper coverage of crime should increase fears of being out of the home at night, as, in his sample of Munich newspapers, more violent offences were reported as occurring in the home than elsewhere, and most occurred during the daytime rather than at night. Unrelated, but relevant, Glassner (1999: 42) points out that television viewers will also see many acts of gratuitous niceness to leaven the occasions of nastiness.

Thirdly, newspaper coverage of serious crimes occurring in places other than where their respondents reside has been shown by at least two studies (Liska and Baccaglini 1990; Heath 1984) to be 'reassuring', as it makes people 'feel safe by comparison'.

Fourthly, as Skogan and Maxfield (1981: 144) put it:

> . . . we may not be able to discern much of an effect of the media because it does not vary much. There is little variation from place to place in terms of media coverage. Newspapers within a city greatly resemble one another in coverage, and both television and the newspapers dispense largely the same message. In one way or another, the bulk of the population is exposed to these messages. When almost everyone receives virtually the same message, studies of individual differences in media consumption and fear cannot reveal its consequences.

Fifthly, the typical failure of the pre-1990s attempts to establish relationships between undifferentiated measures of dependent and independent variables (e.g. between whole samples and total television viewing) has increasingly been replaced by more successful attempts to relate more sophisticated and specialized measures, and 'the more detailed operationalisations lead to stronger relationships between media and fear' (Heath and Gilbert 1996: 382). For example, Bazargan (1994: 105) claims that, following the use of multivariate regression, for his sample

> . . . once all other variables were held constant, Black elderly women, who displayed higher levels of loneliness, who experienced indirect victimization, who frequently watched TV news, and who lived in a semi-highrise building allocated for elderly persons were more likely to report a higher level of *fear of crime outside the home*. (emphasis in original)

As Heath and Gilbert (1996: 382) summarize, research now seeks 'complex patterns rather than simple main effects'. The nature of these complex patterns is summarized as being threefold: 1. characteristics of the message (with sensational, random and local crimes being more fear-inducing, particularly if they are news rather than drama – although, as Cavender and Bond-Maupin (1993) indicate, reality programming can blur the distinction between the two); 2. characteristics of the audience (with those without personal experience of victimization being more vulnerable to media influence); 3. type of dependent measure (measuring fear of urban violence being most likely to elicit a media–fear relationship). Tyler (1980, 1984) and Tyler and Cook (1984) take this further by demonstrating, in a series of experiments and surveys, that people must integrate indirect and direct experiences into a single inference in order to make judgments or attributions. Further, the effect of indirect experience depends on its informativeness, memorability and affectivity, but, crucially, 'exposure to reported crime via the mass media appears to have an impersonal effect; it leads to judgements that the crime rate is high, but not to personal fear of victimisation'.[7] (Tyler 1980: 24–5)

Sixthly, sophisticated measures of media consumption (type, frequency, etc.) are typically adopted, although fear is rarely treated so respectfully. On the one occasion that crime worry frequency has been measured (Farrall and Gadd 2004), it has been shown to be remarkably infrequent, with a mere 8 per cent of their sample, claiming both high levels of past-year worry, and to have experienced such worry more than five times.

The current study

The study reported below differs in two ways from previous research into the relationship between media consumption and the fear of crime. First, the quantitative data included variables relating to long-past (rather than merely immediately past) media consumption, on the basis that people's general anxieties may well have been laid down long before they are surveyed. Secondly, a sub-sample of those surveyed quantitatively was interviewed qualitatively. This is unusual.

Methods

As a preliminary to a major sampling exercise, 167 respondents were interviewed in four Glasgow sampling sites. The sites were selected along two dichotomies (outlying/inner-city and poor/affluent). Following the selection of geographical starting points in each, researchers used a 'random walk' procedure to identify houses (every fifth one was selected), within which an individual aged 16 years or over was identified and interviewed. Further detail is in Farrall *et al.* (1997), where the initial questionnaire is included as an appendix.

Data from these respondents were analysed, and each was classified in terms of their self-defined crime fears and self-perceived victimization risks. Four groups were classified along two dichotomies (high/low fear and high/low risk). Subsequently, 64 respondents were selected for a second interview, 16 from each of the four risk/fear groups. Those chosen were also spread evenly between the four categories of risk/ fear, across the four sites, the two genders, and three age groups (16–29, 30–49 and 50+ years). On this second occasion, a further quantitative instrument, oriented chiefly to media consumption, was administered before tape-recording an open-ended – and wide ranging – qualitative interview.

Analysis

A 'worry' score was created by initially asking each respondent 'on a scale of 1 to 5 (with 1 representing not being worried at all ever; and 5 meaning worrying a lot all the time) how worried are you that somebody might break into your house, or try to break in, and steal things, or try to, or damage things? Steal your vehicle, or things from it, or off it, or do damage to it? Vandalise your home or something outside it? Rob you or assault you or threaten to do either?'[8] Subsequently, individual question scores were squared, summed and the final score was the square root of the sum. The sample worry score was a ten-point one, ranging from 1.0 to 10.0.

In the initial quantitative part of the second interview, respondents were asked which daily newspapers they read and how often. They were given a checklist of 15 national and local daily titles, and invited to nominate others if they read them (a further six titles were volunteered). Responses were coded as 0 = never through to 5 = five or more times a week. Individual nominations were summed, creating 'Tot Newsp', a 19-point scale (0–18; mean (me) = 7.3, median (md) = 6, mode (mo) = 6).

Next, all were asked which crime programmes they currently watched on television. A list of four was offered (nine more titles were volunteered). Responses were coded as 0 = never; 1 = rarely; 2 = some episodes; 3 = don't know; 4 = most episodes; 5 = all episodes. In scale creation, 3 was treated as 0, and the residual nominations summed creating 'NewTV', a 26-point scale (0–25; me = 10.8, md = 10, mo = 5,8).

Further, all were asked which old crime programmes they used to watch on television. A list of four was offered (12 more titles were volunteered). Responses were coded as 0 = never; 1 = rarely; 2 = some episodes; 3 = don't know; 4 = most episodes; 5 = all episodes. In scale creation, 3 was treated as 0, and the residual nominations summed creating 'OldTV', a 24-point scale (0–23; me = 9.2, md = 8, mo = 6,8).

Finally, the three media scales were themselves summed to create 'TotMed', a 70-point scale (0–69; me = 27.2, md = 27, mo = 33).

Results: Part 1

Intercorrelations obtained between the worry and media variables are presented in Table 1. It can be seen that there are no significant correlations between worry and any of the media scores (assuming $p < 0.01$ as a minimum cut-off point for statistical significance). The same is true when the correlations are run separately for males and females, and for those aged 16–42 years (42 being the mean age) and for those aged 43 years and older. At this point, the only legitimate conclusion that can be drawn is that there is no relationship between fear of crime and quantitatively assessed consumption of various types of media, and that this study is similar to most attempts (that fail) to discover such a relationship.

However, the qualitative data offer a different picture. Indeed, they should. Recall that the minority of research studies that discovered a positive relationship between media consumption and the fear of crime only found a weak association. This means that some consumers of large amounts of media were fearless, and some consumers of small amounts were fearful – although this point is typically neglected.

Results: Part 2

Inspection of the qualitative data suggests that the numeric frequency of media consumption is not as critical as the interpretative relevance that individuals place on what they read, see or hear. The perceptions of these respondents are considered below in three worry groups, as measured by their answers to the quantitatively scored questions described above: the low worriers (with worry scores of 1.0–3.9);

Table 1 Worry–media intercorrelations

	Worry
TotNewsp	0.1169
	N (62)
	Sig. 0.365
NewTV	0.1511
	N (62)
	Sig. 0.241
OldTV	0.2595
	N (62)
	Sig. 0.042
TotMed	0.2289
	N (62)
	Sig. 0.074

p = Spearmans.

the medium worriers (scoring 4.2–6.7); and the high worriers (scoring 7.0 and over). Table 2 shows the relevant mean scores for each group.

Total media consumption (TotMed) was dichotomized using the median point 27.00. Those who fell below the median point were classified as low media consumers and those above as high media consumers. Table 3 shows the results of a one-way analysis of variance assessing the difference between the two groups, with worry being the dependent variable. The results show that there was no significant difference in the means between the two groups ($F = 0.216$, $df = 1$, 60, $p > 0.05$), meaning that low and high media consumers, on average, worry about the same amount.

Low worriers

A few samples, quoted in ascending order of worry, illustrate how low worriers deal with the world. One of the very low worriers told us:

> I've never heard of anybody in this area that has been broken into. A car . . . a car has been broken into, but houses, I haven't heard of one yet . . . that's been broken into. My friend, her daughter's car . . . but that's everywhere, you lift the paper . . . that's happening all over the place. . . (57-year-old man from an inner-city poor area; worry = 1.0; media use = 40)

Note how, for him, the very ubiquity of media coverage of crime allows him to dismiss its relevance, and reassert local feelings of safety in its place. An elderly woman from the same area also relied on her own local knowledge, but deliberately avoided watching or reading about crime:

> . . . round here it's not really bad . . . I must say that. This is a good patch here . . . Margaret'll say to me, 'Did you read the paper? Did you read the paper?' But anything that's anyway, anything crime or about it, I don't . . .

Table 2 Worry groups: comparison of means

Means	Low	Med.	High
Worry	2.3	5.7	8.2
NewSp	6	8	7
NewTV	8	12	11
OldTV	8	8	12
TotMed	22	28	30

Table 3 One-way analysis of variance

	TotMed					
Dependent Variables	Total Media Mean	High Media Mean	Low Media Mean	df	F	p
Worry	5.40	5.54	5.26	1,60	0.216	0.644

[I like] nice wee things, nice wee novels and things. . . (86-year-old woman from an inner-city poor area; worry = 1.7; media use = 9)

[...] Another slightly older man from the same area was aware of media sensationalization, but thought that actual risk is not randomly distributed:

I think to me, it's about how you perceive things. . . . I don't . . . I wouldn't say it was all that I'd seen on telly, but the news . . . etc. . . . the papers, you do get an interest in certain types of crime, you do get reporting in certain ways, in terms of, say, people preying on the elderly. So if you were elderly, you might think people are out there to get me, and if you worry about that, and the more you worry about it, the more the tension they pick up on it in the newspapers, and you have a circle, it reinforces it. . . . On the whole, I don't think people get attacked in the middle of the street. I think people have a perception, or maybe they have a false perception, that people out there will just beat people up, and that's how most violence happens. When I would say that's probably most unlikely. We see them because that's what makes them newsworthy. . . . (29-year-old man from an inner-city affluent area; worry = 1.7; media use = 16)

A similarly unworried but much younger woman claimed that the media made her think, not worry:

I think, yeah, of course, you think about that . . . you can't not think . . . I think it's impossible not to think especially if you have multi media, things like the television, newspapers . . . seeing this every day, but I definitely think that think has a different connotation from worry. I don't read the newspaper and worry that it might happen to me. . . . I just don't think there's much point in worrying. Perhaps I do worry, that's a bit rubbished, bit much to say you don't worry, but I definitely don't make a habit of it. Perhaps I probably worry before I go in to do an [academic examination] but I don't worry about things like this. . . . (16-year-old woman from an outlying affluent area; worry = 1.7; media use = 16)

[. . .] An older woman from the same area worried more, but still distanced her own reality from what she read in the newspapers:

It's something that really doesn't bother me. I'm not aware of having read of any muggings in the immediate vicinity, and I don't know personally of anyone who has had trouble. It all seems a bit distant. . . . (45-year-old woman from an outlying affluent area; worry = 3.9; media use = 20)

Low worriers, then, rely chiefly on their own local experience, coupled with a lack of belief in the relevance of media stories of crime to their own lives, to maintain a low worry level.

Medium worriers

With this group, things begin to change. One middle-aged man living in an outlying affluent area claimed not to worry too much, and superficially seems like a low worrier. He said that he didn't worry if he saw crime stories on

> . . . television or anything like that, unless it was in the immediate area. I wouldn't immediately rush round and check all the doors were bolted, and things like that, because I'd have already done that in automatic routine. No, it's only if it's very, very immediate, or very, very local . . . that would make me think again about crime. . . . (50-year-old man from an outlying affluent area; worry = 4.2; media use = 26)

A younger woman appreciated that crimes she worried about happened elsewhere:

> . . . actually, since these rape cases have come from the south side . . . have you seen them on TV? But I thought, 'no', because it can happen anywhere, anytime. . . . (24-year-old woman from an inner-city affluent area; worry = 4.4; media use = 18)

For her, distance from offending seems to increase worry in the same way that it reduced worry for low worriers.

Perched in the middle of the worry range is this 34-year-old woman:

> I think you're just a wee bit mair susceptible when you're in the street, you know, you're hearing it aw the time in the papers, on the telly . . . that people are getting thingmy. An' you know it is a worry if you dae go oot. . . . I think, we've just heard that much I just, on the telly and whatever, that I'm more frightened to walk now . . . I mean I worry about every-thing that you see on the telly or the papers, you know what I mean? You read it, you think 'God, that could happen here'. . . . or whatever. But I'm no' worrying that I'm thinking aboot it all the time. It's just at the time. I think 'Oh, that's terrible'. . . . or whatever. . . . (34-year-old woman from an outlying poor area; worry = 5.0; media use = 23)

[...] Pointing the finger specifically at the media as the ironic sources of worry about crime is this 17-year-old man, who is also a medium worrier. He elaborated at length about the low crime rate in this area, before commenting:

> It happens a lot, you know, the amount of programmes and so on they make about it 'cause I know that CrimewatchUK, you know, helps to solve, you know crimes and so on, but it actually proxies your mind to think . . . what crimes can happen, it makes you think, 'For God's sake! Hope that it doesn't happen to me! I've never seen something like that before'. . . . and things like that . . . so it makes you worry, it makes you actually worry more. I know it's trying to help some people, but I feel if you hadn't seen anything like that, you're like 'Oh my God! They do

things like that!' You think about it. . . . (17-year-old man from an out-lying affluent area; worry = 5.5; media use = 15)

Medium worriers also worry not just about crime, but also about the increase in crime (and, perhaps, about all other things worth worrying about). Take this case:

> Well, maybe not [getting worse in] this district, but you know you seem to hear it on television. Aye, on television, and you see it in the headlines, the news, that people being attacked and you know the drug problem . . . maybe it's kind of reading or listening to the news, I think that makes you a wee bit anxious, because you see things are getting worse, and that's really terrible. You just kind of shake your head, and then everything's kind of . . . the state of the world, all this fighting, Russia, bombing each other, you just kind of feel a bit . . . the world's getting worse and worse. People are not as nice as they used to be. I don't know why they've changed. . . . (74-year-old woman from an inner-city affluent area; worry = 5.9; media use = 28)

Medium worriers, then, begin to reverse the relationship between local experience and media portrayal of crime. Low worriers used their personal knowledge to overrule media imagery. Medium worriers don't know what to think; high worriers do.

High worriers

When asked about the frequency with which she worried, one elderly woman (who had denied ever being a crime victim) replied:

> We, shall we put it this way? When that doorbell rings in the evening, you always say, 'I wonder who that is?' Especially when you see so much, and read so much in the papers . . . see so much on television . . . well, you see, you read the papers and obviously I am a type that worries a great deal. I worry about . . . they always tell me I worry about almost everything. I'm just a worrier, put it that way. . . (75-year-old woman from an inner-city affluent area; worry = 7.1; media use = 16)

High worriers worry, as they feel surrounded by ever-increasing amounts of general and specific nastiness. Here is another:

> Don't know [why she worries about being the victim of practically every type of crime]. . . just because ye see that much on the telly an' ye read that much in the paper . . . this one gettin' mugged an' an auld man, an auld woman an' 80 years'n aw that. Even auld women at 80 gettin' raped! It makes ye . . . yer reading it constantly noo . . . it's no' a case of reading it once in a while, yer reading it aw the time. Every time ye lift a paper or pit on the telly, yer hearin' somethin'. That's aw. It's just kept alive in the brain as far as I'm concerned, d'you know? The media . . . it's a different different world fae when I was young, son, an' I'm no' that auld, I mean,

no' an auld woman, ye know? [when asked if being on her own makes her worry] Don't know, I told you, it's just the media, just the media. Hear that much ae it, ye read that much ae it, s'aw I can put it doon tae. It's no through an experience or anythin' like that, it's no' that. . . . (58-year-old woman from an inner-city poor area; worry = 7.3; media use = 45)

Their relationship with the media is curiously reminiscent of those who send birthday presents to soap opera actors on the occasion of their theatrical birthdays: it is almost 'realer' than life itself. In this way, one 29-year-old man from an outlying poor area (worry score = 7.6; media use = 46), when asked if he knew anybody who had actually been mugged, replied 'only the people I read in the papers, that's about it . . .', and he did not appear to be referring to anybody he knew 'really'.

High worriers act on mediated rather than on real experience, even when acknowledging reality:

Well, I don't know much about any of the other places, just what you read in the paper or what you see on the television about people coming out of their doors and getting shot, all these drug dealers and all that, all thingummy, but they don't live about here . . . . I haven't really seen much violence, but I have heard about it, and like I say, what you read in the paper, and what you see on the television. If we do go into the town, I'm never in alone, there'll always be somebody with me. And whenever we've been coming home, we don't walk it, we jump into a taxi, two or three of us. . . (58-year-old woman from an inner-city poor area; worry = 7.7; media use = 39)

[. . .] Low worriers sometimes do not worry about victimization, even if it seems to occur in their area. Medium worriers are concerned if it happens near them, but not so much if it occurs elsewhere. For this high worrier, where things happen is irrelevant – they happened. As she put it:

I've read in the papers . . . as a matter of fact there was one today again, on the television or wireless, I heard it, unprovoked. The chap was going to his work this morning, and he got attacked, cannot account for it . . . [she was asked where this had happened] . . . somewhere . . . I can't remember whereabouts. . . .

Recall that some of those who worry less believed that the media increased fear of crime. This respondent, conversely, believed that the media increased crime itself:

There's a lot of copy-catting going on, that's what I believe anyway. An awful lot of copy-catting going on. . . . All these rapes that's going on, and all, it's getting worse. I know that happened years ago, but it's getting worse, and I blame the television. . . . (53-year-old woman from an inner-city poor area; worry = 8.6; media use = 37)

Finally, the most worried respondent was a 45-year-old woman who lives in an outlying affluent area (worry score = 10.0; media use = 12). Fear (a good thing), she thinks, is:

> Real. I think fear is based on real events happening. And you can blame the media, maybe we're made more aware of it as well. I'm aware of that, you know, I'm sure things did happen before. . . . I think a bit of fear is a bit like adrenaline, isn't it? It's healthy . . . you need it . . . but we are in danger of becoming a sicker society with fear . . . maybe we should be slowing down the speed with which we go ahead. . . .

Conclusion

[. . .] [W]hile the quantitative data described above reveal some fear of crime (but not that it is related to media consumption), the linked qualitative data reveal that it is not the objectively determined localness, randomness or sensationalism that is important, but rather the interpretation of media content as relevant to and by the consumer. This approach is sometimes referred to as 'reception' research, wherein audiences constitute 'interpretive communities'. These have been defined by Jensen (1991: 13) as 'forms of cultural agency to which individuals are socialized and that generate discursive strategies for making sense of the institutions with which individuals interact on a regular basis'. This approach (and see also Jensen 1990; Fiske 1986) seems more likely to bear future fruit than counting media consumption and attempting to link it statistically with counted fears.

At a more general level, that a connection between media consumption and the fear of crime that is so intuitively obvious cannot convincingly be made decades after the first attempts to do so is a puzzle. The media exist independently of respondents' reporting their reaction to it. The same – more or less – can be said of crime.

It cannot, of course, be said of the alleged fear of it.

Notes

1. Barkan (1997) and Kappeler *et al.* (1996) suggest that 90% of the American population have never been victims of crime.
2. Surette (1998: 114) points out that research is usually into aggression and violence, rather than into crime (and that aggression isn't necessarily criminal, and that crime isn't normally violent). Research investigating the relationship of media consumption to aggression has certainly not died out, as the work of Huesmann *et al.* (2003) testifies.
3. Heath and Petraitis (1987: 99) later qualified Doob and Macdonald's criticisms of Gerbner, and claimed of Doob and Madconald's own findings 'another interpretation of these findings, however, is that television does increase fear of crime but only fear of crime as presented on television'.
4. Concentration on violent programmes neglects the possibility of being exposed to violent commercials inserted into nonviolent programming (Anderson 1997).

5. It can also be inferred that, with the cut-off level set here, 1 in 20 significant relationships will have been created by chance alone.
6. It has been suggested that it is customary with some American journals to report significance at $p < 0.05$, even when actually discovered levels are more significant.
7. There is some evidence in the UK that people overestimate the frequency of crime (particularly of violent crime), underestimate the severity of punishment, and believe that crime rates are rising when they are falling (Hough and Roberts 1998). There is also some evidence that people believe that others are more influenced by media messages than they are themselves (Gunther 1995; Hoffner *et al.* 2001).
8. The 'risk' score is not used in this article.

References

Altheide, D. (2002), *Creating Fear: News and the Construction of Crisis*. New York: Aldine de Gruyter.

Anderson, C. (1997), 'Violence in Television Commercials during Nonviolent Programming', *Journal of the American Medical Association*, 278: 1045–6.

Barkan, S. (1997), *Criminology: A Sociological Understanding*. Englewood Cliffs: Prentice Hall.

Bazargan, M. (1994), 'The Effects of Health, Environmental, and Socio-Psychological Variables on Fear of Crime and its Consequences among Urban Black Elderly Individuals', *International Journal of Aging and Human Development*, 38(2): 99–115.

Cavender, G. and Bond-Maupin, L. (1993), 'Fear and Loathing on Reality Television: An Analysis of "America's Most Wanted" and "Unsolved Mysteries"', *Sociological Inquiry*, 63(3): 305–17.

Chadee, D. and Ditton, J. (forthcoming), 'Fear of Crime and the Media: Assessing the Lack of Relationship' details.

Chiricos, T., Eschholz, S. and Gertz, M. (1997), 'Crime, News and Fear of Crime: Toward an Identification of Audience Effects', *Social Problems*, 44(3): 342–57.

Chiricos, T., Padgett, K. and Gertz, M. (2000), 'Fear, TV News, and the Reality of Crime', *Criminology*, 38(3): 755–85.

Doob, A. and Macdonald, G. (1979), 'Television Viewing and Fear of Victimisation: Is the Relationship Causal?', *Journal of Personality and Social Psychology*, 37(2): 170–9.

Eschholz, S. (1997), 'The Media and Fear of Crime: A Survey of the Research', *Journal of Law and Public Policy*, 9(1): 37–59.

Farrall, S. and Gadd, D. (2004), 'The Frequency of the Fear of Crime', *British Journal of Criminology*, 44(1): 127–32.

Farrall, S., Bannister, J., Ditton, J. and Gilchrist, E. (1997), 'Questioning the Measurement of the "Fear of Crime": Findings from a Major Methodological Study', *British Journal of Criminology*, 37: 658–79.

Fiske, J. (1986), 'Television: Polysemy and Popularity', *Critical Studies in Mass Communication*, 3(4): 391–408.

Gebotys, R., Roberts, J. and Dasgupta, B. (1988), 'News Media Use and Public Perceptions of Seriousness', *Canadian Journal of Criminology*, 30(1): 3–16.

Gerbner, G. and Gross, L. (1976), 'Living with Television: The Violence Profile', *Journal of Communication*, Spring: 173–99.

Gerbner, G., Gross, L., Morgan, M. and Signorelli, N. (1980), 'The "Mainstreaming" of America: Violence Profile No. 11', *Journal of Communication*, Summer: 10–29.

Gerbner, G., Gross, L., Signorelli, N., Morgan, M. and Jackson-Breck, M. (1979), 'The Demonstration of Power: Violence Profile No. 10', *Journal of Communication*, Summer: 177–96.

Glassner, B. (1999), *The Culture of Fear: Why Americans are Afraid of the Wrong Things*. New York: Basic Books.

Gomme, I. (1986), 'Fear of Crime among Canadians: A Multi-Variate Analysis', *Journal of Criminal Justice*, 14: 249–58.

Gordon, M. and Heath, L. (1981), 'The News Business, Crime, and Fear', in D. A. Lewis, ed., *Reactions to Crime*. London: Sage Criminal Justice System Annals, Sage. Chapter 11, pp. 227–50.

Gunter, B. (1987), *Television and the Fear of Crime*. London: J. Libby.

Gunther, A. (1995), 'Overrating the X-Rated: The Third Person Perception and Support for Censorship of Pornography', *Journal of Communication*, Winter: 25–38.

Haghighi, B. and Sorensen, J. (1996), 'America's Fear of Crime', in T. Flanagan and D. Longmire, eds, *Americans View Crime and Justice: A National Public Opinion Survey*. London: Sage. Chapter 2, pp. 16–30.

Heath, L. (1984), 'Impact of Newspaper Crime Reports on Fear of Crime: Multimethodological Investigation', *Journal of Personality and Social Psychology*, 47(2): 263–76.

Heath, L. and Gilbert, K. (1996), 'Mass Media and Fear of Crime', *American Behavioural Scientist*, 39(4): 379–86.

Heath, L. and Petraitis, J. (1987), 'Television Viewing and Fear of Crime: Where is the Mean World?', *Basic and Applied Social Psychology*, 8 (1&2): 97–123.

Hirsch, P. (1980), 'The "Scary World" of the Non-Viewer and Other Anomalies: A Reanalysis of Gerbner *et al.*'s Findings on Cultivation Analysis, Part I', *Communication Research*, 7(4): 403–56.

— (1981), 'On Not Learning from One's Own Mistakes: A Reanalysis of Gerbner *et al.*'s Findings on Cultivation Analysis, Part II', *Communication Research*, 8(1): 3–37.

Hoffner, C., Plotkin, R., Buchanan, M., Anderson, J., Kamagaki, S., Hubbs, L., Kowalczyk, L., Silberg, K. and Pastorek, A. (2001), 'The Third-Person Effect in Perceptions of the Influence of Television Violence', *Journal of Communication*, Summer: 283–99.

Hough, M. and Roberts, J. (1998), *Attitudes to Punishment: Findings from the British Crime Survey*. HORS 179. London: Home Office.

Huesmann, L., Moise-Titus, J., Podolski, C.-L. and Eron, L. (2003), 'Longitudinal Relations between Children's Exposure to TV Violence and their Aggressive and Violent Behaviour in Young Adulthood: 1977–1992', *Developmental Psychology*, 39(2): 201–21.

Hughes, M. (1980), 'The Fruits of Cultivation Analysis: A Reexamination of some Effects of Television Watching', *Public Opinion Quarterly*, 44(3): 287–302.

Jaehnig, W., Weaver, D. and Fico, F. (1981), 'Reporting Crime and Fearing Crime in Three Communities', *Journal of Communication*, 31 (Winter):88–96.

Jensen, K. (1990), 'Television Futures: A Social Action Methodology for Studying Interpretive Communities', *Critical Studies in Mass Communication*, 7: 129–46.

— (1991), 'When is Meaning? Communication Theory, Pragmatism, and Mass Media Reception', *Communication Yearbook*, 14: 3–32.

Kappeler, V., Blumberg, M. and Potter, G. (1996), *The Mythology of Crime and Criminal Justice*. 2nd edition. Prospect Heights: Waveland.

Lamneck, S. (1991), 'Fear of Victimisation, Attitudes to the Police and Mass Media Reporting', in G. Kaiser, H. Kury and H.-J. Albrecht, eds, *Victims and Criminal Justice: Victimological Research – Stocktaking and Prospects*. Freiburg: Max Planck Institut Research Report No. 50. pp. 637–53.

Lane, J. and Meeker, J. (2003), 'Ethnicity, Information Sources and Fear of Crime', *Deviant Behaviour*, 24: 1–26.

Liska, A. E. and Baccaglini, W. (1990), 'Feeling Safe by Comparison: Crime in the Newspapers', *Social Problems*, 37(3): 360–74.

Morgan, M. (1983), 'Symbolic Victimisation and Real World Fear', *Human Communication Research*, 9(2): 146–57.

O'Keefe, G. (1984), 'Public Views on Crime: Television Exposure and Media Credibility', in R. Bostrom, ed., *Communication Yearbook*. Volume 8. Beverly Hills: Sage. Chapter 19, pp. 514–35.

O'Keefe, G. and Reid-Nash, K. (1987), 'Crime News and Real-World Blues', *Communication Research*, 14(2): 147–63.

Perkins, D. and Taylor, R. (1996), 'Ecological Assessment of Community Disorder: Their Relationship to Fear of Crime and Theoretical Implications', *American Journal of Community Psychology*, 24(1): 63–107.

Sacco, V. (1982), 'The Effects of Mass Media on Perceptions of Crime: A Reanalysis of the Issues', *Pacific Sociological Review*, 25(4): 475–93.

Skogan, W. and Maxfield, M. (1981), *Coping with Crime: Individual and Neighborhood Reactions*. London: Sage.

Sparks, R. (1992), *Television and the Drama of Crime: Moral Tales and the Place of Crime in Public Life*. London: Open University Press.

Sparks, G. and Ogles, R. (1990), 'The Difference between Fear of Victimisation and the Probability of Being Victimised: Implications for Cultivation', *Journal of Broadcasting and Electronic Media*, 34(3): 351–8.

Surette, R. (1998), *Media, Crime, and Criminal Justice: Images and Realities*. 2nd Edition. London: Wadsworth.

Tamborini, R., Zillman, D. and Bryant, J. (1984), 'Fear of Victimisation: Exposure to Television and Perceptions of Crime and Fear', in R. Bostrom, ed., *Communication Yearbook*. Volume 8. Beverly Hills: Sage. Chapter 18, pp. 492–513.

Teevan, J. and Hartnagel, T. (1976), 'The Effect of Television Violence on the Perceptions of Crime by Adolescents', *Sociology and Social Research*, 60: 337–48.

Tyler, T. (1980), 'Impact of Directly and Indirectly Experienced Events: The Origin of Crime-Related Judgements and Behaviours', *Journal of Personality and Social Psychology*, 39(1): 13–28.

— (1984), 'Assessing the Risk of Crime Victimisation: The Integration of Personal Victimisation Experience and Socially Transmitted Information', *Journal of Social Issues*, 40(1): 27–38.

Tyler, T. and Cook, F. (1984), 'The Mass Media and Judgements of Risk: Distinguishing Impact on Personal and Societal Level Judgements', *Journal of Personality and Social Psychology*, 47(4): 693–708.

Weaver, J. and Wakshlag, J. (1986), 'Perceived Vulnerability to Crime, Criminal Victimisation Experience, and Television Viewing', *Journal of Broadcasting and Electronic Media*, 30(2): 141–58.

Williams, P. and Dickinson, J. (1993), 'Fear of Crime: Read all about It? The Relationship between Newspaper Crime Reporting and Fear of Crime', *British Journal of Criminology*, 33(1): 33–56.

Winkel, F. and Vrij, A. (1990), 'Fear of Crime and Mass Media Crime Reports: Testing Similarity Hypotheses', *International Review of Victimology*, 1: 251–65.

Wober, J. (1978), 'Televised Violence and Paranoid Perception: The View from Great Britain', *Public Opinion Quarterly*, 42(3): 315–21.

Wober, J. and Gunter, B. (1982), 'Television and Personal Threat: Fact or Artifact? A British Survey', *British Journal of Social Psychology*, 21: 239–47.

Zillman, D. (1980), 'Anatomy of Suspense', in P. Tannenbaum, ed., *The Entertainment Functions of Television*. Hillsdale, NJ: Lawrence Erlbaum. Chapter 6, pp. 133–63.

Critical connections

Ditton *et al.*'s research offers further endorsement of the use of qualitative methodologies as a means of engaging with media reception and influence. Quantitative methods simply cannot deal adequately with the complexity and variability of subjective interpretation. Through qualitative research techniques such as interviews and focus groups, researchers can begin to unpack how texts are actively and differentially interpreted by media consumers, whilst also establishing the importance of other non-media factors in that process. The article excerpted here is drawn from a wider body of research that seeks to problematise the meaning of fear of crime, to reevaluate the connections between fear and various social and cultural factors, and to assess the intensity and, crucially, the frequency of the fear response across different groups and contexts (Farrall and Gadd, 2004).

Discussion questions

- What do we mean by the term 'fear of crime'?
- What are the main theoretical, methodological and empirical problems faced by researchers trying to assess media influence on fear of crime (see also Readings 13 and 32)?
- To what extent do you feel media affect your own fear of crime, and do different forms of media content have different impacts?

References

Farrall, S. and Gadd, D. (2004) 'The Frequency of the Fear of Crime', in *The British Journal of Criminology* 44:, 1: 127–132

Greer, C. (2009) 'Crime and Media: Understanding the Connections' in C. Hale, K. Hayward, A. Wahadin and E. Wincup (eds) *Criminology*, second edition, Oxford: Oxford University Press,

Reiner, R. (2007) 'Media Made Criminality: The representation of crime in the mass media', in M. Maguire, R. Morgan and R. Reiner (eds) *The Oxford Handbook of Criminology* (4th edn). Oxford: Oxford University Press.

Sacco, V. (1982) 'The Effects of Mass Media on Perceptions of Crime: A Reanalysis of the Issues', in *Pacific Sociological Review*, 25, 4: 475–493.

Stanley Cohen

FOLK DEVILS AND MORAL PANICS: THE CREATION OF MODS AND ROCKERS (1972–2002)

Introduction and context

IN 1972, STANLEY COHEN completed a book that began life as his doctoral thesis: *Folk Devils and Moral Panics: The Creation of Mods and Rockers.* Inspired by the more traditionally sociological concepts of symbolic interactionism, deviancy amplification and labelling, Cohen inventively drew from the academic literature on disaster research, among others, to explore the 'social construction' of a particular subcultural phenomenon at a particular place and time (see also Reading 12 on 'social constructionism'). This theoretical innovation was combined with in-depth content analysis, questionnaires, interviews, even voluntary work in the local community, to produce one of the most widely cited pieces of sociological research in the latter half of the twentieth century. Cohen sought to develop and extend the concept 'moral panic', first discussed by Jock Young in his study of drugtakers a couple of years earlier (Young, 1971). The excerpt included here combines sections from two chapters in the book – the first and the last. The first part of the reading establishes the theoretical foundations of the concept, and discusses how we might recognise a moral panic when we see one. The second part of the reading deals with a more frequently overlooked, yet fundamental, element of Cohen's study: why *that* moral panic, in *that* place, at *that* time. It is in this critical exegesis that Cohen's analysis of moral panics becomes a fully sociological account of youth, culture, change and anxiety in post-War Britain.

Societies appear to be subject, every now and then, to periods of moral panic. A condition, episode, person or group of persons emerges to become defined as a threat to societal values and interests; its nature is presented in a stylized and stereotypical fashion by the mass media; the moral barricades are manned by editors, bishops, politicians and other right-thinking people; socially accredited experts pronounce their diagnoses and solutions; ways of coping are evolved or (more often) resorted to; the condition then disappears, submerges or deteriorates and becomes more visible. Sometimes the object of the panic is quite novel and at other times it is something which has been in existence long enough, but suddenly appears in the limelight. Sometimes the panic passes over and is forgotten, except in folklore and collective memory; at other times it has more serious and long-lasting repercussions and might produce such changes as those in legal and social policy or even in the way the society conceives itself.

One of the most recurrent types of moral panic in Britain since the war has been associated with the emergence of various forms of youth culture (originally almost exclusively working class, but often recently middle class or student based) whose behaviour is deviant or delinquent. To a greater or lesser degree, these cultures have been associated with violence. The Teddy Boys, the Mods and Rockers, the Hells Angels, the skinheads and the hippies have all been phenomena of this kind. There have been parallel reactions to the drug problem, student militancy, political demonstrations, football hooliganism, vandalism of various kinds and crime and violence in general. But groups such as the Teddy Boys and the Mods and Rockers have been distinctive in being identified not just in terms of particular events (such as demonstrations) or particular disapproved forms of behaviour (such as drug-taking or violence) but as distinguishable social types. In the gallery of types that society erects to show its members which roles should be avoided and which should be emulated, these groups have occupied a constant position as folk devils: visible reminders of what we should not be. The identities of such social types are public property and these particular adolescent groups have symbolized – both in what they were and how they were reacted to – much of the social change which has taken place in Britain over the last twenty years.

In this book, I want to use a detailed case study of the Mods and Rockers phenomenon – which covered most of the 1960s – to illustrate some of the more intrinsic features in the emergence of such collective episodes of juvenile deviance and the moral panics they both generate and rely upon for their growth. The Mods and Rockers are one of the many sets of figures through which the sixties in Britain will be remembered. A decade is not just a chronological span but a period measured by its association with particular fads, fashions, crazes, styles or – in a less ephemeral way – a certain spirit or *kulturgeist*. [. . .]

At the beginning of the decade, the term 'Modernist' referred simply to a style of dress; the term 'Rocker' was hardly known outside the small groups which identified themselves this way. Five years later, a newspaper editor was to refer to the Mods and Rockers incidents as 'without parallel in English history' and troop reinforcements were rumoured to have been sent to quell possible widespread disturbances. Now, another five years later, these groups have all but disappeared from the public consciousness, remaining only in collective memory as folk devils of the past, to whom current horrors can be compared. The rise and fall of the Mods and Rockers contained all the elements from which one might generalize about folk devils and moral panics. And unlike the previous decade which had only produced the Teddy Boys, these years witnessed rapid oscillation from one such devil to another: the Mod, the Rocker, the Greaser, the student militant, the drug fiend, the vandal, the soccer hooligan, the hippy, the skinhead.

Neither moral panics nor social types have received much systematic attention in sociology. In the case of moral panics, the two most relevant frameworks come from the sociology of law and social problems and the sociology of collective behaviour. Sociologists such as Becker[1] and Gusfield[2] have taken the cases of the Marijuana Tax Act and the Prohibition laws respectively to show how public concern about a particular condition is generated, a 'symbolic crusade' mounted, which, with publicity and the actions of certain interest groups, results in what Becker calls *moral enterprise*: '. . . the creation of a new fragment of the moral constitution of society,'[3] Elsewhere[4] Becker uses the same analysis to deal with the evolution of social problems as a whole. The field of collective behaviour provides another relevant orientation to the study of moral panics. There are detailed accounts of cases of mass hysteria, delusion and panics, and also a body of studies on how societies cope with the sudden threat or disorder caused by physical disasters. [. . .]

The major contribution to the study of the social typing process itself comes from the interactionist or transactional approach to deviance. The focus here is on how society labels rule-breakers as belonging to certain deviant groups and how, once the person is thus type cast, his acts are interpreted in terms of the status to which he has been assigned. It is to this body of theory that we must turn for our major orientation to the study of both moral panics and social types.

The transactional approach to deviance

The sociological study of crime, delinquency, drug-taking, mental illness and other forms of socially deviant or problematic behaviour has, in the last decade, undergone a radical reorientation. This reorientation is part of what might be called the *sceptical revolution* in criminology and the sociology of deviance.[5] The older tradition was *canonical* in the sense that it saw the concepts it worked with as authoritative, standard, accepted, given and unquestionable. The new tradition is sceptical in the sense that when it sees terms like 'deviant', it asks 'deviant to whom?' or 'deviant from what?'; when told that something is a social problem, it asks 'problematic to whom?'; when certain conditions or behaviour are described as dysfunctional, embarrassing, threatening or dangerous, it asks 'says who?' and 'why?'. In other words, these concepts and descriptions are not assumed to have a taken-for-granted status. [. . .]

What this means is that the student of deviance must question and not take for granted the labelling by society or certain powerful groups in society of certain behaviour as deviant or problematic. The transactionalists' importance has been not simply to restate the sociological truism that the judgement of deviance is ultimately one that is relative to a particular group, but in trying to spell out the implication of this for research and theory. They have suggested that in addition to the stock set of *behavioural* questions which the public asks about deviance and which the researcher obligingly tries to answer (why did they do it? what sort of people are they? how do we stop them doing it again?) there are at least three *definitional* questions: why does a particular rule, the infraction of which constitutes deviance, exist at all? What are the processes and procedures involved in identifying someone as a deviant and applying the rule to him? What are the effects and consequences of this application, both for society and the individual? [. . .]

The transactional perspective does not imply that innocent persons are arbitrarily selected to play deviant roles or that harmless conditions are wilfully inflated into social problems. Nor does it imply that a person labelled as deviant has to accept this identity: being caught and publicly labelled is just one crucial contingency which *may* stabilize a deviant career and sustain it over time. Much of the work of these writers has been concerned with the problematic nature of societal response to deviance and the way such responses affect the behaviour. This may be studied at a face-to-face level (for example, what effect does it have on a pupil to be told by his teacher that he is a 'yob who should never be at a decent school like this'?) or at a broader societal level (for example, how is the 'drug problem' actually created and shaped by particular social and legal policies?).

The most unequivocal attempt to understand the nature and effect of the societal reaction to deviance is to be found in the writings of Lemert.[6] He makes an important distinction, for example, between primary and secondary deviation. Primary deviation – which may arise from a variety of causes – refers to behaviour which, although it may be troublesome to the individual, does not produce symbolic reorganization at the level of self-conception. Secondary deviation occurs when the individual employs his deviance, or a role based upon it, as a means of defence, attack or adjustment to the problems created by the societal reaction to it. The societal reaction is thus conceived as the 'effective' rather than 'original' cause of deviance: deviance becomes significant when it is subjectively shaped into an active role which becomes the basis for assigning social status. Primary deviation has only marginal implications for social status and self-conception as long as it remains symptomatic, situational, rationalized or in some way 'normalized' as an acceptable and normal variation.

Lemert was very much aware that the transition from primary to secondary deviation was a complicated process. Why the societal reaction occurs and what form it takes are dependent on factors such as the amount and visibility of the deviance, while the effect of the reaction is dependent on numerous contingencies and is itself only one contingency in the development of a deviant career. Thus the link between the reaction and the individual's incorporation of this into his self-identity is by no means inevitable; the deviant label, in other words, does not always 'take'. The individual might be able to ignore or rationalize the label or only pretend to comply. This type of face-to-face sequence, though, is just one part of the picture: more important are the symbolic and unintended consequences of social control as a whole. Deviance in a sense emerges and is stabilized as an artefact of social control; because of this, Lemert can state that '. . . older sociology tended to rest heavily upon the idea that deviance leads to social control. I have come to believe that the reverse idea, i.e. social control leads to deviance, is equally tenable and the potentially richer premise for studying deviance in modern society.'[7]

It is partly towards showing the tenability and richness of this premise that this book is directed. My emphasis, though, is more on the logically prior task of analysing the nature of a particular set of reactions rather than demonstrating conclusively what their effects might have been. How were the Mods and Rockers identified, labelled and controlled? What stages or processes did this reaction go through? Why did the reaction take its particular forms? What – to use Lemert's words again – were the 'mythologies, stigma, stereotypes, patterns of exploitation, accommodation, segregation and methods of control (which) spring up and crystallize in the interaction between the deviants and the rest of society'?[8] [. . .]

Deviance and the mass media

[. . .] Much of this study will be devoted to understanding the role of the mass media in creating moral panics and folk devils. A potentially useful link between these two notions – and one that places central stress on the mass media – is the process of deviation amplification as described by Wilkins.[9] The key variable in this attempt to understand how the societal reaction may in fact *increase* rather than decrease or keep in check the amount of deviance, is the nature of the information about deviance. As I pointed out earlier, this information characteristically is not received at first hand, it tends to be processed in such a form that the action or actors concerned are pictured in a highly stereotypical way. We react to an episode of, say, sexual deviance, drug-taking or violence in terms of our information about that particular class of phenomenon (how typical is it?), our tolerance level for that type of behaviour and our direct experience – which in a segregated urban society is often nil. Wilkins describes – in highly mechanistic language derived from cybernetic theory – a typical reaction sequence which might take place at this point, one which has a spiralling or snowballing effect.

An initial act of deviance, or normative diversity (for example, in dress), is defined as being worthy of attention and is responded to punitively. The deviant or group of deviants is segregated or isolated and this operates to alienate them from conventional society. They perceive themselves as more deviant, group themselves with others in a similar position, and this leads to more deviance. This, in turn, exposes the group to further punitive sanctions and other forceful action by the conformists – and the system starts going round again. There is no assumption in this model that amplification *has* to occur; in the same way – as I pointed out earlier – that there is no automatic transition from primary to secondary deviation or to the incorporation of deviant labels. The system or the actor can and does react in quite opposite directions. What one is merely drawing attention to is a set of sequential typifications: under X conditions, A will be followed by A1, A2, etc. All these links have to be explained – as Wilkins does not do – in terms of other generalizations. For example, it is more likely that if the deviant group is vulnerable and its actions highly visible, it will be forced to take on its identities from structurally and ideologically more powerful groups. Such generalizations and an attempt to specify various specialized modes of amplification or alternatives to the process have been spelt out by Young[10] in the case of drug-taking. I intend using this model here simply as one viable way in which the 'social control leads to deviation' chain can be conceptualized and also because of its particular emphasis upon the 'information about deviance' variable and its dependence on the mass media.

The case of the Mods and Rockers

I have already given some indication of the general framework which I think suitable for the study of moral panics and folk devils. [. . .] The first and most obvious one derives from the literature on subcultural delinquency. This would provide the structural setting for explaining the Mods and Rockers phenomenon as a form of adolescent deviance among working-class youth in Britain. [. . .]

Another less obvious orientation derives from the field of collective behaviour. I have already suggested that social types can be seen as the products of the same processes that go into the creation of symbolic collective styles in fashion, dress and public identities. The Mods and Rockers, though, were initially registered in the public consciousness not just as the appearance of new social types, but as actors in a particular episode of collective behaviour. The phenomenon took its subsequent shape in terms of these episodes: the regular series of disturbances which took place at English seaside resorts between 1964 and 1966. The public image of these folk devils was invariably tied up to a number of highly visual scenarios associated with their appearance: youths chasing across the beach, brandishing deckchairs over their heads, running along the pavements, riding on scooters or bikes down the streets, sleeping on the beaches and so on.

Each of these episodes – as I will describe – contained all the elements of the classic crowd situation which has long been the prototype for the study of collective behaviour. Crowds, riots, mobs and disturbances on occasions ranging from pop concerts to political demonstrations have all been seen in a similar way to *The Crowd* described by Le Bon in 1896. Later formulations by Tarde, Freud, McDougall and F. H. Allport made little lasting contribution and often just elaborated on Le Bon's contagion hypothesis. A more useful recent theory – for all its deficiencies from a sociological viewpoint – is Smelser's 'value added schema'.[11] In the sequence he suggests, each of the following determinants of collective behaviour must appear: (i) structural conduciveness; (ii) structural strain; (iii) growth and spread of a generalized belief; (iv) precipitating factors; (v) mobilization of the participants for action; (vi) operation of social control. [. . .]

A special – and at first sight somewhat esoteric – area of collective behaviour which is of peculiar relevance, is the field known as 'disaster research'.[12] This consists of a body of findings about the social and psychological impact of disasters, particularly physical disasters such as hurricanes, tornadoes and floods but also man-made disasters such as bombing attacks. Theoretical models have also been produced, and Merton argues that the study of disasters can extend sociological theory beyond the confines of the immediate subject-matter. Disaster situations can be looked at as strategic research sites for theory-building: 'Conditions of collective stress bring out in bold relief aspects of social systems that are not as readily visible in the stressful conditions of everyday life.'[13] The value of disaster studies is that by compressing social processes into a brief time span, a disaster makes usually private behaviour, public and immediate and therefore more amenable to study.[14] [. . .]

The work of disaster researchers that struck me as most useful when I got to the stage of writing up my own material on the Mods and Rockers was the sequential model that they have developed to describe the phases of a typical disaster. The following is the sort of sequence that has been distinguished:[15]

1.   *Warning*: during which arises, mistakenly or not, some apprehensions based on conditions out of which danger may arise. The warning must be coded to be

understood and impressive enough to overcome resistance to the belief that current tranquillity can be upset.

2. *Threat*: during which people are exposed to communication from others, or to signs from the approaching disaster itself indicating specific imminent danger. This phase begins with the perception of some change, but as with the first phase, may be absent or truncated in the case of sudden disaster.

3. *Impact*: during which the disaster strikes and the immediate unorganized response to the death, injury or destruction takes place.

4. *Inventory*: during which those exposed to the disaster begin to form a preliminary picture of what has happened and of their own condition.

5. *Rescue*: during which the activities are geared to immediate help for the survivors. As well as people in the impact area helping each other, the suprasystem begins to send aid.

6. *Remedy*: during which more deliberate and formal activities are undertaken towards relieving the affected. The suprasystem takes over the functions the emergency system cannot perform.

7. *Recovery*: during which, for an extended period, the community either recovers its former equilibrium or achieves a stable adaptation to the changes which the disaster may have brought about.

Some of these stages have no exact parallels in the Mods and Rockers case, but a condensed version of this sequence (*Warning* to cover phases 1 and 2; then *Impact*; then *Inventory*; and *Reaction* to cover phases 5, 6 and 7) provides a useful analogue. If one compares this to deviancy models such as amplification, there are obvious and crucial differences. For disasters, the sequence has been empirically established; in the various attempts to conceptualize the reactions to deviance this is by no means the case. In addition, the transitions within the amplification model or from primary to secondary deviation are supposed to be consequential (i.e. causal) and not merely sequential. In disaster research, moreover, it has been shown how the form each phase takes is affected by the characteristics of the previous stage: thus, the scale of the remedy operation is affected by the degree of identification with the victim. This sort of uniformity has not been shown in deviance.

The nature of the reaction to the event is important in different ways. In the case of disaster, the social system responds in order to help the victims and to evolve methods to mitigate the effects of further disasters (e.g. by early warning systems). The disaster itself occurs independently of this reaction. In regard to deviance, however, the reaction is seen as partly causative. The on-the-spot reaction to an act determines whether it is classified as deviant at all, and the way in which the act is reported and labelled also determines the form of the subsequent deviation; this is not the case with a disaster. To express the difference in another way, while the disaster sequence is linear and constant – in each disaster the warning is followed by the impact which is followed by the reaction – deviance models are circular and amplifying: the impact (deviance) is followed by a reaction which has the effect of increasing the subsequent warning and impact, setting up a feedback system. It is precisely because the Mods and Rockers phenomenon was both a generalized type of deviance and also manifested itself as a series of discrete events, that both models are relevant While a single event can be meaningfully described in terms of the disaster analogue (warning–impact–reaction), each event can be seen as creating the potential for a reaction which, among other possible consequences, might cause further acts of deviance.

Let me now return to the original aims of the study and conclude this introductory chapter by outlining the plan of the book. My focus is on the genesis and development of the moral panic and social typing associated with the Mods and Rockers phenomenon. In transactional terminology: what was the nature and effect of the societal reaction to this particular form of deviance? This entails looking at the ways in which the behaviour was perceived and conceptualized, whether there was a unitary or a divergent set of images, the modes, through which these images were transmitted and the ways in which agents of social control reacted. The behavioural questions (how did the Mods and Rockers styles emerge? Why did some young people more or less identified with these groups behave in the way they did?) will be considered, but they are the background questions. The variable of societal reaction is the focus of attention. [. . .]

It is no less difficult to untangle the reasons for the societal reaction to a form of deviance or social problem than it is to understand why the behaviour or condition is there in the first place. In this concluding chapter, I would like to suggest some of the reasons for the reactions to the Mods and Rockers and place these in the specific historical and cultural context in which the phenomenon developed. The crucial question to ask is not the simple transactional one of why the behaviour was seen as deviant at all – the answer to this is fairly obvious – but why the reaction took the particular form and intensity it did at the particular time. [. . .]

The emergence of the Mods and Rockers

The twin themes of affluence and youth – the second essentially subordinate to the first – have dominated most analyses of post-war social change in Britain. In the popular rhetoric, they have appeared under the Macmillan 'Never Had It So Good' slogan, in the sociological version, under the guise of the embourgeoisement debate. Any analysis, for example, of the way in which the mass media over this period attempted to interpret and make political sense of what was happening, would have to understand the whole theme of the changing styles of life which followed in the wake of 'affluence'. Specifically, one would have to focus on the myth of the classless teenage culture and how this was perpetuated by the mass media. Youth – even when, and perhaps especially when, it was being troublesome – was initially the supreme, the most glamorous and the most newsworthy manifestation of the affluence theme. Justifiably, an important study of the popular press during the period 1935–65 uses the youth theme as a metaphor for social change.[16]

Before the war, the major spending power lay with the over twenties. No age group emerged – in terms of fashion or symbolic allegiance – in a self-conscious attempt at isolation from the dominant culture. In the years between 1945 and 1950 the grounds for change were laid by a constellation of economic arid demographic variables. There was a large unmarried teenage generation (between 15 and 21) whose average real wage had increased at twice the rate of the adults'. This relative economic emancipation created a group with few social ties or responsibilities and whose stage of development could not really be coped with by the nuclear working-class family.

Within a very short time, the ideal teenager was presented in consumption terms. As a reward for full production, he was to be allowed the full spectacle of commodities that the market could offer, and moreover offer and package in a way especially designed for him. This is not to say that he was simply 'exploited' or 'manipulated'; such concepts, particularly when applied to pop music, are too crude to allow for the way in which the adolescent consumer is also an active agent in creating modes of expression which reflect his cultural experience.[17]

Soon, the emerging styles became associated with deviant or publicly disapproved values. The Teddy Boys were the first youth group to mark their symbolic innovation – and it was a considerable one – with defiance, anger or gestures of separation. In exactly the way that occurred later with the Mods and Rockers, such emerging styles became indelibly confused with other phenomena. On the one hand they were confused with the general youth theme: Hot-blooded Youth, It's a Sign of the Times, Affluence . . . On the other, they were perceptually merged into day-to-day delinquency problems, the mundane troubles which make up nearly all the work of the control system and had little to do with (and never have) the headline troubles which are the stuff of moral panics. [. . .]

It is some of the complexities of the relationship between social class, the teenage culture and what I will call *expressive fringe delinquency*, that I would like to refer to. The focus is not on mundane day-to-day delinquency (which consists primarily of property offences) but on behaviour labelled variously as hooliganism, vandalism, rowdyism and which occurs during middle to late adolescence. More specifically, it is on those manifestations of this behaviour associated with collective symbolic styles. Such behaviour should not be explained as being *either* instrumental *or* expressive, but simultaneously as both, and it is these parallel routes to the Mods and Rockers' events that need separate consideration.

A problem and a solution

The instrumental route is that concentrated on by subcultural theorists of delinquency.[18] The argument is that although growing up in industrial society presents certain common problems, the structural and normative diversity of our society allows the problems to be experienced differentially, particularly across class lines, and only makes certain solutions available. A stream of working-class adolescents over the last fifteen years or so have gone through the school system without showing allegiance to its values or internalizing its aspirations. They leave their secondary moderns as soon as possible, accurately perceiving the implications for their future lives of the education they've received. As Downes says, they are not inherently disillusioned about the jobs any more than they are about education: the jobs are dull and tedious. Money becomes – quite rightly – just about the most important occupational criterion. There is a sense of personal redundancy and waste, a drifting from job to job without any real expectation of the next one being any more interesting than the previous one. As Goodman puts it, nobody asks whether jobs are worthy, dignified, useful, honourable: one grows up realizing that during one's productive years one will be spending eight hours a day doing something that is no good.

All this, it might be said, is not new: how many people do feel that their jobs are worthwhile and dignified? And, moreover, when have working-class adolescents not been left out of the conventional educational and occupational races? Over the last fifteen or so years, though, one significant new feature has appeared – the mass teenage culture – to point for some to new aspirations. One must take care not to exaggerate the universality of the culture's effects: it does not serve as a direct shaper of aspirations in the sense of creating specific desires, say, to become a pop star and, indeed, in some traditional working-class areas and whole underdeveloped regions such as the north-east of England, it has hardly permeated through at all. But from the beginning its manifestations were pervasive. The new glossy constellation, in all its guises, had no serious rival: not the traditional working-class culture, not the youth service and not political or community involvement. While the culture is superficially classless, its meaning differs across class lines. The middle-class adolescent has always had other alternatives: satisfaction through education or job, or 'constructive' solutions such as community social work, charity; walks, Duke of Edinburgh-type schemes. (It is only recently that this group has been collectively involved in action that opens it to some public condemnation, for example, drug involvement and organized reaction against the regimentation of school.)

For the working-class adolescent only the town was left. And here – right from the drab cafés of the fifties to the more sophisticated entertainment arenas of the next decade – ways have been blocked. These scenes provided few opportunities for excitement, autonomy and sense of action. Either nothing at all was offered or it was dull and mediocre. He did not have enough money to participate nor the talent, luck or personal contacts to really make it. So, faced by leisure goals he could not reach, with little commitment or attachment to others, his situation contained an edge of desperation.[19] He saw himself as effect rather than cause, he was pushed around by 'them'. Rather than accept all this, rather than do nothing at all, he manufactured his own excitement, he made things happen out of nothing.

It was precisely this form which the happenings on the beaches took. This is not to read into the situation a sophistication and awareness absent in the participants themselves. The Mods in the mid-sixties were all too aware of the absurdity of both their problem and their solution: the drifting, the apparent purposelessness, the ever-present but somewhat desperate hope that something would happen and, in the end, the readiness to make that something happen. If one asked the boy or girl on the street corner, the beach, the Wimpy, the amusement arcade, the pier, the disco, what they wanted to do, they would answer 'nothing'. And this answer had to be taken at its face value. All that was left was to make a gesture, to deliberately enter into risky situations where putting the boot in, throwing rocks around, dumping a girl into the sea, could be seen for what they were. Add to this volitional element the specific desires for change and freedom over the holidays, to get away from home, the romance of roughing it on the beaches or sleeping four to a bed in a grotty seafront boarding-house, finding a bird, getting some pills. One chose these things, but at the same time one was in a society whose structure had severely limited one's choice and one was in a situation where what deterministic forces there were – the lack of amenities, the action of the police, the hostility of the locals – made few other choices possible.

The style

The first signs of all this, the first murmurings of separation later to be expressed so explicitly and vehemently by such groups as the Rolling Stones and The Who, came with the Teddy Boys. They were the first group whose style was self-created, although they were reacting not so much against 'adults' but the little that was offered in the fifties: the café, the desolate town, the pop culture of the dance halls, Locarnos and Meccas aimed at the over twenties.[20] Their style was adapted from a different social group – the Edwardian Dandy – and its exaggeration and ritualization were mirrored in the groups' activities: a certain brutality, callousness, indifference and almost stoicism. [. . .]

The Mods were to emerge in what Nuttall calls the *classic* as opposed to the *romantic* idiom. The Teddy Boy style – born in what was very much the traditional working-class areas of South London – ended up (as clothing styles often do in their last dying moments) in grotesque extremes which gave way to the more 'reformed' drape suit. This was the point at which the new teenager of the end of the fifties, personified perfectly in Colin Macinnes' stylized *Absolute Beginners*,[21] really began to stake his claim. These kids were sharp and self-confident, although unsophisticated and gauche compared to their American equivalents. Even among the middle classes at the time, no type as sophisticated and hip as Salinger's Holden Caulfield could be found. They adopted what was briefly called the 'Italianate' style of dressing, drifted into the world of Expresso bars and were drawn musically to rhythm and blues, particularly small groups, rather than the loud excesses of rock.

Some, like Nuttall, see these kids – and not the Rockers, as was popularly believed – as the real descendants of the Ted. They inherited his vanity, confidence and fussiness; they were too fastidious for the motorway caffs which at that time were attracting another stream. And it was their 'sharp dressing' which led to the modern, the modernist, the Mod. By now, the beginning of the sixties, changes were diffusing rapidly, the youth culture was being opened up to new influences and it was difficult to sort out the types. Already the art school students and college or university drop-outs were appearing on the scene, and the musical focus switched from loud rock, from the brief skiffle craze and from the older conformist ballad tradition, to indigenous groups such as the Beatles, the Kinks, the Pretty Things, the Rolling Stones. A bright hysterical ambience began concentrating in the London clubs such as the Flamingo and the Marquee. This was where the Mod era began and it had reached at least one of its peaks by 1963.

In the meantime, the Rockers were evolving. They could justifiably be seen as similar to the Teds in at least two senses: they were in many respects the *lumpen*, those who hadn't caught on to the new teenage image personified by the Mods; also, they were more outgoing and direct, closer to the butch image of earlier years. But, as Nuttall stresses, they were not just transformed Teds: they leaned towards the romantic stream in their longing for the earlier crudities of pure rock. Their transitional models – like the Italianate styles had been for the Mods – were the ton-up boys of the motorways. These boys saw the Teds becoming too respectable – a few years before the end of the decade, Teddy Boy suits were already being sold at jumble sales – and they went directly to the old American 'Wild Ones' theme: the black leather, the motor-bikes, the metal studs. Away from the city and the coffee bars, they belonged on the motorway and the transport cafés. The more legendary of the cafés, such as the Busy Bee and the Ace on the southern end of the M1, are still, more than ten years later, shrines for the faithful. 'Rockers' – the term, of course, deriving from the loyalty to early rock – was simply the name given and taken by this group.

So, leaving aside all the other significant developments on the youth scene that were beginning to tick over, by 1962–3 the Mods and Rockers division was already there. But – and this is what is missed by all commentators, however sensitive to the nuances of this division – it was *not* a division between all adolescents, nor, more importantly, was the division public knowledge in any significant sense. [. . .]

And the wholly unequal balance between the groups by 1963 must also be understood. The Rockers were left out of the race: they were unfashionable and unglamorous just because they appeared to be more class-bound. The images of lout and yobbo which they had inherited from the Teds hardly made them marketable property. The Mods, on the other hand, made all the running and although the idiom they emerged out of was real enough, it was commercial exploitation which made them completely dominant. This was the Mod era, the manic frenzied years of all-night discos in the West End and the New Towns of southern England, the steel toothed combs, the purple hearts, the peculiar tone of near hysteria caught so perfectly by Tom Wolfe in his description of the 'kinetic trance' of 'Noonday Underground' at Tiles in Oxford Street.[22]

The life in such scenes ('Two hundred and fifty office boys, office girls, department store clerks, messengers, members of London's vast child workforce of teenagers who leave school at fifteen, pour down into this cellar, Tiles, in the middle of the day for a break')[23] was literally and metaphorically underground. On the surface, the intensity of the Mod thing was diluted, but only slightly, by commercialism: Carnaby Street, Cathy McGowan, Twiggy, transistor radios always on to Radio Caroline (opened on Easter Sunday, 1964), boutiques, the extravagant velvets, satins and colours of the more flamboyant of the early Mods. By the middle of 1964 there were at least six magazines appealing mainly to Mods, the weeklies with a circulation of about 500,000, the monthlies about 250,000. There was also *Ready, Steady, Go*, a TV programme aimed very much at the Mods, with its own magazine related to the pro-gramme and which organized the famous Mod ball in Wembley. This was the time when whole streams within schools, sometimes whole schools and even whole areas and housing estates were talked of as having 'gone Mod'. [. . .]

The outsider never saw that this diffusion had produced a considerable and very rigid streaming within, the Mod idiom itself. Almost from the beginning there was a distinction between the more extravagant stream, attracted to the frothy world of the boutiques, the camp, the flotsam of the art school followers. They were very different from the sterner group, with their wide jeans, old army anoraks or combat jackets, canvas shoes. These were the ones who, on their Corgis or Lambrettas, were thought to be involved in the clashes with the Rockers at the resorts. In fact, by 1964–5, the so-called Mod was hardly recognizable. Leaving aside such groups as the beats, the Rockers themselves and the Anglicized plastic flower children, youth workers at Brighton could distinguish at least between *the scooter boys* (dressed in plain but smart trousers and pullovers, plus anoraks, often trimmed with fur; usually uninterested in violence, but involved with the law in a range of driving offences); *the hard Mods* (wearing heavy boots, jeans with braces, short hair, the precursors of the Skinheads, usually prowling in large groups with the appearance of being jumpy, unsure of themselves, on the paranoic edge, heavily involved in any disturbance) and *the smooth Mods* (usually older and better off, sharply dressed, moving in small groups and usually looking for a bird).[24]

To the extent that one could distinguish any core values in this period, these were certainly values congruent with both the style that was selected and the structural problems that had to be faced. There was something more than the rejection of the work ethic which our earlier analysis of the working-class adolescent situation pointed to. These groups – as Dave Laing suggests – had no real conviction about the rationality of the division between work and play, production and consumption. They were not the occupants of the passive consumption role that society had condemned them to and then condemned them for playing: 'Because they no longer believed in the idea of work, but had to submit to the necessity of it, they were not passive consumers as their television and light ale elders were.'[25] Laing goes on to quote from an article in *Heatwave* about the 'furious consumption programme which seemed to be a grotesque parody of the aspirations of the Mods' parents'.[26] What the adult saw on *Ready, Steady, Go* and on the beaches was a stylized version of this programme. They could not see the way in which the clothes, the pills and above all the music were actively used by the kids as catalysts, and modes of expression. Quite rightly, Laing, Nuttall and other such commentators see the essence of the Mods' subversive potential not in the occasional outbursts of violence and still less in drug-taking (an activity which, in its pill form at least, mirrors the bourgeois consumer notion of how to buy solutions to problems) but in their calculated attempt to live in leisure time, not just to consume but to create themselves into Mods. The fact that such erosion of the work ethic occurs in other groups[27] does not make it less significant.

A few lines about some of the music of the time are necessary. By looking at two groups in particular – the Rolling Stones and The Who – as well as using a general stylistic analysis, one arrives at the same roads to the beaches as did theories stressing instrumental solutions. Music was much more important for the Mods than the Rockers – and also than for the Teds who had not grown up as a generation through the whole Rock explosion. If the Beatles tuned in to the ethos in its most general way – and changed as this changed – it was the Rolling Stones who were the first major liberators. As Cohn puts it in two memorable phrases: 'they stirred up a whole new mood of teen arrogance' and they were 'turning into the voice of hooliganism'.[28] The title of one song, 'Get Off My Cloud', could have been the theme of the early years of the separatist youth culture, but more specifically than the separation theme, they managed to convey so many other dominant moods. Theirs was the voice of arrogance and narcissism celebrated by the early Mods; of aggression and frustration (captured especially in 'I Can't Get No Satisfaction' – a song never referring to purely sexual frustration); of cynicism (as in 'Mother's Little Helper') and the occasional hysterical scream at being able to thwart the adult world's attempts at manipulating them. Referring back to Downes's argument, it can be seen how 'right' these moods were for what the kids wanted to use their culture for.

The Stones's background was complicated (ex-art school, Jagger an LSE dropout) and they were to move on to more complicated things, giving up the purist rhythm and blues strand. In contrast, The Who were pure and complete Mod.

They came straight out of Shepherds Bush, 'one of the most major Mod citadels'[29] and they were unambiguously and uncomplicatedly representative of the new consumers. Although they were eventually managed and staged by entrepreneurs of the swinging London scene, who invariably were middle class, they explicitly stood for, sang about and understood (a gift nearly nonexistent in the pop world) their origins.

They shared anger and aggression with the Stones, but there were no cynical attacks on the affluent society and there was none of Jagger's arrogance and certainty. Their dominant mood was uncertainty, the jumpiness and edginess of the hard Mods, and an almost ugly inarticulateness and tension. This started with early songs such as 'I Can't Explain' (their first record) and moved through 'Substitute' ('The simple things I say are all complicated') and reached its convulsive climax with 'My Generation', Pete Townsend's battle hymn of unresolved and unresolvable tensions, which, more than any other song, was the sound of Brighton, Margate and Clacton. Now, six years later, The Who still include this song in most of their live performances and the orgy of smashed instruments and deafening feedback with which it ends, gives the message as much as the words do:

> People try to put us down
> Just because we get around.
> Things they do look awful cold
> Hope I die before I get old.
> This is my generation, baby
> Why don't you all f-f-f-fade away
> Don't try to dig what we all say
>
> I'm not trying to cause a big sensation
> I'm talking about my generation.
>
> This is my generation, baby,
> My generation.

Although The Who have also moved on to some other things, this tone still remains and the stuttering anger has not become much less pronounced. In his classic *Rolling Stone* 1968 interview, quoted by Dave Laing and many others, Pete Townsend testifies to the enduring influence of the Mod experience:

> It really affected me in an incredible way because it teases me all the time, because whenever I think 'Oh you know youth today is never going to make it' I just think of that fucking gesture that happened in England. It was the closest to patriotism that I've ever felt.

This was the same gesture which my analysis of the instrumental problems of the working-class adolescent in the mid-sixties led to. So, by another route, we arrive, on the beaches, the scenes where this book started. By 1964 the Rockers, as Nuttall puts it, 'seemed almost endearingly butch':[30] they were dying out, but fought with the stubborn bitterness of a group left out of the mainstream of social change. Without the publicity that was given to the initial clashes with the Mods, their weakness would have become more apparent and they would have metamorphosed into another variant of the tougher tradition. Their very nature and origins made their chances of gaining strength autonomously (for example, by attracting new recruits) virtually out of the question. Such groups are essentially self-limiting.

In a different way, the reaction also kept the Mods going. Even by 1963 the symbols had not crystallized: newspapers were still using the term 'Teddy Boy' to describe *both* groups or terms such as 'ton-up kids' to describe the Rockers; as in the early days of the Edwardians, the term 'Modernists' appeared more than anywhere else on the fashion pages. It needed a public drama to give each group its identity as folk devils. My argument in this chapter has been that although 'endogenous' factors – the youth culture, the structural position of working-class adolescents – are themselves difficult to separate from the societal reaction, such factors receive their initial importance in the creation of social types. The assignment of negative identities to these types is then dependent on the moral panic.

The sociology of moral panics

Just as the Mods and Rockers did not appear from nowhere, so too must the societal reaction, the moral panic, be explained. Magistrates, leader writers and politicians do not react like laboratory creatures being presented a series of random stimuli, but in terms of positions, statuses, interests, ideologies and values. Their responsiveness to rumours, for example, is not just related to the internal dynamics of the rumour process as described earlier, but whether the rumours support their particular interests.

The foundations of this particular moral panic should be understood in terms of different levels of generality. At the lowest level, there were those peculiar to the Mods and Rockers phenomenon; at the highest, abstract principles which can be applied to the sociology of moral panics as a whole or (even more generally) to a theory of the societal reactions to deviance.

I will not reconsider here some of the lowest order processes already dealt with: how the ambiguity of the crowd situation lent itself to panic rumours, how the media created the news and images which lent the cognitive basis for the panic, how situational pressures conditioned the control culture. A higher level starting-off point must be the same as that which structured our consideration of the Mods and Rockers themselves, namely, the ways in which the affluence and youth themes were used to conceptualize the social changes of the decade.

The sixties began the confirmation of a new era in adult–youth relations. The Teddy Boys (and their European equivalents – the *halbstarke*, the *blouson noir*) were the first warnings on the horizon. What everyone had grimly prophesied had come true: high wages, the emergence of a commercial youth culture 'pandering' to young people's needs, the elevation of scruffy pop heroes into national idols (and even giving them MBEs), the 'permissive society', the 'coddling by the Welfare State' – all this had produced its inevitable results. As one magistrate expressed it to me in 1965, 'Delinquency is trying to get at too many things too easily . . . people have become more aware of the good things in life . . . we've thrown back the curtain for them too soon.'

The Mods and Rockers symbolized something far more important than what they actually did. They touched the delicate and ambivalent nerves through which post-war social change in Britain was experienced. No one wanted depressions or austerity, but messages about 'never having it so good' were ambivalent in that some people were having it too good and too quickly: 'We've thrown back the curtain for them too soon.' Resentment and jealousy were easily directed at the young, if only because of their increased spending power and sexual freedom. When this was combined with a too-open flouting of the work and leisure ethic, with violence and vandalism, and the (as yet) uncertain threats associated with drug-taking, something more than the image of a peaceful Bank Holiday at the sea was being shattered.

One might suggest that ambiguity and strain was greatest at the beginning of the sixties. The lines had not yet been clearly drawn and, indeed, the reaction was part of this drawing of the line. The period can be seen as constituting what Erikson terms a 'boundary crisis', a period in which a group's uncertainty about itself is resolved in ritualistic confrontations between the deviant and the community's official agents.[31] One does not have to make any conspiratorial assumptions about deviants being deliberately 'picked out' to clarify normative contours at times of cultural strain and ambiguity, to detect in the response to the Mods and Rockers declarations about moral boundaries, about how much diversity can be tolerated. [. . .]

As soon as the new phenomenon was named, the devil's shape could be easily identified. In this context, the ways in which the deviance was associated with a fashion style is particularly significant. Fashion changes are not always perceived simply as something novel, a desire to be different or attract attention or as fads which will ultimately die out. They might be seen as signifying something much deeper and more permanent – for example, 'the permissive society' – and historically, stylistic changes have often represented ideological commitments or movements. So, for example, the Sans Culottes in the French Revolution wore long pants instead of conventional breeches as a symbol of radicalism and the American beatnik style became identified with certain signs of disaffiliation.

Mod fashions were seen to represent some more significant departure than a mere clothing change. The glossiness of the image, the bright colours and the associated artefacts, such as motor scooters, stood for everything resented about the affluent teenager. There were also new anxieties, such as the sexual confusion in clothing and hair-styles: the Mod boy with pastel-shaded trousers and the legendary make-up on his face, the girls with their short-cropped hair and sexless, flat appearance. The sheer uniformity in dress was a great factor in making the threat more apparent: the cheap mass-produced anoraks with similar colours, and the occasional small group riding their Vespas like a menacing pincer patrol, gave the appearance of greater organization than ever existed, and hence of a greater threat.

The way in which a single dramatic incident – or, at least, the reporting of this incident – served to confirm the actors' deviant identity is also important. To draw on the analogy already used, the situation was similar to that in which a natural disaster brings to the surface a condition or conflict that previously was latent. The requirement of visibility – and hooliganism is by definition public and visible – so essential for successful problem definition, was met right from the outset.

Mass collective action which before was played out on a more restricted screen, now was paraded even to audiences previously insulated by geographical, age and social class barriers.

This leads on to another major reason for the form of the reaction. The behaviour was presented and perceived as something more than a delinquent brawl and the Mods and Rockers could not be classified very plausibly as the ordinary slum louts associated with such behaviour in the past. They appeared to be affluent, well clothed and groomed and, above all, highly mobile. They had moved out of the bomb-sites in the East End and the streets of the Elephant and Castle. [. . .] These were not just the slum louts whom one could disown, but faintly recognizable creatures who had crawled out from under some very familiar rocks.

Allied to threats posed by the new mobility (the groups' motor-bikes and scooters were obsessively seen as important) and the wider stage on which the behaviour was now being played out, was the image of class barriers breaking down in the emergence of the teenage culture. Traditionally, the deviant role had been assigned to the lower class urban male, but the Mods and Rockers appeared to be less class tied: here were a group of impostors, reading the lines which everyone knew belonged to some other group. Even their clothes were out of place: without leather jackets they could hardly be distinguished from bank clerks. The uneasiness felt about actors who are not quite in their places can lead to greater hostility. Something done by an out-group is simply condemned and fitted into the scheme of things, but in-group deviance is embarrassing, it threatens the norms of the group and tends to blur its boundaries with the out-group.

The Mod was unique in that his actual appearance was far away from the stereotypical hooligan personified by the Teddy Boy or the Rocker. He was also nowhere near as identifiable as the beatnik or hippy. Dave Laing attributes the Mods' subversive potential to this very ordinariness. [. . .]

These were not the sort of people to attract to Brighton and the discouragement they faced was all too obvious. Some were refused service in cafés and pubs, chased away if they were congregating around a shop or seafront stall, even refused accommodation by the landladies of the guest-houses. On the other hand, these were the new 'affluent hordes' and there were no compunctions about exploiting them commercially, for example, by raising prices. It could be seen, though, from the Seaview and Beachside action groups, that the dominant local face was hostile and resentful: these scruffs and hooligans should not be allowed to frighten away the decent holidaymakers, the family groups (who, by this time, were tailing off anyway). There were other new menaces besides the Mods and Rockers: the long-haired Continental youths in the language schools that had sprung up on the south coast and (in Brighton) students from Sussex University who were not only offensive in appearance but partly instrumental in getting Brighton its first Labour MP for generations.

The Mods and Rockers just represented the epitome of these changes; to many local residents, as a Brighton editor put it, '. . . they were something frightening and completely alien . . . they were visitors from a foreign planet and they should be banished to where they came from'. [. . .]

If the Mods and Rockers had done nearly all they were supposed to have done in the way of violence, damage to property, inconveniencing and annoying others (and clearly they did a lot of these things), it does not need a very sophisticated analysis to explain why such rule-breaking was responded to punitively. But threats need not be as direct as this and one must understand that the response was as much to what they stood for as what they did. In one of the few analyses of the relationships between moral indignation and the social structure, Gusfield – looking at Prohibition and the post-Repeal periods – explains the responses of the temperance movement as symbolic solutions to conflict and the indignant reaction to loss of status.[32]

He suggests – directly following Ranulf's classic analysis[33] that moral indignation might have a disinterested quality when the transgression is solely moral and doesn't impinge upon the life and behaviour of the judge; it is a 'hostile response of the norm upholder to the norm violator where no direct personal advantage to the norm upholder is at stake'.[34] This disinterested quality might thus apply to the Bohemian, the homosexual, the drug addict, where questions of style and ways of life are at stake, but not to the political radical, whose action might threaten the structure of society nor to the delinquent who poses direct threats to property and person.

I doubt whether this distinction between 'interested' and 'disinterested' is a viable one, as it seems to imply much too narrow a conception of interest and threat. With groups such as drug-takers and hippies[35] even though little apparent physical or 'political' threat is involved, there is a direct *conflict of interests*. There is certainly a great deal at stake for the norm-upholder if he allows such action to go unpunished and his indignation has only a slight element of the disinterested about it. In the case of the Mods and Rockers, the moral panic was sustained both by the direct threats (in the narrow sense) to persons, property, commercial interests and the gross interests threatened by the violation of certain approved styles of life. Such a combination of interests can be seen clearly in the individuals like Blake. He saw physical dangers, personal disadvantages and the physical threat represented by all the youth culture was supposed to be: prematurely affluent, aggressive, permissive and challenging the ethics of sobriety and hard work. In his case (but perhaps not in all the forms of moral indignation Ranulf tries to explain this way) one might also detect the psychological element of the envy and resentment felt by the lower middle classes, supposedly the most frustrated and repressed of groups. They condemn, that is, behaviour which is secretly craved.

More fundamentally, a theory of moral panics, moral enterprise, moral crusades or moral indignation needs to relate such reactions to conflicts of interests – at community and societal levels – and the presence of power differentials which leave some groups vulnerable to such attacks. The manipulation of appropriate symbols – the process which sustains moral campaigns, panics and crusades – is made much easier when the object of attack is both highly visible and structurally weak.

Notes

1. Howard S, Becker, *Outsiders: Studies in the Sociology of Deviance* (New York: Free Press, 1963), Chaps 7 and 8.
2. Joseph Gusfield, *Symbolic Crusade: Status Politics and the American Temperance Movement* (Urbana: University of Illinois, 1963).
3. Becker, op. cit. p. 145.
4. Howard S. Becker (Ed.), *Social Problems: A Modern Approach* (New York: John Wiley, 1966).
5. The sceptical revolution can only be understood as part of a broader reaction in the social sciences as a whole against the dominant models, images and methodology of

positivism. It is obviously beyond my scope to deal here with this connection. For an account of the peculiar shape positivism took in the study of crime and deviance and of the possibilities of transcending its paradoxes, the work of David Matza is invaluable: *Delinquency and Drift* (New York: Wiley, 1964) and *Becoming Deviant* (Englewood Cliffs, NJ: Prentice-Hall, 1969).

6. Edwin M. Lemert, *Social Pathology: A Systematic Approach to the Study of Sociopathic Behaviour* (New York: McGraw-Hill, 1951) and *Human Deviance, Social Problems and Social Control* (Englewood Cliffs, NJ: Prentice-Hall, 1967).

7. Lemert, *Social Pathology*, op. cit.

8. ibid. p. 55.

9. Leslie T. Wilkins, *Social Deviance: Social Policy, Action and Research* (London: Tavistock, 1964), Chap. 4. I have made a preliminary attempt to apply this model to the Mods and Rockers in 'Mods, Rockers and the Rest: Community Reaction to Juvenile Delinquency', *Howard Journal of Penology and Crime Prevention* XII (1967), pp. 121–30.

10. Young (1971) *The Drug Takers*, op. cit.

11. Neil J. Smelser, *Theory of Collective Behaviour* (London: Routledge & Kegan Paul, 1962).

12. Early journalistic accounts of disasters have given way to more sophisticated methods of data collection and theorization. The body in the USA most responsible for this development is the Disaster Research Group of the National Academy of Science, National Research Council. The most comprehensive accounts of their findings and other research are to be found in: G. W. Baker and D. W. Chapman, *Man and Society in Disaster* (New York: Basic Books, 1962) and A. H. Barton, *Social Organisation Under Stress: A Sociological Review of Disaster Studies* (Washington, DC: National Academy of Sciences, 1963). See also A. H. Barton, *Communities in Disaster* (London: Ward Lock, 1970).

13. Robert K. Merton, Introduction to Barton, *Social Organisation Under Stress*, op. cit. pp. xix–xx.

14. C. F. Fritz, 'Disaster', in R. K. Merton and R. A. Nisbet (eds), *Contemporary Social Problems* (London: Rupert Hart-Davis, 1963), p. 654.

15. From: Barton, *Social Organization Under Stress* op. cit. pp. 14–15; D. W. Chapman, 'A Brief Introduction to Contemporary Disaster Research', in Baker and Chapman, op. cit. pp. 7–22; J. G. Miller, 'A Theoretical Review of Individual and Group Psychological Reaction to Stress', in G. H. Grosser *et al.* (eds), *The Theat of Impending Disaster: Contributions to the Psychology of Stress* (Cambridge, Massachusetts: MIT Press, 1964), pp. 24–32.

16. See Stuart Hall, Introduction to *The Popular Press and Social 1935–1965*. Unpublished MS. Centre for Contemporary Cultural Studies, University of Birmingham, 1971.

17. One of the few serious attempts in this country to deal with both the creative and commercially response aspects of pop music is Dave Laing's *The Sound of Our Time* (London: Sheed & Ward, 1969). His Chapters 9 – 'Notes for a Study of the Beatles'– and 10 – 'My Generation' (which deals with the Rolling Stones and The Who) – are important aids to understanding the Mod phenomenon.

18. This account derives mainly from the work of Dowens, and its elaborations by Peter Willmott, *Adolescent Boys of East London* (London: Routledge & Kegan Paul, 1966), and David H. Hargreaves, *Social Relations in a Secondary School* (London: Routledge & Kegan Paul, 1967).

19. The notion of a mood of desperation preceding the drift to delinquency is used by David Matza in *Delinquency and Drift* (New York: John Wiley, 1964).

20.   For this whole section I am heavily indebeted to the writings of Jeff Nuttall; see
      particularly *Bomb Culture* (London: Paladin, 1970), and 'Techniques of Separation'
      in Tony Cash (ed.), *Anatomy of Pop* (London: BBC Publications, 1970). On the
      earlier period, Ray Gosling is again invaluable; see his autobiography *Sum Total*
      (London: Faber & Faber).

21.   Colin MacInnes, *Absolute Beginners* (London: MacGibbon & Kee, 1959). See also the
      essays, particularly 'Sharp Schmutter' (on the clothing style, at the end of the fifties)
      in MacInnes's *England, Half English* (Harmonndsworth: Penguin, 1966). These are
      among the more noteworthy comments on youth in England during the indefinite
      transitional stage between Ted and Mod.

22.   Tom Wolfe, 'The Noonday Underground' in *The Mid Atlantic Man and Other New
      Breeds in England and America* (London: Weidenfeld & Nicholson, 1968).

23.   ibid, p. 101.

24.   For details on all these types, see *Brighton Archways Ventures Report*, Vol. 3, Chap. 4.

25.   Laing, op. cit. pp. 150–1.

26.   ibid. p. 151.

27.   See, for example, Roger Williams and David Guest, 'Are The Middle Classes
      Becoming Work Shy?', New Society, Vol. 18, No. 457 (1 July 1971), pp. 9–11.
      Quetions about the supposed allegiance of particular groups to the work ethos
      need, of course, to be put in a theoretical context which recognizes the inconsisten-
      cies and contradictions in value systems about leisure. The classic analysis is David
      Matza and Gresham Sykes, 'Juvenile Delinquency and Subterranean Value', *American
      Sociological Review* 26 (October 1961), pp. 712–19.

28.   Nik Cohn, *Awophopaloobop Aloophamboom* (London: Paladin, 1970), p. 141 and
      p. 145. For fuller analysis of The Who see Gary Herman, *TheWho* (London: Studio
      Vista, 1971).

29.   ibid. p. 164.

30.   Nuttall, *Bomb Culture*, op. cit. p. 35.

31.   Kai T. Erikson, *Wayward Puritans: A Study in the Sociology of Deviance* (New York: John
      Wiley, 1966).

32.   Joseph Gusfield, *Symbolic Crusade: Status Politics and the American Temperance Movement*
      (Urbana: University of Illinois, 1963). See especially Chapter 5, 'Moral Indignation
      and Status Conflict'.

33.   Svend Ranulf, *Moral Indignation and Middle Class Psychology* (New York: Schocken
      Books Inc., 1964).

34.   Gusfield, op. cit. p. 112.

35.   For a convincing argument about the bases for the societal condemnation of
      drug-taking, see Jock Young, *The Drugtakers: The Social Meaning of Drug Use* (London:
      Paladin, 1971).

Critical connections

Erich Goode and Nachman Ben Yehuda (1994) developed Cohen's discussion of moral
panic by proposing specific criteria that should be met before suggesting a 'moral
panic' is occurring. They identify five key features of the phenomenon: (i) *concern* (a
reported condition or event generates anxiety); (ii) *hostility* (the condition or event is
condemned and, where there are clearly identifiable individuals who can be blamed

these are portrayed as 'folk devils'); (iii) *consensus* (the negative social reaction is widespread and collective); (iv) *disproportionality* (the extent of the problem and the threat it poses are exaggerated); (v) *volatility* (media attention and the associated panic emerge suddenly and with intensity, but can dissipate quickly too). More recently, Garland (2008) has suggested that two further elements, both crucial but frequently overlooked, are essential to the meaning of the concept that Cohen developed: (i) the *moral dimension* of the social reaction; and (ii) the idea that the deviant conduct in question is somehow *symptomatic* of a wider problem – a threat to established values, or a particular way of life. It is a lack of focus on such constraining definitional criteria that has allowed the term 'moral panic' to be deployed – often by journalists and politicians, but by academics too – in connection with everything from nuclear power, to bird flu, to global warming. These issues can, of course, be moralised, and there are often forceful arguments to suggest they should be. But they are not in and of themselves 'moral', and cannot automatically be analysed as such.

The concept of moral panic lies at one end of a spectrum of ongoing intellectual engagement with the sociology of social reaction. Cohen's most recent book, *States of Denial: Knowing about Atrocities and Suffering* (2001), considers another form of social reaction which, as David Garland (2008) has suggested, lies at the other end of the spectrum. Whereas moral panic theory considers the cognitive processes involved in over-reaction, denial theory explores the palpable lack of reaction to suffering around the world. Thus whilst moral panic theory is about the struggle against stigmatisation, denial theory is about the struggle for stigmatisation, or at least the struggle against the normalisation of pain and suffering. Why, Cohen asks, are there not moral panics about torture, genocide, political massacres, and civil liberties violations? How do we selectively process the endless images of global pain and suffering to which we are exposed on a daily basis? Would it be possible to have, or actively create, a 'good' moral panic, and what might that look like?

Discussion questions

- Outline the theoretical background and underpinning characteristics of Cohen's (1972) notion of 'moral panic', and explain why the moral panic about Mods and Rockers arose in 1960s Britain.
- Researchers have tended to use theories of symbolic interactionism, labelling and social constructionism, along with newspaper content analysis, to explore the creation and path of moral panics. Referring back to Section Two of this Reader, what research methods might be employed to engage with the key protagonists in a 'moral panic'?
- Is it possible to have a positive moral panic, and what might it look like?

References

Cohen, S. (2001) *States of Denial: Knowing About Atrocities and Suffering*. London: Polity.

Goode, E. and Ben-Yehuda, N. (1994) *Moral Panics: The Social Construction of Deviance.*
    Oxford: Blackwell.
Garland, D. (2008) 'On the Concept of Moral Panic', in *Crime, Media, Culture: An
    International Journal*, 4, 1: 9–30.
Young, J, (1971) 'The Role of the Police in the as Amplifiers of Deviancy, Negotiators
    of Reality, and Translators of Fantasy: Some Consequences of our Present System
    of Drug Control as Seen in Notting Hill', in S. Cohen and J. Young (eds), *Images of
    Deviance*, Harmondsworth: Penguin.

Angela McRobbie and Sarah Thornton

RETHINKING 'MORAL PANIC' FOR A MULTI-MEDIATED SOCIAL WORLD (1995)

Introduction and context

DESPITE THE ENORMOUS ATTENTION to and countless applications of moral panic theory by media criminologists over the past three decades, very few people have looked critically at the concept itself, or explored how it might require updating for a twenty-first-century media environment. Further illustrating the parochialism that can afflict exclusively criminological research and theorising, the most significant advances in this regard have not come from criminologists, but from other areas of the social sciences. Angela McRobbie and Sarah Thornton (a cultural theorist and an art historian respectively) argued that, whilst the notion of moral panic has been an extremely influential and useful tool for understanding the social response to a whole range of youth subcultures, styles and deviant(ised) behaviours, the world in the 1990s was a very different place from the world inhabited by the first wave of Mods and Rockers described by Cohen (1972 Reading 34). Their analysis seeks to rethink the concept of moral panic and to relocate it within a multi-mediated world, where signs and symbols are constantly being circulated and recycled, where patterns of power, labelling and influence are less predictable, where 'folk devils' – particularly those drawn from youth culture – have a right to reply, and where neo-liberal corporatism is as likely (re)package and market 'deviant' youth cultures as it is to condemn them.

'Moral panic' is now a term regularly used by journalists to describe a process which politicians, commercial promoters and media habitually attempt to incite. It has become a standard interview question to put to Conservative MPs: are they not whipping up a moral panic as a foil to deflect attention away from more pressing economic issues? It has become a routine means of making youth-orientated cultural products more alluring; acid house music was marketed as 'one of the most controversial sounds of 1988' set to outrage 'those who decry the glamorization of drug culture'. Moreover, as moral panics seem to guarantee the kind of emotional involvement that keeps up the interest of, not just tabloid, but broadsheet newspaper readers, as well as the ratings of news and true crime television, even the media themselves are willing to take some of the blame. Sue Cameron, discussing 'new juvenile crime' on BBC2's *Newsnight*, asks, 'Is it not the media itself which has helped to create this phenomenon?'

Moral panics, once the unintended outcome of journalistic practice, seem to have become a goal. Rather than periods to which societies are subject 'every now and then' (Cohen 1972/80:9), moral panics have become the way in which daily events are brought to the attention of the public. They are a standard response, a familiar, sometimes weary, even ridiculous rhetoric rather than an exceptional emergency intervention. Used by politicians to orchestrate consent, by business to promote sales in certain niche markets, and by media to make home and social affairs newsworthy, moral panics are constructed on a daily basis.

Given their high rate of turnover and the increasing tendency to label all kinds of media event as 'moral panic', we think it is time to take stock of the revisions, then consider the strengths and weaknesses of this key concept. Although both the original model of moral panics and the reformulations which introduced notions of ideology and hegemony were exemplary interventions in their time, we argue that it is impossible to rely on the old models with their stages and cycles, univocal media, monolithic societal or hegemonic reactions. The proliferation and fragmentation of mass, niche and micro-media and the multiplicity of voices, which compete and contest the meaning of the issues subject to 'moral panic', suggest that both the original and revised models are outdated in so far as they could not possibly take account of the labyrinthine web of determining relations which now exist between social groups and the media, 'reality' and representation. [...]

Contesting 'society' and 'hegemony'

British society and media, youth culture and 'deviance' have changed considerably since the 1960s. [...] In original moral panic theory, 'society' and 'societal reactions' were monolithic and, as others have already argued, ultimately functionalist. [. . .] In the 1990s, when social differentiation and audience segmentation are the order of the day, we need take account of a plurality of reactions, each with their different constituencies, effectivities and modes of discourse. [...]

Ethnographies of contemporary youth culture (cf. Thornton 1995) find that youth are inclined *not* to lament a safe and stable past *but* to have overwhelming nostalgia for the days when youth culture was genuinely transgressive. The 1990s youth culture is steeped in the legacy of previous 'moral panics'; fighting mods and rockers, drug-taking hippies, foul-mouthed punks and gender-bending New Romantics are part of their celebrated folklore. Whether youth cultures espouse overt politics or not, they are often set on being culturally 'radical'. Moral panic can therefore be seen as a culmination and fulfillment of youth cultural agendas in so far as negative news coverage baptizes transgression. What better way to turn difference into defiance, lifestyle into social upheaval, leisure into revolt?

Disapproving mass media coverage legitimizes and authenticates youth cultures to the degree that it is hard to imagine a British youth 'movement' without it. For, in turning youth into news, mass media both frame subcultures as major events and disseminate them; a tabloid front page is frequently a self-fulfilling prophecy. Sociologists might rightly see this in terms of 'deviancy amplification', but youth have their own discourses which see the process as one in which a 'scene' is transformed into a 'movement'. Here youth have a point, for what gets amplified is not only a 'deviant' activity, but the records, haircuts and dance styles which *were said* to accompany the activities.

Knowledge of this youth-culture ethos is such that its exploitation has become a routine marketing strategy of the publishing and recording industries. For example, the 'moral panic' about 'Acid House' in 1988, 1989 and 1990 began with a prediction on the back of the album that launched the music genre. The sleeve notes described the new sound as 'drug induced', 'sky high' and 'ecstatic' and concluded with a prediction of moral panic: 'The sound of acid tracking will undoubtedly become one of the most controversial sounds of 1988, provoking a split between those who adhere to its underground creed and those who decry the glamorization of drug culture.' In retrospect, this seems prescient, but the statement is best understood as hopeful. Moral panics are one of the few marketing strategies open to relatively anonymous instrumental dance music. To quote one music monthly, they amount to a 'priceless PR campaign' (*Q*, January 1989)[2]. [...]

In addition to the difficulty we have in excluding rather large social groups and industrial activities from accounts of 'society' or 'consensus', so we can't ignore the many voices which now contribute to the debate during moral panics. In the 1990s, interest groups, pressure groups, lobbies and campaigning experts are mobilized to intervene in moral panics. For example, the spokeswoman of the National Council for One Parent Families, Sue Slipman, played a leading role, on an almost weekly basis over a period of three or six months, in diminishing the demonization by the Tories of young single mothers for having children without being married.

One of the main aims of pressure groups is timely intervention in relevant moral panics – to be able to respond instantly to the media demonization of the group they represent, and to provide information and analysis designed to counter this representation. The effectiveness of these groups and in particular their skills at working with the media and providing highly professional 'soundbites' more or less on cue make them an invaluable resource to media machinery working to tight schedules and with increasingly small budgets. They allow the media to be seen to be doing their duty by providing 'balance' in their reporting. At the same time, they show how 'folk devils' can and do 'fight back'.

This phenomenon of becoming an expert, having been a deviant, has a long history in the field of serious crime, drug abuse and juvenile delinquency. However, the proliferation of groups recently set up to campaign on behalf or with folk devils and the skill with which they engage with media is an extremely important development in political culture. [...]

Although moral panics are anti-intellectual, often characterized by a certain religious fervour, and historically most effectively used by the right, only a predominantly right-wing national press arguably stops them from being amenable to the current left. Of course, government is always advantaged, due to higher number of authoritative news sources and to institutionalized agenda-setting. But, there is always the possibility of backfire. For example, when John Major attempted to build upon the moral panic around 'single mothers' (if not initiated, then certainly fuelled by government spokes-people because it helped legitimize welfare cutbacks) with his 'Back to Basics' campaign, the media, followed by Labour, deflected the empty rhetoric back onto the Tory party, turning the campaign into an ad-hoc investigation into the personal morality and sexual practices of Tory MPs.

The delicate balance of relations which the moral panic sociologists saw existing between media, agents of social control, folk devils and moral guardians, has given way to a much more complicated and fragmented set of connections. Each of the categories described by moral panics theorists has undergone a process of fissure in the intervening years. New liaisons have been developed and new initiatives pursued. In particular, two groups seem to be making ever more vocal and 'effective' intervention: pressure groups have, among other things, strongly contested the vocality of the traditional moral guardians; and commercial interests have planted the seeds, and courted discourses, of moral panic in seeking to gain the favourable attention of youthful consumers.

This leads us to query the usefulness of the term 'moral panic'– a metaphor which depicts a complex society as a single person who experiences sudden fear about its virtue. The term's anthropomorphism and totalization arguably mystify more than they reveal. Its conception of morals overlooks the youthful ethics of abandon and the moral imperatives of pressure groups and vocal experts. In the 1990s, we need to acknowledge the perspectives and articulations of different sectors of society. New sociologies of social regulation need to shift attention away from the conventional points in the circuit of amplification and control and look instead to these other spaces.

Moral panics for every medium

Not only need the attitudes and activities of different social groups and organizations be taken into account and not subsumed under a consensual 'society', but also the disparate perspectives of different mass, niche and micro-media need to be explored. Britain saw a remarkable 73 per cent increase in consumer magazine titles during the 1980s – the result of more detailed market research, tighter target marketing and new technologies like computer mailing and desk-top publishing (*Marketing* 13 August 1993). Crucially, the success of many of these magazines has been in the discovery and effective representation of niches of opinion and identity.

As seen above, moral panic is a favourite topic of the youth press. When the mass media of tabloids and TV become active in the 'inevitable' moral panic about 'Acid House', the subcultural press were ready. They tracked the tabloids, every move, re-printed whole front pages, analysed their copy and decried the *misrepresentation* of Acid House. Some 30 magazines now target and speak up for youth.

Another area of development is the gay and lesbian press who are represented by several national and regional, weekly and monthly papers, magazines and free sheets, some of which have become sub-divided by age, like the long-established *Gay News* which takes a different editorial line from the younger, less political *Boyz*. Of course, these developments are very much dependent on the development of a 'pink economy' and the commercial recognition of the presence and persistence of high levels of gay discretionary income.

Despite their proliferation and diversification, however, the media are obviously not a positive reflection of the diversity of Britain's social interests. This is partly because there are large groups of people in which the media are not economically, and, therefore, editorially interested – crucially, the D and E 'social grades' which are categorized by the *National Readership Survey* as the unskilled working class and 'those at the lowest levels of subsistence', in other words, the long-term unemployed and poorly pensioned. But even here, there are glimmers of hope. The *Big Issue* is now perceived as the newspaper voice of the homeless. Other groups and agencies produce a never-ending flow of newsletters and press releases many of which are written in a house-style customized to the needs of the journalists on national and local media. So-called folk devils now produce their own media as a counter to what they perceive as the biased media of the mainstream. [...]

But one needn't turn to specialist magazines and newspapers to find the plurality and divergences of opinion that characterize today's (and probably yesterday's) 'moral panics'. Even the national dailies have dependably different stances. The paper whose tone and agenda is closest to 1960/1970s-style moral panic is probably the *Daily Mail*. During the Thatcher years, the *Daily Mail* practised and perfected the characteristics of hegemony, in a way which was in uncanny harmony with Thatcherism. It was a daily process of reaching out to win consent through endlessly defining and redefining social questions and representing itself as the moral voice of the newly self-identified middle class as well as the old lower-middle class. The fact that the *Mail* is the only national daily with more female than male readers – if only 51 per cent female – undoubtedly informs its respectable girl's brand of moral indignity. Hence, hysteria about single and teenage mothers is perfect material for a *Daily Mail* moral panic.

Tabloids like the *Sun* prefer to espouse an altogether different brand of moral outrage. With a topless sixteen year old on page 3 and a hedonistic pro-sex editorial line, their moralism need be finely tuned. But that doesn't stop them from being the most preachy and prescriptive of Britain's daily papers, with page after page of the '*Sun* says ...' However, the *Sun*'s favourite moral panics are of the 'sex, drugs and rock'n'roll' variety – stories about other people having far *too much* fun, if only because the paper is set on maintaining a young (and not graying) readership. Moreover, these kinds of story have the advantage of allowing their readers to have their cake and eat it too; they can vicariously enjoy and/or secretly admire the transgression one moment, then be shocked and offended the next. [...]

In the last few years, the broadsheets have not only made use of more visual and colour material, they also seem to have adopted tabloid-style headlines to accompany their tabloid supplements. For example, the covers of the *Guardian* G2 section frequently sport exaggerated, sensational headlines. 'BLOOD ON THE STREETS': They're Packing Pistols in Manchester' announces a story about the increasing use of firearms by young drug dealers on mountain bikes in Manchester's Moss Side (*Guardian* 9 August 1993). Given the more measured copy which follows, the *Guardian* would seem to be using this 'shock horror' language to lighten up the story – the capital letters signifying an ironic borrowing of tabloid style. But, as the *Sun's* language is understood by many of its readers as tongue-in-cheek, the *Guardian's* irony gives it an alibi, but not absolution. Moreover, these mixtures of outrage and amusement point to the 'entertainment value' of moral panics — something mentioned but not really integrated into previous models. [...]

In considering the *Daily Mail*, the *Sun* and the *Guardian*, we've found that each paper has its own style of in-house moralism. As the British press becomes more competitive, one strategy for maintaining healthy circulation figures is for a newspaper to cast itself in the role of moral guardian, ever alert to new possibilities for concern and indignation. It would seem that professional journalistic style, carefully attuned to the popularity of 'human interest' stories, draws on a moralistic voice which, for the purposes of variety, it is willing to undercut with occasional irony, jokes, etc.

Although the multiplicity of contemporary moral panics is perhaps best demonstrated in relation to print media, the same tendencies can be found in radio and television. Even with only four terrestrial channels, new definitions of youth programming have opened a space for counter-discourses. Television producer Janet Street-Porter, drawing on the cut-up graphic style of punk and indicating a new commitment on the part of broadcasters to take youth seriously, pioneered Youth TV, in the mid-eighties through her *Def II* series on BBC2. In keeping with this commitment several of these programmes were explicitly aimed at countering youthful folk devils and moral panics, particularly around drugs. Thus an informative and rational BBC2 *Reportage* programme on the use of Ecstasy in rave culture can be set against the much more traditional sensational and fearful *Cook Report* (ITV) on the same subject (1992).

Mediated social worlds

In addition to unpacking 'society', on the one hand, and the 'media', on the other, the third consideration in updating models of 'moral panic' need be that the media is no longer something separable from society. Social reality is experienced through language, communication and imagery. Social meanings and social differences are inextricably tied up with representation. Thus when sociologists call for an account which tells how life actually is, and which deals with the real issues rather than the spectacular and exaggerated ones, the point is that these accounts of reality are already representations and sets of meanings about what they perceive the 'real' issues to be. These versions of 'reality' would also be impregnated with the mark of media imagery rather than somehow pure and untouched by the all-pervasive traces of contemporary communications. [...]

The strength of the old models of moral panic was that they marked the connection between 'the media' and 'social control'. But, nowadays, most political strategies *are* media strategies. The contest to determine news agendas is the first and last battle of the political campaign. Moreover, the kinds of social issues and political debates which were once included on the agendas of moral panic theorists as sites of social anxiety, and even crisis, could now be redefined as part of an endless debate about who 'we' are and what 'our' national culture is. These are profoundly 'home affairs'. The daily intensity and drama of their appearance and the many voices now heard in the background but in the foreground, punctuating and producing reality, point more to the reality of dealing with social difference than to the unity of current affairs (cf. Hall, Connell and Curtis 1981).

Conclusions

What has been argued here is that the model of moral panic is urgently in need of updating precisely because of its success. While the theory began its life in radical sociology, the strength of the argument quickly found its way into those very areas with which it was originally concerned, influencing social policy and attitudes to deviance generally. As a result, the police, as agents of social control now show some awareness of the dangers of overreaction, while sectors of the media regularly remind viewers of the dangers of moral panic and thus of alienating sections of the community by falsely attributing to them some of the characteristics of the so-called folk devils.

Crucially, the theory has, over the years, drawn attention to the importance of empowering folk devils so that they or their representatives can challenge the cycle of sanctions and social control. Pressure groups, lobbies, self-help and interest groups have sprung up across the country and effectively positioned themselves as authoritative sources of comment and criticism. They now contribute to the shape of public debate, playing a major role in contesting what they perceive as dangerous stereotypes and popular misconceptions.

The theory has also influenced business practice, albeit through an undoubtedly more circuitous route. Culture industry promotions and marketing people now understand how, for certain products like records, magazines, movies and computer games, nothing could be better for sales than a bit of controversy – the threat of censorship, the suggestion of sexual scandal or subversive activity. The promotional logic is twofold: first, the cultural good will receive a lot of free, if negative, publicity because its associations with moral panic have made it newsworthy; second, rather than alienating everyone, it will be attractive to a contingent of consumers who see themselves as alternative, avant-garde, radical, rebellious or simply young. In the old models of moral panic, the audience played a minor role and remained relatively untheorized. With few exceptions, they were the space of consensus, the space of media manipulation, the space of an easily convinced public. A new model need embrace the complex realm of reception – readers, viewers, listeners and the various social groups categorized under the heading of public opinion cannot be read off the representation of social issues.

The moral panics we have been discussing here are less monolithic than those the classic model implied. Recent moral panics do remain overwhelmingly concerned with moral values, societal regularities and drawing of lines between the permissible and the less acceptable. However, hard and fast boundaries between 'normal' and 'deviant' would seem to be less common – if only because moral panics are now continually contested. Few sociologists would dispute the expansion over the last decade of what used to be called, quite simply, the mass media. The diversification of forms of media and the sophisticated restructuring of various categories of audience require that, while a consensual social morality might still be a political objective, the chances of it being delivered directly through the channels of the media are much less certain.

References

Cohen, S. 1972/80 *Folk Devils and Moral Panics*: The Creation of the Mods and the Rockers, Oxford: Basil Blackwell.

Hall, S., Connell, I. and Curti, L. 1981 'The "unity" of current affairs television' in Tony Bennett *et al.* (eds) *Popular Television and Film*, London: BFI.

Thornton, S. L. 1995 *Club Culture: Music, Media and Subcultural Capital*, Oxford: Polity.

Critical connections

The concept of moral panics remains highly pertinent today. Post-September 11, many have argued that the response to the threat of terrorist activities has been 'fundamentally inappropriate' and that the raft of control powers embodied in wave after wave of emergency legislation (Welch, 2006, Hamm, 2004) feeds directly into the notion of the 'authoritarian state'. Some of these ideas are developed in Section Six – on Cybercrime, Surveillance and Risk. Meanwhile, the abundance of studies – often missing much of the depth and sophistication of the original analysis – exploring 'moral panics' shows no sign of letting up. It was never Cohen's contention that young people are powerless against their demonisation, nor that they are always necessarily opposed to it. Much of the exuberance and enthusiasm with which young people challenge authority and 'act out' gender, class, style and identity is overlooked in the more mechanistic applications of the concept. In the preface to the third edition of *Folk Devils and Moral Panics* Cohen acknowledges that things have changed, seeks to address some of the criticisms that have been made, and offers some suggestions of his own regarding how the concept might be developed for the twenty-first century.

Discussion questions

- How might we rethink moral panics for multi-mediated social worlds?
- In what ways are moral panics actively sought out by the promoters of youth-oriented consumer products?
- Given the proliferation of media forms and formats (see also Readings 1, 5 and 6), and the growth in alternative media, is it the case that folk devils of whatever form have greater right to reply than ever before?

References

Cohen, S. (2002) *Folk Devils and Moral Panics: The Creation of Mods and Rockers*, third edition, London: Routledge.

Hamm, M. (2004) 'The USA Patriot Act and the Politics of Fear', in J. Ferrell, K. Hayward, W. Morrison and M. Presdee (eds) *Cultural Criminology Unleashed*, London: Cavendish, p 109–121

Welch, M. (2006) *Scapegoats of September 11th*, New Brunswick: Rutgers University Press.

Cybercrime, surveillance and risk

Introduction

THE LATE- OR POSTMODERN LANDSCAPE is defined by an array of 'new' media technologies capable of both facilitating and constraining communication, interaction, mobility, and the creation and realisation of fluid identities. The rapid spread of digital, computerised and networked information and communication technologies (ICTs) – most notably the Internet – has opened up 'virtual' worlds with their own norms, values and codes of practice. Fundamentally, it has altered the ways in which people engage and interact in time and space, and given new meaning to what it is to be 'social' (see Readings 5 and 7). The parallel emergence of the 'surveillance society' – most vividly encapsulated in the massive expansion of Closed Circuit Television (CCTV) cameras, but involving myriad other forms of information gathering, data processing, categorisation and classification – has likewise transformed how people perceive and navigate their social worlds. These technological transformations, driven and sustained by equally profound shifts in politics and culture, have created new opportunities for crime, violence and victimisation; governance, criminal justice and social control; oppression and resistance, enforcement and defiance. This section on *Cybercrime, Surveillance and Risk* includes key readings on the nature, extent and impact of 'new media' formations, exploring in particular how they relate to crime, control and social order. Collectively, the readings embrace both the distinctiveness of virtual and physical worlds, and the hybrid realities generated by the permeability of the boundaries between them.

It is worth noting that for many young people today there is little 'new' about so-called 'new' media technologies. Many of the students who use this book will not recall a world before the Internet, mobile phones and CCTV surveillance cameras. What have for years been called 'new media' by academics and commentators are simply, for young people, the media. Still, the intention is to mark out these media forms as a more recent developments across the technological landscape. Michel Foucault's hugely influential *Discipline and Punish: The Birth of the Prison* (1977) was one of the first attempts to theorise the significance of the spread of surveillance throughout society, and the implications of this for power, knowledge and social control. Thomas Mathiesen (1997) offers a critique of Foucault's reading of Panoptic surveillance – where the few watch the many – arguing that it is in fact synoptic surveillance – where the many watch the few – that is of greatest importance in producing disciplined bodies fit for the purposes of government. Clive Norris and Gary Armstrong (1999) draw from Foucault and others in their ethnographic analysis of how class, gender, age and ethnicity influence the way CCTV operators interpret footage and make judgements about suspiciousness, criminality and risk. Sheila Brown (2003) considers transformations in the nature and patterning of criminal transgression and victimisation in cyberspace, and problematises notions of law, order, and social control in the virtual world. Katja Franko Aas (2006), drawing from Brown, explores the interrelation between offline and online forms of social governance, and questions the usefulness of conceptualising the virtual and physical worlds as separate entities. Gabe Mythen and Sandra Walklate return to the physical world in their examination of the media communication of terrorist threats in a 'risk society'. Finally, Susan Sontag (2004) presents a damning indictment of the US military and wider administration in her account of the global release of photographs depicting the torture of Iraqi detainees by US military personnel in Abu Ghraib prison.

Michel Foucault

PANOPTICISM (1977)

Introduction and context

MICHEL FOUCAULT (1977) compares and contrasts two seemingly very different modes of punishment: the 1757 public torture and execution of Damiens the regicide, and a day in the life of inmates at a Parisian reform school in 1824. Whereas the first involves the complete destruction of the physical body in a spectacle of suffering for the masses, the second entails the minute regimentation of every aspect of daily existence behind closed doors. Foucault seeks to make theoretical sense of how the nature of punishment could change so radically in such a short period of time. Fundamental to Foucault's explanation of penal development, and a theme which runs throughout his work, is the power-knowledge dyad. Power and knowledge, it is suggested, are inseparable; they are two mutually reinforcing and constituting sides of the same social equation. The dramatic change in punishment described above was, for Foucault, less about growing humanitarianism (though of course this played a role), and more about the generation of a more ambitious project of social control which could be dispersed throughout the entire social body. The aims and purposes of punishment shifted from the spectacular but uneconomical destruction of the physical body to the transformation of the human soul. This is the shift from physical punishment to disciplinary punishment – when punishment becomes corrections.

Key to the effectiveness of this shift in control was the new spatial and social organisation of power. Foucault's major example of this reorganisation is utilitarian philosopher Jeremy Bentham's notion of the Panopticon, an architectural prison design (seldom actually realised), which presented an ideal for surveillance and control and the archetype of the 'disciplinary gaze'. The Panopticon is structured in a manner which enables the few guards to observe the many inmates at all times, without the subjects of surveillance ever knowing when they are being watched. Foucault insisted that if disciplinary power is applied effectively enough, it eventually becomes internalised and is no longer required, as the objects of power become self-disciplining. It was this 'normalisation' of discipline, and the concomitant production of docile bodies, that Foucault saw as a central aim of Panoptic surveillance. From the prison to the factory, the factory to the schoolhouse, and the schoolhouse to the wider 'social body', the dispersal of discipline throughout Western democracies, for Foucault, creates conditions in which citizens effectively act as their own jailers. They internalise the mechanisms of control that permeate and regulate society, thus maintaining the disciplined efficiency of the social system. The reading included here maps out some of Foucault's key ideas, and outlines an approach which has had an enormous influence on subsequent theorising and research on surveillance.

Bentham's *Panopticon* is the architectural figure of this composition. We know the principle on which it was based: at the periphery, an annular building; at the centre, a tower; this tower is pierced with wide windows that open onto the inner side of the ring; the peripheric building is divided into cells, each of which extends the whole width of the building; they have two windows, one on the inside, corresponding to the windows of the tower; the other, on the outside, allows the light to cross the cell from one end to the other. All that is needed, then, is to place a supervisor in a central tower and to shut up in each cell a madman, a patient, a condemned man, a worker or a schoolboy. By the effect of backlighting, one can observe from the tower, standing out precisely against the light, the small captive shadows in the cells of the periphery. They are like so many cages, so many small theatres, in which each actor is alone,

Figure 36.1 The spread and normalisation of the Panoptic gaze. Image © Andy Aitchison

perfectly individualized and constantly visible. The panoptic mechanism arranges spatial unities that make it possible to see constantly and to recognize immediately. In short, it reverses the principle of the dungeon; or rather of its three functions – to enclose, to deprive of light and to hide – it preserves only the first and eliminates the other two. Full lighting and the eye of a supervisor capture better than darkness, which ultimately protected. Visibility is a trap.

To begin with, this made it possible – as a negative effect – to avoid those compact, swarming, howling masses that were to be found in places of confinement, those painted by Goya or described by Howard. Each individual, in his place, is securely confined to a cell from which he is seen from the front by the supervisor; but the side walls prevent him from coming into contact with his companions. He is seen, but he does not see; he is the object of information, never a subject in communication. The arrangement of his room, opposite the central tower, imposes on him an axial visibility; but the divisions of the ring, those separated cells, imply a lateral invisibility. And this invisibility is a guarantee of order. If the inmates are convicts, there is no danger of a plot, an attempt at collective escape, the planning of new crimes for the future, bad reciprocal influences; if they are patients, there is no danger of contagion; if they are madmen there is no risk of their committing violence upon one another; if they are schoolchildren, there is no copying, no noise, no chatter, no waste of time; if they are workers, there are no disorders, no theft, no coalitions, none of those distractions that slow down the rate of work, make it less perfect or cause accidents. The crowd, a compact mass, a locus of multiple exchanges, individualities merging together, a collective effect, is abolished and replaced by a collection of separated individualities. From the point of view of the guardian, it is replaced by a multiplicity that can be numbered and supervised; from the point of view of the inmates, by a sequestered and observed solitude (Bentham, 60–64).

Hence the major effect of the Panopticon: to induce in the inmate a state of conscious and permanent visibility that assures the automatic functioning of power. So to arrange things that the surveillance is permanent in its effects, even if it is discontinuous in its action; that the perfection of power should tend to render its actual exercise unnecessary; that this architectural apparatus should be a machine for creating and sustaining a power relation independent of the person who exercises it; in short, that the inmates should be caught up in a power situation of which they are themselves the bearers. To achieve this, it is at once too much and too little that the prisoner should be constantly observed by an inspector: too little, for what matters is that he knows himself to be observed; too much, because he has no need in fact of being so. In view of this, Bentham laid down the principle that power should be visible and unverifiable. Visible: the inmate will constantly have before his eyes the tall outline of the central tower from which he is spied upon. Unverifiable: the inmate must never know whether he is being looked at any one moment; but he must be sure that he may always be so. In order to make the presence or absence of the inspector unverifiable, so that the prisoners, in their cells, cannot even see a shadow, Bentham envisaged not only Venetian blinds on the windows of the central observation hall, but, on the inside, partitions that intersected the hall at right angles and, in order to pass from one quarter to the other, not doors but zig-zag openings; for the slightest noise, a gleam of light, a brightness in a half-opened door would betray the presence of the guardian.[1] The Panopticon is a machine for dissociating the see/being seen dyad: in the peripheric ring, one is totally seen, without ever seeing; in the central tower, one sees everything without ever being seen.[2]

It is an important mechanism, for it automatizes and disindividualizes power. Power has its principle not so much in a person as in a certain concerted distribution of bodies, surfaces, lights, gazes; in an arrangement whose internal mechanisms produce the relation in which individuals are caught up. The ceremonies, the rituals, the marks by which the sovereign's surplus power was manifested are useless. There is a machinery that assures dissymmetry, disequilibrium, difference. Consequently, it does not matter who exercises power. Any individual, taken almost at random, can operate the machine: in the absence of the director, his family, his friends, his visitors, even his servants (Bentham, 45). Similarly, it does not matter what motive animates him: the curiosity of the indiscreet, the malice of a child, the thirst for knowledge of a philosopher who wishes to visit this museum of human nature, or the perversity of those who take pleasure in spying and punishing. The more numerous those anonymous and temporary observers are, the greater the risk for the inmate of being surprised and the greater his anxious awareness of being observed. The Panopticon is a marvellous machine which, whatever use one may wish to put it to, produces homogeneous effects of power.

A real subjection is born mechanically from a fictitious relation. So it is not necessary to use force to constrain the convict to good behaviour, the madman to calm, the worker to work, the schoolboy to application, the patient to the observation of the regulations. Bentham was surprised that panoptic institutions could be so light: there were no more bars, no more chains, no more heavy locks; all that was needed was that the separations should be clear and the openings well arranged. The heaviness of the old 'houses of security', with their fortress-like architecture, could be replaced by the simple, economic geometry of a 'house of certainty'. The efficiency of power, its constraining force have, in a sense, passed over to the other side – to the side of its surface of application. He who is subjected to a field of visibility, and who knows it, assumes responsibility for the constraints of power; he makes them play spontaneously upon himself; he inscribes in himself the power relation in which he simultaneously plays both roles; he becomes the principle of his own subjection. By this very fact, the external power may throw off its physical weight; it tends to the non-corporal; and, the more it approaches this limit, the more constant, profound and permanent are its effects: it is a perpetual victory that avoids any physical confrontation and which is always decided in advance.

[. . .] Bentham's Preface to *Panopticon* opens with a list of the benefits to be obtained from his 'inspection-house': '*Morals reformed – health preserved – industry invigorated – instruction diffused – public burthens lightened –* Economy seated, as it were, upon a rock – the gordian knot of the Poor-Laws not cut, but untied – all by a simple idea in architecture!' (Bentham, 39).

Furthermore, the arrangement of this machine is such that its enclosed nature does not preclude a permanent presence from the outside: we have seen that anyone may come and exercise in the central tower the functions of surveillance, and that, this being the case, he can gain a clear idea of the way in which the surveillance is practised. In fact, any panoptic institution, even if it is as rigorously closed as a penitentiary, may without difficulty be subjected to such irregular and constant inspections: and not only by the appointed inspectors, but also by the public; any member of society will have the right to come and see with his own eyes how the schools, hospitals, factories, prisons function. There is no risk, therefore, that the increase of power created by the panoptic machine may degenerate into tyranny; the disciplinary mechanism will be democratically controlled, since it will be constantly accessible

'to the great tribunal committee of the world'.[3] This Panopticon, subtly arranged so
that an observer may observe, at a glance, so many different individuals, also enables
everyone to come and observe any of the observers. The seeing machine was once a
sort of dark room into which individuals spied; it has become a transparent building
in which the exercise of power may be supervised by society as a whole.

The panoptic schema, without disappearing as such or losing any of its properties,
was destined to spread throughout the social body; its vocation was to become a
generalized function. The plague-stricken town provided an exceptional disciplinary
model: perfect, but absolutely violent; to the disease that brought death, power
opposed its perpetual threat of death; life inside it was reduced to its simplest expression;
it was, against the power of death, the meticulous exercise of the right of the sword.
The Panopticon, on the other hand, has a role of amplification; although it arranges
power, although it is intended to make it more economic and more effective, it does
so not for power itself, nor for the immediate salvation of a threatened society: its aim
is to strengthen the social forces – to increase production, to develop the economy,
spread education, raise the level of public morality; to increase and multiply.

How is power to be strengthened in such a way that, far from impeding progress,
far from weighing upon it with its rules and regulations, it actually facilitates such
progress? What intensificator of power will be able at the same time to be a multipli-
cator of production? How will power, by increasing its forces, be able to increase
those of society instead of confiscating them or impeding them? The Panopticon's
solution to this problem is that the productive increase of power can be assured only
if, on the one hand, it can be exercised continuously in the very foundations of society, in the subtlest possible way, and if, on the other hand, it functions outside these
sudden, violent, discontinuous forms that are bound up with the exercise of sovereignty. The body of the king, with its strange material and physical presence, with the
force that he himself deploys or transmits to some few others, is at the opposite
extreme of this new physics of power represented by panopticism; the domain of
panopticism is, on the contrary, that whole lower region, that region of irregular
bodies, with their details, their multiple movements, their heterogeneous forces,
their spatial relations; what are required are mechanisms that analyse distributions,
gaps, series, combinations, and which use instruments that render visible, record,
differentiate and compare: a physics of a relational and multiple power, which has its
maximum intensity not in the person of the king, but in the bodies that can be individualized by these relations. At the theoretical level, Bentham defines another way of
analysing the social body and the power relations that traverse it; in terms of practice,
he defines a procedure of subordination of bodies and forces that must increase the
utility of power while dispensing with the need for the prince. Panopticism is the
general principle of a new 'political anatomy' whose object and end are not the relations of sovereignty but the relations of discipline.

The celebrated, transparent, circular cage, with its high tower, powerful and
knowing, may have been for Bentham a project of a perfect disciplinary institution;
but he also set out to show how one may 'unlock' the disciplines and get them to
function in a diffused, multiple, polyvalent way throughout the whole social body.
These disciplines, which the classical age had elaborated in specific, relatively enclosed
places – barracks, schools, workshops – and whose total implementation had been
imagined only at the limited and temporary scale of a plague-stricken town, Bentham
dreamt of transforming into a network of mechanisms that would be everywhere and

always alert, running through society without interruption in space or in time. The panoptic arrangement provides the formula for this generalization. It programmes, at the level of an elementary and easily transferable mechanism, the basic functioning of a society penetrated through and through with disciplinary mechanisms. [. . .]

On the whole, therefore, one can speak of the formation of a disciplinary society in this movement that stretches from the enclosed disciplines, a sort of social 'quarantine', to an indefinitely generalizable mechanism of 'panopticism'. Not because the disciplinary modality of power has replaced all the others; but because it has infiltrated the others, sometimes undermining them, but serving as an intermediary between them, linking them together, extending them and above all making it possible to bring the effects of power to the most minute and distant elements. It assures an infinitesimal distribution of the power relations.

A few years after Bentham, Julius gave this society its birth certificate (Julius, 384–6). Speaking of the panoptic principle, he said that there was much more there than architectural ingenuity: it was an event in the 'history of the human mind'. In appearance, it is merely the solution of a technical problem; but, through it, a whole type of society emerges. Antiquity had been a civilization of spectacle. 'To render accessible to a multitude of men the inspection of a small number of objects': this was the problem to which the architecture of temples, theatres and circuses responded. With spectacle, there was a predominance of public life, the intensity of festivals, sensual proximity. In these rituals in which blood flowed, society found new vigour and formed for a moment a single great body. The modern age poses the opposite problem: 'To procure for a small number, or even for a single individual, the instantaneous view of a great multitude.' In a society in which the principal elements are no longer the community and public life, but, on the one hand, private individuals and, on the other, the state, relations can be regulated only in a form that is the exact reverse of the spectacle: 'It was to the modern age, to the ever-growing influence of the state, to its ever more profound intervention in all the details and all the relations of social life, that was reserved the task of increasing and perfecting its guarantees, by using and directing towards that great aim the building and distribution of buildings intended to observe a great multitude of men at the same time.'

Julius saw as a fulfilled historical process that which Bentham had described as a technical programme. Our society is one not of spectacle, but of surveillance; under the surface of images, one invests bodies in depth; behind the great abstraction of exchange, there continues the meticulous, concrete training of useful forces; the circuits of communication are the supports of an accumulation and a centralization of knowledge; the play of signs defines the anchorages of power; it is not that the beautiful totality of the individual is amputated, repressed, altered by our social order, it is rather that the individual is carefully fabricated in it, according to a whole technique of forces and bodies. We are much less Greeks than we believe. We are neither in the amphitheatre, nor on the stage, but in the panoptic machine, invested by its effects of power, which we bring to ourselves since we are part of its mechanism. [. . .]

We have seen that, in penal justice, the prison transformed the punitive procedure into a penitentiary technique; the carceral archipelago transported this technique from the penal institution to the entire social body. With several important results.

1.   This vast mechanism established a slow, continuous, imperceptible gradation that made it possible to pass naturally from disorder to offence and back from

a transgression of the law to a slight departure from a rule, an average, a demand, a norm. In the classical period, despite a certain common reference to offence in general,[4] the order of the crime, the order of sin and the order of bad conduct remained separate in so far as they related to separate criteria and authorities (court, penitence, confinement). Incarceration with its mechanisms of surveillance and punishment functioned, on the contrary, according to a principle of relative continuity. The continuity of the institutions themselves, which were linked to one another (public assistance with the orphanage, the reformitory, the penitentiary, the disciplinary battalion, the prison; the school with the charitable society, the workshop, the almshouse, the penitentiary convent; the workers' estate with the hospital and the prison). A continuity of the punitive criteria and mechanisms, which on the basis of a mere deviation gradually strengthened the rules and increased the punishment. A continuous gradation of the established, specialized and competent authorities (in the order of knowledge and in the order of power) which, without resort to arbitrariness, but strictly according to the regulations, by means of observation and assessment hierarchized, differentiated, judged, punished and moved gradually from the correction of irregularities to the punishment of crime. The 'carceral' with its many diffuse or compact forms, its institutions of supervision or constraint, of discreet surveillance and insistent coercion, assured the communication of punishments according to quality and quantity; it connected in series or disposed according to subtle divisions the minor and the serious penalties, the mild and the strict forms of treatment, bad marks and light sentences. You will end up in the convict-ship, the slightest indiscipline seems to say; and the harshest of prisons says to the prisoners condemned to life: I shall note the slightest irregularity in your conduct. The generality of the punitive function that the eighteenth century sought in the 'ideological' technique of representations and signs now had as its support the extension, the material framework, complex, dispersed, but coherent, of the various carceral mechanisms. As a result, a certain significant generality moved between the least irregularity and the greatest crime; it was no longer the offence, the attack on the common interest, it was the departure from the norm, the anomaly; it was this that haunted the school, the court, the asylum or the prison. It generalized in the sphere of meaning the function that the carceral generalized in the sphere of tactics. Replacing the adversary of the sovereign, the social enemy was transformed into a deviant, who brought with him the multiple danger of disorder, crime and madness. The carceral network linked, through innumerable relations, the two long, multiple series of the punitive and the abnormal.

2.   The carceral, with its far-reaching networks, allows the recruitment of major 'delinquents'. It organizes what might be called 'disciplinary careers' in which, through various exclusions and rejections, a whole process is set in motion. In the classical period, there opened up in the confines or interstices of society the confused, tolerant and dangerous domain of the 'outlaw' or at least of that which eluded the direct hold of power: an uncertain space that was for criminality a training ground and a region of refuge; there poverty, unemployment, pursued innocence, cunning, the struggle against the powerful, the refusal of obligations and laws, and organized crime all came together as chance and fortune would dictate; it was the domain of adventure that Gil Blas, Sheppard or Mandrin,

each in his own way, inhabited. Through the play of disciplinary differentia-
tions and divisions, the nineteenth century constructed rigorous channels
which, within the system, inculcated docility and produced delinquency by the
same mechanisms. There was a sort of disciplinary 'training', continuous and
compelling, that had something of the pedagogical curriculum and something
of the professional network. Careers emerged from it, as secure, as predictable,
as those of public life: assistance associations, residential apprenticeships, penal
colonies, disciplinary battalions, prisons, hospitals, almshouses. These networks
were already well mapped out at the beginning of the nineteenth century: 'Our
benevolent establishments present an admirably coordinated whole by means of
which the indigent does not remain a moment without help from the cradle to
the grave. Follow the course of the unfortunate man: you will see him born
among foundlings; from there he passes to the nursery, then to an orphanage; at
the age of six he goes off to primary school and later to adult schools. If he
cannot work, he is placed on the list of the charity offices of his district, and if
he falls ill he may choose between twelve hospitals . . . Lastly, when the poor
Parisian reaches the end of his career, seven almshouses await his age and often
their salubrious regime has prolonged his useless days well beyond those of the
rich man' (Moreau de Jonnès, quoted in Touquet).

The carceral network does not cast the unassimilable into a confused hell;
there is no outside. It takes back with one hand what it seems to exclude with the
other. It saves everything, including what it punishes. It is unwilling to waste even
what it has decided to disqualify. In this panoptic society of which incarceration
is the omnipresent armature, the delinquent is not outside the law; he is, from
the very outset, in the law, at the very heart of the law, or at least in the midst of
those mechanisms that transfer the individual imperceptibly from discipline to
the law, from deviation to offence. Although it is true that prison punishes delinquency, delinquency is for the most part produced in and by an incarceration
which, ultimately, prison perpetuates in its turn. The prison is merely the natural
consequence, no more than a higher degree, of that hierarchy laid down step by
step. The delinquent is an institutional product. It is no use being surprised,
therefore, that in a considerable proportion of cases the biography of convicts
passes through all these mechanisms and establishments, whose purpose, it is
widely believed, is to lead away from prison. That one should find in them what
one might call the index of an irrepressibly delinquent 'character': the prisoner
condemned to hard labour was meticulously produced by a childhood spent in a
reformatory, according to the lines of force of the generalized carceral system.
Conversely, the lyricism of marginality may find inspiration in the image of the
'outlaw', the great social nomad, who prowls on the confines of a docile, frightened order. But it is not on the fringes of society and through successive exiles
that criminality is born, but by means of ever more closely placed insertions,
under ever more insistent surveillance, by an accumulation of disciplinary coercion. In short, the carceral archipelago assures, in the depths of the social body,
the formation of delinquency on the basis of subtle illegalities, the overlapping of
the latter by the former and the establishment of a specified criminality.

3.   But perhaps the most important effect of the carceral system and of its extension
well beyond legal imprisonment is that it succeeds in making the power to
punish natural and legitimate, in lowering at least the threshold of tolerance to

penality. It tends to efface what may be exorbitant in the exercise of punishment. It does this by playing the two registers in which it is deployed – the legal register of justice and the extra-legal register of discipline – against one another. In effect, the great continuity of the carceral system throughout the law and its sentences gives a sort of legal sanction to the disciplinary mechanisms, to the decisions and judgements that they enforce. Throughout this network, which comprises so many 'regional' institutions, relatively autonomous and independent, is transmitted, with the 'prison-form', the model of justice itself. The regulations of the disciplinary establishments may reproduce the law, the punishments imitate the verdicts and penalties, the surveillance repeat the police model; and, above all these multiple establishments, the prison, which in relation to them is a pure form, unadulterated and unmitigated, gives them a sort of official sanction. The carceral, with its long gradation stretching from the convict-ship or imprisonment with hard labour to diffuse, slight limitations, communicates a type of power that the law validates and that justice uses as its favourite weapon. How could the disciplines and the power that functions in them appear arbitrary, when they merely operate the mechanisms of justice itself, even with a view to mitigating their intensity? When, by generalizing its effects and transmitting it to every level, it makes it possible to avoid its full rigour? Carceral continuity and the fusion of the prison-form make it possible to legalize, or in any case to legitimate disciplinary power, which thus avoids any element of excess or abuse it may entail.

But, conversely, the carceral pyramid gives to the power to inflict legal punishment a context in which it appears to be free of all excess and all violence. In the subtle gradation of the apparatuses of discipline and of the successive 'embeddings' that they involve, the prison does not at all represent the unleashing of a different kind of power, but simply an additional degree in the intensity of a mechanism that has continued to operate since the earliest forms of legal punishment. Between the latest institution of 'rehabilitation', where one is taken in order to avoid prison, and the prison where one is sent after a definable offence, the difference is (and must be) scarcely perceptible. There is a strict economy that has the effect of rendering as discreet as possible the singular power to punish. There is nothing in it now that recalls the former excess of sovereign power when it revenged its authority on the tortured body of those about to be executed. Prison continues, on those who are entrusted to it, a work begun elsewhere, which the whole of society pursues on each individual through innumerable mechanisms of discipline. By means of a carceral continuum, the authority that sentences infiltrates all those other authorities that supervise, transform, correct, improve. It might even be said that nothing really distinguishes them any more except the singularly 'dangerous' character of the delinquents, the gravity of their departures from normal behaviour and the necessary solemnity of the ritual. But, in its function, the power to punish is not essentially different from that of curing or educating. It receives from them, and from their lesser, smaller task, a sanction from below; but one that is no less important for that, since it is the sanction of technique and rationality. The carceral 'naturalizes' the legal power to punish, as it 'legalizes' the technical power to discipline. In thus homogenizing them, effacing what may be violent in one and arbitrary in the other, attenuating the effects of revolt that they may both arouse, thus depriving excess in either of any purpose, circulating the same calculated, mechanical and discreet methods from one to the other, the carceral makes it possible to carry out that great 'economy' of power whose formula the eighteenth century had sought, when the problem of the accumulation and useful administration of men first emerged.

By operating at every level of the social body and by mingling ceaselessly the art of rectifying and the right to punish, the universality of the carceral lowers the level from which it becomes natural and acceptable to be punished. The question is often posed as to how, before and after the Revolution, a new foundation was given to the right to punish. And no doubt the answer is to be found in the theory of the contract. But it is perhaps more important to ask the reverse question: how were people made to accept the power to punish, or quite simply, when punished, tolerate being so. The theory of the contract can only answer this question by the fiction of a juridical subject giving to others the power to exercise over him the right that he himself possesses over them. It is highly probable that the great carceral continuum, which provides a communication between the power of discipline and the power of the law, and extends without interruption from the smallest coercions to the longest penal detention, constituted the technical and real, immediately material counterpart of that chimerical granting of the right to punish.

4. With this new economy of power, the carceral system, which is its basic instrument, permitted the emergence of a new form of 'law': a mixture of legality and nature, prescription and constitution, the norm. This had a whole series of effects: the internal dislocation of the judicial power or at least of its functioning; an increasing difficulty in judging, as if one were ashamed to pass sentence; a furious desire on the part of the judges to judge, assess, diagnose, recognize the normal and abnormal and claim the honour of curing or rehabilitating. In view of this, it is useless to believe in the good or bad consciences of judges, or even of their unconscious. Their immense 'appetite for medicine' which is constantly manifested – from their appeal to psychiatric experts, to their attention to the chatter of criminology – expresses the major fact that the power they exercise has been 'denatured'; that it is at a certain level governed by laws; that at another, more fundamental level it functions as a normative power; it is the economy of power that they exercise, and not that of their scruples or their humanism, that makes them pass 'therapeutic' sentences and recommend 'rehabilitating' periods of imprisonment. But, conversely, if the judges accept ever more reluctantly to condemn for the sake of condemning, the activity of judging has increased precisely to the extent that the normalizing power has spread. Borne along by the omnipresence of the mechanisms of discipline, basing itself on all the carceral apparatuses, it has become one of the major functions of our society. The judges of normality are present everywhere. We are in the society of the teacher-judge, the doctor-judge, the educator-judge, the 'social worker'-judge; it is on them that the universal reign of the normative is based; and each individual, wherever he may find himself, subjects to it his body, his gestures, his behaviour, his aptitudes, his achievements. The carceral network, in its compact or disseminated forms, with its systems of insertion, distribution, surveillance, observation, has been the greatest support, in modern society, of the normalizing power.

5.   The carceral texture of society assures both the real capture of the body and its perpetual observation; it is, by its very nature, the apparatus of punishment that conforms most completely to the new economy of power and the instrument for the formation of knowledge that this very economy needs. Its panoptic functioning enables it to play this double role. By virtue of its methods of fixing, dividing, recording, it has been one of the simplest, crudest, also most concrete, but perhaps most indispensable conditions for the development of this immense activity of examination that has objectified human behaviour. If, after the age of 'inquisitorial' justice, we have entered the age of 'examinatory' justice, if, in an even more general way, the method of examination has been able to spread so widely throughout society, and to give rise in part to the sciences of man, one of the great instruments for this has been the multiplicity and close overlapping of the various mechanisms of incarceration. I am not saying that the human sciences emerged from the prison. But, if they have been able to be formed and to produce so many profound changes in the episteme, it is because they have been conveyed by a specific and new modality of power: a certain policy of the body, a certain way of rendering the group of men docile and useful. This policy required the involvement of definite relations of knowledge in relations of power; it called for a technique of overlapping subjection and objectification; it brought with it new procedures of individualization. The carceral network constituted one of the armatures of this power-knowledge that has made the human sciences historically possible. Knowable man (soul, individuality, consciousness, conduct, whatever it is called) is the object-effect of this analytical investment, of this domination-observation.

6.   This no doubt explains the extreme solidity of the prison, that slight invention that was nevertheless decried from the outset. If it had been no more than an instrument of rejection or repression in the service of a state apparatus, it would have been easier to alter its more overt forms or to find a more acceptable substitute for it. But, rooted as it was in mechanisms and strategies of power, it could meet any attempt to transform it with a great force of inertia. One fact is characteristic: when it is a question of altering the system of imprisonment, opposition does not come from the judicial institutions alone; resistance is to be found not in the prison as penal sanction, but in the prison with all its determinations, links and extrajudicial results; in the prison as the relay in a general network of disciplines and surveillances; in the prison as it functions in a panoptic regime. This does not mean that it cannot be altered, nor that it is once and for all indispensable to our kind of society. One may, on the contrary, site the two processes which, in the very continuity of the processes that make the prison function, are capable of exercising considerable restraint on its use and of transforming its internal functioning. And no doubt these processes have already begun to a large degree. The first is that which reduces the utility (or increases its inconveniences) of a delinquency accommodated as a specific illegality, locked up and supervised; thus the growth of great national or international illegalities directly linked to the political and economic apparatuses (financial illegalities, information services, arms and drugs trafficking, property speculation) makes it clear that the somewhat rustic and conspicuous work force of delinquency is proving ineffective; or again, on a smaller scale, as soon as the economic levy on sexual pleasure is carried out more efficiently by the sale of

contraceptives, or obliquely through publications, films or shows, the archaic hierarchy of prostitution loses much of its former usefulness. The second process is the growth of the disciplinary networks, the multiplication of their exchanges with the penal apparatus, the ever more important powers that are given them, the ever more massive transference to them of judicial functions; now, as medicine, psychology, education, public assistance, 'social work' assume an ever greater share of the powers of supervision and assessment, the penal apparatus will be able, in turn, to become medicalized, psychologized, educationalized; and by the same token that turning-point represented by the prison becomes less useful when, through the gap between its penitentiary discourse and its effect of consolidating delinquency, it articulates the penal power and the disciplinary power. In the midst of all these mechanisms of normalization, which are becoming ever more rigorous in their application, the specificity of the prison and its role as link are losing something of their purpose.

If there is an overall political issue around the prison, it is not therefore whether it is to be corrective or not; whether the judges, the psychiatrists or the sociologists are to exercise more power in it than the administrators or supervisors; it is not even whether we should have prison or something other than prison. At present, the problem lies rather in the steep rise in the use of these mechanisms of normalization and the wide-ranging powers which, through the proliferation of new disciplines, they bring with them.

Notes

1. In the *Postscript to the Panopticon*, 1791, Bentham adds dark inspection galleries painted in black around the inspector's lodge, each making it possible to observe two storeys of cells.
2. In his first version of the *Panopticon*, Bentham had also imagined an acoustic surveillance, operated by means of pipes leading from the cells to the central tower. In the *Postscript*, he abandoned the idea, perhaps because he could not introduce into it the principle of dissymmetry and prevent the prisoners from hearing the inspector as well as the inspectors hearing them. Julius tried to develop a system of dissymmetrial listening (Julius, 18).
3. Imagining this continuous flow of visitors entering the central tower by an underground passage and then observing the circular landscape of the Panopticon, was Bentham aware of the Panoramas that Barker was constructing at exactly the same period (the first seems to have dated from 1787) and in which the visitors, occupying the central place, saw unfolding around them a landscape, a city or a battle. The visitors occupied exactly the place of the sovereign gaze.
4. Crime was explicitly defined by certain jurists such as Muyart de Vouglans, 1767, 108 and 1780, 3, or Rousseaud de la Combe, 1–2.

References

Bentham, J. (1843) *Works*, ed. Bowring, IV.

Julius, N. H. (1831) *Leçons sur les Prisons*, I.

Touquet, H. du (1846) *De la condition des classes pauvres*.

Critical connections

Foucault's theoretical approach to understanding social and political change did much to eclipse the Marxist explanations of penal development that had dominated throughout the 1970s. Indeed, whilst Hall *et al.*'s (1978, Reading 18) *Policing the Crisis* might be thought of simultaneously as the high point and swan song of a particular period of neo-Marxist theorising about crime and authoritarian control, Foucault's (1977) *Discipline and Punish* constituted the departure point for new developments in criminological theory. His analysis of government – articulated as governmentality theory – moved away from Marxist state-centred, top-down accounts of power and sought to develop a subtler appreciation of the fluid interconnections between governing authorities, social practices, social bodies and, ultimately, social order. Governmentality theory underpins the notion of 'responsibilisation', which describes the neo-liberal state project to motivate citizens to take responsibility for their own security, promote social cohesion, report suspicious behaviours, and *work with* official control agencies for a safer society (Ericson, 2006; Reiner, 2007; Simon, 2006; see also Reading 41). Foucault's analysis of power, knowledge and the dispersal of discipline is evident in accounts of the diversification and spread of formal and informal control agencies, which, as Cohen (1985) so vividly demonstrates, can result in more people being caught in an increasingly expansive criminal justice system for longer periods. And, most significantly within the context of this book, Foucault's discussion of the panopticon has profoundly influenced – though not without criticism – attempts to understand the spread and intensification of surveillance throughout society (Readings 37 and 38).

Discussion questions

- How many forms of Panoptic surveillance can you think of, and how do they impact on your everyday life?
- In what ways might criminals and deviants be 'constituted' by the very professional discourses – for example, psychiatry, medicine, sociology – that seek to understand them?
- Assess Foucault's contention that discipline is dispersed and normalised throughout society.

References

Cohen, S. (1985) *Visions of Social Control: Crime, Punishment and Classification*, Cambridge: Polity Press.

Ericson, E. (2006) *Crime in an Insecure World*, Cambridge: Polity Press.

Reiner, R. (2007) *Law and Order: An Honest Citizen's Guide to Crime and Control*, Cambridge: Polity Press.

Simon, J. (2006) *Governing Through Crime: How the War on Crime Transformed American Democracy and Created a Culture of Fear*, Oxford: Oxford University Press.

Thomas Mathiesen

THE VIEWER SOCIETY: MICHEL FOUCAULT'S 'PANOPTICON' REVISITED (1997)

Introduction and context

INFLUENTIAL THOUGH HIS THINKING has been, even Foucault, who died in 1984, could not have envisaged the extent to which surveillant processes and practices would have spread throughout society. In an article published almost two decades after *Discipline and Punish* was first translated into English, Thomas Mathiesen contrasts Foucault's notion of Panoptic surveillance, where the few watch the many, with an opposite but for Mathiesen equally significant process, Synoptic surveillance, where the many watch the few. With the creation and global marketing of reality television shows like *Big Brother*, web-based social networking sites like MySpace and Facebook, and video sharing sites like YouTube, the parameters of surveillance have changed dramatically. Mathiesen argues that, in fact, whilst Foucault has contributed much to our understanding of surveillance, he made too little of the spread of television. Through comparing and contrasting the functioning of Panoptic and Synoptic, Mathiesen argues that Foucault's account of Panoptic power – systems administered to produce self-disciplining, docile bodies who fit well into the modern capitalist society – more closely describes the function of the Synopticon.

In 1975 Michel Foucault published his widely acclaimed and important book *Surveiller et punir: Naissance de la prison*. The book was quickly translated into a number of languages, and was first published in English by Allen Lane in 1977 under the title *Discipline and Punish: The Birth of the Prison* (Vintage edition, 1979). Through the 1970s and 1980s it exerted a strong influence on the sociology and philosophy of social control in a number of western countries. It also initiated important debates over the issues involved.

The concept and idea of 'panopticon', which Foucault borrowed from Jeremy Bentham, is among the most important in the book. It is also a concept which strongly needs to be supplemented.

Panopticism

The opening chapter of *Discipline and Punish* gives a dramatic and terrifying account of an execution in Paris. The year was 1757, and the man who was executed was a certain Robert François Damiens, who had attempted to murder the King of France, Louis XV. Those who have read the book will remember the account. The execution was brutal to say the least, Damiens was kept alive for a long time and tortured in the most painful manner, and finally torn apart by horses tied to his arms and legs. The horses had to be helped by the executioner to complete the task. The spectacle was attended by large crowds. What Foucault does not tell us is that members of the Court also attended, and that the ladies of the Court wept, not in pity with the culprit, but over the toil of the horses.[1]

This was, to repeat, 1757. The next account in Foucault's presentation – and again this is well known to his readers – implies a complete change of scene. Three-quarters of a century has passed. The year is 1838, and Foucault's source now is the rules for 'the house of young prisoners in Paris'. The life of the young prisoners is regulated by rules down to the most minute details, from the first drum roll in the morning, making the prisoners rise and dress in silence, through prayer, working hours, meals, education, rest, the washing of hands, the inspection of clothes, and finally order, silence and sleep 'at half-past seven in the summer, half-past eight in the winter'. Gone is the open brutality and uncontrolled infliction of physical pain so characteristic of Damiens' execution; instead, there is a carefully developed system of rules regulating life in full and complete detail.

What does Foucault want to illustrate by contrasting the two scenes?

First, he wants to say something about the change in the nature of punishment, from physical punishment to prison. Second, and more importantly, he wants to say something about a change in the content of punishment, from the torture of the body to the transformation of the soul. 'At the beginning of the nineteenth century', Foucault states, 'the great spectacle of physical punishment disappeared; the tortured body was avoided; the theatrical representation of pain was excluded from punishment' (Foucault, 1979: 14). Surely, prison was and is a 'corporal' kind of punishment. But in this context, the body is a tool or a link: 'During the 150 or 200 years that Europe has been setting up its new penal systems, the judges have gradually . . . taken to judging something other than crimes, namely, the "soul" of the criminal' (p. 19). As a correlate, the public character of punishment has disappeared: 'Punishment, then, will tend to become the most hidden part of the penal process' (p. 9).

Third, Foucault wants to say something about a broad historical change of social order. Apparently, this is his most essential point. 'This book is intended', he says, 'as a correlative history of the modern soul and of a new power to judge' (p. 23). Modern penal leniency is actually a technique of power, and by an analysis of it 'one might understand both how man, the soul, the normal or abnormal individual have come to duplicate crime as objects of penal intervention' (p. 24). By the control of the soul, vis-à-vis the control of the body, I understand him to mean the creation of human beings who control themselves through self-control, thus fitting neatly into a so-called democratic capitalist society.

The new prisons had, with variations, an important common form: they were organized so that a few could supervise or survey a large number. They were, in this sense, 'panoptical', from the Greek word *pan*, meaning 'all', and *opticon*, which represents the visual. To Foucault, however, the movement towards the panoptical form was not only a characteristic feature of the modern prison. A new kind of society was implied in the transformation. 'In appearance', he says, panopticism 'is merely the solution of a technical problem, but, through it, a whole new type of society emerges' (p. 216). To Foucault, panopticism represents a fundamental movement or transformation *from the situation where the many see the few to the situation where the few see the many*.

He lets the German prison reformer M.H. Julius describe the transformation. Antiquity had been the civilization of spectacle. 'To render accessible to a multitude of men the inspection of a small number of objects'; this was the problem to which the architecture of the temples, theatres and circuses responded. This was the age of public life, intensive feasts, sensual proximity. The modern age poses the opposite problem: 'To procure for a small number, or even for a single individual, the instantaneous view of a great multitude' (Julius, 1831, in Foucault, 1979: 216). Foucault formulates it this way: 'Our society is one not of spectacle, but of surveillance . . . We are much less Greeks than we believe. We are neither in the amphitheatre, nor on the stage, but in the panoptical machine, invested by its effects of power, which we bring to ourselves since we are a part of its mechanism' (p. 217).

On this background, Foucault describes how panopticism has been transported 'from the penal institution to the entire social body' (p. 298). A carceral society has been developed, in which the principle of panopticism gradually and imperceptibly has invaded ever-larger segments. 'At the moment of its full blossoming', Foucault admits, the new society 'still assumes with the Emperor the old aspect of power of spectacle'. The old monarch may be kept in the new state. But the tendency is that 'the pomp of sovereignty, the necessarily spectacular manifestations of power', gradually yield to 'the daily exercise of surveillance, in a panopticism in which the vigilance of the intersecting gazes was soon to render useless both the eagle and the sun' (p. 217). It is the normalizing gaze of panopticism which presumably produces that subjectivity, that self-control, which disciplines people to fit into a democratic capitalist society.

Synopticism

In what follows, I shall touch on the wider ramifications of Foucault's thesis, notably his perspective – as I understand it – on the control of the 'soul', but rather than providing a full discussion and interpretation of Foucault, which numerous others have provided anyway, I will largely and explicitly limit myself to putting the magnifying glass on one selected aspect of his book: the emphasis on panoptical surveillance as such. There are several good reasons for doing this. For one thing, that aspect is surely there in *Discipline and Punish* as one important component or ingredient; indeed, the French title – *Surveiller et punir* – in itself alludes to it. Second, the same aspect has in a decisive way influenced parts of criminology, notably the study of and debate about the 'widening of the net' of formal control around the prison (Cohen, 1985;

McMahon, 1992). Third, recent historical developments suggest the increasing and politically extremely great importance of the modern surveillance machines as such.

As an observer of the development of modern control systems in Norway and other western countries, I find the panoptical principle, where the few see the many, to be a pronounced aspect of various systems and parts of society. First, in the immediate circle around the prison, organized systems of surveillance of those who are released from prison have grown. Second, further away from the prison, but still within the realm of the criminal control system in a broad sense of the word, organized computer- ized surveillance of whole categories of people rather than just individuals, with a view towards possible future crimes rather than past acts, has grown enormous. In Europe, the recent enormous systems of computerized police cooperation – the Europol Information System, the Schengen Information System, the so-called Sirenes and the European Information System – are cases in point. Third, still further away from the prison, and outside the realm of the police and other formal control systems, it may be said that important social institutions have surveillance functions. It may be maintained that the school system, the medical services, the psychiatric and social systems through their classificatory and diagnostic techniques and scales, are panoptical systems with carceral functions. We certainly live in a society where the few see the many.

Yet, something of crucial importance is missing. Acceleration of surveillance where the few see the many, yes. But is Foucault right in saying that we have developed *from* a situation where the many see the few *to* a situation where the few see the many?

As a striking parallel to the panoptical process, and concurring in detail with its historical development, we have seen the development of a unique and enormously extensive system enabling *the many to see and contemplate the few*, so that the tendency for the few to see and supervise the many is contextualized by a highly significant counterpart.

I am thinking, of course, of the development of the total system of the modern mass media. It is, to put it mildly, puzzling that Michel Foucault, in a large volume which explicitly or implicitly sensitizes us inter alia to surveillance in modern society, does not mention television – or any other mass media – with a single word. It is more than just an omission; its inclusion in the analysis would necessarily in a basic way have changed his whole image of society as far as surveillance goes.

Corresponding to panopticism, imbued with certain basic parallels in structure, vested with certain reciprocal supplementary functions, and – during the past few years – merged with panopticism through a common technology, the system of modern mass media has been going through a most significant and accelerating development. The total time span of this development – the past 150 to 200 years – coincides most remark- ably with the period of the modern growth of panopticism. Increasingly, the few have been able to see the many, but also increasingly, the many have been enabled to see the few – to see the VIPs, the reporters, the stars, almost a new class in the public sphere.

Formulated in bold terms, it is possible to say that not only panopticism, but also *synopticism* characterizes our society, and characterized the transition to modernity.[2] The concept is composed of the Greek word *syn* which stands for 'together' or 'at the same time', and *opticon*, which, again, has to do with the visual. It may be used to represent the situation where a large number focuses on something in common which is condensed. In other words, it may stand for the *opposite* of the situation where the few see the many. In a two-way and significant double sense of the word we thus live in a *viewer society*.

As I have said, the panoptical and the synoptical structures show several conspicuous parallels in development, and they together, precisely together, serve decisive control functions in modern society. Let us first look at some of the parallels, and, by way of conclusion, the control functions.

Parallels

I want to emphasize three parallels:

1   The first one has been alluded to already and strikes the eye immediately: *the acceleration which synopticism as well as panopticism has shown in modern times, that is, during the period 1800–2000.*

The story and history of the media is well known, but has to be sketched briefly in order to place the panoptical development in perspective. Foucault takes the modern prison, which came between 1750 and 1830, as his point of departure for panopticism. Precisely at the same time, between 1750 and 1830, the mass press was born – the first wave of mass media after the printed book. Though we had newspapers in the 1700s, the 1800s was the seminal century, and the 1830s was a seminal decade in what was to become the mass media society par excellence, the USA. In 1833 Benjamin Day founded the *New York Sun*. Two months later, on 3 September 1833, the circulation was 3000, and after five years it was 30,000. James Gordon Bennett's *Herald*, also of New York, was the main competitor. In 1836, Bennett wrote:

> Books have had their day – the theatres have had their day – the temple of religion has had its day. A newspaper can be made to take the lead in all of these in the great movements of human thought and of human civilization. A newspaper can send more souls to heaven, and save more from Hell, than all of the churches or chapels in New York – besides making money at the same time.
>
> (quoted in De Fleur and Ball-Rokeach, 1989: 54)

The growth of the newspaper presupposed a comprehensive scientific and technical development which took place about the same time – the train and the steam ship, which facilitated the distribution of newspapers as well as the interchange of news, and the telegraph, which made rapid communication of news possible. It also presupposed important social conditions: a changed political role of the citizens and the development of a large middle class followed by the growth of trade and consequently of large markets. In a peripheral country like Norway, the same development took place, only a little later.

And, as we know, then came the other media, in a neatly packed row (for details of the development, see De Fleur and Ball-Rokeach, 1989; for Norway, see Mathiesen, 1993), as striking parallels to the development of panopticism. The second wave was the film, also founded on a complex set of technological innovations and social conditions. First silent film, then film with a sound track added, black-and-white film, and finally colour film. The enormous popularity of the film implied the gathering of large crowds of people in large film theatres, blatantly contradicting Foucault's thesis that in modern times we have moved away from the situation where the many see the few, away from synopticism. The popularity of the film presupposed a social structure where mobility, especially out of the family, was possible. In turn, the film probably also facilitated such mobility.

Then came the radio, followed by television, as the third and fourth wave. Television shared the history of the radio as well as its financial basis, its traditions and talents. A large number of complex social circumstances established a need and a search for new communication media which could communicate instantaneous messages over very great distances. An understanding of electricity in the 1900s constituted the foundation of instantaneous communication in its modern form (instantaneous communication was not unknown in earlier times – drum signals and smoke signals in so-called primitive societies, the semaphore stations in Napoleon's France, and so on). The radio was in many ways a by-product of a long, continuous and basic chain of investigations into electrical energy. The 1920s was the great decade for the establishment of regular broadcasting from a number of stations in the United States and other parts of the world.

And, finally, from 1945 in the United States and 1960 in Norway, television, based on a technology developed before and during the Second World War. The basic synopti-cal character of the media was in a fundamental way enhanced by television. As televi-sion developed, millions, hundreds of millions, of people could see the few on the stage, first by the aid of the camera after the event, and more recently on the spot and directly. We may speak of a fifth wave, from the 1980s on, with the enormous technological advances in the form of video, cables and satellites, in Norway and other countries accompanied by privatization of radio and television, as well as digital technology and entirely new pathways of communication. With the plethora of television channels, a decentralization has also taken place, so that there are many synopticons. But there are certainly also many panopticons, many surveillance systems. The decentralized, narrowly oriented panopticons may quickly be combined into large broad-ranging sys-tems by simple technological devices, covering large categories of people in full detail. So may, on given important occasions, the various decentralized synopticons, and in terms of general content the synopticons are strikingly similar.

In his account of society as developing *from* a situation where the many see the few *to* a situation where the few see the many, Foucault fails to take into account all of the major waves of synoptical development briefly outlined above. Perhaps he could not foresee the developments in the 1980s and 1990s, but the major trends were certainly visible in 1975. [. . .]

2   Second, the panoptical surveillance structure and the media structure are parallel in that they are archaic, or 'ancient', as means or potential means of power in society.

Clearly it is Foucault's view that the history of the panoptical structure as a main model commenced in the late 1700s and the early 1800s, though he also mentions historical lines going further back, and he does mention that the panoptical techniques taken 'one by one' have 'a long history behind them' (1979: 224). This historical understanding is expressed through the dramatic *break*, which Foucault emphasized so strongly, from the control policy of the mid-1700s to that of the mid-1800s.

This historical understanding must be wrong. It seems closer to the facts that a panoptical system, though strongly developed during the most recent two centuries, has ancient historical roots; that not only individual surveillance techniques, but the very model of the panoptical surveillance system, goes back to the early Christian era or before. Indeed, in the Gospel of Luke (Luke 2:1) it is stated: 'And it came to pass in those days that there went out a decree from Caesar Augustus that all the world shall be taxed. And this taxing was first made when Cirenius was governor of Syria. And all went to be taxed, everyone into his own city.' The Roman State, in other words, undertook such a large task as to tax, and thereby register, what was at the time 'all the world' in the archives of the state. The surveillance was hardly always successful as a control measure; Herod failed in his search for at least one first-born male child. But this is not the last time surveillance systems have failed to 'hit'; it is indeed a characteristic also of modern data systems. Probably all great state structures in history have had such systems, at least in elementary form. In our own more recent history, three institutions have been particularly important: the church, the Inquisition and the military. I will return to them shortly.

Synopticism is equally ancient, with the emphasis on maximum diffusion from a few leading figures of visual impressions, sound impressions and other impressions. Foucault emphasizes the ancient nature of this structure, though he does not relate it to the media – his point is that it *is* the old form. The older institutions of spectacle differed in several respects from the modern ones. In the older context, people were gathered together; in the modern media context, the 'audience' has increasingly been delocalized so that people have become isolated from each other. In the older context, 'sender' and 'receiver' were in each other's proximity, be it in the ancient theatre or the festivals and image-building of the Colosseum; in the modern media context, distance between the two may be great. Such differences, and especially the general fragmentation which is alluded to here, may have consequences for persuasion as well as protest. Yet, the similarity and continuity is also striking.

The main point here is that the models of both systems go back far beyond the 1700s, and that they have historical roots in central social and political institutions. What has happened in the 1800s, and especially in the 1900s, is that organizational and technological changes have advanced the use of *both models* by leaps and bounds, thus making them into two basic characteristics of modernity.

3   Third, and most importantly, panopticism and synopticism *have developed in inti-mate interaction, even fusion, with each other*. The same institutions have often been panoptical as well as synoptical. Historically we have many examples of this.

The Roman Catholic Church, with the confession during which many isolated individuals confide their secrets one by one to the unseen representative of the Church, has functioned panoptically as a setting in which the few – the priests – have seen and surveyed the many – the people of the town. Simultaneously, the Catholic Church has definitely functioned synoptically, with its enormous cathedrals intentionally placed in very visible locations for synoptical admiration, drawing large masses of people to listen to the sermon, and with the Pope speaking from the balcony of St Peter's on Easter Day.

The Inquisition was panoptical; indeed, panopticism was its very purpose in relation to heresy and witchcraft from the 1200s on: 'As a spider it sat there on guard, watching so that catholicism was not exposed to harmful influences from abroad or from corrupted souls within the country itself' (Henningsen, 1981: 28; translated from the Danish by the present author). But it was also synoptical, with its manifestations of great authority through its many visitations, with the highly visible Inquisitor up front, throughout the communities of the enormous Spanish empire.

The military has always had a strict disciplinary hierarchy providing possibilities for hidden surveillance from the upper echelons of the system. But it has also been synoptical with highly visible military leaders victoriously entering the city after the battle.

Even more clearly the interaction – indeed, fusion – of panopticism and synopticism may be seen in the old prison chapels from the 1800s. They were panoptical in that the minister could see all of the prisoners sitting isolated in their booths, but they were at the same time synoptical in that the prisoners, from their booths, could see only one person – the minister in the pulpit.

In modern times, the interaction has taken new form, and concrete fusion is even more pronounced. First of all, in our century, panopticism and synopticism have developed on the basis of a joint technology. The telegraph and the radio have, as I have already mentioned, been methods on both sides. In our own time, television, video, satellites, cables and modern computer development are joint technological features. In his book *1984* George Orwell described panopticism and synopticism in their ultimate form as completely merged: through a screen in your living room you saw Big Brother, just as Big Brother saw you. We have not come this far, but we clearly see tendencies for panopticism and synopticism to merge into one. A fusion takes place between the two structures in the 'electronic super highway'. Today it is technologically entirely possible to have a large number of consumers synoptically watch television and order and pay for the commodities advertised, as well as undertaking a number of other economic transactions, while the producers of the commodities panoptically survey everyone, controlling the consumers' ability to pay, ensuring that payment takes place, or interrupting the transaction if solvency does not obtain.

Great emphasis has recently been placed on various forms of interactive mass media. The Norwegian author and lawyer Jon Bing has described the 'interactive novel', where the receiver participates with active inputs, thus creating the novel in cooperation and interaction with the original author. His book on the topic has the suggestive title *The Book is Dead! Long Live the Book!* (Bing, 1984). The Internet, World Wide Web and the numerous video games which have entered the market are further cases in point. The receiver actively enters the system and takes out the information needed, combines it with still other pieces of information in numerous novel ways, and actively transmits his own information to others through the Web pages, or in the case of games, activates actors in various ways through the game. [. . .]

What about power?

Before concluding, an elaboration is necessary as far as synopticism goes: is *power* actually represented in the media? This is an important question. To repeat, Foucault wrote that 'the pomp of sovereignty, the necessarily spectacular manifestations of power', have today gradually yielded to 'the daily exercise of surveillance, in a panopticism in which the vigilance of the intersecting gazes was soon to render useless both the eagle and the sun'. The power of visible and concrete rulers was and is fading away. This perspective fits nicely with Foucault's view of power in modern society: the visible actors' power in central institutions of state and society is blurred, indistinct and even unimportant; instead, power is a phenomenon permeating society as invisible micropower.

If this is true, and if those we meet and see in the media are just ornamental figures without power, Foucault's omission of synopticism might not be so serious.

I do not think it is true, and find reason to give an affirmative answer to the question of whether power – indeed, great power – is located in concrete individuals and concrete delimited groups as represented in our mass media. The eagle and the sun have not been extinguished, but are expressed in a different way. This is probably especially so in the most visible media. It does not mean that Foucault's micropower, which cannot be delimited to definite performers but which silently permeates the social fabric, is unimportant. Both perspectives, the perspective of micropower but also that of *the actor's* power, are necessary.

In synoptic space, particular news reporters, more or less brilliant media personalities and commentators who are continuously visible and seen are of particular importance. To understand them just as ornamental figures is to underestimate them. They actively filter and shape information; as has been widely documented in media research, they produce news (for an early documentation, see Cohen and Young, 1973; see also Tuchman, 1978); they place topics on the agenda and avoid placing topics on the agenda (Protess and McCombs, 1991). To be sure, all of this is performed within the context of a broader hidden agenda of political or economic interests, so to speak behind the media (Curran and Seaton, 1988; Murdock, 1988). But this does not detract from the importance and role of the visible actors, on the stage. Stage setters also operate behind and outside the scene. But the visible personalities cooperate with them, contributing significantly in their way – as creative mouthpieces – to the collective and enormously important staging of the great moments in the nation and the world, such as the staging of the Gulf War, so favourable to American interests, in 1991 (see Johnsen and Mathiesen, 1991,1992; Ottosen, 1992), and the Olympic Games in Atlanta and the Republican Party Convention, both in 1996.

It is interesting to see what public opinion polls tell us about people's *confidence* in media personalities. Two nationwide representative Norwegian studies from 1991 and 1993 revealed very great confidence throughout the Norwegian population in prominent television personalities – particular charismatic reporters, commentators and so on. As far as it may be measured through opinions polls of this kind, these reporters and commentators did not only compete effectively, in people's minds, with very central and internationally known and popular politicians. They were even partly ahead in terms of confidence. This brings us to the core of their importance: it appears that the classical and greatly influential 'two step hypothesis' about the influence of the media, in which opinion leaders in outside society are seen as links and transmitters of media messages from the media to the larger population (Lazarsfeld et al., 1948), must be revised. As the Norwegian sociologist Ole Kristian Hjemdal has pointed out,[3] television has produced television personalities who *themselves*, from the screen, function as opinion leaders and links between the media message and people – well known, dear to us, and on the face of it close to us.

But this does not end the story of power. Second, we must add what we know about who are allowed to enter the media from the outside to express their views.

A number of international and Norwegian studies have shown that they systematically belong to *the institutional elites*. Those who are allowed to enter are systematically men – not women – from the higher social strata, with power in political life, private industry and public bureaucracy (a summary of the findings is provided in Mathiesen, 1993: 152–8). From a democratic point of view, the dominance of the television personalities is serious enough through the filtering of information and so on which we know they perform. The problem of democracy is in a decisive way enlarged by the dominance of the institutional elites.

But do not many people with power actively try to avoid the limelight of public attention? Certainly, today as in former times. Nevertheless, they are in an interesting and important way represented by hired information professionals. This point of view has been forcefully presented by the Norwegian sociologist and journalist Sigurd Allern (1992, quotes translated from the Norwegian by the present author). Allern writes that

> . . . the point is not only that the media and journalists *choose* sources. The roles may also be reversed, so that the sources choose the media; they operate professionally and in a goal-oriented way to establish the premises for news production. *The sources* have become constantly more professionalized.

In business, public administration and large-scale organizations there has taken place during the past few decades 'a systematic organizational development to meet the bureaucratic quest for news on the part of the press' (p. 94). 'Information', which in actual fact is influence, has 'become an integrated part of the activity of industrial companies, financial institutions, ministries, police, municipal services and professional organizations' (p. 94). The information professionals have become highly visible and valuable sources of information for the media; informational activity has become an occupation. The information professionals are trained to filter information, and to present images which are favourable to the institution or organization in question. [. . .]

Control functions

Finally, I arrive at the question of control functions. I use the concept here in its simplest possible form, as change in behaviour or attitude in a wide sense, following from the influence of others. 'Control', then, is something more than 'surveillance'; it implies the regulation of behaviour or attitude which may follow for example from surveillance. I use the concept of 'discipline', Foucault's term, as a synonym.

There is an ongoing discussion of whether panopticism and synopticism, surveillance and the media, in fact have the effect of control or discipline (Bottoms, 1983; Waldahl, 1989). The discussion should be taken beyond the effects of isolated, single measures or messages, which has characterized media research in particular. The question is the effects of the total pattern of surveillance measures or media messages. Thus, with regard to the media, the total Gestalt produced by the messages of television is much more important than the individual programme or even type of programme.

The American media researcher George Gerbner and associates have pointed to this in a number of empirical works. As they succinctly put it:

> [The point is a concept of] broad enculturation rather than of narrow changes in opinion or behavior. Instead of asking what communication 'variables' might propagate what kinds of individual behavior changes, we want to know what types of common consciousness whole systems of messages might cultivate. This is less like asking about preconceived fears and hopes and more like asking about the 'effects' of Christianity on one's views of the world or – as the Chinese *had* asked – of Confucianism on public morality.
> (Gerbner and Gross, 1976: 180)

The question is, then, the control or discipline of behaviour and attitude. That aspect of *panopticism* which consists of the growth of a modern veiled and secret surveillance industry, and which preoccupies us here, first of all controls or disciplines our *behaviour*. In this respect the modern surveillance systems are very different from the old panoptical prisons, which are also growing by leaps and bounds. The latter inflict great pain on those who inhabit them. But a vast amount of research shows that they have no effect, or at most a marginal effect, in terms of controlled behaviour (Mathiesen, 1990). Rather, I am thinking of the vast hidden apparatus, and the effect of this apparatus on people in usual or unusual political situations. Well aware of 'the intersecting gazes' of panopticism, but unable to point concretely to them – this is the nature of their secrecy – we arrange our affairs accordingly, perhaps without being fully aware of it. We remain, in our attitude, communists, left-oriented, or what have you, but adjust in terms of behaviour.

Two major examples come to mind. First, the McCarthy period in the US in the 1950s. I experienced the 1950s in McCarthy's own state, at the University of Wisconsin. Communists remained communists, but they became cautious, secretive and partly silent. Second, the activities of the Norwegian secret police from 1945 until the mid-1980s. Extensive unacceptable and illegal surveillance activities have recently been uncovered in an authoritative report delivered by a commission appointed by Parliament (The Lund Report, 1996). The report only verified what communists and other left-oriented groups had said for years. It contains numerous accounts of how communists remained communists and Marxist-Leninists remained Marxist-Leninists, but also of how they adjusted in terms of behaviour, became cautious and secretive, using cover names even for their children when attending political summer camps (it was documented that children down to the age of 11 had been registered). Psychological breakdowns, with repercussions throughout whole families, ensued. The argument that surveillance has negligible effect on behaviour was dramatically contradicted.

Other features of the political situation at the time were no doubt also important in both instances – the Cold War in the wake of the Second World War being one of them. But in the Norwegian case, widespread surveillance as well as the behavioural effects of it continued through the 1970s and 1980s, and to some extent even in the 1990s, and the effects on behaviour are concretely demonstrated.

What I have said here is, as far as it goes, in line with Foucault: to him, the fact that the torture of the docile body came to an end did not mean that the body ceased to be an object of attention. It just took place in a different way: 'The human body was entering a machinery of power that explores it, breaks it down and rearranges it' (1979: 138). But at the same time, as I have said before, he saw his book as 'a correlative history of the modern soul'. To repeat, by the control of the soul, vis-à-vis the control of the body, I understand him to mean the creation of human beings who control themselves through self-control.

My guess is that the souls in our time, and precisely in Foucault's sense as I understand it, above all belong to the other machinery, that of *synopticism*, and that James Gordon Bennett in fact was right when in 1836 he said just that about the mass media. My point is that synopticism, through the modern mass media in general and television in particular, first of all directs and controls or disciplines our *consciousness*. The concept of 'consciousness industry' (Enzenberger, 1974; Tuchman, 1981) is suggestive: to Enzenberger, the modern media encourage the 'industrialization of mind', 'they foster a consciousness conducive to advanced industrialism, just as some fifty years ago, earlier industrialists and efficiency experts transformed the body into an extension of the machine' (Tuchman, 1981: 84), thus – in my words – inducing self-control and making us fit into the requirements of modernity. Max Horkheimer and Theodor Adorno pointed to this process, in the context of their time, half a century ago in their analysis of the culture industry (Horkheimer and Adorno, 1947/1969), and their presentation seems all the more relevant today.

To repeat, it is the total pattern or Gestalt rather than the individual programme or type of programmes which functions this way, à la Gerbner, like Christianity 'on one's views of the world'. Surely, there are variations which are obvious topics for research, and which have been extensively researched: when people have first-hand knowledge, when the issues are close to people's everyday life, and when people have access to alternative information, and so on, the effects are smaller. Indeed, this is also how Christianity worked and continues to work. But the variations should not make us overlook the effect of the total message system. The total message inculcates or produces a general understanding of the world, a *world paradigm* if you like, which emphasizes personal and individual, the deviant, the shuddering, the titillating – as alluded to already, the entertaining in a wide sense (Postman, 1985). The paradigm is successful because it is received in the context of a need – satisfies a need – for escape from the concrete misery of the world, very much like the Church which offered rescue and salvation in the hereafter. It is by satisfying the need for escape that people are made to acquiesce, accept and fit into the requirements of our society. In this sense, the Church and television are real functional alternatives, a relationship which has been explored in such detail and so eloquently by James Curran (1988).

Each from their side, like a pincer, panopticon and synopticon thus subdue or even make silent what Pierre Bourdieu calls 'the heterodox debate' (Bourdieu, 1977: Chapter 4), that is, the debate which raises the basic critical questions concerning the very foundation of our life and existence. We are left, again in Bourdieu's terminology, with 'the orthodox debate', where the answers to the basic questions are taken for granted, and the debate concerns details and remains on the surface. In bold relief: surveillance, panopticon, makes us silent about that which breaks fundamentally with the taken-for-granted because we are made afraid to break with it. Modern television, synopticon, makes us silent because we do not have anything to talk about that might initiate the break.

It does not improve matters that panopticon and synopticon reciprocally feed on each other. Those parts of modern panopticon which I am concerned with here, the secret apparatuses of surveillance, try to keep synopticon at arm's length. After all, they wish to live under cover. But this is precisely where other parts of panopticon, in and close to the old prison, have their function. News from these parts of panopticon – news about prisoners, escapes, robberies, murder – are the best pieces of news which synopticon – television and the tabloid newspapers – can find. Inside synopticon, which devours this news, the material is purged of everything but the purely criminal – what was originally a small segment of a human being becomes the whole human being – whereupon the material is hurled back into the open society as stereotypes and panic-like, terrifying stories about individual cases, thus completely contradicting Foucault's thesis that punishment tends to become the most hidden part of the penal process. The execution in Paris in 1757 becomes, as a spectacle, peanuts compared to the executions (real or metaphoric) on the screens of modern television. This way, a basis is established for more resources to be given not only to the expansion of prisons, but also to the concealed panoptical surveillance systems: the modern European computerized regis-tration and surveillance systems mentioned earlier are, on the formal level, motivated by crime prevention. But empirically we can safely say that they hardly prevent much crime. The 'hit' figures as far as official crime goes are extremely low (Mathiesen, 1996: 28–9). In the light of the mass media image of crime, the low 'hit' figures are taken as a sign that still more resources are needed. And so it continues in a circle.

Taken as a whole, things are much *worse* than Michel Foucault imagined. The total situation clearly calls for political resistance (Mathiesen, 1982). But to muster such double resistance is a difficult task, because the call for resistance may – in line with what I have argued in this article – be silenced by the very panopticon and synopticon which we wish to counteract. In the years to come, much effort and lots of time should therefore be devoted to the search for the roads to resistance.

Notes

1.   Oral information from the Swedish historian Erik Anners.
2.   The concept was first used by the Danish sociologist Frank Henriksen, in a review of a book I had written on the topic I deal with here (Henriksen, 1985; Mathiesen, 1985).
3.   Oral communication to the author.

References

Allern, Sigurd (1992) *Kildenes makt. Ytringsfrihetens politiske økonomi* (The Power of the Sources. The Political Economy of the Freedom of Expression). Oslo: Pax Publishers.

Bing, Jon (1984) *Boken er død! Leve boken! og andre essays om informasjons-politikk* (The Book is Dead! Long Live the Book! and Other Essays in the Politics of Information). Oslo: Norwegian Universities Press.

Bottoms, Anthony E. (1983) 'Neglected Features of Contemporary Penal Systems', in D. Garland and P. Young (eds) *The Power to Punish. Contemporary Penality and Social Analysis*, pp. 166–202. London: Heinemann.

Bourdieu, Pierre (1977) *Outline of a Theory of Practice*. Cambridge: Cambridge University Press.

Cohen, Stanley (1985) *Visions of Social Control. Crime, Punishment and Classification*. Cambridge: Polity Press.

Cohen, Stanley and Jock Young (eds) (1973) *The Manufacture of News. Social Problems, Deviance and the Mass Media*. London: Constable.

Curran, James (1988) 'Communications, Power and Social Order', in Michael Gurevitsch, Tony Bennett, James Curran and Janet Woollacott (eds) *Culture, Society and the Media*, pp. 202–35. London: Methuen.

Curran, James and Jean Seaton (1988) *Power Without Responsibility. The Press and Broadcasting in Britain*. London: Routledge.

De Fleur, Melvin and Sandra Ball-Rokeach (1989) *Theories of Mass Communication*. New York: Longman.

Enzenberger, Hans Magnus (1974) *The Consciousness Industry*. New York: Seabury Press.

Foucault, Michel (1979) *Discipline and Punish. The Birth of the Prison*. New York: Vintage.

Gerbner, George and Larry Gross (1976) 'Living with Television. The Violence Profile', *Journal of Communication* 26 (2): 173–98.

Henningsen, Gustav (1981) *Heksenes advokat* (The Witches' Advocate). Copenhagen: Delta Publishers.

Henriksen, Frank (1985) Anmeldelse av T. Mathiesen: *Seer-samfundet* (Review of T. Mathiesen: The Viewer Society), *Sociolog-nyt* 96: 35–6.

Horkheimer, Max and Theodor Adorno (1947/1969) 'Kulturindustrie. Auf-klärung als Massenbetrug', in *Dialektik der Aufflärung*, Frankfurt: S. Fischer Verlag.

Johnsen, Jan and Thomas Mathiesen (eds) (1991) *Mediekrigen. Søkelys på massemedienes dekning av Golfkrigen* (The Media War. The Media Coverage of the Gulf War under Scrutiny). Oslo: Cappelen.

Johnsen, Jan and Thomas Mathiesen (1992) 'A War in the Name of Freedom', *The Nordicom Review of Nordic Mass Communication Research* 2: 3–19.

Lazarsfeld, Paul F., Bernard Berelson and Hazel Gaudet (1948) *The People's Choice. How the Voter makes up his Mind in a Presidential Campaign*. New York: Columbia University Press.

McMahon (1992) *The Persistent Prison? Rethinking Decarceration and Penal Reform*. Toronto: Toronto University Press.

Mathiesen, Thomas (1982) *Makt og motmakt* (Power and Counter-Power). Oslo: Pax Publishers.

Mathiesen, Thomas (1985) *Tittarsamhället. Om medier och kontrol i det moderna samhället* (The Viewer Society. On Media and Control in Modern Society). Göteborg: Korpen Publishers.

Mathiesen, Thomas (1990) *Prison on Trial. A Critical Assessment*. London: Sage Publications.

Mathiesen, Thomas (1993) *Makt og medier. En innføring i mediesosiologi* (Power and the Media. An Introduction to Media Sociology). Oslo: Pax Publishers.

Mathiesen, Thomas (1996) *Er Schengen noe for Norge? Et bidrag til europeisk politiforskning* (Is Schengen Something for Norway? A Contribution to European Police Research). Oslo: Institute for Sociology of Law Series No. 54.

Murdock, Graham (1988) 'Large Corporations and the Control of the Communications Industries', in Michael Gurevitsch, Tony Bennett, James Curran and Janet Woollacott (eds) *Culture, Society and the Media*, pp. 118–50. London: Methuen.

Ottosen, Rune (1992) 'The Allied Forces' "Media Victory" in the Gulf. Waterloo for Journalism?', *The Nordicom Review of Nordic Mass Communication Research* 2: 31–47.

Postman, Neil (1985) *Amusing Ourselves to Death. Public Discourse in the Age of Show Business*. London: Heinemann.

Protess, David and Maxwell McCombs (eds) (1991) *Agenda Setting: Readings on the Media, Public Opinion and Policy Making*. Hillsdale, NJ: Lawrence Erlbaum.

The Lund Report (1996) *Rapport til Stortinget fra kommisjonen som ble nedsatt av Stortinget for à granske påstander om ulovlig overvåking av norske borgere (Lund-rapporten)* (Report to Parliament from the Commission Appointed by Parliament to Investigate Allegations Concerning Illegal Surveillance of Norwegian Citizens.) Document No. 15, 1995–96, delivered to Parliament 28 March 1996.

Tuchman, Gaye (1978) *Making News. A Study in the Construction of Reality*. New York: The Free Press.

Tuchman, Gaye (1981) 'Myth and the Consciousness Industry: A New Look at the Effects of the Mass Media', in Elihu Katz and Tamás Szecskö (eds) *Mass Media and Social Change*, pp. 83–100. London: Sage.

Waldahl, Ragnar (1989) *Mediepåvirkning* (Media Influence). Oslo: Ad Notam Publishers.

Critical connections

Mathiesen gives close consideration to the role of television in the shift to a 'viewer society'. At the time of writing the article, however, one of the clearest manifestations of this society was yet to emerge. The explosion of 'reality television' programming, exemplified in the global phenomenon that is *Big Brother*, embodies both panopticism and synopticism in a mediatised orgy of surveillant practices (McCahill, 2002). Whilst producers watch the contestants, who never know when they are being 'watched' but know they are being 'filmed' at all times (panopticism), literally millions of television viewers watch the housemates, whose every move (and with each new series this increasingly means *every* move) is caught on camera and broadcast on some channels 24 hours a day (synopticism). The insatiable desire to be watched, to be caught on camera or film, to have one's life not only recorded (by oneself) but shared among others, is perfectly encapsulated in web-based social networking sites like MySpace and Facebook, and video sharing sites like YouTube. This desire is discussed by Susan Sontag in a very different context in Reading 42. With the creation and global marketing of these new forms of communication and social interaction, the parameters of surveillance – scope, direction, intensity, depth, duration – continue to change dramatically.

Discussion questions

- Outline the central characteristics of Mathiesen's 'viewer society' and explain its historical development.
- How many forms of synoptic surveillance can you think of, and how do they impact on your everyday life?
- In what ways to do syntopticism and panopticism converge in popular culture, and in the culture of control?

References

Haggerty, K. & Ericson, R. (2000) 'The Surveillant Assemblage', in *British Journal of Sociology*, 51, 4: 605–622.

McCahill, M. (2002) *The Surveillance Web: The Rise of Visual Surveillance in an English City*. Cullompton: Willan.

Clive Norris and Gary Armstrong

WORKING RULES AND THE SOCIAL CONTRUCTION OF SUSPICION (1999)

Introduction and context

TODAY, VIRTUALLY ALL DEVELOPED and most developing countries across the globe could be described as surveillance societies, if an acceptable definition of such is any society that is 'dependent on communication and information technologies for administrative and control purposes' (Lyon (2001: 1). Of course, some level of surveillance and monitoring is a requirement for the smooth and efficient functioning of society. Banking, credit and financial transactions, travel, attendance at public events, and electronic and digital communication all require the surrendering (whether directly or indirectly) of certain bits of personal data that can reveal the identity, whereabouts and actions of the individual. More fundamentally, universal suffrage requires that every citizen's name, age, sex and residential address is recorded so that people can exercise their right to vote. Surveillance can, then, work as an essential mechanism for protecting individual rights and freedoms. But its relentless spread around the world also brings with it unintended consequences with darker dimensions.

Clive Norris and Gary Armstrong's (1999) *The Maximum Surveillance Society: The Rise of CCTV* takes an in-depth look at how this now ubiquitous technology is deployed and understood by those who use it. They map out and critique the transformations which have occurred in the nature of surveillance, and suggest that, as CCTV surveillance has proliferated, the surveilled have come increasingly to be viewed not as individual private citizens with rights, but as either consumers or criminals. Their theoretical discussion is influenced by Foucault's notion of Panopticon (Reading 36), as well as other key thinkers on surveillance, crime and control. The reading included here is excerpted from their in-depth fieldwork on automated CCTV surveillance systems in Britain. Situated across three different regions, Norris and Armstrong identify seven Working Rules that appear to inform the daily activities of the

CCTV operatives. These rules reveal the significance of class, race, gender and age as important mediators in decision making about what constitutes suspicious behaviour and is therefore worthy of further attention, and what, in contrast, is deemed innocuous and mundane.

The working rules in operation

Rule One – *Given the sheer volume of candidates for targeted surveillance, the operators utilise their already existing understanding of who is most likely to commit crime or be troublesome to provide potential candidates for targeted surveillance.*

It will come as no surprise to anyone who is aware of the literature on police suspicion that CCTV operators adopt similar criteria to construct the targeted population: focusing on the young rather than the old, disproportionately targeting blacks rather than whites, men as opposed to women, and the working rather than middle classes (McConville et al. 1991; Norris et al. 1992). Of course, it may be argued that, since those officially recorded as deviant are disproportionately young, male, black, and working class that targeting such groups merely reflects the underlying reality of the distribution of criminality. Such an argument is, however, circular: the production of the official statistics is also based on pre-given assumptions as to the distribution of criminality which itself leads to the particular configuration of formal and informal operational police practice. As McConville et al. argue, the convicted population 'is a subset of the official suspect population. Whilst convicted criminals may be broadly representative of suspects, there is good reason to believe that they are very dissimilar to the "real criminal population". . . The make up of the convicted population is, therefore, like the make up of the suspect population: a police construction' (1991: 35).

Targeting youth

As we have seen, young men were the main targets of surveillance. This is not surprising given the attitudes that operators displayed towards youth in general and particularly those identified by attire, location or body language as poor or belonging to the underclass. Like the police, operators often referred to such categories as 'toerags', 'scumbags', 'yobs', 'scrotes', and 'crapheads'. As the following two examples illustrate operatives need no special reason to ascribe malign intent merely on the basis of age, particularly if youth are in a group:

> 13.45 – The operator sees and zooms in on four boys walking through a pedestrian precinct. Aged between 10—12 and casually, but fashionably dressed the four in combining age, appearance, location and numbers are suspects for a variety of possibilities. The four gather around in a form of 'conference' and 30 seconds later walk a few yards to their left and enter a shop renowned for selling toys. What the operator sees is not kids entering a shop meant for kids, but sees something else – they are all up to no good and in his opinion have probably just plotted to steal and will be

coming running out any minute with stolen merchandise. In anticipation he fixes a camera onto the shop door and tells the other operator to put the cameras onto the street he presumes they will run into.

Using two cameras and two operators the surveillance lasts six minutes before the boys leave the shop – slowly and orderly and without any apparent stolen goods. Now, the operator informs me, he will zoom in on the four as they walk through town in a search for bulges under their clothing, particularly around the waistline – this according to him is where stolen toys would be concealed. But the boys have jeans and T-shirts on and no bulges are apparent. Still, however, the four are followed by both operators to see if they will pull items out of their pockets – they don't. The four then disappear from view as they enter another department store. The operator looks elsewhere, but comments to his colleague 'They're definitely up to no good.'

16.45 – Impending criminal activity is noticed when three males aged 16 are noticed standing around a market stall displaying watches. The operator zooms in with his camera and gets his colleague to do the same with another camera from a different angle. They then wait . . . but the youths merely walk away having neither purchased nor stolen anything. The operator is left to muse, saying 'I wonder why they changed their minds?' (3 minutes, 1 camera)

While youth is generally seen as suspicious and warranting of targeted surveillance, this would still leave operators with far too many candidates to choose from on the basis of the images alone. Two additional features become salient for further subdividing youth into those who are worthy of more intensive surveillance and those who are not: attire and posture.

The following garments were thought by operatives to be indicative of the criminal intent of the wearer: 'puffer' coats (ski-style fashion), track suit bottoms, designer training shoes, baseball caps (ponytail hairstyles only compounded suspicion) and anything that may conceal the head, be it a woolly hat, hood or cap and football shirts or supporter paraphernalia. Any type of loose-fitting jacket could provoke suspicion because in the operators' eyes it may conceal stolen items or weapons, as would a jacket or headgear worn in warm weather. Young females were only guilty by association, i.e. if seen with 'scrote' boys. Otherwise they were not a category worthy of surveillance unless they were good looking. [. . .]

Colour-coded suspicion

Racist language was not unusual to hear among CCTV operators and, although only used by a minority of operators, the terms 'Pakis', 'Jungle Bunnies' and 'Sooties' when used by some operatives did not produce howls of protests from their colleagues or line managers. Stereotypical negative attitudes towards ethnic minorities and black youth in particular were more widespread and ranged from more extreme beliefs, held by a few operators, about their inherent criminality to more general agreement as to their being work shy, 'too lazy' to get a job and in general 'trouble'.

Given these assumptions the sighting of a black face on the streets of either Metro City or County Town would almost automatically produce a targeted surveillance.

> 14.00 – Whilst surfing the cameras and streets the operator sees two young men standing in a pedestrian shopping precinct both looking into a holdall bag one of them is carrying. Whilst this scene is not remarkable what is unusual is that one of the two is black, a rare sight in the city centre. The two are in their early 20s and smartly dressed. After a minute or so one hands to the other a piece of paper which most onlookers would presume was an address or phone number. Finally, on going their separate ways the two indulge in a fashionable 'high-five' handshake. This alerts both operators.
>
> To these two the 'high-five' was suspicious because it was not done with flat-hands and it 'wasn't firm enough'. In fact according to the second operator one of the men had a distinctly cupped hand. Whilst this was explainable by his holding the piece of paper just given him by the other the operators see only criminality – this could be a surreptitious, yet overtly public exchange of drugs. The youth with the bag is surveilled closely as he continues his walk. He not only has a bag, possibly the mer- chandise, but he is also black – a drug dealer. The suspect then enters a men's fashion store which means that the camera is now trained on the doors whilst the operator awaits a possible hasty reappearance complete with stolen items in shoulder bag. After a few minutes the camera is zoomed into the store and the suspect is visible in a capacity the operators did not consider – he is a sales assistant.

This colour-coded suspicion was intensified when combined with cars, or headgear, or being in places the operators presumed they should not be:

> 15.00 – A black male with dreadlocks, wearing sports gear, and in his mid-20s is inviting the operators' suspicion and surveillance because he is in the wrong place doing the wrong thing. He is in fact crouched by a bicycle rack fiddling about with a bike. Zooming in the operator looks for evidence of a theft – is he looking around him as he fiddles? no, is he forcing something which won't move? no. He then gets something out of his back pocket – this happens to be a bicycle rear lamp. Fitting it on he rides the bicycle, which is obviously his, safely and legally. (4 minutes, 1 camera)

> 23.05 – A group of 12 black youths all in their late teens and casually dressed are noted outside a fast-food outlet. They are doing nothing more than eating and talking to various youths, male and female, white and black, who approach them. However, on the encouragement of the Manager who describes them as 'our ethnic problem' the operator CCTV system surveilles them and follows them when they move up the street. (20 minutes, 1 camera)

[. . .] However, in Inner City, the selection of black youth was not just a matter of operator discretion but a deliberate matter of policy. The first week of operation saw the police officer responsible for setting up the scheme give advice to both shifts on where and what to watch. The priority target was stated to be black youths and the priority crimes drug-dealing and street robbery. This effectively meant that the majority of the cameras were never really monitored, since they covered the more general shopping area, indeed for most of the time only three out of the sixteen cameras were actually watched. For the purposes of target selection, attention was focused almost solely on a junction which housed a row of bus stops and a number of West Indian shops, one of which, Santana's, a general grocers and late-night store, would, from early afternoon to late evening, see groups of youths hang about outside.

Nor can the over-representation be viewed as white operators selecting young black men on the basis of second-hand stereotypes although, as we shall see, some of the white operators targeted blacks with a relish which implied a deep prejudice. Black operators similarly targeted young blacks but their comments directed at the screen were not usually so venomous. The following goes some way to illustrating the point:

Black operatives

19.20 – The night shift have inherited a job from the day shift – namely, a group of 15–20 black males and females, all in their teens and casually/sub-culturally dressed who are standing in a group outside an off-licence and general store called Santana's which is adjacent to a series of bus stops. Zooming in on this group the operator can see nine black males and four black females. The operator is a black man in his late 50s and not impressed by this assortment saying for mine and the other operator's benefit the police should round 'em up and get their mums and dads to come and fetch 'em and shame them. The group are generally standing talking and flirting with the occasional bout of horseplay and dancing, they harass no one. Nearby are standing dozens of people awaiting one of the 12 bus routes which pick up at this point. Even so the camera remains on the group for 30 minutes and notices a group of eight black males in their early 20s who walk through the gathering and continue elsewhere. Two of this group then split off and the operator decides to follow the remaining six, but is thwarted when they walk out of range of the cameras. (51 minutes, 4 cameras) [. . .]

White operatives

10.04 – The first sighting of young black males produces the day's first surveillance. Two 16 year olds, casually dressed, are noticed standing outside a clothes shop talking. The operator zooms in and notices their sub-cultural attire which for one includes a pair of large designer training shoes. The operator comments to no-one in particular 'I wonder where he nicked those trainers from'. The suspects do not enter the store, but resume their walk. The operator looks elsewhere. (2 minutes, 1 camera) [. . .]

Gender blindness?

While women make up 52 per cent of the general population they only accounted for 7 per cent of primary persons surveilled. Women were almost invisible to the cameras unless they were reported as known shoplifters by store detectives or because of overt disorderly conduct. This accords with Bulos and Sarno's observations as they note the views of female operators on whether they viewed the monitors differently from their male colleagues:

> One replied 'no it's exactly the same'. The other two, however, made one or two significant comments. Firstly it was considered that she (female controller) looked more on women as potential criminals. The male controllers tended to see criminal activity as a male preserve and tended to ignore or oversee women acting suspiciously. She (female controller) prided herself in being quick to spot women acting suspiciously. Another female controller commented 'they (men) look at women but not for the right reason!' (Bulos and Sarno 1996: 29).

If they were invisible as suspects they were also invisible as potential victims and were unlikely to become targets by virtue of a protectional gaze, indeed in nearly 600 hours of observation only one woman was targeted for protectional purposes – as she walked to and from a bank cash dispenser. In fact the protectional gaze was more likely be focused on male security guards involved in the transit of cash. Moreover there was evidence that the same attitudes which have traditionally been associated with the police occupational culture surrounding domestic violence continue to inform the operation of CCTV as the following incidents shows:

> 01.20 – With hardly anyone on the streets anyone who is noticed is worth surveilling. An opportunity to break the monotony is provided by a white female in her late 20s who in black leather attire seems to be dressed for an occasion bordering leather fetish. She is first sighted outside a fast food outlet and moments later she climbs into a car – a mini-cab – from the office next door. Sitting in the rear of the vehicle for only half a minute she then gets out and appears to be walking alone down the street. At this point the operator can zoom in and see her attire – black high-heel boots, black leggings, black leather jacket and ribbed and sequined shirt which evokes a laugh and the comment 'What a scrubber' from him. The object of curiosity then stands still and asks two passing females for something – the two appear to ignore her. Less than a minute later the woman then back-tracks to follow a black male (late 20s). Whilst she follows she then gestures towards the bottom of the street whereupon seconds later another white female of similar age appears and joins her friend.
>
> From the other direction appears a small white male in his 20s who is obviously shouting at the first female as the three now walk together back towards the cab firm outside of which other people are gathered. The animated white male continues his rant and attempts to strike the female, this does not connect and is not repeated. The operator does not respond to what he considers a domestic incident, but tells me he is going to zoom in on their faces because as the three now are about to get into a cab they might not pay the driver at the end of the journey! The car drives away at 00.51. (7 minutes, 1 camera) [. . .]

[T]his example gives credence to Brown's assertion that the essentially male gaze of CCTV, has little relevance for the security of women in town centres and may indeed undermine it by offering the rhetoric of security rather than providing the reality (Brown 1998). CCTV also fosters a male gaze in the more conventional and voyeuristic sense, with its pan-tilt and zoom facilities the thighs and cleavages of the scantily clad are an easy target for those male operators so motivated. Indeed, 10 per cent of all targeted surveil-lances on women, and 15 per cent of operator-initiated surveillance were for apparently voyeuristic reasons outnumbering protective surveillance by five to one. [. . .]

Rule Two – *Certain behaviours unquestionably warrant surveillance because they are them-selves criminal or disorderly. However, there is a range of other actions which, whilst not criminal, operators treat as indicative of potential or recently occurring criminality.*

When watching the multitude of screens it is not just particular types of people who warrant surveillance but also certain classes of action. Unsurprisingly if people are noticed engaged in activities that could be construed as fighting, the people are zoomed in on. But as appearances can be deceptive (see Rule 7) and operators are aware that what looked like an assault may actually be a friendly slap on the back, they therefore take cognizance of the contextual features of posture and facial expression to enable interpretation. This is particularly the case with juveniles who are frequently targeted because they appear to be fighting, but on closer inspection turn out to be engaging in 'horseplay' and, as the following incident suggests, at times this may be specifically for the benefit of the cameras:

> 21.07 – Three black youths casually dressed and aged between 16–18 are noticed as they stand outside Santana's talking and laughing. Zooming in the operator tells me that they are 'behavin' . . . just talkin'. While leaving the camera on them the operator shows little interest in this group until a couple of minutes later, the three run off in three different directions and rendezvous a minute later at a phone box. Moments later they run across the road laughing as one takes punches given out by the other two. Then in mock retaliation the 'victim' pulls his trouser belt off and begins to pretend to strike out at his 'assailants'. The horseplay continues and the operator decides to leave them alone. What the operator does not admit is that the three have been playing with the system and him since they were aware the cameras were on them. (13 minutes, 3 cameras)

While displays of fighting warrant surveillance because it is in itself an offence, two types of non-criminal behaviour are seen as potentially indicative of criminality: they are running and loitering.

Running The field notes contain dozens of examples of people being targeted because they are running and, in general, anyone noticed running will be zoomed in on:

> 00.01 – A white male casually dressed and in his early 20s is noted running down the High Street. Because of this behaviour he is zoomed in on and followed. Moments later he reduces speed to a jog then eventually walks. The operator sees that he is not being pursued and that he is not apparently carrying anything upon him and leaves him to walk in peace. (2 minutes, 2 cameras)

09.15 – The operator notices a black male in his late 20s and casually dressed running down the street towards a black woman. Unsure as to whether his intentions are hostile, the operator zooms in, but sees that as the two come into proximity they laugh. The pair stand chatting and a few minutes later go their separate ways. (4 minutes, 1 camera)

[. . .] As the preceding examples illustrate, running is seen as indicative of three possibilities, first, a 'fear and flight' response, in which the operators work to locate who or what provoked such a reaction; second, flight from lawful authority such as a shoplifter being pursued by a store detective and finally as a prelude to an attack. The fact that running turns out to be almost always innocent does not seem to deter the operators. This is perhaps because running provides something concrete to look at which is more interesting than just scanning faces in the crowd. Moreover, it invites an answer to the question 'Why?' and, like all of us, operators like to know the end of the story – even if it has a happy ending. But on one occasion during the research, the targeting of someone running did reveal criminal activity, and operators take solace from these rare successes and use them to temper their experience that, in ninety-nine out of a hundred times, it will indicate nothing more significant than trying to catch a bus.

Loitering with Intent As we have already noted, youths are particularly prone to targeted surveillance especially if they are hanging around in groups on street corners, here it is the 'youth' and 'group' rather than the 'loitering' which provokes operator interest. However when loitering is compounded by place, it becomes indicative of 'loitering with intent' as the following example shows:

10.44 – The operator notices two males standing outside looking into the window display of a jewellers. Both are white and in their late teens wearing casual but stylish clothing. One has a shoulder bag which taken together produce the identikit shop thief in the eyes of the operators. Doing an intensive scrutiny of the display the pair then indulge in horseplay and ridicule and after looking in the window again enter the store.

Upon entering the store the operator switches on the real-time recording facility and waits. They come out after three minutes and walk around the town. As they do so they are watched, the operator looking for evidence of gems appearing out of pockets or bags, but nothing seems untoward. After five minutes they return to the jewellers – a state of alert is provoked in the operators, but this time the pair come out within a minute – their return provoked by the fact that one had left a small parcel in the shop from his first visit. Having retrieved it the two walk away smiling. The operator now sees the pair as not worthy of surveillance. (8 minutes, 4 cameras) [. . .]

Rule Three – *Certain people are immediately worthy of surveillance because they are known by operators to have engaged in criminal or troublesome behaviour in the past.*

It is notable that operators, in the main, did not target people on the basis of personalised knowledge of their past criminality, only thirty cases of targeted surveillance could be directly attributable to personalised knowledge, representing just 3 per cent of the total. There are a number of reasons for this. First, in County

Town and Inner City, there were few ways of learning a person's criminal history. As the systems were not located in police stations, the formal and informal mechanisms which would have enabled them to acquire such knowledge, generally by chatting to police officers, were largely absent. Second, none of the sites had an official 'rogues gallery' (a noticeboard with pictures of suspects attached) which would facilitate identification. Finally the sheer volume of people meant that casual identification when 'cruising' with the cameras would be difficult, the faces are too distant unless they are zoomed in on.

Operators would, however, regularly zoom in on a person or group to see if a person was known, and thus warrant more prolonged surveillance but these attempts were rather hit and miss and generally unsuccessful. For example:

> 10.07 – A white female in her early 20s is sighted walking in the town. Unsure as to whether she is a known drug-user and shoplifter the opera- tor zooms in and realises she is not whom he thought she was and so leaves her. (1 minute, 1 camera)

> 10.30 – A group of six teenagers (white, male, 12–16) are standing in a group in a pedestrian shopping precinct. They are talking and appear calm, but the operator zooms in to see if they include 'known toe-rags'. None of the group are familiar to him but he leaves the camera on them until they walk else- where and he does not bother to follow them. (3 minutes, 1 camera)

When known offenders do come into view they are targeted but, while operators may believe in the adage, 'once a villain always a villain', they know it does not mean that a person is up to villainy today or, if they are, that it will be in view of the cameras. So, unless there are other features which indicate immediate dubious intent the surveillances tend to be short.

> 17.02 – The operator notices two white males (18–20, casually dressed) who are known shoplifters. Informing his colleague of their whereabouts he adds for my benefit that these two are 'general arseholes' who will probably be using tonight's public gathering for pick-pocketing. (2 minutes, 1 camera)

> 19.25 – Surveilling the crowds the operator stops upon a recognised face, a derisory comment is made to the other operator about the vision. The male (26, scruffily dressed) is a known drug-user and shoplifter and is fol- lowed as he walks through the crowd. (1 minute, 1 camera) [. . .]

Rule Four – *Operators must learn to treat locales as territories of normal appearances and against this background variation can be noticed. This involves utilising the temporal and spatial variation of activities within a locale to judge what is both 'out of place' and 'out of time'.*

The operation of this rule creates within CCTV systems a surveillance clock which patterns operators' activities temporally and spatially. To illustrate how it operates we will describe the surveillance clocks in Metro City and County Town.

In Metro City no operator ever spent a full shift engrossed in the task of surveil- lance. The discomfort of watching so many monitors combined with the mind-numbing monotony the job offered meant that operators 'drifted' in their concentration. Moments of intense scrutiny competed with minutes of doing nothing with the mind miles away. Because of this, at times, trying to explain rationally the methods of the operators was at times a futile exercise – even they could not explain why they were moving the cameras the way they were! However there were patterns across the hours of the day, and days of the week which suggested a set of shared assumptions about the spatial and temporal distribution of activities.

The different shifts produced varied modus operandi. The 7.00 a.m.–2.00 p.m. would always see operators spend the first twenty minutes busying themselves with the cameras only to lapse into chat and tea-drinking. As the city centre got busy from 8.30 a.m., cameras would focus on the railway stations and from 10.00 a.m. would generally look for 'suspects' in the pedestrian shopping mall, invariably young males who, by virtue of being that category, were considered potential thieves. Such a category was the main concern until the shift ended. The other regular targets were the homeless and habitual street drinkers.

Arriving fresh the afternoon shift would cruise the cameras for half an hour and then relax and go into a routine. This would see the different operators choose their particular 'favourite' camera view and put it on their dedicated monitor. As the city emptied between 5.00–6.00 p.m., the operators would take breaks and wind down their state of alertness until the young and dressed-up arrived post-8.00 p.m. for nights out in pubs and clubs. The only early evening 'high alert' occurred on Saturdays when four venues held 'Teen-discos' from 8.00–10.30 p.m. before the real thing for adults began at 11.00 p.m. At such times male youths aged between 12–16 were particular targets for surveillance, be they standing outside the disco, or a fast-food outlet or around transport termini.

Night shift offered the operators better opportunities to generate an arrest. The obvious targets for surveillance were pubs and nightclubs, particularly those known as being 'trouble' hot spots. Meanwhile awaiting a fight the cameras would watch anyone seen in a phone box on suspicion they were robbing it and fast-food outlets wherein the operators believed were drunks who having left pubs would seek sustenance and a fight. Post-02.00 a.m. surveillance was usually centred on the 'red light' area of the city centre – a series of six streets which saw street-walkers and kerb-crawlers and other associated entrepreneurs believed to be pimps and drug-sellers. Interestingly for all the hours of surveillance in this area no prostitute was ever arrested for soliciting on the evidence of the cameras and the cars that were stopped by mobile police patrols deployed by the Controller based on camera evidence were not targeted for kerb-crawling, but for a presence which did not accord with 'normal' approaches to women.

From 04.00–07.00 a.m. surveillance focused on anyone seen on cameras. Thus whatever business the person was going about – be it walking home from work or from a disco or a vagrant raking through bins – the cameras followed them. In these tedious hours operators when not snoozing could only articulate their task as one of watching for thefts of newspapers and bread and milk delivered sometimes hours before the small stores opened. This produced one arrest when a vagrant was seen stealing eight copies of a Sunday tabloid. Not all surveillance had an aim or rationale as many an operator explained, the 'cruising' was done out of boredom and 'just because there's someone to look at'. When not wanting to move the cameras, operators could construct a sequence on their monitors; this way sixteen or eight or four set locations would flick around every thirty seconds in front of their eyes. [. . .]

Rule Five – *For operators the normal ecology of an area is also a 'normative ecology' and thus people who don't belong are treated as 'other' and subject to treatment as such.*

This normative ecology goes further than merely signalling 'otherness' as a statistical property but also as a moral property related to conception of the legitimate and illegitimate use of social space. From the operators' perspectives, if a person was defined as 'other', either their moral propensities were unknown, and therefore worthy of surveillance in case they turned out to be malign, or they were already 'known', by reference to stereotypical assumptions contained in media, political and everyday discourses. Operators, of course, had their own common-sense understandings, informed by their localised knowledge, as to which people fall into the category of 'other':

> 12.10 – Seeing two white males in their early 40s walk into a department store, one carrying a suitcase, the operator suspects they could be up to no good. Via retail radio he warns the store detective of their presence. However, the camera which is trained on the shop door shows them leaving the store in less than a minute, the store detective has noticed them in the short time they were in the store and by his reckoning they are two foreigners who are searching for an address. The two are out of place on the Inner City high street, their garments are a long fur coat and long leather coat, respectively, and their suitcases are of the battered leather variety. Followed as they walk down the road they approach no one, but look bewildered as they trudge around. (10 minutes, 3 cameras)

As we have already noted, the surveillance of black people in both County Town and Metro City can in part be explained by the fact that they were seen in the context of a predominately white community, which immediately singled them out as a 'not the norm' but also in part because of the moral properties that operators ascribed to being black. But it was not just blacks who were treated as 'other', as the following illustrates:

> A couple of operators were particularly keen on surveilling the homeless. In Paul's case this was accompanied by verbal abuse towards those standing on the monitors in front of him, and he made clear he did not have much time for: '*Big Issue* scum', 'Homeless low-life' and 'drug-dealing scrotes'. And he would cruise the town, in search of these 'undesirables' and when found he would become agitated and animated in his revulsion. The other operator who did not care for the homeless was Martin who considered most sellers of the *Big Issue* as drug-dealers concealing their true motives behind the façade of poverty. In the Shift Diary he had written for the benefit of other shifts that they were to surveille one seller whom he considered a drug dealer and 'check all weekend and report on Monday'. Underneath this instruction another operator from a different shift wrote

that the suspect had been checked by police 'and he is clean'. Further to this
the System Manager wrote 'surveillance no longer required'.

The concept of 'otherness' is intimately bound up with views as to the appropriate use of social space and who has a right to do what in the city centre. In County Town, for instance, one group that was continuously surveilled was the town centre drunks – not because they caused any trouble but because their activities did not accord with the appropriate use of town centre space.

> A dozen drunks were surveilled on a daily basis in two favoured haunts – the bus station and an alleyway off the market square. Such places were shelter from the elements and a place to exchange bottles and chat away the hours. Whilst unsightly, no offences were committed by them during the observational research and although the operators looked at them regularly they did not see them as a particular problem. The more recent homeless, however, were not tolerated, but this could not be attributed to the operators. As a police visitor to the control room explained because all such people had mortgages and cars and were a fraud, they were not allowed to sell their magazine in the town and operators were requested to bring to police attention any that they found in the centre.

As the above extracts illustrate the targeting of the homeless, the vagrant and alcoholic was a regular feature of both Metro City and County Town. But this was also differentiated by the degree of 'otherness', with *Big Issue* sellers considered as the nadir of the undeserving poor while the ordinary vagrants were merely 'other'. [. . .]

Rule Six – *There is an expectation that just as operators treat territories as a set of normal appearances, so others are expected to treat them as such. And thus if a person appears lost, disorientated, or in other ways at unease with the locale, this will indicate suspiciousness.*

In practice the operation of this rule is often bound up with the other rules of the incongruity procedure. However, what it draws attention to is those whose orientation to the locale through their interaction with both the social and physical environment is 'out of place'. Thus, those who suddenly change direction, or appear to be wandering aimlessly, will become targets or have the suspicion intensified if they are already selected. In the following example, the group has already been selected as warranting surveillance, on the basis of age, number, dress and location. What turns this from a routine targeted surveillance to an extended twenty-five minutes is the youths have not continued in the predicted direction but retraced their original path. It is almost as though operators construct a map of moral progress through the streets which is unidirectional. People of good moral character know where they are going and proceeded to their destination without signs of deviation.

> 16.35 – A group of five black teenagers are noticed walking in the rain down the High Street. The operator immediately zooms in on the three males and two females, all casually dressed, three of them wearing baseball caps. As they walk they look in shop windows then they enter a shop

which specialises in records and stereos, this provokes the operator to shout at the screen 'Get out of there you little devils!'

They come out minutes later and saunter down the street in the rain and after four minutes of this all turn round and retrace their steps. This provokes analysis from the operator who states to me: 'This is how they draw suspicion to themselves . . . when they turn round for no reason . . . they've been to a few shops and now they're going back'.

They had in fact entered only one shop. They were to head towards a grocery store where one entered and bought a can of drink whilst the rest waited outside. Still they are followed as they window shop in the rain until after using four cameras on them over a 25-minute period the operator leaves them alone. [. . .]

Rule Seven – *Operators learn to see those who treat the presence of the cameras as other than normal as other than normal themselves.*

Operators work with the absolute assumption that they have the right to surveille anyone on the street. Anyone who by gesture or behaviour challenges this assumption immediately places themselves in the category of morally suspect and therefore worthy of surveillance. For example:

> 17.11 – The operator resumes his surveillance of Santana's and sees half a dozen of the group board a bus and disappear leaving only four black males who walk across the road and down the High Street eventually disappearing from view. Before they are out of range, however, all four gesture abusively to the camera which angers the operator who says to his colleagues 'I'd love to go down there and run them all over'. (10 minutes, 3 cameras)

Such overt and theatrical resistance to the camera's gaze was not uncommon, especially in Inner City, and token gestures of defiance often accompanied departure from the area. As such, however, they could not be used as the basis of extended surveillance except where the faces were remembered as in the following example:

> 16.00 – The youths outside Santana's provide some entertainment for the operators. Eight casually dressed black males are zoomed in on and one elicits a venomous reaction in the operator. 'That one's a right little shit . . . he knows where all the cameras are'. Whether he does or not the operator has no way of knowing, but he is certain in his dislike of this diminutive 14 year old who is regularly standing with the various gatherings. Others come and go over the next 30 minutes providing a form of intelligence report between the operators. 'He's one of the new ones'. 'He's usually got a mobile phone'. The youths stand and chat occasionally larking about in the pouring rain as they are discussed at a distance. (30 minutes, 1 camera)

If a person is, in the view of the operator, orientating their behaviour to the presence of the cameras this provides a strong warrant for initiating or prolonging surveillance. It is not just overt resistance to the cameras which promotes suspicion but a belief that if a person is demonstrating an awareness of the cameras this may be because they have an immediate criminal intent:

> 11.23 – A black male becomes the object of suspicion because of his appearance and location. In his early 20s and wearing trainers, jeans, leather jacket and baseball cap he is a prime target for surveillance anyway, but to add to his woes he is standing outside the door of the Building Society. The operator tells me that the chap could be waiting for someone, but he is suspicious about his motives because 'he's been looking at the camera'. I watch carefully but do not see him looking at the camera, but still the camera remains on him. Four minutes later a white female in her 40s appears, speaks to the suspect and the pair walk away together crossing the road and joining two other black males, both with baseball caps and casual attire. The four are followed until they go out of range of the camera. (6 minutes, 2 cameras)

While in the previous example merely looking at the camera compounded suspicion, if activities are seen as deliberately aimed at avoiding surveillance, suspicion is further intensified as the following illustrates:

> 13.24 – A group of five black males are now surveilled. All are casually dressed and aged around 15, two wear baseball caps another has a woolly hat. They walk orderly and quietly through the streets, but are followed as they do so and the operator asks for confirmation from his colleague as to whether they are known to him as part of the 'Three O'clock Gang' (those who hang around Santana's after school). The co-operator says they are. The operator continues his surveillance until all five jump onto the back of an open-door bus and disappear up the road. Knowing the direction the bus is going the operator moves his surveillance to a camera opposite the bus stop the bus will next call at. At this stop all five jump off and walk back towards where they had come from. The other operator sees this and tells his new colleague 'This is what they do all the time to avoid surveillance'.
>
> The five then cross the road and stand in a bus shelter. Then, changing their mind they walk to McDonalds so the cameras follow them then await their departure and further journeys. What happens in effect is that having found a group of suspects the operator becomes fixed on following them and so ignores other people and places. The necessity of keeping watch on them is periodically confirmed when one of the suspects is noted to be watching the cameras' movements. The mutual watching has required 5 cameras and taken up 66 minutes.

As the previous examples reveal, operators believe that if those they have already selected as targets change direction, back-track, split up, or move out of camera view this is treated as further evidence of malign intent. But what is apparent from these examples is that rather than trying to avoid surveillance the youths are actually trying to provoke it. Moreover, by demonstrating those behaviours they know will provoke surveillance, they indicate that they are not merely passive objects of a disciplinary gaze. They too can have power, if merely by wasting the operator's time or by subverting

the intentions of the system for their own entertainment. Of course, for the operators this merely compounds their belief that people are up to no good. Displaying a
knowledge of the modus operandi of the system implies knowing what a person
should not be interested in knowing and this knowledge could then be used to
'hoodwink the operators and to neutralise the system'. Indeed a couple of system
managers spoke of how people have created a diversion to concentrate the attention
of the cameras in one area while 'something was happening in another'.

References

Brown, S. (1998), 'What's the Problem Girls? CCTV and the Gendering of Public Safety'
      in C. Norris, J. Moran and G. Armstrong (eds), *Surveillance, Closed Circuit Television
      and Social Control*. Aldershot: Ashgate.
Bulos, M. and Sarno, C. (1996), *Codes of Practice and Public Closed Circuit Television Systems*,
      London: Local Government Information Unit.
McConville, M., Sanders, A., and Leng, R. (1991), *The Case for the Prosecution*, London:
      Routledge.
Norris, C., Kemp, C., Fielding, N. and Fielding, J. (1992), 'Black and Blue: an analysis of the
      effect of race on police stops', *British Journal of Sociology*, vol.43, Issue no. 2, June.

Critical connections

From the control of street beggars in Delhi, India, to the creation of exclusion zones
for the homeless in Paris, France, to the fortressing of middle-class gated communities
in Los Angeles, and the monitoring and marshalling of supporters at football matches
across the world, the CCTV camera has become a key feature of late modern life. And
nowhere more so than in the UK. With over 4.2 million cameras, there is roughly one
camera for every 14 people in the population. In the past decade, the United Kingdom
Home Office has spent over 78 per cent of its crime-prevention budget on CCTV systems, amounting to more than £500 million (see http://www.urbaneye.net). It is now
commonplace to state that the average London citizen may be captured on CCTV
camera up to 300 times in a single day.

   Yet, just as the deepening penetration of surveillance into the fabric of contemporary urban life constrains and controls, so it give rise to resistance, subversion and
alternative meaning. The same surveillance techniques used by state agencies to police
citizens can in turn be used by citizens to police the state. During the 2004 Republication
National Convention in New York city, police arrested more than 1,800 people for public
disorder and related offences. More than 400 cases were dropped on the basis of video
evidence produced by radical collective I-Witness that directly contradicted sworn statements by police officers, in extreme cases exposing police misconduct and perjury. Back
in the UK, Banksy, the infamous British street artist whose work adorns the cover of
this book, recently erected three storeys of scaffolding in central London despite being
watched by CCTV. Then, beneath a huge tarpaulin, spray-painted a stencil depicting a
young boy, watched by a security guard, painting the words 'One nation under CCTV'.
Ironically enough, this satirical comment on the surveillance society, which officially
constitutes a criminal act of vandalism (see Reading 28), would be worth a small fortune if it could be packaged and sold. Those Banksy works which have been packaged

Figure 38.1 A CCTV operator's-eye-view of the world. Image © Andy Aitchison

Figure 38.2 The commodification of the surveillant gaze. Photo by Magnus Arrevad

and sold, many of which mock consumer society, achieve tens of thousands (sterling) at auction, and a raft of celebrity collectors includes Brad Pitt and Angelina Jolie, and Christina Aguilera.

The potential for subversion in an expanding surveillance culture was noted by British subcultural theorist Dick Hebdidge two decades ago (1988: 35): 'Subculture

Figure 38.3 Banksy: One Nation under CCTV. Photo: Author's own

forms up in the space between surveillance and the evasion of surveillance, it translates the fact of being under scrutiny into the pleasure of being watched. It is hiding in the light.'

Discussion questions

- What are the defining characteristics of the surveillance society?
- What can Foucault's Panoptic surveillance (Reading 36) and Mathiesen's Synoptic surveillance (Reading 37) bring to Norris and Armstrong's discussion of 'Working Rules'?
- Discuss the proposition, 'if you've got nothing to hide, you've got nothing to fear'

References

Hebdige, D. (1988) *Hiding in the Light: On Images and Things*, London: Routledge.
Lyon. D. (2001) Surveillance Society: Monitoring Everyday Life, Buckingham: Open University Press.
Urbaneye – accessible at http://www.urbaneye.net.

Sheila Brown

(S)TALKING IN CYBERSPACE: VIRTUALITY, CRIME AND LAW (2003)

Introduction and context

RECENT ESTIMATES INDICATE that more than one in five people across the globe now have access to the World Wide Web, making just over 1.3 billion users (Internet World Stats, 2008). Accepting that these online statistics are trustworthy (certainly, not all online information is – see Reading 14), Internet use increased globally by 265 per cent between 2000 and 2007. In Africa, the growth over the same period was 882 per cent. According to estimates cited by Aas (2007) in Reading 40, the average Briton spends around 164 minutes online every day, and only 148 minutes watching television. The virtual world has for countless surfers and searchers become a routine, everyday reality. The freedoms created by the Internet have, of course, been countered by new dangers and possibilities for crime, violence and social exclusion. Sheila Brown's '(S)talking in Cyberspace, Virtuality, Crime and Law' engages with the 'reality' of the cyber by considering some of the new forms of transgression, and adaptations of old forms, arising in the virtual world, and the implications of these for traditional notions of crime, law and social order.

Brown (2003: 145) notes that the 'spaces and places of the cyber' may be criminogenic, but not in the same way that 'cities and the "real" social are, and not in the way that "real" bodies are'. That said, although there are clear distinctions between the physical and virtual realms, the two realms are not entirely distinct. The dynamics of identity and the rules of being and doing may change significantly in the cyber, but social interaction in the virtual world is still social. As such, it is structured in terms of real social, economic and political dynamics that may have real consequence in the virtual world. Virtual victimisation may be every bit as destructive as victimisation in the physical world.

Cyberspace and cybercultures: approaching the prosthetic

The work of William Gibson [. . .] has to be considered in any discussion of contemporary media culture. This in itself illustrates the theme of this book, since Gibson, the 'cyberpunk' novelist (1984, 1995) – or even the 'father'(!) of cyberpunk – has latterly been feted as a sociological theorist. Burrows (1997), in an essay on Gibson ism, suggests that the novelist has superseded the recent high priests of social theory. In a comment on the processes of sociological '*passeification*', Burrows (1997: 235) writes:

> It is not just technology which appears to be accelerating towards meltdown, so are our cultural and sociological understandings of the world . . . The recent literature on things 'cyber' is a case in point. Reading it makes the latest pile of books on the postmodern, globalisation, reflexive modernisation (last year's model?) and the like appear mellow and quaint. Never mind who now reads Marx? Or even Foucault? Who now reads Baudrillard?

Of course the irony in this is that even when something as allegedly theoretically different as the cyber is concerned, we just seem unable to resist the elevation of someone (male) to the status of 'founding father'. Surely it is partly the addictive allure of Gibson's writing style that makes him preferable to the dry or obfuscating discourses of 'social theorists proper'. Who would you rather spend an evening with, the author of *Das Kapital* or the author of *Neuromancer*? William Gibson is just more *fun*. We need a caveat on Gibson, because allocating him the position of social theorist extraordinaire reduces talking about 'the cyber' to blinkered, linear and elitist (and male-dominated) modernist epistemes. This is the antithesis of the Gibsonian 'vision'. Amongst all the other things that the cyber may be 'about', one of them is the proliferation of voices, which are not particularly amenable to filtering, regulation, or hierarchical orderings of the status of knowledge. It is an interesting shift, which turns to fiction as social theory, and a long overdue one, since as Burrows (1997: 235) also notes

> Our inability to account for our changing world in sociological terms has led, not just to an ontological insecurity but to ever more frantic attempts to provide some sort of sociological frame for a constantly moving target. In the recent conceptual scramble some analysts have begun to turn to sources of inspiration beyond traditional social and scientific discourses.

Cyberhype has been widely criticized for its dystopia, or more commonly utopia (Weinstein and Weinstein 2000), but this hardly seems important since all literatures (whether 'fictional' or not) about the social world have contained dystopian and utopian elements reflecting the difficulty of comprehending change in which we are immersed (for example, Marx and H.G. Wells). 'Futurology' and 'doom' have been endemic in accounts of technological change and the accompanying transformations of the orderings of the social. This is merely an inherent danger of trying to see the world, any world, from the over-and-aboveness that only the sleight of hand available to historians, with their conventions of narrative re-orderings, can really do more or less plausibly. In dealing with the cyber, therefore, it simply has to be accepted that what is said about it must be constantly provisional. Thus I am seeking, as Bell (2000: 1) puts it, to 'understand the ways in which cyberspace as a cultural phenomenon is currently being experienced and imagined'.

'Cyberspace as a "peopled" and "people driven" environment is intricately connected with human agency; yet as we sit in front of the computer terminal we are "simultaneously . . . relocating ourselves in the space behind the screen, between screens, everywhere and nowhere"' (Bell 2000: 3). The nature of cyber*space* is different from the physical spaces of the built environment, and given that the language with which we attempt to delineate it is metaphorical (cf. Lakoff and Johnson 1977) we need to be reflexive about the adequacy of those metaphors. McBeath and Webb (1997: 250) argue that we are prone to adopt 'false analogies', and 'the language we use to try to grasp the structure of cyberspace . . . trades equally on notions of radical difference and sameness'. [. . .]

Crime, law and the cyber

As cities and bodies vanish, and communities and subjects transmutate, so to the same extent does crime, to a large extent their twentieth-century historical correlate, also lose its familiar metaphorical significance. The spaces and places of the cyber are criminogenic, but not in the way that cities and the 'real' social are, and not in the way that 'real' bodies are.

The physical and material force of city crime, the aesthetics of fear in the built environment, is replaced by other forms of victimization. Victimizations of the body are replaced by victimizations of the virtual subject. This does not necessarily increase security, since the spaces of exposure in the cyber are much greater, the ability to find the security bubbles offered in metropolitan oases much less. Nor does it necessarily follow that 'virtual' victimization is less destructive in its effects; arguably, they are much greater and more pervasive. Further, in the power afforded by the human–machine interface, there is a 'value-added' edge to victimization. More people can be affected at once; the possibilities of detection are immeasurably reduced, as is the potential for legal regulation; the potential gains of certain crimes (fraud, hacking, etc.) are huge; and perhaps above all the potential to bring down infrastructures which now rely on the virtual, is no longer merely a sci-fi hacker fantasy. All the goalposts within which crime can be conceptualized are now irrevocably moved, yet with 'one foot in the real' these are hence not only 'new' 'crimes', but also enhancements of old ones (sabotage, stalking, robbery, and so on).

If cities were 'ungovernable spaces' then cyberspace is far more so (Lash and Urry 1994). Then again, given the alterations in the dimensions of space and the nature of the technology, the local is also transformed, raising a whole new series of questions about 'sub' and 'counter' cultures. The expansion of the matrix has not meant the death of the anorak! The sociologies of urban popular (sub)cultures have been in transformation for some time with the increasing globalization, inter-textuality, and virtuality of music culture, for example, and the accessibility of the Internet has transformed the notion of the fanzine, with consequent far-reaching implications for law and popular culture (Redhead 1990). [. . .]

Spam

Stivale (1997: 133) defines 'spam' as:

> That unnecessary data transmission that one participant deliberately produces often simply to fill lines on the recipient's screens, but some-times to communicate aggressive messages as well. 'To spam', then, means precisely to inflict such verbiage on other 'Net' comrades, alone or *en masse*, and is generally taken to be a form of online harassment.

Stivale proposes three levels of 'aggressivity' in spamming, using the example of the LambdaMOO (multi-object oriented) MUD (a multi-user dungeon), a site 'structured like a large house with nearby grounds and community' (1997: 134). Participants in the site are guests in the house and can move around the rooms of the house, engaging in communication with around 8000 other 'guests'. Participants register, choose a character name, a gender, and a personal description, and are then on the road to their virtual identity. The highest level of aggression, 'pernicious spam', is of most relevance here, in that it often 'consists in virtual imitations of "real life" practices of harassment', using sexually explicit verbiage to 'spam unwitting participants in ways that might well be legally actionable in real life' (Stivale 1997: 139, 140). In one instance Dr Jest sent homophobic and sexually violent spam to victims, which spurred a debate as to the status of 'words' as weapons, and whether they 'contain the force of "acts"' (Stivale 1997: 140).

The problem here is that if virtual names are spamming virtual names, then tech-nically there is no 'real' aggressor or victim. The only sanction here is the exclusion of the user from the site, or his or her suspension. A rather different complexion was put on the matter in a case cited by Stivale where a male student was accused of using a female student's real name in a sexual fantasy involving torture, and posting it to a Usenet group. This case came to court on federal charges of transmitting a threat to kidnap or injure by electronic mail, but the judge gave priority to the First Amendment and dismissed the charges (Stivale 1997: 141).

The particular nature of cyberlinguistics poses further problems, since the lan-guage of the LamdaMOO MUD, for example, operates at different communicational levels: to 'say' is to talk directly, to 'emote' is to express a feeling or action indirectly, and to 'whisper' is a private communication between recipients within the same room (Stivale 1997: 141). These levels may be seen as having different relationships to the equivalence or otherwise of the virtual with action, and are therefore contestable textual domains. In addition, spam culprits can reappear in different identities, and the virtuality of identity also calls into question action. For example, in spamming a virtual identity, does it make a difference if misogynist spam is directed towards a female identity yet the 'real' holder of the identity is a man? (This of course is unknowable anyway unless the victim reveals their 'real' gender in complaint.)

It is not just the question of whether the 'virtual' harassment counts as an act, but one of whether the practices in question are regulable. The contrast with the – still mediated – 'real' is clear when one considers that telephone harassment, which is highly actionable, is criminalized, and carries potentially stiff penalties. Spamming thus raises issues that reappear over and again in the cyber: defining victimization as such, apportioning seriousness, and regulating cyberbehaviour. The seriousness of this difficulty is revealed if one considers Appardui's characterization of the imagination 'as social practice' (1990: 5).

MUD wars: virtual practices of violence

If Appardui's phrase is applied to the phenomenon of war games in MUDs, then we arrive quickly at a point of considering whether cyberwars constitute symbolic violence, and what the implications of taking such a position might be. Ito points out that to enter into MUD wars is to be already empowered, since it requires, as with any other cyberjourney, a certain material status in the 'real' world (Ito 1997), that is to say, ownership of or access to hardware and software, telecoms, and the possession of literacy and computer literacy, or cultural capital. However the virtual power struggles that take place in war gaming are, for Ito, as 'real' as the 'real' which enables the gamer to participate. Virtual characters are, he argues, 'alternative reembodiments' which generate questions of 'connection and accountability' (Ito 1997: 96). Pking (killing other characters) is a case in point, and follows the conventions which typically frame killing in the 'real'. MUDmurder would be killing someone, unprovoked, for pleasure or other motives. Self-defence however is MUDpking under provocation; then there is revenge pking for revenge. One of Ito's virtual respondents sees pking as 'almost like killing' in that it ends someone's *extension* of their real selves (1997: 97). Killing a virtual character is delineated from killing a monster because 'a monster is nothing. A monster is an extension of the game. It's not *real*. A person's *real*' (Ito 1997: 97).

Cyber discipline and punishment represent a problematic not comprehended by Foucauldian discourse (Foucault 1977). Multiplicities of virtual identities, and the opportunities offered within the MUD for hiding, make it very difficult to catch an offending MUDder. Punishment relies on the ability to banish an offender, which, because the MUDder can create new characters, is ineffective unless the whole site is banned; even then users with multiple access opportunities can simply re-enter from other sites. Although the 'sheriff' can confiscate properties of offenders (genitalia, physical strength), it does not solve the problem of multiple identities. Thus the dislocation of the virtual subject and the physical body permit the proliferation of offending. While all of this may seem trivial and even insulting to victims of 'real' crime (how could there be comparability between a 'virtual' rape and a 'real' rape?) it raises interesting questions of symbolic domination and violence which feminism has long been tackling in relation to other representational worlds such as fiction and film. The issues of disembodied identities, however, further complicate the symbolic violence of the cyber. In MUDrape it is the virtual identity that is being violated; the 'real' self of which it is an extension or projection is not necessarily embodied in the gender, sexuality, race, or any other dimension of identity of the actual user. Does this therefore make cyberaggression irrelevant (Wall 2001)?

S(talking)

These issues become more 'real' or more embodied when 'talking' on the Internet is considered. While spamming, pking, and MUDrape remain internal to the cyber, whatever their extensions into embodiment through their attachment to embodied identities may be, Usenet groups relate more clearly to 'real' people and would therefore conventionally be regarded as more serious. Frequently heated debates through Usenet groups can generate antipathies that have resulted in some users adopting the identities of others and placing postings in their 'names'. These may be of a pornographic or sexually explicit nature, transforming the identity of the victim into an aggressor. In many other cases motives are not clear, and may involve posting threats to the victim, distribution of defamatory 'information' about the victim, or invitations 'from' the victim, sometimes with details such as the victim's telephone number and/or address. Although this kind of behaviour is legally enforceable, and has resulted, for example, in jail sentences for perpetrators, the 'true' identity of the perpetrator is not always penetrable. Adam (2000: 216–17) cites one instance where the perpetrator did receive a six-year jail sentence:

> Angry that a woman has spurned him, he assumed her identity and posted personal information about her, including her address, in Internet sex chat rooms where he claimed sadomasochistic fantasies in her name. As a result of this a number of men tried to break into her house. The man thought his identity was preserved on the Internet. He was eventually caught after the victim's father spent hours on the Internet posting messages that he hoped would attract the stalker. When the stalker eventually made contact, the woman's father turned the case over to the FBI.

In many more instances, however, the capabilities for hiding real-world 'identities' in the cyber result in non-detection, and in any case, not before the damage has been done. Thus there are two somewhat different scenarios here. While the most obvious one is the case where offline details about another user are revealed, opening them up to embodied threats of victimization, the other, while more contentious, is clearly, under most definitions, threatening behaviour. Even where both perpetrator and victim are anonymous, the symbolic and emotional violence may clearly have 'real' consequences for the online user not dissimilar to those experienced by victims of embodied crime: fear, anxiety, shame, anger, violation, humiliation, and so on. To dismiss stalking where offline details are not revealed is to assume that the victim herself (for most stalking victims, as in embodied reality, appear to be women (Adam 2000)) sustains an unproblematic dissociation of her virtual and actual identities, or that because the threat of embodied violence is not likely to be actualized, then the psychological injury is less.

'Imposture' and power

The complexity of defining virtual victimization is further revealed when one takes into account that the identity of the perpetrator may also be in disjunction from their embodied identity, creating a 'false' situation of trust. Stone's (1996) account of the 'cross dressing psychiatrist' is interesting in this context. As noted above in the example of gaming dungeons, role-playing has long been integral to the cyber, at least since 1972 and the invention of Dungeons and Dragons, the original role-playing game (Stone 1996: 68). Stone's tale concerns a male psychiatrist who opened an account on a CB chat line on CompuServe in 1982. Having been mistaken for a woman, he was attracted to the different, deeply personal and textured ways in which women interacted, and decided to go online as a female. As 'Julie' he impersonated a mute paraplegic neuropsychologist, severely disfigured, who never saw anyone in person. The impostor developed a whole identity around this 'person', started a women's discussion group on CompuServe, and doled out advice. 'She' was even active in detecting men masquerading as women on the Net, and warned other women of the dangers of things not being what they seem (Stone 1996: 70–2). All of this, if disturbing, might not be surprising if Lewin Sanford, Julie's creator, had been remotely like her; but in his 'real' personality online, Sanford was a flop, being a 'devout Conservative Jew' to Julie's atheist, a non-drug taker and almost a non-drinker, compared with Julie's penchant for getting high online, a sexual innocent compared to 'Julie's erotic virtual prowess . . . and fully able-bodied' (Stone 1996: 77). Yet he convincingly inhabited and projected the persona of a severely disabled woman.

One obvious conclusion of this is that to be multiply identitied is not necessarily to be pathologically disturbed; Lewin Sanford consciously and knowingly imposed a 'false' (something of a misnomer, clearly) identity in order to gain the confidence of women online and to be able to communicate with them, his anonymity protected by the system. The only way s/he could be found out was through carelessness.

Was Sanford victimizing women, whether or not he used his insights for gain or to inflict pain? In his (her) erotic adventures, was s/he committing sexual assault? The question of imposture, of course, has since become a highly publicized issue in relation to paedophilia as well as gender. 'Impersonation' of children in order to gain access to 'real' children in chat rooms seems in common-sense terms an obvious form of victimization, even if offline contact does not occur. But *is* this impersonation, in a culture where multiple realities are an acknowledged normal part of social life? The splitting of the body and identity creates an enormous problem for conventional paradigms of harassment and assault. If it is that our bodies give lie to our identities, as typically seen in the case of transgendering in 'reality', then only the surgical alteration of the body (in the case of gender at least) can create 'fit'. In the virtual this requirement is eradicated, freeing up a whole range of identities across ethnicity and the life course which, it could be argued, are no less authentic for their disembodiment. That this process could be a conscious *choice*, that people can choose rather than be innately driven to, achieve virtual cross-dressing through identity-manipulation, makes clear the deeply contradictory nature of attitudes toward trans-identification. On the one hand multiplexing identities is normal and conventional; on the other it raises the problem of consensuality, since those interacting with the multiplexed identities have not knowingly consented to expose themselves to all of those identities. If the multiplexed identity is normal, however, then how can it be imposture? [. . .]

Viral victimization

[. . .] The bogeyman of the virtual world, anyone who has been the victim of a virus attack will know the sense of horror and helplessness as the screen crumbles before them. The sensation of the sender of the virus must be akin to that of the arsonist watching the beauty of a burning building. As apparently random and uncontrollable as an arson attack, ever more sophisticated viruses are an endemic form of attack in the virtual world. Firewall after firewall may be erected, only for the user to discover that they are about as effective as window locks in preventing burglary. The market in viruses ensures their effective circulation, as does their ability to self-replicate. In the age of AIDS and HIV, such metaphors carry a resonant message of menace. This not only includes the connotations of the inability to find a cure, but also of contributory negligence. As Lupton (2000: 479) says,

> there are a series of discourses that suggest that computers which mal-
> function due to 'viral contamination' have allowed themselves to become
> permeable, often via the indiscreet and 'promiscuous' behaviour of their
> users (in their act of inserting 'foreign' disks into their computer, therefore
> spreading the virus from PC to PC).

Some viral threats are even emailed warning of retribution for carelessness. During the writing of this book, I received a warning that the university's computer systems were going to be brought down by a virus which would collapse all the information systems upon which its functioning depended (including, unhappily, the payroll system). This was to be a 'punishment' for 'your laughable security systems. Your firewalls are pathetic and your anti-virus systems come out of the dark ages'. The warning was either a hoax (although it was clear from information given in the email that the 'attacker' had penetrated the university systems as they alleged), or the rapid upgrading of the firewalls and virus scanners succeeded in repelling the onslaught.

Perhaps the scariest thing about viruses, apart from what they can do, is that the discourses of motivation surrounding them are 'irrational', frequently based around notions of 'because I can', 'doing it for fun', or 'punishment'. Insofar as virus culture is linked to hacker culture, it is the culture of the 'terrorist' hacker. Rushkoff reproduces a typical example, Virus 23:

> WARNING:
> This text is a neurolinguistic trap whose mechanism is triggered by you at
> the moment when you subvocalize the words VIRUS 23, words that have
> now begun to infiltrate your mind in the same way that a computer virus
> might affect an artificially intelligent machine . . .
>
> The words VIRUS 23 actually germinate via the subsequent metaphor
> into an expanding array of icy tendrils all of which insinuate themselves
> so deeply into the architecture of your thought that the words VIRUS 23
> cannot be extricated without uprooting your mind . . .

> When you have finished reading the remaining nineteen words this process of irreversible infection will be completed and you will depart believing yourself largely unaffected by this process.
>
> (reproduced in Rushkoff 1996: 251)

Viruses can also be mutated and co-opted, and subsequent mutations of Virus 23 quickly appeared. A 'war of the memes' is generated, essentially a war of the words, since memetic viruses are not about crashing systems but about implanting subversive ideas, or viral manifestos, into your system. Viral hoaxes can be as important as viruses because they are weapons in symbolic warfare, and mirror symbolic warfare in the mediated world generally, where dominant discourses are subverted by counter-cultural messages. Rushkoff (1996) details a number of these, as well as tactics which, like viruses that are launched by disabling the computer systems they wish to over-throw, use guerrilla warfare methods, create a sensation that forces the media to react, thus generating counter-reactions and thrusting the counter-cultural discourse into the limelight. Whether or not this kind of activity is criminal largely depends on how amenable it is to criminalization. Grabosky and Smith (1998) deal with the issue by translating cyberactivity into the language of conventional crime: 'electronic van-dalism' including memetic invasion ('electronic graffiti'). This is a double-edged sword. By substituting a criminalizing set of metaphors ('vandalism'), they place the cyber within the comprehension of traditional criminology; in doing so, they also 'hide' the many difficulties of equating the cyber with the embodied world. This con-tinuing problem is highlighted by the final category of victimization to be discussed in this chapter, that of hate 'crime'.

Cyberhate

This observation brings us back around to the construction of the Other in cyber-space, which finds its manifestation particularly in hate sites, whether misogynist, homophobic, or racist. For example, hatred and patriotism web sites in the UK include Skinheads-UK, White Aryan Resistance, Ku-Klux-Klan, Neo-Nazi, Nation of Islam, Jewish Radicals, Foreign Nationalism, and Antigay. Zickmund (2000) reports a proliferation of US-generated hate sites of similar persuasions. This of course imme-diately deflates the claims of those who see in the cyber a global community, for the 'community', as in the real world, is itself the focus of political and pathological hatred, as subgroups seek to promote the annihilation of other groups. While in the UK 'real' world, incitement to racial hatred, for instance, may be a crime, it is endemic in cyberspace. It is used to 'traffic' in hate to countries where strict hate-censorship laws exist, and Zickmund found that in America,

> members can be easily routed to a variety of groups through a clearing station, such as the Aryan Re-Education Link. This station is a linking serv-ice for thirty-four separate radical Web pages. The groups represented tend towards the skinhead spectrum, but white supremacists are advertised as well.
>
> (2000: 240)

She found that the 'dominant metaphoric association' used by group members was that of war, and particularly the iconic adoption of the Nazi era (Zickmund 2000: 241). Sites are also used to market Nazi products such as military paraphernalia and iconic devices like swastika stick-pins.

The objects of hate function to bind together the hate-community, being represented as contaminating and threatening forces, which require 'containment'. Homosexuals are represented as those who will bring about the collapse of family life, sodomize your sons, and destroy the Church. Third World immigration is described as 'killing our people and our way of life. GET INVOLVED AND STAND UP FOR YOUR WHITE RIGHTS' (Scarborough Skinheads, cited in Zickmund 2000: 243). Displacement (the reversal whereby the hate group see themselves as the dispossessed, robbed of their heritage by the Other) is usual.

The dimensions of cyberhate follow the dimensions of race hate, homophobia and misogyny in general; what is different is its accessibility, pervasiveness, and lack of amenability to regulation. A 'global underground', instantaneously linked through the wires, is hardly an 'underground' in the conventional usage of the term. Cyberhate sites also differ, though, in that they are vulnerable to retaliation, flaming and spamming. The interactivity of the Web means that target groups and libertarians can attempt to subvert the subversion directly. In an ideological and discursive war, this relatively disadvantages the hate groups, whose tactics in the embodied world would also include anonymous attacks on the person and the victimization of property. Conversely, however, Zickmund argues that the participation of oppositional voices provides members of hate groups with a platform, 'factors which increase the opportunities for the enactment of radical rhetoric' (2000: 251).

Although interesting, I find Zickmund's analysis disturbing in that she refers to hate groups as 'radical subversives', and those who confront them as 'antagonists'. Despite Zickmund's obvious oppositional attitude to racism, I find her usage euphemistic, and therefore legitimating. This underlines the dilemma that I have already raised: that the wars of the cyber are essentially wars of words. Policing discursive violence in a cyber environment must prove impossible, because interpretation and interactivity are far more flexible and abstract than with embodied violence. If language is social practice then the complexities of identifying or regulating taxonomies of hate are multiplied in the virtual world, while at the same time the effects of victimization are difficult to establish. The issue of control in general is an ever-present problem in any attempt to apply modernist discourses of 'crime' and 'law' to the cyber.

References

Adam, A. (2000) Cyberstalking: Gender and computer ethics, in E. Green and A. Adam (eds) *Virtual Gender: Technology, Consumption and Identity*. London: Routledge.

Appardui, A. (1990) Disjuncture and difference in the global cultural economy, *Public Culture*, 2(2): 1–24.

Bell, D. (2000) Cybercultures reader: A user's guide, in D. Bell and B.M. Kennedy (eds) *The Cybercultures Reader*. London: Routledge.

Burrows, R. (1997) Cyberpunk as social theory: William Gibson and the sociological imagination, in S. Westwood and J. Williams (eds) *Imagining Cities: Scripts, Signs, Memories*. London: Routledge.

Foucault, M. (1977) *Discipline and Punish*. Harmondsworth: Penguin.

Gibson, W. (1984) *Neuromancer*. London: Victor Gollancz Ltd.

Gibson, W. (1995) *Neuromancer*. London: Voyager.

Grabosky, P.N. and Smith, R.G. (1998) *Crime in the Digital Age*. New Brunswick, NJ: Transaction Publishers.

Ito, M. (1997) Virtually embodied: the reality of fantasy in a multi-user dungeon, in D. Porter (ed.) *Internet Culture*. London: Routledge.

Lakoff, G. and Johnson, M. (1977) *Metaphors We Live By*. Chicago, IL: University of Chicago Press.

Lash, S. and Urry, J. (1994) *Economies of Signs and Space*. London: Sage/TCS.

Lupton, D. (2000) The embodied computer/user, in D. Bell and B.M Kennedy (eds) *The Cybercultures Reader*. London: Routledge.

McBeath, G.B and Webb, S.A (1997) Cities, subjectivity and cyberspace, in S. Westwood and J. Williams (eds) *Imaging Cities: Scripts, Signs, Memory*. London: Routledge.

Redhead, S. (1990) *The End of the Century Party: Youth and Pop Towards 2000*. Manchester: Manchester University press.

Rushkoff, D. (1996) *Media Virus! Hidden Agendas in Popular Culture*. New York: Ballantine.

Stivale, C.J. (1997) Spam: Heteroglossia and harassment in cyberspace, in D. Porter (ed.) *Internet Culture*. London: Routledge.

Stone, A.R. (1996) *The War of Desire and Technology at the Close of the Mechanical Age*. Cambridge, MA: MIT Press.

Wall, D.(ed.) (2001) *Internet Crime*. London: Routledge.

Weinstein, D. and Weinstein, D. (2000) Net game cameo, in D.Bell and B.M. Kennedy (eds) *The Cybercultures Reader*. London: Routledge.

Zickmund, S. (2000) Approaching the radical Other: The discursive culture of cyberhate, in D. Bell and B.M. Kennedy (eds) *The Cybercultures Reader*. London: Routledge.

Critical connections

Brown's discussion of the cyber cuts across a number of the readings in this book. William Gibson's depiction of cyberspace, Jean Baudrillard's notion of hyperreality, and Manuel Castells' related conception of 'real virtuality' (Reading 7, 6 and 5 respectively) are all relevant. Indeed, keen to acknowledge the conceptual roots of the virtual world, Brown is insistent that 'any consideration of the cyber must begin with a consideration of William Gibson's *Neuromancer*, for it was in this book that cyberspace was given its first articulation' (Reading 7). Whilst Sheila Brown focuses primarily on the criminogenic properties of cyberspace and the potential for new forms of criminality online, Katja Franko Aas (Reading 40) is concerned to understand the potential for new forms of online social governance. Both readings include a clear sense of the postmodern in their questioning of the boundaries between the virtual and the real, and seek to develop new lines of enquiry and new directions in criminological research that might encourage a more sustained and serious consideration of the virtual world as a site of crime, governance and control.

Discussion questions

- Identify and discuss some of the main dangers surfing in cyberspace.
- Whose responsibility is it to police cyberspace?
- What are the key methodological, theoretical, empirical and ethical challenges facing researchers of cybercrime and virtual victimisation (see also Readings 6, 14 and 40)?

Katja Franko Aas

BEYOND 'THE DESERT OF THE REAL': CRIME CONTROL IN A VIRTUAL(ISED) REALITY (2006)

Introduction and context

K ATJA FRANKO AAS's (2007) main objective in 'Beyond "the Desert of the Real"', is to explore the relations between offline and online aspects of social governance, particularly as they relate to the control of crime. Aas presents a case for criminologists to engage more fully with the cyber and to integrate cyber concerns and cyber life into the mainstream of criminological research and writing. Drawing from recent work by Sheila Brown (see also Reading 39), and others, she challenges the conventional binary oppositions that have contributed to keeping criminological study of the cyber on the margins. As a number of readings in this collection make clear (Readings 6, 7, 39), the once rigid boundaries separating natural and artificial, technological and social, physical and virtual, represented and real are becoming increasingly permeable and blurred. Thus to continue considering, as many criminologists have, the cyber – and the crimes that take place there – as a distinct realm with distinct rules, is to fail to recognise the 'hybridity' of reality and the varying degrees of virtuality discernible in many contemporary forms of crime and control. Building on the notion of 'simulation' first developed by Jean Baudrillard (1981 – Reading 6), Aas illustrates the significance for contemporary criminology of the blurred distinction between the virtual and the real by systematically considering issues of communities and community safety, surveillance and supervision, extraterritoriality and solidarity, and social and cyber governance.

The 'passion for the Real'

It may no longer be necessary to point out the extent to which information and communication technologies (ICTs) have become engrained into the fabric of our daily lives and have become a cornerstone of the new global economic order (Castells, 2002). According to some reports, the average Briton spends around 164 minutes online every day, compared with 148 minutes watching television (*Guardian*, 8 March 2006). This connectivity has inevitably been a source of vulnerability and insecurity, as pointed out by several contributions in this volume. My children's Internet use and my online eBay and Amazon.com accounts make me feel more vulnerable than if I simply forget to lock my home when leaving for work (see Brenner, this volume). Nevertheless, these risks and insecurities have been somewhat slow to penetrate the canon of mainstream criminology.[1] In that respect criminology may be prone to, paraphrasing Žižek (2002), a certain 'passion for the Real', privileging 'real' life and experiences.

The relative reluctance of criminologists to incorporate the subject of cyber life into their research and writing may partly stem from some central theoretical dualisms and binary oppositions between beings and things, and technology and society, which define the conceptual apparatus of criminology. Brown argues that:

> Criminology has frequently been overly preoccupied with theoretical binary oppositions and this has resulted in a commitment to boundary maintenance strategies within criminological knowledge. The complexities of contemporary technological culture, however, demand precisely the dissolution of binary oppositions and, more particularly, human/technical splitting in the apprehension of the phenomenon of crime. (2006: 223)

This dualist approach, and its inherent tendency to essentialise the technological as instrumental properties of 'things', fails to recognise the transformative qualities of ICTs on the nature of our sociality and subjectivity. Maintaining clear boundaries between the social and the technical, and the 'real' and the virtual, is a strategy wrought with paradox in a world increasingly marked by global communication flows, mediation and simulation (Baudrillard, 1994; Shields, 2003). Nobody inhabits only cyberspace, and increasingly fewer people populate only the physical world as well (Kendall, 2002). However, the perception of life on the screen as an essentially separate realm of existence is not only endorsed by criminological 'realists' but also by many students and participants of cyber life who argue for its unique nature as a space of freedom. As Kendall (2002: 10) notes, 'much of the hype and hope of cyberspace reside in its sovereignty and separation from "real life" and its ability to correct the inequalities existing outside its boundaries'.

On the other hand, inspired by the so-called actor-network theory popularised by Latour and Callon, Brown (2006) proposes developing a 'criminology of hybrids' in order to account for the blurring lines between the technical and non-technical realms. Similarly, Barry (2001) tries to bridge the gap between the social and the technical by suggesting that we should focus instead on concrete arrangements of people and technical products in various forms and circumstances:

> [I]nstead of drawing a line between the social and the technical, one might instead analyse *arrangements*: of artefacts, practices and techniques, instruments, language and bodies. These arrangements make up what we tend to think of as persons and institutions: states, markets, families and

so on. They are collectivities which include technological components. In principle, the complexity of such arrangements is irreducible to their distinct 'social' and 'technical', 'natural' and 'cultural' elements. (Barry, 2001: 9, emphasis in original)

Consequently, Brown (2006) questions the view of cybercrime as a separate realm with its own rules of behaviour. While undoubtedly carrying much leverage, the perception of cybercrime as a *sui generis* category, distinct from 'embodied' crime, further emphasises the boundaries between the virtual and the 'real'. Brown (2006: 236) on the other hand suggests that 'crimes as network activities only contain varying degrees of virtual or embodied monads'. This approach therefore emphasises the blending of the virtual and the physical, and the creation of new hybrid forms of sociality. Similarly, the 'Virtual Society? Get Real!' appeal by Woolgar (2002) not only aptly covers the need to calm down the hype and hyperbole surrounding the alleged exceptionality of the virtual, but also serves as an encouragement to inscribe the virtual into the real-life contexts from which it emerges.

'Look past the flesh and see your enemy'

The previous discussion indicates that the meaning of the virtual is far from obvious. Shields (2003) points out that the term has a long history: from various rituals and ritual spaces to *trompe-l'oeil* simulations in baroque architecture and beliefs in angels and ghosts. As such, the virtual represents 'a long held human capacity for imagination and a perceptual flair for filling in the gaps and flashing out visual images' (p. 71). Today, there is talk of the virtual office, virtual university, virtual relationships, virtual tours and even virtual warfare. Virtualisation is a vital part of the global capitalist economy (Castells, 2002). The digital virtuality of the Internet and of computer games is therefore only one of several forms of virtuality present in contemporary life.

It is also not uncommon (including in academic discussions) to find a phenomenon's importance – and hence 'reality' – illustrated by the number of 'hits' it gets on the Internet. Nor is it uncommon to 'Google' a person or subject to gain an impression of their nature. Therefore, rather than opposing the virtual with the real, Shields (2003) suggests that the virtual should be opposed to the actual and the concrete. Seen from this perspective, the virtual is real, but it is so only in essence and 'not actually so' (ibid.: 43). This view demands that we broaden our understanding of 'reality' and break it down 'into more fine-grained concepts' (ibid.: 20). [I]t is precisely an awareness of the hybridity of 'reality' that enables us to understand the various aspects and degrees of virtuality in many forms of contemporary crime and its control.

Teenagers playing online computer games may not inhabit the same physical space, yet they simultaneously interact in a *social* space, building teams and memories of youthful mastery, conquest and adventure which have as much an effect on their offline friendships as they do online. 'Real-life' embodied friendships are thus built through participation in online environments: 'Just as the virtual becomes more a part of everyday thought process, so everyday life is mixed up in the digitally virtual' (Shields, 2003: 114). Similarly, contemporary sex work and the sex trade in many ways retain their essentially embodied and abusive nature, while at the same time being facilitated and transformed by information and communication technologies such as the Internet and mobile phones (Altman, 2001; Sharp and Earle, 2003). The Internet offers prostitution guides to potential sex tourists and local customers in almost any corner of the world (Monzini, 2005). And while the famous 'electronic cloak' (DiMarco, 2003) enables netizens to experiment with their identity and to free themselves from the constraints of embodiment, some findings suggest that people's online personas often bear a considerable resemblance to their embodied counterparts, and that so-called virtual identities are often strongly connected to the 'real' selves (Kendall, 2002; Woolgar, 2002). Relationships of power, gender, race and global economic inequality are permeating cyber life, and are inscribed in cyber relations, just as they are in terrestrial life (Jewkes and Sharp, 2003; Cunneen and Stubbs, 2004). Kendall therefore argues that:

> People who choose to enter online social spaces do not leave their offline world behind when they do so, but rather begin a process of weaving online communications and activities into their existing offline lives. (2002:16)

This process of 'weaving' is precisely what I want to examine further, the exceptional growth of blogging in recent years being one case in point. Life on the screen is not only a space of freedom from terrestrial constraints and governmental intervention but is gradually becoming an essential medium through which contemporary social mobilisations, including those related to crime and punishment, take place (see also Cere, this volume). Online communication has become 'an important site for the contestation of group values. Indeed, it is through this very contestation that new forms of collectivity are imagined and performed' (Valier, 2004: 93).

It is a telling example that the prime 'public enemies' of our time, Osama Bin Laden and his alleged network, are rendered 'real' primarily through various forms of virtually mediated reality such as videos and recorded messages posted on the Internet. Furthermore, abductions and executions of hostages in Iraq are frequently confirmed to global audiences by online videos. In that respect, 'look past the flesh and see your enemy', yet another *Matrix* line, captures the spirit. The Internet is therefore not only marked by its potential to obscure the face of the Other, but is also increasingly becoming a forum for creating images of the Other – not only criminal offenders, but also members of religious and ethnic groups, or, for that matter, supporters of opposing football teams. And as much as radical Muslim identities tend to be described as primitive and uncivilised by the various 'clash of civilisations' theses, they are sustained by distinctly global networks of communications such as the Internet, mobile phones and global television networks. Online connections are nurturing offline mobilisations by evoking a language adjusted to the cultural ethos of the MTV generation. [. . .]

Virtual or virtualised communities?

In his characteristically radical evaluation of the American condition, Baudrillard suggests that it is beyond the point to look for the 'real' behind the simulation, as simulation *is* social reality. Today, the question is no longer one of false representation of reality but 'of concealing the fact that the real is no longer real, and thus of saving the reality principle' (1994: 13). Baudrillard highlights Disneyland as the paradigmatic representation of the contemporary simulated existence. However, rather than describing Disneyland as exceptional, he claims that 'Disneyland exists in order to hide that it is the "real" country, all of America, that *is* Disneyland' (ibid.: 12). The theme has been taken up in recent years by a number of authors analysing simulated environments such as theme parks, tourist enclaves, shopping malls, restaurant and hotel chains, and the like, which have gradually become a prominent aspect of our daily lives (Cubitt, 2001). In his influential *Disneyization of Society* Bryman (2004) argues that the contemporary world is increasingly converging towards the characteristics of the Disney theme parks.[2]

This literature raises the question of whether we can draw the line between the simulated and the 'authentic', including people's own experiences of their surroundings. In a recent documentary one resident of the celebrated Disney-created town Celebration recounted his experience: 'It was like coming home' (NRK, 2005). Home, however, was in this case a place that had previously never existed and was based on fictional representations. The point here is that staged reality may be experienced as 'authentic', perhaps in some cases even more authentic than the mundane and often dreary surroundings we otherwise inhabit.[3] One could clearly argue that the aforementioned academic perception of the contemporary (particularly American) condition as inauthentic and simulated is itself becoming somewhat of a cliché. Simulation theory is, as Cubitt (2001: 99) points out, open to the accusation that it plays 'a part in the processes through which the world loses its reality'. However, the theory's fundamental redrawing of the concept of 'real' and 'reality' is an important contribution which I want to draw further on.

Hayward (2004) points to the general criminological significance of consumer culture for the transformation of the contemporary urban experience. He raises the question of whether simulated urban spaces, exemplified by Ropongi, Tokyo, represent 'the future for urban spaces based around pleasure and entertainment':

> Groups of young people of differing nationalities staring into multi-sonorous screens, popping strobes and virtual reality headsets, each one obsessively re-playing looped games, prior to heading out into the trance-like world of Ropongi's 'club scene' to experience yet another 'controlled loss of control', this time via a combination of digitally looped dance music and designer drugs. (2004: 193)

Contemporary web-based technologies [. . .] need to be understood within the broader social context of blurring boundaries between the virtual and the real, and of how simulation is inscribed into everyday life. California residents, for example, can obtain information about registered sex offenders in their community on a website operated by the Office of the Attorney General (http://www.meganslaw.ca.gov/). Information provided includes name, aliases, age, gender, race, physical description and photograph, as well as an individual's criminal convictions. Users can search the website by city, county, zip code or individual name. They can also type in the name of a park or school in a community to locate on a digital map sex offenders living in the vicinity. Importantly, the site provides home addresses of about 33,500 of the most serious offenders. Similar, more or less extensive registers are available in the majority of the US states. In this context, the virtually-mediated dangers can be experienced as more 'real' than individuals' actual and concrete experiences of these dangers, thus creating a separate world of hyper-real danger in the community (Shields, 2003).

The 'Megan's Law' mapping system described above can be seen as yet another example of the emerging surveillance society (Lyon, 2001). However, it also provides an insight into the changing notions of community and danger. The system represents by no means the kind of community that first comes to mind when we think of a virtual community. Nonetheless, it is an example of how the new punitive discourse about community safety – represented by the website's motto 'keeping children safe/parents informed' – is appropriating the surveillance potential of the latest technologies. And although the system can be seen as yet another example of the famous American exceptionalism, it needs to be pointed out that online mapping of offline dangers is a far more pervasive phenomenon. Geographic information systems (GIS) are gradually becoming a standard item of police equipment. Besides being a tool for facilitating efficiency and effectiveness of policing and allocation of resources, these systems also offer a simulated construction of community as an 'information hub'. Introducing the language of 'crime hotspots', 'criminogenic areas' and 'yob maps' (Coleman, 2004: 79), these systems provide and create images of low- and high-risk communities to the police and other agencies (Gundhus, 2005). [. . .]

As the examples of GIS and online sex offender registers indicate, the virtual is intricately woven into contemporary (actual and concrete) practices of social exclusion. Many aspects of community safety practices are shot through with virtu-alisation and 'surveillant simulation'. The question therefore arises: what is virtual and what is real? And what, after all, *is* a virtual community?

'We are all Danes now'

In contrast to the calculated risk management aspects outlined above, the Internet also represents a forum for more emotional, often hateful, discourses about deviance and crime control. In her analysis of online communication about crimes, trials and punishment, Valier (2004) shows how the Internet has become a site for various forms of 'technological populism' by encouraging popular participation in web polls and debates about crime and punishment, while framing the discussions in terms of 'tabloid justice':

> The Internet plays an important part in the spread of tabloid justice. It permits anyone to act as reporter or publisher of images and information, to transmit material on any topic to a potentially global audience, as well as allowing people to participate in real-time conversations with distant others. (Ibid.: 97)

Through online communication the 'new punitiveness' (Pratt et al., 2005) finds an additional forum, particularly as the Internet to a large extent transcends the restrictions imposed on print and television by legal and professional journalistic standards. The shift in the balance between populism and professionalism (Garland, 2001) therefore gains an additional dimension through the mushrooming of online forums.

Rather than seeing the Internet as an agent of social anomie and individualism or, alternatively, as an embodiment of the libertarian ideas of cyber tolerance and democracy, Valier (2004) points to emerging forms of online community and solidarity relating to issues of crime and punishment. Online communications 'bring new forms of imagined co-presence and connectedness, which question the Durkheimian association of the passion of punishment with locally or nationally based *communitas*' (p. 109). In highly publicised murder cases, such as that of James Bulger, these communications may obtain a global reach and form 'transnational vengeful networks' (p. 103). What is important here is that the extraterritorial nature of online communication transforms the dynamics of public penal discourse and social belonging, which has been traditionally connected to bounded local and national communities.

The extraterritorial nature of new technologies opens up new and broader forms of solidarity. However, the idea of 'unbounded sociability' promoted by the early virtual community enthusiasts (Rheingold, 1993), clearly has some exclusionary undertones. 'We are all Danes now' was a message emerging on several websites in the aftermath of this year's heated discussions about Muhammad cartoons, first published in a Danish newspaper. The message was reminiscent of the one displayed on the cover of the French newspaper *Le Monde*, in the aftermath of the 11 September attacks, proclaiming that 'We are all Americans now'. Other than expressing global solidarity, the messages are a sign of the emerging 'world risk society', a society connected by its shared awareness and fear of 'de-bounded' global risks (Beck, 2002; Aas, 2006). The so far privileged position of the state and the national as the primary field of criminological reference seems to be increasingly overshadowed by various transnational and subnational configurations (Aas, 2006). Within the context of the network society and the space of flows, racial and religious hatred as well as fear and solidarity transcend national boundaries and increasingly gain transnational dimensions.

Emerging notions of online community need to be understood within the broader context of global transformations and the virtualisation of the transnational into a hybrid online/offline globality.[4] The world of global networks and flows introduces new notions of social ordering and exclusion, as well as challenging the prevailing conceptions of society, community, culture, and social belonging (Aas, 2006). Therefore, the virtual/real dichotomy runs parallel with the more frequently debated global/local division. Robertson's (1995) highly influential term 'glocalisation' may be a useful pointer here, denoting the immanent intertwining of the global and the local, as well as the online and offline hybridity. As Appadurai points out when it comes to the question of virtual neighbourhoods:

> These virtual neighbourhoods seem on the face of it to represent just that absence of face-to-face links, spatial contiguity, and multiplex social interaction that the idea of a neighbourhood seems centrally to imply. Yet we must not be too quick to oppose highly spatialised neighbourhoods to these virtual neighbourhoods of international electronic communication.

The relationship between these two forms of neighbourhood is considerably more complex. (Appadurai, 1996:195)

Appadurai points out that in the case of long-distance nationalism, virtual
neighbourhoods have a considerable impact on locally lived neighbourhoods by
mobilising ideas, opinions, money and social linkages. The perception of the Internet,
and globalisation in general, as the antithesis of local community has shown to be
a truth with many modifications. Even though the technical space of the Internet
appears to be boundless, its social space and effects are not necessarily global, but
rather depend on multiple local contexts and constraints.

Online social environments are not only media for almost unlimited self-expression
and experimentation with identity, although this certainly is the case (Jewkes, 2003),
but also spaces for shaping and maintaining typically 'terrestrial' social mobilisations,
such as national(istic) and diasporic identities and discourses about crime and
punishment. In addition to providing 'a locus for creative authorship of the self'
(Jewkes and Sharp, 2003: 3), through blogs, chat groups and other fora, the Net also
increasingly becomes a locus for constructing the face of our (global) Others, and
thus becomes an integral part of contemporary strategies of social exclusion.
Innumerable Internet marriage marketing sites, for example, offer First World men
essentialised and racialised representations of Third World women as commodities.
These virtually mediated male fantasies can often, as Cunneen and Stubbs (2004)
show, end in a tragically violent reality. Similarly, the process of constructing and
engaging with 'exotic others' through numerous sex tourism websites has made commercial sex an essential part of the contemporary tourist experience (Altman, 2001;
O'Connell Davidson, 2005). These cyber subjectivities therefore precede physical
encounters, often creating images of 'perfect partners' which are impossible to fulfil
in reality (Cunneen and Stubbs, 2004). The virtual tourist and the virtual mail-order
bride are marked by racial, economic and sexual relations whose online and offline
dimensions are hard to untwine (Letherby and Marchbank, 2003).

Governance in a 'borderless' world

> Links to a bloody new Flash videogame called Border Patrol, whose
> object is to kill as many illegal immigrants as possible, are making the
> rounds through email forwards. The game, which comes at a time when
> US leaders are working to revive a sweeping immigration bill in the
> Senate, encourages players to kill targets such as a 'Mexican nationalist',
> 'drug smuggler' and 'breeder' (a pregnant woman with two small
> children) 'at any cost' . . . 'I certainly defend the game,' says self-described
> white supremacist Tom Metzger. 'I told a Mexican activist that he
> better be happy that we're just playing a game on a computer, because
> the temper of thousands . . . is reaching boiling point'. (Newsweek,
> 2006a)

In Bordergames, freely available on the Web at bordergames.org, the player
can take on the role of a young North African immigrant. Having entered

> Spain illegally and settled in Madrid, he must find work, avoid deportation, choose friends wisely and sidestep potential enemies. Social workers can help him integrate or find a job, but telling them his real name and home-town could lead to deportation. Drug dealers may be the wrong types to associate with, but they procure papers in order to find work . . .
> (Newsweek, 2006b)

Terrestrial borders were for a long time seen as the antithesis of cyberlife. The prevailing image of the Internet was of a boundless economic frontier, a realm of freedom, often seen also as an almost complete absence of constraints, resembling a state of nature or the Wild West (Kendall, 2002). This perception of cyberspace as an idealised version of the liberal society – self-regulating, populated by free individuals engaged in communities of common interests – had a clear affinity with the laissez-faire ideology of the 1980s and 1990s and the prevailing ideal of minimal state and other regulatory intervention. In the heyday of neo-liberalism some observers also seemed to think that globalisation would eventually lead to a borderless world (Ohmae, 1990). This enchantment with the notion of a borderless world, however, was considerably longer-lived in the case of cyber-libertarians than it was in the case of terrestrial neo-liberal societies. Borders, and the protection of borders, have become an extremely salient and heated topic in the post-9/11 world (Aas, 2006), as the two computer games described above symbolically illustrate.

More important at this point is that the popular notion of cyberspace as a 'new frontier' and a space of unencumbered freedom has also gone through some funda-mental revisions. One of the most salient criticisms came from Lawrence Lessig's *Code and Other Laws of Cyberspace* (1999). Refuting the popular perception that cyber-space 'cannot be governed', Lessig powerfully argues that the Net is evolving from 'an unregulable space to one that is highly regulable. The "nature" of the Net might once have been its unregulability; that "nature" is about to flip' (p. 25). Consequently, governance of the Internet is increasingly designed to fit the predominant features of the contemporary market societies:

> [T]he invisble hand of cyberspace is building an architecture that is quite the opposite of what it was at cyberspace's birth. The invisible hand, through commerce, is constructing an architecture that perfects control – an architecture that makes possible highly efficient regulation.
> (Ibid.: 6)

Therefore, when it comes to online governance, the focus is gradually moving beyond the abstract debates between libertarians and proponents of state intervention, and acknowledging instead the specific varieties of technologies of governance that invariably develop in any kind of human interaction. We are witnessing not only the introduction of various types of private commercial barriers and surveillance efforts, but also a continuing salience of state surveillance and intervention, justified by a variety of online and offline concerns such as terrorism, pornography, spam, intellectual property rights and free speech (Luke, 1999; Lyon, 2003). Preston (2004) points out that, contrary to popular belief, state policies have been essential to the Internet's genesis, growth, direction and governance (security policy, content regulation and access), and that this political intervention in Internet governance and development can have a potentially positive role. This, of course, is still an intensely debated issue, and disagreements between cyber 'regulators' and 'libertarians' may at times seem as heated as ever, with the former, however, increasingly gaining ground when it comes to dictating practice.

In cyberlife, as in terrestrial life, the notion of freedom from regulation privileges a certain set of social values at the expense of others. Like our terrestrial selves, our cyber selves populate thoroughly regulated and commercialised environments, where democratically elected bodies lose out to private forms of regulation in the name of freedom. One of the major critiques mounted by Lessig is that the architecture of the Internet itself is not neutral and that we need to unveil the normative behind the seemingly 'natural' and technical. 'Code codifies values, and yet, oddly, most people speak as if code were just a question of engineering' (Lessig, 1999: 59). The code regulating cyberspace comes closer to natural laws, making breaches not only illegal but also impossible, just as architectural features of our physical environments enable certain behaviours while precluding others. The blurring lines between the normative and the technical are also gradually becoming a topic of criminological research due to the increasingly code-like language of 'terrestrial' penal governance (Deleuze, 1997; Lianos and Douglas, 2000; Jones, 2000; Aas, 2005). Contemporary governance is adopting the language of computer-mediated technologies. And even though the buzz word of e-governance perhaps hasn't quite lived up to its hype, it is making an unmistakable impact on the ways we govern and relate to social institutions. Understanding the parameters of cyber governance may therefore open up more productive ways of examining and understanding the offline mechanisms of social governance (Jones, 2005).

Conclusion

Acknowledging the blurred lines of distinction between the 'virtual' and the 'real' carries a number of benefits for criminological enquiry. Issues of cybercrime and 'life on the screen' touch on some of the central themes and transformations within the field of criminological interests: from questions of impersonality and disembeddedness of social relations, transnational crime and the changing role of the state in a globalising world, to the issues of postmodernity, subjectivity, technology and control. [. . .]

The extraterritoriality of the Internet and its (perceived and inherent) ingovernability challenge established notions of territorial penal governance. As Valier (2004: 92) observes:

> Penality has conventionally been thought in terms of the bounded entities of local community and nation-state. The penal practices of today however are shaped by the myriad ways in which global networks and flows, exemplified by the Internet, reconfigure the significance of the nation state.

While criminology in general is still in many ways deeply attached to the notion of the territorial nation state, the phenomena it seeks to understand increasingly seem to be global and transnational (Aas, 2006).

There is therefore a need to develop concepts and methods that are sensitive to the complexities of the global. However, a considerable part of criminological research appears in many ways to be guilty of what Beck (2002) terms 'methodological nationalism' – equating social boundaries with state boundaries, and having a nation-state outlook on society, law and justice. This may be partly due to the traditional connection between criminological knowledge and the nation-state apparatus. Consequently, criminology still is theoretically and methodologically badly equipped for understanding the relevance of the emerging space of flows (Aas, 2006). Here, cyber life with its (albeit mistaken) image of a boundless frontier may have much to offer, particularly as the old binary oppositions between the virtual and the 'real', global and local, and technological and social, become fluid and increasingly hard to discern.

Notes

1. The words cyber and Internet do not appear in the prestigious *Oxford Handbook of Criminology* (Maguire et al., 2002), and these topics are only gradually attracting the attention of criminological textbooks.
2. One needs only to think of Dubai, one of the centres of the world economy and tourism, which is a city wrought through with simulation. One can ski in the middle of the desert, shop in immense shopping malls, play golf or tennis high above the sea and reside in gigantic hotels and on palm-shaped artificial islands.
3. Urry (2002: 9) points out that many tourist spaces are organised around 'staged authenticity' and a quest for experiences in other 'times' and other places away from everyday life.
4. I'm grateful to Richard Jones for bringing this to my attention.

References

Aas, K. F. (2005) *Sentencing in the Age of Information: From Faust to Macintosh*. London: GlassHouse Press.

Aas, K. F. (2006) 'Controlling a world in motion: global flows meet "criminology of the other"', *Theoretical Criminology*, 10 (forthcoming).

Altman, D. (2001) *Global Sex*. Chicago and London: University of Chicago Press.

Appadurai, A. (1996) *Modernity at Large: Cultural Dimensions of Globalization*. Minneapolis, MN: University of Minneapolis Press.

Barker, C. (1999) *Television, Globalization and Cultural Identities*. Buckingham: Open University Press.

Barry, A. (2001) *Political Machines: Governing a Technological Society*. London and New York: Athlone Press.

Baudrillard, J. (1994) *Simulacra and Simulation*. Ann Arbor, MI: University of Michigan Press.

Beck, U. (2002) 'The terrorist threat: world risk society revisited', *Theory, Culture & Society*, 19 (4): 39–55.

Beck, U. (2003) 'The analysis of global inequality: from national to cosmopolitan perspective', in M. Kaldor et al. (eds), *Global Civil Society*. London: Centre for the Study of Global Governance, Yearbook 2003.

Brown, S. (2006) 'The criminology of hybrids: rethinking crime and law and technosocial networks', *Theoretical Criminology*, 10 (2): 223–44.

Bryman, A. (2004) *The Disneyization of Society*. London: Sage.

Castells, M. (2002) *The Internet Galaxy: Reflections on the Internet, Business, and Society*. Oxford: Oxford University Press.

Coleman, R. (2004) *Reclaiming the Streets: Surveillance, Social Control and the City*. Cullompton: Willan.

Cubitt, S. (2001) *Simulation and Social Theory*. London: Sage.

Cunneen, C. and Stubbs, J. (2004) 'Cultural criminology and engagement with race, gender and post-colonial identities', in J. Ferrell et al. (eds), *Cultural Criminology Unleashed*. London: GlassHouse Press.

Deleuze, G. (1997) 'Postscript on the societies of control', in N. Leach (ed.), *Rethinking Architecture: A Reader in Cultural Theory*. London: Routledge.

DiMarco, H. (2003) 'The electronic cloak: secret sexual deviance in cybersociety', in Y. Jewkes (ed.) *Dot.cons: Crime, Deviance and Identity on the Internet*. Cullompton: Willan.

Garland, D. (2001) *The Culture of Control*. Oxford: Oxford University Press.

Guardian (2006) 'Britain turns off – and logs on' (online at: http://technology.guardian.co.uk/print/0,,329429230-117802,00.html).

Gundhus, H. (2005) '"Catching" and "Targeting": risk-based policing, local culture and gendered practices', *Journal of Scandinavian Studies in Criminology and Crime Prevention*, 6: 128–46.

Hayward, K. (2004) *City Limits: Crime, Consumer Culture and the Urban Experience*. London: GlassHouse Press.

Jewkes, Y. (ed.) (2003) *Dot.cons: Crime, Deviance and Identity on the Internet*. Cullompton: Willan.

Jewkes, Y. and Sharp, K. (2003) 'Crime, deviance and the disembodied self: transcending the dangers of corporeality', in Y. Jewkes (ed.), *Dot.cons: Crime, Deviance and Identity on the Internet*. Cullompton: Willan.

Jones, R. (2000) 'Digital rule: punishment, control and technology', *Punishment & Society*, 2 (1): 5–22.

Jones, R. (2005) 'Entertaining code: file sharing, digital rights management regimes, and criminological theories of compliance', *International Review of Law, Computers and Technology*, 19 (3): 287–303.

Kendall, L. (2002) *Hanging Out in the Virtual Pub: Masculinities and Relationships Online*. Berkeley, CA: University of California Press.

Lessig, L. (1999) *Code and Other Laws of Cyberspace*. New York: Basic Books.

Letherby, G. and Marchbank, J. (2003) 'Cyber-chattels: buying brides and babies on the Net' in Y. Jewkes (ed.), *Dot.cons: Crime, Deviance and Identity on the Internet*. Cullompton: Willan Publishing.

Lianos, M. with M. Douglas (2000) 'Dangerization and the end of deviance', in D. Garland and R. Sparks (eds), *Criminology and Social Theory*. Oxford: Oxford University Press.

Luke, T. W. (1999) 'Simulated sovereignty, telematic territoriality: the political economy of cyberspace', in M. Featherstone and S. Lash (eds), *Spaces of Culture: City – Nation –World*. London: Sage.

Lyon, D. (2001) *Surveillance Society: Monitoring Everyday Life*. Buckingham: Open University Press.

Lyon, D. (2003) *Surveillance After September 11*. Cambridge: Polity Press.

Maguire, M., Morgan, R. and Reiner, R. (eds) (2002) *The Oxford Handbook of Criminology*. Oxford: Oxford University Press.

Monzini, P. (2005) *Sex Traffic: Prostitution, Crime and Exploitation*. London and New York: Zed Books.

Newsweek (2006a) 'Games without frontiers', *Newsweek International*, 10 April, p. 12.

Newsweek (2006b) 'Over the (border) line' (online at: http://www.msnbc.msn.com/id/12554978/site/newsweek).

NRK (2005) *Celebration*. BBC Productions, 5 November.

O'Connell Davidson, J. (2005) *Children in the Global Sex Trade*. Cambridge: Polity.

Ohmae, K. (1990) *The Borderless World: Power and Strategy in the Interlinked Economy*. London: Collins.

Pratt, J., Brown, D., Brown, M., Hallworth, S. and Morrison, W. (eds) (2005), *The New Punitiveness: Trends, Theories, Perspectives*. Cullompton: Willan.

Preston, P. (2004) *The Meaning of Internet Governance*. Paper presented at the CMC Conference, Oslo, 3–4 November.

Rheingold, H. (1993) *The Virtual Community: Homesteading on the Electronic Frontier*. New York: Addison-Wesley.

Robertson, R. (1995) 'Glocalization: time – space and homogeneity – heterogeneity?', in M. Featherstone et al. (eds), *Global Modernities*. London: Sage.

Sharp, K. and Earle, S. (2003) 'Cyberpunters and cyberwhores: prostitution on the Internet', in Y. Jewkes (ed.), *Dot.cons: Crime, Deviance and Identity on the Internet*. Cullompton: Willan.

Shields, R. (2003) *The Virtual*. London and New York: Routledge.

Urry, J. (2002) *The Tourist Gaze*, 2nd edn. London: Sage.

Valier, C. (2004) *Crime and Punishment in Contemporary Culture*. London and New York: Routledge.

Woolgar, S. (ed.) (2002) *Virtual Society? Technology, Cyberbole, Reality*. Oxford: Oxford University Press.

Žižek, S. (2002) *Welcome to the Desert of the Real! Five Essays on September 11 and Related Dates*. London and New York: Verso.

Critical connections

The phrase 'the desert of the real', which Aas incorporates into the title of the piece excerpted here, was first used by Jean Baudrillard to depict a postmodern landscape on which mediatised images or simulations of reality become more meaningful and relevant, more perfect, more 'real' to people than the physical reality that surrounds them (1981 – Reading 6). In a deliberate nod to Baudrillard's work, it was also used by Morpheus in the Hollywood movie the *Matrix* (1999) to describe the 'reality' Neo encounters when he awakens from the computer simulation which to that point had for him constituted the 'real'. And Slavoj Žižek used the phrase again to describe the events of September 11 2001, suggesting the attacks represented a violent intrusion of 'reality' into the universe of First World citizens – a digital, artificial universe, insulated from the realities of the Third World 'desert of the real'. The terrifying spectacle of the Twin Towers falling – itself like a scene from a Hollywood disaster movie – shattered the illusion that such atrocities could only happen to the 'them' outside the First World, never to the 'us' in it.

Thus Baudrillard (Reading 6), Žižek and Aas, as well as Castells (Reading 5), are all concerned to understand particular aspects of the blurring of the boundaries between the represented and the real. Their respective approaches usefully illustrate how theoretical concepts – for example, Baudrillard's notion of simulation – can be developed, adapted and applied across a range of contexts and situations. In Aas' case, this deliberation extends to cyberspace and, echoing Sheila Brown 's concerns in Reading 39 – proposes that the traditionally straightforward differentiation between the real world and the virtual world may be more problematic than has been previously accepted. The notion of the mediatisation of social governance is taken in a different direction again in Gabe Mythen and Sandra Walklate's analysis of the 'war on terror' (Reading 41).

Discussion questions

- Discuss how contemporary formations of crime and criminal justice blend the virtual and the physical.
- In what ways might the contemporary world be said to be converging towards the characteristics of Disney theme parks?
- Why have some postmodernists described advanced capitalist societies as existing in a digital, artificial and insulated universe (see also Readings 5 and 6)?

References

Baudrillard, J. (2002) 'The Spirit of Terrorism', in *Harpers* [original "L'Esprit du Terrorisme," *Le Monde* November 2, 2001]
Žižek, S. (2002) 'Welcome to the Desert of the Real', London: Verso.

Gabe Mythen and Sandra Walklate

COMMUNICATING THE TERRORIST RISK: HARNESSING A CULTURE OF FEAR? (2006)

Introduction and context

G ABE MYTHEN AND SANDRA WALKLATE (2006) consider the British government's framing of the terrorist threat in media discourses following the bombings in New York, Washington, Madrid and London. Their central argument is that the discourse of 'new terrorism' has 'built upon and escalated a cultural climate of fear and uncertainty', politicising the 'war on terror' in a manner that threatens the integrity of liberal democracy. Through harnessing a culture of fear, the state secures tacit consent for the introduction of increasingly repressive legislation, whilst simultaneously promoting notions of responsibilisation that encourage not only individual vigilance, but also suspicion and mistrust of potentially risky situations and individuals. Within this climate of heightened suspicion, media representations of the terrorist threat both reflect and reinforce simplistic notions of the non-white 'terroristic other', which has negative consequences for ethnic minority groups across the UK.

Mythen and Walklate's analysis is structured around the concept of the 'risk society', originally developed by Ulrich Beck (1992). The risk society thesis has gained much currency within criminology. It features to varying degrees and more or less explicitly across a range of attempts to explain the emergence of a new late modern penology or 'culture of control' which differs markedly from the modernist era of penal-welfarism in terms of its discourses, practices and politics. Though different commentators have interpreted the transition in different ways (see Garland, 2001; O'Malley, 2006; Simon, 2006), the rise in individual 'responsibilisation' is widely acknowledged to be a key characteristic of late modern crime control strategies. Mythen and Walklate's (2006) analysis of responsibilisation as a key element in the political discourse and media representation of the 'new terrorism' thus feeds into this wider discussion of the transition to late modern crime control and social order.

___

Risk, security and new terrorism

Much has been made of the cultural ubiquity of risk within contemporary society and the ways in which risk pervades the lived experience of individuals in western cultures. Within the literature, it has been noted that risk filters through a range of cultural practices and experiences in contemporary society, including work, relationships, food consumption, leisure activities, security and personal health (see Beck, 1992; Culpitt, 1999; Caplan, 2000; Denney, 2005; Mythen, 2005a). The surge of interest in risk has led to the concept becoming a key term of reference for academic debate. Indeed, mimicking the rotation towards culture in the 1980s, it would not be stretching the imagination to talk about the 'risk turn' within the social sciences. In perhaps the best-known contribution to risk theory, Beck (1992) emphasizes both the destructive impacts of risk on the lived environment and the transformatory potential of risk within the public sphere. In a nutshell, the risk society thesis suggests that the axis of social distribution within capitalist societies is rotating away from positive problems of acquiring 'goods' (e.g. income, health care, education, housing) towards negative issues of avoiding 'bads' (e.g. crime, environmental pollution, AIDS and terrorism). Whereas the distribution of goods may be sectoral – some win, some lose – the distribution of bads has universal effects. In short, everybody loses. Accordingly, Beck (1992) holds the view that the pervasiveness of risk – both at the level of harm and cognisance – has facilitated a shift from the acquisition of social goods to the avoidance of social bads. This ideational transformation is encouraged by the intensification of media interest in risk conflicts. For Beck the media serve to 'socially explode' risk issues which would otherwise be secreted from the public. What is more, these fluctuations in media and political discourse have important ramifications for modes of communication between institutions and individuals. Instead of appealing to collective desires for the good life, the language of politics increasingly taps into individualized insecurities and fears. [. . .]

Nowhere is the 'risk turn' more apparent than in the current raft of policy initiatives designed to combat terrorism. In the climate of uncertainty in the UK since the July 2005 suicide bombings it is easy to see why terrorism has featured as an academic and political football. This said, it is worth recognizing that, prior to these events, several theorists had heralded 9/11 as a historical watershed that ushered in a new phase of political struggle, legislative change and military conflict (see Kellner, 2002; McLaren and Martin, 2004; Welch, 2003). Since this time, terrorism has climbed sharply up the political agenda (see Curtis, 2004; Furedi, 2005; Rothe and Muzzatti, 2005). A string of high profile incidents around the globe, including the Madrid train bombings, attacks in Bali and the school siege in Beslan, have catapulted terrorism forward as a crucial issue. At the same time, entrenched conflicts in the Middle East – most notably the Arab–Israeli conflict in Palestine and the 'insurgency' in Iraq – have been sucked into the broader question of how nation states can best manage 'new terrorism'. A variety of commentators have been keen to mark off the activities of radical Islamic networks as fundamentally distinct from the operations of traditional terrorist groups. In the aftermath of 9/11, politicians, political journalists, academics and security experts began to talk excitedly about the emergence of a new form of terrorism.

Although academic debates about the formation of 'new' or 'post-modern' forms of terrorism predate the events of 9/11 (see Lesser et al., 1999; Lacquer, 2000), from this point forth the expression 'new terrorism' began to be used as a popular currency among journalists and politicians seeking to distinguish between the activities of Islamic groups such as Al Qaeda and those of traditional terrorist organizations such as ETA, the IRA and the UVF. A cluster of factors are said to differentiate new from traditional forms of terrorism. Due to a combination of global reach, fluid formation and extensive weapons capability we are told that groups such as Al Qaeda and Jemaah Islamiyah are practising radically different and dangerous types of terrorism (Waugh, 2004). While organizations located in Ireland, Spain (Barbaret, 2005) and Italy (Melossi and Selmini, 2001) have historically operated locally under united ideological objectives and strict hierarchies, new terrorist groups are defined by their amorphous aims, disparate organizational structure and capacity to strike across different continents (Morgan, 2004). Rather than being locally self-financed, new terrorist groups are funded by a diverse range of sympathetic sources around the globe, including private financiers, charities and NGOs (Commission Report, 2004: 57). What is more, the new terrorism is said to be more threatening to human life, with active terrorist cells seeking to launch unannounced and spectacular 'high-lethality acts' which directly target civilians (see Lesser et al., 1999: 42; Field, 2005). These debates within security studies are highly significant given that both international military strategy and domestic political legislation recently enacted in the UK assume and presume that the nature of the terrorist threat has changed markedly in the last decade.

In response to the debate about new terrorism, some academics have been stirred to argue that the 2001 attacks on America serve as a break point in social and political relations. In this oeuvre, Beck (2002b: 9) has talked of living in a 'terroristic world risk society', characterized by political disorientation, and perpetual uncertainty: 'there is a sinister perspective for the world after September 11th. It is that uncontrollable risk is now irredeemable and deeply engineered into all the processes that sustain life in advanced societies' (Beck, 2002a: 46). Indeed, the view that there is something unique and historically significant about the events of 9/11 has been echoed in public opinion findings, with over 75 per cent of British people believing that 'the world has changed forever' as a result of the terrorist attacks on New York and Washington (Worcester, 2001: 7). As Jenks (2003) posits, these events appear to have constituted some form of universal transgression. This said, other thinkers have been more circumspect about the historical significance of 9/11, resisting the temptation to see this incident as a critical interregnum. Furedi (2002), for example, points out that, despite the spectacular quality of the strikes on the United States, terrorism is a culturally ubiquitous phenomenon. Further, amidst fears about sophisticated terrorist attacks involving chemical, biological or radiological weapons, it needs to be remembered that the 9/11 attacks were 'in many ways an old fashioned act of terror, executed with low-tech facilities by a small number of zealots driven by unrestrained hatred' (p. 17). Contra Beck, Furedi believes that the current preoccupation with terrorism is symptomatic of a broader trend of focusing on the negative and destructive features of the modern age. A burgeoning 'culture of fear' has taken root in western cultures, promoted by state institutions and exacerbated by those working within the media and security industries. At the very least in the context of the discussion here – and this clearly chimes more with Furedi than Beck – it needs to be acknowledged that terrorism is a historically embedded entity, regardless of whether it is prefixed as 'new'. [. . .]

Communicating risk: making up the 'war against terrorism'

[. . .] Having aligned itself with the US – both in terms of international military policy and domestic counter-terrorist strategy – the UK government has sought to gain public support for international military excursions and the tightening-up of national law and order measures. In an attempt to gain consent for such practices, politicians and senior civil servants have established and drawn upon the discourse of 'new terrorism'. This discourse is ingrained in the language used by government officials and the political ideals expressed through crime, security and immigration policy. In the words of Tony Blair: 'the rules of the game have changed' (cited in Oborne, 2006: v). Post-9/11 a new language of global (in)security has been adopted by senior politicians, security experts and news journalists. The lexicon of the 'war against terrorism' depicts a titanic battle between good and evil waged against 'terror networks' and 'rogue states' (Mythen, 2005b). The 'war against terrorism' is indubitably a battle for hearts and minds as well as a struggle against a determined enemy. To this end, what is surprising is the indeterminacy of the phraseology and the carelessness with which it has been applied. The very expression 'war against terrorism' is something of a misnomer, suggesting as it does the launching of hostilities against an abstract noun rather than an identifiable nation or nations. Despite this, the vocabulary of 'new terrorism' has been prolific and has drawn heavily on stock wartime metaphors: 'even when the war is not a war . . . the same mechanisms of mobilization are used: a situation of national emergency, a common enemy, recourse to community/patriarchy and warrior/masculinity, mandatory inclusion of all irrespective of interest positions' (Steinert, 2003: 281). In our eyes, the 'war against terrorism' seems not to consist of a coherent and precise set of achievable objectives. Rather, it relates to a potentially disparate collection of ideas, about – among other things – foreign policy, national security, warfare, electronic systems of monitoring and crime prevention. Thus, in the UK the 'war against terrorism' metaphor is not simply extending into national policies about immigration, detention, identity cards, policing and surveillance; it actually appears to be driving them (see Mythen and Walklate, 2005). As Steinert (2003: 266) reasons, it is not far fetched to suggest that regulating the consequences of crime and fighting an enemy have become one and the same thing. [. . .]

At an international level, the stitching together of states and groups classified as aberrant is fuelling a generalized climate of fear and hostility. It is both illogical and ideologically dangerous to lump together states with distinct cultures and histories into a single villainous 'axis of evil'. In so far as the atrocities committed by Islamic fundamentalist groups in the United States, Bali and Madrid need to be condemned, it is specious to equate the actions of a tiny minority with the motivations of huge nation states, or the proclivities of different religious faiths. As Barnaby (2003: 11) reasons, public fears about terrorism are likely to be exacerbated by pronouncements by American and British leaders, connecting the 'rogue states' that form an 'axis of evil' (i.e. Iraq, Iran and North Korea) with international terrorist groups. [. . .] The promotion and/or amplification of certain issues by the media can help set the agenda on a given issue and hence amplify or attenuate a sense of danger (Schlesinger et al., 1991; Kasperson and Kasperson, 1996; Philo, 1999). The news media are dependent upon eye-catching and sensational events, and often report on crises that appeal to both base instincts and a shared sense of morality. As Cottle (2005) posits, in certain instances national media outlets can serve to conduct a moral charge that ripples outwards to stakeholder groups in society. Although different media forms will convey messages in different ways, we would argue that there is a visible moral dimension at play in dominant (re)presentations of the terrorist risk. It is likely that the narrative framing of the terrorist threat has acted as a conduit for establishing what Peelo and Soothill (2000: 136) call 'mass endorsement of morality'. While this strategy is argu-ably more rooted in the news values embedded within the media production process than any ideological conspiracy, the danger is that the representation of the terrorist threat becomes misaligned with the potential degree of harm: 'hardly a week goes by without a new initiative or exercise designed to prepare us for, or defend us against, an attack by Al Qaeda or the like . . . with every incremental reaction by the police or government, so our fear levels creep up another notch' (Duffy, 2003: 1). In both the UK and the USA, government officials have worked hard to keep terrorism high on the political and media agendas, particularly in times of relative calm. A good example of this is George Bush's revelation that Al Qaeda had intended to fly a plane into the tallest building on the west coast, the 73-storey Library Tower in Los Angeles. This planned attack, to be executed by members of Jemaah Islamiyah, was uncovered by intelligence services in 2002. Four years later, in February 2006, President Bush reported the terrorist plot in a press conference, prompting the Mayor of Los Angeles, Antonio Villaraigosa, to complain that this was the first he had heard about it (Webb, 2006).

Of course, the ways in which people respond to terrorist attacks such as 7/7 are only partly determined by the incident itself and/or the scale of the disaster. Acts of terrorism are accorded different meanings in line with what they culturally signify and represent. Although the effects of what Cohen (2002) has called 'meta-images of chaos' are yet to be fully understood, it is clear that terrorist attacks are given meaning through cultural, political, economic and social processes. Culturally proximate events – such as 9/11, 3/11 and 7/7 – become longstanding points of media and political reference, while others such as the Beslan siege in Northern Ossetia fade fast. Public responses to terrorism are shaped not solely by the nature of the emergency but also by pre-existing assumptions, underlying cultural values and political attitudes. The capacity of the mass media to cohere emotions and to appeal to moral notions of what a decent society should look like should not be understated (Cottle, 2005: 50). It does not take a seasoned social scientist to locate the politically loaded discursive construction of a Terrorist Other, pictured and framed through the lens of Anglo-American political elites. It is worth pointing out that, prior to 9/11, relatively little attention was given to the activities of Al Qaeda. Since this time, the Al Qaeda network and its frightening cluster of terrorist cells have received almost permanent political and media exposure. There is more than a sneaking suspicion that the vacuum left by the evaporation of the Cold War enemy has been eagerly filled by the new terrorist (see Curtis, 2004). The enhanced 'visibility' of Al Qaeda echoes Joffe's (1999) sentiments about shifting conceptions of the Other: 'in periods of crisis, when anxiety is raised, the out-group moves from being represented as mildly threatening, a challenge to the core values of the society, to being seen as the purveyor of chaos' (p. 23). Following the political line, dominant media representations of radical Islam have de-humanized and demonized in equal measure, encouraging the public to accept a separation between rational western citizens and a monstrous terroristic Other. This reductivist separation between good and evil is at the heart of George Bush Jr.'s appeal to the American public. In the 2006 State of the Union address, the president called for 'the end of tyranny', urging 'the enemies of freedom' to cease purveying 'an ideology of terror and death' (Bush, 2006). It is axiomatic to state that such either–or reasoning has knock-on consequences for attitudes towards human rights and civil responsibilities:

> The balancing of rights has gone: the only rights that matter for most people are the safety rights of selves and loved ones. The sense of shared risk, shared responsibility has also gone: we cope with risk by a constant scanning of all with whom we come into contact to see whether or not they pose a threat to our security and the only way we can operate this scanning is by adopting stereotypes of safe and risky kinds of people. (Hudson, 2003: 74)

As Hudson reasons, terrorism is an inherently complex and polymorphous phenomenon that should not be reduced to base-level political rhetoric. The Hobson's choice the public have been offered – 'either you are with us, or you are with the terrorists' – is, in reality, a non-choice, given that there is no real possibility of thinking in-between or out of kilter with the dominant position (Goh, 2004: 143). Naturally, the accentuation of difference leaves little room for rational attempts to understand the values, objectives and/or grievances of terrorists and instead reduces the terrorist to an inhuman object of hate. The presentation of the terrorist as abject and ultra-deviant meshes into a wider framework through which moral judgements are decided upon and retributive consequences dished out. Media and political construction of the non-white terroristic Other cannot be disassociated from misguided and unsavoury racist reprisals such as the six-fold increase in religious hate crimes in the three weeks following 7 July 2005. [. . .]

The state, responsibilization and the politics of fear

In addition to vindicating potentially repressive forms of legislation, it is also possible to discern how the ideology of 'new terrorism' demands that citizens are not only fearful of the terrorist Other, but also take on responsibility for managing their safety in the ever presence of this terrorist Other. Pertinent here is Garland's (2001) notion of an emergent 'culture of control' typified by the restructuring of criminal justice policy in the UK and the USA. By using the culture of control paradigm Garland conveys an understanding of the way in which the state has adapted to its failure to solve the problem of crime and in so doing has become centrally occupied with controlling crime, an issue that requires quite a different frame of reference. This process of adaptation has three strands to it: denial, acting-out, and responsibilization. In this article we have already considered some aspects of the first two of these strands. Aspects of denial and acting-out are self-evident in the calls for tightening of the laws in relation to terrorism on the one hand and the emotive language used to denounce terrorist activities and reassure the public on the other. However, strategies of responsibilization arguably have a far more subtle edge. Garland develops this idea as a way of depicting the kinds of policies that encourage citizens into 'victimization avoidance' (Karmen, 1990) and thus invite them to work in partnership with crime-control agencies to ensure their safekeeping. As we shall see, it is possible to discern such a strategy of responsibilization being used in efforts to harness a culture of fear, minimally associated with the criminal socially excluded Other, maximally the new terrorist (Hughes, 2004; Greer and Jewkes, 2005).

Not only does the reductivist thinking associated with the 'war against terrorism' harness our fears, it also invites us to be involved in managing the terrorist risk as a logical step towards ensuring our own safe keeping. In order to fully understand the likely nature of public anxiety generated by the exchanges delineated above it is important to recognize that fears about terrorism are pieced together via cultural and linguistic interactions as well as becoming real through physiological and psychological processes. As Tudor (2003) points out, fear is a macro and a micro response, determined by everyday habitat, cultural practices and social structures on the one hand, and bodies, personalities and social subjects on the other. It follows that, in order to properly grasp fears about terrorism, we need to attend to the cultural networks through which such fears are constructed and actualized. Fear is not free floating. Rather, it is indexed to self-resources, individual experiences and the formation of coping strategies (Lee, 2001; Salecl, 2004). Further, as with crime in general, fears about terrorism will be related to locale and bound up with understandings of place (Banks, 2005; Chadee and Ditton, 2005). The complex dynamics that constitute 'fear' mean that managing it is likely to be a messy process, as Burkitt's (2005) analysis of emotional public responses post the Madrid bombings shows. This said, articulations of anxiety that extend – and are reinforced – over long periods of time are likely to both condition and increase levels of fear among the public. As Welch (2003) persuasively argues, in the USA and the UK, the 'war on/against terror/ism' has deployed a range of discursive techniques. The discourse of 'new terrorism' invites fear at many different levels; from, for example, constructions of risky objects and activities (e.g. airplanes, the underground, shopping, travel) through to the categorization of dangerous classes, creeds and countries. In the latter case, sections of the UK media have bundled together 'asylum seekers', 'economic migrants', and 'illegal immigrants', indicating the potential for any or all of these groups to be inclusive of, or the breeding ground for, terrorists (see Hughes, 2004). But how do these different techniques of harnessing fear join up with the process of responsibilization?

As Garland (2001: 126) suggests 'the state's new strategy is not to command and control but rather to persuade and align, to organise, to ensure that other actors play their part', and key to this encouragement 'are publicity campaigns targeted at the public as a whole' (p. 125). In the case of the UK, it is important to note that such notions of 'choice' and 'responsibility' are firmly entrenched within New Labour ideology. More precisely, the New Labour view of the active citizen as an independent agent contrasts sharply with the undesirable dependent subject reliant on the state (see Clarke, 2005: 450). One good example of responsibilization in action is the 2004 emergency advice campaign implemented to educate citizens about what to do in the event of a chemical, biological, radiological or nuclear (CBRN) terrorist attack. As part of a drive to inform the public about how to respond to emergency situations the UK government launched a national campaign to prepare the public for major incidents. A 22-page emergency advice booklet was launched by government in association with safety pressure groups and the Association of Chief Police Officers. The booklet was delivered to 25 million households at an estimated cost of £8 million, made available on the internet and supplemented by advertisements on radio and television. The booklet provides first aid advice, tips on stocking up with provisions and emergency contact numbers. From a governmental perspective, the dissemination of the booklet was driven by the desire to inform citizens of effective measures for self-protection and to reassure the public about the steps being taken to protect against terrorism. [. . .]

We would argue that the balance of information in the emergency advice booklet is skewed towards the individual – 'what you can do to protect yourself and your community against risk' – and away from the state – 'what we are doing to protect you'. The advice leaflet is decidedly mute about the mobilization and organization of emergency services, information about which agencies would be responsible for which types of incident and the range of equipment and resources available to attend to emergency situations. Moreover, there are several areas in which positive and reassuring information might have been communicated. For example, the public have heard very little about the government's overall counterterrorist strategy, headway made in the so-called 'war against terrorism' or advice about different types of terrorist threat. Instead, the advice offered tends to individualize emergency situations, to responsibilize people for their own risk management rather than clearly laying out institutional security strategies. [. . .]

Commenting on wider changes in public policy, Young (1999) has traced a move from the inclusive to the exclusive society, heightened in recent years by what he refers to as 'vindictiveness' (see Young, 2003 about the rise in religious hate crimes referenced earlier). This shift provides the space in which intolerance can breed and fear of the Other (vindictiveness) can manifest itself. This shift has resonance not only for the character of criminal justice, but also for the balance of responsibility for risk between citizens and institutions. Responsibilization then is not confined to crime and crime prevention. It reflects and taps into the ongoing and changing relationship between the citizen and the state that is ingrained within the shift from liberal to neo-liberal democracy. As Jessop (2002) has convincingly argued, this kind of movement reflects a move from the determined state to the hegemonic state, typified by the predominance of 'hegemonic projects that seek to reconcile the particular and the universal by linking the nature and purposes of the state into a broader – but always selective – political, intellectual, and moral vision of the public interest, the good society, the commonweal or some analogous principle of societalisation' (p. 42). As Hunt (2003) points out:

> Responsibilization is always double sided. It lays down a norm against which indi-
> viduals, groups, or individuals may evaluate their own conduct. But it also opens up
> he possibility of moralisation in so far as others may seek to hold individuals to that

standard, regardless of whether or not they have accepted the responsibility. In this
sense responsibilization always involves moralisation. (p. 183)

It is within this moral vision of the good society or the commonwealth – and the
ideological processes of moralization (who is and who is not Other) that underpin
this – that various forms of responsibilization bid us to do a portion of the state's
safety work not only in keeping ourselves safe but also in evaluating the conduct of
others (Clarke, 2005: 452). As Hudson (2003: 65) reasons, suspect individuals and
groups do not have to perpetrate crimes to be identified as criminal. In the same way,
respectable citizens do not have to encounter crime to identify themselves as victims.
In encouraging 'us' to notice and report the unusual in 'them', the socially acceptable
targeting of 'them' becomes vindicated. [. . .]

The ways in which the terrorist threat has been communicated and the processes
that these mechanisms tap into are a clear example of how responsibility, risk and
control have become embedded in our understandings of fear and security.

References

Banks, M.O. (2005) 'Spaces of (In)security: Media and Fear of Crime in Local Context',
    Crime, Media, Culture 1(2): 169–87.

Barbaret, R. (2005) 'Country Survey: Spain', *European Journal of Criminology* 2(3): 341–67.

Barnaby, F. (2003) *How to Build a Nuclear Bomb and Other Weapons of Mass Destruction.*
    London: Granta.

Beck, U. (1992) *Risk Society: Towards a New Modernity.* London: SAGE Publications.

Beck, U. (2002a) 'The Terrorist Threat: World Risk Society Revisited', *Theory, Culture
    & Society* 19(4): 39–55.

Beck, U. (2002b) 'The Silence of Words and the Political Dynamics in the World',
    Logos 1(4): 1–18.

Burkitt, I. (2005) 'Powerful Emotions: Power, Government and Opposition in the
    "War on Terror"', *Sociology* 39(4): 679–95.

Bush, G. (2006) *State of the Union Address.* Washington: White House.

Caplan, P. (2000) *Risk Revisited.* London: Pluto.

Chadee, D. and J. Ditton (2005) 'Fear of Crime and the Media: Assessing the Lack of
    Relationship', *Crime, Media, Culture* 1(3): 322–32.

Clarke, J. (2005) 'New Labour's Citizens: Activated, Empowered, Responsibilized,
    Abandoned?', *Critical Social Policy* 25(4): 447–63.

Cohen, S. (2002) *'Folk Devils and Moral Panics: The Creation of the Mods and Rockers',* third
    edition, London: Routledge.

Commission Report: Final Report of the National Commission on Terrorist Attacks Upon the
    United States (2004) Washington, DC: National Commission on Terrorist Attacks.

Cottle, S. (2005) 'Mediatized Public Crisis and Civil Society Renewal: The Racist Murder
    of Stephen Lawrence', *Crime, Media, Culture* 1(1): 49–71.

Culpitt, I. (1999) *Social Policy and Risk.* London: SAGE Publications.

Curtis, A. (2004) 'Fear Gives Politicians a Reason to Be', *Guardian,* 24 September.

Denney, D. (2005) *Risk and Society.* London: SAGE Publications.

Duffy, J. (2003) 'Terrorist Threat: Should We Relax a Little?', BBC News Online. Available
    at http://news.bbc.co.uk/1/hi/uk/2968498.stm

Field, F. (2005) 'Without Security Liberty Dies', *Guardian,* 31 August.

Furedi, F. (2002) *Culture of Fear: Risk Taking and the Morality of Low Expectation*. London: Continuum.

Furedi, F. (2005) 'Terrorism and the Politics of Fear', in C. Hale, K. Hayward, A. Wahidin and E. Wincup (eds) *Criminology*, pp. 307–22. Oxford: Oxford University Press.

Garland, D. (2001) *The Culture of Control: Crime and Social Order in Contemporary Society*. Oxford: Oxford University Press.

Goh, I. (2004) 'Dangerous Philosophy: Threat, Risk and Security', *Theory, Technology and Culture* 27(1): 143.

Greer, C. and Y. Jewkes (2005) 'Extremes of Otherness: Media Images of Social Exclusion', *Social Justice* 32(1): 20–31.

Hudson, B. (2003) *Justice in the Risk Society*. London: SAGE Publications.

Hughes, G. (2004) 'Community Safety and "The Stranger": Challenges for Radical Communalism'. Paper presented to New Directions in Community Safety Conference, Birmingham, December.

Hunt, A. (2003) 'Risk and Moralisation in Everyday Life', in R. V. Ericson and A. Doyle (eds) *Risk and Morality*, pp. 192–5. Toronto: University of Toronto Press.

Jenks, C. (2003) *Transgression*. London: Routledge.

Jessop, B. (2002) *The Future of the Capitalist State*. Cambridge: Polity Press.

Joffe, H. (1999) *Risk and the Other*. Cambridge: Cambridge University Press.

Karmen, A. (1990) *An Introduction to Victimology*. San Francisco: Brooks Cole.

Kasperson, R. and J. Kasperson (1996) 'The Social Amplification and Attenuation of Risk', *Annals of the American Academy of Political and Social Science* 545:116–25.

Kellner, D. (2002) 'September 11 and Terror War: The Bush Legacy and the Risks of Unilateralism', *Logos* 1(4): 19–41.

Lacquer, W. (2000) *The New Terrorism: Fanaticism and the Arms of Mass Destruction*. London: Oxford University Press.

Lee, M. (2001) 'The Genesis of Fear of Crime', *Theoretical Criminology* 5(4): 467–85.

Lesser, I., B. Hoffman, J. Arquilla, D. Ronfeldt, M. Zanini and B.M. Jenkins (1999) *Countering the New Terrorism*. San Francisco: RAND.

McLaren, P. and G. Martin (2004) 'The Legend of the Bush Gang: Imperialism, War and Propoganda', *Cultural Studies, Critical Methodologies* 4(3): 281–303.

Melossi, D. and R. Selmini (2001) 'Social Conflict and the Microphysics of Crime', in T. Hope and R. Sparks (eds) *Crime, Risk and Insecurity*, pp. 146–65. London: Routledge.

Morgan, M. (2004) 'The Origins of New Terrorism', *Parameters* (Spring Edition): 29–43.

Mythen, G. (2005a) 'Employment, Individualisation and Insecurity: Rethinking the Risk Society Perspective', *The Sociological Review* 8(1): 129–49.

Mythen, G. (2005b) 'From Goods to Bads? Revisiting the Political Economy of Risk', *Sociological Research Online* 10(3). Available at: http://www.socresonline.org.uk/10/3/mythen.html

Mythen, G. and S. Walklate (2005) 'Criminology and Terrorism: Which Thesis? Risk Society or Governmentality?', *British Journal of Criminology* 45(1): 1–20.

Oborne, P. (2006) *The Use and Abuse of Terror: The Construction of a False Narrative of the Domestic Terror Threat*. London: Centre for Policy Studies.

Peelo, M. and K. Soothill (2000) 'The Place of Public Narratives in Reproducing Social Order', *Theoretical Criminology* 4(2): 131–48.

Philo, G. (1999) *Message Received: Glasgow Media Group Research 1993–1998*. New York: Addison, Wesley, Longman.

Rothe, D. and S. Muzzatti (2005) 'Enemies Everywhere: Terrorism, Moral Panic and US Civil Society', *Critical Criminology* 12: 327–50.

Salecl, R. (2004) *On Anxiety*. London: Routledge.

Schlesinger, P., H. Humber and G. Murdock(1991) 'The Media Politics of Crime and Criminal Justice', *British Journal of Sociology* 42(3): 397–420.

Steinert, H. (2003) 'The Indispensable Metaphor of War: On Populist Politics and the Contradictions of the State's Monopoly of Force', *Theoretical Criminology* 7(3): 265–91.

Tudor, A. (2003) 'A (Macro) Sociology of Fear?', *Sociological Review* 51(2): 238–56.

Waugh, P. (2004) 'Blair: Britain Must Never Be Afraid to Fight Terrorists', *Independent*, 13 March.

Webb, J. (2006) 'Bush Spells out LA Terror Plot', BBC News Online. Available at http://news.bbc.co.uk/2/hi/americas/4697896.stm

Welch, M. (2003) 'Trampling Human Rights in the War Against Terrorism: Implications for the Sociology of Denial', *Critical Criminology* 12(1): 1–20.

Worcester, R. (2001) 'The World Will Never Be the Same: British Hopes and Fears After September 11th 2001', *International Journal of Public Opinion Research*. Available at: http://www.mori.com

Young, J. (1999) *The Exclusive Society*. London: SAGE Publications.

Young, J. (2003) 'Merton with Energy, Katz with Structure: The Sociology of Vindictiveness and the Criminology of Transgression', *Theoretical Criminology* 7(3): 389–414.

Critical connections

In Mythen and Walklate's suggestion that the escalation of a culture of fear can generate acquiescence to authoritarian control measures, there are clear conceptual parallels with Gerbner and Gross's (1976, Reading 32) work on the cultivation of a particular mindset within media consumers for political ends. The theoretical and methodological frameworks that structure their respective analyses differ enormously, but the conclusions are not so wildly divergent. The most significant conceptual difference between their approaches is Gerbner and Gross' (1976) consideration of media discourses (television) in isolation, whilst Mythen and Walklate (2006) treat media as one part of a much wider network of communicative action. That said, where Gerbner and Gross have sought to demonstrate empirically the relationship between media and public perception, for Mythen and Walklate that relationship is illustrated in the abstract. The location of media representations of the threat from 'new terrorism' within the risk society also connects with Reiner *et al.*'s risk-based analysis of changing news and fictional representations of crime and criminal justice in the post-War period (Reading 25).

Discussion questions

- What does it mean to live in a 'risk society?'
- Is it useful, or desirable, to consider the American and European response to the September 11th attacks as a 'moral panic'?

●   Have the putative threat from 'new terrorism', and the corresponding notion of 'responsibilisation', impacted on your crime consciousness, daily routines, or sense of risk and danger?

References

Beck, U. (1992) *The Risk Society: Towards a New Modernity*, London: Sage.

Garland, D. (2001) *The Culture of Control: Crime and Social Order in Contemporary Society*, Oxford: Oxford University Press.

O'Malley, P. (2006) 'Criminology and Risk' in G. Mythen and S. Walklate (eds) *Beyond the Risk Society: Critical Reflections on Risk and Human Security*, Maidenhead: Open University Press.

Simon, J. (2006) *Governing Through Crime: How the War on Crime Transformed American Democracy and Created a Culture of Fear*, Oxford : Oxford University Press.

Susan Sontag

REGARDING THE TORTURE OF OTHERS (2004)

Introduction and context

IN THE FINAL EXTRACT in this Reader, the strategies of governmental
control over the terrorist threat are discussed by Susan Sontag. Originally published
in the *New York Times*, 'Regarding the Torture of Others' discusses the impact of the
global dissemination of torture images from Abu Ghraib prison. The photographs are,
for Sontag, the clearest evidence of the systematic abuse of prisoners in a manner
which directly contravenes international human rights conventions and the protocols
of war.

In an effort to develop an understanding of what happened in Abu Ghraib, a
number of commentators have made connections between these torture photographs
and other examples of documented abuse, for example the public torture lynching of
African Americans that took place across the Southern States of America between
the 1880s and the 1930s (Garland, 2006). At the site of such lynchings, it was not
uncommon for men, women and children to picnic beside the tortured and charred
corpse of a black captive. Photographs would be converted into postcards, perhaps
sent from child to parent elsewhere in the world, happily, even proudly memorialising
the onlookers' attendance at the wilful torture and murder of another human being.
In the lynchings and the abuses at Abu Ghraib the unashamed, boastful poses and
smiling faces of onlookers and participants indicate a particular relationship with the
camera, and with those of us on the other side of the lens. There is little concern about
exposure, still less shame, because it is assumed that those who view the images are
complicit in the abuse. This observation, if accepted, is made all the more striking by
Sontag's reading of the purpose of the photographs and the use made of them. For
Sontag, photographs of lynchings were intended for collection: as mementos from an

event. The images of abuse at Abu Ghraib, by contrast, indicate a shift in the use of the photograph. They were fully intended to be widely shared and disseminated.

For a long time – at least six decades – photographs have laid down the tracks of how important conflicts are judged and remembered. The Western memory museum is now mostly a visual one. Photographs have an insuperable power to determine what we recall of events, and it now seems probable that the defining association of people everywhere with the war that the United States launched preemptively in Iraq last year will be photographs of the torture of Iraqi prisoners by Americans in the most infamous of Saddam Hussein's prisons, Abu Ghraib.

The Bush administration and its defenders have chiefly sought to limit a public-relations disaster – the dissemination of the photographs – rather than deal with the complex crimes of leadership and of policy revealed by the pictures. There was, first of all, the displacement of the reality onto the photographs themselves. The administration's initial response was to say that the president was shocked and disgusted by the photographs – as if the fault or horror lay in the images, not in what they depict. There was also the avoidance of the word "torture." The prisoners had possibly been the objects of "abuse," eventually of "humiliation" – that was the most to be admitted. "My impression is that what has been charged thus far is abuse, which I believe technically is different from torture," Secretary of Defense Donald Rumsfeld said at a press conference. "And therefore I'm not going to address the 'torture' word."

Words alter, words add, words subtract. It was the strenuous avoidance of the word "genocide" while some 800,000 Tutsis in Rwanda were being slaughtered, over a few weeks' time, by their Hutu neighbors 10 years ago that indicated the American government had no intention of doing anything. To refuse to call what took place in Abu Ghraib – and what has taken place elsewhere in Iraq and in Afghanistan and at Guantánamo Bay – by its true name, torture, is as outrageous as the refusal to call the Rwandan genocide a genocide. Here is one of the definitions of torture contained in a convention to which the United States is a signatory: "any act by which severe pain or suffering, whether physical or mental, is intentionally inflicted on a person for such purposes as obtaining from him or a third person information or a confession." (The definition comes from the 1984 Convention Against Torture and Other Cruel, Inhuman or Degrading Treatment or Punishment. Similar definitions have existed for some time in customary law and in treaties, starting with Article 3 – common to the four Geneva conventions of 1949 – and many recent human rights conventions.) The 1984 convention declares, "No exceptional circumstances whatsoever, whether a state of war or a threat of war, internal political instability or any other public emergency, may be invoked as a justification of torture." And all covenants on torture specify that it includes treatment intended to humiliate the victim, like leaving prisoners naked in cells and corridors.

Whatever actions this administration undertakes to limit the damage of the widening revelations of the torture of prisoners in Abu Ghraib and elsewhere – trials, courts-martial, dishonorable discharges, resignation of senior military figures and responsible administration officials and substantial compensation to the victims – it is probable that the "torture" word will continue to be banned. To acknowledge that

Americans torture their prisoners would contradict everything this administration has invited the public to believe about the virtue of American intentions and America's right, flowing from that virtue, to undertake unilateral action on the world stage.

Even when the president was finally compelled, as the damage to America's reputation everywhere in the world widened and deepened, to use the "sorry" word, the focus of regret still seemed the damage to America's claim to moral superiority. Yes, President Bush said in Washington on May 6, standing alongside King Abdullah II of Jordan, he was "sorry for the humiliation suffered by the Iraqi prisoners and the humiliation suffered by their families." But, he went on, he was "equally sorry that people seeing these pictures didn't understand the true nature and heart of America."

To have the American effort in Iraq summed up by these images must seem, to those who saw some justification in a war that did overthrow one of the monster tyrants of modern times, "unfair." A war, an occupation, is inevitably a huge tapestry of actions. What makes some actions representative and others not? The issue is not whether the torture was done by individuals (i.e., "not by everybody") – but whether it was systematic. Authorized. Condoned. All acts are done by individuals. The issue is not whether a majority or a minority of Americans performs such acts but whether the nature of the policies prosecuted by this administration and the hierarchies deployed to carry them out makes such acts likely.

II

Considered in this light, the photographs are us. That is, they are representative of the fundamental corruptions of any foreign occupation together with the Bush administration's distinctive policies. The Belgians in the Congo, the French in Algeria, practiced torture and sexual humiliation on despised recalcitrant natives. Add to this generic corruption the mystifying, near-total unpreparedness of the American rulers of Iraq to deal with the complex realities of the country after its "liberation." And add to that the overarching, distinctive doctrines of the Bush administration, namely that the United States has embarked on an endless war and that those detained in this war are, if the president so decides, "unlawful combatants" – a policy enunciated by Donald Rumsfeld for Taliban and Qaeda prisoners as early as January 2002 – and thus, as Rumsfeld said, "technically" they "do not have any rights under the Geneva Convention," and you have a perfect recipe for the cruelties and crimes committed against the thousands incarcerated without charges or access to lawyers in American-run prisons that have been set up since the attacks of Sept. 11, 2001.

So, then, is the real issue not the photographs themselves but what the photographs reveal to have happened to "suspects" in American custody? No: the horror of what is shown in the photographs cannot be separated from the horror that the photographs were taken – with the perpetrators posing, gloating, over their helpless captives. German soldiers in the Second World War took photographs of the atrocities they were committing in Poland and Russia, but snapshots in which the executioners placed themselves among their victims are exceedingly rare, as may be seen in a book just published, *Photographing the Holocaust*, by Janina Struk. If there is something comparable to what these pictures show it would be some of the photographs of black victims of lynching taken between the 1880s and 1930s, which show Americans grinning beneath the naked mutilated body of a black man or woman hanging behind them from a tree. The lynching photographs were souvenirs of a collective action whose participants felt perfectly justified in what they had done. So are the pictures from Abu Ghraib.

The lynching pictures were in the nature of photographs as trophies – taken by a photographer in order to be collected, stored in albums, displayed. The pictures taken by American soldiers in Abu Ghraib, however, reflect a shift in the use made of pictures – less objects to be saved than messages to be disseminated, circulated. A digital camera is a common possession among soldiers. Where once photographing war was the province of photojournalists, now the soldiers themselves are all photographers – recording their war, their fun, their observations of what they find picturesque, their atrocities – and swapping images among themselves and e-mailing them around the globe.

There is more and more recording of what people do, by themselves. At least or especially in America, Andy Warhol's ideal of filming real events in real time – life isn't edited, why should its record be edited? – has become a norm for countless Webcasts, in which people record their day, each in his or her own reality show. Here I am – waking and yawning and stretching, brushing my teeth, making breakfast, getting the kids off to school. People record all aspects of their lives, store them in computer files and send the files around. Family life goes with the recording of family life – even when, or especially when, the family is in the throes of crisis and disgrace. Surely the dedicated, incessant home-videoing of one another, in conversation and monologue, over many years was the most astonishing material in "Capturing the Friedmans," the recent documentary by Andrew Jarecki about a Long Island family embroiled in pedophilia charges.

An erotic life is, for more and more people, that which can be captured in digital photographs and on video. And perhaps the torture is more attractive, as something to record, when it has a sexual component. It is surely revealing, as more Abu Ghraib photographs enter public view, that torture photographs are interleaved with porno-graphic images of American soldiers having sex with one another. In fact, most of the torture photographs have a sexual theme, as in those showing the coercing of prison-ers to perform, or simulate, sexual acts among themselves. One exception, already canonical, is the photograph of the man made to stand on a box, hooded and sprout-ing wires, reportedly told he would be electrocuted if he fell off. Yet pictures of pris-oners bound in painful positions, or made to stand with outstretched arms, are infrequent. That they count as torture cannot be doubted. You have only to look at the terror on the victim's face, although such "stress" fell within the Pentagon's limits of the acceptable. But most of the pictures seem part of a larger confluence of torture and pornography: a young woman leading a naked man around on a leash is classic dominatrix imagery. And you wonder how much of the sexual tortures inflicted on the inmates of Abu Ghraib was inspired by the vast repertory of pornographic imagery available on the Internet – and which ordinary people, by sending out Webcasts of themselves, try to emulate.

III

To live is to be photographed, to have a record of one's life, and therefore to go on with one's life oblivious, or claiming to be oblivious, to the camera's nonstop attentions.

But to live is also to pose. To act is to share in the community of actions recorded as images. The expression of satisfaction at the acts of torture being inflicted on helpless, trussed, naked victims is only part of the story. There is the deep satisfaction of being photographed, to which one is now more inclined to respond not with a stiff, direct gaze (as in former times) but with glee. The events are in part designed to be photographed. The grin is a grin for the camera. There would be something missing if, after stacking the naked men, you couldn't take a picture of them.

Looking at these photographs, you ask yourself, How can someone grin at the sufferings and humiliation of another human being? Set guard dogs at the genitals and legs of cowering naked prisoners? Force shackled, hooded prisoners to masturbate or simulate oral sex with one another? And you feel naïve for asking, since the answer is, self-evidently, People do these things to other people. Rape and pain inflicted on the genitals are among the most common forms of torture. Not just in Nazi concentration camps and in Abu Ghraib when it was run by Saddam Hussein. Americans, too, have done and do them when they are told, or made to feel, that those over whom they have absolute power deserve to be humiliated, tormented. They do them when they are led to believe that the people they are torturing belong to an inferior race or religion. For the meaning of these pictures is not just that these acts were performed, but that their perpetrators apparently had no sense that there was anything wrong in what the pictures show.

Even more appalling, since the pictures were meant to be circulated and seen by many people: it was all fun. And this idea of fun is, alas, more and more — contrary to what President Bush is telling the world — part of "the true nature and heart of America." It is hard to measure the increasing acceptance of brutality in American life, but its evidence is everywhere, starting with the video games of killing that are a principal entertainment of boys — can the video game "Interrogating the Terrorists" really be far behind? — and on to the violence that has become endemic in the group rites of youth on an exuberant kick. Violent crime is down, yet the easy delight taken in violence seems to have grown. From the harsh torments inflicted on incoming students in many American suburban high schools — depicted in Richard Linklater's 1993 film, *Dazed and Confused* — to the hazing rituals of physical brutality and sexual humiliation in college fraternities and on sports teams, America has become a country in which the fantasies and the practice of violence are seen as good entertainment, fun.

What formerly was segregated as pornography, as the exercise of extreme sado-masochistic longings — as in Pier Paolo Pasolini's last, near-unwatchable film, *Salò* (1975), depicting orgies of torture in the Fascist redoubt in northern Italy at the end of the Mussolini era — is now being normalized, by some, as high-spirited play or venting. To "stack naked men" is like a college fraternity prank, said a caller to Rush Limbaugh and the many millions of Americans who listen to his radio show. Had the caller, one wonders, seen the photographs? No matter. The observation — or is it the fantasy? — was on the mark. What may still be capable of shocking some Americans was Limbaugh's response: "Exactly!" he exclaimed. "Exactly my point. This is no different than what happens at the Skull and Bones initiation, and we're going to ruin people's lives over it, and we're going to hamper our military effort, and then we are going to really hammer them because they had a good time." "They" are the American soldiers, the torturers. And Limbaugh went on: "You know, these people are being fired at every day. I'm talking about people having a good time, these people. You ever heard of emotional release?"

Shock and awe were what our military promised the Iraqis. And shock and the awful are what these photographs announce to the world that the Americans have delivered: a pattern of criminal behavior in open contempt of international humanitarian conventions. Soldiers now pose, thumbs up, before the atrocities they commit, and send off the pictures to their buddies. Secrets of private life that, formerly, you would have given nearly anything to conceal, you now clamor to be invited on a television show to reveal. What is illustrated by these photographs is as much the culture of shamelessness as the reigning admiration for unapologetic brutality.

IV

The notion that apologies or professions of "disgust" by the president and the secretary of defense are a sufficient response is an insult to one's historical and moral sense. The torture of prisoners is not an aberration. It is a direct consequence of the with-us-or-against-us doctrines of world struggle with which the Bush administration has sought to change, change radically, the international stance of the United States and to recast many domestic institutions and prerogatives. The Bush administration has committed the country to a pseudo-religious doctrine of war, endless war – for "the war on terror" is nothing less than that. Endless war is taken to justify endless incarcerations. Those held in the extralegal American penal empire are "detainees"; "prisoners," a newly obsolete word, might suggest that they have the rights accorded by international law and the laws of all civilized countries. This endless "global war on terrorism" – into which both the quite justified invasion of Afghanistan and the unwinnable folly in Iraq have been folded by Pentagon decree – inevitably leads to the demonizing and dehumanizing of anyone declared by the Bush administration to be a possible terrorist: a definition that is not up for debate and is, in fact, usually made in secret.

The charges against most of the people detained in the prisons in Iraq and Afghanistan being nonexistent – the Red Cross reports that 70 to 90 percent of those being held seem to have committed no crime other than simply being in the wrong place at the wrong time, caught up in some sweep of "suspects" – the principal justification for holding them is "interrogation." Interrogation about what? About anything. Whatever the detainee might know. If interrogation is the point of detaining prisoners indefinitely, then physical coercion, humiliation and torture become inevitable.

Remember: we are not talking about that rarest of cases, the "ticking time bomb" situation, which is sometimes used as a limiting case that justifies torture of prisoners who have knowledge of an imminent attack. This is general or nonspecific information-gathering, authorized by American military and civilian administrators to learn more of a shadowy empire of evildoers about whom Americans know virtually nothing, in countries about which they are singularly ignorant: in principle, any information at all might be useful. An interrogation that produced no information (whatever information might consist of) would count as a failure. All the more justification for preparing prisoners to talk. Softening them up, stressing them out – these are the euphemisms for the bestial practices in American prisons where suspected terrorists are being held. Unfortunately, as Staff Sgt. Ivan (Chip) Frederick noted in his diary, a prisoner can get too stressed out and die. The picture of a man in a body bag with ice on his chest may well be of the man Frederick was describing.

The pictures will not go away. That is the nature of the digital world in which we live. Indeed, it seems they were necessary to get our leaders to acknowledge that they had a problem on their hands. After all, the conclusions of reports compiled by the International Committee of the Red Cross, and other reports by journalists and protests by humanitarian organizations about the atrocious punishments inflicted on "detainees" and "suspected terrorists" in prisons run by the American military, first in Afghanistan and later in Iraq, have been circulating for more than a year. It seems doubtful that such reports were read by President Bush or Vice President Dick Cheney or Condoleezza Rice or Rumsfeld. Apparently it took the photographs to get their attention, when it became clear they could not be suppressed; it was the photographs that made all this "real" to Bush and his associates. Up to then, there had been only words, which are easier to cover up in our age of infinite digital self-reproduction and self-dissemination, and so much easier to forget.

So now the pictures will continue to "assault" us – as many Americans are bound to feel. Will people get used to them? Some Americans are already saying they have seen enough. Not, however, the rest of the world. Endless war: endless stream of photographs. Will editors now debate whether showing more of them, or showing them uncropped (which, with some of the best-known images, like that of a hooded man on a box, gives a different and in some instances more appalling view), would be in "bad taste" or too implicitly political? By "political," read: critical of the Bush administration's imperial project. For there can be no doubt that the photographs damage, as Rumsfeld testified, "the reputation of the honorable men and women of the armed forces who are courageously and responsibly and professionally defending our freedom across the globe." This damage – to our reputation, our image, our success as the lone superpower – is what the Bush administration principally deplores. How the protection of "our freedom" – the freedom of 5 percent of humanity – came to require having American soldiers "across the globe" is hardly debated by our elected officials.

Already the backlash has begun. Americans are being warned against indulging in an orgy of self-condemnation. The continuing publication of the pictures is being taken by many Americans as suggesting that we do not have the right to defend ourselves: after all, they (the terrorists) started it. They – Osama bin Laden? Saddam Hussein? what's the difference? – attacked us first. Senator James Inhofe of Oklahoma, a Republican member of the Senate Armed Services Committee, before which Secretary Rumsfeld testified, avowed that he was sure he was not the only member of the committee "more outraged by the outrage" over the photographs than by what the photographs show. "These prisoners," Senator Inhofe explained, "you know they're not there for traffic violations. If they're in Cellblock 1-A or 1-B, these prisoners, they're murderers, they're terrorists, they're insurgents. Many of them probably have American blood on their hands, and here we're so concerned about the treatment of those individuals." It's the fault of "the media" which are provoking, and will continue to provoke, further violence against Americans around the world. More Americans will die. Because of these photos.

There is an answer to this charge, of course. Americans are dying not because of the photographs but because of what the photographs reveal to be happening, happening with the complicity of a chain of command – so Maj. Gen. Antonio Taguba implied, and Pfc. Lynndie England said, and (among others) Senator Lindsey Graham of South Carolina, a Republican, suggested, after he saw the Pentagon's full range of images on May 12. "Some of it has an elaborate nature to it that makes me very suspicious of whether or not others were directing or encouraging," Senator Graham said. Senator Bill Nelson, a Florida Democrat, said that viewing an uncropped version of one photo showing a stack of naked men in a hallway – a version that revealed how many other soldiers were at the scene, some not even paying attention – contradicted the Pentagon's assertion that only rogue soldiers were involved. "Somewhere along the line," Senator Nelson said of the torturers, "they were either told or winked at." An attorney for Specialist Charles Graner Jr., who is in the picture, has had his client identify the men in the uncropped version; according to *The Wall Street Journal*, Graner said that four of the men were military intelligence and one a civilian contractor working with military intelligence.

V

But the distinction between photograph and reality – as between spin and policy – can easily evaporate. And that is what the administration wishes to happen. "There are a lot more photographs and videos that exist," Rumsfeld acknowledged in his testimony. "If these are released to the public, obviously, it's going to make matters worse." Worse for the administration and its programs, presumably, not for those who are the actual – and potential? – victims of torture.

The media may self-censor but, as Rumsfeld acknowledged, it's hard to censor soldiers overseas, who don't write letters home, as in the old days, that can be opened by military censors who ink out unacceptable lines. Today's soldiers instead function like tourists, as Rumsfeld put it, "running around with digital cameras and taking these unbelievable photographs and then passing them off, against the law, to the media, to our surprise." The administration's effort to withhold pictures is proceeding along several fronts. Currently, the argument is taking a legalistic turn: now the photographs are classified as evidence in future criminal cases, whose outcome may be prejudiced if they are made public. The Republican chairman of the Senate Armed Services Committee, John Warner of Virginia, after the May 12 slide show of image after image of sexual humiliation and violence against Iraqi prisoners, said he felt "very strongly" that the newer photos "should not be made public. I feel that it could possibly endanger the men and women of the armed forces as they are serving and at great risk."

But the real push to limit the accessibility of the photographs will come from the continuing effort to protect the administration and cover up our misrule in Iraq – to identify "outrage" over the photographs with a campaign to undermine American military might and the purposes it currently serves. Just as it was regarded by many as an implicit criticism of the war to show on television photographs of American soldiers who have been killed in the course of the invasion and occupation of Iraq, it will increasingly be thought unpatriotic to disseminate the new photographs and further tarnish the image of America.

After all, we're at war. Endless war. And war is hell, more so than any of the people who got us into this rotten war seem to have expected. In our digital hall of mirrors, the pictures aren't going to go away. Yes, it seems that one picture is worth a thousand words. And even if our leaders choose not to look at them, there will be thousands more snapshots and videos. Unstoppable.

Critical connections

In what Sontag (1977) refers to elsewhere as the 'image world', people are evermore inclined to visually document, record and share their lives and experiences in an increasingly media literate world:

> While many people in non-industrialised countries still feel apprehensive when being photographed, divining it to be some sort of trespass, an act of disrespect, a sublimated looking of the personality or the culture, people in industrialised countries seek to have their photographs taken – feel that they are images, and are made real by photographs (Sontag, 1977: 161).

Mark Hamm (2007) has argued that the photographic documentation of the 'sins of Abu Ghraib' presents clear evidence that the torture of Iraqi detainees was not the result of bad apples. Nor, it is suggested, can Zimbardo's famous development of the brutalisation thesis – the Stanford Prison Experiment (1973) – account for the sheer ordinariness with which the torturers appear to be approaching their subjects. The process of de-humanisation appears complete, for such atrocities surely could not be committed on another human being otherwise. Hannah Arendt (1963) wrote of the 'banality of evil' – the extent to which human persecution, including torture, could become so normal, even mundane. It is this characteristic of the images that both Sontag and Hamm find most troubling, and that provides clearest evidence of the institutionalised nature of the abuse in Abu Ghraib.

Discussion questions

- What connections does Sontag make between the abuses at Abu Ghraib and lynching of African Americans in America's Southern States?
- How might the abuse images of Abu Ghraib be 'read' as evidence of systematic, authorised torture of Iraqi detainees, rather than the rogue activities of a few 'bad apples'?
- What can Mathiesen's (Reading 37) theorising of the 'viewer society' add to Sontag's (Reading 42) contention that people 'feel that they are images, and are made real by photographs'?

References

Arrendt, H. (1963) *Eichmann in Jerusalem: A Report on the Banality of Evil*, London: Penguin Classics.

Garland, D. (2006) "Postcards from the Edge: Photographs of Torture in Abu Ghraib and the American South" in R. Behr, H. Cremer-Schafer and S. Scheerer (eds) *Kriminalitats-Geschichten*, Band 41, Lit Verlag: Hamburg.

Hamm, M. (2007) 'High Crimes and Misdemeanors: George Bush and the Sins of Abu Ghraib', in *Crime, Media, Culture: An International Journal,* 3, 3,: 259–284.

Haney, C., Banks, W. C., & Zimbardo, P. G. (1973). Study of prisoners and guards in a simulated prison. *Naval Research Reviews,* 9, 1–17. Washington, DC: Office of Naval Research.

Sontag, S. (1977) *On Photography,* New York: Picador.

Index

Page numbers in *Italics* represent tables.